CONTENTS

Chapter	Page
Introductory	xxi
I.—Genesis of the Polk Family	1
Scotch and Irish History of Family	2
II.—Robert Bruce Pollok	6
The Keys Family	8
III.—Data from Ireland	9
Births and Deaths in Keys Family	11
IV.—Broomfield Castle and Moneen	13
John Polk here in 1680	15
V.—When the Immigrants Arrived	18
James Poke of Barbadoes	19
VI.—The Anglicanism	22
VII.—Emigration of the Polks	23
First Churches on Eastern Shore of M'yland	24
Charles, first Son of Ephraim Polk, 1st	25
VIII.—Robert and Magdalen's Family	28
John Polk's Descendants	29
From the Somerset Records	31
Errors of 1810 Polk Tree	33
IX.—James Polk, Son of Robert Bruce Polk	36
Land Grants to James Polk	36
Will of James Polk	38
X.—David Polk's Will	41
XI.—James Polk's Other Children	45
Emigration to the West	47
The Somerset Records	49
XII.—Letters of Col. Wm T. G. Polk	50
XIII.—Winder and Polk Connection	54
XIV.—Magdalen Polk's Will	59
Grants from Lord Baltimore	61
Additional List of Grants	62
XV.—Will of Robert Bruce Polk	64
Other Polk Wills	65
XVI.—	70

Chapter	Page
XVII —Marriages and Descendants	75
Robert's Children	77
Conclusions	78
XVIII —Wm Polk, Grandson of Robert Bruce Polk	81
Anne Polk, Daughter of John	82
XIX —Joseph Polk and Descendants	84
Lands Granted to Joseph Polk	85
Will of Joseph Pollock	87
Family of Daniel Morris, Sr	91
Martha and Ann Polk	92
Martha Polk's Descendants	93
Numerous Progeny	94
XX —Descendants of William Polk, 3d	95
XXI —Chas Polk, Son of Wm. and Margaret	100
XXII —Margaret Polk McRea	106
XXIII.—General Thomas Polk's Descendants	108
John Paul Jones	112
Major Allen J Polk	114
XXIV —The Mecklenburg Declaration	116
Battle of Allamance	116
Convention Meets	118
The Resolves	118
XXV —Sketch of General Thomas Polk	124
Defeats at Camden and Sumpter	127
Military Organized	128
Escorts Baggage Train to Bethlehem	129
William Polk of Carlisle	131
XXVI —Sketch of Colonel William Polk	133
La Fayette's Visit to North Carolina	141
Death of Colonel William Polk	144
XXVII —Dr William J Polk	147
General Lucius E Polk	147
XXVIII —Dr Thomas G Polk	156
Colonel Cadwallader Polk	157
Captain Rufus J Polk	158
Major Allen J Polk	159
General Thomas G Polk	161
General Lucius E Polk	162

Chapter	Page
XXIX.—Bishop and Lt General Leonidas Polk	169
Civil War	173
XXX—Atlanta Campaign	177
Death of General Leonidas Polk	178
General Johnston's Order	183
Funeral Obsequies and Burial	183
XXXI.—St John s Church, Ashwood, Tenn	188
Interesting Family Letters	191
XXXII—Polk s Serving in Congress	198
Hon Rufus K Polk, M C, from P'sylvania	199
XXXIII.—William Polk, Sr, Son of Immigrants	203
William Polk, Sr, Twice Married	204
XXXIV.—Wrong William made Body of 1819 Tree	207
William Polk and Priscilla Roberts	207
Children of William and Nancy (Knox-Owens) Polk	209
William, Son of Judge David Polk	210
Betsy, Daughter of William Polk	211
Hetty, Daughter of William Polk	211
Gertrude, Daughter of William Polk	211
XXXV—Josiah, Son of William Polk	213
Captain William Son of William Polk	213
Colonel James Polk, Son of William Polk	214
Anne, Daughter of Judge William Polk	215
James Polk, Son of William Polk Sr	215
XXXVI—Samuel Polk's Descendants	224
Colonel Wm Thomas Gilliss Polk's Family	224
Joseph Gilliss Polk's Family	225
XXXVII—Whittington Connection	235
Descendants of Susan Lankford	236
Priscilla Polk Whittington	239
XXXVIII—Sketch of James Knox Polk	241
Jackson and Polk Families	247
Nominated and Elected President	248
Mr Polk's Inauguration	251
Chief Administration Measures	253
Death of James K Polk	254
XXXIX	258

Chapter	Page
XL.—Captain John Polk	312
Taylor Polk's Descendants	312
Capt John Polk's Descendants	316
Judge Alfred Polk	317
Judge Alfred Polk's Family	317
Mary Cynthia (Polk) Davis' Family	318
John ("Jackie") Polk's Descendants	321
Davenports and Cartwrights	322
XLI.—John D Polk and Family	324
Descendants of Emily B Polk	324
John Polk Childres' Family	325
Charles Vaulton Childres' Family	325
John A Polk and Family	325
Benjamin D A Polk's Family	327
"Civil Charley" Polk's Family	328
Descendants of Jackie and Cynthia Polk	332
Rev R O Watkins and Family	334
Sketch of Rev R. O. Watkins	334
Sketch of Judge A B Watkins	335
Memoranda of the Polk Family in Texas	335
XLII.—Children of Chas Polk and Wife Margaret	339
John Polk and Family	340
Colonel William Knox Polk's Descendants	340
Sketch of Headley Polk	343
Warnell Polk	344
XLIII.—Unattached Branches	348
Tragic Death of Rev William Polk	354
XLIV.—Charles Polk, The Indian Trader	355
Will of Charles Polk, Indian Trader	356
Murder of Logan's Kin	359
Capt Charles Polk's Certificate	359
XLV.—Capture of Kincheloe's Station	362
Capt Charles Polk's Family	364
Descendants of Sarah Polk Piety	365
Spoke Indian Tongue Well	372
Polk Land Entries in Kentucky	373
XLVI.—Capture of Capt Chas Polk's Family	374
An Indian Feast	378

CONTENTS

Chapter	Page
XLVII.—Judge William Polk, Son of Capt Chas Polk	390
Judge William Polk and Family	391
Elizabeth (Polk) Spencer	392
Children of Capt Spier Spencer	394
Sally (Polk) Bruce's Descendants	395
Children of Capt Wm Bruce and Wife	395
Joseph Hamilton Scroggin's Family	396
Capt John Scroggin's Family	398
Of Scotch-Irish Blood	398
Quarrel over Baby's Name	399
Nancy Ruby's Family and Chas Polk, 3rd	400
XLVIII—Edmond Polk's Descendants	403
Edmond Polk's Children	106
Grandchildren of Edmond Polk, Sr	108
Grandchildren's Children	108
Children of James Polk	111
Children of James Madison Polk	111
Children of Henry Hamilton Polk	116
Deaths	116
New Salem Church	116
XLIX —Claiborne Polk and Descendants	118
Irwin C Polk's Family	121
Isabella (Polk) Kendle	121
Francis Marion Polk	122
William Albert Polk's Family	122
Caleb Clark Polk's Family	122
Sarah Jane Polk's Family	125
Alexander Hamilton Polk	125
Grandchildren of Alexander H Polk	126
L —Descendants of Rev Isaac M'Coy and Wife	128
Intermarriages	128
The Chick Family	131
Intermarriages of Jno Calvin M'Coy's Children	131
LI —Charles Polk, 3rd. and Family	136
Descendants of Dr Thomas Polk	140
Int.	140
Ske:	143

Chapter	Page
LII —Ephraim Polk, 1st, and Descendants	449
Charles Polk, 1st, Son of Ephraim, 1st	450
Children of Charles Polk, 1st	451
Sketch of Gov John W Hall	452
Judge Charles Polk	455
Gov Charles Polk	455
LIII —Sketch of Gov Charles Polk	461
Sketch of Hon. Albert F Polk	465
Allied Families	469
Minors and Beswicks	470
Beswick Bible Records	473
The Manlove Family	474
Wm Manlove, Sr	477
The Curtis Family	478
Bairatt Family	481
The Clarke Family	482
Brinckles in Military Service	483
Member of Penn's Council	484
The Hayes Family	484
William Polk's Descendants	485
The Luff Family	486
John Polk, Son of Ephraim, 1st	491
LIV —Polk Scroggin Kinship	496
Genesis of American Scroggin Family	496
Gallant Officers of the Revolution	500
Joseph Polk, Sr, Son of Ephraim, 1st	502
Joseph Polk, Jr, Son of Joseph Polk, Sr	502
Robert Polk and Family	505
Children of Wm Reybold Polk	509
LV —Children of Ephraim Polk, 2nd	510
Will of Ephraim Polk, 2nd	510
LVI —Ephraim Polk, 3rd	516
Captain Rhoads' Company	518
Privates	518
Valley Forge	519
Ephraim Emigrates to Kentucky	520
An Indian Raid	522
LVII The Morris Family	528

CONTENTS   xiii

Chapter		Page
	Children of Daniel Morris, Jr	529
	Children of James Morris, Sr	531
	Children of Ephraim Polk, 3rd	532
	Family of Mary Polk Wolf	533
	Children of Polly and Jesse Wolf	533
	Intermarriages	534
	Jesse Wolf's Capture	538
LVIII	—Family of Nancy (Polk) Adams	540
	Nancy Adams' Family	540
	Marriages	541
	Dr James M Ely's Family	541
	Family of Dr James M Adams	542
	Intermarriages	543
	Family of John White	543
	Family of Allen McMichael	548
	Marriages	548
	John H Hufford's Family	550
	Family of Thomas A. Gant	553
	Dr Marcellus M Adams' Family	553
	Fannie Stutsman's Family	554
	Sketch of Dr. Marcellus M Adams	554
	Dr Jefferson J Polk and Descendants	555
	Family of Dr Jefferson J Polk	565
	Martha F Duncan's Family	565
	Family of Dr William Tod Polk	566
LVIX	—Family of Ephraim J Polk	568
	Children of Ephraim J Polk	568
	Children of John M. Polk	573
	Children of Thos J Polk and Wife	574
LX	—Daniel Polk and Descendants	575
	Daniel Polk's Children	576
	Family of David Tanner Polk	576
	Family of David Tanner Polk, Jr	577
	Family of Rhoda Ann Rodgers	577
	Marriages	578
	Family of Ben F Rodgers	581
	Family of Thomas P D Polk	581
		582

Chapter		Page
	Family of Sardius G Polk	587
	Intermarriages	588
	Family of James Knox Polk	588
	Sarah (Kitty) Polk's Family	588
LXI —Family of Hester D Collins		591
	Family of Col John E Collins	592
	Col John Collins Children	592
	Col John Collins' Grandchildren	592
	Descendants of Clement M Polk	593
	Children of Clement Polk	594
	Charles Ephraim Polk	598
	Descendants of Gilead Polk	602
	Children of Gilead Polk	603
LXII —The Johnson Family		610
	The Alexander Family	611
	The Holladay Family	611
	Family of William H. Polk	612
LXIII —William H Polk		617
LXIV —Family of Theodore C Polk		621
	Children of Theodore Clay Polk	621
	Theodore C Polk	622
	Family of John Knox Polk	625
	Sarah Atkins and Ephraim Polk, 5th	626
LXV —Descendants of Jehosephat Polk		629
	Family of Hosea and Sally Polk	630
	Intermarriages	630
	Marcellus Polk's Family	633
	Sketch of Marcellus Polk	633
	Sarah A Deming's Family	634
	James E Polk	639
	Family of Edward M and Melissa Hubbert	639
	Marriages, Births and Deaths	640
	Mary Susan Polk's Family	645
	Margaret Dougherty's Family	645
	Family of Jefferson Scott Polk	645
	Marriages	646
	Sketch of Jefferson Scott Polk	646
	Admitted to Bar in Kentucky	651

CONTENTS

Chapter	Page
Tribute to his Life and Character	652
Sketch of Harry Herndon Polk	659
Herndon Hall, Home of Jefferson Polk	659
LXVI.—Dr. Ed Polk's Branch of Family	665
Dr. Edward T Polk	666
Family of R L Polk	669
LXVII —Robert Polk, Jr , and Descendants	671
Family of Robert Polk, Jr	671
Land Grants to Robert's Line	672
Robert Polk, 3rd, a Colonial Official	673
Children of Robert Polk, 3rd	674
LXVIII —Col William Polk's Descendants	675
Children of Col William Polk	675
Intermarriages	676
William Polk, Son of Col William, Son of Robert Polk, Jr	677
Descendants of Elizabeth (Robinson) Polk	680
LXIX —Trusten Laws Polk's Descendants	691
Children of Wm Nutter Polk	691
Intermarriages	692
Elizabeth Shockley's Family	693
Wm Causey Polk's Family	693
Sketch of Governor Trusten Polk	694
LXX —The White Family	697
Daniel Polk, Sr , of Delaware	699
Daniel Polk, Sr's Family	700
Intermarriages	700
Clayton Family	700
Samuel White Polk's Family	701
Midshipman John Polk	702
Family of Daniel Polk, Jr	703
Family of Elizabeth Powell	704
Family of Kate Powell Tyree	704
Family of Edward B Powell	704
Family of Dr Louis Polk	705
Family of Mrs Landon A Thomas, Sr	705
Family of Landon A Thomas, Jr	706
Family of L	706

Chapter	Page
Peggy Logan's Family	707
The Tilghman Family	708
LXXI.—Capt Robert Polk, Naval Officer	709
Descendants of Capt. Robert Polk	710
Family of Charles Peale Polk	710
Charles Peale Polk, Artist	712
Charles Peale Polk's Letter to Washington	715
LXXII.—Polks of Accomac County, Virginia	717
Intermarriages	717
Sallie Polk's Descendants	718
Margaret Polk's Descendants	719
William Polk's Descendants	724
Capt William Polk's Ancestors	725
LXXIII.—The Pollocks of America	727
Judge John C Pollock's Line	732
James and William Pollock	733
LXXIV.—Dr Thomas Pollock's Descendants	737
Paternal Line of Lt Col Otis Wheeler Pollock	739
LXXV.—Visit to Scottish Ancestral Home	740
The Pogue Family	741

LIST OF ILLUSTRATIONS.

	Page
Frontispiece—W H Polk	
Map of Maryland, Delaware, Pennsylvania, West New Jersey	xxvii
Chart	83
Gen'l Thos G Polk of, North Carolina	109
Col. William Polk, of North Carolina	135
Monument of Col Wm. Polk at Raleigh, N C	145
Dr Wm Julius Polk and Wife, of North Carolina	149
Gen'l Lucius E Polk, of Arkansas	153
Gen'l Lucius Junius Polk of North Carolina and Tennessee	163
Col. Wm H Polk and Wife	167
Bishop Leonidas Polk and Wife	171
Lieut. Gen'l Leonidas Polk	179
St. Paul Episcopal Church, Augusta, Ga	185
St John's Church, Ashwood, Maury County, Tenn	189
Hon Rufus K Polk, M C, from Pennsylvania	201
Col Wm. T G Polk Princess Anne, Md	225
James K Polk and Wife	243
Polk Place, Nashville, Tenn	249
Jas K Polk Monument Raleigh, N C	255
Col Andrew J Polk and Wife	259
Wm Polk and Wife, Alexander, La	263
Col Cadwallader Polk, of Arkansas	271
Rufus J Polk	275
Mrs Lucius J Polk and Madame Paget	279
Col Lucius Junius Polk, Jr, Wife and Two Children, of Texas	285
Col Geo W Polk, Wife and Son, San Antonio, Tex	289
Dr Wm Mecklenburg Polk and Wife, of New York	293
Capt Frank L Polk and Wife, of New York	297
Geo W Polk and Six Sons, of Tennessee	301
Mrs Kenneth Raynor, of North Carolina	305
Antionette (Polk) De Charette and Her Home, near Paris, France	309
Jas N Polk	319

	Page
Mrs Margaret Jane (Polk) Teel, of Texas	329
Judge Albert B. Watkins, of Athens, Tex.	337
Headley Polk, San Marcos, Tex	345
R C Ballard Thruston, of Louisville, Ky	369
Amiee J. and Edna B. Ruby, of La Fayette, Ind	401
Hon Jas Guthrie, of Louisville, Ky	409
Claiborne Polk and Alexander Hamilton Polk, of Indiana	419
Agnes and Jessie Pringle	423
Benjamin F Polk, Princeton, Ind	437
Gov John W. Hall, of Delaware	453
Dr Thos. Jefferson Pyle, Wife and Daughter	457
Gov Charles Polk of Delaware	463
Hon Albert F Polk, of Georgetown, Delaware	467
John W Hering, of Milford, Delaware	475
Dr J M Luff, of Felton, Delaware	487
John P R Polk, of Wilmington, Delaware	507
Old Ephraim Polk Homestead, on Lain's Run, Scott County, Kentucky	523
Mrs Mary (Polly) Wolfe	535
Elizabeth Tyner White, of La Fayette, Indiana	545
Dr M M Adams and Wife, of Greenfield, Indiana	551
Ellen, Mary, Olive, and Nettie Adams, of Greenfield, Indiana	555
Dr Jefferson J Polk, of Perryville, Kentucky	559
Dr Wm Tod Polk, of Perryville Kentucky	563
Wm Goddard Polk, of Louisville Kentucky	569
Roy Rodgers 2nd U. S A	579
Willis W Polk and Wife	583
Chas E Polk and Wife	595
Walter B Manny and Wife, Ella Tatum Manny	599
Edw Hubbert Tatum	603
Chas W Polk and Sister Maud, of Pelatuma, California	607
Mary (Polk) Bouldin and Wm C Polk, of Lexington, Kentucky	613
Theodore C Polk, Jr, Thomas Barlow Polk, James Williams, Margaret Williams	619
John Milton Polk, of Denver Colorado	623
Mrs Sarah (Polk) Atkins, of Liberty Indiana	627

LIST OF ILLUSTRATIONS   xix

	Page
Jehosephat Polk and Wife, Sallie Ann Polk	631
Marcellus Polk and Wife, Ella Samuell Polk, and Six Children	635
Sarah Ann Deming and Husband, Joseph G. Deming	637
James E. Polk and Wife, Maggie (Payne) Polk	641
Melissa (Polk) Hubbert and Husband, Edw. S. Hubbert	643
Jefferson S. Polk and Group	647
Jefferson Scott Polk and Wife, Julia (Herndon) Polk	649
John S. Polk and Wife	653
George B. Hippee and Wife, Minnie (Polk) Hippee	655
Mrs. Sallie (Polk) Maish and Husband	657
Harry Herndon Polk and Wife	661
Herndon Hall	663
R. L. Polk, Detroit, Michigan	667
Mrs. Josephine Polk Cumins	683
Dr. Mahlon N. Hutchinson and Wife	687
Governor and United States Senator Trusten Polk, of Missouri	695
Portrait of Washington	713
Mrs. Sabra Polk Joynes and Daughter, Mrs. Tabitha Joynes Laurence	721
Col. Otis W. Pollock, San Francisco	729

"A people which takes no pride in the noble achievements of remote ancestors will never achieve anything worthy to be remembered by remote descendants"—Lord Macaulay

INTRODUCTORY —

The first efforts toward the compilation of a history of the Polk family appear to have been made about 1824 by Colonel William Polk, of North Carolina, a grand-son of William and Margaret (Taylor) Polk who went from Pennsylvania to North Carolina and settled West of the Yadkin about 1750, or earlier, in what was then Anson County, now Mecklenburg In the spring of 1824 Colonel Polk, strongly impressed with the idea of preserving the family history, opened a correspondence with General William H Winder, of Baltimore, a kinsman by blood, who had married his cousin Gertrude, daughter of Judge William Polk of Maryland

After outlining his purpose to General Winder, Colonel Polk informed him of his intention to visit the North that year, and during such visit he would see and consult with him regarding the matter of the preparation of a history of the family To this proposition General Winder heartily acceded, the various members of the family in Maryland and Delaware also evincing a lively interest in the matter This initial movement, however, was greatly retarded by the death of General Winder, which event occurred on May 24, 1824, in the forty-ninth year of his age, and shortly before Colonel Polk's contemplated visit

Among those who also took an active and enthusiastic interest in the proposed history was Josiah F Polk, Chief Clerk to the Second Auditor of the Treasury, and later Chief Clerk of a division of the State Department at Washington Josiah was a native of Somerset County, Maryland, the locality in which Robert and Magdalen Polk, the immigrants, settled and he had a large acquaintance with the various branches of the family.

After the death of General Winder in 1824, the members of his family, together with Josiah F Polk, set about accumulating what data they could find, and while so engaged in 1825 .... ashington and .... Josiah and others interested in the matter of the family history giving them such data as he possessed about his particular branch after their emigration from near Carlisle, Pa., to North Carolina. This work of collecting data was still in progress but unfinished at the time James K. Polk was elected President in 1844. After this event the work was invested with additional interest, Bishop Leonidas Polk, of Louisiana, a son of Colonel William Polk, and Col. Wm. H. Winder, of Philadelphia, a son of General Wm. H. Winder taking an active part in the accumulation of data, as did, also, the President. The original purpose of Colonel William Polk and the early projectors of the enterprise seems to have been a complete history of all the branches of the Polk family. As a result of their accumulation of data, a finely engraved "tree" of the descendants of John Polk (eldest son of Robert and Magdalen), including all the southern Polks, was published in 1849.

Further work in the matter appears to have abated then, so far as the southern Polks were concerned, but Josiah F. Polk and other members of the Maryland branch continued for some years longer to gather data. Josiah was the most active of the Maryland branch in the matter of securing data for a full history, but after his death the scheme again fell into abeyance.

Shortly before the Civil War Bishop Polk renewed his efforts in the matter, applying for assistance to Colonel Wm. T. G. Polk, of Princess Anne, Md. The latter, born and residing all his life in Somerset County, was peculiarly qualified for the duty of assisting Bishop Polk, and set about the accumulation of facts to send to him. The Civil War coming on shortly after, before Colonel Polk could forward his data to the Bishop, it was never sent, and was finally lost by the burning of Colonel Polk's house, in which the entire contents were consumed. Bishop Polk, entering the Confederate army at the beginning of the war, rose to the rank of Lieutenant General and was killed by a cannon shot at Pine Mountain, Georgia, June 14, 1864.

Nothing more was done in the matter of a family history until 1873, when the present writer had occasion to visit

Washington City on official business. Having business with the Second Auditor of the Post Office Department, Hon. J. Bozman Kerr, he called on that gentleman. Upon introduction to Mr. Kerr, who at one time (1849 to 1851) represented the Princess Anne District in Congress, the latter inquired: "What branch of the Polk family do you belong to?" In reply, the writer stated that all he knew of his family was that his grand-father, Ephraim Polk 3d, a native of Sussex County Delaware, served during the Revolutionary War in a Philadelphia regiment commanded by Colonel Wm Wills. That after the war Ephraim 3d went back home, was married in 1792, and in the fall of 1793, during Wayne's campaign against the Indians, emigrated to Kentucky.

In reply Mr Kerr stated that all the Polk's in the United States sprang from Robert and Magdalen Polk, who settled in Maryland about 1660 or a little later, that he knew a great number of them, and by writing to Col Wm T G Polk of Princess Anne, who for many years was Clerk of the Court at that place, much interesting history of the family could be learned.

Mr Kerr later wrote out and mailed to the writer an interesting sketch of the Polks of Maryland, and of the contemporary history of their time, in which it was shown that the ancestors of Henry Clay had first settled in Somerset County later emigrating to Virginia. It was also pointed out by Mr Kerr as a striking coincidence that, at that early day in Somerset County, the Polks were known as a "Democratic" and the Clays as a 'Whig' family, and further, that at a future time, there should contend for the Presidency of the United States two men from these respective Somerset County families.

Acting on the suggestion of Mr Kerr, and desirous of learning more about the Polk family, the writer opened a correspondence with Colonel Wm T G Polk and other members of the family in Maryland and Delaware, from whom he received much information. To Colonel Wm T G Polk, particularly is he indebted for the greater part of the facts here in .... children, he .... he history of the family, not only from personal acquaintance and association for years with many of its members, but also because of his long official charge of the county records. This correspondence with Colonel Polk was kept up until his death, during which he was prompt and indefatigable in assistance with valuable data.

A correspondence was also opened with Mrs Aurelia W Townsend, of Oyster Bay Long Island, who furnished much matter concerning the Maryland branches, that had been collected by her family, the Winders with Mrs Lucy E Polk, of Warrenton, North Carolina, widow of Col Wm H Polk, of Tennessee brother of James K Polk, with Hon Horace M Polk, of Bolivar, Tennessee, with Major Allen J. Polk, of Helena, Arkansas, with John P R Polk, of Wilmington, Del, with Daniel Polk, of Denver, Colorado, formerly of Shelby County, Kentucky, with Judge William Polk and Judge Alfred Polk, of Texas, and Chas I Polk and C G Polk, of Memphis, Tennessee, with Jas V Polk, Beaumont, Tex, Col Geo W Polk, of San Antonio, and various other Polks in California, Missouri, Illinois, Indiana, and other western states Many of the latter descended from "Charles Polk, the Indian trader," whose son, Capt Charles Polk and family, of Frederick County, Maryland, descended the Ohio to Louisville in 1780 Some of the latter afterwards went to Indiana between 1800 and 1810—and were members of the first Constitutional Convention of that State territorial officers and Indian fighters under Harrison, at Tippecanoe and on other fields

To Mrs Wm H Polk Hon Horace M Polk, and Major Allen J Polk, (since deceased) was the writer indebted for much data concerning the southern branch of the family Major Allen J Polk, particularly, evinced the deepest interest in the family history, and gave great assistance in the preparation of data. He was a courtly, educated, highly intelligent gentleman, a Chesterfield in manners, and charmed all with whom he came in contact Much credit is also due to Col George W Polk, of San Antonio, Texas, for a full and careful arrangement of data regarding the southern branch of the family From these various sources, during a period of more or less active investigation for thirty-eight years, the writer accumulated the data from which he now essays the publication of a family history; a work begun by Colonel William Polk and others in 1824, renewed at different periods, but never completed. In so long a time many members of the family have passed away, including many valuable sources of information, and in that way much has been lost. Many others have come onto the stage of life whose names must be added to the family rolls.

In explanation of his own long delay, or apparent dilatoriness in completing the work begun by him in 1873, the writer will state that in April, 1876, he emigrated to the Southwest, continuing there three years and returning to Kentucky. During that period of absence his work on the history rested. Engaging next in active journalism which occupied all his attention for a period of many years, he had no time to take up again the history with a view of finishing it.

Among those deeply interested in the work, and most urgent for its completion was the late Jefferson Scott Polk, of Des Moines, Iowa, a Kentuckian by birth and grandson of Ephraim Polk 3rd, who emigrated from Delaware to Kentucky in 1793. He manifested from the first a deep interest in the matter, and when the writer suspended the work for a time, he took it up and applied himself to the further collection of matter, accumulating much before his death. A lawyer by profession, and a man of great business capacity, at his death in 1907 he was accounted a multi-millionaire. Aided by the writer, he endeavored to complete a history of the family, and among the last requests to his children was one to the effect that the history be completed. In accordance with that wish, the present writer resumed the work and herewith presents the result of his labors in that direction at various periods between 1873 and the present time. That it lacks many names that ought to be recorded, is unquestionable. That, however, is due to the lack of interest shown by some and the dilatoriness of others in furnishing data asked for.

Such a history should appeal to the just pride of every one descended from Robert and Magdalen Polk. In their descendants they have left .... need be ashamed. A family t....... , ... list of statesmen soldiers, and men prominent in all walks of life, men who have made their mark and left their impress on their day and generation. Of virile Scotch-Irish blood, from the ancient roof-tree in Maryland they have gone forth into every section of the country, in every place taking leading parts in the concerns of their fellowmen. Their dominant racial characteristics have found expression in various prominent forms of public recognition. Such a book will be a memorial that can be handed down to future generations of the family, growing more valuable and more highly appreciated as time passes.

Realizing the uncertainty of life, doubtful as to whether any other member of the family might feel inclined to finish the work before he, also is called to join the "great majority," remembering the inscription "*Tempus edax rerum*," on the face of the old clock brought by Robert and Magdalen from Ireland and still ticking off in Maryland the seconds that go to make up centuries, and aware that Time might also consume him within a short time, the writer has sought to finish his task as soon as possible, leaving to those who may come after him the correction of any mistakes discovered. He has laid the foundation and now commits to future generations of the family the work of extending the history on through the coming years.

WILLIAM HARRISON POLK,

Lexington, Kentucky,
November 28, 1912.

MAP OF MARYLAND, DELAWARE, PENNSYLVANIA AND WEST NEW JERSEY.

POLK FAMILY AND KINSMEN.

CHAPTER I.

GENESIS OF THE POLK FAMILY.

Whether or not the biblical account of the origin of man, or the scientific claim that he came by progressive evolution from a protoplasm be true, can make little difference to most people concerned in the activities of the human family. The never ending procession that is constantly coming out of the shadows of the Past brings no proof as to where or whence it started. They can only say, "We are here," and so with reference to present human families. They are here, and but few of them know their genesis. Excepting the Jewish accounts of their origin, as set forth in the Old Testament, the human race has kept little record of its lines of descent. Out the darkness of the Middle Ages have come accounts of the origin and descent of some of the leading characters that have shaped the world's events, but little has been handed down concerning the family genesis of the greater masses of the peoples of various nations.

The history of the Polk family is traceable back into what is called the Dark Ages, when the progress of civilization was arrested and obscured for several centuries by a cloud of war and destruction, evoked by superstition. From members of the family in Ireland and Scotland, and from official records in Maryland, have come down to us the Polk family history, beginning in the year 1053, during the reign of Edward the Confessor. "Fulbert the Saxon," the first recorded progenitor of the family, had come over to England before Harold was overthrown at Hastings by William the Conqueror. He is said to have been Chamberlain to the latter, and one of his beneficiaries.

From British genealogical sources, and from descendants of Fulbert in Scotland and Ireland, we obtain the pedigree down to the emigration of Robert Bruce Polk, immediately to America. From official records of Maryland and Delaware, and from family documents, this history of the family has been continued down to the present. We thus have presented a view of the family history during a period of 858 years, a length of retrospect possessed by but few families in America.

Fulbert the Saxon, a native of Normandy, in France was an uncle of Heloise, whose love of Abelard, and its finale of sorrow constitute one of the most pathetic human stories of the Middle Ages. As stated above, he was Chamberlain to William the Conqueror. He accompanied him to England and was engaged with him in the battle of Hastings (1066). Shortly after he received from William a large grant of land in Scotland, which became known later as the Barony of Pollok.

SCOTCH AND IRISH HISTORY OF FAMILY.

A. D. 1073

In the reign of King David 1st, the vast feudal barony of Pollok, in Renfrewshire, was held by "Fulbert the Saxon," a great noble and "Territorial King," who had come from Normandy, France, to England as Chamberlain of William the Conqueror.

DIED 1153

Fulbert died in 1153, at the beginning of the reign of Malcolm 4th, and was succeeded by his son Petrus.

PETRUS

The son of Fulbert (in 1153) succeeded his father. Petrus assumed as a surname, (which at that time only came to be used) instead of a patronymic, the name of his great hereditary lands of Pollok. The Lord Baron Pollok of this feudal kingdom, was a man of great eminence in his time, and a benefactor of the Monastery of Paisley, which donation was confirmed by Jocelme, Bishop of Glasgow, who died A. D. 1190. Petrus was "a law unto himself," and equalled the Sovereign in wealth, rank and power. He was the ancestor of many brave warriors and Crusade Knights who joined in the mighty struggle of Europe during the eleventh and twelfth centuries, to free the Holy Sepulchre from the grasp of the Moslem.

Petrus de Pollok was greatly distinguished for "valor in arms and prowess in the chase" and his exploits in them were the subject of many minstrel lays. His next brother, Helias, gave to the same Monastery the church of Mears, the next parish to eastward.

Besides the vast estates in Renfrewshire, the chevron of which barony is still borne on the shield of arms of the Prince of Wales, he held the great barony of Rothes in Aberdeenshire, which he gave to his only daughter, Mauricle, who married the celebrated Sir Norman de Lesley. Mauricle de Rothes was the ancestress of the great Earls of Rothes and Lords of Lesley. The 8th Earl of Rothes was constituted after the Restoration Marquis of Ballenbriech, Duke de Rothes, President of the Council and Lord High Chancellor of Scotland.

The "State Records" show that many inter-marriages have taken place between the Lesleys, Polloks and Royal Stuarts.

Sir John Pollok Leslie (Knight) was Receiver General to King James 4th, and married a grand-daughter of that Monarch.

On the death of Petrus de Pollok, his ancient patrimonial estates of Pollok being settled on heirs male, passed to his brother Robert de Pollok (1175), and it is noticeable how the name of Robert has been handed down from father to son to the present generation.

Robert 1st was witness in the donation of the Kirks of Strathgry and Ninerwick, by Walter, founder of the Monastery of Paisley in the beginning of the reign of William the Lion. He is also witness in several of the Charters of Allen, the son of Walter. Robert de Pollok 1st, was succeeded by his son Robert 2d.

ROBERT DE POLLOK 2d

Contemporary with Alexander 2d (A D 1214) mortified a yearly rent to the same Monastery for the soul of Petrus de Pollok, and Robert, son of Fulbert, his father. Alexander 2d, reigned from 1214 to 1249, and was succeeded by his son Th m t-

THOMAS DE POLLOK

Thomas de Pollok was witness to sundry charters of donation to the Abbey of Paisley (A. D. 1249). He was contemporary with Alexander 2d and Alexander 3d of Scotland Alexander 3d reigned from 1249 to 1286. Thomas was succeeded by his son Petrus de Pollok 2d.

PETRUS DE POLLOK 2d.

Was one of the persons of rank who, in A D. 1296, gave a forced submission to Edward 1st of England, in the bond known as the "Ragman's Roll" He was succeeded by his son Robertus.

ROBERTUS DE POLLOK

Married Agnes, daughter of Sir John Maxwell, Lord of Caerlaverok and was succeeded by his son John

JOHN DE POLLOK

Who, in A D 1372 obtained from his grandfather, the said John, Lord Maxwell, a charter of certain lands, dated at Caerlaverok, was succeeded by his son Brucii or Brucis de Pollok

BRUCII DE POLLOK.

Left a son John de Pollok

JOHN DE POLLOK

Is designated in a charter by James 2d of Scotland, of date 12th December, A D 1439, as "Nobilis Sir Johannes de Pollok, *filius et heires* Brucii de Pollok" He fought on Queen Mary's side at the battle of Langside, for which he was forfeited His son—

JOHN DE POLLOK

Was killed at the faction fight of Lockerbie (in 1593), when assisting his kinsman, Lord Maxwell, against the Laird of John's Stone. From this (A. D. 1439) famous noble sprang the illustrious line of Pollok of that ilk. His successor was—

CHARLES DE POLLOK

Of that ilk. John de Pollok last mentioned had another son besides Charles. This other son was—

ROBERT DE POLLOK

Who became Sir Robert de Pollok of Ireland, and who received from King James 2d (about 1440) the great land grant of "Vetus Scotia," or "New Scotland," as Ireland was then called. This Sir Robert's eldest son, Sir John, inherited the hereditary estates in Old Scotland. Sir Robert's younger son, Robert, inherited the estates in Ireland, and became Sir Robert

SIR ROBERT DE POLLOK (2d)

Of Ireland, inherited the estates in Ireland and became the founder of the family in Ireland (where the name to this day is often spelled and pronounced P-o-l-k, as of one syllable, by the natives) and whose American descendants, the Polks, still preserve the 'lineal memorial' of their noble and knightly ancestors.

A. D. 1640

In 1640, Sir Robert of Ireland joined the Scotch Convenanters whose Commander-in-Chief and Governor of Dunbarton Castle was a relation, General Sir Alexander Leslie, one of the most famous soldiers of his time.

1646

In 1646, Sir George Maxwell, of the Nether Pollok, was married to Lady Annabella Stuart, lineal descendant of King Robert 3d, and their granddaughter Annabella, married her cousin, Sir Robert Pollok of Upper Pollok, grand nephew of Sir Robert of Ireland, whose nephew, Ezekiel Stuart married Debora Annerly.

Sir Robert Pollok was succeeded by his son, Thomas Pollok. **This Sir Robert also had a second son, Robert Bruce Pollok.** Thomas, eldest son of Sir Robert 2d, succeeded to the Irish estates, located on Lough Neagh, not far from Londonderry.

CHAPTER II.

ROBERT BRUCE POLLOK.

Robert Bruce Pollok, second son of Sir Robert 2d of Ireland, was a Captain in Col Porter's Regiment, which served under Cromwell. Porter married Magdalen Tasker, youngest of the two children of Col Tasker, a distinguished Chancellor of Ireland, whose seat was "Castle Hill," near the village of Ballindrate, commanding a view of the river Dale 'Moneen," another estate belonging to Col. Tasker, lying in the parish of Liftord, near Strabane, on the river Foyle, consisted of six hundred acres These he divided between his two children, Barbara Keys, wife of Capt John Keys, and Magdalen Magdalen first married Col Porter, who died not long afterward Col Porter died without issue by Magdalen and she next married Robert Bruce Polk (Pollok) a Captain in his regiment and an intimate friend, it is said

Magdalen was related to the Countess of Mornington and her sister Prudence, aunts to the Duke of Wellington.

Capt Robert Bruce Polk died (1703-4) as shown by his will of date May 6, 1699 probated June 5, 1703-4, on record at Annapolis, Anne Arundel County, Md

Before the American Revolution a double record was kept of all wills, one in the county of residence of decedents, and another in the office of the Chief Commissary" (Clerk) of the Colony, at its capital The will of Magdalen, dated 1726 is of record in Somerset County, Maryland, but not that of her husband, Capt Robert Bruce Polk Why the latter does not also appear on the records of Somerset County, is not certainly known To this absence (the document of record at Annapolis having only been discovered within a few years past) was no doubt due the long prevalent opinion that Capt Robt. Bruce Polk did not accompany his family to America but died in Ireland Later and fuller investigation cleared up this doubtful point by the discovery of his will on file at Annapolis and of land grants to him from Lord Baltimore (the first, of which was Polk's Folly,') and other documents

It is indisputable now, in the light of these modern discoveries, that Capt. Robert Bruce Polk came with his family to Maryland, near about 1672, that they landed from a ship at "Damn Quarter" (now called Dame's Quarter) and planted their new home in that locality, between Manokin and Nanticoke rivers, and near the junction of those streams with Chesapeake Bay. Here they occupied adjoining tracts of land for which they later acquired patents from Lord Baltimore. Just how many children Robert and Magdalen had when they came to America is not certainly known. Evidently a portion of them, the first five, were born in Ireland. According to latest records, their children were ¹John, ²William, ³Ephraim, ⁴James, ⁵Robert, ⁶David, ⁷Joseph, ⁸Martha, and ⁹Anne. That they had a son David was not known until Capt. Robert's will was found a few years ago on file at Annapolis, wherein he is mentioned. Judging from various circumstances, Joseph was the youngest son.

THE KEYS FAMILY

Barbara the eldest daughter of Col. Tasker, married Capt. John Keys, who was also an officer in Col. Porter's regiment and an intimate friend of Capt. Pollok. Some of Barbara's descendants still own a part of the ancestral estates formerly called "Moneen Hall" and "Broomfield Castle." The old building of the latter falling into decay, a new one called "Castle Keys" was erected by Lieutenant Tasker Keys, about 1780 and hence the change of name to the latter designation. Old Broomfield was among the most interesting seats in Ireland, according to a statement to the writer by a gentleman who was born and reared near it. Capt. John Keys and wife went with the British army to India, where he accumulated a large fortune. On their return to Ireland they again occupied their ancestral estates and later Barbara purchased from Joseph Polk of Maryland, Magdalen's youngest son, and devisee, the estate of "Moneen" near Strabane.

Magdalen Tasker, it is said, was of French descent, and inherited in m... ... ... incorrectly ... ... pers of record in Maryland, the difference in name evidently caused by careless entries on the part of court clerks and scribes executing official papers. This estate is described in Magdalen's will as "lying in the Kingdom of Ireland, in the Barony of Raphoe, the County of Donegal and the Parish of Lifford."

During the years 1874 to 1877 while the writer was actively engaged in the collection of data for this history of the Polk family, he wrote to the post-master at Strabane, who gave him the names of distant kinsmen in that neighborhood. These were also written to for information concerning the family. In reply he received answers from several Irish kinsmen by the names of Pollok, Polk and Keys. He also wrote to Scotland receiving in reply a letter from Andrew Pollok, proprietor of the ancient Scottish homestead. Under date of "Moorhouse," Eaglesham, Scotland, 13th March 1876, Andrew Pollok, wrote: I am a cousin of the author of "The Course of Time," who was born on the farm I now occupy, and which has been traditionally possessed by our family for five hundred years.

I have also looked over Crawford's History of Renfrewshire, in which a detailed account of the family of Pollok of that ilk is given, tracing it back to the beginning of the 12th Century, but after all this I have not been able to find any mention of how the Boar was slain which gave rise to the Pollok Crest."

The fact is indisputable however from authentic records derived from both Ireland and Scotland, that Sir John de Pollok, owner of the estates of Pollok, in Scotland, a part of which Andrew Pollok occupied at the time he wrote, had a son Charles, who inherited the Scotch estates under the then existing English law of primogeniture. Also, that Robert de Pollok, a younger brother of Charles, received (about 1440) from James 2d, a large grant in Ireland of lands forfeited or escheated to the Crown by reason of the warlike acts of the Irish under their various leaders. And this Sir Robert of Ireland had a son, **Sir Robert de Pollok 2d,** who became the founder of the family in Ireland and had sons Thomas and Robert Bruce Pollok, the latter being the emigrant to Maryland during the proprietorship of Lord Baltimore.

CHAPTER III.

DATA FROM IRELAND

A very interesting letter concerning the family, was of date Oct 17, 1877, to the author, from John Keys, sixth in descent from Captain John Keys and Barbara Tasker. In this letter, Mr. Keys says, "My father requests me to answer your very welcome letter, he giving me all the information he could. I am sorry I did not get your letter before my grandfather, John Keys, died. He was an interesting old fellow and knew a great length back. He was over in your country twice and knew how to enjoy himself. I often think of the tales he used to tell me about his father, Lieutenant Tasker Keys.

I am not able to give you much information about Colonel Tasker. He was a Chancellor of Ireland and a man much renowned for wealth and honour. His word of command was "Death or Liberty." He distinguished himself in many ways—command, horsemanship, valour. He always rode a white horse, and died after the "Derry Spree." His life was well spent. Then he had just the two daughters, Barbara and Magdalen. It is said they were very good songsters, having good voices.

Barbara, the eldest got married to Captain John Keys, who was under Colonel Tasker. She had only one of a family and that was a son Tasker, after her own name, which exists in our family since. Magdalen, the younger, was married to Colonel Porter. He died some time before the "Derry Spree." Then she ran off with one Polk, who was a companion or friend to Colonel Porter. The Porters were a strong connection in this country at that time. It appears that the Porters threatened Polk, and she having no family to Col Porter, his family obtained most of the property in the estate of "Moneen." There is only one of that family alive. He is now out in your country. He was over here last fall and gained a great lawsuit, which will help him. He claims connection to our family

There is only one Pollok connected with our family at present. He is married to a first cousin of father's, but there are several others at a distance that I know. They are all Presbyterians. The Keys are all Protestants. There are none of the old books with marriages and births of that far back to be found. They were all burned. I can only furnish you with dates five generations back, from what my grandmother tells me. I will go as near as I can to the others. I mean the two first.

BIRTHS AND DEATHS IN KEYS FAMILY.

1—Capt. John Keys, born about 1640, died about 1725

2—Tasker Keys (son of John) born about 1682, died about 1752.

3—William Keys (son of Tasker) born 1712, died 1793

4—Lieutenant Tasker Keys (son of William) born 1745, died 1840

5—John Keys (son of Lieut. Tasker) born 1790, died 1874

6—Tasker Keys, (son of John) born 1827, alive yet

7—John Keys, (son of Tasker) born 1853, alive yet

Lieutenant Tasker Keys was married to Jane Riddle, sister to Judge Riddle, who died out in your country. Lieutenant Tasker had one brother, Dr. Roger Keys, who died in India, and great legacies came home. He sent for two of his brothers' daughters, as there were four of them, Lieutenant Tasker being their father.

As soon as they arrived the Doctor held a party of officers of the army. They were asked to sing and sang "Erin-go-bra." So they got married at once, one to Capt. Munroe and the other to Capt. Taylor. The remaining two married also, one to Attorney Keys, of Enniskillen, the other to a Mr. Snell, a merchant. The two latter are alive yet.

Lieutenant Tasker Keys was Grand Master of the Orangemen here in that society. He squandered and mortgaged all the property, which left a knot unloosed ever since. He came through several battles, the most remarkable being on Berry Hill, in County Tyrone between the Protestants and the Catholics. He put them to flight after a long fight. He rode a King William and fell off and broke a leg. It grew crooked, and when he saw that he went directly to the cow-house, put it behind a stake, and broke it over again. He said he wouldn't walk on a bandy leg. So it grew straight. Lieutenant Tasker was a great man for building. He built two fine houses. One of them is the largest castle in our parish, called Broomfield Castle. People at a distance call it Castle Keys.

John Keys, the only son, was married to Martha Rodgers, who is still alive. When they were in the church, about to be married, his father, Lieutenant Tasker, not satisfied with the match, entered the church with a good stick and dispersed the wedding party in different directions. The Rector got out of a window and did not appear until the following Sunday. The bride's brother being Curate of the same church married them the next day. From them are Robert, Tasker, Roger, Jane and Margaret. Robert is married to Anne Atchison, they have two boys and two girls. The eldest boy Robert, is Dispensary Doctor of this parish. Catherine is married to Dr. J. Matthews. Thomas and Sarah Anne are the remaining two. Tasker, my father, married Jane Weir a very strong connection in this parish. I am the eldest, John; then come Maggie, James, Tasker, Minnie, Martha, Rebecca, Roger. Roger Keys is a doctor in Philadelphia. He has been married twice. He has six of a family, four sons and two daughters. Margaret and Jane are in New York City. Margaret is a widow, her husband's name was Hannaman. She has no family. Jane is single.

I forgot to mention that Lieutenant Tasker was married secondly to Honoria Keys, no family by her. She died in 1867. I took a tour to Dublin Castle to see if I could find anything worth mentioning, but all the old books were destroyed."

The foregoing letter is a little lengthy, but is here given in extenso in order to show who were the descendants of Barbara, the only sister of Magdalen Polk. From the recital regarding Lieutenant Tasker Keys, it appears that he was somewhat of a "wild Irishman," irascible, impetuous, fearless and obstinate, qualities which commonly are l fine to lead in battle, or to head a procession of Orangemen.

Another letter to the author, dated Broomfield, Sept. 1, 1877, from Tasker Keys, says: "Hugh McMenamin, postmaster of the Lifford office, gave me a letter from you dated June 11, 1875, asking him for information about "Moneen" My name is Tasker Keys, son of John Crayton Keys, and grandson to Lieutenant Tasker Keys, who was a great grandson of Capt. John Keys whose wife was daughter to Colonel Tasker and sister to Magdalen, who married Colonel Porter, and next a Mr Pollock

I do not know anything about that family, but would like to know from you There is none of them in this vicinity I am the only member of the old stock in this neighborhood now "Moneen" is an estate which is in the parish of Lifford It was divided between those whom I have mentioned (Barbara and Magdalen), and I hold part of it yet All the old dwellings are down The house Colonel Tasker lived in is near a little village called Ballindrate The name of his residence was "Castle Hill," commanding a view of the river Dale From him I hold that renowned name, Tasker "Moneen" in size is about 600 Cunningham acres

I am sorry to say they all lived too fast. For instance, my grandfather, Lieutenant Tasker Keys, was grandmaster of the Orangemen He mortgaged the property and married secondly, and bound her a jointure that was a heavy yoke on our family I have eight of a family, four boys and four girls The two eldest boys intend to visit your country shortly, as I have a great number of friends out there '

CHAPTER IV.

BROOMFIELD CASTLE AND MONEEN.

When Col Tasker, of Donegal County, Ireland, died, he was possessed of two fine estates lying near the river Foyle, above Londonderry—"Broomfield Castle" and "Moneen Hall." The first was a famous estate, and, according to a statement to the writer by one who was born near it, had on it "one of the finest old castles in Ireland." At his death Col Tasker devised Bloomfield to his eldest daughter Barbara and Moneen to Magdalen they being his only two children it is said

As stated by one of the Keys family to the author in 1874 "Moneen embraced six hundred Cunningham acres," with a fine mansion on it It lay close to the little village of Strabane, with the postmaster of which place, Hugh McMenamin, the author also corresponded in 1874, and from whom he derived interesting facts regarding Col. Tasker's two estates

At the same time, by reason of information derived from Postmaster McMenamin the author opened correspondence with some of the Pollocks and Keys still resident in Donegal and retaining parts of the old estates From them he also derived much interesting data respecting the family before Robert and Magdalen emigrated to Maryland and founded the Polk family of America

In their correspondence with this writer, some of the Keys and Pollocks, who still retained portions of the estates named, told of the ups and downs of their ancestors One of these, Lieutenant Tasker Keys Grand Master of the Orange men of Ireland, crippled by the fall of his horse at the battle of Berry Hill, entered the church where his daughter was about to be married to a man whom he did not approve, and with a stick compelled the parson who was about to perform the ceremony to jump out a window. The Lieutenant the writer said, also "bound a heavy jointure on the estate." in favor of his wife which s of the family. The ved too fast, losing most of their property." This was particularly true of the Keys branch, descended from Capt John Keys of the British Army, a distinguished officer of the service in India, who married Barbara, the eldest daughter of Col. Tasker, and sister of Magdalen Polk, wife of Capt Robert Bruce Polk

The long established tradition in the Polk family is, that after the death of Magdalen Polk in 1727. leaving her estate of "Moneen" in Ireland, to her youngest son Joseph, the latter returned to that country, sold the property to his Aunt Barbara Keys, and came back to America. How long Joseph remained in Ireland, we know not Possibly ten or twelve years According to Col Wm T G. Polk, his name did not appear on the records of Somerset County for some years after the probate of his mother's will in 1727

Joseph was doubtless married to Miss Wright, daughter of Thomas Wright of Somerset, some years before his mother's death, and had children by her Born about 1681, he would have been about 46 years old at the time his mother died. It is quite likely that his wife and all the children by her accompanied him to Ireland and continued for some years at "Moneen" before the "emigration fever" again attacked him His reappearance in Maryland was about 1739-40, for the Dorchester records show that on Jan 21st of the latter year John Handy, of Somerset County, deeded to Joseph Pollock of the same County, planter, 300 acres of land called 'Little Goshen," in Dorchester County To this purchase Joseph undoubtedly moved and there died in 1751, aged about seventy years

On Nov 9, 1742, Joseph Pollock asked the Court to appoint processioners to re-establish or mark the bounds of "Little Goshen," which was done Joseph's will is dated Sept 12, 1751, and was probated June 10th, 1752, so he must have died a short time before the document was put to record in Dorchester In his will he mentions his children as Robert Zephaniah, James and Ann He also requests that Robert "dwell with his 'mother-in-law' (stepmother?) till he arrives at the age of 18 years, or till the day of her marriage"

This indicates that Robert was by a former wife, and possibly also Ann whom he calls his 'eldest daughter"

James he calls his "youngest son," evidently by his second wife Ann born about 1740-41, may also have been the eldest child by his second wife.

JOHN POLK HERE IN 1680.

There is documentary evidence that one John Polke the son of Robert and Magdalen, was here in 1680, the same year that Hottens Register records the presence of "James Poke" and family at St Michaels, Barbadoes

In a letter to the writer, of date October 31, 1874, Col Wm T. G Polk says

'Since I last wrote to you I have discovered an entry where John Polke entered the ear marks of his cattle to be recorded, on the 8th of September, 1680. This is the earliest record I can find relating to the Polks

I agree with you that Robert, Sr , was a stern old Covenanter and that he instilled his principles and religion into his children, Robert alone excepted, who looks, from reading the records, like he was somewhat obstreperous William my ancestor, has transmitted his Presbyterian principles to his posterity to this day Every male of his line, so far as I know, without an exception of his numerous posterity, has either been a member of that church or manifested a preference for it Some of the females marrying into other denominations have gone with their husbands, but quite as many have carried their husbands with them I can count seven who have been, or now are, ruling elders Five of them, my grandfather and one of his brothers, my great grandfather, myself and one of my brothers, in a church that was fully organized as appears by authentic records, in 1705, and tradition says it was organized twenty or twenty-five years before that time by Reverend Frances McKeemie Another one in the old Rehoboth Presbyterian church also organized by McKeemie in this neighborhood which I have heard Dr Robert J Breckinridge say he believed to be the oldest Presbyterian church on this continent

I have examined the Register's office and can find no will of a Polk that will be of special use to you beyond the two you have those of Magdalen and Ium all others all relate to William and his posterity There can be no doubt that Joanna was the last wife of John Polk, Sr., and that she survived him I have shown that John was dead before March 10, 1708 Among the proceedings of the court begun and held on the 11th of August, 1708, it is recorded that 'the widow Polke brought into Court a servant" to be adjudged of his age, etc And the Clerk of that date, in making his index, calls her "Joanna Polke" Here we have the widow Joanna Polk transacting business in Court after John's death, and this fixes the point unless it can be shown that there was another person called the widow Joanna Polk about the time of John's death

I know nothing personally about that branch growing out of Daniel Polk, who was born in 1750 They were in Delaware It seems to me that some of those letters that were destroyed, said something about Senator John M Clayton, of Delaware being related to the Polks.

John Polk, son of Robert and Magdalen, died between October 8, 1707, and March 10, 1708, for on the former day he executed a deed to Alexander Hall, and "Joanna his now wife" joined with him, on the latter date his brother William was applying to be appointed guardian to his children William, John's son, died comparatively young, for he was a minor needing a guardian in 1708, and eighteen years afterward "Priscilla Polk, executrix of William Polk,' was prosecuting a suit to recover a debt, viz in 1726 and so he must have died before he was thirty-eight, probably before he was thirty-five His will is not recorded here, why, it is hard to say

William, the immigrant, my ancestor, died about January, 1740, aged about 79 His will is on record here James, as you know by his will, died about the beginning of 1727 As John must have been at least twenty-one in 1680, my ancestor William and his brother Ephraim over twenty-one in 1687, the immigrants at the time of James' death must have been between sixty and seventy years

Ephraim died before 1739, for in that year Charles Polk, his son, seem to have closed out his real estate in this county, making three deeds in the 16th of October of that year, be sides several others on other days. He conveyed to John Laws 'Long Delay' and "Golden Quarter,' and he and Patience, his wife, executed a deed to Joseph Polk, in which he recites the grant to Ephraim Polk for "Clonmell." And then to show that he had a full right to convey, says he is 'the son and lawful heir of said Ephraim." He doubtless sold out and removed to Sussex county, Delaware about 1740, and was the father of your great grandfather Ephraim 2d. for his name disappears from the record after that date

Robert and Joseph I cannot find out what became of them."

After this letter was written by Col Polk it was discovered that Robert, Jr, the immigrant, did leave male issue—David, Thomas, Daniel, William and Robert, the latter commanding the privateers 'Black Jake" and 'Montgomery" in the Revolution and being killed in action William, another one of his sons, was the father of Trusten Laws Polk. whose son, Wm Nutter Polk, was father of Governor Trusten Polk of Missouri Robert also had five daughters. Joseph probably settled in Delaware before he acquired any real estate here, and purchased there Robert, Jr's, children may have been daughters and the property have gone into other names Continuing Col Polk says

'I find the spelling of the name has been both ways down to the beginning of the present century Many of the deeds are written Pollock, and signed Polk, and vice versa Many years ago I saw a Scotchman who said he knew persons of the name in his native land The name on places of business would generally be spelled 'Pollock,' but would invariably be pronounced "Polk"

Col James Polk's brother Josiah had two sons. William and John but they removed with their mother, after their father's death, to the western part of this State I do not know whether they are alive. If they are, they are now old men, for they were both boys with me Col James Polk has a son James, another named Lucius and a third whose name I do not now recollect They reside in Baltimore Their father gathered up ... itive to the family I ha...

CHAPTER V.

WHEN THE IMMIGRANTS ARRIVED.

The question of what year Robert Bruce Polk and family reached America has often been discussed, but it has never been definitely settled. That it was some time between 1672 and 1680 admits of no doubt. According to Josiah F. Polk, "there is documentary proof that some of the Polks were in Maryland as early as 1672." Robert Bruce Polk did not, however, according to the records of the Maryland Land Office, receive a grant of land until March, 1687. Why he did not, and by what sort of title he held his place of abode for fifteen years before he was accorded a grant, does not appear.

One tradition handed down in the family is that they "came shortly after the siege of Londonderry." This cannot be correct, for that event did not take place until 1689, two years after Robert was granted "Polk's Folly" and "Polk's Lott," as appears by the Land Office list of grants.

Charles 2d died on February 6, 1685 and was succeeded by James 2d. The latter proved to be a most arbitrary and unpopular monarch, both at home and in the British colonies. By his direction unjust taxes were imposed on his subjects, and to escape his persecutions large numbers of them emigrated to America. Seeking to reduce the colonies to direct dependence on the Crown, James cancelled the Charter of Massachusetts and ignored that of Maryland granted to Lord Baltimore. During the first year of his reign a great number of Scotch, Irish and English emigrated to the American colonies. Over a thousand prisoners taken in Monmouth's Rebellion were sent to Virginia to be indentured as servants for years, but the latter design was not carried out and in this way Virginia received many useful citizens. The reign of James, however, was a brief one; in December 1688, he was compelled to abdicate.

During the reign of Charles 2d, the predecessor of James, the American colonies received their greatest accessions of population. Thousands who had become weary of Charles' oppressions turned their faces to the New World, hoping that by going beyond the Atlantic they could find some respite from the exactions of kingly power. This desire for emigration was rendered still stronger by the excessively arbitrary course of James during his short reign. Hence it was that, from 1660 to 1689—during the reigns of these two monarchs—the American colonies received tremendous accessions of the best and most virile blood of the British Kingdom.

In addition to voluntary emigrants who arrived during that period, there were also sent to the colonies, by the government, large numbers of political rebels, also serving men to be sold for a term of years, apprentices and single women. The better class of emigrants, beside the political rebels, was composed of persons of quality, freeholders and religious exiles. This stream of settlers continued to flow to American Colonies steadily from 1660 to 1700.

JAMES POKE OF BARBADOES.

A very great number of those who emigrated possibly the majority, came by the 'Southern Route' to the West Indies, touching at the Barbadoes, where many landed and remained for a number of years before coming on to the colonies. A careful and exact record was kept by the British officials of each person on the ship, the name of the vessel, where embarked, deaths, births, etc. In Hotten's highly interesting book "Our Early Emigrant Ancestors," published at New York in 1880, is given a list of emigrants who arrived in the American Colonies between the years 1600 and 1700. A great number of these, particularly during the reign of Charles 2d and James, came to St. Michaels, in the Barbadoes, and from thence to the Atlantic Colonies.

On page 440 of Hotten's collection, following the caption "A list of the inhabitants in and about the town of St. Michaels, Barbadoes, Anno Domini, 1680, with their children, hired servants, prentices, bought servants and negroes," is a lengthy list of names, persons residing here, most of whom, making it only a temporary abode.

In this list of residents "in and about St Michaels" appears the entry "James Poke and wife, 6 children 2 hired servants, and apprentices, 1 bought servant and 4 slaves"

Here we find the name of Polk written "Poke," at an unlooked for place in America, but on the direct line of travel and the commonly used one at that time. Assuming that this James married at the age of 21; allowing 13 years for the birth of his six children, then deducting these 34 years from 1680, when he was at St Michaels, it would put the date of his birth at about 1646, or near about the time of the reputed date of the birth of Robert Bruce Polk, as estimated by the Keys family in Ireland.

There is no discovered record to show when James Poke left Barbadoes, or that he ever did so, but the presumption is strong that he remained there but a few years, if that long, and then came on to Maryland. The strong inference that St Michaels was his abode but a short time, and that he came on and settled in Somerset county, Maryland, is borne out by documentary proof in the shape of a will of one James Polk, of record at Princess Anne. This will is dated November 8, 1726, and was probated May 11, 1727, on testimony of John Pollett and Mary Pollett, witnesses to the instrument. In this will James mentions eleven children, four boys and seven girls, and one yet unborn.

The will of Magdalen Polk, dated April 7, 1726, was probated March 20, 1727, and witnessed by David Polk, Wm Pollett and Magdalen Pollett. Both wills, therefore, were made and probated in the same years—1726 and 1727.

According to the records, Robert and Magdalen Polk had two daughters, Martha and Anne. Anne married Thos. Pollett and had issue William, Magdalen, John, Mary, and others. Some of these persons appear as witnesses to both wills, and this establishes the fact that Magdalen Polk and James Polk were nearly related, but how near? Was he a brother, or a son of Robert Bruce Polk? If the latter, he must have been an elder son coming first to Barbadoes, remaining there for a short period, and thence to Maryland to join the other members of his family. A clause in the will of James Polk of Somerset has suggested to some a doubt that he was a son of Robert and Magdalen, but the weight of evidence is to the effect that he was Robert Bruce Polk may have been born earlier than the Keys family estimated it. James' will, executed and probated in the same years that Magdalen's will was (1726-1727) has as witnesses to it several persons who testified to hers He also mentioned in it his Cousin Charles (Polk), the son and heir-at-law of Ephraim 1st, and his "Cousin Edward Roberts,' husband of Nancy, daughter of John and Joanna Polk.

The exact time of Robert and Magdalen Polks arrival in America is of minor importance, in view of the fact that it has been so nearly approximated by creditable evidence It is of record that John was in Maryland in 1680 that James was at St. Michaels, Barbadoes, in the same year, and it is but reasonable to assume that Robert and Magdalen were also here at the same time, and had arrived several years before, or about the period when Scotland and Ireland, under Charles 2d, were torn with dissensions by the tyrannical conduct of Lauderdale and the Duke of York Though prelacy had been abolished and the Presbyterian form of worship established soon after the Reformation, yet an exact compliance with the Episcopal forms was now enforced with such vigorous and severe penalties that the people rose in arms and put to death one of the principal bishops English soldiers were dispersed over the country and power was given to all commissioned officers to compel every one they met to take a prescribed oath, and instantly to shoot any person that refused It was just about this period of religious tyranny and oppression that Robert and Magdalen Polk came to Maryland to find an asylum from trouble and oppression in their native land

CHAPTER VI

"The Anglicanism which in England had a meaning," says Froude, "In Ireland was never more than an exotic, and until the new comers in the North of Ireland had introduced another spirit the church of Ireland had existed only to give point to the sarcasm of the Catholics." Even Irish Episcopacy had taken a certain Puritan and Evangelical tinge from its Presbyterian neighbor, which created a strong antipathy to everything that savored of sacerdotalism.

After the death of Cromwell and the accession of Charles II in 1660, there began a long period of difficulty and danger. Vindictive measures were at once instituted by Charles against all those who had been leading actors in the drama that brought the head of his father, Charles I, to the block. Many of the "Regicides," as were termed those who had been active in bringing about the death of Charles I, in order to escape the wrath of his son, fled to foreign parts, many coming to America and changing their names in order to conceal their indentity. The new parliament of 1661 consisted mostly of high churchmen and royalists. It restored ancient oppressive laws and instituted efficient measures to prevent even the smallest degree of toleration to all who refused conformance with the liturgy of the court. This state of unrest continued throughout the reign of Charles II, and in 1679 drove the people of Scotland into rebellion.

CHAPTER VII.

EMIGRATION OF THE POLKS

It was during this period, in the middle of the reign of Charles II that Capt Robert Bruce Polk and his family decided to emigrate to America in order to obtain immunity from further persecution at home, and the entire company which came in the ship with them consisted of persons who were coming to the New World for like reasons—the exercise of civil and religious liberty Such an asylum they found on the "Eastern Shore" of Maryland, lying between Chesapeake Bay and the Atlantic and in the Colony of Lord Baltimore who, though himself a Catholic, was a man of the most generous impulses and liberal views His colony was rapidly settled by not only emigrants from abroad but it also became an asylum for those who were driven out of New England by Puritan persecutions, and from Virginia by the tyrannical measures and impositions of the Established Church against all dissenters Many ministers were thrown into jail for preaching the Gospel

This sketch of the conditions and transactions that obtained, especially in Ireland, between the settlement of Ulster from Scotland and the middle of the reign of Charles II, is here given in order that the reader may have some conception of the reasons which induced Robert Bruce Polk and his family to emigrate to America Here they planted their rooftree; and here they found that which they sought—civil and religious freedom

As early as 1668 we hear of a Presbyterian minister from Ireland at work in Maryland, but the name of this avant courier of that faith is lost In 1683, a few years after the coming of Robert Bruce Polk and family, Rev Francis Mackeemie arrived from County Donegal, Ireland—the same locality from which came the Polks, and he organized the first group of Presbyterian churches in America Of these, several points on the Eastern Shore. In one of this group Robert Bruce Polk and family deposited their membership, and for 225 years, almost without interruption, numerous individuals of the family have been members and some of them ruling elders.

FIRST CHURCHES ON EASTERN SHORE.

Under date of August 24, 1875, Col. Wm. T G Polk continues his interesting narrative regarding the family as follows

"Taking Princess Anne as the center, a radius of eighteen miles would describe a circle in which would be included four or five Presbyterian churches which the records of our county clearly show were fully organized before 1705 The general impression is they were planted in the decade between 1639 and 1690, and within a few years of each other by Reverend Francis McKeemie Of this family of churches Dr Robert J Breckinridge thought Rehoboth was first planted, but it was long before conceded by general consent The one at this place is called 'Manokin Church,' from the stream on which it stands.

It is not probable that Robert and Magdalen worshipped at Rehoboth, for it is fifteen miles east of this place, and Pidgeon House neighborhood is fifteen or eighteen miles west So they would be thirty odd miles distant, which would have made it inconvenient for them to attend There is no certain evidence, documentary or traditional, that will show they were members of any church, that I know of But the presumption is violent that they were members of the Manokin church and worshipped at this place

In the first place, the old Bible which was destroyed in my brother's house about thirty years ago, which tradition says was brought by them from Ireland, and was used by them then, and which was hid by them during the persecution that prevailed from the Restoration to the Revolution, in a hollow tree, bore the marks of being wet frequently This would indicate that they were of a religious turn of mind. And, besides, this turn seems to have been impressed upon their children The records of the Manokin church are lost before

1746, but in that year James Polk appears as a ruling elder in the church and continued a prominent and active one to the end of his life. A few years after James' son William appears as a ruling elder, and contemporary with him William's Cousin Benjamin, and about the same time Gilliss, the brother of Judge Polk and so on down to this generation. I have never known a Polk descended from William and remaining in this County, except one, but who was a decided Presbyterian. Hence, I infer that Robert Polk and his wife, Magdalen were not only Presbyterians and members of the Manokin Church, but that they were very decided and have instilled that form of religious faith to the remotest generation, so far as their son William was concerned.

I have no doubt that if the records of the Manokin church could be found, they would appear as active in promoting the interest of the church from its planting to 1744, as they have been from 1744 to 1873. There has been scarcely a time in those 129 years that the family has not furnished one or more ruling elders to this church.

There is nothing strange in the fact that Covenanters should settle in Lord Baltimore's Colony. Although he was a strict Catholic himself, he was a very liberal man toward the religious views of others. He passed laws protecting all denominations, in consequence of which the Western Peninsula of this state was settled almost entirely by Romanists, and it is still the prevailing creed. This Eastern Peninsula was settled entirely by Protestants and that creed still prevails to such an extent that I do not believe there is a Catholic family in the county, and probably not more than one dozen of individuals that hold to that faith. There is no church or chapel in it, and I believe never has been.

CHARLES, SON OF EPHRAIM POLK.

I supposed I had lost sight of Charles, son of Ephraim, but I found a deed executed by Charles in 1764. I examined it and found it was for several tracts, among them "Locust Hammock," granted to John in 1685, and given by John's will to William Kent of the Territories of Pennsyl.... "(Delaware) and conveyed by Kent to Ephraim Polk in 1700. All this was recited in the will, and it was further recited that Charles was "the son and heir-at-law of Ephraim." Now in his deed of 1739, he is described as of Somerset County, but in 1764—twenty-five years later—he is described as of Worcester County, Maryland. It is a fact that in 1739 Worcester County was a part of Somerset, but in 1742 a strip of Somerset bordering on the Atlantic Coast, and abutting the southern boundary of Delaware, was erected into a new county called Worcester, after the Earl of Worcester. From this southern boundary of Delaware to Georgetown, in Sussex, is only fifteen miles, so that Charles might have resided in Worcester County, Maryland and yet settle his brother Ephraim, your great grandfather, near Georgetown in Sussex County and near himself. I think this settles the point very clearly that Charles is the lost link in your lineage, and James' "Cousin Charles," mentioned in his will. The governor of that name must have been a much younger man.

I thought that Charles might have left a will in Worcester, so I wrote to Snow Hill, the county seat, inquiring for it. He seems to have left no will or anything by which we can determine what became of him. There is an administration on one James Polk in that county in 1773, by Sarah Polk his administratrix, but there does not appear to be any distribution, or anything by which we could ascertain the name of his family.

One of the deeds of Charles in 1739 was to Joseph Polk. In 1748 Joseph Polk conveys this land, together with "Polk's Folly," 100 acres, and "Bally Hack," to Wm and John Shores, and he recites that "Polk's Folly" and "Bally Hack" were granted to Robert Polk.

This "Polk's Folly" remained in the Polk family until 1748, sixty-one years, when it was sold to Wm and John Shores, and it no doubt remained with the Shores' one hundred and twenty years. For when Mr Dashiell and I bought it in 1868, we purchased of the Trustee to sell the real estate of Thomas Shores. In 1739 Joseph was of Somerset County, but in 1748 he was of Dorchester. The latter county lies along the north bank of the Nanticoke, and is very accessible to Dame's Quarter by water which was in those early days the principal highway. What became of Joseph afterwards, I know not. He may have gone to Pennsylvania and been the father of the John Polk of Carlisle a copy of whose will of October 27, 1772 you sent to me; or to Delaware, and have been the father of Daniel about whom you have been inquiring. So far as I can learn, there is not one of the name in Dorchester, and not one in Worcester, except three young men who went there within the last ten years from this county. Although the Polks acquired very large quantities of land on both sides of the Nanticoke, there is not one of the name left, so far as I can learn, and although they acquired thousands of acres of land in Dame's Quarter, there is not one, and has not been one, of the name in the old stamping ground for more than fifty years, nearer than I, and I am about eighteen miles distant. Such are the mutations of this life.

That William Polk, son of Robert and Magdalen, was mixed up with the Owens' in business transactions, the records clearly show, for he purchased the old homestead of Wm and John Shores. That William's wife's name was Anne, (or Nancy) the records also show.

Mr Winder gives you the names of my father's brothers correctly, so far as they go, viz; Dr John, of Laurel, Delaware Josiah and Samuel, but he leaves out James, who married and had a family, and William, who died a young man Betsy and Nancy married two Harcums and went to Northumberland County Virginia, to reside.

William's tribe has stuck to the old manor ground better than any of the others. There are many wills here, but they all relate to his descendants, except the two you have, those of Magdalen and James. It seems to me from reading the records here that Robert, Sr, and Robert Jr. John, William and Ephraim, the immigrants, lived and died in this county. If James, whose will you have, was not one of the immigrants, I cannot tell what became of him. The sons of the maker of the will which you have, removed to Dorchester, sold their lands here, and I know not what became of them. There are none of them now in Dorchester. Joseph, no doubt, followed the Nanticoke into Th... ... 's not appear t...

CHAPTER VIII.

ROBERT AND MAGDALEN'S FAMILY.

At this remote date it is not ascertainable how many of Robert and Magdalen's children were born in Ireland, and how many in America. That most of them, came to America with their parents, seems certain. John must have been of age in order to register the ear-marks of his cattle in 1680. James, of Barbadoes, had six children at the same date, which would evidently put the date of his birth as far back as 1746, and that of John's birth near the same time. This would allow thirty-four years for the birth of the nine children of Robert and Magdalen, and sustains the assumption that most of them were born in Ireland.

Until the discovery of Robert Bruce Polk's will a few years ago, in the Colonial Land Office at Annapolis it was believed that the children of the immigrants numbered but eight, viz: ¹John, ²William, ³Ephraim, ⁴James, ⁵Robert ⁶Joseph, ⁷Martha, and ⁸Anne, and it was also assumed that they were born in this order, for which assumption there is no positive proof.

The text of Robert Polk's will shows that he had another son, by the name of David, though there is nothing to indicate his numerical position in the line of births. The order in which Robert, Sr., mentions them in his will is: ¹Robert, ²David, ³Martha, ⁴Joseph, ⁵James, ⁶Ephraim, ⁷John and ⁸William. Anne, supposedly the youngest child, is not mentioned at all. Why, it does not appear. That she was born after her father's death, is not likly, for Magdalen must have been over sixty years of age at his demise. The omission of Anne's name from the list of his devisees may have been because she was dead before he executed his will. It is possible, but not certain, that Robert Bruce Polk, in his will, mentioned his children in their proper numerical order, Robert coming first, David next, Joseph fourth, and John and William last. But we shall accept them in the old order so long recognized by members of the family, beginning with John as the eldest son ending with Joseph as the youngest

JOHN POLK'S DESCENDANTS.

John Polk, eldest son of Capt. Robert Bruce Polk and Magdalen (Tasker) Porter, was born in Donegal county, Ireland, about 1662, or the beginning of the Restoration under Charles 2d

According to the Polk tree compiled by Col W H Winder, Josiah F. Polk, Bishop Polk and others, in 1849 John Polk, Sr , had two wives, the first Joanna Knox, and the second, Jugurtha Hugg, a Swedish girl But the record of old Monie Presbyterian Church in Somerset, where births and deaths are recorded, gives John's first wife as Jane (————?) and she was the mother of his three children. William, Anne and John, the latter dying a week after his birth and his mother the day before him After Jane's death (Oct. 28, 1700) John married Joanna Knox, said to have been a sister of Nancy (Knox) Owens, wife of John's brother William Polk, Sr of Somerset.

William and Ann (Nancy) grew to maturity and married John Polk died, as collateral records show, in 1707, leaving his second wife, Joanna (Knox) Polk, a widow Not long after John's demise his grief stricken widow, it appears, as most young widows are prone to do, assuaged her sorrow by taking as a second husband, Thomas Hugg a widower by whom she had issue John's daughter Ann (generally called Nancy), married her cousin Edward Roberts, and in her marriage the Polk name ceased being continued to posterity in his branch by her brother William The descendants of the latter, however, are not near so numerous as those of William Polk, Sr , Ephraim and others

After the death of John, his brother William applied in 1708 to the Somerset court and asked to be appointed guardian of William and Nancy, stating in his petition that before death his brother John had requested him and his wife to take care of his children and see t... ...ught up and to give them ... ...sked that the portion of these children coming from their father's estate in "moveables," personal property, be delivered to him, which was done. In a deed from William Kent, (or Cent) and wife to Ephraim Polk, for a tract of land that had belonged to John, "Locust Hammock," lying on the east side of Chesapeake Bay and South of the Wicomico, in Damn Quarter Neck, it is recited that John's will bore date of December 20, 1702, by which he devised 'Locust Hammock" and other lands to William Kent, (or Cent) who lived in 'St John's County, in the Territories of Pennsylvania" afterwards Delaware These lands were later transferred by Ephraim to John's children, William and Nancy, after they had reached their majority John's will is not of record in Somerset County, and this recital is the only evidence of it to be found

From these facts it appears that John Polk, dying in 1707, at rather an early age, and probably anticipating that his wife Joanna might marry again, transferred by will his lands in trust to William Kent, most likely a kinsman. By Kent they were transferred to Ephraim Polk, and by the latter back to the heirs of John, after they became of legal age The personal property of the children, as shown by William's petition to court in 1708, was placed in his charge and by him applied to their use and benefit

The reasons that moved John to transfer his real estate through William Kent to Ephraim, and to request that his brother William receive and use the personal property for the benefit of his children, does not now appear, and is only inferential But this the records show he did, and it is fair to assume that the motive influencing him was that his widow might marry again, and her second husband might dissipate the property if an opportunity presented Such precautions are not unusual even at the present day

The deed from William Kent to Ephraim Polk (for lands devised to him by John in 1702) is dated November 2, 1716 Joseph Polk was witness to power of attorney and made affidavit to same on November 20th following It is likely that William, the son and heir-at-law of John, came of age about this latter date, and that he and his sister Anne (Nancy) then received their respective portions of their father's estate.

Anne, sister of William married Edward Roberts, of Somerset County, and William married Edward's sister, Priscilla Roberts. The descendants of Edward and Nancy have not been traced.

William Polk, who appears by Kent's transfer to Ephraim in November 1716, to have attained his majority about that time died in Maryland in 1726. His widow Priscilla next married Robert Clarkson, of Somerset County and by him had issue.

A very large number of emigrants from Maryland and the other colonies settled in the vicinity of Carlisle, Pa., about 1750, and also, in subsequent years, and the town soon became a center of frontier trade and a point of distribution. Other members of the Polk family also settled there; among them John Polk, who died there in 1772, leaving a life estate in his property to his "aged mother Margaret Polk, now residing on the Eastern Shore of Virginia." To Carlisle also came Wm Polk, a son of Wm Polk, Sr., son of Robert and Magdalen.

FROM THE SOMERSET RECORDS.

In a letter to W. H. Polk, Lexington, Ky., of date October 31, 1874, Col Wm T G Polk, of Princess Anne, Md., who was for many years Clerk of the Orphan's Court of Somerset County, in which court was recorded the legal transactions of Robert and Magdalen Polk and their children says

"Since I last wrote you I have discovered an entry where John Polk entered the ear-marks of his cattle to be recorded on the 8th of September 1680."

"There can be no doubt that Joanna was the last wife of John Sr., and that she survived him. I have shown that John was dead before 10th of March 1708. And among the proceedings of the Court begun and held on the 11th August 1708 it is recorded that 'the widow Polke brought into Court a servant,' to be adjudged of his age, etc. And the clerk of that date in making his index, calls her 'Joanna Polke.'"

"Here we have the widow Joanna Polke transacting business in Court after John's death and unless it can be shown that dow

Joanna Polke, about the time of John's death."

Exhaustive investigation of the records of that Court since Col. Wm T. G. Polk penned the above, has failed to discover any other Joanna Polk than the widow of John, and these investigations have proven that she was his second wife and evidently not the mother of his children William and Nancy, who were, on June 9, 1708 committed by the Court, at John's dying request, to the care, custody and guardianship of his brother William Polk and wife, to be reared and educated by them

This request of John, on the application of his brother William, the Court granted, without protest from Joanna No objection on her part is of record Had she been their mother, it would have been natural for her to have entered objection to a separation from the children

Order of the Court.

June 9, 1708 Petition of Wm Polke and Order of Court, etc., appointing him Guardian of Wm and Anne Polke, children of John Polke, deceased

To the Worshipfull ye Justices of Somerset County now in Court sitting Wm. Polk humbly sheweth That whereas your petitioners Brother Jno Polke late of this County, Dec'd left two children behind him towit Wm & Anne Polke wch upon his death bed he requested of your petitioner & wife to take care of them to see them educated and brought up Christian like & alsoe to bring up ye boy to learn a trade wch your petitioner humbly craves yt we may have ye two children ordered unto him pr your worships and he shall be willing to doe by them as his Brother John Polke requested & what your Worships shall in your Prudence & discretion think fitt to be done (Reasonably) for ye Orphans and your petitioner as in duty bound shall ever pray

William Polke

The petition being read & considered by ye Court have ordered yt ye two children Wm & Anne Polke be delivered to sd Wm Polk their uncle with all yt belongs to them yt is to say their parts of ye portion left them by their dead father

John Polk as moveables & yt ye sd Wm Polke give good security to preserve ye same for ye use of ye sd William & Anne Polk orphans and to learn ye sd Wm Polke a Trade and to read & Writte // at wch day came Wm Polke & James Polke & entered into recog. each in ye sum of tenn pounds sterling to be levied on their goods and chattles Lands & Tennements for ye use of ye Orphans Wm. & Anne Polk // the condition of wch recog is such yt if Wm Polk uncle to ye Sd Orphans Wm & Anne Polke shall doe his best endevor to preserve what parts is delivered to him of their portions left by their deceased father till of agge & then to return ye same with their increase if any & doe take care to learn ye sd William Polke a Trade & to read & writte and doe allow ye sd Wm & Anne Polke all necessarys convenient till they shall be of agge then this recognizance to be null and void otherwise to be and remain in full power force and verture in ye Law taken in oppen cort.

Continuing, Col Wm T. G Polk says 'John died between Oct 8, 1707 and March 1708 for on the former day he executed a deed to Alexander Hall, and "Joanna his now wife" joined with him; on the latter date his brother William was applying to be appointed guardian to his children

William, John's son, died comparatively young, for he was a minor needing a guardian in 1708, and eighteen years afterward "Priscilla Polke, executrix of William Polke," was prosecuting a suit to recover a debt, viz in 1726, and so he must have died before he was 38 probably before he was 35 His will is not recorded here in this County, why it is hard to say"

ERROR OF 1849 POLK TREE

Careful examination of the Somerset County records by Earle B. Polk, present Assistant Deputy Clerk, and others confirms the statement that John Polk died about 1707-8 leaving a widow Joanna Polk, and that his children, William and Nancy were placed by Court under guardianship of his (John's) brother, William P. II Sr, who had pt   from Joanna   That his son William grew to man   ried Priscilla Roberts and died   low.

Priscilla, next married Robert Clarkson, by whom she had issue.

Hence, John Polk and Joanna, and William and Priscilla, as shown on the Polk "Tree" compiled by Col Wm H Winder, Josiah F Polk and others in 1849, were not the progenitors of the Southern or North Carolina branch of the family The error made was doubtless due to insufficient examination of the Court records of Somerset and other counties

The William Polk who was ancestor of the North Carolina branch and who went there from Carlisle, Pa , about 1750, and "died west of the Yadkin," as stated by old Mrs Smart in a letter to Bishop Polk, was the son of another son of Robert and Magdalen.

The weight of evidence indicates that the William Polk who married Margaret Taylor, was a son of Wm Polk, Sr , second son of the immigrants, Capt Robert Bruce and Magdalen Polk It is said that Wm Polk Sr , was twice married first to Nancy (Knox) Owens, and second to a widow Grey, who had a son Allen Grey. Both wives died before Wm. Sr , executed his will in Jan 1739-40, as in that he mentions the "decease of my wife," and makes a bequest to Allen Grey, a member of his family, who was, inferentially, his stepson

The much discussed question of how many children John Polk had who was their mother, and when they were born, has been conclusively settled by Mr Earle B Polk, of Princess Anne, Md , who made an examination of the records of old Monie Church, in Dame's Quarter, Somerset County, the neighborhood of John's residence

From this church record Mr Polk copied and transmitted to the author the following:

(From the Records of Old Monie Church.)

William Polk, son of John Polk, born of Jane, 11 July, 1695.

Ann Polk, daughter of John Polk, born of Jane, 27 January, 1698.

John Polk, son of John Polk, born of Jane, 22 Oct., 1700 and died 29 Oct inst

Jane Polk, the wife of John Polk died 28 Oct , 1700

This record shows that John Polk and his wife Jane, had

three children born to them, William, Ann and John the latter dying a week after birth, and his mother the day before he died This old church record puts to rout a flood of assertions and deductions that have attached to this question since 1849, during earnest efforts by various members of the family to arrive at the truth as to John, his wife, and his children

CHAPTER IX.

JAMES POLK, SON OF ROBT. BRUCE POLK.

James Polk fourth son of Capt Robert Bruce Polk (or Pollock) and his wife Magdalen Tasker (Porter) Polk, was born about 1673, near about the time his parents came to America, and he died in 1727, as his will of that year indicates He grew to manhood on the farm in Somerset County, Md, and in due course of time, about 1700, fell a victim to cupid's wiles and married Mary Williams, said to have been a sister to Elizabeth Williams, who married his brother Ephraim Polk

Judging from the list named in his will, James' children appear to have been one of the principal crops that he raised on his plantation He acquired by grants from Lord Baltimore several tracts of land in Dame's Quarter, Somerset County, adjoining or close to the lands located and patented by his father and brothers He appears to have been by trade a ship carpenter, or builder, and no doubt found occupation in building small vessels like those in use at that day Most of the sons of the early Presbyterian immigrants into America at that time had been taught, or were put to some useful trade

LAND GRANTS TO JAMES POLK.

The record of land grants on file in the Land Office at Annapolis, Maryland, to members of the Polk family, commence with the grant of "Locust Hammock," 125 acres, and "Front of Locust Hammock," to John Polk, June 1, 1685

The next grant was to Robert Bruce Polk, John's father for "Polk's Folly," 100 acres, and "Polk's Lott," 50 acres, on March 7, 1687 Both of these grants to Robert Bruce Polk are described as "Lying in Somerset County, on the north side of Manokin River near the head of Broad Creek." On this record Robert's name is written Polke

The next grant was on Nov 8 1700, to Robert Polk, Jr, for "Bally Hack,' 200 acres Marsh ground, lying in Somerset county, and on Sept 20 following, Ephraim Polk received an adjoining tract, ' Clonmell," 100 acres Both these two tracts lay between Manokin Branch and Pidgeon House or Little Creek "

The first entry by James Polk, fourth son of Capt Robert Bruce Polk was of 'James Meadow,' 200 acres June 1. 1705, and described as "lying in Somerset County, in Dame's Quarter, N E, of Williams' Creek, Two adjoining tracts, 'Chance" and 'Poak's Chance," of 200 acres each, were granted to Ephraim Polk, in 1715

Two other grants are also of record in the name of James, viz

Feb 27, 1728, to James Polke, Green Pasture," 200 acres, West side of an island, Dame's Quarter, Somerset County "

' Nov 23, 1730 White Oak Swamp, 100 acres, north side Manokin River, Somerset County, to James Pollock "

These three tracts aggregating 500 acres, are all the lands shown by the Land Office records to have been granted by Lord Baltimore to James Polk, fourth son of Robert and Magdalen

In those days there seems to have been much delay in the issue of patents to land claimants Many immigrants came in and marked out and claimed tracts, for which they did not receive patents until years later Robert Bruce Polk settled on and occupied a tract for which he did not receive a patent until twelve or fifteen years later

The first patent to James Polk, as above recited, was for "James Meadow," June 1 1705 The next two were issued in 1728 and 1730 The will of James Polk, on record in Somerset County is dated Nov 8 1726 and was probated May 11, 1727 Therefore he must have died early in the latter year Hence the grants of "Green Pasture" and ' White Oak Swamp" were not issued u   the L nd Off   ' after James' decease to his w re nd of th   t l   leted the purchase price n s

Magdalen Polk's will is dated April 7, 1726, and was probated March 20, 1727. The will of James Polk is dated Nov 8, 1726 and it was probated May 11, 1727. So Magdalen and her son James executed their wills in the same year, and both died the following year, 1727. Though dying when a little over fifty years of age, James left a family of eleven children and a twelfth one was born to his wife after his death, for which he also made provision in his will. An official copy of James' will, secured by the writer from the Somerset County Clerk's office, reads as follows:

WILL OF JAMES POLK

In the name of God Amen the Eight day of November in the year Anndm 1726 I, James Polk of Somerset County in the Province of Maryland, Ship Carpenter, being very Sick and weak of body, but of perfect mind and memory thanks be given therefor unto God, therefore calling to mind the mortality of the body and knowing that it is appointed once for all men to die, I do make and ordain this my last Will and Testament that is to say principally and first of all I recommend my soul to the hands of Almighty God, that gave it, and for my Body I recommend it to the Earth, to be buried in a Christian-like & descent manner, at the discretion of my Executors, nothing doubting but at the resurrection the same to receive again, by the might power of God, & for such worldly estate as it hath pleased God to bless men in this life, I give, devise & dispose of in the following manner and form

Item—I give to my son David my now dwelling plantation to him and his heirs forever

Item—I give unto my son David the one half of all that Land & Marsh that I have on Pidgeon House

Item—I give unto my sons John & James the other half of the aforesaid Land & Marsh on Pidgeon house. Likewise I have a Warrant for one hundred acres of Land and one hundred acres of Land which my Cousin Charles is to make over, both which Land and warrant I give and bequeath to my son David one half of both Land & warrant, and the other half I give to my sons John & James to them and to their heirs forever

Likewise I have two hundred acres of Marsh Lying on Samuel Jones Island. One hundred acres thereof I give and bequeath unto my Son Henry and the other Hundred acres of the aforesaid Marsh I give and bequeath unto my Cousin Edward Roberts, and to his heirs forever on the provision my Cousin Edward do deliver up the Bond that I past to him

Item—I give unto my sons Henry & John & James all that Land I purchased of Thomas Layfold likewise all that Land I purchest of Richard Taton, both Tracts of Land lying on the head of Mintocrakinanock called John's Neck, to them my sons and their heirs forever, to be equally divided among them, and Likewise I give and bequeath my sons Henry, John & James all that parcel and Track of Land lying on or near the black walnut Landing at ye mouth of ye Norwest fork to them and their heirs forever, to be equally divided among them.

Item—I give and bequeath unto my daughters Mary & Sary & Margaret & Elizabeth & Magdalen & Jane & Anna ten pounds to each of them Likewise I give and bequeath unto the Child my wife is now with ten pounds if please God it lives And Likewise I will that my well beloved wife may have full Privilege of my dwelling plantation and Marshes during the time of her widowhood. And likewise I leave my sons David, Henry & John to be my Executors in full and do hereby utterly disannul all other wills or Testaments and Legaceys by me in anywise before this time named, ratifying and allowing and confirming this and no other to be my last Will and Testament, in witness whereof I have hereunto set my hand and seal the day & year first above written

Signed sealed and delivered   James Polk (Seal)
in the presents of us
William Polk, John Pollet, Mary Pollet

May ye 11th 1727 Then came John Pollett & Mary Pollett subscribing evidences to ye within Will, who made oath upon ye Holy Evangelist of Almighty God that they see ye within named James Polk the Testator sign and seal ye within instrument as his last will ... him publish and declare ...

doing he was of sound disposing mind & memory, to ye best of their knowledge

Sworn before me ye day & year above written

John Tunstall, Depty Com'y of Som-st County, per Geo Plater Reg'r

Examined Tes Esme Bayly, Reg. W S Co

The Wm Polk who witnessed the foregoing will was most likely James' brother, who was the second son of Robert and Magdalen. The other witnesses—John and Mary Pollett, were no doubt James nephew and niece, children of his sister Martha Polk, who married Thomas Pollitt. A number of people by the latter name still live in Somerset County, but are untraced. It is said that Thomas Pollitt lived to be quite an old man and that he was well acquainted with the family history of the Polks. Like the Polks, the Pollitts emigrated to other Colonies and States both before and after the Revolution, and quite a number of that name are to be found in the Middle West, to which so many Maryland and Delaware people came in the early days of its settlement.

It will be noticed that James in his will does not give his wife's name, an omission observable in nearly all the old wills of that time. Josiah F Polk, born and reared in Somerset, and the most active collector of data for the Polk Tree, in 1848-9, stated that James and Ephraim Polk married sisters named Williams, and later investigations show that James' wife was Mary Williams, and that Ephraim's was Elizabeth Williams. At that day it was a very frequent occurrence for several brothers of a family to marry sisters of another family.

Woven in with the numerous facts collected during the compilation of the Polk family Tree of 1849 were also many errors, and a large part of the work performed by this writer has been to discover and eliminate these errors that crept into the family record.

Of the history of James Polk's children, little has been obtained. David appears to have been the oldest, born about 1700 and died 1773. His will is dated Feb 21, 1773 and was probated March 11 the following month. The fact that he received from his father the home plantation, would indicate that he was the oldest son. In his will David does not mention any wife and presumably she was then dead.

CHAPTER X.

DAVID POLK'S WILL.

The will of David Polk, eldest son of James Polk of record in Dorchester County, Md., is as follows:

IN THE NAME OF GOD AMEN I, David Pollock of Dorchester County and Province of Maryland being sick and weak of body but of sound and perfect mind and memory, blessed be God for the same, do publish this my last will and Testament in manner and form following, that is to say:

Imprimis I give and devise to my grandson David Pollock the dwelling plantation where I now live and all lands laying and being on the East side of the Great Road from Cratchett's Ferry to the head of said county, and all the lands joining of said dwelling plantation; also twenty acres of land lying on the Westmost side of said road and parilile with said road, being part of a tract of land called "David's Hope," to him the said David Pollock during his natural life, and after his decease to his lawful heirs and so on from heir to heir while there may be an heir found lawfully born

Item I give and bequeath to my said grandson David Pollock one negro boy called Mingo to him and his heirs forever Farther it is my will and desire that my grandson David Pollock shall have my great or large looking glass also one mahogany desk, also two mahogane tables, to him and his heir forever

Item I give and devise to my grandson William Pollock all the remainder of my lands that lays on the West side of the above mentioned road, and the rest of the lands joining the quarter plantation, during his natural life, and after his decease to his lawful heirs, and so on from heir to heir while there may be an heir found lawfully born

Item I give and bequeath to my grandson Priscilla Pollock, all the lands and plantations where I now dwells on during her natural life, and after her decease to my granddaughter Esther Pollock and her heirs forever

Item My will and desire is that if my two grandsons David Pollock and William Pollock should both die having no lawful heirs, then it is my will and desire the lands devised to my grandson David Pollock shall be the right and property of my granddaughter Esther Pollock, and her heirs forever

Item My will and desire is that the lands devised to the above mentioned William Pollock, him having no lawful heir as above mentioned, shall be the right and property of my four daughters viz Elizabeth Roberts, and Mary Duett, Love Collins and Emelia Laws, to them and their heirs forever

Item I give and devise unto Elizabeth Roberts one tract of land laying and being in Somerset County called and known by the name of Green Pasture, to her and her heirs forever

Item I give and devise unto Mary Duett one tract or parcel of land laying and being in Worcester County called and known by the name of "Crowney's Folly," to her and her heirs forever

Item My will and desire is all the negroes by me given to each of my several daughters before or after their marriage shall descend to their heirs forever

And lastly as to all the rest, residue and remainder of my personal estate, goods and chettels of what kind or nature soever, I give and bequeath to my beloved children, to be equally divided amongst them And farther it is my will and desire that my daughter-in-law Priscila Polk shall have the tuition of my two grandchildren, viz William Pollock and Esther Pollock, and said Priscila Pollock shall have the benefits from their and each of their estates, both real and personal, until of age to receive their and each of their estates either real or personal.

And further it is my will and desire that John Collins of Andrew Collins and Alexander Laws shall and is hereby appointed sole Executors of this my Last Will and Testament hereby revoking all former Wills by me heretofore made, and

In Witness whereof I have hereunto set my hand and seal this 21st day of February 1773

David Pollock (Seal)

Signed sealed published and declared by the above named David Pollock to be his last Will and Testament in presence of us who have hereunto subscribed our names as witnesses, in the presence of the testator

Robert Mitchell,
Levin Fallon,
Lucilla Polk

At the foot of the foregoing Will was thus written, viz Dorchester County, Sct On the 11th day of March Anno Domini 1773 John Collins and Alexander Laws of Worcester County made oath on the Holy Evangels of Almighty God that the aforegoing Instrument of Writing is the true and only Will and Testament of David Pollock late of Dorchester County, deceased that hath come to their hands or possession and that they do not know nor ever heard of any other Will made since by the said Testator

Certified per Jno Goldsborough,

Dy Com'sy Dor Co

Dorchester County Sct On the 11th day of March Anno Domini 1773, Robert Mitchell and Levin Fallen two of the subscribing witnesses to the aforegoing Will, duly and solemnly sworn on the Holy Evangels of Almighty God, depose and said that they saw the Testator David Pollock sign the aforegoing Will and heard him publish and declare the same to be his last Will and Testament That at the time of his so doing he was to the best of their apprehension of sound and disposing mind and memory, and that they, together with Lucilla Polk the other subscribing witness to the aforegoing Will, subscribed their respective names as witnesses thereto in the presence of the Testator and at his request

Certified per Jno Goldsborough,

Dy Com'sy Dorch County

The foregoing will shows that David Pollock (Polk) was a man of enterprise and had accumulated quite property in lands and slaves he was died leaving four daughters—Elizabeth Roberts, Mary Duett Love Collins and

Emelia Laws, but no sons. Had there been a son, there is little doubt that he would have received the bulk of the property left to the two grandsons, David and William. The name of the son who was the husband of Priscilla Pollock (David's "daughter-in-law") is not known. Probably he was then dead and she a widow. The tract of land called "David's Hope," lying in Dorchester County, was granted to David Pollock Nov 11, 1742. His daughter Elizabeth had evidently married a cousin, one of the sons of Ann Polk and Francis Roberts, and he was also dead, it appears, and Elizabeth a widow. As to his daughters Mary Duett, Love Collins and Emelia Laws, it will be noted that John Collins and Alexander Laws appear as witnesses to the will. No doubt they were the husbands of Love and Amelia. As to who Lucilla Polk, one of the witnesses to will was, the instrument affords no clue. Possibly an aunt or near kinsman. Had she been a daughter of David, she would no doubt have been one of his devisees and named in the will as such. The request that his daughter-in-law Priscilla Polk should have the tuition of his two grandchildren, William Pollock and Esther Pollock, indicates that she was most likely their mother.

CHAPTER XI.

JAMES POLK'S OTHER CHILDREN.

The other children named by James Polk in his will, and the time of their births as approximated from insufficient data, were:

  2 Henry Pollock, born about 1703, died ?
  3 John Pollock, born about 1705, died ?
  4 James Pollock, born about 1707, died ?
  5 Mary Pollock, born about 1709, died ?
  6 Sarah Pollock, born about 1711, died ?
  7 Margaret Pollock, born about 1713, died ?
  8 Elizabeth Pollock born about 1715, died ?
  9 Magdalen Pollock, born about 1717, died ?
10 Jane Pollock, born about 1721, died ?
11 Anna Pollock, born about 1724, died ?
12 ——————————, born about 1727-8, died ?

What became of the foregoing eleven children, whom they married and who were and are their descendants, the writer is not informed nor does the large mass of data in his possession from hundreds of the Polk family throw the least light upon their pathways through life. To some other Polk family historian this task is committed, with the hope that all of them can be induced to answer roll call.

There were a number of Pollocks at and adjacent to Carlisle, Pa, between 1730 and the Revolutionary War. Some changed their names to Polk, while others adhered to the older form—Pollock.

Of persons named Pollock, at Carlisle just before the Revolution, there was one James Pollock, possibly the James Pollock (No 1) of the above list. This Carlisle James appears to have been born somewhere between 1700 and 1710, and hence the date of birth of the de— James would about fit him. This Carlisle James——————————— 25

1773, in which he mentions six children: ¹John; ²Jean, who married Mr Hinchman, ³Martha, who married Mr Dobson, ⁴James, ⁵William, ⁶Robert. The probable date of the birth of James, son of James Pollock (or Polk) and of this Carlisle James, as stated, was about the same time, but that is not positive proof that they were one and the same person. Some contend that the Carlisle James belonged to the Pennsylvania Pollock family, (whose ancestors came to America from Coleraine, Ireland, considerably later than Robert Bruce Polk) of whom Oliver Pollock the Revolutionary patriot, and the late Governor Pollock, were distinguished members

There is also on file at Carlisle the will of one John Polk of date Oct 27, 1772. He appears to have been unmarried and devised his property to his "aged mother Margaret Polk," and brothers James, William and Robert, "now living on the Eastern Shoar of Virginia." This will was probated June 11 1774, and it is quite probable that the testator was John the second named of the above James Pollock of the 1773 will. Definite proof of this, however, is lacking, and the work of unravelling this knot is left to others who may wish to attempt the task

Joseph Pollock, of Dorchester County, Md., in his will of Sept 12, 1751, probated June 10, 1752, appoints his "friend John Pollock, son of James Pollock," to divide certain lands between his sons Robert and Zephaniah Pollock.

Of Henry Pollock, Mary Pollock, Sarah Pollock, Margaret Pollock, Elizabeth Pollock, Magdalen Pollock, Jane Pollock Anna Pollock, and the one mentioned by James Pollock in his will as yet unborn, the records are silent and concerning them deponent saith not

Concerning this James Polk, whose identity as a son of Robert and Magdalen Polk has in a measure been questioned by some, attention is called to two points in his will. One of these is where he speaks of "my cousin Charles," the other where he mentions "my cousin Edward Roberts." The latter unquestionably was the son of Francis and Ann (Polk) Roberts, who married his cousin Ann or Nancy, daughter of John Polk by his first wife Jane ———

But who was his "Cousin Charles?" Was he the first son of Ephraim Polk? Or, was he the Chas Polk who appears to have been a son of William Polk by a first wife? This Charles (of William) was born somewhere about 1700 to 1707 it appears, and going to the upper Potomac frontier, became an Indian trader and died in 1753.

In Hotten's "List of Emigrants to America" on page 440, we find the following:

"A list of the Inhabitants in and about the town of St Michaels, Barbadoes, Anno Domini 1680, with their children, hired servants, prentices, bought servants and negroes."

In this census, comprising a long list, appears:

"James Poke and wife, 6 children, 2 hired servants, and apprentices, 1 bought servant and 4 slaves."

This James Poke seems to have been a man of some consequence, for he had two hired servants and apprentices, one bought servant, and four slaves or negroes. Evidently he carried on some constructive work, as he had "apprentices."

It is likely also that he later came on to America, but it is not certain that he was the James Pollock who died in Somerset County, Md, in 1727, reputed son of Robert and Magdalen. This Somerset James was married about 1700 and apparently was only about seven years of age at the time Barbadoes James had a wife and six children.

This completes, as far as known, the line of James Polk (or Pollock), fourth son of Robert and Magdalen Polk.

EMIGRATION TO THE WEST.

The chief trend of westward emigration 1730 to 1750 was to the vicinity of Carlisle and thence across the southern line of Pennsylvania, and down the Valley of Virginia to the Yadkin River section of North Carolina. The rich and fertile lands of the West, lying beyond the Alleghanys, and on the Ohio and its tributaries, were not then accessible because of the hostility of the Indian tribes, who presented a barrier to the encroachments of the whites in that direction. The French however, from their posts in Canada, had long before established an extensive trade in the Ohio Valley with various Indian tribes and it was their policy to send maps of the Alleghanys, any encroachments into their domain by Anglo-Saxon traders and prospectors.

This bar to the progress westward of American settlers was maintained until 1770 by the assistance of the Indians, when the alert Scotch-Irish riflemen on the frontier crossed the barrier and spread out into the fertile plains of Tennessee Kentucky and Ohio, the firing line of a mighty host that followed close after them. This intrusion of the whites into their favorite hunting grounds was fiercely resisted by the Indians, under French prompting, and the infamous murder of the family of Logan at Yellow Creek, below Pittsburg, in March 1774, by Daniel Greathouse and a company of other "white savages," precipitated a general Indian war, which culminated in a fierce battle, October 10th of the same year, at Point Pleasant, the Indians being defeated after a severe struggle with the frontiersmen under Col. Andrew Lewis.

Had William Polk, son of William Sr., and his family remained at Carlisle until 1774, there is but little doubt he would have emigrated to and settled at some point in the Ohio Valley. Some of the family in after years did this; among them his nephew, Capt Charles Polk, who came to Louisville in 1780 and William Pogue (Polk) who emigrated to Southwest Virginia and soon after to Kentucky, and was killed at Harrodsburg, by Indians in 1776.

But the westward progress of William Polk and family, it is said, was halted at Carlisle from 1723 until 1750, then, following the lead of the Boone's and other pioneers, they moved forward and down the trough of the Alleghanys to the Yadkin, joining the Scotch-Irish pioneers of the Carolinas who had before spread westward from the Atlantic Coast. By and through this contact and union with other colonists of like religious faith and political aspirations, was strengthened and moulded into definite form and direction those principles of freedom which found expression in the Mecklenburg Resolutions of May 20, 1775, the first Declaration of Independence ever enunciated in America, preceding the Philadelphia Declaration by more than a year. Mr Jefferson and carping critics to the contrary notwithstanding.

In this great event at Mecklenburg the sons of William

Polk and his wife, Margaret Taylor, took a leading part, a fact of which their descendants and relatives are justly proud Here they and their kinsmen, the Alexanders and the Brevards, planted the foundation of a superstructure that afterward became the Temple of Liberty on the Western Continent, after the sore travail of the Revolution had tested their principles by the arbitrament of a long and bloody war

William, however, did not live to witness or take part in those transactions which eventuated in war, and in which his sons bore such conspicuous and distinguished part He died west of the Yadkin about 1753-4 His wife, Margaret (Taylor) Polk, whom he married at Carlisle, and who accompanied him to North Carolina, survived him and lived to a great age

THE SOMERSET RECORDS.

Among those longest and most deeply interested in the preservation of the family history, was the late Col Wm T G Polk, of Princess Anne, Maryland Col Polk was born and lived all his life in Somerset County, near the spot where Captain Robert Bruce Polk and family settled He owned at his death, "Polk's Folly," the original grant in 1687 by Lord Baltimore to Capt Robert Bruce Polk lying in Dame's Quarter, between Manokin and Nanticoke rivers, and this tract has descended to Ephraim Polk, the present owner, son of Col Polk

Col Polk, as stated, took great interest in the family history, and a regular correspondence on the subject, between him and the author, begun in 1874, was carried on up to the time of his death, ———————— This correspondence, on his part, was of such an interesting character that it is here given with but slight omissions as to the letters copied Born and reared on the old stamping ground," where Robert and Magdalen Polk first settled, familiar with the history and traditions of the locality, for many years Clerk of the Court of Somerset County, with free access at all times to the records, no one was better qualified to pursue the work of uncovering the past history of his family Being also a man of the highest standing and of undoubted veracity, what he has stated may be relied on with the utmost confidence

CHAPTER XII

LETTERS OF COL WM T G POLK.

Under date of October 3d, 1871, Col Polk says "Some thirteen or fourteen years since I commenced collecting the very matter which you desire and had obtained a good deal Some of it would, I think, have answered the very questions which you have put to me especially about the Delaware branch of the family This was intended for Bishop Polk afterwards a General in the Confederate Army, who was trying to preserve, as you are now doing, whatever was interesting in the family of Polks in the United States.

"But the war broke out and it was never sent, and last year I had the misfortune to have my dwelling destroyed by fire and everything personal to myself and wife, except the clothes on our backs, together with those papers, was destroyed It will be difficult to reproduce them, as they were in the shape of letters from persons, some of whom are dead and others whose names I have forgotten If the Bishop's papers have been preserved, I suppose there is more information in them than can be found in any one place There was Josiah F Polk, who, with his three sisters, removed many years ago from this county to Washington, D. C He had a great deal of information, and I had several letters from him, some of them thirty years ago, but he and his sisters never married and all are now dead

"In your letter you state that Robert and Magdalen landed at "Dame's Corner" It is Dame's Quarter, formerly called "Damn Quarter," and so written in all the old records This is a low, flat strip of land but little above tidewater, about four or five miles in length, lying on the south side of a stream now called Wicomico, emptying into the Chesapeake Bay And just east of it is another tract one or two miles long, called "Pidgeon House" Just west of Dame's Quarter, and toward the Bay, separated from it by a small stream called the Thoroughfare, is an island two miles long and a half or three-fourths of a mile wide, formerly called Big Devil's Island, now softened down to "Deal's Island." Just west of this is a smaller island, containing a few acres, which was called "Little Devil's Island."

"These names recall a story that is told of one of our immigrant vessels. There being no large towns then, the vessels came into our streams and landed their passengers just where they expected to live. I tell the story as I have heard it told, without vouching for its truth. The ship came up the Chesapeake Bay, and on its way took on board as a pilot, a person who knew the way to this neighborhood of Dame's Quarter. It was a hot day in June or July, and as the vessel left the Bay to turn into this stream the mate took his position about nightfall near the pilot, who was directing them how to steer.

"Pointing to the little island, the mate asked what place it was. The pilot answered 'Little Devil's Island.' After passing it, the mate inquired what place the larger island was, the pilot responding 'Big Devil's Island.' After the ship had passed this also, the mate waved his hand toward the shore of the river and asked its name. 'Damn Quarter,' grimly responded the pilot. Just ahead was a low marsh and from it were rising in the air myriads of fireflys, peculiar I suppose to such low places, and which must be seen for one to have an adequate idea of them, for they cannot be described. Suffice it to say that their vast numbers, on a hot night, especially after a rain, seem to completely illuminate the atmosphere.

"The story goes that the mate, now thoroughly alarmed, excitedly called to the man at the helm and implored him to put the ship about. 'For,' said he, 'we have just passed the Little Devil's Island, and the Big Devil's Island. We are now abreast of Damn Quarter, and h——ll must be the next place, for I see the sparks and can almost hear the roar.'

"I never saw any one bold enough to assert that this incident, handed down to us through tradition, happened on the vessel that brought our ancestors, Robert and Magdalen Polk, to this continent, but it has been told in such close proximity to their landing as to leave that impression. Would one or false, the scene is laid at the very place, and about the very time of their arrival. The particular spot where they landed, tradition says, was at "Pidgeon House," and it retains its name to this day.

"There is a tract of land near this place called "Polk's-Folly," taken up no doubt by one of the family. I asked a man, since your letter, if he knew anything about it. It is a singular coincidence that it included a place which I and my son-in-law bought a few years ago without knowing anything of the patent name of the land. Ex-Governor Trusten Polk, of Missouri, misunderstood me when he wrote you that I said there is a farm in this county that has been in the possession of my family since 1690. That, I think, ante-dates the advent of our fathers, but it has been continuously in our family more than one hundred and sixty years, having been purchased by one of the first settlers, and passed by devise from father to son, and there has been but one deed in the whole time for it which is the last occupant, whose father died intestate.

"I will also state in this connection that there are three articles of personal property, two of them, at least, in our possession, which were brought from Europe by our family. The first was a large quarto Bible, containing the Old and New Testaments, and an old version (Rouse's probably) of the Psalm's. The spelling was antique and the punctuation queer * * * The date on the title page was 1669. That on the Testaments was different. Evidently printed separately and bound up together. Seventy years ago the book was in a dilapidated condition as to the binding, and my father had it substantially rebound in calf. It was said that our ancestors hid it in a hollow tree, in the days of the Persecution, after the Restoration, to prevent it from being taken from them. It is said that while one read it, others of the family would stand guard to give warning of the approach of Papists. And truly, it seems that this might have been probable, as the book was very much stained, as though it had been thoroughly saturated with water many times. It was destroyed in 1847, together with the dwelling of my brother, and all the ancient records it contained.

"The second article is a case containing fifteen square

bottles, each holding over two and a half gallons. Since my recollection, the bottles were all perfect, and when all full contained about forty gallons. But General Temperance, causing King Alcohol to retire, these bottles have been used for vinegar and other liquids that would freeze. Hence all have been cracked and most of them lost. I have but two or three of them left, useless except as a connecting link between the present and the past. My nephew, Ephraim G. Polk, who owns the old homestead, has the old case.

"The third article is a large brass clock, which, in the case stands eight or nine feet high, with great leaden weights of ten or twelve pounds each. In addition to keeping the hours of the day, it keeps the day of the month and the phases of the moon, and is a repeater. A string may be attached to a lever inside the clock and carried to the foot of your bed. At any hour of the night, if the string is pulled, she will repeat the last stroke, unless it is within a half hour of the next strike. So you can know within a half hour the time, without rising from your bed. Seventy years ago it was given by my grandfather to my father, with the old homestead. When he took possession of them he found the old clock in a lumber room covered with dust. Supposing it to have finished its work, he proposed to a clock-maker to trade it in part payment for a new clock, if there was any value to it. It was sent, and when my father saw the clock-man, the latter told him that no man need want a better clock. He cleaned it up for a few dollars. I left it thirty years ago on a farm which has been in my immediate family one hundred and nine years, with some servants, and although it has not been cleaned in that time, when I have occasion to spend a few days on the farm, or when I send mechanics to repair or build houses, if she is wound up, she will run eight or nine days and keep excellent time. My father laid aside the old case and had a new one of mahogany made. This clock was made, I suppose by ' W. Nicholson, White Haven " which is inscribed on a plate screwed to the face, and there is an inscription also on the face—"*Tempus edax Rerum*" and I find it true in reference to our family, for Time has consumed almost everything relating to its early history."

CHAPTER XIII.

WINDER AND POLK CONNECTION

Respecting the connection between the Winder and Polk families, Col Polk states in the same letter: "Mrs. Winder was Gertrude Polk, a daughter of William Polk, son of David, son of William the immigrant, who was a son of Robert and Magdalen He (William) was Chief Judge of one of the judicial circuits of Maryland, and consequently a member of our Court of Appeals He was esteemed in his state a man of fine intellect and a well read lawyer. He died in 1814, aged about 63 years.

Mrs Winder's mother was a Winder, and she married Gen'l Wm H Winder, her first cousin She was a well educated lady, of rare accomplishments, and I think she died within the current year, about 88 years of age She had a brother by her father's second marriage, Col James Polk, Register of Wills for this County for twenty-five years, and subsequently Naval Officer in connection with the customs at Baltimore, during the administration of President James K Polk He was a man of fine parts and rare conversational powers He died in 1868, in Baltimore, is buried in this place and was 75 years of age He left many children One of them, Esther, married Ex-Governor E Louis Lowe, of Maryland, and is now living with her husband in New York City. Mrs Winder also had a sister by the third marriage of her father, named Anne Anne's mother, after the death of her father, married Dr Savage and they removed from this county to Georgia and there she became the wife of Hon Herschel V Johnson who, you know, was a candidate for Vice President on the ticket with Stephen A Douglass, in 1860 Judge Polk had many children one called William, who was either in the Naval or Revenue service of the United States Another son, Josiah, was Clerk of this County and died young, probably in

1814, about the time his father died. His widow with her children, moved to the Western Shore of this state.

I am descended from William, his son James, his son William, his son Samuel, his son Wm. T G, the writer of this aged nearly seventy. My son Wm T G Jr is a youth nearly twenty, four other sons dead.

"There is documentary evidence here to show that the six brothers, John, William, Ephraim, James, Robert and Joseph, were all here in this county. To John, a deed from Henry Smith, 15th March, 1692. To William, a deed from John Goldsmith, 12th July, 1697. To Robert a deed from Augustine Standford 12th August, 1697, for land in Pidgeon House, near 'Damn Quarter'. To Ephraim, from William Kent or Cent (spelled both ways) 2d November 1716. Joseph was witness to power of attorney and made affidavit to same, 20th November, 1716, about a tract of land called Locust Hammock, in "Damn Quarter Neck". To James a deed from James Snell and wife for a mill, 24th of April, 1721. And these are not all by many, as, for instance To William from William and John Owens, 1st August, 1713. This is the land Ex-Governor Trusten Polk of Missouri, alluded to as being so long in our immediate family etc.

The most important of the documents I have mentioned I think, is the deed from Wm Kent or Cent and wife to Ephraim. In deducing this title it is recited in this deed 'Yt whereas, ye Right Honorable Charles of Noble Memorie late Lord and Proprietory of ye Province of Maryland and Avalon Lord Baron of Baltimore, by his deed of grant under ye greater Seale used in ye said Province of Maryland, for granting of Land, these bearing date ye first day of June Anno Domini one thousand six hundred and eighty-five, did for consideration therein mentioned grant unto John Poalke, late of Somerset County a parcel or tract of land called Locust Hammock, scituate, lying and being on ye east side of Chesapeake Bay, on the south side of Wicco-Comico (now Wicomico) in Damn Quarter Neck.'

This record establishes the fact that the family was here anterior t̲ ̲ ̲ ̲ ̲ ̲ ̲ ̲ ̲ ̲ ̲ ̲ ̲ ̲ ̲ that John's will ̲ ̲ ̲ ̲ ̲ ̲ ̲ ̲ ̲ ̲ ̲ ̲ ̲ ̲ e de vised this Locust Hammock and other lands to this William Kent, or Cent, who lived in St John's County, in the territories of Pennsylvania And in 1708, William Polk prefers his humble petition to the Court, asking to be appointed guardian to William and Anne, children of his brother John, alleging that his brother, on his death-bed requested him (William) and his wife to take care of his children and see that they were properly brought up, and to give them a christian education, and also asking that the portion of these children, coming from their father's estate in moveables, be delivered to him, which was done, etc, etc

"These two facts prove that John's death occurred between 1702 and 1708, probably 1707 or the early part of 1708. John's will is not recorded in this county There is a traditional account that he moved to Pennsylvania to reside, and if so, he may have died there and his will may be recorded there The recital in this deed is the only evidence we have of its existence This land was conveyed from Kent (or Cent) by William to Ephraim, by virtue of a power of attorney from Kent, and Joseph Polk was one of the witnesses to it and made affidavit to it before two Justices of the Peace, on the 20th of November, 1716, and this proves that Joseph was also here present, and is the only documentary evidence of his presence that I can find To Joseph there is no deed for lands and it looks as if he was less thrifty and prosperous than the others, and that may have been the reason moving his mother to give him her land in Ireland, as you will find she did, by the copy of her will you have

It has been the generally received opinion that Robert Polk, husband of Magdalen, died in Ireland I had adopted that opinion myself, but since your letter to me I have been looking over the old records to refresh my memory, and I have had that opinion much shaken. The belief that Capt Robert Bruce Polk died in Ireland was doubtless induced by the fact that while his wife's will is of record in Somerset County, his own is not After a long search, it was found of record at Annapolis, Anne Arundel County executed May 6, 1699, and probated June 5, 1702 It was filed in the office of the Chief Commissary of the Colony, at Annapolis, and settles the fact that he did not die in Ireland.

On the 10th March, 1697, Robert Polk, Senior, petitions Court, alleging that he had purchased a tract on Monie near Damn Quarter, had cleared a cornfield, and that the horse road passed right through his field, and asked permission to turn the road around his fence. Now, this looks as if there were two Robert Polks doing business here, and that for the sake of distinguishing them, one of them was called "Senior." Who could these two Roberts be at this early date but the husband and son of Magdalen?

Magdalen must have been very aged when she died, for if we suppose John to have been twenty-five when Lord Baltimore granted him Locust Hammock, it would fix his birth at 1660. And supposing him to have been the eldest of her children, and she to have been twenty at his birth; it would carry her birth back to 1640. Now, you know by her will that she died in the last of 1726 or first of 1727, or within thirteen years of a century from her birth. The probabilities are that she was more than 87 years of age at her death.

Continuing, Colonel Polk writes: "At this distance of time I cannot account for John's giving his lands to Kent (or Cent) who, from all that appears of record to the contrary, was a stranger to his blood, when he left two children, William and Anne, especially as it seems probable they were poor, as their uncle William, only asks to have possession of the "moveables." But there were other lands deeded to John, and he may have given them to his children. It is probable that he was married twice, and his wife, who was named Joannah, survived him, as appears from the records, and is called the "widow Polk." She could not have been the mother of William and Anne, or he would not have requested his brother William and his wife to take care of them. What became of Margaret and Anne, the two daughters of Robert and Magdalen Polk, does not certainly appear, particularly as to one of them. I think one of them married Thomas Pollitt. The Pollitts claim relationship to the Polk family and there is a Magdalen Pollitt mentioned in the records. Some years ago I remember there was a Tuley Pollitt in the

The highly interesting character of the foregoing letter must be the author's excuse for copying it here so fully, and the same excuse must also apply to further copious quotations from the letters of Col. Wm. T. G. Polk, who was peculiarly qualified by age, residence, and contiguity to the landing place of the Polks in America to give information concerning them. He did not, however, nor did any of those who investigated the family history, discover that Robert and Magdalen Polk had nine children, instead of eight, and that this other one was named David, who appears to have died unmarried, as he devised his property to his namesake, a son of his brother William. In his will of date 1699, Robert Polk, Sr., mentions this son David.

Magdalen Polk is said to have lived to be over ninety years old, dying at her home place "White Hall" in Somerset County, between April 7, 1726, and March 20, 1727, the respective dates of the execution of her will and its probate or admission to record.

* It will be noticed that the letter of John Keys, of Ireland, dated October 17, 1877, to W. H. Polk gives the approximate birth of Capt. John Keys (who married Barbara Tasker, the sister of Magdalen) as "about 1650" and his wife was likely near the same age. Magdalen was also very near the ages of Capt. Keys and Barbara.

CHAPTER XIV

MAGDALEN POLK'S WILL

In the name of God Amen

I, Magdalen Pollock, being weak and sick of body, yet of perfect mind and memory, praise be to Almighty God, do make and ordain this my last will and Testament, in manner and form as followeth

First:—I give my soul into the hands of Almighty God, hoping through the merits of my Savoir Jesus Christ to receive full pardon of all my sins. And my body I commit to the Earth from whence it was taken, to be buried in Christian burial, at the discretion of my Executor hereafter nominated

Item—I give and bequeath a tract of land called Moneen lying in the Kingdom of Ireland, in the Barrony of Rafo and County of Donegal and in the Parish of Liford, unto my son Joseph Pollock and to the heirs of his body forever, with all the rest of my moveable estate, and him to be whole Executor of this my last Will and Testament, hereby Revoking all other Wills and Testaments by me made by word or writing

In Testimony whereof I set my hand and seal this 7th day of April, 1726

      Magdalen Polk Seal

Signed, sealed and delivered in sight and presents of us David Polk, William Pollet, Magdalen Pollet

March ye 20th, 1727. Then came David Polk, William Pollett & Magdalen Pollett, subscribing evidences to ye within Will, who made oath upon ye Holy Evangelist of Almighty God that they see ye within named Magdalen Polk, ye Testator, sign and seal ye within Instrument as her last Will and Testament, and that they heard her publish and declare ye same as so to be, and that at ye time of her so doing she was of sound, disposing mind and memory. Sworn to before me the day and year above written

      John Cunst[?]ll, Deputy [...]
         Sussex County

The Exr hath not got letter of Administration on this Estate nor doth not design   Pr Geo Plater, Reg'r
Examined   Test Esme Bayley, R W S C

This official copy of Magdalen's will was procured by W H Polk from the Clerk of Somerset County on January 6, 1873 It will be noticed that at the beginning of the document she calls her name "Pollock" but signs it Polk She also calls her son Joseph "Pollock" This will is also recorded at Annapolis, in the office of the "Chief Commissary," or Colonial Recorder It will further be noticed that Magdalen made Joseph, the youngest son, her sole devisee As suggested by Col Wm T G Polk, the reasons moving her to do this may have been because Joseph, judging by the records, appears to have been less thrifty in the gathering of worldly possessions than his brothers all of whom seem to have been men of good business qualities and to have accumulated fine landed estates, either by grant from Lord Baltimore or by purchase Just what disposition Joseph made of this Irish property bequeathed to him by his mother is not certainly known Family tradition says that he went to Ireland, sold "Moneen" to his aunt, Barbara Keys and returned to Maryland and died in Somerset County

The assumption that Joseph was less enterprising than his brothers, is strengthened by the fact that all the other sons of Robert and Magdalen received numerous grants of land from Lord Baltimore, as shown by the records of the Colonial Land Office, while but one appears in the name of Joseph Polk and that of date November 15, 1738, consisting of ninety acres located "on the South side of Wicomico River," under the patent name of "Forlone Hope's Addition" This patent title is suggestive of a lack of enterprise by Joseph, who probably was blessed with a "restful" inclination It will also be noticed that the date of the grant to him (1738) was about ten years after the devise of "Moneen" to him under his mother's will and this fact goes to prove the likelihood of the tradition that he went to Ireland, sold the land to his aunt, and returned to America

GRANTS FROM LORD BALTIMORE

Following is a list of the principal and first land grants to Robert Bruce Polk and his sons, by the Lords Baltimore, between the years 1687 and 1712.

"Robert Polke," "Polke's Lott," 50 acres, lying in Somerset County, on the North side of Manokin River, March 7, 1687 Recorded in Liber 221, folio 356

Robert Polke—"Polk's Folly," 100 acres, lying in Somerset County, on the North side of Manokin River, near the head of Broad Creek, March 7, 1687. Recorded in Liber 22, folio 356

Robert Poalk, Jr., "Bally Hack," 200 acres, lying in Somerset County, Marsh Ground, Nov 8, 1700. Recorded in Liber D D No 5, folio 73

Ephraim Poalk, "Clonmell," 100 acres, lying in Somerset County, between Manokin Branch and Pidgeon House, or Little Creek, September 20th, 1700 Recorded in Liber D D, No 5, folio 73

Ephraim Poalk, "Long Delay," 214 acres, lying in Somerset County, in Damn Quarter, on west side of Ball's Creek March 26, 1705. Recorded in Liber D D No 5, folio 366.

James Poalk, "James' Meadow" 200 acres, lying in Somerset County, in Damn Quarter, on the N E side of Williams Creek, June 1, 1705 Recorded in Liber D D No. 5, folio 368

Ephraim Poalk, "Chance," 200 acres Lying on E side Chesapeake Bay, in Dorchester County, May 27, 1715 Recorded in Liber E E No 6, folio 235

The foregoing list of the earliest grants made to sons of Robert and Magdalen was procured in 1873 It will be noticed that the two first entries were to Robert Polke, Sr, husband of Magdalen, and comprised 150 acres By the name "Polk's Folly," he possibly referred to what he considered to be his "folly" in coming to the New World

The names of the other grantees are written Poalk, evidently a clerical freedom which seems to have been common at that time, with entry clerks and others engrossing or handling legal documents The seven foregoing grants foot up 1,124 acres of land received by Robert Sr., Robert, Jr., Ephraim, and James David, John, William and Joseph's names do not appear in this list as acquirers of public domain

ADDITIONAL LIST OF GRANTS.

A few years later a second and larger list was procured from the Maryland Colonial records, which is as follows

"Polks chance," 200 acres E side Chesapeake Bay, Dorchester County, Ephraim Polack "Chance," 10th Sept, 1715, (the dates of these entries being different, the last was no doubt an addition to the first)

"Monen" 100 acres, E side Main branch Nanticoke River, in John's Neck. Wm Polk Somerset County, 10th July, 1725

"Denigall," 100 acres E side Main Branch Nanticoke River, in John's Neck, Wm Polk, 10th July, 1725

"Romas," 100 acres, E side Main Branch Nanticoke River, in John's Neck William Polk, 10th Sept, 1725

Richmond," 200 acres, Southermost side Main Branch Nanticoke River Somerset County, Wm Polk, 6th March, 1728

"Charles Purchase," 100 acres, E side do, do, do, Charles Polk 14th March, 1728

"Green Pasture," 200 acres, W side on Island Damn Quarter, Somerset County, James Polke, 27th Feb, 1728

"Polk's Privilege," 50 acres, N E side Main branch Nanticoke River, Somerset County, Charles Polk, 2d Nov, 1730

"White Oak Swamp," 100 acres, N side Nanticoke River, Somerset County, James Pollock, 23rd Nov, 1730

"Charles' Advantage," E Side Main Branch Nanticoke River, Somerset County, Charles Polk, 2d Nov, 1730

"Plimouth," 290 acres, in Dorchester County, David Pollock, 11th Oct, 1730

"Addition " 200 acres, do do, do 3d Dec, 1732

"Second Purchase," 400 acres, E side of Branch of Main N E. Branch Nanticoke River, Somerset County, Charles Polk, 24th July, 1733

"C . . . ." . . . acres, 2 miles from head Wicomico Creek . . . . . . , Wm Polk and Thomas Polint, 4th December, 1735

"Forlorn Hope's Addition," 90 acres, S side Wicomico River, Somerset County, Joseph Polk, 15th May, 1738

"Margaret's Fancy," 50 acres, E side Chesapeake Bay, Dorchester County, Robert Polk 7th July, 1739

"Hogg Yard, 134 acres, Dorchester County, Ephraim Pollock, 10th Dec., 1740

"Dublin's Advantage," 184 acres, do. do, do, John Pollock, 20th December, 1741

"John's Venture," 200 acres, do, do, do, John Pollock, 20 December, 1741

"David's Hope,' 450 acres, do, do, do, David Pollock, 11th November, 1742.

This second list of grants, embodying 3,128 acres, when added to the first list, make 4,152 acres granted to the Polks from Mar 7, 1687, to Nov. 11, 1742, a period of fifty-five years There were many others beside, at later dates, to various Polks as the records show From the foregoing lists it appears that Ephraim secured the largest quantity of land, 908 acres being entered in that name It is apparent, however that the last grant "Hogg Yard," was to Ephraim 2d, as Ephraim 1st died in 1718 William Polk's entries amounted to 500 acres, Charles secured 600 acres. Charles Polk, the oldest son and heir at law of Ephraim 1st, was a man of great enterprise and accumulated a good sized fortune for that day He sold his lands in Somerset County, amounting to 600 acres, and moved to Dorchester County He was the ancestor of a distinguished branch of the family in Delaware among whom were Govenor Trusten Polk, of Missouri, and Governor Charles Polk of Delaware His nephew, Ephraim Polk 3d was a soldier of the Revolution, in Col Wm. Will's Philadelphia regiment, and after the close of the war emigrated to Scott County, Kentucky (1793) where he died in 1814 after again enlisting to serve under Jackson at New Orleans.

CHAPTER XV.

WILL OF ROBERT BRUCE POLK.

The belief prevailed for many years in the Polk family, even in the very neighborhood where the immigrants landed, that Capt Robert Bruce Polk had died in Ireland, and that only his family, Magdalen and her children constituted the original immigrants

It is evident that this impression first arose about 1848, while Col W H Winder, of Baltimore. Josiah F Polk, of Washington, D C and others interested, were engaged in getting up a history and "tree" of the family. Finding no record proof of the presence in Somerset County of Robert Bruce Polk, and ascertaining that his wife, Magdalen was long a widow before her death, the conclusion was that he had died in Ireland before the emigration of his family The will of Magdalen, and of others of the family, was of record in Somerset County, but that of Robert Bruce Polk did not appear They doubtless were unaware, or did not remember, that in the early existence of the Colony of Maryland, there was a "Chief Commissary " as he was called, and that this officer had in each county a "Deputy Commissary," by whom all wills were probated and put on record, a copy of same being then forwarded to the Chief Commissary for re-entry and filing thus insuring greater security in case either office should be burned

Robert Bruce Polk evidently did not die at Annapolis, where his will was discovered a few years ago by a descendant of the Polks, Mr R C Ballard Thruston of Louisville, Ky. The copy of his will that should have been of record at Princess Anne, Somerset County was evidently lost or mislaid That Robe t . - living in Somerset County when he executed his will on M a b h 1 " c proven by the instrument itself, for in the 4th section in bequeathing his house and plantation to his wife Magdalen, he speaks of it as "my now dwelling place and plantation."

The procurement by the author, in 1875, from the Maryland Land Office, of a list of twenty-seven grants of land from Lord Baltimore to the Polk family, two of which were to Robert Bruce Polk himself, settled the fact that he did come to America with his family, and the subsequent discovery of his will at Annapolis further proves it beyond all question

Robert's Will

In the Name of God. Amen

This sixth day of May in the year of our Lord 1699, I Robert Polke of Somerset County in the Province of Maryland being of good health and Perfect memory at this present thank be to Almighty God for the same yet knowing the uncertainty of this present life and being desirous to settle my affairs doe make this my last will and Testament in manner and form following·

First and principally I commend my soule to God who gave it to me, assuredly believing that I shall receive full and free pardon of all my sins and be saved by the pretious Death and Merritts of my Blessed Savior and Redeemer Jesus Christ and my Body to the Earth from whence it was taken to be buried after a decent and Christian manner at the discretion of my Executor hereafter named and as touching such worldly estate as God in his mercy hath bestowed upon me It is my will that it be disposed of as hereafter is expressed

2ndly I leave to my son Robert Polke a parcel of land called Lone Ridge being part of a tract of land called Forlone Hope, formerly belonging to Augustine Standforth but now conveyed to me the said land called Lone Ridge beginning at a marked pine standing in a slash next to my said Son's House and from thence running north east the number of poles specified in the pattent soe leaving to my son Robert what land belongs to the said pattent on the north east side of the said Slash to him the said Robert Polke and his heirs forever

3rdly I leave to my said son David Polke the remainder of the above said tract of Land called Forlorn Hope as also one hundred acres of land called Polks Folly bounded as per

Pattent will appear both said tracts of land to him the said David and his heirs forever

4thly I leave to my Beloved Wife Magdalen Polke my now dwelling house and plantation during her natural life as also a third of what goods and moveables I am possed with or shall hereafter to the day of my death the said Goods and moveables to be at her dispossing at her decease. Another third of my Goods and moveables I leave to my daughter Martha be it little or much here and her heirs forever and as for the other third It is my will it be equally divided between my sons David and Joseph, and if it should please God to Remove me before I purchase a seat of Land after my son Joseph, this my will that my son David give unto my son Joseph four thousand pounds of Tobacco in the leu of the above said tracts of Land left to my son David and as for what Cattle I have given to my son Joseph they being in his proper Mark it's my will that he enjoy and possess the same he and his heirs forever for this boy Christopher must live with Magdalen Polke during her life time then.

5thly I leave to my son James an Orphan Boy called Christopher Little to him the said James and his heirs during the time of his Indre

I leave unto my son Ephraim the choice of what stear I have or may have at the day of my death

I leave to my sons John and William Polke to each of them twelve pence

I constitute and appoint my son David Polke and my wife Magdalen Polke to be Executors of this my last will.

Codicil—I constitute my sons Ephraim and James Polke to be Executors of this my last will and testament disannulling and making voide all former Will or Wills by me made either by word or written

In Witness whereof I have hereunto set my hand and seal the day and year above written this being altered the eighth day of August, 1703

                        Robert Polke   Seal

Richard Ison, hi
Mary O Furgh h
Richard Whittley

And I desire that Martha Poock may have liberty let her cattle run on the plantation until she gets plantation and as to Sarah Powers she must have a heifer at her freedom day."

Signed, Sealed and delivered in the presence of us
Robert Polk
Richard Whittley
Richard Knight
Mary O English

On the back of said will was thus written "Vizt —Memorandum this 5th day of June the within will was proved to be the Act and Deed of the within named Robert Polke by the oaths of Richard Whittley, Richard Knight and Mary English before

                      Peter Dent, Depty Com'y

Test
R McKendree Davis,
Dept Register Orphans Court
Anne Arundel County
  State of Maryland
Annapolis Wills T B. 1701-3, folios 416-418

The quaint capitalization and spelling of some of the words of the instrument were characteristic of the times. Many well-to-do people could but indifferently write or spell, as opportunities for acquiring an education were scarce The spelling of some words in Robert's will remind us of the inscription cut on a tree by Daniel Boone, to the effect that he "Cilled a Bar on this Tree"

It is deducible from the will of Robert:

1st —The tract of land which he bequeathed to his sons 'Lone Ridge," was a part of "Forlorn Hope," (to which Joseph added 90 acres by a later entry on Nov 15, 1738) which he had purchased from Augustine Standforth, probably the original grantee

2d —That one of his two daughters was named Martha, not Margaret, as some have given it

3d —That he certainly had a son David, making his children nine in number John, W⸺, Ephraim, James, Robert, David, Joseph, Martha and S⸺. The inference of several sources is that D⸺ ⸺ ⸺ they unger is Joseph be-

ing the youngest and the legatee of his mother in her will
It is inferable, also, that David may have died between the
time his father's will was executed (May 6, 1699) and the time
the codicil was added, (August 8, 1703), by which codicil the
first named executors—Magdalen and David—were supplanted
by the sons Ephraim and James. It also appears that David
died a bachelor, for, in his will, he bequeaths his property to
his nephew and probable namesake, David Polk, Jr, son of
William, son of Robert and Magdalen.

4th—That tobacco must have been extensively raised in
Maryland, for it was used as a medium of exchange, under certain conditions of the will David being required to pay to
Joseph 4,000 lbs of the weed

5th—That the orphan boy Christopher Little was indentured to Robert until he should attain to his majority 'If
Robert had any African slaves he did not mention the fact,
which he would likely have done had he possessed any.

6th—Ephraim, John and William received but slight bequests It is evident that they already possessed comfortable
estates and did not need anything from the estates of their
parents Hence the latter sought to equalize, as far as possible, the conditions of their children by making David and
Joseph their principal legatees

7th—That Robert Bruce Polk died between May 6th, 1699,
and June 5th, 1704, most likely in May of the latter year, as
it has long been the custom to offer wills for probate shortly
after the death of decedent

From Magdalen's will it is deducible·

1st—That the person who drew up her will wrongfully
wrote the name of her estate in Ireland, bequeathed to Joseph
as "Moning," when it should have been Moneen, as shown by
correspondence with members of the Keys family, who still
own a part of it

2d—That of the witnesses to her will, David was her son,
and William and Magdalen Pollitt her nephew and niece,
children of Thomas Pollitt, who married her daughter Martha

OTHER POLK WILLS

Beside the will of Robert and Magdalen Polk which are

here given in full, there are a great many of record in Somerset Anne Arundel, Dorchester and Worcester Counties, Maryland, in Newcastle, Kent and Sussex Counties, Delaware, and also in Pennsylvania, the Eastern Shore of Virginia, North and South Carolina, Georgia, Alabama, Mississippi, Texas, Missouri, Arkansas, Iowa, Illinois, Indiana, Kentucky, Tennessee In fact, there is hardly a state in the Union in which Polks are not found and Polk wills recorded

Among others in possession of the writer are: Will of Wm Polk, Sussex County Delaware, Nov 20, 1786 Will of Wm Polk, Somerset County, Maryland, Jan 23, 1739. Will of Ephraim Polk 2d, Sussex County, Delaware, Jan 5, 1789 Will of Charles Polk, Frederick County, Maryland, March 19, 1753 Will of John Polk, Cumberland County, Pa, Oct 27, 1772 Will of Emanuel Polk, Sussex County, Delaware, Sept 6, 1793 Will of James Polk, Somerset County, Maryland, November 8, 1726

CHAPTER XVI

OBSERVATIONS OF R C. B THRUSTON

Respecting some of the foregoing points discussed, Col R C Ballard-Thruston of Louisville, Ky, a member of the Polk clan, has arranged consecutively a number of official transactions, followed by his "Conclusions" respecting the same They are

JOHN POLK SON OF ROBERT BRUCE POLK
(Index to Authorities Quoted)

("W T G P"—Col Wm T G Polk, Princess Anne, Md)
("W H P"—Wm H Polk, Lexington, Ky)
("E. B. P"—Earle B Polk Princess Anne, Md)
(" M W G "—Miss Mary Winder Garrett, Williamsburg Va.)
(" A. H M "—American Hist. Magazine)

INFORMATION.

1680, Sept 8,   John Polke entered the ear marks of his cattle. (WTGP Oct 31 1874 WHP Aug 15, 1899.)

1685 June 1,   John Poalk patented "Locust Hammock" in Somerset Co, Md on the east side of the Chesapeake Bay and south side of the Wiccocomico River in Dames Quarter Neck (WHP Aug 15, 1899. See deed from Wm Kent or Cent, to Ephraim Polk, dated 1716)

1689,   The names of Robert Polk and John Polk appear on a list of loyal subjects of Somerset County, who addressed a letter to King William and Queen Mary (Baltimore Sun 660 Sept 1 1901 .

1692, Mar. 15,   Deed from Capt. Henry Smith to John Polk of Somerset (WHP Aug 15, 1899) for "Bellendrett" 150 acres part of Smith's Recovery a 700 acre patent to said Smith dated April 22 1684 (See copy of deed Polk to Hall)

1695, Dec. 6,   John Polk was witness to the will of William Porter, of Somerset, dated December 6, 1695 and proven June 10, 1696 (Md Calendar of Wills II, 103)

1698, Mar. 27,   In will of Wm Owens of Somerset, dated Mar 27, 1698, John Polk and Wm Knox were named as overseers (Md Cal of Wills II 181)

1699, May 6,   In will of his father, Robert Bruce Polk, John was devised 12 pence

1702, Dec. 20,   John willed "Locust Hammock" and other lands to William Kent, of St John's County in the Territories of Pennsylvania (See recital in deed from Wm Kent to Ephraim Polk dated November 2, 1716 (WHP August 15 1899; EBP April 3, 1909)

1707, Oct 8,   John Polke, of Somerset County, "coopper," and Johanna his "now wife," made deed to Alex Hall of the same county, conveying Bellendrett, 150 acres, that was deeded by Capt Henry Smith to him March 15, 1692, and which was a part of Smith's Recovery, a 700 acre patent to said Smith dated April 22 1684 (See copy of deed). John Polk seems to have signed this deed in person, but Johanna made her mark

1707-8, Mar. 10,   Deed from Matthew Wallis, of "ye county of New Castle upon Delaware yeoman," to John Polk of Somerset County, cooper, conveys 100 acres in Somerset County, being 2 miles back in ye woods 'from ye forks of Rockiaemkin River, where ye "said River divides itself into branches and on head of Rockawackin River (later spelled Rockawakin River)." This 500 acres in two tracts, 1st, 300 acres called "Friends Denyall," which recital in deed shows was patented to Thos. Cox, October 26 1681, deeded by him and wife, Rebecca, to Phenix Hall, October 3, 1684. Deeded by Hall and wife, Elizabeth to Matchew Wallis, October 31, 1687. The other was a 200 acre tract called "Kirkminster," which the recital shows was patented to Matthew Wallis, October 9, 1694.

1708, June 9, William Polk petitioned the court asking to be appointed guardian to Wm & Anne (Nancy), children of his brother John, alleging that 'his brother, on his death bed requested him (William), and his wife, to take care of his children and see that they were properly brought up and to give them a Christian education." Wm also asked that "the portion of these children coming from their father's estate, moveables, be delivered to him,' which was done.

Col Wm T G Polk, October 31, 1874, gives this date as May 10, 1708, by error, (WHP August 15, 1899. EBP February 26, 1909, see copy of petition and order of court)

1708, Aug. 11, The Somerset County records show that the "widow Polk" brought a servant into court to be judged of his age, etc. This was indexed Joannah Polk (WTGP 10, 31, 1874, EBP 4 3, 1909.)

The "widow Polk" is again mentioned under the same date in connection with a boy that ... and to John Polk now deceased" (BP April 3, 1909)

1708, Sept. 2, — Inventory of John Polk's goods—a very long list—summing up £ 66-9-1. (EBP April 3 1909).

1710, Dec. 6, — Account of Thos Hugg and Joannah his wife "relict of John Polk" in reference to the estate of John Polk (EBP Apr 3, 1909)
The records of Somerset Co show that Joanna widow of John Polk, married a man named Hugg. Also there is pretty good circumstantial evidence that John had a son, John, younger than his son William (Josiah F. Polk to W H Winder, Feb 15, 1849, quoted by W. H Polk Aug. 20, 1899) Josiah stated "In tracing more particularly the descendents of John, the eldest son of Robert and Magdalen, I learn that he did leave children by his second wife, Jugga Hugg, and from that union springs one of the Delaware family" (WH Winder to Jas K. Polk, Sept 23, 1848, quoted by WHP, Aug. 20 1899) If John also married Jugurtha Hugg, she was his first wife and mother of his children, William and Nancy see h c f p

1716, Nov. 20, — Deed from Wm Kent, of the Territories of Pennsylvania, to Ephraim Polk, conveying "Locust Hammock," etc. This deed recites a patent to "John Poalke, late of Somerset." dated June 1, 1685, also that said John's will bears date Dec 20, 1702, in which he willed this tract to Wm Kent for the benefit of his two children Wm. and Ann   (WHP Aug 15, 1899)

1723 Sept. 28, — Deed from Thos Hugg and wife Joanna to John Caldwell recites conveyance "to John Poike the late husband of the said Joanna" and conveyed her dower rights in the following two tracts

1723-4 Jan 7, Deed from "William Polk of Dorsett and province of Maryland, blacksmith, and Prisela his wife" to John Caldwell, of Somerset Co. (conveys two tracts of land "Friends Denial" 300 acres, "Kirkminster" 200 acres. Recites the grants of the above two tracts to Thos. Cox and Matthew Wallis and their conveyance to John Polk, deceased. That they "descended to his son Wm. Polk as heir-at-law to the said John Polk," and that the grantor is the said Wm. Polk. Both Wm. Polk and wife seem to have signed the deed in person.

1726-7, Will of Thos. Hugg, of Somerset, dated Feb 17, 1726-7, proven May 11, 1729, in which he devised the home plantation to wife Johanna during her widowhood, and makes bequest to eldest daughter, Jane, and youngest daughter, Mary, and to his son William by his former wife. Leaves his wife executrix and makes his mark to his signature. (EBP 3/13/1909.)

1740, Nov. 5, Deed from Patrick Caldwell and wife Mary to John Polk, conveys a tract of land "in Somerset Co. on the east side of the Nanticoke River, at a Red Oak about 100 yards from where the county road crosses the head of a branch of Broad Creek called Rossaketoms Branch, about a mile below Johanna Huggs." (EBP 3/13/1909.)

CHAPTER XVII.

MARRIAGES AND DESCENDANTS.

John Polk married Joanna Knox and left two children, William and Ann, or Nancy (AHM Oct 1897 p 382) William Polk brother of John, married Ann or Nancy Knox (then the widow Owens) (AHM Apr 1898 p 230). Ann Polk, sister to John & William, married Francis Roberts and had two children, Edward and Priscilla Roberts who married their first cousins, Wm & Ann Polk children of John (AHM Oct 1897 1, 383)

1722, Matthew Harmanson and wife, Easter, Northampton Co ,deeded to Wm Polk of Dorchester Co, a 250 acre tract of land called "Collier's Adventure," that was patented to Robert P. Collier, of Somerset Co in 1674, lying on the north side of Nanticoke River. Conveyance was by John Pollet, as attorney, and witnessed by James Pollock and James Bruckshor.

1726, Will of William Polk, of Dorchester, dated Nov 25, 1726, proven Feb 21, 1727-8, bequeaths to son John Polk, dwelling plantation, etc
To oldest daughter, Jane, two adjoining tracts of land, Low Ridge and Polk's Folly.
To youngest daughter, Ann, 50 acres on head of Dames Quarter Creek
To John Pollett a tract of land
To wife (not named) all of his land during her widowhood

of John

1727, May 20,   Inventory of estate of Wm Polk filed by Robert Clarkson, who married Priscilla, widow of William Polk. It was signed by James Cannon, John Pollett, Robert Polk and Thomas Polk, as creditors and next of kin (MWG Aug 2nd & 30th, 1899.) Priscilla married Clarkson about 3 months after her husband Wm Polk died, as above shows

1727, June 11,   The account of Priscilla Polk, executrix of William, late of Dorchester, deceased (Acc Lst 9, Vol 382 Aug 2 1899, (MWG)

1728, July 30,   John Pollett, Sr, of Dorchester, gave a bond to Priscilla Polk of Dorchester, relict and executrix of Wm Polk deceased. Said bond recited

D-4,   If John Pollett his heirs &c shall at any time "or times hereafter happen to run out his or her "lands and should by that means intersect the "Upper fencing of the said Priscilla Polk, her "heirs &c as it now stands, that then the said "John Pollett, his heirs &c shall be obliged to "make over his or their Right, title and interest "unto" &c Witness
Ester V. (x) Whitty, Rachel C (x) Samuel, daughter of John Samuel & John Phipps

1740, Nov. 5,   Deed from Patrick Caldwell and wife Mary to John Polk, in which these words appear "In Somerset Co on the east side of the Nanticoke River, at a Red Oak about 100 yards from where it crosses the head of a branch of Broad Creek called Rossaketoms Branch, about a mile below Johanna Hugg's (LRP Mar 13 1903)

1743, Jan. 5,   Deed from David Pollock of Dorchester, to Thomas Wright for parcel of land and marsh, seven acres, taken out of a patent called "Contention," beginning at a marked pine bounder of tract formerly surveyed for Thomas Bloyce, on east side of Little Creek, etc , etc Consideration 1000 pounds of tobacco (See Liber X No 1 folio 93)

1750, Dec. 28,   John Polk, of the Territories of Pennsylvania deeded to Wm Turpen, of Dorchester, Colliers
D-19,   Adventure containing 250 acres

ROBERT'S CHILDREN.

1726,   Will of James Polk, of Somerset County, dated Nov 8th 1726, proven May 11, 1727, makes a bequest "unto my cousin Edward Roberts on the provision my cousin Edward do deliver up the bond that I passed to him " (See copy of will under James Polk line)

1773,   Will of David Pollock, of Dorchester, dated Feb 21, 1773, proven March 11, 1773 He makes bequests to his daughter Elizabeth Roberts, to his daughter-in-law, Priscilla Pollock; to his grand-children, David, William and Esther Pollock. (See copy of will under James Polk line)

1773,   Will of Pricilla Pollock, of Dorchester, dated Feb 26, 1773, proven Apr 5, 1773; names son David, daughter Esther Pollock; brothers William and Francis Roberts, and sister Nancy Nellums (See abstract of will recorded in book 9, page 711 in Land Office at Annapolis Maryland)

CONCLUSIONS.

All traditions make John Polk the eldest son of Robert Bruce Polk. This I accept as correct, although I have no proof of it.

From my investigations, I am inclined to think that at a very early age—16 or possibly even at 14—boys were, under proper conditions, given all the rights of freemen unless it was that of voting. The idea that they must have been 21 years of age to even deal in real estate was erroneous. They certainly could witness instruments and even trade in cattle, recording their ear-marks, etc., at a much earlier age. The date of John's birth as 1659, or earlier, was assumed on the theory that he must have been 21 in 1680 when he entered the ear-marks of his cattle. This, I am inclined to think he could have done possibly at the age of 12, which would place his birth somewhere between 1659 and 1668. Under William Polk, it will be seen that he, (William) died 1740, aged about 78, therefore born about 1662. If this is correct, and if John Polk were older than William, then John must have been born about 1660. If younger than William, then he was born from 1664 to 1668, depending upon the relative ages of John and his sister Ann. I incline, however, to the view that John was the eldest child and born about 1659 or 1660.

The deed from John Polk and Joanna, his "now wife," to Alex Hall in 1707, would indicate that he had been previously married. Again it is claimed that his will or bequest of land in Dec., 1702, to Kent was for the purpose of providing for his children William and Anne, presumably by a wife earlier than the one which he then had. The petition in court by his brother Wm in June 1708 would also indicate that the wife who survived him was not the mother of William and Anne or she would have been the natural guardian and custodian of her own children.

There is a persistent claim that John and his brother, Wm married sisters whose maiden names were Joanna and Nancy Knox. Certain it is that Anne (or Nancy) married Wm Owen, and later Wm Polk, second son of Robert Bruce

Polk In his will dated Mar 1698, this Wm Owens named John Polk and Wm Knox (presumably brothers-in-law) as overseers

John's children, William and Nancy, were evidently named for their uncle and aunt, Mr and Mrs Wm Polk, which was an additional incentive for the interest Wm Polk took in these two children And whilst it should not be accepted as conclusive proof that John had no other children by his first wife, still the records that I have seen do not even intimate that there may have been more than the two children mentioned It is claimed that the deed or bequest to Wm Kent in 1702 was to insure provision for his two children William and Nancy The records show that their uncle William acted as their guardian The deed from Kent to Ephraim Polk in 1716 has been assumed as evidence that Ephraim also acted as guardian I am inclined to think that this is a mistake, that William had then reached his majority and sold Locust Hammock to his uncle, hence the deed from Kent, who was merely a trustee, to Ephraim Polk

If this view is correct, it would also serve to locate the birth of Wm Polk as 1695 unless he were under 21 when he made the sale. Summing up the evidence on John Polk, I should say that he was born 1659 to 1660, that he married in 1694, at the age of about 35, and had only two children, William and Nancy In Dec 1702 he made a will, or a deed, in favor of Wm Kent, making provision for his children, William and Nancy, the presumption being that he was then married to, or about to marry, his second wife, though we have no proof of this second marriage until Oct 1707 At first he lived in Somerset County, Md, he may have moved to St John's County, Pa, (now Kent County, Del) and there married Joanna ————; but apparently he was a resident of Somerset County, Md at the time of his death in 1708 In this connection it must be noticed that at that time the territorial claims of Somerset County, Md, extended to and included the present Sussex County, Del

There is nothing to show where John was living at the time of his death, nor where his family lived afterwards It is probable, however, that he resided on the ——— bought from Matthew Wallis in 1708, known as "Friends Denial" and "Kirkminster," and that his family continued to reside there until his son William, the blacksmith, sold the property in 1723 to John Caldwell. I incline to the idea that Thomas Hugg and wife lived near this property and that it was a portion of this same 500 acres that was deeded by Patrick Caldwell to John Polk in 1740.

Thomas Hugg left a will dated Feb. 17, 1726/7, just four days before the will of Wm Polk, the blacksmith, was proven. It was, therefore, probably written after the death of Wm Polk. By this will, Hugg shows that he had been previously married and that he had a son William by his first marriage, and two daughters, Jane and Mary, by his second. He does not mention any step-children and to my mind the presumption is that he had none.

I have not been able to locate the date of the death of Joanna, widow, first of Jno Polk and later of Thos. Hugg. She does not seem to have left any will of record. My conclusion is that she had no children by Jno Polk, and by Thos Hugg, only two, who were living in 1726/7; and that she, herself, was the one referred to in the deed from Patrick Caldwell and wife to John Polk dated Nov. 5, 1740, and therefore was living at that time.

CHAPTER XVIII

WILLIAM POLK, GRANDSON OF ROBERT BRUCE POLK.

William Polk, son of John Polk, eldest son of Capt Robert Bruce Polk was probably born 1695. He was certainly very young in 1702, when his father made provision for the maintenance of him and his sister, Anne, by devising "Locust Hammock" to Wm Kent He was left an orphan somewhere between March 10, 1707/8 and June 9, 1708, for, on the latter date his uncle, William, was appointed guardian for him and his sister, Anne or Nancy, with instruction that William be taught a trade He was probably of age Nov. 20, 1716, on which date, Wm Kent deeded Locust Hammock to Ephraim Polk 1st I believe as the result of a sale of that property by Wm Polk, blacksmith, to his uncle Ephraim In 1722 he purchased from Matthew Harmanson and wife a 250 acre tract called Collier's Adventure, on the north side of the Nanticoke River, upon which he probably lived

There is a tradition in the family that William married his cousin Priscilla Roberts, which is probably correct, for in 1723 he and his wife Priscilla, his step-mother and her second husband, Joanna and Thos Hugg, sold the 500 acres known as "Friends Deniall" and "Kirkminster" to John Caldwell, at which time he is recorded as being of "Dorsett Co."—Dorchester

William died about Nov 25, 1726/7 leaving a son, John and two daughters, Jane and Anne. These children were presumbly named for their grand parents, John Polk and his wife Jane, and Anne Polk, who married Francis Roberts His wife did not long remain single, for on May 20, 1727, the inventory of his estate was filed by her and her second husband, Robert Clarkson The singular feature about this inventory is that it was signed by James Cannon John Polk Robert

Polk and Thos Polk as "creditors and the next of kin" Robert and Thomas Polk were probably his first cousins, sons of Robt Polk and Grace Guillette. John Pollet was also probably his first cousin, a son of his aunt Martha. How James Cannon came to be next of kin, I do not know, but I am inclined to think that both he and John Pollet married two of the daughters of Robert Polk and Grace Guillette, that Wm Polk, the blacksmith, had purchased from his uncle Robert, Low Ridge and Polks Folly and had not completed the payment for same, therefore, his uncle Robert's sons and sons-in-law appear as creditors and next of kin

It is singular that his widow, Priscilla, should appear as the wife of Robert Clarkson May 20, 1727, and three weeks later, on July 30, 1728, she as Priscilla Polk, "relict and executrix of Wm. Polk deceased, should have received a bond from her husband's uncle, John Pollet, Sr regarding the possible conflict of land lines

What became of his daughters, Jane and Anne, does not appear.

John Polk, Jr, (of that line) son of Wm Polk, blacksmith, was certainly the one who in Dec 1730 conveyed Colliers Adventure, which his father William had purchased in 1722 Nothing further is known of this John for certainty, but I am inclined to think that he was the same one who in 1740 made purchase from one Patrick Caldwell of certain lands in Somerset County on the east side of Nanticoke River, about a mile below Joanna Hugg, whose first husband was John Polk, Sr

ANNE POLK, DAUGHTER OF JOHN

According to persistent tradition, Anne Polk, daughter of John, married her first cousin, Edward Roberts, the son of Francis Roberts and Ann Polk She was probably born about 1698 and married by the time she was 18 or 20, say in 1715 I believe it is her children who are mentioned under the James Pollock line, of whom there were four, viz: William Francis, Priscilla and Nancy. Priscilla married a son of David and grandson of James Pollock The first name of her husband does not appear, but he had a son David and a daughter Esther, named in his will of 1773

One of these sons of Edward Roberts (William or Francis, it does not appear), married his cousin Elizabeth, daughter of David and granddaughter of James Pollock. The remaining child was called Nancy Nellums in the will of her sister, Priscilla Pollock, dated Feb. 1773.

The intermarriage of the children and grandchildren of John Polk, James Pollock and their sister Anne Polk Roberts are graphically shown by the following chart:

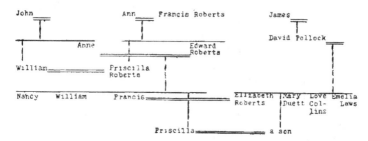

The descendants of John Polk seem to have settled either in the southern part of Delaware or the adjacent portion of Maryland. Unless they had intermarried with some other descendants of Robert Bruce Polk, their lines of descent are not known, and in fact so far as I can see, I have seen no evidence that is to my mind conclusive proof of descent from John Polk's line.

There was one Wm. Polk who married Margaret Taylor. Some of his descendants claim that he was a son of John Polk and Joanna Knox; that he married twice, first his cousin Priscilla Roberts, and second Margaret Taylor; that he sold out his land in Maryland in 1723 and removed to Carlisle, Pa., from which point, with his wife and most if not all of his children, he moved about 1750 to North Carolina. This claim, however, is negatived by a closer examination of the records than was made by those who compiled data for the Polk Tree published in 1849.

Certain it is that the Wm. Polk, who married Priscilla Roberts had but three children and died in 1726-7; and that he was not the one who married Margaret Taylor, and was the ancestor of the southern Polks.

CHAPTER XIX.

JOSEPH POLK AND DESCENDANTS

Joseph Polk (or Pollock) according to all family tradition and record evidence the youngest son of Robert Bruce Polk and his wife Magdalen Polk, was born about 1681 and died in 1752, aged 71 years, at his home in Dorchester County, Maryland. His parents having come to America some years before the date of his birth, it is evident that Joseph was a native of Somerset County.

In his will of May 6, 1699, Robert Bruce Polk, naming his several children, writes their names Polke, and so signs his own name to the instrument. Joseph, it appears, was about twenty-two years of age at the time his father deceased. To Joseph and David, Capt. Robert Polk devised one-third of his "goods and movables," and also to David a part of the tract of land called "Forlorn Hope." And in case of his death before he could purchase a seat for Joseph, then David was to give unto him four thousand pounds of tobacco, in lieu of the land. He also confirms unto Joseph the cattle he had given to him, "they being in his proper mark." This shows that Joseph, even before he had attained to his majority, owned cattle on the range and had legally registered his brand.

Joseph evidently continued to live with his mother at "White Hall," the manor plantation, until her death in 1727. During most of that time—as is generally the case with mothers and sons so situated—Joseph was no doubt a petted, much humored darling of his doting mother, and likely influenced by that partiality she, in her will of 1726 devised to him the Irish estate which she had inherited from her father, Col. Tasker. Another inducement thereto is inferrable from the fact that Joseph's brothers had all acquired substantial estates in Maryland before her death.

In her will of 1726, Magdalen, at the beginning, calls herself "Pollock," but signs it Polk, omitting the terminal letter "e" that her husband had used in his will of 1699

"Moneen Hall," her Irish estate consisting of 600 acres, was evidently all the landed property owned in fee simple by Magdalen before and at her death. After her demise her personal property was divided among her children, and under the English law, the eldest son inherited the manor plantation John, said to have been the eldest son, had died in 1707-8, and the next son William, was the eldest son living in 1727, when his mother Magdalen died. As such, therefore, he inherited "White Hall" and it continued in his line for many years afterward.

Joseph appears to have taken unto himself a helpmeet in the person of a Miss Wright, daughter of Col Thomas Wright, of Dorchester County, by whom he had several children It also appears that he had a second wife, whose maiden name is not known, and that she was alive when he executed his will of Sept 12, 1751 In this will he does not call her by name. In making her his sole executrix, he calls her "my well beloved wife" He also wants his son Robert to "dwell with his mother-in-law" (evidently meaning stepmother) until he is 18 years old or until her marriage

LANDS GRANTED TO JOSEPH POLK

The records of the Maryland Land Office show that Capt Robert Bruce Polk and his sons received at various times grants of land from the Lords Baltimore and that the aggregate of these amounted to about five thousand acres, or more These grants began in 1685 with a considerable tract to John Polk, followed in 1687 with grants to Robert Polk Sr of "Polk's Folly" and "Polk's Lott," amounting to 150 acres In 1700 Ephraim Polk received 374 acres Robert Polk Jr. 200 acres In 1705 James Polk received 200 acres, and in 1715 Ephraim got 200 acres more The records show numerous other grants to the family up to 1713

In this long list of grants there was but one to Joseph Polk, viz "Forlorn Hope's Addition" 90 acres South Side of Wicomico River

Joseph is said to have returned from Ireland, whither he had gone shortly after the death of his mother in 1727, to assume charge of the estate of "Moneen Hall" that she devised to him, and which he finally sold to his aunt Barbara Keys. He therefore appears to have remained in Ireland about nine or ten years before he returned to America. During that interim his name does not appear on the records of Maryland.

When he got back to Maryland, however, Joseph proceeded to acquire a grant from Lord Baltimore, which he did in "Forlorn Hope's Addition." It appears, though, that with the proceeds derived from the sale of the Irish estate to his aunt Barbara Keys, Joseph purchased other lands, already improved by first owners. Among these the Dorchester records show the sale by John Handy Gentleman of Somerset, to Joseph Pollock, Planter, of Somerset,' All of "Little Goshen," 300 acres, in Dorchester, about 8 miles from the head of the N E branch of Nanticoke river and about 2 miles westward of a plantation of Christopher Nutter, called "——— alias Ruffe" Surveyed April 23, 1684, and patented to George Loffield July 15, 1695."

On March 16, 1743, Thomas Nutter of Dorchester conveyed to Joseph Pollock of Dorchester

"All that part of a tract called "Dublin," about 8 miles from the head of the N E branch of Nanticoke river, and about 2 miles westward of a plantation of Christopher Nutter, in Dorchester, and containing 50 acres'

This tract adjoined Little Goshen and together they gave Joseph a homestead of 350 acres, on which it appears he proceeded to "grow old gracefully" during the balance of his days. He did not, like his father and brothers, change his name to Polk but adhered to the ancient and correct form— Pollock As Joseph Pollock, he was devisee in his mother's will of her estate in Ireland. By that name he sold and transferred the estate, and ever afterwards he adhered to the ancient and proper form

Joseph Polk was one of the devisees of his brother Robert Polk Jr (fifth son of Robert and Magdalen) in his will of Feb. 21, 1725 probated May 10, 1727. One item of this will is

"I give and bequeath unto my brother Joseph Polk part of "Forlorn Hope," on the Northern end, being a certain tract of land formerly surveyed for Augustin Stanford, and likewise a certain tract of land called "Bally Hack," lying near the head of a creek called "Pidgeon House Creek" to him and the heirs of his own body forever."

It will be observed that Robert Polk Jr., as shown by the probate of his will, died the same year (1727) in which his brother James and his mother Magdalen Polk deceased.

WILL OF JOSEPH POLLOCK

(Dated Sept 12 1751, probated June 10, 1752.)

In the Name of God Amen, this twelfth day of September Anno Domini one thousand seven hundred and fifty-one, I, Joseph Pollock, of Dorchester County and Province of Maryland, Planter, being sick and weak of body, but of perfect mind and memory, and knowing it is appointed for all men to die, do make and ordain this my last Will and Testament

First I commend my soul to Almighty God that gave it and my body to be buried in a Christianlike manner at the discretion of my Executors hereafter named. As touching such worldly estate wherewith it hath pleased God to bless me with in this world I give, devise and dispose of the same in manner and form following

Imprimis I give and bequeath to my well beloved son Robert Pollock the westermost end of a tract of land called "Little Goshen," and likewise a tract of land called "Horsey's Swamp," containing one hundred acres of land, to him and his heirs forever, and in case he dies without heirs, then to fall to my youngest son James Pollock and his heirs forever, upon the condition of him the said James Pollock paying my daughter Ann Pollock the sum of fifty pounds current money of Maryland in lieu of the land when he shall arrive at the age of twenty-eight years age I likewise give and bequeath to my son Robert Pollock a young negro boy called Sam, being in full for his part of my estate.

Item—I give and bequeath to my well beloved son Zephaniah Pollock the Eastermost end of a tract of land called "Little Goshan" to him and his heirs forever, and in case he dies without heirs then to fall to my youngest son James Pollock and his heirs forever Likewise my will and desire is that the tract of land called "Little Goshan" be equally divided between my two sons Robert and Zephaniah Pollock, at the discretion of my friend John Pollock son of James Pollock, and in case the said Eastermost end of "Goshan" should be lost by means of a suit of law then in lieu thereof I give unto him a young negro girl named Fender, but in case he obtains the land then the said negro girl Fender to be equally divided among my other children I likewise give and bequeath to my son Zephaniah Pollock a gun, in full for his part of my estate

Item —I give and bequeath to my eldest daughter Ann Pollock a young negro girl named Rose, in full for her part of my estate

Item —My will and desire is that my trusty friend John Pollock after my death may prosecute the suit of law now pending between myself and Christopher Nutter and the charges thereof to be defrayed out of my estate

Item.—I give and bequeath to my son James Pollock all my smith tools and the remainder of my estate to be equally divided among my other children

Item —I likewise leave my well beloved wife full and whole Executrix of this my last Will and Testament and my Will and Desire is that my son Robert Pollock may dwell with his mother-in-law till he arrives at the age of eighteen years or till the day of her marriage, and I do hereby utterly disannul and make void all other Wills and Testaments before this by me in any wise named, ratifying and confirming this and no other to be my last Will and Testament

In witness I have hereunto set my hand and Seal the day and year above written

Joseph Pollock (Seal)

Signed, sealed, pronounced and declared by the said Joseph Pollock to be his last Will and Testament, in presence of us

 Charles Rawlins,
 Jacob Layton,
   his
 John J Neal
  mark.

On the 10th day of June Anno Dom 1752 Charles Rawlins and John Neal two of the subscribing witnesses to the aforegoing Will, being duly and solemnly sworn on the Holy Evangels of Almighty God depose and say that they saw the Testator Joseph Pollock sign the aforegoing Will and heard him publish and declare the same to be his last Will and Testament. That at the time of his so doing he was to the best of their knowledge and apprehension of sound and disposing mind and memory, and that they, together with the above Jacob Layton subscribed their respective names as witnesses to the said Will, in the presence of the said Testator and at his request, which Oath was taken by the said Witnesses in the presence of John Pollock as friend and Trustee to the heir at law appointed by the Dec'd which same John Pollock did not object to the probate of the said Will etc

      Certified per
       Jam Auld,
        D COM D. C.

From the above instrument it will be observed that the testator Joseph Pollock left a wife, most likely his second one, at his death That she was probably not then an old woman, and likely to marry again, as he wishes his son Robert to "dwell with his mother-in-law" (meaning stepmother) "until he arrives at the age of eighteen years, or, till the day of her marriage" Joseph does not call the name of his wife, an omission noticeable in nearly all the wills of that period. That Robert was his eldest son is evident from the fact that he gave to him and to Zephaniah, equally, the lands of "Little Goshan" (the manor plantation) and "Horsey's Swamp," with reversion, in case of leaving no heirs, to the youngest son James Pollock. It is quite likely by the second wife. Ann he calls his "eldest daughter," and evidently she also was by his first wife, Miss Wright. The inference is that, by his use of the words "eldest daughter," he had other female children. But, if so, he did not call their names.

Unquestionable proof that Joseph Pollock's first wife, Miss Wright, was the mother of his eldest children, Robert and Ann, is afforded by the will of Col Thomas Wright, dated Feb 8, 1753, and probated Feb. 27th, following, in Somerset County. In this will he gives to his grandchildren Ann Polk and Robert Polk, 1 shilling each." It is observable that he does not call them Pollock, but Polk. The bequests to them were paltry sums and their only value is in the record they have helped to preserve of the line of Joseph. Had the other two children of Joseph Zephaniah and James, also been children of Miss Wright, Col Wright would have given them a shilling each, as his purpose seems merely to have been compliance with a legal requirement, without which the grandchildren would have had greater claims on his estate. As Col Wright did not mention Zephaniah and James, it is evident that they were by Joseph's second wife who survived her husband.

About two years after her father's death Ann left the parental roof, being married on Dec 24 1754, to Daniel Morris, Jr, who resided near the eastern boundry of Dorchester and close to the Sussex County Delaware line. With Daniel Morris, Jr, her husband, and others of the Morris, Hopkins, Nutter and Polk families Ann emigrated to Kentucky in Nov, 1793. Among the slaves she brought was this negro girl Rose who is called "Old Rose" in the will of Ann's husband Daniel Morris Jr, of record in the Clerk's office of Fayette County, Kentucky. This will is dated May 1, 1802, and was probated at Lexington, at December Court, 1806. In it he directs that "Old Rose" have her choice as to which of his children she should wish to live with.

Ann (Pollock) Morris died in June, 1816, near Payne's Depot, Scott County, and was buried beside her husband Daniel Morris Jr, in the Morris family graveyard. For further information of her come under head of Ephraim Polk 3d, who married her daughter Rhoda Ann Morris

What became of Joseph Pollock's three other children named in his will—Zephaniah, Robert and James—we have no knowledge. The name Zephaniah has come down the line for more than a century, cropping out a number of times in the Kentucky and Indiana Morris families. Likewise the name Robert and James, still more frequently.

By those who knew her, Ann (Pollock) Morris is described as a large woman, with great energy individually and in matters of business. She reared a family of twelve children to maturity, and most of these marrying, have left a numerous progeny in Kentucky and other Central Western States.

FAMILY OF DANIEL MORRIS SR.

The following record of the family is copied from the old Morris family Bible.

Daniel Morris Sr. born in Sussex County, Del. 17—, died there about 1785. Among his children were

1. Daniel Morris Jr., b. 17—; married Ann Pollock Dec. 24, 1754.

2. A daughter, b. abt. 17—, married Wm. McNitt, in Del. They also emigrated to Kentucky about 1793.

3. David Morris, b. abt. 17—, married Miss Shotwell, emigrated to Kentucky in 1788, and settled at Mayslick, Mason County where he established a tavern for the entertainment of the great number of emigrants arriving at Limestone (now Maysville) and bound for Central Kentucky.

Concerning the marriage of a cousin of David Morris' wife, Collins History of Kentucky, under the chapter on Mason County, says the first five settlers at Mayslick in 1788 were Abraham, Cornelius and Isaac Drake, of Plainfield, N. J. (brothers), David Morris and John Shotwell, with their families. David Morris' wife was a sister of Shotwell and Isaac Drake's wife and her grown sister, Miss Lydia, their cousins, daughters of Banjamin Shotwell. Isaac Drake had two children, Daniel, (afterwards the celebrated Dr. Daniel Drake) and Elizabeth, afterwards Mrs. Glenn. "They came together by boat Landing June 10, 1788, at Log Point,"

Maysville, thence to their new purchase and future home Here they built five cabins, each of which was one story high, with wooden chimney, puncheon floor, clapboard roof, and portholes. The Indians at that time were making frequent incursions into Kentucky and the pioneers were kept constantly on the alert. In the spring of 1790 the savages fired on some campers near Mayslick and one man was killed.

"In 1791, Miss Lydia Shotwell was married (the first marriage in Mayslick) a number of friends from Washington and others coming to the wedding armed. During the wedding, an alarm was given—of an Indian attack on a wagon, five miles out on the Lexington road. The armed men mounted their horses and galloped off rapidly to the scene. It proved to be a false alarm—the first wedding sell in Mason County, and rather serious to be appreciated."

It will be noticed that the children of Ephraim Polk 3d trace back to Robt. and Magdalen Polk through two branches. First Ephraim third, Ephraim second, Ephraim first, Robert and Magdalen. Second—Rhoda (Morris) Polk (wife of Ephraim 3d) daughter of Daniel Morris Jr. and his wife Ann Pollock, daughter of Joseph Pollock (youngest son of Robert and Magdalen) and his wife Miss Wright of Maryland.

MARTHA AND ANN POLK

Capt. Robert Bruce Polk and his wife Magdalen (Tasker-Porter) Polk's family was composed of seven sons and two daughters, according to all family traditions and other evidence. These two daughters, as shown by Robert Bruce Polk's will of 1699, were Ann and Martha. All the old compilers of the Polk family records and the 1849 Polk Tree give the name Margaret instead of Martha, and this error was accepted until the discovery a few years since of Capt. Robert's will, showing daughters Ann and Martha, but no Margaret.

Of the lines and descendants of these two daughters, we have obtained but little account from those to whom we applied. Their families seem to have scattered afar from the old stamping ground their trails being lost in the mazes of the en... we learn yet remain in Somerset

What we have been able to learn of these two daughters can be quickly related, viz

Ann Polk was presumably the third child—at least one among the eldest—of Robt and Magdalen Polk She was born about 1669, in Ireland, and was a little tot when her parents emigrated to America in order to secure a larger field for the exercise of political and religious liberty

It appears also that Ann died before reaching middle life. She was married about 1690 (maybe sooner) and presumably she was dead in 1699, judging from the fact that she is not mentioned in her father's will, while her sister Martha is given a devise.

The first husband of Ann was Francis Roberts, a planter, of Dame's Quarter, by whom she had children Edward and Priscilla Edward grew to manhood and married his first cousin, Nancy, daughter of his uncle John Polk, first son of Robert and Magdalen Priscilla Roberts married William Polk brother of Nancy The names of William and Priscilla (Roberts) Polk erroneously appear on the Polk family tree compiled and published in 1849 The wrong William was inadvertently gotten into the line

Francis Roberts died but a few years after marriage to Ann and she appears of record as Executrix, to settle his estate, with Thomas Pollitt and John Polk as bondsmen As a second husband, Ann chose John Renshaw, Jr., who subsequently joined in Ann's bond concerning the estate of Francis Whether or not Ann had issue by this latter union we cannot say. It is more than likely that she did

MARTHA POLK'S DESCENDANTS

Martha Polk, second daughter of Robert and Magdalen Polk, was born in Maryland about 1679, and married Thomas Pollitt of Somerset As she was called "My daughter Martha" by Capt Robert Polk in his will of 1699, and given one third of his 'moveables,' it is probable that at that time she was still single and a member of his household In a codicil to his will, he says "and I desire that Martha Poock (Polk) may have liberty to let her cattle run upon pasture until she gets a place"

The witnesses to the will of Magdalen Polk, of April 7, 1726, were David Polk, William Pollitt and Magdalen Pollitt. The two latter, no doubt, were children of Martha and Thomas Pollitt. She also had two other children, John and Mary as the records show.

Thomas Pollitt dying, Martha took as a second husband Richard Tull, of Dame's Quarter, and the official records show that she was his wife in 1710. If they left issue, we have no record of the fact.

A NUMEROUS PROGENY.

The records, and the investigations made in 1849, and recently by the present writer, show that of Robert and Magdalen's sons, William has the greatest number of descendants and Ephraim next. Those of the former largely reside in Maryland and include the Winders and other noted families of that section. Those who emigrated to North Carolina were also exceedingly prolific and are scattered all over the South and Southwest. The descendants of Ephraim are found principally in Delaware, Kentucky, Indiana, Missouri and other states of the West, and everywhere they have gone to the front and become leaders in civic and military affairs.

Wm. Polk, 2nd, appears to have been the eldest son of William Polk, Sr., and his wife Nancy (Knox) Owens, who was the widow of William Owens of Somerset County, and the reputed sister of Joanna Knox, the second wife and widow of John Polk, Sr. By Nancy, William Sr., had another son, Charles Polk, who became an Indian trader on the Maryland frontier and died in 1753. One of the latter's sons, Capt Charles Polk, a noted border officer, emigrated to Kentucky in 1780, and thence to Indiana in 1808, dying there in 1823.

Wm. Polk, 2d, after a sojourn of some years at Carlisle, Pa., married there Miss Margaret Taylor, and between 1740 and 1750 emigrated to North Carolina, dying there about 1753, according to the statement of Mrs. Susan Smart to Bishop Polk in 1818.

CHAPTER XX.

DESCENDANTS OF WILLIAM POLK, 3d

William Polk 3d (eldest son of William Polk and Margaret Taylor Polk), was twice married. The names of his wives are not preserved. By his first marriage he had two sons, ¹Thomas and ²John. By his second marriage, he had a son Ezekiel. The latter became an Ensign in one of the infantry regiments of the United States Army and died in 1791, as appears by Heitman's Register.

Thomas Polk, eldest son of William Polk by his first wife was generally called "Colonel" Thomas Polk. He married Mary Shelby, a sister of Reese and Thomas Shelby, and said to have been a sister of General Evan Shelby, father of Governor Isaac Shelby, hero of King's Mountain and the Thames, and twice Governor of Kentucky. The parents of Mary Snelby, says Miss Garrett in her Polk sketches, resided just across the South Carolina line, in the Chesterfield District (now county), and died there. Thomas Polk and his wife Mary, lived on Watson's Creek, but later removed to Richardson's Creek, at what was called Little Mountain. After his settlement there it became known as "Polk's Mountain," and he died there in 1842. In 1880 the name of the mountain was changed to "Gibraltar." Colonel Thomas and Mary (Shelby) Polk had issue: ¹Shelby, ²Andrew, ³Thomas, ⁴Jobe, ⁵Hannah, ⁶Dicy, ⁷Patsy, ⁸Mary, ⁹Elizabeth.

The eldest, Shelby Polk, married Winnifred Colburn. He emigrated to Tennessee in 1813 and left numerous descendants, some of whom went to Texas in the days of the Republic. Shelby died about 1847 leaving issue: ¹Esther, ²Headley, ³Thomas, ⁴William, ⁵Shelby, ⁶Mary, ⁷Eliza.

Esther (daughter of Shelby and Winnifred Polk), married Whitman Colburn, and had issue: Harriet and Winnifred (twins), James Polk, William Headley, Henry, Linda married John Grayham and they emigrated to Texas, having issue ¹Randolph, ²Ophelia, ³Thomas, ⁴Price, ⁵Headley and ⁶Elilur Grayham. Winnifred Colburn (twin sister of Lucinda) married Andrew Webb and emigrated to Arkansas. They had issue: ¹Lucinda, ²James, and several more children.

James Leroy Colburn (son of Esther and Whitman Colburn) married Margaret Bradford. He removed to Tennessee and left children.

William Headley Colburn (son of Esther Polk and Whitman Colburn), married Margaret Doyle. They removed to Tennessee and left children.

Headley Polk, second child and eldest son of Shelby Polk and Winnifred (Colburn) Polk, was born in North Carolina in 1812, and removed to Texas in 1845. He married Eliza Sebastian, of the well known Sebastian family of Tennessee. She was a cousin of Hon. W. K. Sebastian, U. S. Senator from Arkansas. The children of Headley Polk and Eliza (Sebastian) Polk were: ¹James Dallas, ²John Robert, ³Martha O. ⁴Anna S., ⁵Sally E., and ⁶Mary F. Polk.

John Robert Polk married Kate Woods and they had issue: ¹Iver May, ²Katie B., ³Annie, ⁴Euphia, ⁵Dallas L., and ⁶Headley Polk.

Martha O. Polk (daughter of Headley Polk and Eliza Sebastian Polk), married B. Harris and had issue ¹Robert P., ²Headley Bruce, ³Lena and ⁴Evan Harris.

Sallie E. Polk, daughter of Headley Polk and Eliza (Sebastian) Polk, married E. A. Brackney dying and leaving one child, Ladie Polk Brackney.

Mary F. Polk, daughter of Headley Polk and Eliza (Sebastian) Polk, married B. Lyell.

Thomas Polk, son of Shelby Polk and Winnifred (Colburn) Polk, married Elizabeth Braddy. They had issue: ¹Citizen, ²Charles, ³Wallace, ⁴Dora and ⁵Sallie Polk. Charles and Citizen Polk were soldiers in the Confederate Army, in the Civil War, and were killed in battle.

Dora Polk, daughter of Thomas and Elizabeth (Braddy) Polk, married Mr. Tillman. Her sister Sallie Polk married Mr. Wilson when issue not learned.

William Polk, son of Shelby and Winnifred (Colburn) Polk, married Elizabeth Bradford. He was a soldier in the Confederate Army. Issue ¹Winfora, ²Shelby, ³Marchal, ⁴Thomas, ⁵Robert. Winafora married Richard McKinney and had several children. Shelby Polk, second child of William Polk and Elizabeth (Bradford) Polk, married a Miss Lockman. Anna Polk, daughter of Headley and Winnifred Polk died unmarried.

Shelby Polk (fifth child of Shelby Polk and Winnifred Colburn Polk), died unmarried.

Mary Polk, sixth child of Shelby Polk and Winnifred (Colburn) Polk, married Nathan Rodgers: Issue ¹Winnifred M, ²Mary A, ³Oclatia, ⁴Charles E, ⁵Ella, ⁶Octavia.

Eliza Polk seventh child of Shelby Polk and Winnifred (Colburn) Polk, married William G Nackolls. They had issue ¹Charles E, ²Mary O, ³William L and ⁴Lenora Z Nackolls.

Charles E. Nackolls married ————, and had issue.

Mary O Nackolls married R V Vinson and had issue ¹Carl and ²Nora.

William L Nackolls married Georgia Fan and had one child, William C. Nackolls.

Lenora Z Nackolls, youngest child of William G Nackolls and Eliza (Polk) Nackolls, married James Barnett and died leaving one child, William G Barnett.

Andrew Polk, second son of Col Thomas Polk and Mary (Shelby) Polk, was twice married, first to Miss Caraway. He settled on Big Brown Creek (later Polkton) where three children were born to him by his first wife ¹Thomas J, ²James K and ³Marshall Polk. Thomas married and left several children, who reside in North Carolina. James K emigrated to Texas and died there. Marshall Polk married and resides at Polkton, N C. He has several children. One of them Miss Ella Polk, resides at Columbia, S C.

Andrew Polk's second wife was Lorena Autery, by whom he had one child, the late Col L L Polk, of Raleigh, N C, President of the National Farmers' Alliance. He also established a newspaper to advocate the principles of the Farmers' Alliance and was a man of marked ability, …… and speaker He died in 1891, in Washington City. He married Miss Gaddy, of North Carolina.

Thomas Polk (third son of Col Thomas Polk and Mary Shelby Polk), married Sarah Brooks and inherited his father's old homestead Of his sons, two of them, Marshall and Shelby, were killed in the Confederate Army, and two died after the war—William and Andrew Thomas J inherited the homestead and there are several other children who reside in Anson and Union Counties, N C

Jobe Polk (son of Col Thomas and Mary Polk), never married

Hannah Polk (eldest daughter of Col Thomas Polk and Mary Shelby Polk), was twice married Her first husband was a Mr Sides, by whom she had one child, Hannah Her second husband was Adam Long, by whom she had three sons, Thomas Henry and Adam Long, also several daughters Hannah (Polk) Long lived to the age of ninety years

Dicey Polk, second daughter of Col Thomas Polk and Mary (Shelby) Polk, married Francis Colburn They emigrated to Tennessee, in which state such a large number of the Polks and their connections had previously settled

Patsy Polk, third daughter of Col Thomas Polk and Mary (Shelby) Polk, married William Crittenden They also removed from North Carolina to Tennessee

Mary Polk, fourth daughter of Col Thomas Polk and Mary (Shelby) Polk, married Aaron Little and settled in that part of Anson County now known as Union She died in 1862, leaving a family of ten children Armstead Little was killed at the battle of Sharpsburg, Md, in 1862, leaving a widow and six children Lina Little, second child of Aaron Little and Mary (Polk) Little, married Jabez Williams and died in 1855, leaving one daughter

Martha Little, third child of Aaron Little and Mary (Polk) Little, married Tillman Green They left a numerous family

Elizabeth Little, fourth child of Aaron Little and Mary (Polk) Little, married Archibald Helms They had several children

⸺ ⸺ ⸺, ⸺ ⸺ of Aaron Little and Mary (Polk) Littl⸺ ⸺ ⸺ ⸺ ⸺ They had several children

Thomas B and James L. Little, were twins of Aaron and Mary (Polk) Little. Thomas B removed to Arkansas, James L married in North Carolina and had several children, one of whom Mary E P. married Alfred J Austin Rosana and Penelope Little (twins), and Sarena and Minerva Little (twins) of Aaron and Mary (Polk) Little

Penelope Little, daughter of Aaron and Mary (Polk) Little, married W H Austin and had ten children who attained maturity, viz [1]Henry W Austin, unmarried, [2]Mary Lavenia Austin, married U A Davis, [3]Belinda Victoria Austin, married Jacob C. Griffin, and had four sons; [4]Francis Penelope Austin, married E L Helms and had three sons, [5]John Aaron Austin married Hattie Austin, and had four sons, [6]Sarah Austin, [7]James C Austin; [8]Ida Serena Austin; [9]Alexander T Austin; [10]Daisy B. Austin

Sarena Little, daughter of Aaron and Mary (Polk) Little married J. H Little and at her death left a large family

Elizabeth Polk, youngest child of Col Thomas Polk and Mary (Shelby) Polk married Richmond McManus of South Carolina At her death she left two daughters

John Polk, second son of William Polk (by his first wife) married and located on Crooked Creek in that part of Anson now known as Union County, where he died leaving several daughters. One of them, Margaret, married J Peter Hager; another married John Hager, and their descendants reside in North Carolina and other states

CHAPTER XXI.

CHAS. POLK, SON OF WM AND MARGARET.

Charles Polk, second son of William Polk and Margaret (Taylor) Polk, was married in 1750 (the year the family emigrated from Pennsylvania to North Carolina) to Polly Clark, by whom he had five sons, viz: [1]Thomas Polk, [2]Charles Polk, [3]Shelby Polk, [4]William Polk and [5]Mike Polk

Debora Polk, second daughter of William Polk and Margaret (Taylor) Polk, married Samuel McLary and left issue

Charles Polk, second son of Charles Polk and Polly (Clark) Polk, was a soldier in the Revolution from North Carolina. He married and had three sons; Col Wm Polk Charles Polk and another son left descendants

Susan Polk, third daughter of William Polk and Margaret (Taylor) Polk, married Benjamin Alexander, by whom she had six children. [1]Thomas, [2]Charles, [3]Susan, [4]William, [5]Benjamin, [6]Taylor William Alexander was a Captain and a distinguished officer of the North Carolina Line, in the Revolutionary War On account of his dark complexion he was called "Black Bill" and was noted for his valor on the field.

John Polk, fourth son of William Polk and Margaret (Taylor) Polk, was born near Carlisle, Pa, about 1740—possibly earlier He was a soldier in the Revolution and acquitted himself with gallantry He married Eleanor Shelby, a daughter of Major Evan Shelby, son of Gen'l Evan Shelby. Eleanor was a kinswoman of Mary Shelby, who married Col Thos Polk John Polk and his wife Eleanor (Shelby) Polk had issue [1]Charles Polk, [2]Shelby Polk, [3]Taylor Polk, [4]John Polk, [5]Eleanor

Taylor Polk, third son of John and Eleanor (Shelby) Polk, married Jency Walker, a daughter of Alexander Walker of Kentucky They had seven children, viz: [1]Benjamin Polk, [2]Tay[lor] [3]J[ohn] [4]Evan P[o]lk [5]Cumberland Polk, [6]William Polk [7]Alfr[ed] [8]L[ucy] P[ol]k

Benjamin Polk, eldest son of Taylor Polk and Jency (Walker) Polk, married Peggy Boatright and had issue ¹Jency Polk, ²Benjamin Polk, ³James Polk, ⁴Charles Polk ⁵William Polk, ⁶Richard Polk ⁷Priscilla Polk They all died in childhood

Taylor Polk, second son of Taylor Polk and Jency (Walker) Polk, married Prudence Anderson and had ten children viz ¹Anderson Polk, ²Eleanor Polk, ³Cumberland Polk ⁴Sarah Delaney Polk, ⁵Mitchell Polk, ⁶Sylvester Walker Polk, ⁷Henry Clay Polk, ⁸Taylor Polk, ⁹Prudence Polk, ¹⁰Alfred Polk

Anderson Polk, eldest son of Taylor Polk and Prudence (Anderson) Polk, was married three times By his first wife, Eliza Epperson, he had children ¹Henry Polk, who married Ellen Deathrow, ²Sarah Polk, who married John Huddleston, ³Jane Polk, who married Thomas Huddleston, ⁴Sylvester Polk, who married Sarah Intz

Anderson Polk's second wife was Martha Martin, by whom he had issue, ⁵Texana Polk, who married Thomas Williamson, ⁶Matilda Polk, who married James Joplin; ⁷Thomas Polk, who married Annie Matlock, ⁸Prudence Polk who died unmarried.

Anderson Polk's third wife was Susan Laughey and they had issue ⁹Martha Polk, who married Jefferson Bugg; ¹⁰Almeda Polk who married Charles Cruger

Eleanor Polk, second child of Taylor Polk and Prudence (Anderson) Polk, married Daniel Huddleston and had issue ¹Prudence who married Joseph Story, ²Daniel, who married Miss Stemson; ³Jane, who married Moses Waterman ⁴Rachel who married Jefferson Cunningham, ⁵T J Huddleston, who married Jane Polk ⁶Katherine, who married James Stevens.

Cumberland Polk third child of Taylor Polk and Prudence (Anderson) Polk, married Almeda Blackwood and had issue ¹Prudence, who married James Stanford; ²Taylor, who married Ellen Griggs, ³Caldona, who married Robert Priest, ⁴Lucinda, who married [illegible] ⁵[illegible] who married Pend [illegible], and

⁷John, ⁸Sylvester, ⁹Henry and ¹⁰Wesley, all of whom died unmarried.

Sarah Delany Polk, fourth child of Taylor Polk and Prudence (Anderson) Polk, married Capt T G Epperson and had issue ¹Henry Peyton, who married Miss Rowles, ²Mary, who married Blount Bullock, ³Taylor, who married Victoria Bush, ⁴Isabella, who married George Jacobs, ⁵Emma, who married Ira Cobb.

Mitchell Polk, fifth child of Taylor Polk and Prudence (Anderson) Polk, died unmarried

Sylvester Walker Polk, sixth child of Taylor Polk and Prudence (Anderson) Polk, married Sarah Large and had issue ¹Isom, who married Lucy Miller, ²Victoria, who married H O Brockmann, ³Paschal, who married Hannah Jones, ⁴Isadore, who married W R Copps; ⁵David, who married Jane Burnett, ⁶Laura, who married L D Burnett, ⁷Alpha, who married John Lindsey, ⁸Maud, who married W L Kothmann, ⁹Claude

Henry Clay Polk, seventh child of Taylor Polk and Prudence (Anderson) Polk, married Mary A. Dickson and had issue· ¹Henry, who married Anne Gould, ²David, who died single, ³Emma, who died single, ⁴Alice, who married Dr G B Green; ⁵John, who married Susan Brown, ⁶Anna, who married John Hawkins, ⁷Lela, who married Dr. John Brown, ⁸Betty, who died single, ⁹Roxy; ¹⁰Leon

Taylor Polk, 3rd, eighth child of Taylor Polk and Prudence (Anderson) Polk, married Mary Petty and had issue ¹Laura, ²Augusta, ³Mollie, who married T W. Poole, ⁴James, who married Mary Allison, ⁵⁶Leta and Lota, twins, ⁷Henry, ⁸Leon ⁹Myrtle, who married Richard Shegog, ¹⁰Beverly

Prudence Polk, ninth child of Taylor Polk and Prudence (Anderson) Polk, married Benjamin R Dickson and had issue ¹Charles, who married Carrie Young, ²Minnie, who married Dr Oscar Smith, ³William, ⁴Pearl, who married Russell Williams, ⁵Ethel, who married George Holland

Alfred Polk, tenth child of Taylor Polk and Prudence (Anderson) P H, married Sarah Wilson and had issue, ¹Sylvester, ²Burt Mable Lanie Polk.

James Polk, third child of Taylor Polk, 1st, and Jency (Walker) Polk, was twice married, first to Miss Trammell; second to Miss Sallie Cox, and had issue ¹Jency, ²Bettie, ³Franklin, ⁴James, ⁵Cumberland.

Jency eldest child of James Polk by his first wife, married Fielding Tweedle Issue one son William Tweedle, who died single

Bettie Polk, second child of James Polk by his first wife, married Martin Newman and had issue ¹Jas F Newman, ²Mary Newman

James F Newman married Josephine Rushing and had issue ¹Alfred, ²Arthur, ³Ira

Mary Newman married Thomas Trammell and had issue ¹James P, ²Walter T, and ³Bertie Trammell

James P Trammell married his cousin Mattie L Polk and had issue, Thos G Trammell

Franklin Polk, son of James Polk by his first wife, married Jane Rider and at his death left issue

James Polk, fourth son of James Polk, and eldest son by second wife, Sallie Cox, married Lizzie Roberts and left issue

Cumberland Polk son of James and Sallie (Cox) Polk, married Laura Kirk and had issue: ¹James, ²Lizzie, ³Annie, ⁴Frank, ⁵Mattie, ⁶Louis, ⁷Minnie

Lizzie, second child of Cumberland Polk and Laura (Kirk) Polk, married D L Norman and had two children ¹Cecil, ²Ross

Mattie Polk, fifth child of Cumberland Polk and Laura (Kirk) Polk, married James P Trammell, her cousin

Cumberland Polk, fourth child of Taylor Polk and Jency (Walker) Polk, married Nancy Cox, (sister of Sallie Cox who married James, brother of Cumberland Polk) Nancy and Sallie were daughters of Joel Cox and Frances (Bartlett) Cox of Kentucky Cumberland and Nancy (Cox) Polk had issue. ¹Lucinda, ²Lucretia, ³Marshall Alexander, ⁴Elias Rector, ⁵William Jackson, ⁶Louisa Jane, ⁷Louis Taylor, ⁸Jency, ⁹Prudence ¹⁰Mary ¹¹Martha, ¹²James Knox Lucinda, eldest child of Cumberland and Nancy (C x) Polk, died in infancy

Lucretia, second child of Cumberland and Nancy (Cox)

Polk, married Edmond Cearley (spelled Kerley in colonial times) and had issue

Samuel Reyburn, who died unmarried; Newton Fleming who died unmarried.

Mary Jane and Cumberland who died in infancy

⁵Louisa Elizabeth, who married George Babcock, but left no issue, ⁶Cyrus Granville, who died unmarried, ⁷John Brackville, ⁸Emma Cornelia, who married Judge F. M. Angellotti, of San Rafael, California, and had issue ¹Frank L. Angellotti, who died in infancy, ²Marion Polk Angellotti

⁹Charles Talent, who married Jennie Mangrum and had one child, Mila Mangrum Cearley Polk

Marshall Alexander Polk, third child of Cumberland Polk and Nancy (Cox) Polk, died in childhood. Elias Rector Polk fourth child of Cumberland Polk and Nancy (Cox) Polk, died unmarried. He was a Confederate soldier in Kenard's regiment, and died from wounds received in battle

William Jackson Polk, fifth child of Cumberland Polk and Nancy (Cox) Polk, married Esther Woodward, and had issue: ¹Thomas, ²Julia. William Jackson was also a Confederate soldier and died from disease contracted in the army

Louise Jane Polk, sixth child of Cumberland Polk and Nancy (Cox) Polk, married Rev E. J. Billington and had issue ¹Lucretia, ²Ezekiel Jackson, ³Julia

Louis Taylor Polk, seventh child of Cumberland Polk and Nancy (Cox) Polk, died unmarried. He was killed in 1862 in the Confederate Army, at the battle of Arkansas Post. He was a member of Col Nelson's regiment

Jency Polk, eighth child of Cumberland Polk and Nancy (Cox) Polk, married William O'Neal, and had issue: ¹Nancy, who married Robert Ross, ²Gussie, who married Elisha Ross, ³Prudence, who married William Ross; ⁴John, unmarried at last accounts, but on the lookout for a Ross

Prudence Polk, ninth child of Cumberland Polk and Nancy (Cox) Polk, married Frederick Jones and had two children: ¹Mary, who married William White, ²William.

Mary Ann, tenth child of Cumberland Polk and Nancy (Cox) Polk, married Jacob Jackson but had no issue

M... P... ... P... ... ... child of Cumberland

Polk and Nancy (Cox) Polk, married Handy Walker and had issue. ¹Jency ²James, ³Ella

James Polk twelfth child of Cumberland Polk and Nancy (Cox) Polk, never married.

William Polk, fifth child of Taylor Polk and Jency (Walker) Polk married two cousins, Misses Griffith By the first he had two sons Levi and Cumberland Both of these young men joined the Confederate army and fell in battle By his second marriage William Polk had no issue and his line became extinct

Alfred Polk, sixth child of Taylor Polk and Jency (Walker) Polk, married twice, first to Irene Chandler, second to Mrs Ricketts By the first he had issue ¹James ²Josiah ³Mary J who married W. W Garner, ⁴Mitchell A, ⁵Caroline, who married L Dennis, ⁶Benjamin, ⁷Samuel, ⁸Almeda who married J N Stancill, ⁹Young C Polk

By his second marriage, to Mrs Ricketts, Alfred Polk had issue ¹⁰Robert L ¹¹Wm P, ¹²Richard T Polk

Jency Polk, seventh child of Taylor Polk and Jency (Walker) Polk, married Mitchell Anderson, a brother to Prudence Anderson, who married Taylor Polk, 2nd Issue ¹Fannie, ²James, ³Mitchell, ⁴Benjamin, ⁵Abraham ⁶Eliza, ⁷Stacy, ⁸Jane, ⁹Henry, ¹⁰Taylor Anderson

James Mitchell, Benjamin and Abraham Anderson, all quite young, enlisted in the Confederate army and were all killed in battle The other children of Mitchell Polk have not been traced The God of Battles certainly laid a heavy hand on this family

CHAPTER XXII.

MARGARET POLK McREA.

Margaret Polk, sixth child of William Polk and Margaret (Taylor) Polk, married Robert McRea, of North Carolina, and had eleven children ¹William, ²Debora, ³James P., ⁴Susan, ⁵Dinah, ⁶Margaret, ⁷Thomas, ⁸Harriett, ⁹Richard, ¹⁰William, ¹¹Mary McRea

William McRea, eldest son of Robert McRea and Margaret (Polk) McRea, married and had issue: ¹William, ²David, ³James, ⁴Margaret, ⁵Banks, ⁶Richard, ⁷Robert, ⁸Josephine McRea

Debora McRea second child of Robert McRea and Margaret (Polk) McRea, married Wm Campbell and had nine children, viz ¹Mary, ²Jane, ³Debora, ⁴Robert ⁵Margaret, ⁶William, ⁷Harriet, ⁸John, and ⁹Andrew Campbell.

James P McRea, third child of Robert and Margaret (Polk) McRea, married and emigrated to Tennessee, and had a family of ten children, viz ¹Margaret, ²Robert, ³Sarah M ⁴Mary, ⁵Adam, ⁶James, ⁷William ⁸Eugene, ⁹Rebecca, ¹⁰Julia McRea. MARIAH REBE :A MELISSA BREVARD

Sarah, the third child of James P. McRea, of Tennessee, 1831 married Jno. W. M. Clay and left issue: ¹Margaret, ²James, ³William, ⁴John L, ⁵Leonidas, ⁶Sarah, ⁷Martha Clay, ¹⁰ IOLA.

Susan McRea, fourth child of Robert McRea and Margaret (Polk) McRea, married William Barnett and had issue. ¹William, ²Susan, ³Margaret, ⁴Ann, ⁵Jack, ⁶Jane, ⁷Robert Barnett

Dinah McRea, fifth child of Robert McRea and Margaret (Polk) McRea, married ———— Hart, and had issue. ¹Mary, ²Margaret, ³Isabella, ⁴William, ⁵David Hart

Margaret McRea, sixth child of Robert McRea and Margaret (Polk) McRea, married ———— Spratt and had issue ¹Thomas, ²Robert, ³Margaret, ⁴Susan, ⁵James, ⁶Elizabeth, ⁷Martha, ⁸Leonidas Spratt

Thomas McRea, seventh child of Robert McRea and Margaret (Polk) McRea, married ———————— and had three children, viz. [1]William, [2]Robert, [3]Margaret McRea

Harriet McRea, eighth child of Robert McRea and Margaret (Polk) McRea, married ———————— Taylor and had issue [1]Mary, [2]Robert, [3]John Taylor

Rachel McRea, ninth child of Robert McRea and Margaret (Polk) McRea, married ———————— Vance and had issue. [1]Robert, and [2]James Vance

William McRea, tenth child of Robert McRea and Margaret (Polk) McRea, died unmarried

Mary McRea, eleventh child of Robert McRea and Margaret (Polk) McRea, married ———————— Barnett and had issue· [1]Mary, and [2]William Barnett.

CHAPTER XXIII.

GENERAL THOMAS POLK'S DESCENDANTS

Gen'l Thomas Polk seventh child of William Polk and Margaret (Taylor) Polk married Susan Spratt, a daughter of Thomas Spratt, a prominent citizen of Mecklenburg County, by whom he had: [1]Thomas, [2]Col William, [3]Ezekiel, who was lost at sea says Mr. Smart in 1849 in a letter to Bishop Polk, [4]Charles, [5]Margaret, [6]Mary [7]Martha [8]James, [9]Debora Polk

Thomas Polk, eldest child of General Thomas Polk, and Susan (Spratt) Polk, never married. He was a Captain in the Revolution, in the Fourth North Carolina regiment, commanded by his father and was killed by a bullet in the forehead at the hard fought battle of Eutaw, Sept 8, 1781 where the gallant patriots under General Nathaniel Greene contended for five hours with an army of veteran British soldiers under General Stuart the engagement being a drawn battle in which both sides suffered a heavy loss of officers and men

Colonel William Polk second child of General Thomas Polk and Susan (Spratt) Polk was twice married, first to Grizelda Gilchrist, second to Sarah Hawkins. By his first wife he had two sons [1]General Thos G Polk [2]Dr William Julius Polk By his second wife he had eight children, viz. [3]Lucius Junius Polk, [4]Lieutenant General Leonidas Polk, Confederate States Army, who was killed during the Civil War by a cannon shot at Pine Mountain, Ga, June 14 1864, while reconnoitering the Federal lines, [5]Mary B Polk, [6]Alexander Hamilton Polk, [7]Col Rufus K Polk, [8]George W Polk, [9]Susan S Polk, [10]Col Andrew J Polk Lucinda another child of Col Wm Polk, born Jan 12, 1804, died when a little over a year old, as did also another child, John Hawkins Polk

General Thomas G Polk, eldest son of Col William Polk and G   Polk w   nuary 22, 1791 and marri   h n b u 1 is hildren t live to

GEN'L THOS. G. POLK,
of North Carolina.

THE NEW YORK
PUBLIC LIBRARY

ASTOR LENOX AND
TILDEN FOUNDATIONS

maturity, viz : ¹Mary A Polk, ²Jane Polk, ³William Polk ⁴Richard Polk. ⁵Emily Polk, ⁶Thomas Polk The three last named died unmarried

Mary A. Polk, first child of General Thomas G. Polk and Mary (Trotter) Polk, married Hon George Davis, of Raleigh, N C, a distinguished lawyer and Attorney General of the Confederate States, under President Jefferson Davis Six of their children lived to maturity, viz· ¹Junius Davis, ²Mary Davis (who died unmarried), ³Emily Davis, ⁴Louis Davis, (who also died unmarried) : ⁵Isabella Davis, ⁶Margaret Davis

Junius Davis. eldest child of Hon George Davis and Mary (Polk) Davis, married twice; first to Mary Orme Walker, second to Mary Cowan By them he had eight children ¹Mary Polk Davis, ²Thomas Davis, ³Junius Davis, ⁴George Davis, ⁵Platt Davis, ⁶Louis Davis, ⁷Robert C Davis, ⁸Eliza Davis, the two last named by his second wife.

Emily Davis, third child of Hon. George Davis and Mary (Polk) Davis, married June Crowe and had issue: ¹George Crowe, ²Fairfax Crowe, ³William Crowe ⁴Emmet Polk Crowe

Isabella Davis, fifth child of Hon George Davis and Mary (Polk) Davis, married Spencer Shotter, by whom she had one child, Isabella Davis Shotter

Margaret Davis, youngest child of Hon. George Davis and Mary (Polk) Davis married George Rountree and had issue ¹Isabella Rountree, ²Cynthia Rountree, ³Meta Rountree.

Jane Polk, second child of General Thomas G. Polk and Mary (Trotter) Polk, married Dr A Buchelle and died without issue

Colonel William Polk, third child and eldest son of General Thomas G. Polk and Mary (Trotter) Polk, born in Mecklenburg County, N C. ———— 1822, now a resident of Alexandria La . is a sugar planter and enterprising business man. He is a member of the Order of the Cincinnati, by descent from his grandfather, Col William Polk, of the Revolution Col Wm. Polk first married Miss Flower, who died leaving one child, a son ———— — — ——— His second wife was Miss Rebecca Evaline Lamar of Georgia, a cousin of

Justice Lamar, and niece of General M B Lamar, a President of the Republic of Texas Col Polk has three children · ¹Alice Polk, ²William Polk, ³Eloise Polk.

Alice Polk, eldest child of Col Wm Polk and Rebecca Evaline (Lamar) Polk, married Wm P Flower, a sugar planter of Louisiana, by whom she had one child, William Polk Flower, Jr

William Polk, second child of Col Wm, Polk and Rebecca Evaline (Lamar) Polk, married Miss Baillio. He is also a sugar planter and large landholder in the Parish of Rapides He had one child, Lamar Polk

Eloise Polk, third child of Col Wm Polk and Rebecca Evaline (Lamar) Polk, married David S Ferris of New York, and they have one son, Coldon Livingston Ferris

Dr William Julius Polk, second son of Col William Polk and Grizelda (Gilchrist) Polk, was born March 21, 1793 He married Mary R Long, a granddaughter of General Allen Jones of Halifax, North Carolina Issue: ¹Grizelda, ²Allen J ³Dr. Thomas G , ⁴Mary Branch, Gen'l Lucius E , Col Cadwallader, and Col Rufus K Polk

JOHN PAUL JONES.

John Paul, the young Scotchman who was called the father of the American Navy, and whose naval exploits during the American Revolution startled the world, shortly after coming to America lived long in the Jones families, in North Carolina Prompted by his affection for them, he added their family name to his own and ever afterward was called John Paul Jones One of this Jones family was General Allen Jones, of Halifax, N C , and Willie Jones, an attorney in connection with the settlement of the estate of his brother, William Paul, of Virginia whose heir he became on the latters death. General Allen Jones was the grandfather of Mary R Long who married Dr Wm. Julius Polk, son of Col. Wm Polk, of Raleigh, N C

In her sketch of the John Polk branch of the family, published in the January, 1908, number of the American Historical Maga   Mr Mary Winder Garrett says of Mrs Mary (Long) P H   ife Dr Wm. J Polk. This lady had the brave, undaunted spirit of the Roman matron and, when in the late Civil War General Buell offered it, declined protection for herself and home while her sons were exposed to the dangers of the field."

In this connection it may also be stated that when the Federal Army occupied Nashville, General Buell made a similar offer of protection to Mrs James K. Polk, which she also declined But General Buell, notwithstanding her refusal, gave that protection to her home which he deemed requisite and necessary Illustrative of the high spirit which characterized the females of the Jones family during the Revolutionary War, we quote the following from Mrs Ellet's "Women of the Revolution" "When Cornwallis and his army were at Halifax, on their way to Virginia, Col Tarlton was at the house of an American In the presence of Mrs Willie Jones Tarlton spoke of Col William Washington as an illiterate fellow, hardly able to write his name 'Ah, Colonel " said Mrs. Jones,' You ought to know better for you bear on your person proof that he knows very well how to make his mark'"

At another time, Tarlton was speaking sarcastically of Col Washington, in the presence of Mrs Jones' sister, Mrs Ashe "I would be happy to see Colonel Washington, he said, 'with a sneer" Mrs Ashe instantly replied "If you had looked behind you, Col Tarlton, at the battle of the Cow pens, you would have enjoyed that pleasure."

"Stung with this keen wit, Tarlton placed his hand on his sword General Leslie, Tarlton's superior, who was present, remarked 'Say what you please, Mrs Ashe, Colonel Tarlton knows better than to insult a lady in my presence"

The children of Dr William J. Polk and Mary (Long) Polk, that attained to maturity, were [1]Grizelda Gilchrist Polk, [2]Major Allen J Polk, [3]Thomas G Polk, [4]Lucius E Polk, [5]Mary J Polk, [6]Cadwallader Polk and [7]Rufus K Polk

Grizelda Gilchrist Polk, eldest child of Dr William J Polk and Mary (Long) Polk, married Judge Russell Houston a native of Tennessee a talented and prominent lawyer, and at one time Chief Justice of his native state For a quarter of a century he held the position of Chief Counsel to the Louisville & Nashville R. R. Judge Houston was a

Whig, and when the Civil War came on as a result of the contention over slavery, he espoused the cause of the Union. The children of Judge Russell Houston and Grizelda (Gilchrist) Polk, were [1]Mary R Houston, [2]Allen P Houston, [3]Lucius E Houston, [4]Elise, [5]Houston

Mary Russell Houston, eldest child of Judge Russell Houston and Grizelda (Polk) Houston, married Lytle Buchanan

Allen P Houston, second child of Judge Russell Houston and Grizelda (Polk) Houston, married Mattie Belle Shreve, and they had issue [1]Russell Houston, [2]Bell L Houston, [3]Allen P Houston, Jr.

Lucia E Houston, third child of Judge Russell Houston and Grizelda (Polk) Houston, married George H Hull and had five children, viz [1]Grizelda H Hull, [2]George H Hull, [3]Lytle B Hull, [4]Russell H Hull, [5]Lucia H. Hull

Elise Houston, fourth child of Judge Russell Houston and Grizelda (Polk) Houston, married John L. Ferrell Issue [1]Grizelda H Ferrell (deceased), [2]Mary Russell Ferrell

MAJOR ALLEN J. POLK.

Major Allen J Polk, second child and eldest son of Dr William J Polk and Mary (Long) Polk, was twice married, first to Miss Mary Clendennin, in 1846 His second wife was Miss Anna Clark Fitzhugh of Louisville, a very beautiful woman, daughter of Judge Dennis Fitzhugh, third husband of Francis Eleanor Clark, youngest sister of General George Rogers Clark, Conqueror of the Northwest Territory in 1778

By his first wife, Miss Clendennin, Major Allen J Polk had one child to reach maturity, Mary Polk, who married Frank Hemphill and had issue. [1]Mary, [2]Allen, and [3]Polk Hemphill By his second wife, Anna Clark Fitzhugh, Major Polk had issue [1]Susie H. Polk, [2]Anna Lee Polk [3]Zelda Polk [4]Robin Allen Polk

Susie H, daughter of Major Allen J Polk and Anna Clark (Fitzhugh) Polk, married T W Keesee January 13, 1887, and has issue [1]Zelda Polk Keesee, born January 31, 1889, [2]Thomas Woolfin Keesee, born July 13, 1891: [3]Allen Polk Keesee

Anna Lee Polk, daughter of Major Allen J Polk and Anna Clark (Fitzhugh) Polk, married Samuel A Pepper and had issue [1]Allen Polk Pepper (daughter) born December 5, 1888, [2]Zelda Fontaine Pepper, born March 27, 1889, [3]Anna Fitzhugh Pepper, born February 7, 1895.

Zelda Polk, daughter of Major Allen J Polk and Anna Clark (Fitzhugh) Polk married Capt D T Hargreaves, of Memphis, Tennessee, November 12, 1890.

CHAPTER XXIV.

THE MECKLENBURG DECLARATION.

No political transaction in America has provoked more controversy than that of the Mecklenburg Declaration of Independence, at Charlotte, North Carolina, on June 20th, 1775, more than a year previous to the Declaration formulated by the Continental Congress and enunciated at Philadelphia on July 4, 1776.

It is a well known fact that jealousy and ambition play no inconsiderable part in many of the affairs of mankind, and that they often give color and support to false assumptions regarding human transactions. And these influences, jealousies and ambition, lie at the bottom of all that has been written and spoken against the authenticity of the Mecklenburg Declaration.

Historians and writers of the Northern colonies of Massachusetts, New York, Connecticut, New Jersey, Pennsylvania, and also of Virginia, have earnestly endeavored to preserve their Revolutionary records, and they have not been backward in claiming for their respective colonies the lion's share of honors attending the performance of the struggling patriots. Particularly is this true of the historians and writers of Massachusetts and Virginia. It is true that the initial blow that precipitated the active conflict was struck at Lexington, Massachusetts, on April 19th, 1775. One month later, May 19th, 1775, the patriots of Mecklenburg County, North Carolina, assembled at Charlotte, to deliberate on what was best to be done to escape the political ills to which they had long been subjected by British power, and on the following day issued their declaration of independence.

BATTLE OF ALLAMANCE.

Four years before the affair at Lexington however, a blow had been struck by the people of North Carolina, at Allamance, in which a large number of patriots, then styled "Regulators," were killed and wounded, and a considerable number of the force of Governor Tryon, the Colonial Executive were also placed *hors de combat*.

The occasion of this sanguinary clash between the Royal Governor's forces and the North Carolina Colonists was the repeated exactions and hardships imposed on the people by his Lordship, through his rapacious agents and officials. After an exciting train of events had happened, the contention eventuated in bloodshed.

The battle of Allamance has well been called the "reveille drumbeat of the Revolution," because it was the first armed conflict to take place in America between the colonists and their British oppressors. This conflict occurred on May 16, 1771, near the head-waters of Cape Fear river. Therefore it antedated the affair at Lexington Massachusetts, by almost four years. It also preceded the Mecklenburg Declaration the same length of time, and the Philadelphia Declaration by more than five years. Yet, in spite of these incontrovertible facts partial historians have for a century tried to obscure them and accord all the honors to a later conflict and a later Declaration of Independence.

Although the Regulators were defeated at Allamance, leaving a large number of their dead and wounded on the field, Tryon was given a test of patriot mettle and shown that Americans would not tamely submit to the oppressions of George III and his tyrannical henchmen. The principles for which the North Carolina patriots fought Tryon, a short time later found expression in the Mecklenburg Declaration. This conflict served to intensify the state of feeling then existing, and for four years following the public mind was kept tense and expectant by numerous incidents of outrage, bad feeling and contention.

Out of these feelings and opinions grew the Mecklenburg meeting and pronouncement of independence. The town of Charlotte was the chief point at which was held a series of meetings to discuss the condition of affairs in that section of the colony. These meetings were at first irregular and without system. It was finally agreed that C. J. Thomas Polk, who commanded the Mecklenburg Militia regiment, a large property holder, a man of great excellence of character, extensive knowledge of his people, and deservedly popular, should be authorized to call a convention of the representatives of the people whenever circumstances should appear to require it Col Polk was a brother of Capt. Ezekiel Polk, grand-father of James K Polk It was also agreed that the Convention, when called, should consist of two men from each captain's company chosen by the people of the several militia districts of the County, and that their decisions should be binding upon the people of Mecklenburg Governor Martin, who had succeeded Tryon as Royal Governor of the Colony, sought to prevent the assembling of the Provincial Congress at Newbern, and great excitement followed his action

CONVENTION MEETS.

Believing that the time for action had arrived, Col Polk issued notice to the elected committeemen of the County to assemble at the court house in Charlotte. This they did on May 19, 1775 Abraham Alexander was chosen chairman and Dr Ephraim Brevard, secretary of the meeting The latter was a son-in-law of Col Thos Polk, having married the latter's daughter Martha. Dr. Brevard was a graduate of Princeton, a man of good education and scholarly attainments, and it is said that on him as secretary of the resolutions committee devolved the duty of drafting the resolutions prepared by the committee and reported to the convention The Alexanders were also related to the Polk's by intermarrriage During the first, and most of the second day, the subject of independence was discussed The news of the battle of Lexington reached Charlotte during the convention, it is said and it prompted the delegates to decisive action The committee thereupon reported the resolves, which were as follows

THE RESOLVES.

1st Resolved, That whosoever directly or indirectly abetted, or in any way form or manner countenanced the unchartered and dangerous invasion of our rights as claimed by Great Britain, is an enemy to this Country, to America, and to the inherent and inalienable rights of men

2d Resolved, That we, the citizens of Mecklenburg County, do hereby dissolve the political bands which have connected us to the mother country, and hereby absolve ourselves from all allegiance to the British Crown, and abjure all political connection, contract, or association, with that nation, who have wantonly trampled on our rights and liberties, and inhumanly shed the blood of American patriots at Lexington

3d Resolved, That we do hereby declare ourselves a free and independent people, are, and of right ought to be, a sovereign and self-governing Association under the control of no power other than that of our God, and the general government of the Congress, to the maintenance of which independence, we solemnly pledge to each other our mutual co-operation, our lives, our fortunes, and our most sacred honor

4th Resolved, That as we now acknowledge the existence and control of no law or legal officer, civil or military, within this country, we do hereby ordain and adopt as a rule of life, all, each, and every of our former laws—wherein, nevertheless, the Crown of Great Britain never can be considered as holding rights, privileges, immunities, or authority therein

5th Resolved, That it is further decreed, that all, each and every militia officer in this county is hereby reinstated in his former command and authority, he acting conformably to these regulations. And that every member present, of this delegation, shall henceforth be a civil officer, viz a Justice of the Peace, in the character of a Committeeman, to issue process, hear and determine all matters of controversy, according to said adopted laws, and to preserve peace, union and harmony in said county; and to use every exertion to spread the love of country and fire of freedom throughout America, until a more general and organized government be established in this province

Abraham Alexander, Chairman
John McKnitt Alexander, Secretary.

Ephraim Brevard,	Charles Alexander,
Hezekiah J Balch,	Zaccheus Wilson,
John Phifer,	Waightstill Avery,
James Harris,	Benjamin Patton,
William Kennon,	Matthew McClure,
John Ford,	Neil Morrison,
Richard Barry,	Robert Irving,
Henry Downs,	John Flannegin,
Ezra Alexander,	David Reese,
William Graham,	John Davidson,
John Queary,	Richard Harris,
Hezekiah Alexander,	Thomas Polk, Sr.
Adam Alexander,	

A vote was then taken and the resolves were unanimously concurred in By-laws and regulations for the government of a standing Committee of Safety were then adopted

These resolutions, which were drawn up by Dr Ephraim Brevard, chairman of the committee, were read by him to the delegation The resolves, by-laws, and regulations were read by John McKnitt Alexander The chair then put the question and the vote was a unanimous approval. Shortly after the vote of the convention on the resolutions and complying with the vociferous demands of those outside who were unable to get into the house, Col Thomas Polk standing on the court house steps, read the resolutions and other resolves to the assemblage of citizens, who also gave sanction to the same by lusty cheers and throwing up of hats, some of which fell on the roof of the courthouse

A copy of all the transactions was then made and dispatched by Captain James Jack to Philadelphia, requesting him to present them to Congress, which body was then in session

Another copy was sent to Samuel Johnston, Moderator of the Provincial Congress at Hillsboro and was laid before that body long before it arrived of Capt Jack at Philadelphia, he delivered the resolutions to Messrs Caswell, Hooper and Hewes, delegates in Congress from North Carolina. These gentlemen, it is reported, considered the resolutions premature, or radical, and did not offer them to Congress It is said that they were shown to some of the members of Congress who held advanced views on the question of independence among them Thomas Jefferson That the latter saw the resolutions there can be little doubt, in view of the fact that some of the exact verbiage of the Mecklenburg Declaration is used in the declaration drawn up by Jefferson at Philadelphia in July, 1776 The friends of Jefferson however claim that the coincidence was only accidental and that Jefferson never saw the copy carried to Philadelphia by Capt Jack

As the historian Jones observes, in the defense of the Mecklenburg Declaration "Whilst the sage of Monticello was pondering on the various projects of a reconciliation with the mother country, and never for once looking beyond 'that desirable end,' while Virginia and even Massachusetts were continually vowing allegiance to the Throne, and North Carolina herself, through the medium of her Congress, was declaring that independence was not her object, the people of Mecklenburg, with the sagacity of an honest and injured race, recoiled at once on the power that oppressed them, and dissolved forever the unhallowed union of British domination and American allegiance

Among those present at the Mecklenburg meeting and giving their enthusiastic approval to its transactions, were a number of other Polks, including Capt Ezekiel Polk, brother of Col Thomas Polk. Every member of the family was an earnest and devoted Whig and used every possible effort to advance the cause of independence

A number of years afterward, the original copy of the transactions of the Mecklenburg Convention were consumed by the burning of the house of John McKnitt Alexander, the Convention's Secretary. Thomas Jefferson, having his attention called to them by Mr Adams, denied that such a declaration ever took place In his egotism and jealousy, for he possessed these qualities in an eminent degree, Mr Jefferson yearned to appropriate to himself all the honors of the American Declaration of Independence. The Legislature of North Carolina appointed a committee to examine and report on the matter, and among those giving depositions regarding the transactions were a number of aged citizens who were present at the meeting and heard the declaration read. The transaction was conclusively proven, but the carping critics yet continue to deny that such an event ever occurred on May 20th, 1775, contending that the only resolutions adopted were those of May 31, following.

The Polk family are justly proud of the distinguished part taken in that historic event by their kinsmen, Col. Thos. Polk, Ezekiel Polk, and others of the family. In a speech delivered at Raleigh, in Oct., 1905, Theodore Roosevelt said "It was in North Carolina that the Mecklenburg Declaration of Independence foreshadowed the course taken in a few short months by the representatives of the thirteen colonies assembled at Philadelphia. North Carolina can rightfully say that she pointed us the way which led to the formation of a new nation. In the Revolution she did many memorable deeds; and the battle of King's Mountain marked the turning point of the Revolutionary war in the South."

While all those concerned in the Mecklenburg Declaration proceedings did their whole duty, the prime movers in the affair are said to have been Dr. Ephraim Brevard, Waightstill Avery, a distinguished lawyer, Col. Thomas Polk and Rev. Hazekiah Balch, the latter, like Dr. Brevard, a graduate of Princeton.

The historian Jones says: "Tradition ascribes to Thomas Polk the principal agency in bringing about the declaration. He appears to have given the notice for the election of the Convention, and, being Colonel of the County, to have superintended the election in each of the militia districts. He had been for a long time in the service of the Province as a surveyor, and as a member of the Assembly, and was thus intimately acquainted not only in Mecklenburg, but in the counties generally. Dr. Ephraim Brevard (the author of the Declaration) and Waightstill Avery, were men of the highest cultured attainments, and, contributing their enlightened resources to the shrewd native enthusiasm of Thomas Polk produced a Declaration at that time unrivalled, not only for the neatness of its style, but for the moral sublimity of its conception "

In a letter dated June 22, 1829, to Thomas Jefferson, calling his attention to the almost forgotten declaration, (and in reply to which Mr Jefferson denied the authenticity of that transaction) John Adams said What a poor, ignorant, malicious, short-sighted crapulous mass is Tom Pain's Common Sense in comparison with this paper The genuine sense of America at the moment was never so well expressed before nor since."

When the news of the Mecklenburg Conventions action reached the Royal Governor, Martin, he denounced it as a treasonable transaction, "most tratoriously declaring the entire dissolution of the laws, government, and constitution of this country, and setting up a system of rule and regulation repugnant to the laws, and subversive of His Majesty's Government. And these views, more fully expressed, he transmitted to the Crown, along with a copy of the Cape Fear Mercury, containing the Meeting's proceedings and resolutions

CHAPTER XXV.

SKETCH OF GEN'L THOMAS POLK.

Thomas Polk, son of William Polk and Margaret (Taylor) Polk, was born near Carlisle, Pa., about 1730, and died at Charlotte, N. C., in 1793, where he was buried. His father removed to the Yadkin Country about 1750, and settled at Sugar Creek, a few miles south of the present town of Charlotte, close to the South Carolina line. His neighbors and associates, therefore, comprised people of both colonies who were alike animated by a spirit of resistance to British Tyranny.

On Sugar Creek Thomas Polk erected a large mill and also became an extensive planter, acquiring a large body of land. He had received in Pennsylvania a good English education and fitted himself for the profession of a surveyor. In this occupation he was quite active for some years after settling in his new home, often assisted by his son William, as the latter approached manhood. By reason of such experience William also became a skilled surveyor.

Being a man of great force of character, keenness of vision in public affairs, and an ardent advocate of right and justice, Thomas Polk soon took a leading position among his neighbors and was consulted on all matters of moment.

In 1755 Thomas Polk married Susan Spratt, a daughter of Thomas Spratt. In 1769 he was chosen a member of the Provincial Assembly of North Carolina. Under his influence and patronage was founded "Queen's College," at Charlotte, the alma mater of many distinguished Southern men and statesmen. The Crown of Great Britain disallowed the charter, but it prospered nevertheless until British troops burned its building. By the founders it was called, "The Southern Cradle of Liberty."

In the capacity of surveyor Thomas Polk was frequently employed by the Colonial Government of his colony. He was often a member of the Colonial Assembly, serving with credit to himself and constituency. He was a member of that body when Husbands with his "Regulators" made war upon Governor Tyron and later fought the battle of Allamance. Thos Polk is said to have sympathized with the Regulators.

He was a member of the Colonial Congress in 1775, and Colonel of Minute Men in the Salisbury District. In the same year he was made Colonel of the Mecklenburg Militia Regiment and in 1776, Colonel of the 4th Regiment North Carolina Continentals, which the following year became a part of General Francis Nash's Brigade that joined Washington's army at the north.

A short time after the meeting of the Convention at Charlotte, word came that a number of Tories had embodied themselves at Cross Creek (now Fayetteville) to oppose the American cause. Col Thomas Polk promptly raised a regiment of infantry and cavalry, the latter corps commanded by his brother, Capt Charles Polk. But when Col Polk and his force reached the scene the Tories had dispersed, and the troops returned home.

In 1771 Thomas Polk was again a member of the Provincial Assembly with Abraham Alexander from Mecklenburg, in the Lower House. Joseph Martin was then Royal Governor of the Province. Thomas took a leading part in all the movements to oppose the aggressions of the Crown. As stated by Joseph Seawell Jones, the North Carolina historian, "Thomas Polk was the first to maintain the necessity of dissolving the political ties which bound the colonies to Great Britain. His feelings and opinions were decided, his expressions outspoken and courageous." And Jones adds: "Out of these feelings and opinions grew the Mecklenburg Declaration of Independence."

The feeling for independence was much more pronounced in the Southern than in New York and some other Northern colonies, where opinions were very much mixed as to the advisability of resistance. The war was largely settled by Southland troops to the last regiments of kingly encroachments. There were also a large number of Scotchmen in the Province, the greater proportion of whom were Loyalists, bearing arms against their neighbors who adhered to the cause of freedom. One regiment of these was headed by Donald McDonald, who later was made a prisoner when his regiment was defeated by the patriots.

Cornwallis pronounced the town of Charlotte, "The Hornet's Nest of North Carolina." In his Memoirs, p 159, Col Tarlton says "It was evident, and had been frequently mentioned to the King's officers, that the counties of Mecklenburg and Rowan were more hostile to England than any others in America."

Col Thomas Polk was a born leader of men, and recognized as a master spirit in the community in which he lived His policy was one of uncompromising resistance to the encroachments of the British ministry After the collision on April 19th, 1775, between the King's troops and Massachusetts patriots, he was called on, as Colonel of the County, to call a meeting of the people of Mecklenburg, such convention to be composed of two delegates from each company of his regiment This he did, and thus was organized the body which enunciated the famous Mecklenburg Declaration

From the court house steps Col Polk read to the assembled throng outside the resolutions adopted, and which had been drawn up by his son-in-law, Dr. Ephraim Brevard, Secretary of the Committee on Resolutions

On July 30, 1775, Governor Martin wrote to the Colonial Secretary, in London "The resolves of the Committee of Mecklenburg, which your lordship will find in the enclosed newspaper, surpass all the horrid and treasonable publications the inflammatory spirits of this continent have yet produced."

Only nine days later Gov Martin, fleeing from the gathering storm and taking refuge on a British warship in the harbor, issued a proclamation in which he denounced the newspaper account as an "infamous publication," and the resolution as most traitorously declaring the entire dissolution of the laws, government and constitution of this country, and setting up a system of rule and regulation repugnant to the laws and subversive of His Majesty's government."

The Tories of South Carolina, attacked the patriots under Col Williamson, at Cambridge and Ninety-Six, compelling him to capitulate. In retaliation, the South Carolina Council of Safety ordered out troops, among them Thompson's Mounted Rangers, in which Capt Ezekiel Polk, a brother of Col Thomas Polk, commanded a company Nine hundred North Carolina troops under Col Thomas Polk Rutherford, Morten and Graham, went to their assistance, and in a severe engagement defeated the Royalists

Col Polk's Regiment, the 4th Continentals, was brigaded under General Francis Nash, and formed a part of that command when it was ordered in 1777 to the North to reinforce Washington For three years Col Polk remained under Washington, participating in the battle of Brandywine and other engagements. It also suffered at Valley Forge

In Nov , 1779, the North Carolina troops returned to the South to reinforce General Lincoln, and, except Col Polk's regiment, were added to the garrison of Charleston, where they were captured in May 1780

DEFEATS AT CAMDEN AND SUMPTER.

General Gates, the much heralded "Hero of Saratoga," was then chosen to command the Southern Department Through Pinkney, the aide to Baron de Kalb, Gates offered Col Thos Polk (Aug 3), the double position of Commissary General of the State, and Commissary of Purchases for the army This tender he accepted, but soon after occurred the disastrous defeat of Gates at Camden The latter was panic-stricken and fled to Hillsboro, the then seat of government Two days after Camden, Sumpter was also defeated Cornwallis had started on his march to Charlotte, with a view of utterly destroying the "Hornets' Nest " As he neared the town the family of Col Thomas Polk fled to a place of safety

On Sept 26th Cornwallis entered Charlotte and appropriated Col Polk's residence for his headquarters, it being the only painted house in the town at that time, it is said There he remained until the American victory at King's

Mountain, Oct. 7, 1780, when he decamped. Before leaving he confiscated all of the property of Col. Polk that he could find. Four days after the King's Mountain affair Col. Polk wrote the following to the Board of War.

"Camp Yadkin River, Oct. 11, 1780.

Gentlemen —

I have the pleasure to inform you that on Saturday last the noted Col. Ferguson, with 150 men, fell on King's Mountain, 800 taken prisoners and 1,500 stand of arms. Cleveland and Campbell commanded. A glorious affair. In a few days we will be in Charlotte, and I will take possession of my house, and his lordship take the woods.

I am, Gentlemen, With Respect,

Your humble servant
Thos. Polk

To the Board of War Hillsboro."

Riding from house to house in Western North Carolina, and also across the border in South Carolina, Col. Polk encouraged all to enlist in the patriot ranks. He was highly esteemed by General Greene, and after the death of General Davidson at the battle of Cowan's Ford, the field officers of the Salisbury District strongly urging his appointment, Col. Polk was commissioned in Davidson's stead. In consideration of the claim of Col. Locke, the commission was not confirmed.

THE MILITARY ORGANIZED.

In August, 1775, the Colonial Congress addressed itself to the question of resistance. Two Continental Regiments the 1st and 2d, were raised, commanded respectively by Colonels Moore and Howe. The Minute Men and Militia were also well organized into companies and regiments, each county contributing a Militia Regiment. In all the Militia Regiments numbered thirty-five.

The field officers of the Mecklenburg Regiment were Thomas Polk, Colonel; Adam Alexander, Lieut. Colonel; John Phifer, 1st Major; John Davidson, 2nd Major. In a short time it was discovered that some of the Militia officers selected were Loyalists and they were displaced and some of them prosecuted

In April, 1776, the Militia system was reorganized by the Congress, care being taken to enlist none but true patriots Francis Nash (who fell in Sept, 1777, at Germantown, near Philadelphia) succeeded to command of the 1st North Carolina Continentals, and Alexander Martin to command of the 2nd regiment. Col Thomas Polk was also advanced to the Continental Line, four more regiments of that branch of service being raised He was chosen Colonel of the 4th Regiment with James Thackston as Lieutenant, Colonel and Wm Davidson Major This regiment constituted a part of Nash's Brigade, which afterward marched North to the aid of Washington, and saw hard service in numerous engagements, and suffered and starved with the devoted Forlorn Hope of American cause at Valley Forge

ESCORTS BAGGAGE TRAIN TO BETHLEHEM.

Just before the battle of Germantown, when the advancing British force under Lord Howe was nearing Philadelphia, Washington ordered Col Thos Polk to take two hundred men—a battalion of his mounted regiment—and escort a baggage train of seven hundred wagons, loaded with all the army stores, to a place of safety On these wagons were also loaded all the bells of the city, in order to prevent the British from casting them into cannon balls Among these bells was that on the State House, known as "Liberty Bell," rung on July 8, 1776, to proclaim the Declaration of Independence This bell was cracked on July 8, 1835, when tolled for the last time, on the occasion of the funeral solemnities of Chief Justice John Marshall To his children and grandchildren Col Polk often related the incidents of his escort of the baggage train to a place of safety

Leaving Philadelphia, the train journeyed North to Bethlehem, a quiet village on the Lehigh, settled by Moravians, and arrived there on Sept 23d

In his book entitled "Leonidas Polk Bishop and General," an interesting life of his father Lt Wm Mecklenburg Polk relates the life of Gen Polk as follows

"Among other services entrusted at this period to this active officer (Col Thomas Polk) was the command of the force which removed the heavy baggage of the army to a place of safety"

"With these went the bells of Philadelphia, which on the near approach of the British had been taken down from their airy homes in tower, steeple, and belfry, hurried upon wagons and sent lumbering over the stony roads, first to Trenton, N J, and afterwards to the sleepy old village of Bethlehem, Pennsylvania"

"At this period Bethlehem was inhabited only by a colony of German Moravians, and these were governed in things temporal as well as spiritual by the counsel of their priestly head, so the only public records are to be found in the seemingly most carefully kept diaries of the various bishops, who, as was much the custom in the Teutonic lands from whence these pious wanderers had come, ruled in Bethlehem"

The Moravian church diary of that period contains these entries

"Sept 23, 1777 The whole of the heavy baggage of the army, in the continuous train of seven hundred wagons direct from camp, arrived under escort of two hundred men commanded by Col Polk of North Carolina

They encamped on the south side of the Lehigh and in one night destroyed all our buckwheat and the fences around our fields.

"The wagons after unloading return to Trenton for more stores Among the things brought here were the church bells from Philadelphia, and the wagon in which was loaded the State House bell broke down in the street and had to be unloaded."

Under date of September 24th is recorded: "In the afternoon Cols Polk and Thornbury arrived with 700 wagons containing the heavy baggage, and guarded by two hundred men, who encamped on the banks of the Lehigh Here everything was unloaded, and a guard left for protection Besides the army stores was brought the bells of Philadelphia"

"While passing through the town the wagon containing

the "State House Bell," (that was called the "Liberty Bell,") broke down and the bell had to be unloaded "

'The Highland prisoners with their guard left for Reading on their way to Lancaster, and from thence are to be taken to West Virginia No sooner were their old quarters cleared than the Doctors of the Hospital took it for their store. We heard that the army was expected here, for Baron de Kalb with a corps of French engineers has commenced to survey the heights in and around the town Col Polk has received orders to hold himself in readiness to cross the river and occupy the southern acclivity of the town."

The absence of Col. Thomas Polk on this duty prevented his participation in the battle of Germantown (Oct 4, 1777) where Nash's Brigade, under Lord Stirling, bore a distinguished part, and in which Col Polk's son, Lieut Col Wm Polk, was severely wounded by a bullet through his cheeks In the same engagement also were Delaware kinsmen (of the Ephraim Polk line) and the powder-horn carried by one of them is now in possession of the writer, his grandson.

WILLIAM POLK OF CARLISLE.

On the family "tree published in 1849 from data furnished by Col Wm H. Winder, Josiah F Polk, Jas K Polk Col. Wm Polk, Horace M Polk Bishop Leonidas Polk, and others, the names of the children of William Polk, who emigrated from Carlisle, Pa, to North Carolina about 1750, appear in the following order ¹Wm Polk, who married twice (wives names unknown), ²Charles Polk, who married Polly Clark, ³Debora Polk, who married Sam'l McLeary, ⁴Susan Polk, who married Benjamin Alexander: ⁵Margaret Polk, who married Robert McRea, ⁶John Polk, who married Eleanor Shelby: ⁷General Thomas Polk, who married Susan Spratt, ⁸Ezekiel Polk, who married first Miss Wilson, and afterward Mrs Lennard

This order of birth is most likely correct, agreeing with the statements of Mrs Susan Smart, in a letter to Bishop Polk in 1849 Mrs Smart was the eldest child of Susan Barnett, daughter of Margaret Polk and Robert McRee and at the time of her statements to Bishop Polk she was eighty-seven years of age. She was born, therefore in 1762 and was twelve or thirteen years of age when her mother's (Susan Barnett's) grand-father, William Polk, emigrated from Pennsylvania to North Carolina in 1750 or 51. She "well knew all the members of the family," as she stated in her letter to the Bishop, but gave no dates of births or deaths of William Polk's children.

Some of the family data handed down differs from the order of the names as printed on the family tree but as it was compiled during the life of Mrs. Smart Col Wm Polk (son of Gen'l Thomas Polk) and others, we accept the order given on the tree as most likely correct.

Concerning the two wives of William Polk (eldest son of William of Carlisle), the tree does not give their names, but later data shows that after being twice married, he died after becoming an old man, leaving a numerous progeny. One of his sons was the Col Thomas Polk, who married Mary Shelby, daughter of Evan Shelby, Jr., son of General Evan Shelby Sr. Nor does the tree tell who Debora married, but later information shows that she married Samuel McLeary, of Mecklenburg County, by whom she had a considerable family. All the old family bibles of those early generations seem to have been destroyed by the mutations of time. The loss of many records of the family, generally by the burning of dwellings, has to a large extent hampered the writer's searches after facts. The burning of a number of county office buildings in Maryland, Delaware and Pennsylvania, has also destroyed much family data that once existed in the shape of wills, deeds, and other official documents of record. It is evident that the children of William Polk were all grown when he moved from Carlisle to the Yadkin, and there is a tradition that some of his sons preceded him by several years to North Carolina. Mrs Smart clearly states that he "died in North Carolina, west of the Yadkin, at least twenty-five years before the Revolution." So he must have been born about 1705 to 1712 a son of Col. Wm Polk, Sr., of Somerset County, Md., by his first wife, Nancy (Knox) Owens widow of Wm Owens of Somerset Co

CHAPTER XXVI.

SKETCH OF COL. WILLIAM POLK.

Colonel William Polk second son and child of General Thomas Polk, was quite as distinguished as his father in the transactions of the Revolutionary War. He was born in Mecklenburg County, N. C., July 9, 1758. At fourteen he attended a Grammar School and acquired the rudiments of an English education. He afterwards, when seventeen, entered Queen's college, at Charlotte, where he remained for three years, or until he lacked but one year of his majority. He also, like his father, studied surveying and became proficient in that calling. As the armed conflict between the Colonies and the mother country drew apace, and his college duties becoming irksome, he left the institution and took steps to participate in the cause of Liberty.

In April, 1775, the month before his father read the Mecklenburg Declaration from the courthouse steps in Charlotte, William was appointed a Second Lieutenant in the Third South Carolina Regiment, under Col Wm Thompson popularly known as "Old Colonel Danger." William was assigned to the Second Company of the Regiment, the members of which were about equally enlisted from North and South Carolina. The company was rapidly recruited to full strength and shortly after with another Company of the Regiment, was ordered to Ninety-Six, S. C., to curb the insolence of the Tories in that quarter.

Col. Thompson had a high opinion of Lieutenant Wm Polk and gave him command of several expeditions on one of which he captured Colonel Fletcher, a noted South Carolina Tory Leader.

On Dec 22, 1775, four hundred Loyalists were surprised on Reedy river by Colonel Thompson and made prisoners Hearing that Capt York and thirty men had left the Loyalist Camp the day before on a foraging expedition Colonel

Thompson sent Lieutenant William Polk with thirty men and a number of volunteer militia to intercept him York and all his party except two were captured The two escaping Tories were pursued by Lieutenant Polk and William Henderson (who afterwards succeeded General Sumpter in command of the South Carolina Brigade), and in the struggle Polk was shot through the shoulder Another account handed down is that Polk's guide was a professed American patriot but at heart a Tory. named Soloman Deason, who led him into an ambush of the enemy, a volley from the latter badly wounding Polk in the shoulder.

It has been stated, and never controverted, that Lieutenant Wm Polk was "the first man wounded in the Revolution after the battle of Lexington, April 19 1775."

At the time Lieutenant Wm. Polk was wounded a foot of snow was on the ground and he was carried one hundred and forty miles to his father's home at Charlotte where he lay under the treatment of a surgeon for ten months before he was able to resume his duties in the field During this absence from duty the National Declaration of Independence was promulgated at Philadelphia and war was formally declared. Charleston had been besieged and the battles of Long Island, White Plains and other conflicts had taken place It was with joy that Lieut. Wm Polk, now able to rejoin the ranks of his struggling countrymen, repaired again to his regiment for duty, taking part in all its strenuous work against the British

On Nov 26, 1776, having demonstrated his soldierly qualities he was chosen by the Provincial Congress of North Carolina to fill the office of Major of the Ninth Regiment of North Carolina troops raised on Continental Establishment his father, Thomas Polk, already being Colonel of the Fourth Regiment of Continentals William joined his regiment at Halifax, in March, 1777 The Colonel and Lieutenant Colonel of the Regiment being at the time detailed on other duties Major Polk took command of the Regiment, drilling and disciplining it Though not yet attained to his majority in years, Major Polk soon convinced his fitness for command and gained the full confidence of his superiors Not long after

COL. WM. POLK,
of North Carolina, Revolutionary Officer.

THE NEW YORK
PUBLIC LIBRARY

ASTOR LENOX AND
TILDEN FOUNDATIONS.

Colonel Francis Nash being promoted to Brigadier General, was placed in command of the Brigade of North Carolina Continentals, and ordered to the North to reinforce Washington. The Ninth was one of the Regiments composing this Brigade. And Nash being joined by the Third Division of the North Carolina Line proceeded to the Jerseys and united with the army of Washington, then on the march to oppose Lord Howe's troops at the headwaters of Elk river Major Polk was engaged with his regiment in the battles of Brandywine and Germantown, which took place shortly after. Near the close of the latter action, while giving a command, a British musket-ball passed through his cheeks, knocking out his upper teeth and wounding his tongue so that he was unable to talk.

About the same time General Nash, his Brigade commander, received a mortal wound, from the bursting of a British shell, and his eyesight also was destroyed The parting between Major Polk and his dying general was pathetic one In 1826, speaking of it to a friend, Colonel Polk said

"The last time I ever saw General Nash was on the battlefield of Germantown He was being borne from the field on a litter. I had just been shot in the mouth and could not speak I motioned to the bearers of the litter to stop They did so, and I approached to offer my hand to Nash He was blind and almost in syncope from loss of blood, but when he was told that Wm Polk was standing near him, so wounded that he could not speak, Nash held out his hand and said. "Good-bye, Polk, I am mortally wounded"

In spite of his wound, Major Polk remained near his command and went into winter quarters with the army at Valley Forge Thus, with his father, Col. Thomas Polk he was one of that guard of faithful Continentals who clung to the fortunes of Washington through the want and misery of that dreadful winter

In March, 1778, the nine North Carolina regiments serving with Washington were so reduced by death and expiration of short terms of enlistment that the state consolidated them into four regiments retiring the supernumerary officers by lot. It was the misfortune of Major Polk to lose his command in this way

On his return to the South, Major Polk engaged in the recruiting service, and also in expeditions against the Tories in North and South Carolina During this service he became associated with Andrew Jackson and they became fast friends, that friendship lasting through life

When Gates was assigned to command of the Southern Army, Major Polk became a member of the staff of Major General Caswell, and was present with him at the disastrous defeat at Camden. After the fall of Baron de Kalb, and the rout was complete, through his knowledge of the country he guided successfully the retreat of the regular and militia troops through the woods and by-ways

Major Polk next joined General William Davidson After the retreat of Cornwallis from Charlotte, following the victory of King's Mountain, Major Polk was sent to Gates, and afterwards to Governor Thomas Jefferson of Virginia, and to the Maryland Council, to inform them of the deplorable condition of affairs in Charlotte and Salisbury

In 1780, when Greene relieved Gates of command of the army at Charlotte, he ordered Major William Polk to accompany and assist General Kosciusko in selecting a better camping district for the army, one where provisions were more plentiful. The army was then established on the Pedee Major Polk then returned to Charlotte to help General Davidson raise a force of militia from Mecklenburg, Iridell, Rowan and Lincoln Counties With eight hundred men enlisted, Davidson in January following marched to the assistance of General Morgan on his hurried retreat from the success of Cowpens. As the British under Cornwallis were crossing the Catawba at Cowan's Ford, in pursuit of the Americans, Davidson and his new troops attacked them. Cornwallis' horse was killed under him Davidson, mortally wounded, fell into the arms of Major Polk who was riding by his side. The Militia then gave way and scattered Major Polk rallied as many as he could, led them to Salem, and reported for service to General George Pickens before Green crossed the Dan, skirmishing with the rear of Cornwallis' army and afterwards following Tarlton and the Royalist Colonel Pyle into the country of the Dan. Major Polk was conspicuously gallant and distinguished in the hard fought battle at Guilford, C. H.

Soon after the battle of Guilford, C. H., and the retreat of Cornwallis to Wilmington, Major Polk received a commission as Lieutenant Colonel from Governor John Rutledge, of South Carolina, and was ordered to raise a regiment of Swordsmen and Mounted Infantry, to be called the Fourth Regiment, South Carolina Horse. Inside of a month he had enlisted two-thirds of the regiment and reported to General Sumner, operating between the British posts of Camden and Ninety Six. Joined with the force of Colonel Wade Hampton, they marched sixty miles in seventeen hours, surprised the British outpost at Friday's Ferry, on the Congaree, killing twenty-seven and burning the blockhouse in sight of Fort Granby.

Col. Polk next joined Sumpter at the siege of Orangeburg, helping to capture that post. He was then ordered to report to General Francis Marion, before Fort Mott, but before his arrival there the British garrison had surrendered. He took an active part in the operations against the British posts near Charleston. At Eutaw Springs the brigade was composed of Hampton's, Middleton's and Polk's regiments. This brigade, with Lee's Legion, covered the advance of Greene's line of battle and took position on the left, opposite the Light Infantry of Major Majoribanks, one of the best officers in the British army. During the battle the Militia wavered, but Hampton, Polk and Middleton rallied them.

During an obstinate hand-to-hand fight with the British cavalry, Col. Polk's horse was shot dead and fell on him. A British soldier started to bayonet him, when a Sergeant with a stroke of his saber cut down the Briton and saved his Colonel's life. It was a desperate battle and in it Col. Wm. Polk's brother, Lieutenant Thomas Polk, was killed by a ball in the forehead.

In his official report of the battle General Greene said: "Lieutenant Colonels Polk and Middleton were no less conspicuous for their good conduct than their intrepidity, and the troops under their command gave a specimen of what may be expected from men naturally brave, when improved by proper discipline."

The British retreating to Charleston, left nothing for the American cavalry to do but skirmish and picket, and in such service Col. William Polk and his command engaged until peace was made and the army disbanded.

Among the interesting incidents of Colonel Wm. Polk's military career was an encounter with the gallant British dragoon Tarlton, then a mere lad like himself, in his raid upon the Waxhaw. But beyond a few words of Andrew Jackson, relating to a surprise of Polk and himself by British cavalry under the dashing young Englishman, we have little knowledge of the circumstances of the meeting. It appears to have occurred upon an occasion when the British cavalry caught the 'Rebels' defiling through a long lane bordered by high rail fences. That good use was made of the opportunity is shown by the straits to which Jackson and Polk were put in order to make their escape, and may be inferred from Tarlton's well known capacity as a commander of cavalry.

Though but a lad when he was commissioned, William Polk was a stalwart man, six feet four inches in height, and of great strength. Sabres were difficult to obtain in the American colonies, and his sword was made for him from a scythe blade. He was often engaged at the head of his troops in hand-to-hand encounters with the enemy's cavalry. In one of these a sturdy British soldier singled him out and made a furious assault upon him. For a time the issue was doubtful, but Polk, beating down his adversary's guard, struck the gallant fellow squarely upon the crown of his head and clove him almost to the chin.

In 1783, after the close of the war, Colonel Polk served his State and County in various civic capacities. The Legislature of North Carolina appointed him Surveyor General of the Middle District, now in Tennessee. He remained there until 1786, and was twice elected a member of the House of Commons, representing Davidson County in that body. In 1787 he was elected to the General Assembly of North Carolina, from his native county of Mecklenburg, which he continued to represent until he was nominated by President

Washington and confirmed by the Senate, as Supervisor of the Revenue for the District of North Carolina. This office he held for seventeen years, through the administrations of Washington, Adams and Jefferson, and until the Internal Revenue laws were repealed.

In 1789 Col. Wm. Polk, then thirty-one years of age, married Grizelda Gilchrist, daughter of a Scotch gentleman, and granddaughter of Robert Jones, a prominent lawyer of Halifax. Two children were born to them. Mrs Polk died in 1799. Col Polk soon after moved to Raleigh, where in 1801 he married Sarah, daughter of Col Philemon Hawkins and a sister of Governor Hawkins. Of this second union twelve children were born, one of whom was Leonidas Polk, Bishop of Louisiana and Lieut General Confederate States Army, who fell during the Civil War at Pine Mountain, Ga., June 14, 1864.

In 1811 Col Wm Polk was made a director of the State Bank of North Carolina and was chosen President by the Board. He filled this office until 1819, resigning in order to devote his attention to his estate in Tennessee, comprising 100,000 acres of land

On March 25, 1812, Col. Wm Polk was appointed by President Madison, with consent of the Senate, a Brigadier General in the Army of the United States. This commission, much to his subsequent regret, he declined on political grounds, thinking—erroneously as he afterwards saw—that his position as a staunch and very prominent Federalist forbid his acceptance of the flattering but well earned distinction from Mr Madison's administration

LA FAYETTE'S VISIT TO NORTH CAROLINA.

When LaFayette returned to America in 1824, and made his memorable tour through the states in that and the following year, Col Wm Polk was one of the commissioners appointed to assist in doing the honors of the State to his old comrade in arms. By request of Governor Burton, Col Polk raised a military escort of cavalry from Mecklenburg and Cabarrus counties. At Halifax the cortege was met by General Daniel Col Polk, the military companies, and many citizens on horseback. It had been arranged that the ladies were to waive their handkerchiefs as soon as LaFayette came in sight, and when General Daniel exclaimed: "Welcome, La-Fayette!" the whole company was to repeat the welcome after him Unluckily, the ladies misunderstood the programme, waited too long, and were reminded of their duty by a stentorian command of 'Flirt ladies, flirt, flirt, I say!" from General Daniel as he walked down the line to meet La-Fayette "Great country! great country!" exclaimed La-Fayette to Col Polk, who was vainly trying not to smile.

Col. Polk and LaFayette rode together in a barouche drawn by four iron-grey horses The Governor received him in the vestibule and escorted him to the reception chamber, where he was welcomed in a formal address.

At the conclusion the company was amused with a spectacular scene La Fayette and Col Polk, both had been wounded at Brandywine At the conclusion of Col Polk's address, from the steps of the Capitol, LaFayette turned to him and before the old soldier knew what he was about, threw his arms around his neck and tried to kiss him on the cheek Col Polk straightened himself up to his full height of six feet four, instinctively throwing his head back to escape the osculatory act, but LaFayette, being a dapper little fellow tiptoed and hung on to the grim giant, while a shout of laughter burst from the spectators and was with some difficulty turned into a cheer.

LaFayette spoke but little English, and he undestood less He had retained a few phrases, which he would utter, generally in an effective manner, but sometimes ludicrously malapropos. "Thanks, my dear friend! Great country! Happy man! Oh, I member!" were nearly his whole vocabulary.

During a stay of three days at Raleigh, LaFayette was abundantly feted and was very gracious. Tradition says he had a voracious appetite On shaking hands his invariable salutation would be "How do you do, my son? How do you do?" When old soldiers were presented he would invariably ask the question: "Are you married?" If the reply was "Yes, sir," he would reply "Happy man, happy man!"

If the reply was "No, sir," he would reply "Lucky dog, lucky dog!" An immigrant from France, being presented, informed him of the recent death of his wife, and received the mechanical reply "Happy man! happy man!"

Of Col Wm Polk's influence on the State of Tennessee, Governor Swain of North Carolina said

"He was the contemporary and personal friend and associate of Andrew Jackson, not less heroic in war, and quite as sagacious, and more successful in private life It is known that Col Polk greatly advanced the interests and enhanced the wealth of the hero of New Orleans by information furnished him from his field notes as a surveyor, and in directing Jackson in his selection of valuable tracts of land in the State of Tennessee; that to Samuel Polk, the father of the President, he gave the agency of renting and selling his (Wm. Polk's) immense and valuable estate in lands in the most fertile section of that state, that as first President of the Bank of North Carolina, he made Jacob Johnson, the father of President Andrew Johnson, its first porter, so that of the three native North Carolinians who entered the White House through the gates of Tennessee, all were indebted alike for benefactions, and for promotion to a more favorable position in life, to the same individual, Col Wm. Polk

Col. Wm Polk took a prominent part in the ceremonies of unveiling Canova's statue of Washington, at Raleigh, in 1821. The statue reached that city on Dec 24th, and the Raleigh Register published a lengthly account of the proceedings attending its acceptance and dedication. On the Fayetteville road, south of Raleigh, the statue was met by a concourse of State officials, members of the Assembly, and other citizens A procession was formed at 3 o'clock, on the ground where the statue was halted As the procession moved the artillery drawn up in front of the Capitol fired a salute of twenty-four guns The Adjutant General of the State was Marshal of the Day and had charge of all the details of business

When this imposing pageant had reached the Capitol, Col Wm Polk delivered an oration to the assembled multitude

DEATH OF COL WM. POLK.

Colonel William Polk died at his residence in Raleigh on January 4th, 1834, in the seventy-sixth year of his age, his life having been one of great activity and filled with many exciting episodes His splendid services to the cause of freedom during the Revolution his talent for command and his fearlesness in battle, had endeared him to every patriot in North and South Carolina His funeral was attended with military honors He was an ardent member of the patriotic order of the Society of the Cincinnati, founded at the close of the Revolution and composed of officers of the patriot army He was the last surviving field officer of the North Carolina line in the war for independence

MONUMENT OF COL. WM. POLK,
at Raleigh, N. C.

CHAPTER XXVII.

DR WILLIAM J. POLK.

Dr William J Polk. second child of Colonel William Polk and Grizelda (Gilchrist) Polk, was born in Mecklenburg County, N C, March 21, 1793 He graduated at the University of North Carolina, in 1813, at the age of twenty years; studied medicine and took his degree of M. D. at the Philadelphia Medical University He first settled in Fayetteville, N. C., and began practice, but soon afterwards marrying Miss Long, a grand-daughter of General Allen Long, of Halifax, he moved to Mecklenburg County and commenced planting His father leaving him a large body of land in Tennessee, he removed to that state in 1835 and made Columbia his future home

"Dr Polk's life," said his son, Major Allen J Polk, in a letter to the writer: "Was calm, uneventful, cultivated, high-toned and honorable Possessed of ample means he preferred the quiet of home and his books to the pursuit of office and political honors It was with reluctance that he even accepted the Presidency of the Bank of Tennessee at Columbia" He was for years a member of the Episcopal church, and died happily, before he could see his country torn by Civil War, in 1861.

GENERAL LUCIUS E. POLK.

Gen Lucius Eugene Polk, fourth son of Dr. William J Polk and Mary (Long) Polk, was one of the bravest and most distinguished officers of the Confederate Army in the Civil War, and a worthy descendent of gallant and distinguished Revolutionary ancestors who fought under Washington, Greene, and other noted leaders.

General Lucius E Polk was born July 10, 1833 in Salisbury, N. C. He was educated at the University of Virginia, and settled in Phillips County, Arkansas, near Helena, where he engaged in planting, his plantation being near that of his brother, Major Allen J Polk When the Civil War came on, he enlisted as a private in a company raised by Capt Patrick R Cleburne. This company was named the "Yell Rifles," in honor of the distinguished Col Yell, of that State, who gained prominence in the Mexican War. The "Yell Rifles" became distinguished, not only for intrepid conduct under the lead of Captain "Pat" Cleburne, but because of the number of generals it turned out—Cleburne, Hardeman, Polk and Govan.

Shortly after Lucius E. Polk joined Cleburne's Company, he was made Third Lieutenant, a position formerly designated as Ensign in the old army organization Cleburne being elected Colonel of the regiment, Lieutenant Polk commanded his company in the battle of Shiloh, being in the hottest of the fight, and losing a fourth of his men in killed and wounded. Lieutenant Polk also received a wound in the face Colonel Harris, commander of the regiment, and also the Lieutenant Colonel, being killed, the Major wounded and made a prisoner, Lieutenant Polk was unanimously chosen as Colonel of the regiment, a few days after the battle.

In the retreat from Corinth, when hard pressed by the Federal Army under Halleck and Grant, Col Lucius E Polk's regiment covered the Confederate rear and strenuously resisted the enemy's advance, destroying the corduroy bridges across the deep, unfordable streams, compelling the Federals to construct others in order to maintain a steady advance.

It is said that there were forty-five Polks, on the Confederate side, in the battle of Shiloh, and there was several of the same name, from Kentucky, Illinois, Indiana and other states, among the Union troops engaged.

Cleburne's Brigade soon became the most famous fighting corps in the Southern Army, and was noted at all times for its headlong bravery in action It was with General E Kirby Smith in September, 1862, when he advanced from Knoxville, flanked the Federal General George W Morgan's division, out of Cumberland Gap, and invaded Kentucky

DR. WM. JULIUS POLK AND WIFE,
of North Carolina.

With General Kirby Smith, and generally in the advance was Cleburne's brigade, including the regiment of Col Lucius E Polk At the battle of Richmond, August 30, 1862, Col Polk's regiment bore a conspicuous part and he was wounded in the head As he fell from his horse, General Cleburne dismounted to see if he was dead, also received a wound in the face They were both in the saddle again a few weeks later, at the battle of Perryville, October 8th, where, after desperate conflict with Buell, Bragg's army retreated

The Confederate forces in this battle were commanded by General Lucius E. Polk's uncle, Lieutenant General Leonidas Polk. Bragg's and Kirby Smith's armies, now united, retreated out of Kentucky by way of Danville, Harrodsburg, Crab Orchard, London and Cumberland Gap, to Knoxville From the latter place most of it went to Chattanooga and there awaited the approach of General Rosencranz, who had superseded Buell in command of the Federal forces after the battle of Perryville.

At the battle of Perryville, Col Polk received another wound, his third one, in the foot General Cleburne, who was at his side, was also wounded, being shot in the leg They were both disabled for several weeks Meantime Col Polk was promoted to the rank of Brigadier General and placed in command of Cleburne's old brigade, that officer being made a division commander

The battle of Stone River (or Murfreesboro, as it is called by the Confederates) took place on December 30th and 31st, 1862, and January 1st, 1863 It was one of the most sanguinary battles of the war and was ended by the retreat of the Confederates In this battle, as it did on every occasion, Cleburne's Division performed conspicuous service, Polk's Brigade increasing the military renown of its leader

After the battle of Ringold Gap, General Cleburne wrote to Brigadier Generals Polk and Long and Colonels Govan and Granberry: "I must return my thanks Four better officers are not in the service of the Confederacy. The conduct of officers and men in this fight needs no comment; so far as I know, every man did his whole duty "

In appreciation of their services, the Confederate Congress, by joint resolution, returned thanks to Major General Cleburne and the officers and men under his command. After the defeat of the Confederates at Lookout Mountain and Missinary Ridge, General Polk's Brigade and the rest of Cleburn's division, retired in good order. In the retreat General Polk covered the rear with his veteran brigade, and at Ringold Gap, where Hooker's Corps was launched heavily against him, he made a stout resistance and gave it a bloody repulse after which the pursuit by the Federals ended.

General Polk was also with General Jos. Johnston in his masterly retreat to Atlanta, in which was verified the maxim of Fabius that "A good retreat is better than a doubtful victory."

The battle of Chickamauga, the most sanguinary conflict of the war, according to the number of troops engaged, was fought on September 19th and 20th, 1863. Here General Lucius E. Polk again distinguished himself. Major General John C. Breckinridge said of Cleburne's division, of which Polk's brigade formed a part. "Having received permission from Lieutenant General Hill to make another charge, the division advanced with intrepidity, under a severe fire, and dashed over the left of the intrenchments. In passing them, I saw on my left the right wing of Major General Cleburne, whose brave division turned the center."

This right wing of Cleburne's division was the brigade of General Lucius E. Polk. In his report of the battle, General Cleburne said: "I have already incidentally called attention to the gallant conduct of Brigadier General Polk, but it is due him and the country, which wishes to appreciate its faithful servants today, that to the intrepidity and stern determination of purpose of himself and men I am principally indebted for the success of the charge on Sunday evening, which drove the enemy from the breastworks and gave us the victory."

Sherman being assigned to command of the Federal army, concentrated his troops, amounting to ninety thousand men, at Tunnel Hill, Ga., in order to advance on Atlanta. In all the fighting, from Tunnell Hill to Kenesaw Mountain,

GEN'L LUCIUS E. POLK,
of Arkansas, Major Gen'l C. S. A.

General Lucius E Polk's brigade was conspicuous for its gallantry At Kenesaw Mountain, where Sherman made a desperate assault on the Confederate intrenchments and was bloodily repulsed, General Lucius E Polk's horse was killed under him, by a fragment of a shell General Polk also received a severe wound in one of his legs—his fourth one He refused to allow the surgeons to amputate his leg, suffered from it for a long time, and never entirely recovered its use

General Lucius E. Polk rose by his own merits and services He was a handsome, distinguished looking man, brave, modest and disinclined to talk about his deeds He was averse to discussing the events of the war, except with old comrades. So modest was he, it is said, that he refused even to write or furnish a sketch of his life when urged to do so by his alma mater. Covered with wounds that attested his valor on the field, beloved by all who knew him, he died at his home near Columbia, Tennessee, in October 1894 The last years of his life were devoted to planting

CHAPTER XXVIII.

DR. THOMAS G. POLK.

Dr Thomas G. Polk, third child of Dr William J Polk and Mary (Long) Polk, was born in Mecklenburg County, N C, December 5, 1825; died at Decatur, Alabama, June 14 1877 He graduated from the Jefferson Medical College, Philadelphia, and was an Assistant Surgeon in the Mexican War On account of poor health during the Civil War, being unable for the more active field duties, he was a volunteer aid on the staff of General J C Tappan, at Banks' defeat on Red River, and also served at the battles of Vicksburg, Mansfield and Pleasant Hill

Dr Thomas G. Polk married, in 1851, Miss Lavenia C Wood, a descendant of the distinguished Mason family of Virginia, by whom he had issue. [1]Mary Polk, [2]Caroline Polk, [3]Grizelda Polk, [4]William J Polk

Mary, the eldest child of Dr Thomas G Polk, married William Littlejohn, of Memphis, Tennessee, and had issue: [1]Thomas, [2]Margaret, [3]Lavenia Margaret married William Spright.

Caroline, second child of Dr Thomas G Polk and Lavenia (Wood) Polk, married Hamilton S Homer, of Helena, Arkansas, and had two children. [1]John Sidney and [2]Minnie Polk Homer.

Grizelda Polk, third child of Dr Thomas G Polk and Lavenia (Wood) Polk, married Henry R Stirling, of Lower Louisiana, and had one child Mary B Stirling

William J Polk, fourth child of Dr. Thomas G. Polk, and Lavinia (Wood) Polk, married Euola Greenleaf and has one child, Magdalen Tasker Polk

Mary Jones Polk, daughter of Dr William J Polk and Mary (Long) Polk, married Col Joseph G. Branch, of Arkansas by whom she had four children: [1]Mary Branch [2]Lucia Branch [3]Lawrence Branch [4]Joseph Branch.

Mary Branch married Dr Chas Winn, and they have one child, Lawrence Branch Winn

Lucia Branch married William Howard, of St. Louis They have also, one child Gerald Howard

General Lucius E Polk, son of Dr William J. Polk and Mary (Long) Polk, married his cousin, Sallie Moore Polk, daughter of Rufus K. Polk and Sarah (Jackson) Polk, and they had issue ¹Rufus King Polk, ²Rebecca Polk, ³Lucius Polk ⁴William Polk, ⁵James K Polk

Rufus King Polk married Isabella Greer, of Pennsylvania, and they had two children· ¹Emma Polk, ²Porter Polk

Rebecca Polk married Scott Hardin of Tennessee, and had issue ¹Sarah P, ²Benjamin, ³Lucius The other three children of General Lucius E Polk, at last accounts, were unmarried.

COLONEL CADWALLADER POLK

Another Polk who attained to distinction as a soldier in the Civil War, and by his gallantry shed additional lustre on a family of soldiers, was Col Cadwallader Polk, a brother of General Lucius Polk, and nephew of Major General Thomas G. Polk and Lieutenant General Leonidas Polk

Here we have, in this branch of the family emenating from William Polk and Margaret Taylor seven descendants, who attained to eminent military distinction, viz General Thomas Polk and his son Colonel William Polk, of the Revolution General Thomas G Polk and his brother Lieutenant General Leonidas Polk, sons of Colonel William Polk; General Lucius E Polk, Colonel Cadwallader Polk and Capt Rufus K Polk, all brothers and grandsons of Colonel William Polk

Colonel Cadwallader Polk, was the sixth child of Dr. William J Polk and Mary (Long) Polk, and was born in Columbia, Tenn , October 11. 1838 He graduated at the University of North Carolina and was among the first to join the colors of the South at the outbreak of the Civil War, as a Second Lieutenant in Manny's First Tennessee Infantry His regiment being sent , I ... ...

under Stonewall Jackson in his numerous marches and battles in Virginia and West Virginia On the return of his regiment to the Western army, he was with it at Shiloh. After his term of enlistment expired, he joined Hindman's Legion and campaigned in Northern Arkansas and Southern Missouri, being commissioned a Major in one of the new regiments.

He was next promoted to the rank of Lieutenant Colonel and in the battle of Prairie Grove, in Arkansas, was desperately wounded and left on the field for dead Placed in a Federal hospital, he slowly recovered from his wound and was exchanged Under General Holmes, he participated in the battle of Helena, part of which was fought on the Polk plantations After the promotion of his old Colonel, he was elected to the command of his regiment and led it in the battles of Little Rock and Jenkins' Ferry, serving until the surrender of the Confederate Army at Appomattox. He then settled down to the life of a planter, near his brothers, Allen J. Polk and Rufus K. Polk, near Helena

Colonel Cadwallader Polk married Miss Carrie Lowry, of Louisiana and they had issue [1]William J, [2]Anna T, [3]Walter, [4]Cadwallader, [5]Nina, and [6]Edwin M

William J Polk, eldest child of Colonel Cadwallader Polk and Carrie (Lowry) Polk married Lulu Donnell, in January, 1891, and had issue [1]George Polk, [2]Caroline Polk

Anna T Polk married Christopher Agee, Nov 19, 1890, and had issue: Walter Polk, born September, 1891.

Nina Polk, married William Crolidge, November, 1893, and had issue. [1]William, born January, 1895; [2]Elizabeth, born January, 1897.

CAPTAIN RUFUS J. POLK.

Captain Rufus J Polk, seventh child of Dr William J Polk and Mary (Long) Polk, was born in Columbia, Tennessee, in 1844 When the Civil War began he was eighteen years of age and a student at the University of North Carolina. Leaving that institution as soon as hostilities began at Fort Sumpter, he joined the Confederate Army, was made a

Second Lieutenant of Artillery, and assigned to Hume's Battery at Island No. 10, in the Mississippi, where his guns were principally engaged against the ironclad vessels of the Federal navy under Commodore Foote, Ellet, and others. On the capture of the Island by the Federal army and navy, Captain Polk was made a prisoner and sent to Camp Chase, later transferred to Johnson's Island, where he remained six months, when he was exchanged at Vicksburg and appointed Adjutant of Col. Baker's regiment. A short time afterward he was appointed to the position of Captain and Aide-de-Camp on the staff of his brother, General Lucius E. Polk, serving with him through the Georgia Campaign and until the end of the war. He was with General Forrest on his raid into Middle Tennessee. After his brother was wounded, he served on the staff of General Armstrong, and at the battle of Selma, the last but one of the Civil War, he was wounded in the arm.

Captain Rufus J. Polk was married in 1867 to Miss Cynthia Martin, daughter of Geo. W. Martin and Narcissa (Pillow) Martin, of Tennessee. He removed to Little Rock, Arkansas, and they had issue [1]Lucien Eugene Polk, [2]Rufus J. Polk, [3]William Julius Polk, [4]Charles Leonidas Polk.

MAJOR ALLEN J. POLK.

Major Allen J. Polk, second child of Dr. William J. Polk and Mary (Long) Polk, was born March 5, 1824, at Farmville, N. C. and died at Helena, Ark., 1897. He was educated at the University of North Carolina, at Chapel Hill, the alma mater of so many of his kinsmen. After graduation, he studied law with his brother-in-law, Judge Russell Houston, at Columbia, Tenn. At the age of twenty-one he removed from Columbia to Helena, Ark., where he engaged in cotton planting with marked success, accumulating a fortune estimated at over $200,000. This he lost during the Civil War, a large part of it being in slaves. Carpet-bag domination in the South after the war created conditions that were unbearable to the whites, forcing many of them to move to states further North in order to secure protection to themselves and families. In

Major Polk's county the population numbered 5,000 whites and 15,000 negroes. Quitting his plantation, Major Polk moved to Louisville, purchasing a home at St. Matthews, near that city, where the writer visited him and was most hospitably entertained during the '70's. Here he remained for several years, until Carpetbag rule was expelled from the South, when he returned to Arkansas, resumed planting, and resided there until his death.

A man of high intelligence, genial, courteous, courtly in manner, and a delightful conversationalist, Major Polk charmed all with whom he came in contact. No one understood better than he the art of entertaining friends. In her sketch of Major Polk, published in the American Historical Magazine, Miss Mary Winder Garrett says of him: "He spent much time in Washington. He was a man widely known for his brilliant social qualities, high culture, genial disposition and personal magnetism, numbering many of the most noted men of the day among his personal friends. Major Allen Polk derived his title from the commission he held during the Civil War, in General Hindman's Arkansas Legion. He was never in active service, but used his means and influence, with untiring zeal, in behalf of the South."

In 1859 Major Allen J. Polk married Miss Anna Clark Fitzhugh, of Louisville, daughter of Judge Dennis Fitzhugh, and grand-niece of Gen'l George Rogers Clark, and Gov. William Clark of Missouri. She was also related to the Fitzhugh family of Virginia. She possessed an ample fortune, which united with that of her husband, made them a very wealthy couple.

Major Allen Polk cared little for political honors, but made several "experiments," as he termed them, in Arkansas, making the race for the Legislature in 1854 and 1856, and for the Constitutional Convention in 1868. Speaking to the writer about these "experiments," he said: "My popularity was not sufficiently great to elect me in the first two instances; my color and nativity were against me in the last."

GENERAL THOMAS G. POLK.

General Thos G Polk, eldest son of Col William Polk and Grizzie Gilchrist, was born Feb. 22, 1791, in Mecklenburg County, N C He graduated at the University of North Carolina in the class of 1809. He studied law and obtained a license to practice, but possessing an ample fortune, he did not pursue his profession He represented his native county in the House of Commons, in the years 1823, 1824 and 1825 He moved to Salisbury, S C, where he married Miss Mary Trotter He represented Rowan County in the House of Commons in the years 1829, 1830, 1831 and 1832 He was Senator for that district in 1835 and 1836 In 1833 he was a candidate for Governor. There were three candidates in the field, and no one having a majority of the votes cast, Gov David S Swain was chosen by the Legislature.

General Polk was for many years Major General of Militia of his district In 1838 he moved to Tennessee and settled at La Grange, where he resided but a short time, removing thence to Holly Springs, Miss. General Polk was said to have been an effective political speaker. He was a Whig in politics He was tendered the nomination for Governor of Mississippi but declined so hopeless a race.

In the Mexican War, General Polk offered his services to President Polk, and was recommended by most of the leading men of both parties in that State for an appointment as Brigadier General It was not then esteemed a virtue to fill offices with relatives, and President Polk declined giving him the appointment, as he also did in a similar application in behalf of his own brother, Col Wm H Polk, who was highly endorsed

General Thos G Polk died during the Civil War at Holly Springs, Mississippi His children who survive him, or who have left issue, are: Wm. Polk, of Louisiana; Mary, wife of Hon George Davis, of Wilmington N C; and Emily, of Holly Springs, Miss

GENERAL LUCIUS J. POLK.

General Lucius Junius Polk, third son of Colonel William Polk, by his second wife, Sarah (Hawkins) Polk, was born March 16, 1802, and was twice married. His first wife was Miss Mary Easten, a niece of General Andrew Jackson, the marriage ceremony taking place in the White House while Jackson was President of the United States. She presided there for President Jackson, up to the time of her marriage. The second wife of General Lucius J. Polk was Mrs. Ann Pope (nee Erwin) widow of Wm. Polk. Ten of his children reached maturity, eight by the first and two by the second marriage.

General Lucius J. Polk was an elegant gentleman, cultivated, refined, and courtly. His mother was a sister of Governor Hawkins, of North Carolina. He graduated at the University of North Carolina in 1822, and located in Maury County, Tennessee, where he resided until his death. He lived in elegant style and entertained most hospitably. He made an exciting canvass for Senator from Maury County, against General Littlefield, an old politician, and fine speaker, and defeated him. Satisfied with public life, he could never again be induced to enter the policital field. He obtained his title of General from Governor Brown, of Tennessee, in the militia.

General Lucius J. Polk's children were. By first wife, Miss Easten: ¹Sarah Rachel Polk, ²Mary Brown Polk, ³Emily Donaldson Polk, ⁴William Polk, ⁵Eliza Easten Polk, ⁶Frances Anne Polk, ⁷Susan Rebecca and ⁸George Washington Polk (twins). By his second wife, Mrs. Ann (Erwin) Pope, he had: ⁹Lucius Julius Polk, ¹⁰Elvira Juliet Polk.

Sarah Rachel Polk, eldest child of General Lucius J. Polk, married Capt. Robin Cadwallader Jones, of Hillsboro, N. C. He was killed in the Civil War, at Brandy Station, Va. He was an officer in General Wade Hampton's command. Five of their children attained to maturity, viz: ¹Mary Polk Jones, ²Rebecca Edwards Jones, ³Robin Jones, ⁴Sarah Polk Jones, ⁵Lucy C. Jones.

GEN'L LUCIUS JUNIUS POLK.
of North Carolina and Tennessee.

Mary Polk Jones, the eldest child, married Col D. B. Cooper, of Nashville, Tenn. She died in 1893, leaving five children. [1]Sarah Polk Cooper, [2]William F Cooper, [3]Robin Jones Cooper, [4]Mary Brown Cooper, [5]Duncan Brown Cooper

Sarah Polk Jones, fourth child of Capt. Robin Cadwallader Jones, married J C Bradford, Attorney-at-law, Nashville Tenn., issue [1]Thomas Bradford, [2]Sarah Polk Bradford.

Lucy Cadwallader Jones, youngest child of Capt Robin Cadwallader Jones, married Stanley B Herndon, of Mobile, Ala. They had issue: [1]Robin Jones Herndon, [2]Virginia Herndon, [3]Jones Herndon

Mary Brown Polk, second child of General Lucius J Polk, married Col Henry C Yeatman, an officer on the staff of General Leonidas Polk She died in 1891, leaving issue: [1]Mary Badger Yeatman, [2]Henry Clay Yeatman, who died December 20, 1896, [3]Russell Houston Yeatman, died 1892, [4]Tryvant Player Yeatman, [5]Jane Bell Yeatman; [6]Lucia Polk Yeatman.

Emily D Polk, third child of General Lucius J Polk, married Major J Minick Williams, also a staff officer with General Leonidas Polk and J B Stuart She died in 1891, leaving issue [1]Henry Yeatman Williams, who married Louisa Pileber, of Nashville, no issue, [2]James Minick Williams, attorney-at-law; [3]Lucius Polk Williams of Texas; [4]Nannie M. Williams, died in 1890, [5]Eliza Polk Williams, died in 1892, [6]Priscilla Shelby Williams

William Polk, fourth child and eldest son of General Lucius J Polk, married Rebecca Mayes and had one child that died in infancy William was a soldier in the Confederate army, was wounded in one of the battles in which he was engaged, and by his gallantry and good conduct rose to the rank of Major

Frances Anne Polk, fifth child of General Lucius J Polk, married Col Edward Dillon, of Indian Rock, Botetourt County, Virginia Before the Civil War he was an officer in the Regular Army, afterwards a Colonel in the Confederate Army, serving in Van Dorn's command, in the Trans-Mississippi Department Their children were [1]James R Dillon, of Galveston Texas, [2]Edward Dillon [3]Lucius Polk Dillon [4]Jno

C Dillon, ⁵Eliza Polk Dillon, ⁶Frances Polk Dillon, ⁷Frank C Dillon

Eliza Polk, sixth child of General Lucius J. Polk, untraced Her name appears on the Polk tree published in 1849

Susan Rebecca Polk, seventh child of General Lucius J Polk, born July 7, 1847, married Major Campbell Brown, a cultivated gentleman of large fortune, living near Spring Hill, Tennessee He was a grandson of Governor Campbell, United States Minister to Russia, and also related to Col William Campbell, of Virginia, one of the captors of Col Ferguson at Kings' Mountain Major Campbell Brown served in the Confederate Army, on the staffs of General Ewell and General Joseph E Johnston He died in August 1893 The children of Major Campbell Brown and Susan Rebecca Polk were. ¹Lucius Polk Brown, born August, 1867, married Jessie Roberts, daughter of Albert Roberts of Nashville, and great niece of Prof T H Huxley, the English scientist They have one son Campbell Huxley Brown, born October 25, 1896, ²Richard Ewell Brown, born January 12, 1869, a practicing physician in New York, and unmarried, ³George Campbell Brown, born September 25, 1871, unmarried, a farmer and resides near Spring Hill Tenn ⁴Percy Brown and ⁵Lizinka Brown (twins), born April 6, 1873.

George Washington Polk, eighth child of General Lucius J Polk, married Jane Jackson, of Florence, Ala He resides in San Antonio, Texas, and is land agent for the Southern Pacific Railroad He has three children ¹George Washington Polk, ²Jane Jackson Polk, ³Henry Jackson Polk

Lucius Junius Polk, Jr, ninth child of General Lucius J Polk and Ann Pope (his second wife) was born in Tennessee and resides at Galveston, Texas, where he is General Manager of the Gulf, Colorado & Santa Fe Railroad He married Miss Daisy Cantrell, of Little Rock, Arkansas, and they have six children, viz ¹Armour Cantrell Polk, ²Ann Leroy Polk ³Lucius Junius Polk ⁴Margaret Wendell Polk, ⁵Daisy Cantrell Polk ⁶Ellen Cantrell Polk, dead

Elvira Juliet Polk tenth and last child of General Lucius J Polk and Ann Pope (his second wife) married Horace Cooper of Nashville Tennessee and has one child, Horace Cooper

COL. WM. H. POLK AND WIFE.

CHAPTER XXIX.

BISHOP AND LT. GENERAL LEONIDAS POLK.

Leonidas Polk, fourth son of Col. William Polk (second by his marriage with Miss Sarah Hawkins), was born at Raleigh, N. C., April 10, 1806. His early education was receiived at the Academy conducted by Rev. Dr. McPheeters, of that city.

During his boyhood Leonidas was a leader in all the sports of his companions. In 1821 he matriculated in the University of North Carolina, at Chapel Hill, where he soon became exceedingly popular with his fellow students. He was a handsome, well grown boy at that time and a great singer of patriotic songs. At the end of his second year at Chapel Hill he was appointed a cadet at West Point, which institution he entered in June, 1823.

One of his closest friends among the cadets was Albert Sidney Johnston, of the class before him. They were room mates until the latter graduated in 1826, and their friendship was strong and constant until Johnston's death on the bloody field of Shiloh, in the early days of the Civil War.

In January, 1824 he passed his first examination, and in a class of ninety-six he stood fourth in mathematics; in French, twenty-seventh. He graduated July 4, 1827. The year before, in 1826, he returned home on a furlough from the Academy, deply impressed with religious feelings and convictions. One evening he was seated on the porch conversing with a friend, - ...rice Waddell, a grandson of General Francis Nash, who fell at Germantown in 1777. Col. Wm. Polk, who was present, spoke with enthusiasm of Nash, the Mecklenburg Declaration, and of those who had fought and died for their country.

Leonidas remarked that the principles of honor could only be strengthened and enforced by the principles of religion As soon as that view of the subject was presented, the old soldier rose, and, without a word, left the porch

A year later, Leonidas announced his intention to cast aside all the advantages he had earned at West Point, to abandon a military career, and exchange his uniform for a surplice Col Polk was deeply disappointed He could not understand the motive for such a resolve To him the life of a soldier was the noblest life to which a gallant man could devote himself, and it had been his pride to think that Leonidas was destined to continue, and perhaps to add lustre to, the many military traditions of his family

To the intense regret of his father, Lieut Leonidas Polk's resignation was forwarded to the Secretary of War, by whom it was accepted, and he prepared to enter upon his studies for the ministry In May 1828 he became engaged at Raleigh to his former schoolmate, Frances Devereux, and on Nov 1th of the same year he began his studies for the ministry in the Seminary at Alexandria Completing his studies, he was ordained deacon at Richmond, Va, on Good Friday, April 9, 1830.

On May 16th following he was married to his affianced and returned to Richmond to enter on his duties as Assistant to Bishop Moore, in the Cure of the Monumental Church On Jan 27th, 1831, his first child, Alexander Hamilton, was born He was ordained a priest in May 1831, at the Diocesan Convention at Norfolk, and the following August visited Europe for the benefit of his health

In April, 1833 he removed to Tennessee on May 15th reaching his brother Lucius' residence in Maury County His father Col Wm Polk, owned a tract of five thousand acres of land, known as "Rattle and Snap," which he divided between his four sons, Lucius J, Leonidas, Rufus K, and George W Early in 1834, Col Wm Polk, his father, died in Raleigh nearly four score years of age

It is but little know, and is rather an odd fact that Leonidas Polk's mother was one of the earliest railway promoters in the United States; a line projected in North Carolina, though it open a tramway costing $2,250 per mile, running it in the city portion of the Capitol at Raleigh to a

BISHOP LEONIDAS POLK AND WIFE.

stone quarry. It was called the "Experimental Railway,' and was finished in 1833, when a handsome passenger car was put on the track 'for the accommodation," as the directors announced, "of such ladies and gentlemen as desired to take the exercise of a railroad airing."

Crowds of people flocked in from the surrounding country and adjacent counties to avail themselves of the privilege, and it is recorded that no accidents occurred, the directors having prudently provided as the motive power of the train a safe old horse that was warranted not to run away!

Mrs Polk was not only the projector of the "Experimental Railway," but was also one of the principal stockholders, and the soundness of her judgment was amply vindicated when the profits of the enterprise were found to amount to three hundred per cent of the original investment When the success of the Experimental Railway led to other railway enterprises of greater magnitude, Mrs Polk was not forgotten; and at a banquet given in honor of the first train drawn by steam power into Raleigh, a special toast was drunk. 'To the distinguished lady who suggested the construction of the Experimental Railway, she well deserves a name among the benefactors of the State"

In 1834 Leonidas Polk went to Raleigh, and the following Spring took charge of the Episcopal church at Columbia In 1835 on account of failing health, he traveled in Kentucky He was next made Bishop of the Southwest, his field embracing Arkansas, the Texas Republic, Indian Territory, Mississippi, Louisiana and Alabama As such he was consecrated by Bishops Smith, Meade, Otey and McIlvane. In the summer of 1856 Bishop Polk announced his plan for founding a University at Sewanee, Tenn In this he was ably seconded by Bishop Stephen Elliott, and on Oct 6, 1860, the corner stone of the University of the South was laid at Sewanee by Bishop Polk Bishop Otey, of Tennessee, presided, and the orator of the day was Col John S Preston, of South Carolina

THE CIVIL WAR.

The approaching mighty conflict of arms which during its progress drenched the land in fratricidal blood now absorbed the attention of the people. The son and grandson of soldiers, and himself educated for that profession, Bishop Polk naturally took special interest in the approaching struggle.

On May 14, 1861, Bishop Polk wrote to Jefferson Davis, President of the Confederate States, about the exposed situation of the Mississippi Valley States. In reply Mr. Davis wrote from Montgomery, Ala., on May 22d, closing his letter with the sentence: "It would gratify me very much to see you."

Bishop Polk next visited Virginia, held services, and did what he could to sustain the cause of his people.

Mr. Davis offered him command of the Department of the West, but he declined it. Shortly afterward he offered him a commission as Brigadier General, to have command of the land and water defenses of the Mississippi, above the mouth of Red River. A few days later Mr. Davis sent him an urgent request to accept the commission of Major General, with practically the same duties. Several delegations from the Mississippi Valley went to Richmond to urge Bishop Polk's acceptance of the tender and finally he consented. His commission as Major General was issued June 25, 1861, and a few days later he proceeded to take command of the department, with headquarters at Memphis. Neither Missouri nor Kentucky were included in his command. On July 28 General Pillow occupied New Madrid, Mo., with 6,000 men, and Gen'l Hardee had 7,000 at Pocahontas. In Sept. 1861 Missouri and all Arkansas were added to Gen'l Polk's department.

On August 28th General Fremont, the Federal Commander in Missouri, assigned Brigadier General U. S. Grant to the command of Federal forces in Southeast Missouri, to operate against Gen'l Polk's forces. A land and naval force was dispatched under Col. Wagner to occupy and hold Belmont, opposite Columbus. It landed there on Sept. 2d. On Nov. 7th, a little more than four days later, occurred the battle of Belmont, at the close of which Gen'l Grant's force was driven from the field and escaped by boats.

March 5, 1862, Gen'l Beauregard assumed command of the First Division of the Western Department and placed Gen'l Polk in command of the forces at Humboldt. The designation of the army was now changed to that of the Army of the Mississippi, and the army was divided into four corps, with Albert Sidney Johnston as Commander-in-Chief, Beauregard second in command, and Bragg Chief of Staff. The four corps were commanded respectively by Polk, Bragg, Hardee and Breckinridge—Bragg adding command of a corps to his duties as Chief of Staff.

At Shiloh, April 6, 1862, the Confederates had a force of Polk's Corps, four brigades, 9,136 men; Bragg's Corps, six brigades, 13,589 men; Hardee's Corps, three brigades, 6,789 men; Breckinridge's Corps, three brigades, 6,439. Total 35,953.

We omit here description of the sanguinary struggle that occurred at Shiloh, between the Federal forces under Generals Halleck and Grant, and the Confederates under Generals Albert Sidney Johnston and Beauregard, except to state that Johnston the room-mate and intimate friend of Leonidas Polk while they attended the U. S. Military Academy at West Point, was mortally wounded. In the same battles Capt. Marshall T. Polk, of Polk's Battery, lost a leg. On June 21st, following, Gen'l Bragg succeeded Beauregard in command of the Confederates and at once planned an invasion of Kentucky with the hope of capturing Louisville. Then ensued the long "foot race" for that city, between Bragg and Buell, the latter reaching there first. After rest and the reception of fresh troops, Buell faced about and struck the Confederate at Perryville, on Oct 8th, where Gen'l Leonidas Polk was in command. After the battle was about concluded Bragg arrived on the field and ordered a retreat, his army going out of the State through the mountains and Cumberland Gap, to Knoxville. Gen'l Buell was supplanted in the Federal command by Gen'l Rosecranz. After pursuing the Confederates as far as London, Rosecranz turned his columns south to Nashville. The heavy assaults on the Federals at Perryville were made by the troops of Polk's Corps, which, after the retreat, reached Knoxville on Oct 31st. Bragg then transferred the Army of the Mississippi at Murfreesboro, to oppose Rosecranz.

The battle of Murfreesboro (called Stone River by the Federals) took place on Dec 31 and Jan. 1, 2, 3, 1863, and was one of the most sanguinary struggles of the war, the Federals losing 13,249 men, and the Confederates 10,266. The loss of Polk's Corps was 31⅓ per cent. For the first two days success attended the Confederates but on the third they were forced to retreat.

In Oct., 1863 President Davis assigned General Polk to relieve Gen'l Hardee at Enterprise, Miss., the latter to take Polk s Corps, under Bragg Gen'l Joe Johnston relieved Bragg at Dalton, in Dec 1863 Gen'l Polk at the same time assigned to the department of Alabama, Mississippi and East Louisiana

CHAPTER XXX.

ATLANTA CAMPAIGN.

General Wm T Sherman having been appointed to the command of the Federal forces, on May 5, 1864, he moved forward with over one hundred thousand men against Johnston, who was posted at Dalton with a force of less than 50,000 men Johnston asked Polk to come to his assistance with his troops and the Confederate government ordered him to go, with all the troops he could take. Polk hurried to Johnston's assistance with three divisions of infantry and Jackson's Cavalry, in all about 19,000 men and relieved Hood at Resaca

After Dalton followed the battles of Resaca, Calhoun, Kingston, Adairsville, Cassville, New Hope Church, Marietta, Lost Mountain and Kenesaw Mountain, ending in the capture of Atlanta

Col. Henry Watterson, then with the Confederate Army, thus described Gen'l Leonidas Polk as he appeared on the battlefield:

'Wrapped in his old gray hunting shirt with slouched hat and saber, he sat his horse and received the leaden compliments of the enemy with complacent yet not indifferent good humor He had a habit of shrugging his shoulders when a Minie ball came too close to his ear But he never got out of the way for them. In battle he was a daring old man, with his heart in the fray, and his best faith on the result, riding through shot and shell from point to point, unconscious of danger At Shiloh, at Perryville, at Murfreesboro, at Chickamauga, at Resaca, he was to be seen constantly at the front, at every point of his line, supervising the progress of events with his own presence. He was kind and considerate of his men; he was approachable and self-denying in his own person; and he did not know the name of fear He was proverbial for getting into hot places His staff loved him most fondly He was every inch a gentleman, without mannerism or assumption simple and innocent, yet dignified and imposing"

DEATH OF GENERAL LEONIDAS POLK.

On the 25th, at New Hope Church, Sherman's army made a heavy but unsuccessful assault on the Confederate lines On the night of June 5th the Confederate army again fell back On the 9th Gen'l Polk rose at daylight, rode to the front, then back to confer with Gen'l Johnston On the 10th he sent his headquarters to the house of Mr. Hardige, a mile nearer Marietta, and there was heavy skirmishing all day June 11th was rainy and gloomy Gen'l Polk's headquarters were almost under the shadow of Kenesaw Mountain The next day Sunday 12th, was also foggy and rainy. It had been raining for twelve days and the roads were almost impassable

During this time Gen'l Polk seemed more abstracted than usual, often reading his bible and tracts prepared by Dr Quintard, a substitute for the book of Common Prayer An occasional shot from the skirmish line punctuated his reading About 10 o'clock Gen'l Polk came out of his room and said to one of his staff that he would like to read the church service In a few minutes the room was full and grizzled men in gray bowed their heads, many also standing near the doors and under the dripping eaves The General read the service throughout and joined in the singing of a psalm and hymn In a voice trembling with emotion he read the concluding prayer, and, asking a blessing, sat down in profound silence.

This was the last time that Bishop Leonidas Polk ever read the service of the church

The morning of June 13th was again foggy and rainy, and all was quiet at the front, the two armies watching and waiting for developments. Gen'l Polk remained indoors, writing most of the time During the day however, he rode to the headquarters of Gen'l Johnston who expressed a desire to make a personal inspection the following morning of an advanced position held by the division of Major General Bate, on Pine Mountain and he requested Gen'l Polk to accompany

LIEUT. GEN'L LEONIDAS POLK,
C. S. A., at death.

him and assist in the examination An appointment for that purpose was made and Gen'l Polk returned to his headquarters

Tuesday morning, June 14th, dawned clear and the sun shone out brilliantly Gen'l Polk ate an early breakfast, at the conclusion of which he sent the following, his last order, to Major General French.

"June 14th, 1864 8 A M

General

General Polk desires you to extend your present line, at once, to the left, so as to cover the recent line occupied by Gen'l Canty

Respectfully,

Major Gen'l French THOS N. JACK, A A G"

Gen'l Polk then dispatched his son, Capt Wm M Polk, a member of his staff (and now a distinguished physician of New York City) with a verbal message to Gen'l French regarding his skirmish line

Gen'l Johnston arrived soon after 8 o'clock, and Gen'l Polk mounting his horse, they rode to the headquarters of Gen'l Hardee, who was also invited to join in the examination Each General was attended by several members of his staff, Gen'l Polk by Lieut Col Jack, A A G, Col W D Gale, A D C, Major Frank McNairy, Volunteer A, D C, and Lieut Hopkins of the Orleans Light Horse The party reached Gen'l Hardee's headquarters about 10 o'clock and dismounted Holding a short consultation, they mounted again and rode forward In a few minutes they reached the main line of the intrenchments, through which they passed, continuing for nearly a mile, and dismounting behind a sharp hill known as Pine Mountain They moved cautiously over the top and then down a short distance to a small earthwork occupied by a battery and its supports

Reaching the crest of the hill they had a full view of the country before them, over which sunshine and shadows moved, keeping pace with the slowly drifting clouds Both lines of battle were plainly visible and bodies of men could be seen busy with axe and spade

Guns were being placed in position and the fields were white with the covers of a thousand wagons. In the distance to the front, lay the hills of the Etowah, to the right, the peaks of Kenesaw. The constant firing of the heavy skirmish line, reinforced at intervals by the guns of some battery, all combined to make the scene one of unusual beauty and grandeur. Some of the younger officers stood on the parapet and exposed themselves to the sharp gaze of the enemy. The men of the battery warned them of the danger. While they were speaking there was a flash, a puff of smoke, a sharp report from a rifled gun, and the shot striking near was buried in the parapet, scattering rocks and dirt around. One of the officers observed that the enemy seemed to be getting their range and suggested a change of position. Generals Johnston and Polk moved to the left and stood for several moments behind a parapet, in earnest conversation. Several other shots followed, going higher, one striking the crest of the hill. Generals Johnston and Polk, completing their talk, began to retrace their steps. Gen'l Johnston fell a little back and Gen Polk ascended to the crest of the hill, on which was a signal station. Facing about again as if to take a farewell view, Gen'l Polk folded his arms across his breast and stood silently gazing on the scene below.

While thus he stood there was a puff of smoke in the valley below, a sharp report, and a cannon shot crashed through the breast of General Polk, killing him instantly. He fell upon his back, with his feet to the foe. Immediately upon the fall of the beloved General, the flag corps on the crest signalled to the rear for an ambulance, stating that Gen'l Polk had been killed. As he fell his faithful escort rushed to his side, gathered up the mutilated body and bore it to the rear of the hill. In a sheltered ravine his sorrow-stricken comrades, silent and in tears, gathered around his mangled corpse.

General Hardee, bending over the body, said to Gen'l Johnston: "General, this has been a dear visit. We have lost a brave man, whose death leaves a vacancy not easily filled." Then kneeling beside the body, he exclaimed "My dear, dear friend, little did I think this morning that I should be called upon to witness this."

General Johnston, with tears in his eyes, knelt and laid his hand upon the cold brow of the fallen hero, saying "We have lost much! I would rather anything but this."

The news flew along the line that Gen'l Polk had fallen, reaching the pickets, it passed from them to the Federal l.nes Before his limbs were become rigid, the news had been telegraphed to Washington as well as to Richmond His body being placed in an ambulance, and escorted by the mournful cavalcade, was conveyed back to headquarters 'Jerry," the noble roan ridden by him in all his battles and marches, was led riderless in front

Thus fell on the battlefield Leonidas Polk, Bishop, and Lieutenant General, a worthy son of Col. Wm. Polk, and grandson of Gen'l Thos Polk, Revolutionary officers of credit and renown Peace to his memory!

GENERAL JOHNSTON'S ORDER

The same afternoon General Joseph E Johnston issued the following general order to the army.

"Headquarters, Army of the Tennessee.
In the Field, June 14, 1864
General Field Orders No 2

Comrades: You are called to mourn your first captain, your oldest companion in arms Lieutenant General Polk fell today, at the outpost of this army—the army he raised and commanded, in all of whose trials he shared, to all of whose victories he contributed.

"In this distinguished leader we have lost the most courteous of gentlemen the most gallant of soldiers.

"The Christian, patriot, soldier, has neither lived nor died in vain His example is before you, his mantle rests with you.

J E Johnston, General"

Kinlock Falconer, A A G

FUNERAL OBSEQUIES AND BURIAL.

The body of Gen'l Polk was taken to the railway station during the afternoon, for removal to Atlanta On arrival at that city it was received by a committee of the city and placed in the chancel of St. Luke's Church. Clothed in Confederate uniform it rested, with a cross of white roses upon the breast, and by the side of the coffin lay his sword. During the morning large numbers came to pay the last tribute of affection. At noon an appropriate service, followed by an address, was conducted by Rev. Dr. Quintard. The military escort, arriving at an early hour, was drawn up in front of the church. At the conclusion of the services the body was placed in a field ambulance and escorted to the station followed by the dead general's personal staff, by Generals Smith, Wright, Ruggles and Reynolds, Col Ewell, and other officers, and by citizens.

The members of staff and the Atlanta Committee were met at Augusta the following morning by the rectors and vestry of the Church of the Atonement and St Paul's. The body was conveyed to the latter, where a guard of honor received it. After lying two days in the church the body was placed in the City Hall, where it was viewed by a vast number of citizens.

On the 29th the military force of Augusta, consisting of a regiment of infantry, a battery of artillery and a company of cavalry, was drawn up at the City Hall. At half past 9 o'clock the casket was draped in the Confederate flag, covered with wreath of laurel and bay, and placed upon the hearse by the guard of soldiers. Headed by a band, and preceded by the Mayor of the city, the solemn march began. Wardens and vestrymen from St Paul's and Church of Atonement, Augusta, and from St John's of Savannah marched on either side of the pall-bearers. Then came the military family of General Polk, the clergy, officers of the army and navy, Confederate Civil officers, and various other organizations. Through streets thronged with mourning spectators, the procession moved to St Paul's church. All business houses were closed, and the only sounds that were heard was the dirge of the band and the monotone of tolling bells.

At the church the body was met by the bishops of Georgia, Mississippi and Arkansas in full canonical robes,

ST. PAUL'S EPISCOPAL CHURCH,
Augusta, Ga., tomb of Gen'l Leonidas Polk and wife within.

with a company of surpliced priests. Through files of soldiers the body was conveyed into the church, the Senior Bishop (Bishop Stephen Elliott) repeating the words of the service for the burial of the dead. Entering the chancel, the body was met at the foot of the steps. Then anthem "Lord let me know mine end," was chanted, to organ accompaniment. The Bishop of Arkansas read the lesson and the people united in the singing. The Senior Bishop then delivered the "Burial Address," from the text "The Master is come and calleth for thee." It was a magnificent address and deeply stirred the hearts of all who heard it.

At its conclusion the body, under military escort and preceded by the bishops and priests, was carried to the grave in the rear of the church, and with concluding ceremonies was interred. As the words 'Earth to earth, ashes to ashes, dust to dust," were uttered, earth was cast upon the body by the Bishop of Louisiana, Bishop of Arkansas and Lieut. Gen'l Longstreet. As the concluding words of the service were uttered, the guns of the battery gave forth the last salute to the soldier-priest who on Pine Mountain, "gave his body to that pleasant country's earth, and his pure soul unto his captain, Christ, under whose colors he had fought so long."

CHAPTER XXXI

ST JOHN'S CHURCH, ASHWOOD, TENN.

In Maury County Tenn, upon the road leading from Columbia to Mt Pleasant, and about six miles from the former place, in a grove of majestic and towering oaks, stands a neat brick church of chaste and simple Gothic architecture, its interior, plain but beautiful, capable of seating, with a small end gallery, about five hundred persons

This building was erected in 1842, by the joint liberality of Right Reverend Bishop Polk and his three brothers, and with the lot of six acres was presented to the church in that diocese The lot was chosen from the most eligible part of the Bishop's plantation, and but a short distance from his residence It was built for the accommodation of a few Episcopal families in the neighborhood, who, with a large number of slaves, upon their plantations, made up quite a large congregation. For the latter class the Bishop had been in the habit of holding regular services in his own house

On Sunday, Sept 4th, 1842, the Church was consecrated an immense congregation being present to witness the ceremonies, which were conducted by Bishop Otey In the chancel with him were Rt Rev Bishop Polk, Revs Smith, of Columbia, Leacock Horrell and Saunders Seven candidates were confirmed during the services by Bishop Polk After the administration of the sacrament by Bishop Otey the services closed

Standing a few hundred yards back from the turnpike among a forest of towering trees, this church is one of the most attractive in the United States and in it services have been regularly held ever since, except for occasional omissions during the Civil War, when the presence of armies prevented It is an object of the greatest interest to every person who visits that section of Tennessee, and a lasting

ST. JOHN'S CHURCH.
Near Ashwood, Maury County, Tenn.

monument to the christian zeal, piety, and liberality of the sons of Col William Polk, the patriot soldier of the Revolution.

INTERESTING FAMILY LETTERS.

During the work of compiling the Polk tree that was published in 1849, the following letters were written by Mrs Susan Smart to Bishop Polk and by the latter to President James K Polk:

Bishop Polk's Letter.

Thibodoux, La,
Jan 17, 1849

My Dear Sir —In reply to your letter on the subject of our ancestors, I regret to say I have misplaced and cannot find a memorandum I made several years ago, which contained a good deal of the information which Col Winder wants It contained the names of the children of William (the son of John, the son of Robert Polk), of whom your grandfather and mine were two That William was he who first emigrated from Maryland and settled in the county of Anson, out of which he and his descendants, and their associates, caused Mecklenburg County to be formed I may yet find it, if so, I will transmit it to you or Mr. Winder.

As it is a matter of some importance to us, I have addressed a letter to old Mrs. Smart, an old relative of ours, who was a contemporary of my father, and who, I believe still lives (under cover to Julius Alexander) requesting her to give me the names of the children of William Polk, of Maryland and to inform me what became of them So soon as I hear from her I will forward you her letter. She was a well informed old lady, and if living will give us some interesting facts

I have been much interested in the letter you have caused to be copied and sent me, from Ireland I have not a doubt that the writer is of the same family, as well from the name of the locality for that was the precise region from which I have always be he is h ever deceived in the

I can lay my hand on a single sheet, only of the memorandum I have spoken of, and that contains an account of the relationship of the Polks and Alexanders. From it I learn that William Polk (son of John, son of Robert) who removed from Maryland (our great grandfather) married a Miss Taylor, who was the mother of our grandfathers. She was one of five sisters, one other of the five married a Mr Ruse and was the mother of Rev. David Ruse. The other three married Alexanders, who were the progenitors of all those of that name in Mecklenburg. These grades of relationship I find on that sheet, but as it is aside from Mr. Winder's purpose, I say no more of it.

You are right in saying that William Polk, our great grandfather, had sons named Charles and John. That Charles was the father of the celebrated "Old Charley, the Hunter," of the Western District of Tennessee, in the early settlement of it, and since that day of Texas, where I think he still lives. He (the hunter) was father of Col William, whom I knew as post-master at Holly Springs Miss, and who, I presume, to be the William Polk, the distiller, spoken of by Mr Winder as living near La Grange Tenn. He once lived there. He has another son living at this time near Shreveport, Caddo Parish, La, named Charles, a highly respectable planter, who is married and has a family; and another son, with whom he removed to Texas, whose name I do not now recollect.

When I saw "Old Charley," many years ago he showed me a powder-horn which he prized highly, from having carried it through the Revolutionary War, in which he was a soldier in the North Carolina Line, under command of his uncle General Thomas Polk. He mentioned to me an incident in regard to the horn which added to its interest in his eyes, and which illustrated the primitive manners as well as the gallent feeling of the times.

Just before the forces were to move towards the North he discovered he had lost his horn, and on reporting the fact to his General and kinsman the morning following, when the troops were under arms the General requested him to accompany him two or three of the lines, during the inspection saying, "I thought that it was not impossible the horn might make its appearance He did so, and to his very great delight, and the profound discomfiture of the luckless wight who had appropriated it, shot-pouch and all duly garnished the neck and shoulder of one of the host An examination was instituted forthwith, which terminated in convicting the party upon whom it was found, of having appropriated it wilfully and knowingly, and the penalty was dismissal from the service, with a refusal even to allow him to serve in such a cause

The old fellow told the anecdote with great interest and pride in the gallantry and the high sense of honor which distinguished his day and command.

Old John Polk had a son, I think, called Benjamin, who lived in Maury County, Tenn., and who, I think, was father to Armstead of the same county

General Thomas Polk, my grandfather, married Miss Susan Spratt, by whom he had William, Thomas, Ezekiel Charles and James, five sons, and Mary, Deborah, Margaret and Martha, four daughters Of the conspicuous part taken by General Thomas Polk in the celebrated Mecklenburg Declaration of Independence, Mr Winder is, I presume, informed from the public accounts of that transaction. All of his sons followed him into the war that ensued and were more or less actively engaged. Thomas was killed in the battle of Eutaw, by a ball in the forehead He bore at the time a Lieutenant's commission It has so happened that I have recently seen some unpublished manuscript of a distinguished officer of the Revolution, in which there was mentioned among the killed, at the same battle, a Lieutenant Ezekiel Polk, who must have been the son of one of the other brothers; which, I know not

Since beginning this letter I remembered having on my estate an old and highly intelligent negress, who belonged in early life to my grandfather, General Thomas Polk, and upon sending for her and questioning her, she promptly informed me that she well remembered our great grandmother, Miss Taylor, that was the wife of William Polk of Maryland She was very often at her master's (General Thomas Polk's; was a small woman and lived to a great age Upon asking if he had a daughter named Debora she replied in the affirmative, and added that she "married Sam McLeary," confirming your impression She also stated there were two other sisters Margurette, who married David McRee, and Mary, who married John Barnett She does not know whether the two former had children, but knows that the latter was the mother of Mrs Smart, the old lady I have mentioned having written to, and also of Col Jack Barnett, a very noted man in Mecklenburg, of his day, and father of Susan Barnett, whom you may remember having seen while you were at Chapel Hill, at my father's in Raleigh

She also mentioned the names of four of her master's brothers, whom she often saw with their sisters, the ladies mentioned, at her master, viz Charles, James, William and Ezekiel She knew them all perfectly well, as servants are in the habit of knowing the members of their master's families She states that she "remembered perfectly well the night that master Sam. Polk was married to Miss Jinny Knox" As to whether there was a brother of her master's named John, she does not know, but "the others she knew as well as she knows me"

Her statements have refreshed my own memory upon some of the facts to which she testifies, and I place the fullest confidence in her testimony It has occurred to me that Charles of Caddo, La, the son of "Charles the Hunter," and grandson of Charles, brother of General Thomas Polk, might be in possession of some facts as to his own and other branches of the family, and I have concluded to write him upon the subject, which I will do and enclose you what he may furnish through his father. I have made out hastily, but accurately, a genealogy of the family from William of Maryland, downward, (excluding only the descendants of Col. Ezekiel Polk, which can be better furnished by you) so far as I am informed, and send it to you herewith If my correspondence shall enable me to furnish more particulars, I will send them to you

With my kindest regards to Mrs Polk, I remain,

Very truly your friend and Kinsman,

Leonidas Polk

Letter of Mrs. Smart

As stated by Bishop Polk in the foregoing letter to President Polk, he wrote for information to Mrs. Smart, an aged kinswoman, who replied as follows

Charlotte, N. C., Feby 15, 1849

Dear Sir —

Your letter, enclosed in one to Mr Alexander, I have received, and will answer it as well as I can I never saw your great-grandfather, William Polk, but was informed by your grandfather, and my parents, that he died several years before, at least twenty-five years before the Revolutionary War His wife was a Taylor (Margaret) and he married her at the North, in Pennsylvania, and removed to North Carolina and settled west of the Yadkin, where he died He left the following children: Thomas, your grandfather; William, who was the oldest son, John, Charles, Ezekiel, who was grandfather of the President The following daughters Susan, who married Benjamin Alexander; Debora, who married Samuel McCleary, and died without issue: Margaret, who married Robert McRee, leaving a large family, among whom is James P. McRee, of Tennessee

Susan Alexander left a large family, many of whom now live in this county She was the mother of William Alexander, a Captain, commonly called "Black Bill," a distinguished soldier in the Revolutionary army. John Polk married Eleanor Shelby, a daughter of Col Isaac Shelby He had three sons and one daughter, the sons by name Charles, John and Taylor; the daughter Eleanor. Those now living, belonging to the family, reside in the West.

William married a woman whose name I do not remember They removed to Tennessee many years ago and had many children Charles married Polly Clark, a full cousin of your father's on the mother's side They removed to the West, having a large family Ezekiel married Nanny Wilson, the mother of Samuel Polk and the grandmother of the President, and after her death was married twice By his second wife he had no children that lived any time; by his third wife, whom he married in Tennessee, I am informed he had several children

Your grandfather, Thomas Polk, who was the most distinguished man in the family, married Susan Spratt, my mother's sister. They had the following children. Your father, Thomas, who was killed at the battle of Eutaw, by the side of my brother, John Barnett; Ezekiel, who died at sea; James who married the daughter of Col Moore; Charley, who married the daughter of Hezekiah Alexander died, leaving two children, one now living in Tennessee, Thomas I Polk, Martha, the eldest daughter, married Dr Ephraim Brevard, who had one daughter, Martha, who married Mr Dickerson, of South Carolina, leaving one son, the late Col James Polk Dickerson, who was killed in Mexico; Margaret, the second daughter, married Governor Nathaniel Alexander, and died without children; Polly, the fourth, married Daniel Brown, a distinguished lawyer of South Carolina. They had three children who died young. The third daughter, Debora, died at the age of fourteen.

My aunt, Susan Spratt, who married your grandfather General Thomas Polk, was the daughter of Thos. Spratt, who was an excellent man and died highly esteemed by every one. Your father, with whom I was very intimate, was always proud of his Spratt blood and often boasted of it. Col. Thos Neal, of South Carolina, married Jane Spratt, a daughter of Thomas Spratt, by whom he had several children, among others Andrew, a Colonel in the Revolutionary Army, who resembled your father very much. He was killed at the battle of Eutaw, and Thomas, a Major, who fell shortly after the battle of Eutaw.

I have mentioned your grandmother, Susan Spratt, and her family, although you did not ask of them, which I think you should have done. I am now eighty-seven years of age and although infirm of body, am yet able to visit my friends and converse with them, and am now writing this letter at the house of Wm. J Alexander, who, with his wife, I consider among my best friends. This letter of course I am not able to write myself, but have procured the services of Mrs Alexander's sister. I should be glad to hear from you, and remain

Yours respectfully,
Susan Smart

In the foregoing letter of Mrs Smart, she states that William Polk removed from Pennsylvania, where he married Margaret Taylor, settled West of the Yadkin, and died there, "at least twenty-five years before the Revolution." This would fix his death about the year 1751 or one year after it is said he emigrated from Pennsylvania to North Carolina.

As stated in the foregoing two letters, the children of William Polk (emigrant to N Carolina) were: Mary, William, Charles, James, Debora, Susan, Margaret, John, Thomas and Ezekiel The two latter sons attained to great distinction in the events which preceded the Revolutionary War, and in the transactions of that great and successful struggle for American Independence

CHAPTER XXXII.

POLK'S SERVING IN CONGRESS.
From Dictionary of U S Congress, 1864

James Knox Polk was born in Mecklenburg County, North Carolina, November 2, 1795 He removed with his father, in 1806 to Tennessee, and lived in the Valley of Duck River, a branch of the Cumberland He graduated at the University of North Carolina in 1815, studied law in Tennessee with Felix Grundy, and was admitted to the bar in 1820. He was a member of the House of Representatives in Congress from 1825 to 1839, and Speaker in that body from 1835 to 1837, and was elected Governor of Tennessee in 1839, for two years. In December, 1844, the Electors chose him President of the United States, and during his eventful administration the Oregon question was settled, Texas annexed, war with Mexico declared, and New Mexico and California were acquired He died at Nashville, Tenn., June 15, 1849

Col. William H Polk was born in Maury County, Tennessee, May 24, 1815. He was educated at Chapel Hill, North Carolina, and the University of Tennessee He studied law and was admitted to the bar in 1839. In 1841 and 1843, he was elected to the State Legislature; was appointed by President Tyler Charge d' Affaires to Naples, where he negotiated a treaty with the Two Sicilies. He served as a Major in the Ninth Dragoons, in the Mexican War, was a Delegate to the Nashville Convention in 1850; and a Representative in Congress, from Tennessee, from 1851 to 1853 He was a brother of President James Knox Polk and opposed to the secession of the South from the Union He died at Nashville, Dec 16 1862

Trusten Polk was born in Sussex County, Delaware, May 29, 1811; graduated at Yale College in 1831, studied law at the Yale Law School, and in 1835 he emigrated to Missouri, where he commenced the practice of his profession

In 1845, while absent from Missouri for the benefit of his health, he was elected a member of the Convention called to remodel the State Constitution In 1856 he was elected Governor of Missouri, and inaugurated January, 1857, but soon resigned for a seat in the United States Senate, to which he was elected for the term of six years, from March 4, 1857, his chief opponent being Thomas H Benton He was a member of the Committee on Foreign Affairs, and of Claims Following a charge of treason preferred against him, because of his strong sympathy with the South, he was expelled from the Senate on Jan 10, 1862 Returning to St Louis, he resumed his practice of the law, which he continued until his death

RUFUS K. POLK.

Rufus King Polk, son of Gen'l Lucius E Polk, of Helena, Ark., was born August 23, 1866 in Maury County, Tenn , on his father's plantation a few miles from Columbia

Rufus Polk's youth was passed on the old plantation until he was started to school at a local academy and fitted for college. He entered Lehigh University, in Pennsylvania, and graduated with the class of 1887 with the degree of Bachelor of Science, and then took a post-graduate course in mining engineering. After leaving college he located at Danville, Pa , and was employed as chemist by the Montour Iron and Steel Company. With the exception of a few months during which he had charge of the furnaces of the Hocking Valley Coal and Iron Company in Ohio, he engaged in business in Danville, as Assistant Superintendent of the Montour Iron and Steel Company, General Manager of the North Branch Steel Company and finally became a partner in the firm of Howe & Polk, manufacturers of structural iron in which business he was engaged at the time of his death. His business the year preceding his death, as he stated, exceeded one million dollars of product.

In the spring of 1898, when the United States declared war against Spain, Rufus Polk, with his associates in the National Guard, left his wife, family and large growing business interests and was mustered in as First Lieutenant of

Company F, Twelfth Regiment of Pennsylvania Volunteers, serving until his muster out and honorable discharge after peace was declared.

On his return home he was nominated as a Democrat to represent the 17th District of Pennsylvania, composed of the counties of Columbia, Montour Northumberland and Sullivan, in the Fifty-sixth Congress, and although that district was then represented by a Republican, his majority was nearly 2,000. Two years later he was re-elected to the Fifty-seventh Congress with an increased majority of nearly 1,500, so popular had he become, and he would have been elected to the Fifty-eighth Congress had he lived and not positively refused to run again because of his large business interests.

Rufus K. Polk died at his home in Danville, Pa., March 5th, 1902. His funeral was attended by an immense concourse of people, as all loved him. His pall-bearers were eight stalwart employes of the firm of Howe & Polk. (See Record No. 113.)

HON. RUFUS K. POLK, M. C.,
of Pennsylvania, son of Gen'l Lucius E. Polk.

THE NEW YORK
PUBLIC LIBRARY

ASTOR LENOX AND
TILDEN FOUNDATIONS

CHAPTER XXXIII.

WILLIAM POLK, SR., SON OF IMMIGRANTS.

William Polk, the second son and child of Capt Robert Bruce Polk and his wife Magdalen (Tasker-Porter) Polk, was born about 1664-7, in the County of Donegal, Ireland, a short distance from Londonderry and Coleraine It was in the vicinity of the latter place that the first Pollok emigrants from the South of Scotland settled when James, after the death of Elizabeth, planted strong Scotch colonies in the country in order to nullify the warlike enterprises of the Catholic hosts in that quarter which had, under Hugh O'Neil and other active leaders, so long defied the repressive efforts of Queen Elizabeth

John, William, Anne, Ephraim, and possibly James were all born before Robert and Magdalen emigrated to America William was probably a child of seven or eight years of age when his parents left Ireland.

His father settling at a place then called Damn Quarter," (now softened down into Dame's Quarter), on the Eastern Shore, and in the county of Somerset, it was there that William grew to manhood

Capt Robert Bruce Polk does not appear to have patented a tract of land very soon after arrival in Maryland, but to have waited awhile, securing a patent for "Polk's Folly," a tract of one hundred acres, and "Polk's Lott," fifty acres, on March 7, 1687 His sons Ephraim and Robert in 1700 also secured patents John, the eldest son of Capt Robert Bruce Polk, was the first one of the family to obtain a grant. On June 1st, 1685, Lord Baltimore patented to him a tract called Locust Hammock," described as "lying on the East side of Chesapeake Bay on South side of the mouth of Wiccocomicoe River, in Damn Quarter Neck."

William Polk's first patents were for

"Moneen," 100 acres   n east side Main ' in h   Nanticoke River, in John's Neck, Somerset County," July 10, 1725.

Donigall," 100 acres (do do do.)

"Romas," 100 acres, September 10, 1725

In partnership with his brother-in-law, Thomas Pollitt, William also patented "Come by Chance," 20 acres, ' two miles from head of Wicomico Creek," December 4, 1735.

Under the then existing law of primogeniture, and being the eldest son of Magdalen Polk at her death in 1727, William inherited the manor plantation, "White Hall," making it thereafter his regular abiding place, and at his death in 1740 it descended to his eldest son, Judge David Polk. It was a noted Colonial mansion and in it was dispensed a generous hospitality by its various occupants. Having large orchards of various fruits, and a distillery on the place, William was in a position to practice "hospitality."

It will be noted that William made no entry of land—or, rather, he secured no patent to such—until 38 years after his father's, and forty years after his brother John's patents. Why he deferred the matter so long does not at this time appear. It is certain however that he purchased one or more tracts from others who had secured patents for same, and hence the records relative to such do not appear on the books of the Colonial Land Office at Annapolis. He took charge of the ancestral home after the death of his mother.

WM POLK, SR., TWICE MARRIED.

Tradition says, and facts and inferences support the statement, that William was twice married, first to Nancy (Knox) Owens, a widow, and was a widower at the time he made his will in 1739-40. The latter is distinctly shown in the document wherein he bequeaths to his son David, among other personal property, "a lot of linen, left in the house at the decease of my wife." This deceased wife seems to have been his second wife, and, inferentially she was a "widow Gray" when he married her, with a son named Allen Gray. Such a youth was a member of William Polk's household, at his death, for, in his will he says, "I give and bequeath unto Allen Gray one little black mare, one black cow and her calf, to the only proper use of him the said Allen Gray." The inference is strong that Allen was William's stepson That his mother dying while she was the second wife of William, the boy continued in the home of his stepfather, who became attached to him and was thereby moved to remember him in his will The traditions handed down, together with the facts obtained by the Polk tree compilers of 1849, give Nancy (Knox) Owens, as the mother of William Polk's children— David, James, Elizabeth Williams, and Jane Strawbridge. It seems, however, that these compilers failed to discover the two of the children of William one of whom appears to have been Charles Polk, who became an Indian trader on the Maryland frontier, at the North Bend of the Potomac, in Frederick County, where he died in 1753, and the other William Polk, who went to Carlisle, Pa, married there Miss Margaret Taylor one of a numerous family of daughters and moved to North Carolina about 1750, becoming progenitor of the Southern branch of the Polk family

These sons, William and Charles, were doubtless the eldest of Williams' children, born somewhere between 1700 and 1710, and likely received from their father what he estimated would be their fair share of his property, and then went forth in quest of broader and more active fields of effort One of them, William, moved to the Allegheny frontier and located at Carlisle, Pa., where he married Margaret Taylor After some years here, following the trend of emigration at that time, he moved down to the sunny banks of the Yadkin, where several of his sons afterward became famous participants in America's first Declaration of Independence, enunciated at Charlotte, N C, May 20, 1775

The other son Charles, appears to have bent his course to the westward branches of the Potomac, where he embarked in trade with the Indians accumulating a competency before his death in 1753 In this trade he became thoroughly acquainted with the Indian character and acquired their friendship.

Charles appears to have married near his frontier station What was the name of his wife, is not certainly known, but the strong inference is that it was Christian Matson, for in his will of March 19, 1753, he calls her "Christian my dearly beloved wife," and makes her and Ralph Matson (presumably her brother) executors of his will, his sons all being too young at that time for such duties Some of the Matsons accompanied Capt Chas Polk to Kentucky and Indiana

CHAPTER XXXIV.

WRONG WILLIAM MADE BODY OF TREE.

The long held traditionary statement that the William Polk who moved from Carlisle to North Carolina was a son of John Polk and Priscilla Roberts, has been irrefutably proven to be incorrect by exhaustive examinations of the official records of Maryland, Delaware, Pennsylvania, Virginia and North Carolina

John Polk, eldest son of Robert and Magdalen, reputed progenitor of the Southern Polks, married Jane ——————— as shown by the old Monie church records, in Somerset County, and she was the mother of his two surviving children, William and Nancy. Jane died October 28, 1700, six days after the birth and death of her infant child, named John These facts the Monie church records show after a careful examination made by Mr Earle B Polk, of Princess Anne, Deputy Circuit Clerk of Somerset County

John Polk next married Joanna Knox, said to have been a sister of Nancy (Knox) Owens, William Polk's first wife, and he died in 1707-8. The court records of Somerset speak of her as the "widow Joanna Polk."

John and Jane's children, William and Nancy, were committed by the said Court, shortly after their father's death to the care and guardianship of William Polk, Sr., (John's brother) who, on August 11, 1708, preferred a petition to Court for the purpose, in obedience, as he stated, to his brother's dying request. After John's death, his widow Joanna married Thos Hugg, and had issue by him

WILLIAM POLK AND PRISCILLA ROBERTS.

William, son of John and Jane, grew to manhood, married Priscilla Roberts, his cousin, and died in Maryland in 1726, his widow later marrying Robert Clarkson These statements are supported by official records and they entirely dissipate the long held tradition that the William who married Priscilla Roberts was the progenitor of the Southern Polks, as stated on the Polk "Tree" published in 1849

Of the seven sons of Robert Bruce Polk and Magdalen Polk, one of them, David, was not discovered by the 1849 compilers Neither did they discover Capt Robert's will of 1699 else they would have found David in the list of children named therein. The finding of this document within a few years past, on file in the Colonial Office at Annapolis, Md, revealed the name of David It also showed that one of Robert and Magdalen's daughters, reputed to have been named Margaret, was named Martha

David presumably died single, or intestate He acquired several tracts of land, as the records show, but no will has been found to tell of its disposition, or of the names of his children if he had any

An inference from some of the records is that David married a daughter of Christopher Nutter, of Somerset, but proof is lacking There is also a tradition that he moved to Pennsylvania, where a number of Pollock kinsmen from about Coleraine, a few miles from Londonderry, Ireland, settled between 1735 and the Revolutionary War That David refused to change his name, like the others did, to Polk, and stuck to the original Pollock, is a tradition that has been handed down in the family

The children of Robert and Magdalen Polk's other sons —John, William, Ephraim, Robert and Joseph—are apparently pretty fully accounted for by past family chroniclers, and by more recent and careful examination of official records Very recently discovered records show Jane ———, as wife of John Polk, when she died, and the names and dates of birth of their children Another discovery was the will of Joseph Polk, youngest son of Robert and Magdalen, showing his death to have occurred in Dorchester County in 1752, and the names of his children

The children of the William Polk, who married Margaret Taylor at Carlisle, Pa, and moved to North Carolina about 1750, where he soon afterward died "about 25 years before the Revolutionary War" (as related by old Mrs Smart to Bishop

Polk), were as stated on the Polk Tree of 1849, their names being furnished at that time by contemporary kinsmen and near relatives like General Thomas, Col William, and Bishop Polk, Mrs Susan Smart, et al (See these names under head of descendants of Wm Polk and Margaret Taylor, on another page)

CHILDREN OF WILLIAM AND NANCY (KNOX-OWENS) POLK.

In addition to William and Charles Polk, who appear to have been his eldest children, Wm. Polk, Sr , had four children These four were [1]Elizabeth, [2]James, [3]David, and [4]Jane

It appears that the first named, Elizabeth generally called "Betsy" was a full sister of William and Charles, and possibly also their elder in years, judging from the date of her birth, as given These four are named in William's will of 1739-40 Their dates of birth, marriage and death are given as follows [1]Elizabeth (Betsy) Polk, born about 1695, died ———, married John Williams of Somerset, [2]James Polk born May 17, 1719, died 1770, married 1st Mary Cottman, 2nd Betty Cottman, [3]Judge David Polk born 1721, died 1778, married Betsy Gilliss; [4]Jane Polk, born 1723, died ———, married James Strawbridge

Elizabeth and John Williams had issue [1]Mary, who married Wm. Polk, her first cousin, son of James Polk, [2]Capt John Williams, a Revolutionary soldier, who died in 1798. He was a prominent business man of Somerset County And two other sons, who are said to have emigrated to the Carolinas Names not known

Rev. Arthur P Brown, pastor of the First Baptist church at Fresno, Cal , writing to Paul M. Polk of Vicksburg, Miss , on March 20, 1905, concerning the Polk family, says of Robert Bruce Polk "His son was the father of Charles Polk of Frederick County, Md , whose history you have "

Rev. Brown was a descendant of Charles Polk of Frederick County, Indian trader on the North Branch of the Potomac, and made extensive researches into the genealogy of his branch of the Polk family extending over a number of years

His statement above, referring to Wm Polk Sr, (son of Robert and Magdalen Polk), being the father of Charles Polk the Indian trader, is additional proof of other statements coming from that line, that Capt Charles Polk, was a cousin of Ezekiel Polk, grandfather of James K Polk

Referring to the personal appearance of many of the Polks—especially the female portion of her branch—Mrs Aurelia Winder Townsend, deceased, of Oyster Bay, Long Island who gathered a great deal of data concerning the family, and also was the custodian of much that came to her from Josiah F Polk, Col W H Winder, and others of the 1848-9 compilers, says

"I have never known any Polks but the descendants of my great grandfather, except a brother of General Polk Of those whom I know personally, and by tradition, sixteen have been people who would be remarkable anywhere for beauty Of my grandfather's seven children, Mrs. Fromentine was the only one not noted for beauty, but she was a very good looking woman My uncle Josiah I never saw but every one who knew him agreed that he was in face, figure and carriage absolutely faultless Uncle William was very handsome. Uncle James the handsomest man I ever saw. My mother was a very handsome woman, and her sisters, Mrs Stuart and Mrs Johnson, very beautiful Morris Polk, cousin Josiah's brother was very handsome, and his daughter the most beautiful creature I ever looked at It stirs my blood to think of her, though I have not seen her for thirty-five years"

WILLIAM, SON OF JUDGE DAVID POLK.

(By his granddaughter, Mrs Aurelia W. Townsend)

William Polk (son of David Polk and Betsy Gilliss), was born December 11, 1752, and married February 1775 to Esther (daughter of Wm Winder and widow of Isaac Handy), who was born October 9, 1751 She died April 1790 and he next married Nancy Purnell (widow of ———— Dennis), who died in 1794 In 1809 or 10 he married Anne Hubbell Issue by the

BETSY, DAUGHTER OF WM. POLK.

Betsy Polk was born May 19, 1776 and died October 6, 1822. She was married about 1800 to Elegius Fromentine, a French refugee. When Louisiana was bought by the United States they settled at New Orleans, where Mr. Fromentine became a distinguished lawyer, and U. S Senator. They both died of yellow fever, she on the 5th, he on the 7th of October 1822. No issue.

HETTY, DAUGHTER OF WM. POLK.

Hetty Polk was born April 9, 1779, died ——— She married 1st April 1797, Col. Nehemiah King, who died in a few years, and then she married her cousin, Dr Chas. Winder, who died a few months after their marriage. Several years later she married Major Alexander Stuart, U S A, who died April 1824.

Issue by the first husband: ¹Charlotte (who died in infancy), ²Henry. Henry married 1st Aurelia, a daughter of his mother's half brother, Richard Handy, 2d Matilda Handy Issue by the 1st: ¹Charlotte, ²Laura, ³Aurelia, by the 2d Henry

GERTRUDE, DAUGHTER OF WM. POLK.

Gertrude Polk was born April 13, 1781; married May 9, 1799, to her cousin General Wm H Winder In 1802 they settled in Baltimore, where he died at the head of the Bar, May 24, 1824. She died December 28, 1872 Issue ¹John H., ²Wm H, ³Charlotte, ⁴Aurelia, ⁵Wm H, ⁶Charlotte, ⁷Gertrude, ⁸Wm Tasker, ⁹Gertrude, ¹⁰William, ¹¹Charlotte, ¹²Aurelia. The first two Williams, the first Gertrude and Tasker died in infancy. The first Aurelia died May, 1819, aged 13 The second Gertrude on June 21, 1841, unmarried John H Winder was born February 21, 1800, at Rewston in Somerset County, Md, the residence of his grandfather Winder He was educated at West Point, and remained in the army until his marriage in 1823 to Elizabeth, daughter of Andrew Shepherd of Georgia At her death in 1827 he returned to the service and while stationed at Smithville N C, married Mrs. Caroline A Eagle, widow of Joseph Eagle, a planter on Cape Fear river, and daughter of Thos Cox of Edenton, N C He servid all through the Florida and Mexican wars and at Gen'l Scott's recommendation was brevetted Lt Colonel for his services in the last. He resigned April 20, 1861, and was appointed Brigadier General in the Confederate Army, June 21, 1861 For the first three years of the war he was General Commanding the Department of Henrico The last year of the war he was Commissary General of Prisoners East of the Mississippi He died very suddenly at Florence, S C, Feb 8, 1865, of disease of the heart, brought on by excessive fatigue and anxiety in the discharge of his duties

Issue by the first wife. [1]Wm A Winder By the second [2]John C, [3]Wm Sidney, [4]Thos. P, [5]Gertrude The last two died in infancy Wm A married Abby, daughter of Gov I Goodwin, of Portsmouth, N H., Issue [1]Wm John C., married Octavia Bryan, daughter of John H Bryan, of Raleigh. N C, where he resides He is a civil engineer, Superintendent of the Raleigh & Gaston and Raleigh & Augusta Air Line railroads. Issue [1]Mary B, [2]Caroline, [3]John H, [4]Gertrude, [5]Aurelia, [6]Octavia

Wm Sidney is a prominent lawyer in Baltimore, unmarried Wm H 3d is living in New York, unmarried

Charles H married Mary H, daughter of Gen'l Joseph Sterett of Baltimore, who died Jan, 1876. Issue: [1]Wm H, [2]Josephine S, [3]Mary H. The first died in infancy. The third Sept. 1, 1861, unmarried.

Josephine S married Stewart Darrell, of Bermuda, a merchant in Baltimore Issue. [1]Cavendish and [2]Josephine

CHAPTER XXXV.

JOSIAH, SON OF WM. POLK.

Josiah Polk was born Nov. 17, 1783, died 1814. He married Rebecca, daughter of Dr John Troup. He practiced law in Princess Anne, Somerset Co Md where he died in 1814 Issue ¹Henry, ²William, ³James, ⁴John ⁵Mary. Henry and William died unmarried. John, a physician in Hartford Co. Md, married Elizabeth Billingsley. Issue ¹Lizzie, ²Emma. Lizzie married Eugene Pomeroy, a lawyer in New York Emma married Sidney Simon, U S N. Mary E married 1st Dr Samuel Carr, 2d, David Dudley Field, a lawyer of New York. She died April, 1876. Issue by 1st ¹Lizzie and ²Charles. Lizzie married Wm Brown of New York, and died soon after without issue. Chas H married Mary Virginia, daughter of Dr Sims of New York. Issue ¹Constance, ²Addie, ³Emmet.

CAPT. WILLIAM, SON OF WM. POLK.

Capt Wm Polk was born Aug. 9, 1786, died Feb 13, 1856 He married Nov. 29, 1811, Almy, daughter of Wm Townsend of Oyster Bay, L I. He died on the morning, she in the evening of Feb 13 1856. Issue. ¹Wm Winder, ²Mary T., ³Margaret H, ⁴James B, ⁵Frank, ⁶Gertrude, ⁷Louise D Frank and Gertrude died in infancy. Wm Winder and James B died unmarried. Mary T married 1st July 16 1840, Victor Monroe, of Frankfort, Ky., 2d Albert Iverson U. S. Senator from Georgia. Issue by first ¹Wm Winder, ²Frank Adair, ³Mary. William Winder, living in Kentucky, married Miss Lavenia Berry, daughter of H K Berry of Nelson County, Ky, and sister of Capt. Anderson Berry, C. S A now of Lexington, Ky

²Frank, a lawyer in New Orleans, unmarried

³Mary married George Vincent of Louisiana. Issue Wm Monroe

Louie D married J Bannister Hall, a merchant of Baltimore, Dec 11, 1860 Issue. ¹Wm. W , ²Annie G , ³I. Bannister, ⁴Louis, ⁵Marguerite Wm W died in infancy

COL JAMES, SON OF WM. POLK.

Col James Polk was born March 1793, died 1868. He married Ann Stuart, in 1816, and died in Baltimore in Dec 1868. Issue. ¹William, ²Esther, ³Mary, ⁴Ariana, ⁵James, ⁶Lucius, ⁷Joseph B The latter became a distinguished actor in comedy, reaching a high station in his profession. Col James Polk was Register of Wills for Somerset County. Later in 1845, he was Naval Officer in Baltimore, and in 1848 was Collector for that port.

William married in Texas a Miss Estes and has three sons, ¹Wm. E , ²Stuart and ³James She resides in San Antonio, Texas.

Esther married Gov E Louis Lowe, of Md Issue ¹Adelaide, ²Annie, ³Paul, ⁴Vivian, ⁵Victoria, ⁶Louie ⁷Esther, ⁸Mary Adelaide married E Austin Jenkins, a very wealthy merchant of Baltimore Issue ¹Austin, ²Louis Lowe, ³Edmond Joseph, ⁴Martin Spaulding, ⁵Mary.

Mary married Onno Goitei, of Amsterdam, Holland. Dutch Consul at Baltimore and a merchant of that city Issue· ¹Onno, ²Albert, ³Meta, ⁴Judge James P., ⁵Dr. Nathan, ⁶Marie.

Onno married Alice Edmonson. Issue· ¹Alice and ²Arthur Edmonson.

Ariana married Lucillius Briscoe, of Georgia Issue. Mattie Briscoe They reside at Griffin, Ga.

James Polk, son of Col. James Polk, married Nannie Maddox, by whom he had issue: ¹Anna, ²Kate, ³James ⁴Wm Maddox, ⁵John Lucius, ⁶Mary Stuart, ⁷Herschel V J

Anna married J. Leland Busch, Sup't of Public Schools, Norfolk, Va No issue

Kate married W. M. Nixon, a merchant of Augusta, Ga , Issue ¹John, ²William.

James married Florence Queen, an attorney of Washington, D C. Issue: ¹Kenneth, ²John

Wm Maddox married Emma S Hudson, of Newport News, Va   No issue

John Lucius died in 1890, and Herchel V J in 1878.

John Lucius married Mary Clark and left a son Clark Polk, who married and has two children

ANNE, DAUGHTER OF JUDGE WM. POLK.

Anne, daughter of Judge Wm Polk, married 1st, Robert Walker of Georgia, 2d, Hon Herschel V Johnson, of Georgia   Issue by 1st   [1]William   By the second, [2]Robt Emmet, [3]Tallulah, [4]Winder, [5]Anne, [6]Gertrude, [7]Herschel [8]Tomlinson.

William married Virginia Estes and died without issue

Robt Emmet Johnson died soon after he reached maturity.   Tallulah married ——————————— and lives in Georgia   Winder, by profession a lawyer, married and lives in Georgia   Gertrude is unmarried   Herschel, a physician, lives in Georgia, and Tomlinson, a planter, in the same state

JAMES POLK, SON OF WM. POLK, SR.

James Polk, second son of William Polk, Sr, and the widow Nancy (Knox-Owens) Polk, was born May 17, 1719 and died in 1771   His will was dated January 30, 1771, and probated April 16, 1771   James was twice married and his second wife also deceased before him   He first married Mary Cottman, secondly, her sister, Betty Cottman   His will is of record in Frederick County, Maryland   In it he mentions his wife, Betty Polk, sons, Benjamin and William; three daughters, Nancy, Leah and Mary Polk, grandson, James Polk, and granddaughter, Betty Whittington   Leah and Mary appear to have been children by the last wife, Betty Cottman

James Polk, son of William Polk, Sr, by his 1st wife, Mary Cottman, had issue   [1]Virginia, born 1736, died unmarried, it is said, [2]Benjamin, born 1738, died ——————, married Sarah Whittington, daughter of Southey Whittington and Mary Parker; Priscilla born 1740 died 1804, married C I Wm Whittington [4]Nancy born about 1, 2, died unmarried, it is said; ⁵William, born 1744, died ———, married his cousin Mary Williams, daughter of Elizabeth Polk and John Williams, ⁶Leah, born about 1746, untraced, ⁷Mary, born about 1748, died ——, married James Bratton.

By his second wife, Betty Cottman, who was left executrix of his will, James Polk is said to have had the two last named children, Leah and Mary. His will is dated Jan 30, 1771, and was probated April 16th following

The children of Benjamin and Sarah (Whittington) Polk were ¹James, ²Benjamin, ³Joshua, ⁴Whittington, ⁵Southey, ⁶Jane, ⁷Mary (Polly), ⁸Nelly, ⁹Isaac, ¹⁰Eleanor, ¹¹Elizabeth, ¹²Sarah, ¹³Daniel—a 'baker's dozen."

James Polk, the first son of Benjamin and Mary Cottman Polk, was at one time Surveyor of Somerset County

Benjamin Polk, second child of Benjamin and Sarah (Whittington) Polk, married ——————————, and left two children, Southey and Eliza.

Whittington Polk, son of Benjamin and Sarah (Whittington) Polk, married first the widow A. Chapman, second ————————————, and left issue

Eleanor, daughter of Benjamin and Sarah (Whittington) Polk, untraced   Said to have died unmarried

Jane, daughter of Benjamin and Sarah (Whittington) Polk, married 1st, Wm H Harper; 2d, her first cousin, Dr. Jno Polk, son of Wilham and Mary (Williams) Polk   Dr Polk was a skilful physician and one of the founders of the Delaware Medical Society. He removed to Laurel, Del, died there, and his family returned to Somerset

Mary, daughter of Benjamin and Sarah (Whittington) Polk, married Stephen Collins, an elder in the old Rehoboth Presbyterian Church, (first church of that faith in America) and a brother of Rev. I Collins.

Daniel Polk, son of Benjamin and Sarah (Whittington) Polk, untraced

Isaac, son of Benjamin and Sarah (Whittington) Polk married Rebecca Dashiell and left one child, Sarah, who married W H Stephens

Betsy, daughter of Benjamin and Sarah (Whittington)

Polk, married Michael Cluff, of Worcester County, and they had several children.

Sarah (Sally), daughter of Benjamin and Sarah (Whittington) Polk, married John Whittington

Rebecca, daughter of Benjamin and Sarah (Whittington) Polk, untraced

Norah, daughter of Benjamin and Sarah (Whittington) Polk, untraced.

Nelly, daughter of Benjamin and Sarah (Whittington) Polk, married W. H Harper. She was his first wife His second and third wives were Jane Bristow, of New York, and Rebecca Covington, of Md

Joshua Polk, son of Benjamin and Sarah (Whittington) Polk, died at the age of nearly 78 years He was the eldest child His early life was spent in Caroline County, Md., but later he emigrated to Ohio, where he died He was born Oct 31, 1761, died Dec 7, 1839 He was thrice married; first to Elizabeth Rush She died in August, 1820. No issue Joshua's second wife was Elizabeth Williams, and his third Margaret Payne No issue by latter. His children by the second wife, Elizabeth Williams, were six in number, viz ¹Elizabeth Polk, who married ———— Clouser. No issue ²Joshua Whittington Polk, born Dec 22, 1812, untraced ³Mary Collins Polk, born April 5, 1814, died Nov 12, 1814 ⁴Malinda Polk, born Feb 6, 1816, died ————, untraced ⁵Maria Louisa Polk, born Jan. 19, 1818, untraced ⁶Josiah Polk, born Aug 21, 1820; died in infancy.

These children were born in Maryland, before their parents' removal to Ohio in the winter of 1827.

Joshua Whittington Polk, son of Joshua and Elizabeth (Williams) Polk, is a citizen of Clinton County, Ohio, and is a prominent farmer of that section. He is nearly four score and ten years of age, and is noted for having always been a man of moderation in all things He was married in October, 1836, to Elizabeth Leaverton, of Highland County, Ohio, and had by her twelve children, viz ¹Robert Thompson Polk, ²Leyda Catharine Polk, ³Samuel Judkins Polk, ⁴Hannah Elizabeth Polk, ⁵Wm Alexander Polk, ⁶Andrew Newton Polk, died unmarried; ⁷Josiah Polk ⁸Jason Polk.

⁹Ruth A Polk, ¹⁰Phoebe Jane Polk, ¹¹Lettice Alma Polk, ¹²Thomas Whittington Polk Phoebe, Jane and Thomas Whittington are unmarried

Robert Thompson Polk, the first child of the above list, is a Universalist minister He lives at Towanda, Pa He married Julia Hadley and they had seven children, viz ¹Herbert James, ²Alvar Whittington, ³Mary, ⁴Murry Sheply, died young, ⁵Cora Alma, ⁶Robert Hadley, ⁷Elery Channing Polk

Herbert James Polk, the eldest married Etta Turner, two children Mildred and Bertha. Herbert James Polk and family reside in Boston He is connected with the Old Colony Trust Company, of that city

Alvar Whittintgon Polk lives in Boston He married Annie Greenleaf They have one child. Hadley Greenleaf Polk

Mary Polk, third child of Robert Thompson Polk, is married and also lives in Boston

Cora Alma Polk is unmarried, as is also her brother, Robert Hadley Polk They live in Towanda.

Elery Channing Polk is unmarried and a student at college

Leyda Catharine Polk married John Eddingfield, and they have two children, Nancy Elizabeth and Mary Whittington, unmarried

Nancy Elizabeth married Tennyson Saunders, no issue

Samuel Judkins Polk, married Rachael Larkin, and had seven children, viz ¹Jno Thompson, ²Sarah Elizabeth ³Evelyn Mattie, ⁴Charles Whittington, ⁵Frank, ⁶Julia Moorman, ⁷Burch Polk

John Thompson Polk, eldest son of Samuel Judkins Polk, married Mary Denny. No issue.

Hannah Elizabeth Polk, daughter of Joshua Whittington Polk married Joseph E Powell and they have four children, viz ¹Elizabeth, ²Sarena Lavenia, ³Lettice Alma, ⁴Anna Frances Powell

Elizabeth, eldest child of Joseph E. and Hannah (Polk) Powell, married John Carlisle, a professor in Versailles, Miss She died leaving three children, ¹Bessie Lucille ²Phoebe Grace,

Sarena Lavenia Powell, married Edgar Edwards

Wm Alexander Polk married twice First to Margaret Larkin by whom he had four children, viz: ¹Joshua Whittington Polk, died unmarried, ²Fannie Larkin Polk, ³Robert Thompson Polk, ⁴Earnest Polk, died unmarried

Wm Alexander Polk's second wife was Isaphene Orr, one child

Josiah Polk, son of Joshua Whittington Polk, married Celeste Ann Shockley, and had five children, viz: ¹Walter ²Charles, ³Elsie, ⁴Elizabeth, ⁵Winifred, ⁶Alma Burnett.

Walter Charles Polk, son of Josiah and Celeste Ann (Shockley) Polk, is a civil engineer and resides at Indianapolis, Indiana. He married Eva Purdy; no issue.

Jason Polk, son of Joshua Whittington Polk, married Cordelia Huff and had four children, viz ¹Cordelia, ²Ada, ³Mary Jane, ⁴Burley Polk.

Ruth A. Polk, daughter of Joshua Whittington Polk, married Albert Carey and had issue: ¹Bertha, ²Chilton O'Neal, ³Bessie, ⁴David, ⁵Mary Carey.

Lettice Alma Polk, daughter of Joshua Whittington Polk, married Emerson Groff Polk, her cousin, a banker and prominent business man of Pocomoke City, Md. They have no issue.

Malinda Polk, daughter of Joshua and Elizabeth Williams Polk married Wilson Leaverton, and dying, left seven children, viz ¹Sarah Leaverton, unmarried, resides in Illinois: ²Maria Leaverton, married Orlando Paddry, no issue: ³Wesley Leaverton, unmarried, lives in Illinois; ⁴Jason Leaverton, untraced, ⁵William Leaverton, died unmarried; ⁶Dexter Leaverton, unmarried, lives in Illinois; ⁷Albert Leaverton, married and left children in Illinois

Maria Polk, daughter of Joshua and Elizabeth (Williams) Polk, married Thomas Leaverton, and left eight children viz: ¹Lettice Leaverton, ²Mary Leaverton, ³John Leaverton, ⁴Annie Leaverton, ⁵Dora Leaverton, ⁶Thomas Leaverton, dead, ⁷Lydia Leaverton, ⁸Sarah Leaverton.

Lettice above named married James Dyer, of Kansas and they have children

Mary Leaverton married Aaron Fink, no issue.

John Leaverton married Emma Hoxworth, of Illinois They have several children

Annie Leaverton married Nelson P Merrill of Iowa; two children: [1]Cora Merrill, [2]Major Merrill

Dora Leaverton married ———— Hoxworth, one child, Nellie

Thomas Leaverton died unmarried

Lydia Leaverton married a Mr. Easter; no issue.

Sarah Leaverton married ———————— and has one child and resides in Illinois

Capt Whittington Polk, fourth child of Benjamin and Sarah (Whittington) Polk, was born Sept 9, 1769, died Oct 21, 1859, aged ninety years He was an elder in old Rehoboth Presbyterian Church, the first church of that creed established in America, and in which so many of the Polks have been officers He was married twice first to Rebecca Collins, by whom he had no issue Second, to Rebecca Adams, by whom he had six children, viz. [1]Sarah Elizabeth Polk, [2]Whittington Polk, [3]Rebecca Collins Polk, [4]William Stephens Collins Polk, [5]Joshua Polk, who died in youth, [6]Emerson Groff Polk.

Of the above, Sarah Elizabeth Polk married Wm Whittington, son of James and Sally (Coulburn) Whittington, and they have two children, Alice Coulburn and Sarah Rebecca Whittington

Alice Coulburn Whittington married Wm Scott and they had issue [1]Alice, [2]William

Sarah Rebecca Whittington, daughter of William and Sarah Elizabeth (Polk) Whittington, married Revel Patterson, and had one child, Wm Williams Patterson, who married Ruth Long, no issue

Whittington Polk, son of Capt Whittington and Rebecca (Adams) Polk, married twice; first Sarah Ann Stevenson, second Grace Stevenson By the first he had issue [1]Upshur Whittington Polk, unmarried, [2]Marion Clement Polk, unmarried, Wm James Polk, married Josephine Lawson, one child

By his marriage to Grace Stevenson, Whittington Polk had one child, Ethel Polk.

Rebecca Collins Polk, daughter of Capt Whittington Polk and Rebecca (Adams) Polk, married Thomas Whittington, son of James and Sally (Coulburn) Whittington. Their only child, Mary Zippora, married Henry P Merrill and died leaving two children

William Stephens Collins Polk, fourth child of Capt Whittington Polk, was twice married His first wife was Maggie Powell, his second wife was Sarah Adams By the first he had issue [1]Wm Lee Polk, [2]Eva Polk, [3]Florence Polk, [4]Joshua Polk.

William Stephens Collins Polk and his wife, Sarah (Adams) Polk had issue: [1]Ada Rose, [2]Hattie Polk, unmarried

Wm Lee Polk, son of Wm. Stephens Collins Polk and Maggie Powell Polk, married Nellie Clark and they have Carl and another child

Eva Polk, second child of Wm Stephens Collins Polk, and Maggie (Powell) Polk, married Edward Dixon and had three children: [1]Howard, [2]Lee, [3]Milton

Florence Polk, daughter of Wm. Stephens Collins Polk and Maggie (Powell) Polk, married Jesse Crockett and they had five children. [1]Edward, [2]Idabelle, [3]Jesse Polk, [4]Merwin, [5]Alma Polk Crockett

Joshua Polk, second son of Wm Stephens Collins Polk and Maggie (Powell) Polk, married Mary Pierce and they have one child, Allen Miller Polk.

Emerson Groff Polk, sixth child of Capt Whittington Polk and Rebecca (Adams) Polk, married three times First to Adeline O Dryden, by whom he had one child, Adeline, who died young By his second wife, Louisa Dorsey, he had three children [1]Annie Dorsey, [2]Emerson Whittington, [3]Carrie Hargis Polk.

Annie Dorsey Polk, eldest child of Emerson Groff Polk, married Wm Schoolfield and left at her death three children, viz. [1]Allen Polk Schoolfield, [2]Emily Louisa Schoolfield, [3]Wm Emerson Schoolfield

Emerson Whittington Polk, second child of Emerson

Groff Polk and Louisa (Dorsey) Polk, married Edna Frasier; no issue.

Emerson Groff, for his third wife, married his cousin, Lettice Alma Polk, daughter of Joshua Whittington Polk and Elizabeth (Leaverton) Polk; no issue. (See Benjamin Polk's descendants, of Wm. Polk branch).

Jane Polk, sixth child of Benjamin and Sarah (Whittington) Polk, married her cousin, Dr John Polk of Somerset County, Md, and later of Laurel, Del, where he died. Dr. John Polk was the eldest son of Col Wm Polk, son of Wm Polk Sr. Dr. John and his wife Jane Polk, had four children ¹Harriet, ²Clarissa, ³Margaret, and Dr. Wm T. Polk. The two first never married. Margaret married Wm Stewart and died without issue. Dr. Wm T. Polk married his cousin, Mary Ann Harcum, of Northumberland County, Virginia. He married secondly Louisa Jane Harcum, a sister of his first wife. Mary A Polk, by the first marriage married Wm. Broughton.

Isaac Polk, son of Benjamin and Sarah (Whittington) Polk, married Rebecca Dashiell and had one child, Sarah Polk, who married W H Stevens and had five children. The first died in childhood. The others were ¹Rose, ²Wm. Sidney, ³Ephraim, and ⁴Ella Stephens. Rose married Mr Townsend and had three children ¹Mattie, ²John, ³William. Sidney married Mary Ellen Mutt and died leaving four children ¹Hartley, ²Mary, ³Wm Sidney, ⁴Rose.

Ephraim Stephens, third child of Wm H Stephens and Sarah (Polk) Stephens, married a Miss Mills and had three children.

Ella Stephens, youngest child of John and Sarah (Polk) Stephens, married James Fedderman and left no issue.

Betsy Polk, daughter of Benjamin and Sarah (Whittington) Polk, married Michael Cluff and left one child, Whittington Cluff.

Sarah Polk, daughter of Benjamin and Sarah (Whittington) Polk, married John Drummond Whittington, a cousin, by whom she had, ¹Southey Whittington, ²Edward Whittington, ³Hester Whittington.

Southey Whittington married twice, first to Ann Rider, no issue Second, to Jane Rider, a sister of Ann, by whom he had one child, Ella Whittington

Edward Whittington, second child of Jno Drummond Whittington, married Martha Bayless, one child, Anna Whittington

Hester Whittington, third child of John Drummond Whittington, died unmarried

Ella Whittington, daughter of Southey Whittington and Jane (Rider) Whittington, married twice First, to Thomas Powell, by whom she had one child, Emma Powell; second, to Levin Dashiell; no issue

Anna Whittington, daughter of Edward Whittington and Martha (Bayless) Whittington, married Charles Wetherell, and at her death left three sons: [1]Charles, [2]Edward, [3]Samuel

Rebecca Polk, twelfth child of Benjamin and Sarah (Whittington) Polk, married Stephen Collins and died without issue

Nora Polk, youngest child of Benjamin and Sarah (Whittington) Polk, married Ephraim White and had several children.

CHAPTER XXXVI.

SAMUEL POLK'S DESCENDANTS.

Samuel Polk, third son of William Polk and Mary (Williams) Polk daughter of John and Elizabeth Williams, was born April 10, 1780 and died October 30, 1826. Samuel was married July 10, 1804 to Sarah Irving Gilliss (daughter of Capt Joseph Gilliss and Elizabeth (Irving) Gilliss) who was born September 13, 1783, and died September 28, 1842.

Samuel Polk and wife had issue: [1]William Thomas Gilliss Polk, born May 18, 1805, died December 17, 1875, [2]Caroline Gilliss Polk, born June 24, 1807, died August 12, ——, [3]Joseph Gilliss Polk, born December 29, 1809, died November 8, 1870, [4]Littleton Robins Polk, born June 17, 1813, died ——, [5]Ellen Gilliss Polk, born June 16, 1816, died ——, [6]Eliza Esther Ann Polk, born April 13, 1819, died January 9, 1897, [7]Mary Williams Polk, born February 23, 1823, died December 26, 1906.

COL. WM THOMAS GILLISS POLK'S FAMILY.

Col Wm T G Polk, of Princess Anne, Md., was a leading merchant and business man of that place, a man of great probity of character, pure and exalted life, and an earnest, consistent Christian who held fast to the Presbyterian principles brought from Ireland to America by his ancestors. He was for many years an elder in the church and a recognized leader in his local congregation. He was for a number of years Clerk of the Circuit Court of Somerset County, and was appointed a Colonel on the staff of one of Maryland's Governors. Hence his title. No man in Maryland stood higher, or enjoyed in a greater degree the respect and confidence of his people. To him, especially, is the author of this book indebted for early information traditional, documentary and official concerning Robt Bruce Polk and Magdalen Polk, their children, and much history of the Maryland Polks

COL. WM. T. G. POLK,
Princess Anne, Md.

Col. Wm T G Polk was twice married. His first wife, to whom he was united February 22, 1832, was Elizabeth Gilliss Woolford. She died April 8, 1851. His second wife was Mrs Mary Ann Henry of Berlin, Md., whom he married June 1, 1853.

By his first wife he had issue   1John Woolford Polk, born January 24, 1834, died April 23, 1869, 2Samuel Woolford Polk, born July 13, 1836, died February 2, 1841; 3Sarah Ann Woolford Polk, born December 6, 1838, died February 14, 1841 4Elizabeth Williams Woolford Polk, born March 10, 1841 died October 24, 1870

By his second wife, Mrs Mary Ann Henry, who died April 7, 1891, Col Polk had seven children, viz   5William Thomas Gilliss Polk, born January 7, 1855. Residence Princess Anne, 6Addie Henry Polk, born March 29, 1856 Residence Columbia, Mo, 7Edward Henry Polk, born December 25, 1858, died December 5, 1867; 8Caroline Woolford Polk born June 22, 1862, died April 22, 1863, 9Mary Bredelle Polk, born January 1, 1864 Residence Princess Anne; 10Samuel Polk, born December 18, 1866, died July 4, 1867, 11Elizabeth Polk, born September 18, 1870, died August 2, 1871

Caroline Gilliss Polk (second child of Samuel and Mary (Williams) Polk), married John Woolford, being his second wife They had no issue

JOSEPH GILLISS POLK'S FAMILY.

Joseph Gilliss Polk (third child of Samuel and Mary Henry Polk), married October 3, 1830, Imogen Gilman of Washington, D. C., daughter of Ephraim and Anna (Crawford) Gilman She was born September 20, 1812 and died March 1897

Joseph Gilliss Polk held the offices of Sheriff of Somerset county, and of School Commissioner He was for a number of years an elder in the Presbyterian Church at Princess Anne

Joseph Gilliss and Imogen (Gilman) Polk has issue 1Joseph Littleton Polk, D D Ph D., born August 12, 1837, died ———, 1905, 2Sarah Ann Polk, born December 21, 1838, died December 21, 1840, 3Imogen Gilman Polk, born November 27, 1840, died December 8, 1840, ⁴Samuel Polk, born August 25, 1842, died September 9, 1866, ⁵Ephraim Gilman Polk, born October 6, 1844, died October 10, 1899, ⁶Imogen Gilman Polk, 2d, born September 21, 1846, died December 22, 1905, ⁷Anna Crawford Polk, born September 27, 1848, resides at Ridley Park, Pa., ⁸Wm Thomas Gilliss Polk, born August 2, 1850, residence Princess Anne, ⁹Laura Augusta Polk, born August 14, 1855, died August 8, 1873.

Littleton Robins Polk, fourth child of Samuel Polk, died unmarried

Ellen Gilliss Polk (fifth child of Samuel and Mary Polk), married John Woolford and was his first wife, his second being Caroline Gilliss Polk, a sister of Ellen. John and Ellen had issue ¹John Woolford, born ———. Residence Princess Anne; ²Thos Gilliss Woolford, born ———; ³Ellen Woolford, born ———

Eliza Ann Polk (sixth child of Samuel and Mary Polk), married April 14, 1852, Dr John Washington Dashiell, born January 30, 1817. They had issue ¹Robert Kemp Whittingham Dashiell, born April 20 1854, died June 12, 1894, ²Sarah Gilliss Dashiell, born November 30, 1855. Residence Princess Anne. ³Ella Bell Anna Maria Dashiell, born May 29, 1859. Residence Princess Anne

Mary Williams Polk (seventh and youngest child of Samuel and Mary Polk), born February 23, 1823, married December 3, 1846, John Henry Bell, and they had eleven children, viz ¹Mary Bell, born August 29, 1847, died September —, 1847, ²Carrie Polk Bell, born September 22, 1848, died in infancy; ³Ellen Stewart Bell, born November 12, 1850. Residence Hampton, Va., ⁴Jane Meckelhenny Bell, born October 22, 1852 died in infancy, ⁵Sarah Eliza Bell, born September 28, 1853, living in New Jersey; ⁶Littleton Polk Bell, born March 26, 1855, died ———, ⁷Annie Rebecca Bell, born February 26, 1857, died in infancy, ⁸Julia Bell, born January 7, 1859, died in infancy, ⁹John Henry Bell, born February 7, 1860, died in infancy, ¹⁰William Polk Bell, born September 18, 1863, died in infancy, ¹¹Addie Henry Bell, born March 21, 1870 residence Baltimore, Md

Leon Woolford Polk (eldest son and child of Col Wm

T. G. Polk and Elizabeth Gilliss Woolford) never married. He served as a soldier in the Confederate Army, in the Civil War

Elizabeth Williams Woolford Polk (third child of Col. Wm. T. G. Polk and his first wife, Elizabeth Gilliss Woolford), married June 13, 1861, Hayden Heyne Dashiell, and had issue. [1]Edwin Polk Dashiell, born May 23, 1863, died May 10, 1867; [2]John Woolford Dashiell, born November 18, 1866, living; [3]Louis Dashiell, born August 31, 1868, residence Bel Air, Md., [4]William Henry Dashiell, born October 19, 1870, residence Princess Anne.

Wm Thomas Gilliss Polk, Jr. (son of Col. Wm T. G. Polk, Sr.), married November 21, 1905, Elizabeth Elzey Woolford No issue

Addie Henry Polk (daughter of Col Wm T G. Polk and Mary Ann (Henry) Polk), married July 13, 1882, Richard Henry Jesse, of Columbia, Boone County, Mo Issue [1]Richard Henry Jesse, born January 4, 1884, [2]Mary Polk Jesse, born October 22, 1885, [3]Caroline Elizabeth Jesse born August 12, 1887; [4]William Polk Jesse, born March 14, 1891; [5]Adeline Jesse, born August 23, 1892; [6]Henry Bredelle Jesse born October 14, 1894

Mary Bredelle Polk, (daughter of Col Wm. T. G Polk and Mary Ann Henry), married November 20, 1886, Henry Lawrence Brittingham Issue [1]Henry Lawrence Brittingham, born December 3, 1888, [2]William Polk Brittingham, born July 26, 1892; [3]James Francis Brittingham, born July 4, 1894 These all reside at Princess Anne, Md

Joseph Littleton Polk, D. D Ph. D (eldest child of Joseph Gilliss Polk and Imogen Gilman), married Mary Wilson of Canonsburg, Pa., daughter of Thomas McKean Wilson and Elizabeth (Murdock) Wilson. They had twelve children, viz. [1]Mary Wilson Polk, born ———. Residence Wilmington, Del : [2]Alexander Murdock Polk, born ———; [3]Imogen Gilman Polk, born ———, [4]Samuel Polk, born ———. Residence Calore, Md, [5]Joseph Gilliss Polk, born ———, died in childhood; [6]Elizabeth Murdock Polk, born ———, died in childhood; [7]Laura Gilman Polk, born ———, residence Fagg - Manor Pa ; Lyde Wilson Polk, born ———, unmarried   Lives at Coatsville, Pa, with mother; [9]Thomas McKean Polk, born ———   Residence Martinsville, Pa , [10]Annie Polk, born ———, [11]William Thomas Gilliss Polk, born September 6, 1869   Residence Fagg's Manor, Pa , [12]Elizabeth Murdock Polk, born October 12, 1882, unmarried   Lives with mother at Coatsville, Pa

Samuel Polk (fourth child and son of Joseph Gilliss Polk and Imogen Gilman), never married   He was a soldier in the Confederate Army, in the Civil War.

Ephraim Gilman Polk (fifth child of Joseph Gilliss Polk and Imogen Gilman), married February 15, 1871, Mary Oliver Culbreth, daughter of Thomas B and Elmire (Redden) Culbreth   She was born November 4, 1852, and died June 14, 1881. Ephraim was a colonel on the staff of one of the Governor's of Maryland, a member of the Maryland Legislature in 1878; served as a School Commissioner of Somerset county was editor of The Marylander, a newspaper published at Princess Anne   Ephraim Gilman Polk and wife had issue [1]Earle Brodie Polk, born January 3, 1872, residence Princess Anne, where he is Deputy Circuit Clerk of Somerset county Like Col Wm T. G Polk, he was a most valuable aid to the author in collecting ancient Polk data in that State   It was he who discovered from the official county, and the Monie Church records that John Polk's second wife, Joanna Knox, was not the mother of William and Nancy, John's two children, (as long claimed and as shown on the Polk Tree of 1849) but a first wife whose given name was Jane

Anna Crawford (seventh child of Joseph Gilliss and Imogen Polk), married October 1, 1868, Arthur George Woolford and had issue   [1]Arthur Woolford, born August 2, 1869, residence Suffolk, Va , [2]Joseph Woolford, born January 21, 1871, died November 26, 1883; [3]Levin Woolford, born November 21, 1872, residence Sunbury, N C ; [4]Eliza Atkinson Woolford, born August 16, 1874, residence Crisfield, Md , [5]Samuel Woolford, born March 29, 1876, residence Norfolk, Va

Imogen Gilman Polk (sixth child of Joseph Gilliss and Imogen Gilman Polk), married October 3, 1867, Wm Charles Fontaine   They had issue   [1]Joseph Gilman Fontaine, born July 4 1868, died October 12, 1869, [2]Imogen Polk Fontaine, born June 27, 1870, residence Princess Anne; ³Ann Crawford Fontaine, born August 23, 1872, residence Princess Anne; ⁴Laura Polk Fontaine, born October 9, 1874, residence Princess Anne; ⁵Berkley Douglass Fontaine, born January 13, 1884, residence Philadelphia, Pa ; ⁶Ephraim Polk Fontaine, born February 7, 1886, residence Philadelphia, Pa , ⁷William Gilman Fontaine, born July 1, 1889, residence Philadelphia, Pa

William Thomas Gilliss Polk (eighth child and son of Joseph Gilliss Polk and Imogen Gilman), went to the West in 1871 and has not been heard of since

Laura Augusta Polk (youngest child of Joseph Gilliss Polk and wife), never married

John Woolford, Jr (eldest son of John Woolford, Sr, and Ellen Gilliss Polk, by his first wife), never married Nor did his brother or his sister, Thomas Gilliss and Ellen Woolford, both of whom are dead

Robert Kemp Whittingham Dashiell never married

Sarah Gilliss Dashiell married November 30, 1880, Francis Henshaw Dashiell and they had two children ¹Eliza, born April 1883; ²Olive, born December 27, 1894, residence Princess Anne

Ella Bell Anna Maria Dashiell married June 27, 1888, Edward Ornick Smith No issue

Ellen Stewart Bell, married October 14, 1874, first Scott Covington, second, October 6, 1889, Capt William Mitchell By the first she had ¹Ernest Covington, born August 14, 1875, died in infancy; ²Frank Harold Covington, born January 20, 1878 By her second husband, Capt. Mitchell, she had one child, Elizabeth Raleigh Mitchell, born September 28, 1890, residence Hampton, Va

Sarah Eliza Bell, married September 15, 1869, Alfred Joseph King of Pottsville, Pa., and they had: ¹Pauline King, born April 2, 1870; ²Estelle King, born December 10, 1871, ³Edith C King, born November 5, 1873, ⁴Marian Alice King, born January 6, 1888, dead All of the family reside at Philadelphia

Littleton Polk Bell never married

Addie Henry Bell, married April 12, 1898, George Allen Kelly, of Baltimore, Md No issue

John Woolford Dashiell, unmarried.

Louis Dashiell, unmarried.

William Henry Dashiell, unmarried.

None of Addie Henry Polk Jesse's children are married

None of Mary Bredelle Polk Brittingham's children are married.

Mary Wilson Polk, married Wm S Prickett, of Wilmington, Del, and they had issue: [1]Josephine Mary Prickett; [2]Emily May Prickett, died in infancy, [3]William Sharp Prickett; [4]Florence Elizabeth Prickett. They reside at Wilmington, Del

Alexander Murdock Polk, M D , married Annie Meredith Hurlock, of Church Hill, Md No issue

Imogen Gilman Polk, married P A. H. Armstrong, now deceased, a Presbyterian minister. One child, Henry Pleasant Armstrong

Samuel Polk (son of Joseph L Polk) minister, married September 14, 1893, Mary Amos of Muddy Creek Fork, York county, Pa., daughter of Dr. James B. Amos and Rebecca Mitchell. They have issue: [1]Joseph Littleton Polk, born July 20, 1894, died January 29, 1906; [2]Rebecca Amos Polk, born October 26, 1896; [3]James Murdock Polk, born November 19, 1902.

Laura Gilman Polk married William McClellan of Fagg's Manor, Pa Issue unknown

Lyde Wilson Polk is unmarried

Rev Thos. McKean Polk married Gertrude Edwards of Fagg's Manor.

Annie Polk, married Charles Cook, of Fagg's Manor.

Wm Thomas Gilliss Polk (son of Joseph L Polk), married, name of wife and of issue, not known

Elizabeth Murdock Polk is unmarried.

Earle Brodie Polk (son of Ephraim Gilman Polk and Mary Oliver (Culbreth) Polk, married December 22, 1897, Garnet Alma Chelton, of Somerset county, Md, daughter of Zachary Taylor Chelton and Annie (Ford) Chelton. Issue: [1]Earle Brodie Polk, born October 12, 1898; [2]Fulbert Culbreth Polk, born March 7, 1905 residence Princess Anne, Md

Arthur Woolford, married June 21, 1893, Missouri Kelby Withers, of Suffolk, Va. Issue. [1]Zouzie Woolford, born April 2, died April 13, 1894; [2]Austin Withers Woolford, born August 21, 1895, [3]Nannie Polk Woolford, born October 24, 1897; [4]Arthur Thompson Woolford, born June 30, 1900, [5]John Riddick Woolford, born December 31, 1901, [6]Missouri Taylor Woolford, born December 5, 1908

Levin Woolford. (son of Arthur George Woolford and Anna Crawford Polk), married September 14, 1905, Fannie Smith Costen, of North Carolina. No issue.

Eliza Atkinson Woolford (daughter of Arthur George and Anna Crawford Polk), married April 27, 1900, Albert Goodrich They had issue: [1]Albert Edwin Goodrich, Jr, born September 19, 1902; [2]Gilman Granger Goodrich, born November 5, 1905; [3]Lila Woolford Goodrich, born August 19, 1908. The family resides at Crisfield, Md

Samuel Woolford (son of Arthur George Woolford and Anna Crawford Polk), married April 28, 1907, Emma Ashbee. One child, Samuel Woolford, born February 29, 1908 Residence Norfolk, Va.

Imogen Polk Fontaine, married June 12, 1906, George Hammond Myers of Hagerstown, Md One child, George Hammond Myers, Jr, born June 14, 1907 Residence, Princess Anne, Md.

Annie Crawford Fontaine is unmarried

Laura Polk Fontaine, married October 22, 1903, George Barton Fitzgerald, of Princess Anne Issue one child, Geo Barton Jr, born July 5, 1908

Berkley Douglas Fitzgerald, married October 28, 1908, May Agnes Wildes Guy, of Philadelphia, Pa. No issue

Ephraim Polk Fontaine is unmarried.

Wm. Gilman Fontaine, married August 10, 1907, Lucille Jane Mullendore, of Hagerstown, Pa One child, Wm Gilman Fontaine, Jr, born October 10, 1908 Residence, Philadelphia, Pa.

Eliza Polk Dashiell and Olive Dashiell are unmarried.

Frank Harold Covington, married April 6, 1904, Alice Harper Burton One child, Harold Peyton Covington, born January 17, 1905 Residence Baltimore, Md.

Elizabeth Raleigh Mitchell is unmarried

Pauling King (daughter of Alfred King and Sarah Eliza Bell), married Joseph N Short, of Philadelphia No issue

Estelle King is unmarried.

Edith C King, married Dr. Harry Thatcher, of New Jersey. One child, Lawrence Smith Thatcher.

Marion Alice King died in childhood.

None of Mary Wilson Polk Prickett's children are married

Rev Thomas McKean Polk (son of Joseph Littleton Polk, D D Ph. D. and Mary Wilson), married October 24, 1903, Gertrude Edwards, of Fagg's Manor, Pa. Residence Martinsville, Pa., where he is pastor of a church. They have issue. [1]Thomas McKean Polk, Jr, born October 10, 1904, died October 1904, [2]Katharine Edwards Polk, born March 17, 1906; [3]McKean Edwards Polk, born May 30, 1908

Annie Polk (daughter of Joseph Littleton Polk, D D. Ph D), married April 29, 1905, Charles S Cook, of Fagg's Manor. Issue: [1]Mary Wilson Cook, born January 16 1907 [2]Lindley Ewing Cook, born April 1, 1908.

Wm Thomas Gilliss Polk, of Fagg's Manor (son of Joseph Littleton Polk, D D. Ph. D), married September 23, 1903, Anna Pierce Miller of Pennsylvania, born February 14, 1881, daughter of Aaron and Rachael Emma (Kimbel) Miller, of Cochranesville, Pa. Wm T. G. Polk is engaged in farming They have two children [1]Wm Thomas Gilliss Polk, Jr, born July 6, 1904; [2]Arthur Miller Polk, born August 18 1907

CHAPTER XXXVII

WHITTINGTON CONNECTION.

One of the leading families of Maryland with which the Polks became connected by marriage was that of Whittington Col Wm Whittington came from England during the early settlement of the country, locating in Northampton County, Virginia, close to the Maryland line where he resided and became a leading and influential man in Colonial and local affairs He first settled at Cherrystone, moving thence to Indian Town, Worcester County It is said that at his birth he was so small that his nurse put him into a quart measure and closed the lid When grown to manhood, he measured seven feet in height He was a strict Presbyterian The maiden name of his wife is not known His children were [1]William Whittington, Jr, who married Elizabeth Taylor, [2]Esther, who married Isaac Morris; [3]Hannah, who married ——— Huff; [4]Atalanta, who married Stephen White [5]Southey, who married Mary Forsett

Children of Atalanta and Stephen White: [1]Mary, who married ——— Brinkley, [2]Esther, who married A. Sterling, [3]William Whittington White.

Priscilla (Polk) Whittington, wife of William Whittington Jr, lived to a great age and was regarded as most remarkable woman in many ways She was a daughter of James Polk, son of William Polk and Nancy Owens, and reputed the youngest child. Born in 1740, she died in 1834, aged 94 years Several of her husband's kinsmen also intermarried with Polks of other branches, and their kinsmen of Somerset County, Maryland and Sussex County, Delaware During the Revolutionary War, a party of British burned her residence on their approach she mounted a horse and with one small child in front and another behind her, rode twenty miles to the home of her brother William Polk

Southey Whittington, who married Mary Forsett, had issue ¹²Isaac and Stevenson (twins), ³Tabitha, ⁴Priscilla and ⁵Sarah Isaac married Miss E Wishart, Stevenson married Miss Sarah Coulburn, and Sarah married Benjamin Polk, a brother of Priscilla Polk, who married William Whittington, son of Southey.

The children of Sarah Whittington and Benjamin Polk were ¹Joshua, who died December 7, 1839 in Sussex County, Del, aged 78 years, ²James, who was lost at sea, ³Benjamin, Jr., married Miss ——— and left issue Southey and Eliza, ⁴Whittington, married twice, first a widow Chapman, second a Miss ———; ⁵Elenora, untraced. ⁶Southey, untraced, ⁷Isaac, married Rebecca Dashiell, ⁸Nellie, married Wm. H Harper; ⁹Jane, married Dr John Polk, her cousin; ¹⁰Mary, married Stephen Collins, an elder in old Rehoboth Church, the first Presbyterian church in America, no issue; ¹¹Sally, married John Whittington; ¹²Betsy, married Michael Cluff, of Worcester, ¹³⁻¹⁴Rebecca and Norah, untraced; ¹⁵William, who married first the widow Chapman and second a Miss Collins No issue

Isaac Whittington (son of Southey and Mary Forsett) by his wife E Wishart had issue ¹Hannah, married Hanly Handy, of Somerset Co, Md, ²Ann, married Wm Cox, of Maryland, ³Joshua, married Mary Marshall, ⁴Lyttleton, married Sarah Hearne, daughter of Jacob Hearne, of Sussex They had issue ¹William Wishart, married Ann Handy, of Maryland; ²Isaac, married Matilda Pusey, of Kentucky; ³Milcah, married James Smith, of Versailles, Ky, son of Wm Smith and Deborah Hearne, ⁴Jennie married Warren Hearne, of Kentucky; ⁵Betsy, married Col Graham, of Kentucky, ⁶⁷James and Nannie (twins); James married Miss Lillard, of Kentucky; Caroline married Richard Taylor, of Kentucky; ⁸Edward married Cordelia Taylor

The children of Milcah and James Whittington Smith were ¹Amanda Jane Smith, born ———, died August 1, 1838; ²James Whittington Smith, ³C Cordelia Smith.

James Whittington Smith married Viola McCorkle. March 1 1880 Issue ¹Wm Walker, ²Bessie, ³Milcah ⁴David Duke ⁵Cordelia

Besides the foregoing, there are a number of other younger descendants of Sarah Whittington and Benjamin Polk, and Wm Whittington 3d, and Priscilla Polk, but they are untraced. Many of them are in Kentucky and the Western States.

DESCENDANTS OF SUSAN LANKFORD.

(By Henry Fillmore Lankford, Princess Anne.)

Susan (Porter) Lankford was the daughter of John Porter and Mary Jane (or Polly) Porter, and Mary Jane or Polly Porter was the daughter of Priscella (Polk) Whittington and William Whittington. The first husband of Mary Jane (or Polly) the mother of Susan, was William Strawbridge, the second William Davis Allen, and the third John Porter.

Susan Porter married Benjamin Lankford on the 24th of January, 1822. They are both dead. Susan died in 1883, and Benjamin in 1886.

The issue of Susan and Benjamin Lankford are as follows:

(1) Henry Smith Lankford, eldest child, born 30th January, 1823. First wife, Martha Riggin. They had Emma Florence Lankford, born 11th June, 1852, married Charles E Gunby. He is dead. Issue [1]Paul Lewis Gunby born 18th July, 1882, [2]Harry Porter Gunby, born 22nd July, 1884; [3]Carrie Lankford Gunby, born 3rd August, 1887, and [4]Florence Martha Gunby, born 30th September, 1889. Paul Lewis Gunby married Jessie A Wilkins; issue [1]Paul Benjamin Gunby, born 7th April, 1906.

The second wife of Henry Smith Lankford was Mary Dameron Pinckard, of Lancaster County, Virginia. They are both dead. Their issue is as follows: [1]Henry Fillmore Lankford, born 21st April, 1856; married Dec ——, 1908, Alice Catherine Fitzsimmons of Independence, Mo. [2]Clarence Pinckard Lankford, born 8th February, 1864, married Emily Estella Marshall. Issue Priscilla Pinckard Lankford, born 11th January, 1896; Marion Daisy Lankford, born 31st January, 1870; married Benjamin James Barnes. Issue, [1]Mary

Louise Barnes, born 8th February, 1892, ²Marion Frances Barnes, born 21st September, 1896, and ³Benjamin Lankford Barnes, born 11th October, 1902.

(2.) Julia Anne Lankford, second child, born 25th February, 1825, married George Washington Lankford, both dead Their issue ¹James F Lankford, born ———————, died unmarried. ²Susan Lankford, born ———————, married Samuel D Lankford. Their issue. George W Lankford, born ———————, and Samuel D Lankford, born ——————— ³Sallie A Lankford, born ——— ———————, died unmarried

(3) John Louis Lankford, third child, born 14th October, 1826, married Mary A Lankford Their issue ¹Annie Frances Lankford married Charles A. Miller, (she was born 1st March, 1857) Their issue ¹Mollie Jane Miller, born October 3d, 1883, ²Elizabeth Lankford Miller, born December 9th, 1894 ³Roman Davis Lankford, born January 3rd, 1859, died unmarried ⁴Mary Lankford, born February 2nd, 1861 married Robert F. Maddox, and died without issue ⁵Charles Anthony Lankford, born 28th April, 1863; married Nancy Leach issue Mary Priscilla Lankford, born February 2nd, 1902 ⁶Benjamin Franklin Lankford born June 21st, 1865 unmarried ⁷Susan Lewis Lankford, born July 15th, 1867; married William J Hall Their issue. ¹Henry Louis Hall, born January 7th, 1892; ²Mary Elizabeth Hall, born June 23rd, 1897; ³William J Hall, Jr, born November 3rd, 1899, and ⁴Virginia Hall, born September 29th, 1906

(4) Benjamin Franklin Lankford, fourth child, born 25th ———, 1827 His first wife was Amanda E Porter Issue as follows ¹Susan Ella Lankford, born 1st October, 1860, married George W. Lankford, of Marshall, Mo They have no issue. ²William Franklin Lankford, born February 1st, 1862, married Emma A Hargis Issue: Amanda E. Lankford, born November 23rd, 1888 ³Benjamin Louis Lankford, born February 4th, 1864, married Helen Sudler Maddox No issue ⁴Sallie Virginia Lankford, born May 5th 1866; married John M Shields of Petoskey Michigan No issue. ⁵Milton Stewart Lankford, born October 5th, 1873; married Florence C Whitman Issue ¹Milton Stewart Lankford, Jr, born

Sept. 17, 1906, and ²Dorothy Leavitt Lankford, born August 21, 1908.

The second wife of Benjamin Franklin Lankford was Matilda A Sudler, who survived him. No issue by this marriage.

(5) Sarah Anne Lankford, fifth child, was born August 29th, 1831; married Samuel G Miles. Issue Clara Miles born October, 1854, married Thomas S Hodson.

(6) Charles A Lankford, sixth child, born March 17th, 1837, died unmarried.

(7) Mary Martha Lankford, seventh child, born October 5th, 1839, married Robert Henry Miles. Issue. ¹Edward Everett Miles, born November 25th, 1861 His first wife was Susie R Pitts No issue living. His second wife is Lotta Bagwell No issue

(8) Susan Frances Lankford, eighth child, born January 11th, 1842, married Thomas W. Taylor. Issue: ¹Fannie Lankford Taylor, born October 4th, 1873, ²Bessie Porter Taylor, born August 12th, 1876; ³Constance Snead Taylor born June 9th, 1878, ⁴Thomas W Taylor, born April 6th, 1885, died unmarried August 16, 1906.

(9) Cornelia Josephine Lankford, ninth child, born June 14th, 1849, married William T Lankford Issue ¹Robert Eugene Lankford, born February 6th, 1886, ²Mary Suzanne Lankford, born June 10th, 1890

PRISCILLA POLK WHITTINGTON.

Priscilla Polk, third child of James Polk and Mary (Cottman) Polk, was born in 1740, and died in 1834. She married Col William Whittington, of "Chance," Somerset County, Maryland Col Whittington was a brother of Sarah Whittington who married Benjamin Polk, the brother of Priscilla Polk. Priscilla is mentioned in the will of her father, James Polk.

The children of Col William Whittington and Priscilla (Polk) Whittington were: ¹Elizabeth, ²Margaret, ³James, ⁴William, ⁵Ann, ⁶Mary Jane Elizabeth Whittington married Mitchell Russum Margaret Whittington, sometimes called "Peggy," married William Porter and moved to Woodford County, Kentucky. James Whittington married a Miss Lawson. Their children were: [1]John, [2]Harry, [3]Theodore, [4]Aljah, [5]Franklin, [6]Eliza, [7]Jane, [8]Sarah Anne, [9]Cornelia, [10]Mary, [11]Martha. Mary Jane Polk Whittington, sometimes called "Polly," married three times. Her first husband was Dr. William Strawbridge, (son of William Strawbridge, Sr., and Jane Polk), to whom she was married on the 7th of May, 1788. The only issue of this marriage, Jane, was killed in childhood by the kick of a horse. Mary Jane's second husband was William Davis Allen, to whom she was married on the 26th of March, 1793. There were two children by this second marriage: [1]William Allen, whose descendants are living in Wicomico County, Maryland. [2]Elizabeth Allen, sometimes called "Betsey" Allen, who married three times; first, a Jones; second, a Louis; third, a Griffith.

After the death of her second husband, William Davis Allen, the widow, Mary Jane Polk-Whittington-Allen, married John Porter in 1801.

The children of Mary Jane and John Porter, her third husband, were: [1]Jane, [2]Sarah Ann, [3]Susan. Jane Porter married Peter Gillette. Their descendants are living in Dewitt, Carroll County, Missouri.

Sarah Ann Porter married Anthony Brattan. No descendants.

CHAPTER XXXVIII

SKETCH OF JAMES KNOX POLK.

James Knox Polk, eleventh president of the United States, was born in Mecklenburg County, North Carolina, November 2, 1795, and died in Nashville, Tenn. June 15, 1849. He was the eldest of the ten children of Samuel Polk, a son of Capt Ezekiel Polk, one of the leading Revolutionary patriots of North Carolina, and a signer of the celebrated Mecklenburg Declaration of Independence

Samuel Polk was an enterprising and prosperous planter, but yearning for a wider field and better opportunities for his children, he emigrated with his family in 1806, to the valley of Duck River in Tennessee, whither a great number of North Carolians had preceded him His wife, whom he married in 1794, was Jane Knox, a daughter of Col James Knox, after whom her eldest son was named Col Knox, as he was called, was a resident of Iridell County and a Captain in the war of the Revolution

Beside James Knox Polk, Samuel Polk and wife had five sons and four daughters. Of these, Marshall T married and settled in North Carolina, and died there Franklin, John and Samuel W, all died unmarried William H, was appointed in 1845, by President Tyler, Charge d' Affaires to the Two Sicilies, where he was on duty when the Mexican War broke out Eager to serve his country, he at once tendered his resignation and returned to the United States and offered his services to the government, backed by the recommendations of numerous influential persons The President, loth to take advantage of his position to advance officially a near kinsman, demurred to his appointment but later yielded to strong influences, and Wm H Polk was commissioned a Major in the Third Dragoons, a new cavalry regiment, organized for service in the war

The school advantages of James Knox Polk during the first eleven years of his life until his father moved to Tennessee, were small, including only the simpler branches. The same conditions pertained to his new home in Tennessee, but yearning earnestly for knowledge, he applied himself assiduously and made rapid and thorough advancement in his studies. Samuel Polk was followed to Tennessee by many of his kinsmen, a number locating in the fertile region now included as a part of Maury County, and others, including his father, Col. Ezekiel Polk, in Western Tennessee, about LaGrange. In his new home Samuel prospered and he gave to his son, James K. Polk, the best obtainable school advantages.

While conducting the operations of a clearing and cultivating a large plantation Samuel Polk at intervals engaged in surveying. By industry and economy he acquired in time a handsome fortune. He lived to witness the brilliant triumphs of his first born son in his professional career, and to mark his manly bearing as he advanced steadily along the road to greatness and fame. Respected as one of the first pioneers of Maury County, and esteemed highly as a man and citizen, Samuel Polk died in 1827. His wife, Jane (Knox) Polk, a most excellent and pious woman, afterwards married a gentleman named Edens, of Columbia. She was revered and loved by all who knew her.

James Knox Polk's boyhood was nearly all passed on the farm, and here were imbibed those habits of industry and sterling principles which characterized all his after life; principles of self-reliance, industry, integrity and virtue, which adorned his ripened manhood. He assisted his father in the management of the farm, and was his almost constant companion in his surveying excursions. They were frequently absent for weeks together, traversing the forests and canebrakes which then covered the face of the country. On these excursions it was the duty of James to take care of the pack horses and camp equipage and prepare the scanty meals. He also assisted in chaining the tracts surveyed. He was very fond of reading and was of a very reflective turn of mind. Principally for the recreation they afforded, he engaged in the pastimes and sports of boyhood. It was his greatest desire to obtain a liberal education and toward this object he bent all his energies. The profession of law was the goal of his

JAMES K. POLK AND WIFE.

ambition and he read with avidity, the few law books that he could procure

James K. Polk was greatly distinguished for his correctness and punctuality in all things. He had great industry and application, and true native talent that seized upon and analyzed every proposition presented to his thoughtful and analytical mind

During the infancy of the State of Tennessee, as is usual in all new settlements, school facilities were quite limited The father of James K. Polk, though not at the time wealthy, was able to give all his children a good education He contemplated with pride the inclination of his son's mind toward study and kept him pretty constantly at school. Though suffering for years from a painful affliction that required a surgical operation to cure it, he completely mastered the English studies, after which his health began to give way. His father, alarmed by his son's failing health, placed him with a merchant with the view of fitting him for commercial pursuits

This change from his books to the counting room was a severe blow to the ambition of James. He had no taste for his new calling and the duties were irksome to him in the extreme He had an antipathy to the mercantile profession, almost as great as that of John Randolph, who could not endure "a man with a quill behind his ear." After a few weeks with the merchants, by much entreaty and persuasion, James induced his father to allow him to return home, and in July, 1813, then eighteen years of age, he was placed under the tuition of Rev Dr. Henderson. Later he attended the Murfreesboro Acadamy, then conducted by Samuel P Black, a celebrated classical teacher of Middle Tennessee. No obstacle now stood in the way of James and under the promptings of his earnest desires he made rapid progress in his studies In two and a half years he had prepared himself for an advanced class in college, and in the autumn of 1815, being then in his twentieth year, he matriculated in the University of North Carolina, at Chapel Hill, at the beginning of the sophomore year.

This noted University, at which so many of the eminent statesmen and divines of the South have received their education, was then under charge of Rev Dr. Joseph Caldwell, justly styled the father of the University." Col. William Polk, of Raleigh, a first cousin of the father of James K. Polk, was an influential and active member of the board of trustees, and had been from the beginning of the institution.

While at the University James redoubled his energies and quickly and easily went to the head of his classes. It is said of him that he never missed a recitation or a religious service in chapel. He was thorough in everything he undertook. Of the exact sciences he was very fond, and also an excellent linguist. At all the semi-annual examinations he bore off first honors.

In June, 1818, James K. Polk graduated with the highest distinction, which was assigned to him alone, as the best scholar in both the mathematics and classics, and delivered the Latin Salutatory Oration. At the Annual Commencement of the University in 1847, the honorary degree of Doctor of Laws was conferred on Mr. Polk, together with John Y. Mason, subsequently Secretary of the Navy and later distinguished as a Confederate statesman.

In 1819 Mr. Polk entered the law offices of Hon. Felix Grundy, of Nashville, who was at that time head of the Tennessee Bar. In 1820 he passed the regular examination and was admitted to the bar. He at once returned to Maury County, established an office at Columbia, and a good practice soon came to him. His first public service was that of Chief Clerk to the Tennessee House of Representatives. In 1823, by a heavy majority, he was elected to the Legislature, where he remained for two years. One of his most conspicuous acts was a bill to prevent duelling at that time an all too common practice in the South and West.

In January, 1824, he was married to a charming young woman, Miss Sarah Childress, daughter of a wealthy merchant of Rutherford County. To the charms of a fine person she united intellectual accomplishments of a high order, and was well fitted to adorn any station. In 1825 Mr Polk made the race for Congress, in the Duck River district, and was elected by a substantial majority. He was repeatedly returned for fourteen years. A warm personal regard existed between him and General Andrew Jackson, and he was often a welcome guest at the Hermitage.

JACKSON AND POLK FAMILIES.

The Jackson and Polk families had been intimate for years, in Mecklenburg County, N. C. During the Revolution, Andrew Jackson's father being dead, he and his two brothers joined the army. The eldest was killed at the battle of Stono, and the second died from a wound received, which was aggravated by British neglect in the hospital. During the absence of her sons in the army, Mrs. Jackson was often hard pressed for the necessaries of life, and was relieved in numerous instances by Col. Thomas Polk, who owned several mills in that section. This kindness to his mother Andrew Jackson never forgot, and hence he entertained an abiding friendship for the Polk family. In a speech in 1849, telling how he joined the army, he said that he was inspired to the act by seeing Col. Wm. Polk (son of Col. Thomas), wounded, bleeding and covered with dust, urging his men forward at the battle of Guilford C. H.

While serving his district and State in Congress, James K. Polk continued to be distinguished for his punctuality and promptness. His speeches were always to the point, clear and forcible. He made his debut as a speaker in advocating an amendment to the Constitution giving the choice of President and Vice-President directly to the vote of the people. Among the recommendations of Mr. Adams which he strongly opposed, were the Panama Mission, an extensive system of internal improvements, and a high protective tariff. His adherance to the principles of the Democratic creed was steadfast and unyielding. He stood firmly for General Jackson previous to and during his entire administration, and was one of the earliest opponents of the recharter of the United States Bank.

On the assembling of the Twenty-fourth Congress, in December, 1835, James K. Polk was selected as Speaker and was elected by a large majority. He continued in the Chair of the House for five sessions.

In adjourning the House on March 4, 1839, and terminating his connection forever with that body, Mr Polk delivered a farewell address of some length, characterized by deep feeling, and which made a profound impression

On his return to Tennessee he was urged to make the race for Governor and did so. The canvass was a warm one and as a stump speaker Mr Polk was invincible. He was elected over Governor Cannon by upward of twenty-five thousand majority, and on October 14th, took the oath of office at Nashville and entered upon his executive duties. In August, 1841, he was a candidate for re-election, but the political storm which swept the country and prostrated the Democratic party in 1840 throughout the Union, made his success impossible In 1843 he was again a candidate but was beaten by nearly four thousand majority

The great political issue of the Presidential campaign of 1844 was the annexation of Texas That territory had just been wrested from Mexico by General Sam Houston, a son of Tennessee, with his brave following of Texas patriots. Being organized into an independent republic, Texas asked admission into the Federal Union The Northern States strongly opposed such admission, fearing as a result the extension of slavery The Southern States favored admission, and the contest was hotly waged over an issue that would not down, and which a few years later precipitated the great Civil War.

Replying to a committee of citizens of Cincinnati, who asked his views on the subject, Mr. Polk made such a strong impression upon the people that he at once became a popular favorite for the highest office in the gift of the people

NOMINATED AND ELECTED PRESIDENT.

Mr. Polk's views, as expressed in his reply to the Cincinnati Committee, made a great impression on the National Democratic Convention, which met at Baltimore on May 24, 1844. After a dead lock over other candidates named, Mr Polk was brought forward on the eighth ballot as a candidate for the Presidency, and harmony at once followed confusion On the following ballot, the ninth, he received nearly all the

POLK PLACE.

THE NEW YORK
PUBLIC LIBRARY

ASTOR, LENOX AND
TILDEN FOUNDATIONS.

votes of the delegates and the nomination was next made unanimous. A strong factor in the result, it is said, was the advocacy of Mr. Polk's selection, by General Jackson. George M. Dallas was then chosen as the party's candidate for Vice President, and "Polk and Dallas" became the Democratic war cry.

The opposition party, the Whigs, nominated Henry Clay, of Kentucky, for President, and Theodore Frelinghuysen, of New Jersey, for Vice President. The canvass was a spirited one, and mass meetings and processions filled the land with political exuberance and enthusiasm. Campaign songs of Whigs and Democrats were heard on every hand.

As the time for Mr. Polk's inauguration approached he prepared for his journey to the National Capital, accompanied by Mrs. Polk, his adopted son, and Col. J. Knox Walker, his nephew and private secretary. His progress was everywhere greeted with the most unbounded enthusiasm. At Louisville he was escorted to his boat by military companies and a vast throng of citizens. At Cincinnati a like demonstration awaited him, and after a splendid banquet the party took carriages for the balance of the trip, over the National Road. Three other carriages beside that of Mr. Polk composed the procession. The second contained the Kentucky delegation; the third that of Louisiana; and the fourth Tennessee gentlemen. At Wheeling there was also a great demonstration for "Young Hickory," as his admirers called him. The same enthusiasm attended him during the rest of the route.

MR. POLK'S INAUGURATION.

On March 4, 1845, James K. Polk was duly inaugurated as President of the United States. He delivered an appropriate and excellent address on the occasion, in which he set forth his views on questions at issue, and enunciated the principles that would guide him in the discharge of his duties. He chose his cabinet from among the most distinguished men of his party. The paramount question at that time was that of our title to Oregon, which the Baltimore National Democratic Convention had declared to be "clear and unquestionable." By a firm course on the part of the President, this bone of contention with Great Britain was amicably settled. It is estimated that thirty thousand people witnessed Mr Polk's inauguration.

The President and Mrs Polk received visitors at the White House the day following the inauguration. Mrs. Polk's ease, grace and simple dignity won the admiration of all. Mrs. Polk was assisted in her social duties by Mrs Walker, wife of her husband's private secretary, a notably beautiful woman. On one occasion Mr. Clay, being at a White House reception, remarked to Mrs Polk that, "although some had expressed dissatisfaction with the administration of her husband, not one seemed to have found fault with hers."

Immediately after the treaty of annexation of Texas was concluded with the United States, Mexico officially pronounced the treaty to be "a declaration of war between the two nations," and Santa Anna, President of Mexico, in June, 1844, declared it to be the firm determination of Mexico to re-conquor Texas. He called for an army of 30,000 men and four millions of dollars for that purpose. The Mexican forces were hurried into the field and pushed to the Northern frontier.

On the part of the United States, the military forces under General Zachary Taylor advanced to the Rio Grande, to prevent invasion by Mexican troops. Congress a short time afterwards declared war against Mexico and called for fifty thousand volunteers. These volunteers were furnished principally by Kentucky, Tennessee, Mississippi, Arkansas, Missouri, Illinois, Indiana and Ohio. The brave riflemen of the West were hurried to Mexico and at the ensuing battles of Palo Alto, Resaca de la Palma, Monterey, Vera Cruz, Chapultepec and City of Mexico, they carried the Stars and Stripes to victory, giving to the United States not only Texas but also New Mexico and Upper and Lower California. As has been truthfully said:

"When Americans today look upon the great and wealthy territory secured thereby, it is not probable that any one will fail to thank Mr Polk for his firm position in bringing on the cc... ... ... California can never be ad... ... ..."

Mr. Polk's Cabinet consisted of James Buchanan, of Penn., Secretary of State; Robert J. Walker, of Miss., Secretary of the Treasury, William L. Marcy, of New York, Secretary of War; George Bancroft, of Mass., Secretary of the Navy till September 9, 1846, afterward John Y. Mason, of Va., Cave Johnson, of Tenn., Postmaster General; Nathan Clifford, of Maine, and Isaac Toucey, of Conn., successively Attorneys General.

CHIEF ADMINISTRATION MEASURES.

The chief measures which distinguished the administration of James K. Polk, besides those already enumerated, were the adoption of the low tariff of 1846, replacing the protective one of 1842, the establishment of the independent treasury system, by which the revenues of the government are collected in specie without the aid of banks; the creation of the Department of the Interior, and the admission of Wisconsin as a state of the Union.

As one of his biographers, Jenkins, said of him:

"Mr. Polk could not have said, with Augustus Caesar, that he found the capital of the republic built of brick, and left it constructed of marble; but he might have claimed that he found her territories bounded on the south by the Sabine and the 42d parallel, and her authority west of the Rocky Mountains existing only in name; and when he transferred the government to other hands, New Mexico and California were annexed to her domain, and her flag floated in token of sovereignty on the banks of the Rio Grande, on the shores of the Straits of Fuca, and in the bay of San Francisco."

The acquisition of this territory served to fill out and complete the vast and comprehensive plan of national empire inaugurated by Thomas Jefferson and the American people in the purchase of Louisiana Territory from France in 1806. And the wisdom of both these transactions is attested by the magnificent development in those regions since their acquisition, adding wealth and strength to our country by the discovery of vast stores of gold and silver, and the settlement of millions of enterprising citizens.

The adjournment of Congress at the close of Mr. Polk's administration, took place March 3, 1849. The 4th being Sunday, the inauguration of his successor, Gen'l Zachariah Taylor, took place on Monday the 5th. On the same day Mr and Mrs Polk took leave of their friends and started to their home in Tennessee. All along the route through Richmond, Wilmington, Charleston, Savannah, New Orleans, and every place they passed, a grand ovation and welcome was awaiting him from vast crowds of admiring citizens. Reaching his beautiful home in Nashville which he had but a short time before purchased, he retired to the comforts and pleasures of his home, and devoted his time to its improvement.

DEATH OF JAMES K. POLK

Some time before his return to Tennessee, Mr Polk purchased the mansion and grounds formerly owned by his friend and preceptor, Hon Felix Grundy, in the city of Nashville. Here, in this elegant Colonial home, surrounded by every comfort, he settled down to spend the rest of his life in ease and quietude, in the sweet companionship of his devoted wife, his books, and of his devoted friends.

The year of 1849 was made memorable by a second visit to the United States of that dread disease, Asiatic cholera, and many deaths occurred from it in the Mississippi Valley. On his way up the Mississippi River from New Orleans, in the month of March, Mr Polk had suffered what was considered a moderate attack of the disease, which was warded off by the physicians who attended him. He was very much enervated but was thought to have entirely recovered. But on his arrival at Nashville he became more enfeebled, though giving his constant attention to the improvement of his home, in which work he was often assisted by Mrs. Polk. These constant labors seem to have brought on again his old affliction of dysentery and he was prostrated on his bed. For several days no apprehension was felt by his friends and kinsmen. Dr Hay, his brother-in-law and family physician for twenty years, came from Columbia to attend him, aided by other skillful medical men. But all that medical skill could do proved futile and Mr Polk continued to sink day by day

JAS. K. POLK MONUMENT,
Raleigh, N. C.

and he died without a struggle on June 15, 1849 About a half hour before his death his venerable mother entered his chamber and kneeling by his bedside offered up a beautiful prayer to the "King of Kings and Lord of Lords," committing the soul of her son to his holy keeping. Mr Polk's death occurred in the fifty-fourth year of his age

The funeral exercises took place on the following day and his body was laid to rest in a grave in one corner of the residence yard. Over the grave was erected an imposing structure of marble that long stood and was only removed when the remains were transferred to the State House yard to give place for a large flat building The funeral was attended by nearly the entire population of Nashville and adjacent country Upon the coffin plate the inscription consisted simply of his name and the dates of his birth and decease Thus passed from the stage of human action one who was an honor to his family, not only because of his intrinsic merits as a man, but also by reason of the fact that he had attained and filled with advantage to his fellow citizens the highest office in the gift of his country.

CHAPTER XXXIX.

NUMBERED RECORD OF POLKS.

The following numbered record of Polk families was prepared and is constantly being added to by Col Geo W. Polk, of San Antonio, Texas It includes principally the descendants of Col Thos Polk, of Mecklenburg County, N C.

RECORD No 1—Col William Polk, son of Col Thomas Polk and Susan Spratt Polk, b July 9, 1758, in Mecklenburg County, N. C. Occupation or profession, Officer of the Revolutionary Army, Bank President, Capitalist. Col Polk married 1st Grizelda Gilchrist, Oct. 15, 1789. He married 2nd, Sarah Hawkins Jan 1st, 1801.

Issue by his 1st marriage: [1]Thomas G ; [2]Dr. William Julius; 2nd marriage: [3]Lucius Junius, [4]Lucinda Davis, b Jan 12, 1804, d May 9, 1805; [5]Leonidas, [6]Mary Brown, [7]Alex Hamilton, b Sept. 19, 1810, d Sept 8, 1830; [8]John Hawkins, b Aug 15, 1812, d Oct 28 1813, [9]Rufus King, [10]George Washington, [11]Philemon Hawkins, b Mar 26, 1820, d Aug 27, 1820; [12]Susan Spratt; [13]Andrew Jackson; [14]Sarah Hawkins, b Mar 16, 1826, d Sept 11, 1826; [15]Charles Junius, b Oct 8, 1828, d Oct 16, 1831

Col Wm Polk d July 14, 1834, and was buried at Raleigh, N. C. His first wife d Oct 22, 1799; his second wife d Dec. 10, 1843

Grizelda Gilchrist, first wife of William Polk, was the daughter of Thomas and Martha Gilchrist, whose maiden name was Jones Grizelda was b the 24th day of October 1768, in the town of Suffolk, Va

Sarah Hawkins, second wife of William Polk, was the daughter of Philemon and Lucy Hawkins, whose maiden name was Davis Sarah was b in Warren County, N. C, on the 6th day of March, 1784

RECORD No. 2 - Thos G Polk, son of Wm Polk and Grizelda Gilchrist, b Feb 22, 1791 at Raleigh, N C., was a

COL. ANDREW J. POLK AND WIFE.

lawyer by profession. He was married Oct 30, 1812 to Mary Eloise Trotter.

Children ¹Jane; ²Mary; ³William; ⁴Emily, d. Nov. 3, 1907, ⁵Thomas, (died young), ⁶Richard; ⁷Gilbert.

Gen'l Thos. G. Polk d. Mar 16, 1869 at Holly Springs, Miss His wife d May 25, 1870

Gen Thomas G Polk was a graduate of "Yale" Also of the celebrated Law School at Litchfield, Conn A courtier in manner and person, full of the chivalry of his race Married a noble woman, celebrated for her learning and piety

RECORD No 17—Jane Polk, daughter of Gen'l Thos. G Polk and Mary Trotter Polk, married Dr Bouchelle

RECORD No. 18—Mary A Polk, daughter of Thos G Polk and Mary Trotter Polk, married George Davis. Issue. ¹Junius; ²Mary (died unmarried); ³Emily; ⁴Louis; ⁵Isabella; ⁶Margaret

RECORD No. 24—Junius Davis, son of George Davis and Mary Polk Davis, profession lawyer, was twice married First to Mary Orme Walker, second to Mary Cowan Issue· ¹Mary; ²Thomas; ³Junius; ⁴George; ⁵Platt; ⁶Louis; ⁷Robert; ⁸Eliza

RECORD No 26—Emily Davis, daughter of George Davis and Mary Polk Davis, was married to Jno Crowe Issue ¹George; ²Fairfax; ³William; ⁴Emmett

RECORD No. 27—Louis Davis, son of George Davis and Mary Polk Davis, untraced

RECORD No. 28—Isabella Davis, daughter of George Davis and Mary Polk Davis, was married to D. Shotter Issue: Isabella

RECORD No 29—Margaret Davis, daughter of George Davis and Mary Polk Davis, married Mr ————, and had issue ¹Isabella; ²Cynthia; ³Meta

RECORD No 19—William Polk, son of Thos G Polk and Mary Eloise Trotter, was b Nov. 17 1821, d - 1909 Sugar planter, Ashton Plantation near Alexandria, La Married Jan. 20, 1853 to Rebecca Jardine Long by whom he had issue ¹Alice, b March 11, 1858, ²William, b Feb 6, 1862, ³Mary Eloise, b Sept 4, 1864

William Polk d Jan 24, 1898 at New Orleans and was buried at Alexandria, La His wife died in 1909

William Polk resided from early manhood to his death in Louisiana He was a man greatly esteemed and beloved and an authority on cane culture He married into the distinguished Lamar family, of Georgia, whose name like the Polk name, is of national fame

RECORD No. 46—Alice Polk, daughter of William Polk and Rebecca Lamar Polk, b March 11, 1858 at Holly Springs, Miss, married Aug 4, 1890 at Asheville, N C, to Wm F Flower Issue. ¹Wm Polk Flower, Jr, b May 26, 1891

This oldest child of William Polk and Rebecca E Lamar, Alice Polk a beautiful and accomplished woman, was educated in Stanton, Va, at Dr Phillips' celebrated Church School She lived for a number of years at Flenerton Plantation, La, later in New Orleans, La.

RECORD No. 47—Wm Polk, Jr., son of Wm. Polk and Rebecca Lamar Polk, b Feb 6, 1862, at Ashton Plantation, Rapides Parish, La Residence Alexandria, La., is a prominent sugar planter and was married Aug 8, 1893 to Miss Ella Bailho Hayes Issue ¹Lamar, b at Rosalie Plantation La, May 4, 1894; ²Ella b in Alexandria, La, on June 5, 1904

The only son of William Polk and Rebecca E Lamar, Wm Polk, Jr, was educated at the University of Louisiana, Baton Rouge He was a man of influence and was several times elected to the Legislature, where he served with ability He married a beautiful woman, of an aristocratic French family

RECORD No. 48—Mary Eloise Polk, daughter of Wm Polk and Rebecca Lamar Polk, b Sept 4, 1864 in Texas, was married Jan 20, 1885 to David S Ferris Issue: ¹Livingston Polk, b Aug 30, 1886, West Chester County, New York, the ancestral home of the Ferris family

This second daughter of William Polk and Rebecca E Lama   u   b exquisite blonde type, was educated at Dr Bo I   .   Institute in Columbia, Tenn She

COL. WM. POLK AND WIFE.
Alexandria, La.

is noted for a sweet benevolence of character and rare social graces.

RECORD No. 3—Dr Wm Julius Polk, son of Wm Polk and Grizelda Gilchrist, b March 21 1793, at Raleigh, N C, residence in Maury County, Tenn He was a wealthy planter He was married June 1, 1818 to Mary Rebecca Long. Issue ¹Grizelda Gilchrist; ²Allen J; ³Thomas G; ⁴Mary Jones, ⁵Lucius Eugene; ⁶Cadwalader Jones, ⁷Rufus J. Dr. Wm. Julius Polk d at his home Buena Vista, Maury County, Tenn, June, 1860 Mary Rebecca Long was b in 1797, at Mt Gallant, N C, the home of her grandfather, Gen'l Allen Jones, from whom she inherited it She d in 1886 at Columbia, Tenn

RECORD No 54—Grizelda Gilchrist Polk, daughter of Wm J. Polk and Mary Long Polk, b March 8 1819 at Mt Gallant, Northampton County, N C, was married June 4 1844 to Russell Houston, of Louisville Issue ¹Mary Russell, ²Louise Ross, d Aug 10, 1850; ³Allen Polk ⁴Lucia Eugene; ⁵Elise She d April 27, 1901 and was buried in Cave Hill Cemetery, Louisville, Ky. Her husband Russell Houston d Oct. 1, 1895 For thirty years Mr. Houston was chief attorney for the L & N. R R.

RECORD No. 61—Mary Russell Houston, daughter of Russell Houston and Grizelda Polk Houston, b March 27 1845, was married April 21, 1874 to Lytle Buchanan, of Louisville No issue She d May 10, 1907

RECORD No. 62—Allen P Houston, son of Russell Houston and Grizelda Polk Houston b ———, married Mattie Belle Shreve, of Louisville, Ky. Issue ¹Russell, ²Belle L, ³Allen P

RECORD No. 63—Lucia Polk Houston, daughter of Russell Houston and Grizelda Polk Houston, married George H Hull. Issue· ¹Grizelda H.; ²George H, ³Lytle B.; ⁴Russell H; ⁵Lucia H Residence, Tuxedo, N Y

RECORD No 64—Elise Houston, daughter of Russell Houston and Grizelda Polk Houston married 1st Joseph L

Ferrell, 2nd Theodore Presser. Issue. By first, ¹Grizelda H ; ²Mary Russell Residence, Philadelphia

RECORD No. 65—Russell Houston, son of Allen P Houston and Mattie Shreve Houston, was born at Louisville, Ky Residence. Chicago He married Dec. 14, 1898 to Flora P. Harris. Issue. ¹Mattie Belle Houston, ²Russell Houston, Jr , ³John Harris Houston

RECORD No 66—Belle S. Houston, daughter of Allen P Houston and Mattie Shreve Houston was born at Louisville, Ky. She married Ralph Goher Hubbart. Issue. Mattie Belle Shreve.

RECORD No 68—Grizelda Hull, daughter of George H. Hull and Lucia Houston Hull was married May 28, 1905 to Capt Richmond Pearson Hobson of Merrimac fame Issue: ¹Lytle, ²George, ³Russell, ⁴Lucia

RECORD No. 55—Major Allen Jones Polk son of Wm J Polk and Mary Long Polk, was b March 5, 1824, at Farmville, N C., and died at Helena, Ark. He was a leading planter. Major Polk was twice married, first to Mary Clendenin Issue ¹Wm (d young), ²Mary His second wife was Anna Lee Clark Fitzhugh, whom he married June 16, 1859 By the latter he had issue ¹Allen Jones, b March 22, 1860, ²Clark Fitzhugh, b May 10, 1861; ³Susan Huntington, b. Jan. 1, 1864, ⁴Anna Lee, b Nov 28, 1866, ⁵Grizelda Houston, b Dec 8, 1868; ⁶Robin Ap Allen, b June 8, 1879

Maj. Allen J Polk died March 17, 1897 Anna Fitzhugh Polk d Dec 3, 1902 Allen J Polk, Jr. d Feb 13, 1875 Clark Fitzhugh d May 6, 1885

RECORD No. 76—Mary Polk, daughter of Allen J Polk and Mary Clendennin, b Oct 18, 1852 at Columbia, Tenn married Dec 18, 1877 to Frank B Hemphill Issue ¹Mary Polk, ²Franklin b Aug 15, 1890, ³Allen Polk, b Oct 26, 1893

RECORD No 79—Susan H. Polk, daughter of Allen J Polk and Anna Clark Fitzhugh, b Jan 1, 1864 at Terre Haute, Ind , married Jan 14, 1883 to T. W. Kessee. Issue: ¹Zelda

Polk, b Jan 31, 1889; ²Thos. Woolfin, b July 13, 1891, ³Allen Polk, b Oct 1, 1896 Residence Helena, Ark

RECORD No 80—Anna Lee Polk, daughter of Allen J. Polk and Anna Clark Fitzhugh, b Nov 28, 1866 at Louisville, Ky, was married Feb. 17, 1887 to Sam'l A Pepper. Issue ¹Allen Polk, b Dec 5, 1888, ²Zelda Fontaine b. March 27, 1889, ³Anna Fitzhugh, b Feb 7, 1895, ⁴Samuel Alexander, b Sept 28, 1897 Residence, Memphis

RECORD No. 81—Grizelda Houston Polk, daughter of Allen J Polk and Anna Clark Fitzhugh, b Nov 8, 1868, at Louisville, Ky., married Nov. 12, 1890 to D T Hargraves Issue ¹David Thompson, b July 3, 1900; ²Grizelda Polk, b May 29, 1904, ³Anna Lee, b Oct 27, 1907

RECORD No. 82—Robin Ap Allen Polk, son of Allen J Polk and Anna Clark Fitzhugh b June 8, 1879 at Helena, Ark., by profession a Civil Engineer. All single

RECORD No. 56—Dr Thos. G. Polk, son of Wm J Polk and Mary Long Polk, was b Dec 5, 1825, in Salisbury, N C He was married in 1851 to Lavinia C Wood Issue ¹Mary, ²Carrie; ³Grizelda, ⁴Wm J

Dr. Polk died in 1877, and was buried at St Johns Church, Maury County, Tenn His wife died in 1887 (See Chapter 28 for sketch)

RECORD No. 93—Mary Polk, daughter of Thos G Polk and Lavinia Wood Polk, b March 12, 1852 in St Marys Parish, La She was married April 10, 1872 to W W. Littlejohn Issue: ¹Thomas; ²Margaret, ³Wm Whitson, b. March 30, '83, d June, 7, '84; ⁴Lavinia Polk Her husband died Feb 8, 1907, buried at Decatur, Ala

RECORD No 97—Thomas Littlejohn son of W W Littlejohn and Mary Polk Littlejohn, b March 22, 1873 at Memphis, Tenn Wife's name unknown Issue: ¹Margaret, b April 13, '97

RECORD No 98—Margaret Littlejohn, daughter of W W. Littlejohn and Mary Polk Littlejohn b April 14, 1875 at Memphis, Tenn She married Sept 8, 1896 to W Si Spright She d May 29, 1902 at Decatur, Ala

RECORD No. 99—Lavinia Littlejohn, daughter of W W Littlejohn and Mary Polk Littlejohn, was born at Decatur, Ala., ————.

RECORD No. 94—Caroline Polk, daughter of Thos G Polk and Lavinia Wood Polk, b Sept 7, 1853, at Milliken's Bend, La Married May 6, 1873 to H S Horner. Issue ¹John Sidney, ²Mabel, b Aug 11, 1876, d Sept 3, 1877, ³Mimi Polk.

RECORD No. 101—John Sidney Horner, son of H S Hornor and Caroline Polk Hornor, b. Dec. 14, 1873, at Helena, Ark, is a banker He was married Jan. 3, 1900, to Frances May Moore Issue ¹Robert Moore, ²Carolyn Polk

RECORD No. 102—Mimi Polk Horner, daughter of H S Hornor and Caroline Polk Hornor, was b. at Helena, Ark She married Dec 17, 1900, to Wm B Pillow Mr Pillow died May 23, 1904, at Helena

RECORD No. 95—Grizelda Polk, daughter of Thos. G Polk and Lavinia Wood Polk, b Dec. 8, 1855, near Greenville Miss, residence near Burton, Ala, married July 5, 1877, to Joseph Sterling Issue Mary Ruffin Grizelda d Oct 25, 1906, at Helena, Ark.

RECORD No. 96—Wm. J. Polk, son of Thos. G Polk and Lavinia Wood Polk, b June 14, 1862, was married Jan 2, 1893, to Enola Greenleaf Issue ¹Magdalen Tasker Wm J Polk, d April 12, 1902, at Decatur, Ala

RECORD No. 57—Mary Jones Polk, daughter of Dr. Wm J Polk and Mary Long Polk, b. Nov 28, 1831, at Salisbury N C She married Jos Gerald Branch, of Florida. Residence, St Louis, Mo Issue ¹Mary Polk; ²Lawrence, ³Lucia Eugenia, ⁴Joseph Gerald

RECORD No. 107—Mary Polk Branch, daughter of Jos Gerald Branch and Mary Polk Branch, was born at Buena Vista, Maury County, Tenn Residence, St Louis, Mo Married Ju.. 16, 1... to Dr Charles Winn w.. d. 1893 at Nashville

RECORD No. 108—Laurence Branch, son of Jos Gerald Branch and Mary Polk Branch, b. at Buena Vista, Maury County, Tenn. Residence, St Louis, Mo Occupation, wholesale merchant. He is unmarried

RECORD No. 109—Lucia Eugenia Cadwallader Polk Branch, daughter of Jos Gerald Branch and Mary Polk Branch, was born at Columbia, Tenn. Residence, St Louis, Mo She was married Dec. 11, 1888 to J William Howard Issue ¹Gerald Branch, b in Columbia, Tenn, Dec 31, 1889, ²Lawrence Branch, b in St. Louis Mo, Aug 20, 1900

RECORD No 110—Joseph Gerald Branch, son of Jos Gerald Branch and Mary Polk Branch, was b. at Columbia, Tenn Residence, Chicago, Ill Profession, Mechanical and Electrical Engineer He is unmarried.

RECORD No 58—Gen'l Lucius Eugenia Polk, son of Dr Wm. J Polk and Mary Long Polk, b. July 10 1833, at Salisbury, N C Residence, Maury County, Tenn He was a planter, and was married Aug 19 1863 to Sallie Moore Polk Issue ¹Rufus K (M C of Pa), ²Mary Rebecca, ³Lucius E; ⁴Wm Julius; ⁵James Knox Gen l Lucius E Polk d Dec 1, 1892 and was buried at St Johns Church, Maury County, Tenn

RECORD No. 113—Rufus K. Polk, son of Gen'l Lucius E Polk and Sally Moore Polk, b Aug 23, 1866, in Maury County, Tenn. Profession, Mining Engineer and Metallurgist (M C of Pa See Congr memorial addresses), at his death was a M. C from the 17th Pa District He was married Oct 27 1892 to Isabella Grier. Issue ¹Emma Grier, b Nov 12, 1893, ²Porter Grier, b Feb 24, 1895, ³Rufus King, b Sept 2, 1896, ⁴Isabel Grier, b. Sept 22, 1897; ⁵Sarah Moore and Mary Rebecca, b May 15, 1900 Rufus K Polk d. March 5, 1902 and was buried at Danville Pa

RECORD No. 114—Mary Rebecca Polk, daughter of Lucius E Polk and Sally Moore Polk, b. May 20, 1868, at West Brook, Maury County, Tenn She was married Feb 4, 1900 to Scott P. Harlan Issue ¹Scott Polk, b Dec 29, 1891, ²Benjamin Joseph, b. Aug 9, 1892, ³Lucius Polk, b Jun 2 24 1895, ⁴Katherine Scott b Jan 11 1898

RECORD No. 115—Lucius E Polk, Jr, son of Gen'l Lucius E Polk and Sallie Moore Polk, b March 23, 1870, at West Brook, Maury County, Tenn He is a Civil Engineer Also served as First Lieut 4th Regt. Tenn Vol Inft and Captain 43d Regt U. S. V. I. during Spanish-American War He was married Aug 30, 1898 to Blanche Clements Issue. Lucius Eugene, b. Feb 14, 1900, at Knoxville, Tenn Lucius d May 18, 1904, and was buried at St Johns Church, Maury County, Tenn

RECORD No. 116—Wm J Polk, son of Lucius E Polk and Sally Moore Polk, born June 13, 1875, at West Brook, Maury County, Tenn He is a planter and lives in Maury County. He was married June 21, 1899 to Willie May Glass Issue [1]Mary Rebecca, b July 16, 1901; [2]Sarah Glass, b July 1, 1904

In June, 1895 Wm J Polk graduated from Battle Ground Academy, Franklin, Tenn Entered LaFayette College, Pa, in September 1895 In September 1896 entered Medical Department Vanderbilt University of Nashville, Tenn. Joined Medical Department of First Tenn Reg Vol May 1, 1898. Served until disbanded in San Francisco, Cal Took special hospital work in Tulane Hospital, New Orleans, La, from January 1899 until following May, 1899

RECORD No. 117—James Knox Polk, son of Lucius E. Polk and Sally Moore Polk, b Jan 14 1882, at West Brook, Maury County, Tenn, d. Feb 13, 1912, at Paris, Tex. Buried at St John's Church Maury County, Tenn Profession, that of Journalist He was married March 10, 1907 to Lottie Schwartz

RECORD No. 59—Col Cadwallader Polk, son of Dr. Wm J and Mary Long Polk, b Oct 16, 1837, at Columbia, Tenn. Residence Helena, Ark He is a planter, and was married March 29, 1864 to Caroline Lowry Issue. [1]Wm J, [2]Annie T; [3]Rufus Walter; [4]Cadwallader Long, [5]Nina (Cornelia) Lowry, [6]Edwin Moore, [7]Cleora Lawrence, b Aug 28, 1866, d July 15, 1867

RECORD No. 130 Wm J Polk, son of Cadwallader Polk and Caroline Lowry Polk b Jan. 15, 1865 at Camden,

COL. CADWALLADER POLK,
of Arkansas, son of Dr. Wm. J. Polk.

THE NEW YORK
PUBLIC LIBRARY

ASTOR LENOX AND
TILDEN FOUNDATIONS

Ark Commission Merchant Married Lulu Donnell. Issue. ¹George Donnell, ²Carry May, ³Ellis Riven, b Aug. 1, 1898, d June 6, 1900

RECORD No 136—George D. Polk, son of Wm. J Polk and Lulu Donnell, b. Jan 27, 1893, at Helena, Ark

RECORD No. 137—Carry May Polk, daughter of Wm J Polk and Lulu Donnell Polk, b. Nov. 19, 1899, at Helena, Ark Married Nov 19, 1890 to Christopher Agee Issue: ¹Watkins

RECORD No. 131—Annie T. Polk, daughter of Cadwallader Polk and Caroline Lowry Polk, b Dec 8, 1867, at Helena Ark

RECORD No. 132—Rufus Walter Polk, son of Cadwallader Polk and Caroline Lowry Polk, b. Jan 27, 1869, at Helena, Ark Residence, Little Rock, Ark, real estate agent Married in 1898 to Sue Louise Powell. Issue· ¹Edward Winfield; ²Rufus Walter; ³Caroline

RECORD No. 133—Cadwallader Long Polk, son of Cadwallader Polk and Caroline Lowry Polk, b May 12, 1870, at Helena, Ark., Merchant. Married in 1897 to Lucille Quarles Issue· ¹Greenfield, b April 12, 1898, d. Dec 23, 1902; ²Cadwallader; ³Lucille, b June 21, 1906, d June 1907

RECORD No. 134—Cornelia Lowry Polk, daughter of Cadwallader Polk and Caroline Lowry Polk, b. March 19, 1874, at Helena, Ark Married in 1903 to Wm Coolridge Issue· ¹William; ²Elizabeth, ³Annie Agee

RECORD No. 135—Edwin Moore Polk, son of Cadwallader Polk and Caroline Lowry Polk, b March 31, 1880, at Helena, Ark. Commission Merchant, unmarried

RECORD No. 60—Rufus J Polk, son of Dr Wm J Polk and Mary Long Polk, b July 30, 1843, in Maury County, Tenn. Residence, Little Rock, Ark Married Dec 2, 1867 to Cynthia Martin Issue: ¹Lucius Eugene, b. Nov 20, 1868; ²Rufus Junius, b. April 4, 1873; ³Wm Julius, b. March 12, 1874, ⁴Charles Martin b June 28, 1875 (See Chapter 28 for sketch.)

RECORD No 151—Charles M Polk, son of Rufus J. Polk and Cynthia Martin, b June 28, 1878, at Helena, Ark Residence, St Louis, Mo Profession, lawyer Married Nov. 6, 1906 to Nannie Lee Issue ¹Wm. Lee, b Sept 11, 1907

RECORD No 4—Gen'l Lucius J Polk, son of Wm Polk and Sarah Hawkins Polk, b March 10, 1802, at Raleigh, N C Sarah Hawkins Polk, b March 10, 1802, at Raleigh, N C Residence, Maury County, Tenn Planter Married 1st April 10, 1832 to Mary Ann Eastin, 2nd Sept 15, 1853 to Mrs Anne Pope Issue ¹Sarah Rachael, ²Mary Brown, ³Emily Donelson, ⁴William ⁵Eliza Eastin, ⁶Frances Anne; ⁷Susan Rebecca, and ⁸George W twins Issue by second wife: ⁹Lucius Junius, ¹⁰Ella Juliet Lucius J Polk, d Oct 3, 1870 and was buried at St John s Church Maury County, Tenn First wife, Mary Eastin Polk, d Aug 1, 1847, buried at St. Johns Church, Maury County, Tenn

RECORD No. 152—Sarah Rachel Polk, daughter of Lucius J Polk and Mary Eastin Polk, b Jan 24, 1833, at Hamilton Place, Maury County, Tenn Married at Hamilton Place, April 24, 1855 to Robin Ap C Jones Issue ¹Mary Polk Jones, b at Hillsboro, N C, Jan 18, 1856, ²Rebecca Edwards, b at Hamilton Place, Jan. 16, 1857; ³Robin Ap Robin, b at Hamilton Place, Feb 18 1859; ⁴Sarah Polk b at Hillsboro, N C, Oct 10, 1860, ⁵Lucy Cadwallader, b at Hillsboro, N. C, Feb 3, 1862 Sarah Rachel Polk Jones died June 12, 1905 and was buried at St Johns Church, Maury County, Tenn Her husband died June 9, 1862 and was buried at Hillsboro, N C

RECORD No 163—Mary Polk Jones, daughter of Robin Ap C Jones and Sarah Polk Jones, b Jan 18, 1856, at Hillsboro, N C Residence, Nashville Tenn Married Jan. 18, 1877 to Duncan B Cooper Issue: ¹Sarah Polk, ²William ³Robin Jones, ⁴Mary Polk, ⁵Duncan Brown Mary Polk Jones d Dec 20, 1893.

RECORD No. 168—Sarah Polk Cooper, daughter of Duncan B Cooper and Mary Jones Cooper, b. June 5, 1878, at Mulberry Hill, Maury County Tenn Residence, Nashville

RUFUS J. POLK.
Son of Dr. Wm. J. Polk.

Tenn. Married Nov 8, 1899 to Lucius Burch   Issue: John Christopher Burch, b. July 21, 1900, in Nashville, Tenn

RECORD No. 169—Wm Cooper, son of Duncan B. Cooper and Mary Jones Cooper, b Jan 24, 1880, at Spring Hill, Maury County, Tenn   Unmarried

RECORD No. 170—Robin Jones Cooper, son of Duncan B Cooper and Mary Jones Cooper, b Aug. 15, 1881, in Maury County Tenn   Residence, Nashville, Tenn   Lawyer. Married Dec 15, 1910 to Eva Lee Smith, daughter of President Milton H Smith of the L & N R R

RECORD No. 171—Mary Polk Cooper, daughter of Duncan B Cooper and Mary Jones Cooper, b Nov 18, 1884, at East Nashville, Tenn.   Residence, Mobile, Ala.   Married Nov 2, 1904 to Beverly Risque Wilson   Issue   Mary Polk Wilson, b Aug 21, 1905, Mobile, Ala

RECORD No. 172—Duncan B. Cooper, Jr, son of Duncan B. Cooper and Mary Jones Cooper, b Aug 28, 1887, at Nashville, Tenn   Married Nov 28, 1909 to Dorothy Crowe

RECORD No. 164—Rebecca Edwards Jones, daughter of Robin Ap C Jones and Sarah Polk Jones, b. Jan. 16, 1857, at Hamilton Place Maury County, Tenn   Residence, New Orleans, La

RECORD No 165—Robin Ap Robin Jones, son of Robin Ap C Jones and Sarah Polk Jones, b Feb 18, 1859, at Hamilton Place, Maury County, Tenn   Residence, Nashville, Tenn

RECORD No. 166—Sarah Polk Jones, daughter of Robin Ap C. Jones and Sarah Polk Jones, b Oct 10, 1860, at Hillsboro, N C. Residence, Nashville, Tenn.   Married June 27 1888 to J C Bradford   Issue: [1]Thomas H Bradford, b Feb 28, 1890, [2]Sarah Polk Bradford, b March 5, 1891, m Alfred Thos. Shaughnessy, Montreal, Can , April 30, 1912

RECORD No. 167—Lucy C Jones, daughter of Robin Ap C Jones and Sarah Polk Jones, b Feb 3, 1862, at Hillsboro N C   Residence, Mobile, Ala   Married Stanley Bell Herndon   Issue [1]Robin Cadwallader Lee , b March

13, 1889 ; ²Virginia, b. Nov 20, 1890; ³Rebecca Jones, b Jan 2, 1893, ⁴Lucy, b April 4, 1899. Stanley Bell Herndon died Nov. 16, 1908

RECORD No. 153—Mary Brown Polk, daughter of Lucius J Polk and Mary Eastin Polk, b March 25, 1835, at Hamilton Place, Maury County, Tenn Married Sept 2, 1858 to Henry C. Yeatman Issue: ¹Mary Eastin, b May 25, 1861; ²Henry C, b. March 2, 1866, d Aug. 7, 1897, ³Russell H., b April 25, 1869, d. April 26, 1893, ⁴Trezevant P , b Oct 13, 1871; ⁵Jenny Bell, b March 3, 1875; ⁶Lucia Polk, b Aug 7, 1877, d May 2, 1908 Mary Brown Polk died March 27, 1890 Buried at St Johns Church, Maury County, Tenn

Col Henry C Yeatman was killed Aug. 1, 1910, by a railroad train near his home in Maury County, Tenn. Buried in St. John's Churchyard.

RECORD No 181—Mary Eastin Yeatman, daughter of Henry C Yeatman and Mary Polk Yeatman, b May 25, 1861, at Hamilton Place, Maury County, Tenn. Residence, near Knoxville, Tenn Married Aug 7, 1897 to Thos S Webb. No issue.

RECORD No. 182—Henry C. Yeatman, Jr , son of Henry C Yeatman and Mary Polk Yeatman, b March 2, 1866, at Hamilton Place, Maury County, Tenn Residence, Mexico Occupation, Civil Engineer, d Aug 7, 1897 Buried at St Johns Church, Maury County, Tenn

RECORD No 183—Russell H. Yeatman, son of Henry C Yeatman and Mary Polk Yeatman, b April 25, 1869, at Hamilton Place, Maury County, Tenn , d April 25, 1893

RECORD No. 184—Trezevant P. Yeatman, son of Henry C Yeatman and Mary Polk Yeatman, b. Oct 13, 1871, at Hamilton Place Residence same Planter

RECORD No. 185—Jenny Bell Yeatman, daughter of Henry C. Yeatman and Mary Polk Yeatman, b. March 3, 1875, at Hamilton Place, Maury County, Tenn

RECORD No. 186—Lucia Polk Yeatman, daughter of Henry C Yeatman and Mary Polk Yeatman, b Aug. 7, 1877, at Hamilton Place Maury County Tenn., d. May 2, 1908

MRS. LUCIUS J. POLK AND MADAME PAGET,
Wife of British Minister to United States.

THE
PUBLIC LIBRARY

ASTOR LENOX AND
TILDEN FOUNDATIONS.

RECORD No. 154—Emily D Polk daughter of Lucius J. Polk and Mary Eastin Polk, b March 29, 1837, at Hamilton Place Residence, Nashville, Tenn Married Nov. 13, 1860 to J Minnick Williams Issue [1]Henry Yeatman; [2]J Minnick unmarried, b Feb 8, 1866; [3]Lucius Polk unmarried, b Nov. 1867; [4]Nannie M , b July 1870, d April 9, 1890, [5]Eliza Polk, b April 1872, d. July 3, 1891; [6]Priscilla Shelby, b Jan 4, 1878

RECORD No. 187—Henry Yeatman Williams, son of J Minnick Williams and Emily Polk Williams, b March 29, 1863, at Hamilton Place Residence, San Antonio Tex Traveling Passenger Agent of Santa Fe R R Married March 8, 1894 to Louise Pitcher. No issue

RECORD 192—Priscilla Shelby Williams, daughter of J. Minnick Williams and Emily Polk Williams, b Jan 4, 1878, at Ashwood, Tenn Married March 7, 1901 to Geo. S Briggs Issue, George Shelby, b March 7, 1902, Norfolk, Va

RECORD No. 155—William Polk, son of Lucius J Polk and Mary Eastin Polk, b Feb 1, 1839, at Hamilton Place Planter. Married Rebecca Mayes No issue William d April 5, 1905

RECORD No. 156—Eliza E Polk, daughter of Lucius J Polk and Mary Eastin Polk, b April 15, 1841, at Hamilton place., d July 3, 1897.

RECORD No. 157—Frances Anne Polk, daughter of Lucius J. Polk and Mary Eastin Polk, b. Aug. 4, 1844, at Hamilton Place. Residence Indian Rock, Va Married Nov. 29 1866 to Edward Dillon Issue [1]James Royall; [2]Edward, [3]Lucius Polk: [4]John Cunningham, [5]Eliza Polk, [6]Frances Polk; [7]Francis Cunningham Frances Anne Polk d March 26, 1912, at Lexington, Va Her husband d Aug 11 1887, at Lexington Va

RECORD No. 194—James Royall Dillon, son of Edward Dillon and Frances Polk Dillon, b Sept. 2, 1869, at Richmond, Va. Residence, Galveston Tex   Must n Belt & Terminal Ry

RECORD No. 195—Edward Dillon, son of Edward Dillon and Frances Polk Dillon, b Oct 19, 1871, at Buchanan, Botetourt County, Va. Residence, Indian Rock, Va. Manufacturer of lime. He married Oct 6, 1896 to Susan S Pendleton. Issue: 1Edward Dillon, b. July 26, 1898, 2Edmund Pendleton, b. April 27, 1900, 3Mary Unity, b Nov 12, 1902, 4William Polk, b May 13, 1905, 5Susan Strachan, b Jan 1, 1909.

RECORD No. 196—Lucius Polk Dillon, son of Edward Dillon and Frances Polk Dillon, b June 8, 1873, at Indian Rock, Va Manufacturer. Married April 25, 1899 to Mary Evelyn Morton. Issue 1Lucius Polk Dillon, b May 26 1909, 2Charles Morton, b Feb 4, 1911, 3Francis Ann, b Jan 2, 1912

RECORD No. 197—John Cunningham Dillon, son of Edward Dillon and Frances Dillon, b May 17 1875, at Indian Rock, Va. Manufacturer. Married Jan. 18 1911 to Miss Mae McClurg Childress.

RECORD No. 198—Eliza Polk Dillon, daughter of Edward Dillon and Frances Polk Dillon, b July 30, 1878, at Indian Rock, Va Married April 4, 1907 to Robert Scott Spillman Issue. Frances Polk Spillman and Robert Scott Spillman, twins, b Jan 6, 1908, 3Edward Dillon, b May 31 1909

RECORD No 199—Frances Polk Dillon, daughter of Edward Dillon and Frances Polk Dillon, b Jan 25, 1880, at Indian Rock, Va Unmarried.

RECORD No. 200—Francis Cunningham, son of Edward Dillon and Frances Polk Dillon, b Sept. 17, 1885, at Indian Rock, Va

RECORD No. 158—Susan Rebecca Polk, daughter of Lucius J Polk and Mary Eastin Polk, b July 7, 1847, at Hamilton Place Residence, Spring Hill Maury County, Tenn Married Sept 11, 1866 to Campbell Brown Issue 1Lucius Polk, 2Richard Ewell, 3George Campbell; 4Percy, 5Lizinka Campbell Brown, d Aug 30, 1893

RECORD No. 207—Lucius Brown, son of Campbell Brown and Susan Polk Brown, b Aug 1, 1867, at Hamilton Place. Residence, Nashville, Tenn. He was twice married, 1st Jan 30, 1895 to Jessie Roberts. 2nd, Dec 12, 1903 to Susan Massie Issue [1]Campbell Huxley, b Oct 25, 1896, [2]Susan Massie Polk, b Feb 11, 1906, [3]Lizinka Campbell, b Sept 2 1908, [4]Lucia Cabell, b Oct 28, 1910. His first wife, Jessie Roberts, d July 2, 1897

RECORD No. 208—Richard Ewell Brown, son of Campbell Brown and Susan Polk Brown, b Jan 12, 1870, at Nashville, Tenn Residence, New York City Physician He married Sept 10, 1901 to Marion Lee Issue: [1]Marion Lee Brown, b. July 29, 1905, d May 10, 1906, [2]Richard Ewell Brown, Jr, b Feb 10, 1908; [3]Marion Lee Brown, 2d, b March 19, 1911

RECORD No. 209—George Campbell Brown, son of Campbell Brown and Susan Polk Brown, b Sept 25, 1871, in Maury County, Tenn He d Jan 23, 1912, at Nashville, Tenn in the 41st year of his age He was a planter and unmarried

RECORD No. 210—Percy Brown, son of Campbell Brown and Susan Polk Brown, b April 6, 1874, in Maury County, Tenn Farmer Married Aug 6, 1907 to Gertrude Plunket Issue [1]Jas Plunkett Brown, b No 1, 1909; [2]Percy Brown, Jr, b April 12, 1912

RECORD No. 211—Lizinka Brown, daughter of Campbell Brown and Susan Polk Brown, b April 6, 1874, in Maury County, Tenn Died Aug 28, 1899

RECORD No. 159—George W. Polk, son of Lucius J Polk and Mary Eastin Polk, b July 7, 1847, at Hamilton Place, Maury County, Tenn. Residence, San Antonio, Tex Civil Engineer, and formerly Assistant Land Commissioner Southern Pacific Company Married Oct 29, 1885 to Jane Jackson Issue [1]Kate Jackson, b Jan 13, 1887; d. Aug. 23, 1888; [2]George W., b May 13, 1889 [3]Jane Jackson, b Jan 20, 1893; [4]Harrison Jackson, b May 10, 1896

RECORD No. 160—Lucius J. Polk, son of Lucius J Polk and Anne Irving Polk, b Aug. 14, 1854, at Hamilton Place, Tenn Residence, in Texas. Railroad service Married Nov 28, 1878 to Daisey Cantrell Issue. ¹Armour Cantrell, b Sept 12, 1879; ²Anne Leroy, b Dec. 16, 1881; ³Lucius Junius, b March 19, 1886; ⁴Margaret Wendell, b. Jan. 13, 1888, ⁵Daisey Cantrell, b July 29, 1890, ⁶Ellen Harrell, b March 15, 1893, d May 15, 1895

RECORD No. 219—Armour C. Polk, son of Lucius J Polk and Daisey Cantrell Polk, b Sept. 12, 1879, at Little Rock, Ark. Residence, New Orleans, La and Mobile, Ala. Civil Engineer Married Sept. 29, 1907 to Charlotte Payne

RECORD No 220—Anne Leroy Polk, daughter of Lucius J Polk and Daisey Cantrell Polk, b Dec. 16, 1881, at Little Rock, Ark Residence, Danville, Va. Married Oct 10, 1903 to Allen Cuculla Issue ¹Allen Polk, b Aug. 1, 1904, ²Anne Polk. Sept 9, 1908

RECORD No. 161—Elvira Juliett Polk, daughter of Lucius J. Polk and Anne Irving Polk, b Sept. 5, 1856, at Hamilton Place Tenn Residence, Nashville, Tenn Married Jan 13, 1881 to Horace Steven Cooper. Issue. Horace Polk Cooper, b Jan 2, 1887.

RECORD No. 6—Leonidas Polk, son of William Polk and Sarah Hawkins Polk, b April 10, 1806, at Raleigh, N C. Bishop of Louisiana, Lieut General in the Confederate States Army Married May 6, 1830 to Frances Devereux Issue. ¹Alex Hamilton; ²Frances Devereux, ³Katherine; ⁴Sarah; ⁵Susan R, ⁶Elizabeth; ⁷Dr Wm. Mecklenburg; ⁸Lucia Leonidas Polk was killed at Pine Mountain, Ga , June 14, 1864 and was entombed in Epicopal church at Augusta, Ga His wife d April 16 1875, and was laid beside him

RECORD No. 229—Alex Hamilton Polk, son of Leonidas Polk and Frances Devereux Polk, b. Jan 27, 1831, at Richmond, Va Residence, Mississippi and North Carolina Planter Married June 15, 1854 to Emily N. Beach Issue ¹Alex Hamilton, b Nov 23, 1855, ²Frank, b. March 17 1858; ³George, b Nov 12, 1861, ⁴Hamilton, b Sept. 15, 1863, ⁵Leo-

COL. LUCIUS JUNIUS POLK, JR., WIFE
AND TWO CHILDREN,
of Texas.

nidas, b Nov 27, 1865; ⁶Beach, b Sept 15, 1868 Alexander Hamilton Polk, d Oct 2, 1872, at Hartford, Conn. His wife d March 9, 1902, at same place and both were buried there.

RECORD No. 238—Frank Polk, son of Alexander Hamilton Polk and Emily Beach Polk, b. March 17, 1858, at New Orleans, La. Residence, North Carolina and Baltimore. Md Planter He married Nov 23, 1897 to Margaret Callaway Issue ¹Emily Hamilton, b Aug 23, 1880, ²Leonidas Charles, b July 19, 1883, d Dec 30; ³Francis Devereux, b Nov 6, 1885, ⁴Magdalen Tasker, b. Feb 25, 1887 · ⁵Alex Hamilton b July 16 1889. Magdalen Tasker d July 19, 1887, at Asheville, N C Frank Polk, d Sept 25, 1891 and was buried in Louden Park, Baltimore, Md

RECORD No. 239—George B. Polk, son of Alex H Polk and Emily Beach Polk, b. Nov 17, 1861, at Nashville, Tenn Residence Oxford Md.

RECORD No. 241—Hamilton R. Polk, son of Alex H. Polk and Emily Beach Polk, b. Sept 15, 1863, at Raleigh, N C Residence, North Carolina and Baltimore, Md Druggist. He married May 4, 1896 to Margaret Callaway Polk No issue He d Nov 9 1906 and was buried at Louden Park, Baltimore, Md

RECORD No. 242—Leonidas Polk, son of Alex H Polk and Emily Beach Polk, b Nov 27, 1865, at Hartford, Conn Residence, Asheville, N C. and Baltimore, Md. He married June 10, 1901 to Charlotte H. Zimmerman. Issue ¹Leontine Adele, b March 10 1902; ²Charlotte Patricia, b Pan 3, 1905

RECORD No. 243—Nichols Beach Polk, son of Alex H. Polk and Emily Beach Polk, b Sept 19, 1868, at Asheville, N C Residence, Asheville, Baltimore and New York. He is a bank clerk and unmarried

RECORD No 230—Frances Polk, daughter of Gen'l Leonidas Polk and Frances Devereux Polk, b. Nov. 27, 1835, at Ashwood Tenn Residence New Orleans La. and Oxford, Miss. Married Nov 27, 1866 to Peyton H Skipwith.

Issue ¹Kate, b Sept 18, 1867, ²Frank, Oct 10, 1872 Frances d March 15, 1884 Her husband d March 13, 1898

RECORD No. 251—Kate Skipwith, daughter of Peyton H. Skipwith and Frances Polk Skipwith, b Sept 18, 1867, at Sewanee, Tenn. Residence, Oxford, Miss Unmarried

RECORD No. 252—Frank Skipwith, son of Peyton H Skipwith and Frances Polk Skipwith, b Oct 10, 1872, at Oxford, Miss Residence Oxford Cotton buyer.

RECORD No. 231—Katherine Polk, daughter of Gen'l Leonidas Polk and Frances Devereux Polk, b Aug. 16, 1838, at Ashwood, Tenn Residence, Nashville, Tenn Married Dec 14, 1858 to Col Wm D Gale Issue ¹Frances, ²Wm D, ³Katharine; ⁴Leonidas, ⁵Josephine, ⁶Ethel Col Gale d Jan 30, 1888 and was buried at Nashville, Tenn.

RECORD No. 253—Frances Gale, son of Col. Wm D. Gale and Katherine Polk Gale, b April 1, 1860, near Nashville Residence, Nashville and New York Married April 30, 1895 to Frank W Ring No issue Mr Ring d July 17, 1896 at Portland, Me

RECORD No. 254—Wm Dudley Gale, son of Col Wm D Gale and Katherine Polk Gale, b April 22, 1861, at Yazoo River, Miss Residence, Nashville, Tenn Insurance Married Jan 18, 1894 to Meta Orr Jackson Issue ¹William Dudley, b. Feb 1, 1897, ²George Jackson, b Sept 3, 1902

RECORD No 255—Katherine Gale, daughter of Col Wm D. Gale and Katherine Polk Gale, b Aug 29, 1862, near Jackson, Miss. Residence Nashville, Tenn Never married She d November 24, 1889 at Nashville, Tenn

RECORD No 256—Leonidas P. Gale, son of Col Wm D Gale and Katherine P Gale, b May 10, 1864, at Asheville, N C Residence, Nashville, Tenn Unmarried and d Sept 16, 1890

RECORD No. 257—Josephine Gale, daughter of Col Wm D Gale and Katherine Polk Gale, b Jan 22, 1867, at Nashville, Tenn He was un married and d Nov 13, 1876, at Nashville, Tenn

COL. GEO. W. POLK, WIFE AND SON.
San Antonio, Tex.

RECORD No. 258—Ethel Gale, daughter of Col Wm D. Gale and Katherine P Gale, b Nov 19, 1869, at Nashville, Tenn. Unmarried and d June 13, 1870

RECORD No. 232—Sallie H. Polk, daughter of Gen'l Leonidas Polk and Fanny Devereux Polk, b ———— Married Frank Blake. One child, Frank Residence New Orleans La

RECORD No. 233—Susan R Polk, daughter of Gen'l Leonidas Polk and Frances Devereux Polk, b April 16, 1842 at Raleigh, N C. Residence, New Orleans, La. Married June 21, 1870 to Dr Joseph Jones Issue ¹Hamilton, ²Fanny, ³Laura Dr Jones d Feb 16, 1896, at New Orleans, La

RECORD No. 262—Hamilton Jones, son of Dr. Joseph Jones and Susan Polk Jones, b Oct 26, 1872, at New Orleans, La, is a physician He was married June 25, 1901 to Caroline E Merrick Issue ¹Joseph Merrick Jones, b Aug. 31, 1903

RECORD No. 263—Fanny Jones, daughter of Dr Joseph Jones and Susan Polk Jones, b May 8, 1871, at New Orleans La.

RECORD No 264—Laura M Jones, daughter of Dr Joseph Jones and Susan Polk Jones, b Aug 26, 1876, at New Orleans, La Unmarried

RECORD No. 234—Elizabeth D. Polk, daughter of Gen'l Leonidas Polk and Frances Devereux Polk, b June 29, 1843, at Ashwood, Tenn Residence, New Orleans, La She was married April 27, 1864 to W. E. Huger Issue: ¹Frances, ²Lucia ³Emily; ⁴John ⁵Arthur, ⁶William; ⁷Leonide, b July 3 1865, d Aug 11 1866 Mr Huger d July 3, 1901 at New Orleans Birth dates of first six children not given

RECORD No. 266—Frances Huger, son of W E Huger and Elizebeth Polk Huger, b March 24, 1867, at New Orleans, La Married Jan 10 1895 to H Legrand Issue ¹William, b March 22, 1896 ²John W. b N c 24, 1899, ³Henry Richardson, b Feb 11, 1904

RECORD No. 267—John Middleton Huger, son of W E Huger and Elizabeth Polk Huger, b May 1, 1868, at New Orleans, La Cotton broker. Married Dec 18, 1900 to Louise Woeste. Issue ¹Louise Polk, b March 3, 1903; ²John Middleton, b March 2, 1907

RECORD No. 268—Lucia Polk Huger, daughter of W. E. Huger and Elizabeth Polk Huger, b October 29, 1870, at New Orleans, La. Residence, New York, N Y Married Jan 31, 1894 to Joseph Hardie Issue ¹Joseph, b Oct 23, 1900; ²William Huger, b. Sept. 26, 1904.

RECORD No. 269—Emily H Huger, daughter of W E. Huger and Elizabeth Polk Huger, b Jan 11, 1876, at New Orleans, La Art teacher.

RECORD No. 270—Arthur Middleton Huger, son of W. E. Huger and Elizabeth Polk Huger, b Aug 26, 1878, at New Orleans, La Cotton buyer Married April 24, 1903 to Lillie Charbonnet Issue ¹Killian L, b Aug 3, 1904

RECORD No. 271—William Elliott Huger, son of W E. Huger and Elizabeth Polk Huger, b Oct. 22, 1882, at New Orleans, La. Residence, New Orleans, La Insurance business

RECORD No. 235—Dr Wm Mecklenburg Polk, son of Gen'l Leonidas Polk and Frances Devereux Polk, b Aug 15, 1844, at Ashwood, near Columbia, Tenn Residence, New York City Physician. He was married Nov 14, 1866 to Ida Lyon Issue ¹Leonidas, b. Feb 24, 1868, d. April 29, 1877; ²Frank Lyon, b Sept. 24, 1869; ³John Metcalf, b May 6, 1875, d. March 29, 1904; ⁴Serena Devereux, b. March 19, 1877, d May 8, 1878

RECORD No. 280—Capt Frank Lyon Polk, son of Dr William Mecklenburg Polk and Ida Lyon Polk, b Sept. 24, 1869, in New York Residence, 129 East 36th St. New York City. He was married Feb 28, 1908 to ~~Mrs.~~ Miss Elizabeth Sturgis Potter Issue ¹John Metcalf, b Nov 18, 1908; ²Elizabeth Sturgis, b Jul 31, 1910; ³Frank Lyon, b Nov 3 1911

DR. WM. MECKLENBURG POLK AND WIFE,
New York.

RECORD No. 236—Lucia Polk, daughter of Gen'l Leonidas Polk and Frances Devereaux Polk, b Oct 22, 1848, at Leighton Plantation, La Residence New Orleans, La, and Philadelphia, Pa She married Jan 8, 1870 to Edward Chapman. The latter d March 19, 1883, at New Orleans, La

RECORD No. 7—Mary B Polk, daughter of William Polk and Sarah Hawkins Polk, b May 28 1808, at Raleigh, N. C Married March 9, 1826 to Hon. George E Badger Issue ¹Katherine M, ²Sally Polk Mary B, d March 1, 1837 at Raleigh, and her husband on May 11 1866, at the same place

RECORD No. 284—Katherine M Badger, daughter of Hon George E Badger and Mary Polk Badger, b. Aug 9, 1827, at Raleigh, N C Married May 6, 1846 to Wm Haigh Issue: ¹Geo. B, b Mar 24, 1847, d June 1, 1886; ²Sallie, b Aug 9, 1849, d May 31, 1905; ³Mary Polk, b June 24, 1852, d June 14 1860 Katherine, d July 4, 1905, at Fayetteville, N C, and her husband in June, 1870 Both buried at Fayetteville, N. C

RECORD No. 286—Geo B Haigh, son of Wm Haigh and Katherine Badger Haigh, b. March 24, 1847, at Raleigh N. C He was married June 20, 1882 to Dora Williamson. Issue ¹Kate Mallon, b Oct 9, 1883 ²George B, b June 1, 1886, at Graham, N C

RECORD No. 289—Kate Mallon Haigh daughter of George B. Haigh and Dora Williamson Haigh, b Oct 9, 1883 at Burlington N C Residence, Reidsville, N C Married June 21, 1905 to John Newton Walt. Issue ¹John Newton Walt, Jr, b Oct 3, 1906.

RECORD No. 287—Sally Haigh, daughter of William Haigh and Katherine Badger Haigh, b. Aug. 9, 1849, at Fayetteville, N. C. Married Jan 25, 1866 to Jos B Underwood Issue ¹William Haigh, b Nov 23, 1866, d July 16, 1870, ²John, b Feb 5, 1868; ³Joseph Boykin, b July 9, 1870, ⁴George Badger, b. May 4, 1872; ⁵Kate Haigh, b. Sept 16, 1874, ⁶Mary Polk, b N v ? 1876, d March 1, 1892; ⁷Ellen Hale b. March 23, 1879, ⁸Elizabeth Hinsdale b Sept 20 1881, ⁹Devereux

Haigh, b Feb 2, 1889, d Oct 1, 1889; ¹⁰Hamilton Polk, b Jan 18, 1891 Sally Haigh d May 31, 1905, at Fayetteville, N C., and Mr Haigh on Jan 6, 1907

RECORD No. 292—John Underwood son of Jos Boykin Underwood and Sally Haigh Underwood, b Feb 5, 1868, at Fayetteville, N C. Real estate and insurance business. He was married Jan 26, 1898 to Annie Montgomery Kyle Issue ¹John Williamson, b July 30, 1899, ²Laura Kyle, b Oct 25, 1902, ³William Emmett b Jan 23 1905

RECORD No. 293—Joseph Boykin Underwood, son of J B Underwood and Sallie Haigh Underwood b July 9, 1870, at Wilmington, N C Residence, Fayetteville, N C. Commission merchant and broker Married April 30, 1875 to Nelly McGill Pemberton. Issue ¹Janie McRae, b. May 21, 1896, ²Sally Haigh, b Oct 30, 1899, ³Nellie Pemberton, b April 10, 1894

RECORD No. 294—Geo Badger Underwood, son of Joseph B Underwood and Sally Haigh Underwood, b May 4, 1872, in Sampson County, N C Residence, Fayetteville, N C In railroad service

RECORD No. 295—Kate Haigh Underwood, daughter of Joseph B Underwood and Sally Haigh Underwood, b Sept 16, 1874, at Fayetteville, N C. Residence, Tarboro and Fayetteville, N C Married Dec 26, 1900 to James A Moore Issue. ¹James H., b Dec 1, 1901; ²Joseph Underwood, b Jan 18, 1904

RECORD No. 288—Mary Polk Haigh, daughter of William Haigh and Katherine Badger Haigh, b June 24, 1852, at Fayetteville, N C, d June 14, 1860.

RECORD No 297—Ellen Hale Underwood, daughter of Joseph Boykin Underwood and Sally Haigh Underwood, b March 23, 1879, at Fayetteville, N C Married Dec 30, 1903 to Dr David G. McKethan No issue

RECORD No. 298—Elizabeth Hinsdale Underwood, daughter of Joseph B Underwood and Sally Haigh Underwood, b Sept 10, 1881 at Fayetteville N C Married Oct

CAPT. FRANK L. POLK AND WIFE,
of New York.

THE NEW YORK
PUBLIC LIBRARY

ASTOR LENOX AND
TILDEN FOUNDATIONS.

28, 1903 to Henry M. Pemberton. Issue ¹Henry Marshall, b Dec 14 1901, ²Jo- Boykin Pemberton, b May 22, 1908

RECORD No. 285—Sally Polk Badger, daughter of Hon Geo. E Badger and Mary Polk Badger, b May 28, 1833, at Raleigh N C Married Sept 25, 1854 to Montford McGehee Issue ¹Thomas, ²George Badger, ³William Polk, ⁴Lucius Polk Sally d. Dec. 19, 1903, at Raleigh, N. C. Her husband d March 31, 1895, at Raleigh, N C

RECORD No 311—Thomas McGehee, son of Montford McGehee and Sally Badger McGehee. b June 9, 1857, at Milton, Caswell County, N C Residence Davidson College, N C where he graduated in 1876. Was cashier of the Mississippi Valley Bank, Vicksburg Miss, and afterwards went into railroading He d Nov 12, 1886, in New York City and was buried at Oakwood Cemetery, Raleigh, N C

RECORD No. 312—George Badger McGehee, son of Montford McGehee and Sally Badger McGehee, b March 8 1861, at Milton, Caswell County, N C Residence, Fletcher Henderson County, N C, near Asheville Farmer He was married Feb 12, 1892 to Eliza M Skinner Issue ¹Annie Ludlow, b Feb 6, 1893, ²Mary Polk, b July 3, 1894; ³George Badger, b Aug 3, 1904

RECORD No. 313—Wm Polk McGehee, son of Montford McGehee and Sally Badger McGehee. b. July 14, 1865, at Milton, Caswell County, N C. Residence, University of N C and Davidson College, N C Present residence, Denver, Col Traveling salesman in drugs Married Dec 3, 1903, at Kansas City, Mo, to Elizabeth DeVeaux Wilson

RECORD No. 314—Lucius Polk McGehee, son of Montford McGehee and Sally Badger McGehee, b. May 14, 1868, at Woodburn, Person County, N C Residence, Capel Hill. N. C. Profession, lawyer, Professor of Law in University of N C Married Jan 28, 1903, at Digby, Nova Scotia to Julia Leslie Covert b. July 6, 1876. His wife d Aug 24, 1903, at N thers N Y and was buried in Oakw l Cemetery, Raleigh, N C.

RECORD No 10—Rufus King Polk, son of William Polk and Sarah Hawkins Polk, b May 15, 1814, at Raleigh, N. C Residence, Maury County, Tenn Planter Married Sept 2 1840 to Sarah Jackson Issue ¹Sally Moore Rufus, d Feb. 25, 1843 and was buried at St. Johns Church, Maury County, Tenn His wife d. July 11, 1888, and was buried beside him.

RECORD No. 318—Sally Moore Polk, daughter of Rufus King Polk and Sarah Jackson Polk, b Sept 1, 1841, at Fork of Cypress, Ala. Residence, Westbrook, Tenn. She was married Aug 19, 1863 to her kinsman, Gen'l Lucius E Polk, C S A Issue ¹Rufus King, b Aug 23, 1866, ²Mary Rebecca, b May 20, 1868; ³Lucius Eugene, b March 22, 1870, ⁴William Junius, b June 13, 1875, ⁵James Knox, b Jan 14, 1882 Gen'l Lucius E Polk, d Dec 1, 1892, and was buried at St John's Church, Maury County, Tenn

RECORD No 319—Jas Hilliard Polk, son of Geo W. Polk, and Sally H. Polk, b Jan 8, 1842 in Maury County, Tenn. Residence, Ft. Worth, Texas He was married Nov 24, 1885 to Mary Demoville Harding. Issue. ¹Lt Harding Polk 8th U S Cav, b in Maury County, Tenn, March 16, 1887; ²George W. Polk, b Nov 18, 1888

RECORD No. 11—George W. Polk, son of Wm Polk and Sarah Hawkins Polk, b July 12, 1817, at Raleigh, N C Residence, Maury County, Tenn Planter Married Nov 24, 1840 to Sally L Hilliard Issue ¹James Hilliard; ²Rufus King, ³Sally H , ⁴Mary Murfree; ⁵George B M , ⁶Susan S ⁷Lucius Junius, ⁸Isaac Hilliard, ⁹Leonidas Polk, ¹⁰William H., ¹¹Carolina. Geo W Polk, d Jan. 8, 1892 and was buried at St John's Church, Maury County, His wife d July 2, 1894

RECORD No. 320—Rufus K Polk, son of George W Polk and Sally Hilliard Polk, b. Oct 31, 1843, in Maury County, Tenn Married April 28 1881 to Margaret Philips. Issue· ¹Mary Elizabeth Polk, b. July 30 1883, in Davidson County, Tenn Rufus K , d. Aug 25, 1902 and was buried at St. John's Church

GEO. W. POLK AND SIX SONS, of Tennessee.

RECORD No 321—Sally H Polk, daughter of George W Polk and Sally Hilliard Polk, b June 18, 1845, in Maury County, Tenn

RECORD No. 322—Mary Murfree Polk, daughter of George W. Polk and Sally Hilliard Polk, b June 25, 1847, in Maury County, Tenn Residence, Berkeley, Cal Married Nov 29, 1870 to Julius J DuBose Issue [1]Juliet B, b Nov 29, 1871, d. in infancy; [2]Tasker Polk, b Jan 4, 1873, [3]Mary Hilliard, b Dec 26, 1875; [4]Alfred Bishop, b Sept 30, 1877, [5]Jessie McIver, b Nov 24, 1879, [6]George W Polk, b. July 4, 1881; [7]Sarah Camilla, b. June 17, 1883, [8]Julius Jesse, b. Aug 18, 1889; [9]Juliet Brevard, b. Nov 29, 1871 Mary Murfree Polk was buried at St John's Church

RECORD No. 326—Isaac Hilliard Polk, son of Geo. W Polk and Sally L. Polk, b. Aug 8, 1854, in Maury County Tenn Residence, Los Angeles, Cal Isaac was twice marred First, on April 13, 1889 to Ella Martha Cook; Second, on April 19, 1897 to Minerva J Bradbury By the first he had issue: [1]Sally Hilliard, b Feb 24, 1891 By the second, [1]Isaac Hilliard, b. April 6, 1898; [2]Lewis Bradbury, b July 30 1899

RECORD No. 330—Harding Polk, son of Jas. H Polk and Mary Harding Polk, b March 16, 1887, in Maury County, Tenn Lieutenant 8th Cavalry, U. S. Army He was married Dec 29, 1910 to Marie Esther Fleming, of Burlington, Iowa. Issue: [1]James Hilliard, b Dec. 13, 1911, at Manilla, P. I

RECORD No. 334—Tasker P DuBose, son of Julius J DuBose and Mary Polk DuBose, b Jan 4, 1873 in Maury County, Tenn. Residence, California Married July, 1905 to Carrey Van Horn Culbert

RECORD No. 336—Alfred B. C. DuBose, son of Julius J DuBose and Mary Polk DuBose, b. Sept. 30, 1878, at Memphis, Tenn Alfred Bishop Cassells DuBose d April 23, 1892, and was buried in Elmwood Cemetery, Memphis, Tenn.

RECORD No. 336—Sarah C DuBose, daughter of Julius J. DuBose and Mary Polk DuBose, b June 17, 1882, at Memphis, Tenn   Residence, Los Angeles, Cal, is a lawyer She was married Dec 22, 1906 to George F a m g Hockley

RECORD No. 323—Geo B. M. Polk, son of Geo. W. Polk and Sally Hilliard Polk, b Dec 15, 1848, in Maury County, Tenn., d March 25, 1877

RECORD No. 324—Susan Spratt Polk, daughter of Geo. W Polk and Sally L Hilliard, b June 23, 1851, in Maury County, Tenn. Residence, St Louis, Mo She was married March 4, 1877 to Jas Yeatman Player. Issue [1]Susan Polk, b. Oct 25, 1878, d July 24, 1879; [2]George Polk, b Jan 21, 1880, [3]Jas Yeatman, b March 30, 1882, [4]Susan Trezevant, b. Aug 8, 1884, [5]Thomson Trezevant, b Sept 7, 1886, [6]Sally Hilliard, b March 28, 1889

RECORD No. 342—Geo Polk Player, son of Jas Yeatman Player and Susan Polk Player, b Jan 21, 1880, at St Louis Mo. Residence, St Louis He was married June 17, 1902 to Eva Frank Lumnen. Issue: [1]Geo Polk, b July 11, 1903.

RECORD No 343—Jas Yeatman Player, son of Jas. Yeatman Player and Susan Polk Player, b March 30, 1882, at St. Louis, Mo Residence, San Antonio, Tex He was married Nov 1, 1911 to Lucile N Harris

RECORD No. 344—Susan Trezevant Player, daughter of Jas Yeatman Player and Susan Polk Player, b. Aug. 8, 1884, at St Louis, Mo Married Jan 12, 1907 to Wm Preston Graves

RECORD No 325—Lucius Junius Polk, son of George W Polk and Sally Hilliard Polk, b April 21, 1853, in Maury County, Tenn. Residence, Ft Worth, Tex

RECORD No. 328—Wm H Polk, son of George W. Polk and Sally L Polk, b Jan. 27, 1859, in Maury County, Tenn Residence, California Married Mable Vanderbogart. Issue: [1]Anna Leah. Wm H. Polk d March 26, 1896 and was buried at Riverside, Cal

RECORD No. 329—Carolina Polk, daughter of George W Polk and Sallie Hilliard Polk, b. June 26, 1861, in Maury County, Tenn Residence, Asheville, N C Caroline was twice married, first to Isaac Hilliard, second, to Joseph H Horton. No issue

MRS. KENNETH RAYNOR.
Daughter of Col. Wm. Polk. of North Carolina.

RECORD No. 13—Susan Spratt Polk, daughter of Col Wm. Polk and Sarah Hawkins Polk, b May 25, 1822, d. July 10, 1909, at San Antonio, and was buried at Fort Worth, Texas. She was b at Raleigh, N C Residence, Raleigh, N. C , Washington, D C and in Texas for some time before her death She was married July 12, 1842 to Hon. Kenneth Rayner Issue. ¹Sally Polk, ²Henry A ; ³Kenneth; ⁴Fanny, ⁵Susan Polk, ⁶William Polk, ⁷Hamilton Polk Raynor.

RECORD No. 351—Sallie Polk Raynor, daughter of Hon Kenneth Raynor and Susan Polk Raynor, b March 30, 1845, at Raleigh, N. C Residence, Fort Worth, Tex Married Nov 13, 1867 to Jos H. Hyman Issue: ¹Susan Polk: ²Harry, ³Mary Raynor, ⁴Sally Josephine Kenneth Raynor, ⁵Joseph H Sally Polk Raynor d Feb 10, 1905 Joseph H Hyman d Feb 6, 1901.

RECORD No. 358—Susan P Hyman, daughter of Jos Hyman and Sally Raynor Hyman, b Aug 19, 1868, at Memphis, Tenn Residence, Fort Worth, Tex Married Dec. 3, 1902 to A L Matlock No issue.

RECORD No. 359—Harry Hyman, son of Jos Hyman and Sally Raynor Hyman, b Jan 2, 1872, at Forest Home, Miss. Residence, Washington, D C He is a lawyer and was married March 22, 1906 to Minna Scott No issue

RECORD· No. 360—Mary Hyman, daughter of Jos Hyman and Sally Raynor Hyman, b May 30, 1875, at Stephenville, Texas. Residence, Stephenville Married Nov 30, 1898 to Silas Lee King Issue: ¹Kenneth Raynor, b. Aug 19, 1902; ²Sallie Raynor; ³Avery Lenoir Matlock, b Jan 24, 1909

RECORD No. 361—Sally J Hyman, daughter of Jos. Hyman and Sally Raynor Hyman, b Feb 2, 1878, at Stephenville, Texas

RECORD No. 362—Kenneth R Hyman, son of Jos Hyman and Sally Raynor Hyman, b. Dec. 5, 1881, at Stephenville, Texas Grocery merchant. Married April 29, 1908 to Meltona Benavides Issue ¹Kenneth Raynor Hyman, Jr, b Oct 14, 1909.

RECORD No 363—Joseph Hyman, son of Joseph Hyman and Sally Raynor Hyman, b. March 19, 1883, at Stephenville, Tex Stenographer and bookkeeper

RECORD No 353—Kenneth Raynor, son of Hon Kenneth Raynor and Susan Polk Raynor, b August 1, 1847, at Raleigh, N C Married Dec 16, 1878 to Eugenia Leach They have one child, Mary Leach

RECORD No. 355—Susan P Raynor, daughter of Hon Kenneth Raynor and Susan Polk Raynor, b March 26, 1855, at Raleigh N C Married twice, first, April 28, 1881 to Dr Arthur Glennan, second, to Mr McMillan Issue [1]Arthur W ; [2]Susie Polk, [3]Kenneth Raynor; [4]Pansy

RECORD No. 356—Wm. P Raynor, son of Hon Kenneth Raynor and Susan Polk Raynor, b Dec 10, 1857, at Raleigh N C Residence, El Paso Tex Married Jan. 30, 1879 to Lula Ragsdale

RECORD No. 357—Hamilton P Raynor, son of Hon Kenneth Raynor and Susan Polk Raynor, b at Raleigh, N C He married first, Eliza Nelms, second, Anna W Armand Issue by first marriage, Kenneth

RECORD No. 14—Col Andrew J Polk, son of William Polk and Sarah Hawkins Polk, b August 10, 1824, at Raleigh, N C Residence Ashwood, Tenn He was an extensive planter and was married January 14, 1846 to Rebecca VanLeer Issue [1]Antionette; [2]VanLeer, [3]Rebecca Col Andrew J Polk, d March 10, 1867, at La Tour de Peilz, Canton de Vaud, Switzerland His wife d at Cannes, France They were buried at LaTour de Peilz, Canton de Vaud, Switzerland The eldest child, Antionette, married in Paris, France (Dec. 12, 1877) at the Papal Nuncio Baron de Charette (later Marquis), Commander of a division in the French Army. Also of the Papal troops of Rome when the Italian army took the city.

RECORD No. 373—Antoinette Polk, daughter of Col Andrew J Polk and Rebecca VanLeer Polk, b Oct 27, 1847, at Nashville, Tenn Residence, France She married Dec 12, 1877 to General Baron Athana-c de Charette de la Contrie. Issue [1]Ant... de Charette de la Contrie

ANTIONETTE (POLK) DE CHARETTE AND HER HOME,
Near Paris, France.

RECORD No. 374—Van Leer Polk, son of Col Andrew J Polk and Rebecca Van Leer Polk b July 9, 1850, at Ashwood, Maury County, Tenn Attorney and journalist He marred Dorothy Bodine No issue

RECORD No. 375—Rebecca Polk, daughter of Col Andrew J Polk and Rebecca VanLeer Polk, b Aug 26, 1858, at Nashville, Tenn Residence in France

RECORD No. 376—Antoine de Charette de la Contrie son of Gen'l Baron Athanase de Charette de la Contrie, Marquis de Charette, was b at Nantes, France, Sept 3, 1832, d at La Basee Motte Chateau Neuf, Ille Et Vilaine, France, Oct 10, 1911 Antoine de Charette de la Contrie 2nd, married Nov 11, 1909 to Miss Susanne Henning, of Louisville, Ky

Now Marquis

CHAPTER XL.

CAPT JOHN POLK

Capt John Polk, third son of William Polk and Margaret Taylor Polk, was born somewhere close to 1740, as he was several years older than his brother Ezekiel, who was born in 1747. In the spring of 1765, John Polk was residing on the vast Selwyn land grant in Mecklenburg county, and was the author of a petition to the Governor and Council complaining of the oppressive conduct of Henry Eustace McCulloh, Selwyn's Chief Agent

On "June ye 7th, A D 1766," we find John Polk enrolled in the Clear Creek Company of Mecklenburg Colonial Militia, Captain Adam Alexander commanding, Charles Polk (John's elder brother), being First Lieutenant By acts of the General Assembly, John Polk was a member of commissions charged with the duty of laying out roads connecting the western counties with the towns of Wilmington and Brunswick, the latter being the capital of the province These commissions were created by acts of the General Assembly of the Province in 1766, 1771 and 1773 In 1778, while the Revolutionary War was in progress, the name of John Polk appears as one of the militia officers (rank not given) serving in Colonel Francis Locke's regiment from Rowan county, that county then adjoining Mecklenburg

These facts are taken from Colonial Records of North Carolina, Vol VII, pp 6, 11, 12, 13, 34 and 35; the State Records of North Carolina, Vol XIII, pp 389 and 390, Ibid Vol XXII, pp 395, Vol XXIII, pp 751, 870 908 and 920

TAYLOR POLK'S DESCENDANTS.

Taylor Polk, son of John Polk and Eleanor Polk, married Jency Walker daughter of Alexander Walker, descended from John Walker and Cathe ine Rutherford, his wife, of the 'Creek

Nation" of Walkers, who came from Wigton, Scotland, and settled in Rockbridge County, Virginia, in 1741. Taylor Polk and Jency had seven children: [1]Benjamin; [2]Taylor, [3]James; [4]Cumberland, [5]William Walker, [6]Alfred, [7]Jency, [8]Warnell.

Benjamin, eldest child of Taylor Polk and Jency his wife, married Peggy Boatright, and had issue: [1]Jency, [2]Benjamin, [3]James, [4]Charles, [5]William [6]Richard, [7]Priscilla. All died in childhood and the Benjamin Polk line became extinct.

Taylor Polk, second son of Taylor Polk and Jency his wife, married Prudence Anderson. Issue [1]Anderson [2]Eleanor, [3]Cumberland, [4]Sarah Delaney, [5]Mitchell; [6]Sylvester Walker, [7]Henry Clay, [8]Taylor; [9]Prudence, [10]Alfred.

Anderson Polk, eldest son of Taylor Polk 2nd and Prudence, married, first, Eliza Epperson, and had issue [1]Henry, married Ellen Deathrow, [2]Sarah, married John Huddleston, [3]Jane, married Thomas Huddleston; [4]Sylvester, married Sarah Intz. Anderson Polk, married second Martha Martin, and had issue [5]Texanna, married Thomas Wilhamson, [6]Matilda, married James Joplin; [7]Thomas, married Annie Matlock, [8]Prudence, d. unmarried. Anderson Polk married, third Susan Langley, and had issue [9]Martha, married Jefferson Bugg, [10]Almeda, married Charles Cruger.

Eleanor Polk, second child of Taylor Polk, 2nd and Prudence (Anderson) Polk, married Daniel Huddleston and had issue [1]Prudence, married Joseph Story, [2]Daniel, married Miss Stinson; [3]Jane, married Moses Waterman, [4]Rachael, married Jefferson Cunningham, [5]T J, married Jane Polk; [6]Katherine, married James Stevens.

Cumberland Polk, third child of Taylor Polk, 2nd and Prudence (Anderson) Polk, married Almeda Blackwood and had issue: [1]Prudence, married James Stanford, [2]Taylor, married Ellen Griggs, [3]Caldona, married Robert Priest, [4]Lucinda married John Houston, [5]Lawrence, married Penelops Rose, [6]Sarah, married Alonza Tracy; [7]John, d unmarried; [8]Sylvester, unmarried; [9]Henry, unmarried; [10]Wesley, unmarried. It is possible that the latter was the Wesley Polk, who removed from North Carolina to Missouri about the date of formation of the latter state, but we are unable to name his descent.

Sarah Delaney Polk, fourth child of Taylor Polk 2nd and Prudence (Anderson) Polk, married Capt G T Epperson and had issue. ¹Henry Peyton, married Miss Rowles, ²Mary, married Blount Bullock, ³Taylor Polk, married Victoria Bush, ⁴Isabella, married George Jacobs, ⁵Emma, married Ira Cobb

Mitchell, fifth child of Taylor Polk 2nd and Prudence (Anderson) Polk, died unmarrred

Sylvester Walker Polk, sixth child of Taylor Polk 2nd and Prudence (Anderson) Polk, married Sarah Large, and had issue ¹Isom, married Lucy Miller; ²Victoria, married H O. Brockmann, ³Paschal, married Hannah Jones; ⁴Isadora, married W R. Capps, ⁵David, married Jane Burnett; ⁶Laura, married L D Burnett, ⁷Alpha, married John Lindsay; ⁸Maud, married W L. Kothmann, ⁹Claude

Henry Clay Polk, seventh child of Taylor Polk, 2nd and Prudence (Anderson) Polk, married Mary A Dickson and had issue· ¹Henry, married Annie Gould, ²David, d unmarried; ³Emma, d unmarried, ⁴Alice, married Dr G. B. Green; ⁵John, married Susan Brown, ⁶Anna married John Hawkins; ⁷Lela, married Dr John Brown; ⁸Betty, d. unmarried, ⁹Roxy; ¹⁰Leon

Taylor Polk, 3d. eighth child of Taylor Polk, 2nd and Prudence (Anderson) Polk. married Mary Petty and had issue· ¹Laura, ²Augusta, ³Mollie, married T W Poole ⁴James, married Mary Allison, ⁵Leta and ⁶Lota twins, ⁷Henry; ⁸Leon, ⁹Myrtle married Richard Shegog, ¹⁰Beverly

Prudence Polk, ninth child of Taylor Polk, 2nd and Prudence (Anderson) Polk, married Benjamin H. Dickson and had issue ¹Charles, married Carrie Young; ²Minnie, married Dr. Oscar Smith; ³William, ⁴Pearl, married Russell Williams; ⁵Ethel, married George Holland

Alfred Polk, tenth child of Taylor Polk, 2nd and Prudence (Anderson) Polk, married Sarah Wilson and had issue: ¹Sylvester; ²Burt, ³Mable; ⁴James

James Polk, third child of Taylor Polk, 1st and Jency (Walker) Polk, married, first, Miss Trammell, second, Sallie Cox The children were ¹Jency, married Fielding Tweedle; ²Bettie married Martin Newman· Franklin, married Jane

Rider, [4]James, married Lizzie Roberts; [5]Cumberland, married Laura Kirk.

Cumberland Polk, fourth child of Taylor Polk, 1st and Jency (Walker) Polk, married Nancy Cox, daughter of Joel Cox and Frances Bartlett his wife, of Kentucky Nancy Cox was a sister of Sallie Cox who married James, brother of Cumberland The issue of this marriage was: [1]Lucretia; [2]Lucinda, d. in infancy, [3]Marshall Alexander, [4]Elias Rector, [5]William Jackson, [6]Louisa Jane, [7]Jency; [8]Louis Taylor, [9]Prudence; [10]Mary, [11]Martha [12]James Knox

Lucretia Polk, eldest child of Cumberland Polk and Nancy (Cox) Polk, married Edmund Cearley, and had issue: [1]Samuel; Reyburn, d unmarried, [2]Newton Fleming, [3]Mary Jane, d in infancy, [4]Cumberland, d in infancy, [5]Louise Elizabeth, married George Babcock, no issue, [6]Cyrus Granville, d unmarried, [7]John Brackville, [8]Emma Cornelia, married Hon Frank Marion Angellotti, Justice of the Supreme Court of California since 1902, and had issue Frances Louise, d. in infancy, and Marion Polk, [9]Charles Lalant, married Rhoda Jeanette Mangrum and has one child, Mila Mangrum Cearley

Marshall Alexander Polk, third child of Cumberland Polk and Nancy (Cox) Polk, d in childhood.

Elias Rector Polk, fourth child of Cumberland Polk and Nancy (Cox) Polk, d unmarried from the effect of wounds received in the Confederate Army He belonged to Col Kennard's regiment

William Jackson Polk, fifth child of Cumberland Polk and Nancy (Cox) Polk, married Esther Woodward, and had two children [1]Thomas; [2]Julia

Louisa Jane Polk, sixth child of Cumberland Polk and Nancy (Cox) Polk, married Rev E J Billington, and had three children [1]Lucretia, [2]Ezekiel; [3]Julia

Louis Taylor Polk, seventh child of Cumberland Polk and Nancy (Cox) Polk never married. He was killed in the Confederate Army, at Arkansas Post.

Jency Polk, eighth child of Cumberland Polk and Nancy (Cox) Polk, married William O Neal and had four children. [1]Nancy, [2]Gussie [3]Prudence [4]Jim

Prudence Polk, ninth child of Cumberland Polk and Nancy (Cox) Polk, married Frederick Jones and had two children ¹Mary, ²William

Mary Ann Polk, tenth child of Cumberland Polk and Nancy (Cox) Polk, married Charles Jackson. No issue

Martha Robinson Polk, eleventh child of Cumberland Polk and Nancy (Cox) Polk, married Handy Walker and had three children ¹Jency; ²James; ³Ella

James Knox Polk, twelfth child of Cumberland Polk and Nancy (Cox) Polk never married.

William Polk, fifth child of Taylor Polk, 1st and Jency (Walker) Polk, married two cousins, the Misses Griffith Two sons by the first marriage. ¹Lewis; ²Cumberland Both were killed in the Confederate Army.

Alfred Polk, sixth child of Taylor Polk, 1st and Jency (Walker) Polk, married, first, Irene Chandler, second Mrs Ricketts Issue by first marriage ¹James, ²Josiah, ³Mary J, married W W. Garner; ⁴Mitchell, ⁵Caroline, married L Dennis, ⁶Benjamin. ⁷Samuel; ⁸Almeda, married J. N Stancell. ⁹Young By his marriage with Mrs. Ricketts, Alfred Polk had issue ¹⁰Robert, ¹¹William Part. ¹²Richard

Jency Polk, seventh child of Taylor Polk, 1st and Jency (Walker) Polk, married Mitchell Anderson brother to the wife of Taylor Polk, 2nd The children of this marriage were ¹Fannie; ²James, ³Mitchell; ⁴Benjamin, ⁵Abraham, ⁶Eliza, ⁷Stacey; ⁸Jane, ⁹Henry; ¹⁰Taylor James, Mitchell, Benjamin and Abraham Anderson enlisted when mere boys, in the Confederate Army, and were all killed in the war

CAPT JOHN POLK'S DESCENDANTS.

Charles Polk, eldest son of John Polk and Eleanor (Shelby) Polk, was a soldier in the Revolution He married Margaret Baxter and had issue ¹John ("Jackie"); ²Jennie; ³Andrew, ⁴Col Wm, ⁵Charles, ⁶Cynthia, ⁷Isaac, ⁸Judge Alfred Polk John ("Jackie") married Elizabeth Allen, and had a daughter, Amanda M. Polk, who married Rev Dr. R O Watkins. Judge Albert B Watkins, son of the latter, is a leading attorney at law at Athens Tex Jennie married 1st, a Mr.

Fowler, second, John Potts, and settled in Alabama. Andrew married Martha Kimball, moved to Missouri, and later to Cherokee County, Tex. Col. William married Nancy Petty and settled at Holly Springs, Miss. Charles married Elizabeth Haynes. Cynthia married her cousin John Polk, son of John Polk and Elizabeth Oldson. Judge Alfred Polk married Nancy McIvor.

JUDGE ALFRED POLK.

Judge Alfred Polk removed from Tennessee to Texas in 1837, and lived to be 83 years of age. He settled in San Augustine County, to which locality he was followed by his father, "Civil Charley" Polk, and others of the name. Alfred Polk, being a man of superior mental attainments, soon took high rank in his community. He was chief Justice during the Texas Republic, a position similar to that of District Judge of the present day, with concurrent jurisdiction in both civil and criminal cases.

After Texas entered the Union, Judge Alfred Polk continued in the office of Judge for nine years longer. After a total service of eighteen years in public life he retired to his farm and lived quietly the balance of his days maintaining to the end, however, a deep interest in all political affairs. He was the father of ten children, including two sets of twins. Three of his children were born before, and the others after his removal to Texas. All of his six sons served in the Confederate Army. The youngest son, Drew, was killed in the battle of Thompson's Station, and was buried in the Polk cemetery, near Columbia, Tenn., where so many of the family are interred.

JUDGE ALFRED POLK'S FAMILY.

Judge Alfred Polk, youngest son of "Civil Charley" Polk (son of John Polk and Eleanor Shelby), married Nancy McIvor and had ten children, viz: ¹Charles I Polk, b. ——, married Victoria Thomas; ²John K. Polk, b. ——, d. 1902, married Issti Mary Thomas. She d. 1ee Charles I and Jno K. were twins. Ann Elizabeth Polk ——, married Ben E.

Smith, ⁴Silas G Polk, b ——, married Althea McKnight, no issue, ⁵Drew S Polk. b ——, killed in C S A during Civil War; ⁶Margaret C Polk. b ——, married Dr Wm Browning, ⁷William A Polk. b ——, ⁸Mary Cynthia Polk. b 1841. d ——, married Ludwell R Davis, b 1828. (Wm A and Mary C were also twins), ⁹Andrew Tyler Polk, b ——, married Mary Ann Simmons, Oct 1, 1874, ¹⁰Isabella Polk. b ——, married George Smith

Judge H K Polk, married Ella Burleson and had issue: ¹Charles I ; ²Jamie, ³Hallie, ⁴John, ⁵Carlo; ⁶Kate, ⁷Mamie, ⁸Henry

James V Polk is unmarried and is a prominent business man and real estate operator at Beaumont. Texas

John K Polk and wife, Mary (Thomas) Polk, had issue ¹Sudie Gertrude, b ——, 1882, married Murray B Thomas in 1905 They had issue ¹John Elbert,, b 1906; ²Charles Wesley, (daughter), b 1886, married 1907 to Chas Francis Sossman, issue: ¹Rubie Estelle, b 1908, ²John D Polk, b 1892, d 1901

Ben E. Smith and wife, Ann Elizabeth (Polk) Smith, had issue: ¹Silas, ²Polk; ³Eva; ⁴Ben E , Jr , ⁵L. H., ⁶Nannie; ⁷M C.; ⁸B B The first three named are dead

Silas G Polk and wife Althea had no issue

Margaret C Browning had issue ¹Annie Robert; ²Kate Priscilla

MARY CYNTHIA (POLK) DAVIS' FAMILY.

Mary Cynthia Polk and Ludwell Rector Davis had issue: ¹Dr Drew S b 1868, married Effie May Greer 1901; ²William Thomas, b 1870, married Fannie B Price 1892, ³Elias Kincheloe, b 1872 married Anna Hill, 1909 No issue, ⁴Margaret Isabella, b. 1874, unmarried, ⁵Annie Browning, b. 1876, unmarried, ⁶Mary Johnnie, b 1878 unmarried, ⁷Alfred Polk, b. 1880, unmarried, ⁸Ludwell R Jr, b 1882, married Hattie Anderson. 1905, ⁹Winnie, b 1885 d 1887

Dr Drew B Davis and Effie May Greer married 1901 and had issue: ¹Nellie Vance b. 1902; ²Drew S Jr, b 1904; ³Kitti ——, ⁴Annie Belle, b 1907, ⁵Wm Thomas, Jr., b 1911

JAS. V. POLK,
of Beaumont, Tex.

William Thomas Davis and Fannie Bernard Price had issue ¹James Ludwell, b 1893; ²Mary Isabella, b 1896, ³Drew S Jr., b 1898, ⁴Johnnie Adeline, b 1900; ⁵Ellen Elizabeth, b. 1902; ⁶Wyatt Garrett Foster, b 1904

Ludwell Rector Davis married Hattie Anderson and had issue: ¹Mildred Wayne, b 1906, ²Edward Rector, b 1909

Isabella Polk and husband, George Smith, had issue ¹Charles P, ²Maggie, ³Jamie, ⁴Dr G M ; ⁵Gussie ⁶Robert B, ⁷B. J.; ⁸T. H., ⁹T. T ; ¹⁰Anna May Jamie and Gussie are dead

Andrew Tyler Polk and Mary Ann Simmons were married Oct. 1, 1874 Their children were ¹Sophia Lula, b Dec 25 1876, ²John Simmons, b Aprl 29, 1879; ³Tyler Vernon, b May 28, 1881, ⁴Samuel Clarence, b May 7, 1885

John Simmons Polk and Catherine B Thomas were married Nov 14, 1901 Their children were ¹Walter Earl, b Nov 26, 1903; ²Leland Thomas, b Dec 14 1905, ³Annie May, b April 13, 1908, ⁴Gladys, b March 4, 1912

Tyler Vernon Polk and Mattie Virginia Thomas were married Dec 14, 1902 Their children ¹Aaron Gordon, b. Jan 12, 1904; ²Annie Blanche, b Sept 1, 1904, ³Margaret Ruth, b June 22, 1909

JOHN ("JACKIE") POLK'S DESCENDANTS.

John Polk (generally called "Jackie" and also "Colonel"), was b Oct. 25, 1798, and d Feb 16, 1864 Cynthia Springs Polk, b Feb 25, 1801, d Aug 28, 1855 John and Cynthia were married Oct. 28, 1825 They had issue ¹Isaac Carlo, b Oct 15, 1826; ²Margaret, b April 22, 1829, ³Elizabeth Jerome, b Jan 20, 1832, ⁴Eugenia, b July 27, 1834, d Jan 24, 1864; ⁵John DeKalb, b Nov 10, 1839, ⁶Benjamin C, b Feb 20, 1843.

John Polk's second wife, to whom he was married July 30 1856, was Mrs. Mary S McLenny, nee Floyd She d June 22, 1859. They had twins, Erasmus and Bettie Georgiana, b July 18, 1857. The first d Aug. 11, 1857 Bettie grew to womanhood and married Frank Hudgeons about 1881. They moved from Parker County, Texas to Marthaville, La Untraced since.

John Polk's third wife was Nancy Newsom, b in Georgia They had one child, Almonte Lee, b Sept 12, 1863, after her father's death Almonte married Frank Wilder, of San Antonio, Tex, Nov. 27, 1894, and they have one child, Greta Wilder, b Nov. 6, 1897 Mr. Wilder was born in Illinois.

DAVENPORTS AND CARTWRIGHTS

Thomas Byser Davenport, b Feb 7, 1831, d Dec 11, 1863. Eugenia Polk, b July 27, 1834, d Jan. 24, 1864. They were married Oct. 13, 1855 and had issue. [1]Mary Cynthia b July 18, 1856, [2]John Polk, b July 7, 1858, d. Oct 27, 1859, [3]Eugene Beauregard, b April 15, 1861, d. Oct 30, 1863, [3]Elizabeth DeKalb, b May 11, 1863

Mary Cynthia Davenport, married Matthew Cartwright, July 24, 1876, and had the following children and grandchildren

(1) Leonidas Davenport Cartwright, b May 9, 1877, married Justa Joiner and had issue [1]Terrill Joiner, b Oct 25, 1900, [2]Leonidas D, b Nov 29, 1902; [3]Justa, b. July —, 1909; [4]Jerome Broocks, b. July 16, 1911

(2) Amanda Holman Cartwright, b March 21, 1878, married Lane Taylor, Dec 20, 1900 They had issue [1]Eugenia Polk, b Sept. 11, 1901; [2]Maria Louisa b Dec. 29, 1903

(3) Eugenia Polk Cartwright, b. Dec 3, 1880, married James I Cartwright, Nov 8, 1904 They had issue: [1]Matthew, b Aug 15, 1905

(4) Estelle Cartwright, b July 20, 1882, married Wm Bartle Lupe, Nov 4, 1903, and they have issue· [1]Mary Davenport, b Feb 1905, [2]Estelle, b July —, 1907, d May —, 1909; [3]William B, b March 17, 1910

(5) Jerome Broocks Cartwright, b Nov 3, 1883, married William Preston Head, March 26, 1907 Residence, Sulphur, Okla.

(6) Mary Davenport Cartwright, b May 13, 1885, married Clarence S Pickerell, Jan. 7, 1909.

(7) John H Reagan Cartwright b Feb 22, 1888, married Isabel B, u ii ·, 1910

(8) Holman Cartwright, b March 26 1889
(9) Matthew Cartwright, b Jan 17, 1892
(10) Bourke Cartwright, b Jan 21, 1894

Elizabeth DeKalb Davenport daughter of Thomas B. Davenport, married Dr Samuel Miller Gladney, Oct 3, 1881 They had issue ¹Donald Ross, b. April 27, 1885, ²Mary Eugenia, b. June 25, 1891; ³Jane Ross, b. March 31, 1895; ⁴Samuel M, b Nov 25, 1898

Mrs Eugenia Broocks, married secondly M. George C Greer. Her children by her second husband were ¹Louis V ; ²John B ; ³George C

Mrs Greer's three brothers, John H, Lycurgus and Benjamin Polk, were all in the Confederate army and the latter fell in battle

Moses Lycurgus, generally called "Curg," was elected to Congress from his district and died after serving one term John H is a prominent lawyer and business man, and resides in Beaumont, Texas.

Margaret, daughter of Cynthia and John Polk, married James Burleson, a prominent planter and stockman, and they have issue. ¹Joe, ²Carlo, ³James; ⁴Pip; ⁵Jerome Joe and James, the only survivors, are noted planters and stockmen of San Augustine.

CHAPTER XLI.

JOHN D. POLK AND FAMILY.

John D Polk (second son and fifth child of John and Cynthia S Polk), was born in San Augustine, Texas, Nov 10, 1839 and married Miss Elizabeth Beles, in Leon County, Texas, Nov 10, 1857 John D served through the Civil War as Captain of Company D, Gould's Battalion, Texas Cavalry (dismounted) Walker's Division, Trans-Mississippi Department, C S A The children born to John D Polk and wife were. ¹James H, b in Leon County, Sept 1858, d in Louisiana, 1906, ²William, b in Leon County, 1862, d at Eagle Pass, Tex, in 1886, ³Benj C., b in Leon County, 1865, killed in train wreck near Austin, in 1898, ⁴Fessonia, b in Titus County, Oct 27, 1869

Fessonia married David A Blake, Oct 27, 1886, and they reside at Lometa, Texas Their children were: ¹Elizabeth, b at Eagle Pass, Dec 18, 1887 ²Lucile b at Dallas, July 27, 1889; ³David A, Jr, b at Brenham, Feb 14 1892; ⁴Roscoe, b at Temple, Oct. 9, 1900, ⁵Alef, b at Brownwood, July 19, 1902

Elizabeth, the eldest daughter, married Edward W Passow at San Angelo, Jan 20, 1907 One child, Edward Blake, b Nov 2 1907 Residence of family, Chicago, Ill

Lucile Blake married Vancourt Kelly, at San Angelo, June 23, 1909. They have one child, Vancourt Jr, b May 30, 1910

DESCENDANTS OF EMILY B POLK.

Emily B Polk (daughter of "Jackey" Polk and Elizabeth Allen), b Feb 25, 1823, and d Jan 3, 1877 Emily was married Feb 25, 1846 to J T Childres, b June 21, 1817, and d. Dec 10 1879. Emily B Childres and husband had issue. ¹Mar th beth b Feb 9 1846 married L. F. Branch, Oct. 3, 186   E P H b Feb 8 1849 married Jennie Gilbert,

Dec 27, 1874; ³Chas. Vaulton, b Aug 23 1851 married Julia Matthews Dec 2, 1879, ⁴Joseph William, b Dec 17, 1853, ⁵James Micajah, b Aug 22, 1856, married Leta Kirksey, Aug 29, 1880, ⁶Richard Jackson, b April 8, 1859, ⁷Margaret Benia, b. Aug 9, 1861, married Frank Powell, ⁸Emily Blanche, b June 21, 1864, married J. W. Gilbert, in Jan 1881, ⁹Alfred Lee, b Aug 13, 1867, married, d Oct 10 1872, ¹⁰Ophelia Amanda, b June 19, 1873, d June 24, 1894.

Emily B. (Polk) Childres and husband, Josiah T Childres b in Tennessee, emigrated to Texas in 1837.

JOHN POLK CHILDRES' FAMILY.

(1) Willie, b Dec 30, 1876, d July 15, 1878

(2) Clive, b. May 20, 1878; married Kate Smith, Feb —, 1904 Issue ¹Mary, b June —, 1906; ²Smith b 1909

(3) Ruby b Jan, 1881 married T E Collins, Dec, 1901. Issue ¹Milton, b July, 1903, ²Ruby, b 1905.

(4) Verna, b 1883; married her cousin, I V. Childres

(5) Elmer b Aug 22, 1886, married Cornelia Harrell, Oct, 1909 Issue ¹Verdell, b Nov 10, 1910

(6) Milton, b March 13, 1896; d Dec —, 1892

(7) Earl, b Sept —, 1893

CHAS. VAULTON CHILDRES' FAMILY.

Chas. Vaulton Childres and wife, Julia Anne Matthews, had issue ¹Inlow Vaulton, b ——; married Verna S Childres, ²Joseph Jackson b ——; married Lillian Ashley; ³Emily Jennett, b ——; ⁴Charley Lee b ——

JOHN A. POLK AND FAMILY.

John A. Polk, fourth son and child of John Polk and Eleanor (Shelby) Polk, was born in Mecklenburg County, North Carolina and was a soldier under his father in the Revolutionary War, and d in Texas in 1855

Shortly after peace was declared, large numbers of the sons of North Carolina moved to Tennessee, settled in Tennessee, ... irley,"

Shelby and Taylor, were a part of the emigrating host, as were also his kinsmen, Col Ezekiel Polk, the latter's son Samuel, (father of James K Polk), Col. William Polk, (son of Gen. Thomas Polk), and others of the family Prompted by the inherent aggressiveness of the Scotch-Irish character, the Polks kept up to the firing line of civilization as it swept over the mountains and deployed into the fertile valleys of the Tennessee region Along with his brothers, and kinsmen Ezekiel and Samuel Polk, John settled in the Western section of Tennessee, near Bolivar

Though located in a fertile and attractive region, from the vast section lying between Red River and the Rio Grande, came marvelous accounts of fertility of soil and opportunities for wealth. Yielding to these influences, John A Polk and his brother "Civil Charley," started with their families for the new Eldorado about 1840, and located in San Augustine County, where he died in 1855 Like his brother Charles, John A had married a number of years before he emigrated to Texas The maiden name of his wife was Elizabeth Oldson They had issue

(1) Benjamin D A Polk, b Jan. 1, 1790, d June 2, 1840

(2) Nancy Polk, b ——, d ——, married Ethelbert Kirby

(3) Evan Polk, b ——, d ——; married Jannie Miller

(4) Robert Polk, b ——, d ——; married Malvina Porter

(5) Elizabeth Polk, b ——, d. ——; married Robert Campbell

(6) John (generally called "Jackie."), who married three times He first married Cynthia Polk, a cousin, daughter of "Civil Charley" Polk, second, Mrs Mary (Floyd) McClenny, third, Nancy Newsom, of Alabama

(7) Armstead Polk, youngest child of Benj D A Polk, untraced

John A. Polk's children were all born in Tennessee, and some of them emigrating to Texas, died there

BENJAMIN D. A. POLK'S FAMILY.

Benjamin D. A Polk, oldest child of John A Polk and Elizabeth (Oldson) Polk, b. Jan 1, 1790, married Sept 26, 1816, Margaret R Moore, daughter of James and Catharine Moore She was b. Oct 10, 1797

Benjamin D. A and Margaret (Moore) Polk had issue. [1]Elizabeth Ann, b Oct 19, 1817, d Oct 14, 1843; [2]James M, b March 19, 1820, d. March 24, 1840; [3]John A, Jr, b May 12, 1822; d. June 1, 1822, [4]Lucius B, b June 2, 1823, d. Feb. —, 1910, married Maggie Miller; [5]Viola C., b Sept 4, 1825, d July 7, 1840, unmarried, [6]Franklin A, b Dec 1, 1827; d June 24, 1843; unmarried, [7]Mary Ophelia, b Oct 13, 1829, d. July 28, 1836, [8]John Thadeus, b. March 17, 1832; d Oct. 16, 1832; [9]Margaret Jane, b Nov 1, 1833; living at Teneha, Texas, in Jan, 1913, married George Teel one of Austin's Texas colony; [10]Robert Green, b April 13, 1836; d Aug 5, 1852; [11]Sarah Robina, b Oct 19, 1838

Of the foregoing, Lucius B Polk was married to Maggie Miller, and they had issue [1]Benjamin, d unmarried, at 30 year of age, [2]Matthew, [3]Kate, [4]Jane, [5]Edna, [6]Mollie

Margaret Jane Polk, daughter of Benjamin D A Polk and wife, married Wyatt Teel, and had a family, one of whom, John Teel, a commercial traveler, resides at Teneha, Texas John Teel married Alef Collins, and has issue [1]Yvonne, b Dec 4, 1903, [2]Ydelle, b Nov. 3, 1906

Mrs Margaret Jane (Polk) Teel, widow of George Teel, a Texas pioneer of Austin's colony, living on her farm near San Augustine, near where she and her husband located in early days Among relics in her possession, says a sketch of her in the Houston Post of November 20, 1910, is a Bible presented to her by her kinsman, James K. Polk; a large Bowie knife given by its inventor, Col James Bowie, to her husband, in Arkansas in 1821, with walnut handle, decorated in silver, broad blade, finely tempered; and a long rifle with heavy stock, that was shattered against the door of the old stone fort in Nacogdoches when the Texans were rushing it

"CIVIL CHARLEY" POLK'S FAMILY.

"Civil Charley" Polk, eldest son of John Polk and Eleanor Shelby, was born Jan. 18, 1760, in Mecklenburg County, North Carolina. This date he gave in 1846, in his application for a pension, under the Congressional act of 1832, granting pensions to Revolutionary soldiers.

In his declaration, after stating his name, place and date of birth, he says he "served at various times during the Revolution in the North Carolina troops, under Captains James Jack, John Polk (his father), Charles Polk (his uncle), Oliver, Wiley and Fletcher and Colonels Adam Alexander and Thomas Polk (his uncle); also served as Sergeant in a mounted Spy Company for five months and twenty-eight days in 1814."

His application was filed, but no pension was allowed probably on account of a lack of confirmatory documentary proof, the Revolutionary records of North Carolina being exceedingly incomplete and, in many instances, entirely lost. He stated, however, to his family in after years, that it never was his intention to try to collect a pension, but only to secure an official record of his services.

From his declaration of service it is certain that his father, John Polk and his uncle, Charles Polk, were both Captains in the army, though well advanced in age—probably between forty-five and fifty years old.

Colonel Adam Alexander was a near kinsman of the Polks, as were all of that name in Mecklenburg. Several of the Taylor girls, of Pennsylvania, (sisters of Margaret Taylor, who married Wm Polk), intermarried with the Alexanders, as did also some of the Polk women. All of the Alexander men by these intermarriages joined with their kinsmen and neighbors in the Mecklenburg Declaration of May 20, 1775, and in active army service in the Revolution that followed.

C. G. Polk, of Tennessee, writing concerning his grandfather, says "I have heard ever since I was a boy that my grandfather who was called 'Civil Charley' and Thomas, Samuel and Ezekiel Polk were the boys that raised the

MRS. MARGARET JANE (POLK) TEEL,
of Texas.

THE NEW YORK
PUBLIC LIBRARY

ASTOR LENOX AND
TILDEN FOUNDATIONS.

Liberty Pole at Charlotte, North Carolina." The night before the Mecklenburg Declaration, May 19, 1775, it is traditionally stated, was the time the pole was raised by enthusiastic young patriots of Charlotte.

As stated, Charles was a soldier in the Revolution, and was twice captured by the British. He had very white hair, and by some was called "Whiteheaded Charley." After his second capture by the enemy, the British officer exclaimed "Ah, my whiteheaded fellow, we have caught you again, have we?" For four days he was given no food, and was half starved when a former slave of his father's, who had gone to the British army expecting freedom, threw him an ear of corn as he passed to feed the stolen stock. On account of his agreeable manner and disposition, he was generally called "Civil Charley" Polk, in contradistinction to his cousin, "Devil Charley," son of General Thos Polk and Susan Spratt, who was noted for his daredevil pranks.

Possessed of a remarkably vigorous constitution, "Civil Charley" Polk attained to a great age. After many years' residence in Western Tennessee, he again decided to emigrate and went to Texas, where he spent the balance of his days, and died.

Most of Charles' sons accompanied him to the Lone Star State, in which had also located other Polks, some in Austin's colony. The principal one of the latter was Dr Thomas Polk, from Indiana, son of Capt Charles Polk, the Indian fighter, and grandson of Chas Polk, the Indian trader, at the North Bend of the Potomac, who was a son of Wm Polk, Sr, of Maryland and brother of that Wm Polk who emigrated from Carlisle, Pa, to North Carolina and founded the Southern branch of the Polk Tree.

"Civil Charley" Polk emigrated to Tennessee, and thence to Texas, about 1842, had issue. ¹Jane; ²John ("Jackey"), ³Andrew, ⁴William Knox, who married Nancy Petty, ⁵Cynthia, who married her cousin, John Polk, son of John, brother of "Civil Charley," ⁶Charles, who married Elizabeth Hayne, ⁷Judge Alfred, who married Nancy McIvor.

John (or "Jackey") Polk, eldest son of "Civil Charley" Polk and Margaret (Baxter) Polk, married Elizabeth Allen about 1814, and they had issue: [1]William A., who married Martha Barrett and remained in Tennessee; [2]Charles Grandison, who married Mary Ann Massey and remained in Tennessee; [3]Benina, who married Wm Massey brother of Mary Ann; [4]Amanda M., who married Rev. Richard Overton Watkins; [5]Emily, who married Josiah Childres; [6]Nancy, who married Norman Branch; [7]Victoria, who married Wm Birdwell. The latter have two children—Charles and Willie

"Jackey" Polk and all of his family, except the boys Wm A and C G Polk, emigrated from Tennessee to Texas, going to San Augustine County and later settling at Linn Flat, Nacogdoches County.

Jennie Polk married John Potts and they settled in Alabama

Andrew Polk and wife went to Missouri, removed thence to Cherokee County, Texas, and later to Waco, Texas

Cynthia and her husband, John Polk, removed from San Augustine County to Leon County. Their children married and remained in San Augustine County. John was married three times, and by his third wife has a daughter living in San Antonio

Mrs Ann Smith (daughter of Judge Alfred Polk), who married Benjamin Smith, lives at Silver Valley, Coleman County, Texas. Most of Judge Alfred Polk's children married and located permanently in San Augustine County, leaving many descendants who are prominent and influential citizens

DESCENDANTS OF JACKIE AND CYNTHIA POLK.

Eugenia Polk, daughter of 'Jackie" and Cynthia Polk, married Dr Thomas B Davenport, and to them were born two children, [1]Mary Cynthia and [2]Elizabeth. Mary Cynthia Davenport was b July 20, 1857, married July 26, 1876, Matthew Cartwright, b Aug 11, 1856, and to them were born ten children, as follows

(1) Leonidas Davenport Cartwright, b May 9, 1877, who married Justa Joiner, (b ——, 1879), in December 12, 1899. They have four children, [1]Lorel, b Oct 26, 1900, [2]Leonid.. b J.. . 29 1902 [3]Justa b July 12 1909,

⁴Jerome, b July 7 1911 They live in San Antonio, Texas.

(2) Amanda Holman Cartwright, b March 12, 1879, married James Lane Taylor, of Sherman, Texas, Dec 20 1900 They now live in San Antonio, Texas, and have two children. ¹Eugenia Polk, b Sept 11, 1901, ²Maria Louise, b Dec 29 1903.

(3) Eugenia Polk Cartwright, b. Dec. 3. 1880, married James Ingram Cartwright. Nov. 8 1904. They are now living in Uvalde, Texas, and have one child, Matthew, b Aug 14 1905.

(4) Estelle Cartwright, b July 19, 1881 married Wm B Lupe, Nov 4, 1903 They are living in San Antonio, Texas, have two living children and one dead ¹Mary Davenport b Feb 3, 1905, ²Estelle, (deceased), ³William, Jr, b March 17, 1910

(5) Jerome Broocke Cartwright, b Nov 3, 1883, married William Preston Head March 26, 1907 Living now in Sulphur, Okla.

(6) Mary Davenport Cartwright b May 13, 1885, married Clarence I Pickrell, Jan 7, 1909 Now living in El Paso Texas.

(7) Reagan Cartwright, b Feb 22 1887 married Isabel Branson, of Coatesville, Pa, Nov 9, 1910 Now living in Alpine Texas

(8) Holman Cartwright, b March 20, 1890

(9) Matthew Cartwright, b Jan 7, 1893

(10) Broocke Cartwright, b Jan 20 1895

Elizabeth DeKalb Davenport, second daughter of Eugenia Polk and Dr. Davenport, married S. M. Gladney, and they have four children. ¹Donald; ²Eugenia, ³Jane Ross, ⁴Samuel They live at Torrell Texas

Jerome Polk, who married Col John Broocke, had four children ¹Margaret Eugenia, who married George C. Greer and they have three sons, Lewis V Second Lieutenant in U. S A. stationed at Fort Bliss Wyoming, John H. and George Jerome, ²John H of San Augustine, Texas, ³Moses Lycurgus Broocke, (deceased) former U S Congressman from Beaumont Texas married Laura Allen ²Ara;

³Elizabeth John H Broocke married the widow Laura Allen Broocke and they have one child, Jerome

John D. Polk, son of Cynthia and John Polk, is now living in San Angelo, Texas, and is about 76 years of age He has one daughter, Elizabeth, who married David Blake, and they have several children Elizabeth, who married Mr Passow; Lucile, who married Wm. H Kelley; David and others

REV. R. O. WATKINS AND FAMILY.

The children born to Rev R O Watkins, and Amanda (Polk) Watkins, were.

(1) John Polk Watkins, b Dec. 22, 1840, d Jan 30, 1908, married to Lorena McColium Issue. ¹Edward; ²Elizabeth; ³Finis, ⁴Jewel; ⁵A B

(2) Jesse A Watkins. b May 1, 1843, married Dora Harr Issue · ¹Nettie; ²Charles; ³Archibald, ⁴Elzabeth. Residence, Kemp Texas.

(3) Richard O Watkins, b Aug 6, 1846, unmarried Residence, Kemp, Texas

(4) Dr William Archibald Watkins, b June 4, 1849, married Jennie Nobles Issue · ¹Genivieve, ²Chailiie, ³Mary, ⁴Elizabeth, ⁵Willie J Residence, Kemp, Texas

(5) Robert Smith Watkins, b Jan 31, 1852, married Murphia Collins No issue Residence, Kemp, Texas

(6) M E. Watkins. b. Oct 31, 1854, d Jan. 14, 1870

(7) Judge Albert Bacon Watkins b. Aug. 4, 1857, married Laura Murchison Issue · Royal R, only child. Residence, Athens, Texas

John Polk Watkins and his brother, Jesse Watkins, were Confederate soldiers in the Civil War.

SKETCH OF REV. R. O. WATKINS.

Rev Richard Overton Watkins, who married Amanda M Polk, daughter of John Polk and Elizabeth Allen, in March, 1842, in San Augustine County, Texas, was a native of Tennessee He was born near the town of Clarksville, on the Cumberland River March 31, 1816 He was educated

at Sharon, Miss., and removed with his father to Texas in
1833, and settled first near Clarksville, Texas, and later at
Nacogdoches, Texas. He was the first Protestant minister
ordained in the Republic of Texas, the Presbytery meeting
at the time in old Fort Houston. He was a soldier in the
early Indian and Mexican wars, in Texas. He was a son of
Capt. Jesse Watkins, who was killed by the Indians in Texas
in November, 1838. He lived at Kemp, Texas, and died there
on May 27, 1897, in his eighty-second year. He spent his
life continuously in the ministry, and was much interested in
the higher educational matters of his church in the State.

SKETCH OF JUDGE A. B. WATKINS.

Albert Bacon Watkins, son of Rev. R. O. Watkins and
Amanda (Polk) Watkins, was born at Kemp, in Kaufman
County, Texas, Aug. 4, A. D. 1857. He was educated at
Trinity University, graduating there in 1877. He studied
law at Kaufman, Texas, with the law firm of Manion & Adams,
who were at the time well known throughout the State. He
was admitted to the bar at Kaufman in September, 1879, and
shortly afterwards became a member of the firm and moved
to the town of Athens and continued with the firm until the
death of one of its members. He was District Judge of the
Third Judicial District of Texas, including Houston, Anderson and Henderson Counties, in 1892, and afterwards, but
has never held any other office. He has engaged in the active
practice of the law ever since. He was Most Worshipful
Grand Master of Masons in Texas for the years 1896 and 1897.

MEMORANDA OF THE POLK FAMILY IN TEXAS.

(By Judge A. B. Watkins, Athens, Texas.)

Two of the sons of John Polk and Eleanor (Shelby) Polk
emigrated from Tennessee to Texas, namely: Charles ("Civil
Charlie"), and his brother John Polk. Both of them settled
at first in San Augustine County. They moved to Texas
about the year 1840. Charles, the elder, came with his four
sons, John ("Jacky"), Arthur, Charles, and Alfred, and also

his daughter, Cynthia, who was then married to her cousin, John Polk, son of his brother John above mentioned.

Charles Polk was born in Charlotte, N. C., January 18, 1760. He fought in the war of the Revolution, and told my father that his father, who was at the time a middle aged man, was also a soldier and an officer.

Charles Polk married Miss Margaret Baxter, in North Carolina, later moved to Maury County, Tennessee, and not long afterwards moved over near Bolivar, Tenn., where he resided until he moved to Texas in 1840. He lived to be quite an old man and died in San Augustine County, Texas, about the year 1846 or 1847. He was rather a small sized man, light haired and blue-eyed, and quite active and vigorous almost up to the date of his death.

John Polk, his brother, also came, with at least one son, John. My information is that he was two years younger than his brother Charles. He lived in San Augustine County several years with or near his son, John, who had married Cynthia Polk, before coming to Texas, and they each afterwards moved to Leon County, Texas. He died there, as I have been informed, about 1849 and his son John died about six years later.

Taylor Polk, their other brother, is said to have moved to Arkansas, and the Texas people know but little of his family, although I am told that the Corsicana Polks are some of his descendants.

JUDGE ALBERT B. WATKINS,
Athens, Tex.

THE NEW YORK
PUBLIC LIBRARY

ASTOR, LENOX AND
TILDEN FOUNDATIONS.

CHAPTER XLII.

CHILDREN OF CHAS. POLK AND WIFE MARGARET.

Of the children of Charles Polk and his wife, Margaret, I add briefly as to all except John.

Jane, the oldest daughter, ~~first married~~ 2nd a Mr Fowler, and afterwards John Potts, and moved from Tennessee down into Alabama I can give but little of her family history

William married Miss Nancy Petty and moved from LaGrange, Tenn., to Holly Springs, Miss He lived and died in that State. All the other members of the family came to Texas

Andrew, married a Miss Martha Tindle, and afterwards moved to Missouri and thence later to Texas, and settled in Cherokee County He had several children One of them, a daughter, married James Anderson, a distinguished attorney They lived at Rusk, and later at Waco. They left children who reside now in Waco and in Austin, Texas.

Cynthia Polk (daughter of "Civil Charley" Polk), married her cousin, John Polk, and they moved to Texas about 1840, and settled near the town of San Augustine. With my mother, at least, she had the reputation of being the brainiest of the Polks in this part of the country

Charles Polk, sixth child of Charles and Margaret (Baxter) Polk, married Elizabeth Hayne, and moved to Leon County, Texas I can give but the least information possible about his family I know he had one son He died there, and I am of the impression that he did not have a very large family.

Alfred Polk, youngest child of "Civil Charley" Polk and Margaret (Baxter) Polk, married Nancy McIvor They moved from Tennessee to Texas with several of the other members of the family and settled about one mile ... own of

San Augustine. They raised a large family. Alfred Polk or Judge Polk, as he was most commonly known, represented the highest type of good citizenship. For fifty years he commanded the undiminished love and esteem of the people of his part of the State. It might be added that his good wife, Nancy, claimed also an abiding place in the hearts of her neighbors and friends.

JOHN POLK AND FAMILY

John Polk was the second child and eldest son of Charles Polk and Margaret Baxter.

John married Elizabeth Allen, who at the time resided in Kentucky. All of their children were born and most of them married while they resided near Bolivar, Tenn. They came to Texas with the others of the family and settled first near San Augustine, and afterwards moved up into Nacogdoches County, and lived there until they both died. He died in 1866, at about 84 years of age. His wife, Elizabeth, died when 70 years of age. He was, like all the other Polks, in Texas, a slave owner. All of their children came with them to Texas except the two older ones, William A. Polk and Charles Grandison Polk, who remained in Tennessee, near where they were born.

COL. WILLIAM KNOX POLK'S DESCENDANTS.

(By Mrs. Grace Hemingway, Jackson, Miss.)

Col. Wm. Knox Polk, of Holly Springs, Miss., (son of Civil Charley Polk and Margaret Baxter, of North Carolina, and grandson of John Polk and Eleanor Shelby), emigrated at an early day from Tennessee to Mississippi. In his new location he became a planter, raising cotton principally. He was married to Nancy Petty, by whom he had six children: [1]Isabella Polk, b. Oct. 7, 1815, married 1834 to Dr. C. S. Bowen, d. 1896; [2]Emeline Polk, b. about 1817, married Peter B. Jones, d. ——; [3]Jane Polk, b. about 1819, married Dr. R. S. Lucas, d. 1865; [4]Laurentine S. Polk, b. about 1821 d. at 27, at Memphis; [5]Amanda Polk, b. about 1823, also died young, [6]William I.

Polk, b about 1825, d ——, married 1st Maggie Coopwood, 2nd Mattie E Moore

Isabella Polk, (b Oct 7, 1815), married Dr. C S Bowen 1831, d 1896 They had eleven children viz

(1) Emily Bowen, b 1835, married in 1853 to Dr S P Lester, of Batesville, Miss Emily d in 1865 leaving four children. ¹Belle, b 1855, married J. M Cox, in 1871, they had issue. ¹Lillian, b 1876, d about 1894 ²William b 1879, married Lois Jackson, in 1905, they had issue. ¹William Jr, b 1908, ²Lois, b 1910 ³Lester, b 1884, married Estelle Kinchloe ⁴Louise, b 1887, married Jules Tombs in 1905, they had issue ¹Bessie, b 1906, ²Mary Alice, b. 1907, d 1908; ³John Dudley, b 1910, ⁴Bowen, b Dec, 1889 ⁵Leonard, b Jan 1897 ²Bowen, b. 1857, not married. ³Maude, b. 1860, married G H Watkins, d 1897. ⁴Jessie, b. 1864, married Rev R. A N Wilson, 1892, they had issue ¹Gerald, b 1893, d 1898, ²Lester, b. 1895, ³Robert, b. 1898, ⁵Dorothy, b 1901, ⁶William, b 1904

(2) Eliza Bowen, daughter of Dr C S Bowen, b. Sept 13, 1837, married Dr Wilbur F Hyer, April 21, 1861, d Oct 11, 1909 Issue ¹Lucy, b. Sept. 5, 1862, d. 1873. ²Jane, b Dec 21, 1864 married Richard P Moore, Aug 29, 1889, they had issue ¹George, b June 28, 1890, ²Richard P Jr, b June 16, 1892, ³Grace, b. Dec. 4, 1894, d. June 8, 1896; ⁴Elise b June 10, 1897; ⁵Marshall, b May 18, 1899, d May 16 1900; ⁶Frances, b Nov 30, 1903, ⁷Wilbur, b April 21, 1906 ³Emily, Frances Bowen, b. March 25, 1867, married James H Price, April 26, 1904 ⁴John McRaven, b March 15, 1869, d 1876 ⁵Grudchen, b Nov. 11, 1871, married Charles V Akin, June 1, 1893, d Dec 31, 1900, they had issue ¹Lois, b April 7 1894, ²Miriam, b Sept 21, 1896, d Dec 1896, ³Gladys, b Sept 5, 1897 ⁶Grace Bowen, b Jan. 21, 1874, married Wm Hemingway June 19, 1901, they had two chidren who died in infancy ⁷Wilbur F Jr, (called "Tom"), b. Jan. 22, 1877, unmarried ⁸Eric Bowen, b Nov 14, 1881, unmarried.

(3) David Bowen, b 1839, married Emma Kay in 1870, d 1895 Issue ¹Stella, b 1869, d 1873 ²Wm. Bates, b 1872, d 1912. ³Paul Kay, b 1875, married and had two children, and d. in 1908 ⁴Emma, b 1880, married 1900 had two children, married 2nd time 1909 —— — ⁵Annie Rose, b 1883 d 1885

(4) Amanda Bowen, b 1841, married Van Potts, 1865 Issue ¹William b 1866, d. 1867. ²James, b 1868, married Mamie Barlow, 1899, d about 1903, they had two children ³Robinson, b 1870, unmarried ⁴Bowen, b 1872, d 1878 ⁵Van, b 1875, married Virgie Lester 1897, they had issue ¹Melvin, b 1898; ²———, b. 1900, d 1901, ³Aubrey, b 1902; ⁴Noel, b 1905; ⁵Twins, b 1907, d. 1908; ⁶T. W, b 1909.

(5) William Polk Bowen, b 1844, married Alice Bost, in 1866 Lives in Texas Issue: ¹Alfred, b 1868; ²Charles, b 1871, ³Cliff, b. 1880

(6) Mattie Bowen, b 1846, married James S Taylor, 1869 Issue ¹Katie, b 1870, d. 1871 ²J. G b. 1872, d. about 1906, unmarried. ³Christopher, b. 1875 ⁴Ernest, b. 1880, married Effie Tucker, 1906, they had issue: ¹Ernestine, b 1908 ⁵Guy, b 1882 is unmarried

(7) Robert Bowen, b 1848, unmarried.

(8) Christopher Strong Bowen, b 1850, married Georgia Mims 1879, d 1885. Issue: ¹Annie, b 1880, married Walter Knotts 1899, three children: Ned, Elizabeth and Walter ²Mims, b 1881, unmarried ³Sarah, b 1883, unmarried.

(9) Charles Bowen, b. 1852, d. 1858.

(10) Alice Bowen, b 1856, unmarried

(11) Edward Reese Bowen, b. 1862, married Rosa Eddins in 1891 Issue one child, Christopher Strong Bowen, Jr

Emeline Polk, second child of Col. Wm Knox Polk, married Peter Jones. They had issue:

(1) Laura Jones, married Van H Potts.

(2) Kate Jones, married Van H. Potts (2nd wife). For his third wife he married their cousin, Amanda Bowen, daughter of Isabella Issue by first two wives ¹Kate May, married Howard Harris, and had issue Robert Lois, Van, Karen, Lily, Flavia.

(3) Marshall Branch Jones married Ellen Nesbit. He is long since dead and she lives in Memphis Their children were. ¹Anna, not married, ²May, ³Lelia, married during the winter of 1911-12, husbands name unknown; ⁴Nina, married Dr Miller and lives at Hillsboro, Tex, they had two children Dorothy Flyer and Lutie Stairs; ⁵Evelyn, married E. B Williams and lives in Meridian, Miss, they had issue Evelyn,

and a son, I think, ⁶Lutie Polk married Mr. Stairs and lives in New York City.

(4) Lucas Polk, married Virginia Spencer. He is dead and she resides in the West. Issue: ¹Stanley Branch, ²Alma, ³Lon Neal; ⁴Marshall Drane.

(5) Mollie Jones, married W. W. Perkins and d. 1897. Issue: ¹Howard, married Floy Potts, one child, Mary Ann, ²Florence, unmarried; ³Louis, married Louise ———, ⁴Clift, unmarried, ⁵Fred married Ethel Fuqua, ⁶Gladys, unmarried.

(6) Katie Jones, married Marshall Bouldin. One child Marshall Jones Bouldin. He is married and lives in Clarksdale.

(7) Lily Jones, married W. D. Porter, of Oxford, and d. several years ago. One child, Earl, who married Miss Moore.

(8) Sue Jones, unmarried, lives in Memphis.

Jane Polk daughter of Col Wm Knox Polk, b. 1819, d. 1865 married Dr R S Lucas and had two daughters, Mollie J and Baza, who d unmarried.

Laurentine S Polk, b about 1821, d unmarried aged 27 years.

Amanda Polk, b about 1823, also died young.

William I Polk, b about 1825, married first Maggie Coopwood, second Mattie E. Moore. He had issue: ¹William C. Polk, by first wife, ²Jessie Lee Forrest Polk, ³Frank Polk, ⁴Allie L Polk. William I. Polk resided in Memphis, Tenn, and was engaged in the stock trade.

SKETCH OF HEADLEY POLK.

(By his daughter, Miss Annie Polk, San Marcos, Texas.)

Headley Polk's father was Shelby Polk and his mother, Winifred Colburn of Mecklenburg County, N C. He was a grandson of Col Thomas Polk, of South Carolina, and Mary (Shelby) Polk, grand-daughter of the famous General Evan Shelby, of North Carolina. Headley's great grandfather was William Polk, eldest son of William Polk and Margaret Taylor, and brother of General Thomas, Capt Ezekiel, Capt Charles and Capt John Polk, all of whom bore conspicuous parts in the struggle for Independence.

Headley Polk was born in N Ca on ——— 6, 1812

and moved with his parents, when but a child, to West Tennessee, then a new and undeveloped country, where he grew to manhood. He was born at a time when men were tested as to what sort they were. Having lost his father when young, Headley nobly assumed the responsibility of earning and providing for the family, and though he had all his life longed to "go West," he would not do so until he had secured his mother, brothers and sisters a home.

On June 3, 1845, Headley was married to Miss Eliza Sebastian, of Maury County, Tenn., and in the fall of the same year he moved to Texas, where he, as one of her noblest citizens, ever afterward identified himself with her interests. By his indomitable energy and great perseverance he overcame the great obstacles that he had encountered, and was a success in the commercial world.

Notwithstanding he was about ninety-five years old when he died, Headley was strong in body and mind, and while quiet in his manners, his Christian life and walk exerted a powerful influence upon all who knew him. His pastor, in speaking of him, said: "It was a joy and an inspiration to be associated with him."

WARNELL POLK.

Respecting Warnell Polk, who settled in Texas, and whose ancestry it was somewhat difficult to ascertain, Col. George W. Polk, of San Antonio, says: "In a letter received from J. M. Sears, of San Marcos, this state, one of the family says: 'Your inquiry has been handed me by my uncle, Frank M. Polk, of Fentress. In reply I am sending you all the information that he knows in regard to his family. Warnell Polk, son of Taylor Polk, was born in Ark. Taylor Polk died when Warnell was seven years old; his mother died four years later. After his mother's death Warnell came to Texas and stopped in Bastrop County with Jim Weaver, but left him when fourteen years old and was taken by Dr. D. F. Brown, of Prairie Lea, Tex., and lived with Dr. Brown until he married Miss Irene Myers. Warnell L. Polk and wife had eight children. Following are their names in order, and present post office addresses: 'Laura G. married G. C. Eustace, (P. O. Luling),

HEADLEY POLK,
San Marcos, Tex., at 90 years old.

²Frank M , married Miss M. A Chamberlain (P O Fentress); ³Mollie, married Lev. Watts (P O Dale), Mr Watts died several years ago, ⁴McIver, married B E Barber (P. O. Fentress), ⁵Ida P., married J. Will Sears Mr and Mrs Sears are both dead, ⁶Ada L , married W J Blackwell, Mrs Blackwell d in 1888 (P. O W J. Blackwell, Lockhart), ⁷C W , married Miss Annie Hampton (C W was killed in 1904), ⁸Clara Virginia, married Charles P Smith (P O Lockhart)

CHAPTER XLIII.

UNATTACHED BRANCHES.

During the early part of the past century, a great many of the Polks emigrated to Western and Southwestern territories and States, most of them going from North and South Carolina and Tennessee. Nearly all of these, presumably, have been located by the writer and placed in their proper positions on the family tree. A few, however, by reason of failure on their part to preserve or to remember who their great grand-parents were now constitute detached limbs. Various traditions, however, are remembered by them, and these traditions serve to indicate pretty accurately their relation to the parent stock.

The principal of these detached branches, in point of the number of its members, appears to be located in Southeast Missouri, between Iron Mountain and the Arkansas line, all descended from one William Wesley Polk, who is reputed to have gone to Missouri from Georgia. The first of these heard of by the writer was one William Polk, a Baptist preacher, during the early part of the Civil War, who was murdered by three Federal soldiers. In no border State of the Union was so much political bitterness manifested, or so many people ruthlessly murdered by guerilla bands, bushwhackers, and other combatants, as in Missouri. In Southeast Missouri, particularly in the Ozark Range of mountains, these conditions existed to a most alarming extent.

Data relative to this branch was procured from Capt. Charles K. Polk, of Iron County, a prominent and influential citizen who has filled several positions of honor and trust at the hands of his people. In response to enquiries by the writer, Capt. Charles K. Polk said:

"I've long since been sure that the Polk family sprung from one parent stock. I have never yet met a Polk but what claimed a relationship with James K. Polk and Charles Polk, of Tennessee, commonly known as "Devil Charley." I am not sure of my grandfather's name, but my impression is that it was William Wesley Polk In talking to an old friend after my father's death, he referred to him (my grandfather) as Wesley Polk I never saw him, as he died before I was born. He came from Georgia and settled in Madison County, Mo He may have stopped in Tennessee awhile before he came to Missouri, but of this I am not sure He had two sons and one daughter I have no knowledge of any others—John W, the older and William the younger, and the daughter Sarah William was the Baptist preacher, of whom you heard when at Ironton during the war Our family record was burned, and for that reason I cannot give dates of births, marriages and deaths

My father John W Polk, married Christina Yount. She was German, American born They had four children to live until grown and to marry and raise families, three daughters and one son

"Matilda, the eldest, married James McDowell. To them were born three sons Mr McDowell and one of the sons died, and she, with her two other sons, returned to her father's home. James the younger boy, died about the age of eighteen John W. McDowell, the other, lived to be married to Flava Harris The Harris family emigrated from Kentucky. John W and Flava (Harris) McDowell had two daughters, Ada and Matilda McDowell. After this Matilda, James' wife, and her son John W McDowell died, and Flava, widow of the latter with her two daughters went to Oregon with the Harris family and settled near Summer Lake Ada, the eldest, married Fred Foster and they live at Summer Lake. Matilda married William Barnes.

'Rebecca, second daughter of John W Polk and Christiana Yount, married Leroy Matkins To this union was born fourteen children six of whom survive The oldest is Wm Matkin, of French Mills, Mo, the second S A Matkin, of Arcadia, Mo; the third James Leroy Matkin, of Arcadia, the fourth Mary Ann Dunn, of Grandon, Mo, the fifth Benjamin I Matkin, the sixth Ira Matkins, of Arcadia

"Lahd c P lk th daug c P lk and Christin Y un P k m t l th th are dead Two children survive them, George Miller, French Mills, Mo., and Mary Simmons, of Brunot, of Wayne Co., Mo.

"Charles K. Polk, was born Oct 16, 1839 He was married Nov. 29, 1859 to Miss Sarah Christ, who died in 1860. On July 1, 1861 he enlisted in the Missouri State Guard for six months, to co-operate with the Confederates. A short time after the organization, the Second Lieutenant resigning, Charles was chosen in his place At the expiration of six months they were disbanded at Pitman's Ferry, near Arkansas Line He then re-enlisted in the Confederate States service, in a Cavalry Company, for a term of 'during the war' At the organization of the company he was elected First Lieutenant They were formed into a regiment of ten companies and designated as the Third Missouri Cavalry, Col Colton Green commanding. Later they were assigned to General Marmaduke's Brigade On Nov. 1, 1863, Capt Surridge was elected Major and Lieut Polk was promoted to Captain. shortly after Col Solomon Kitchen was ordered to North Arkansas with twelve commissioned officers, Capt Polk being one of the number, to collect stragglers left behind and to recruit others While in North Arkansas on his duty, he became acquainted with one Wm. H Polk, who had immigrated from Tennessee His wife, also from Tennessee, was formerly Mary Emerson. Mrs Polk had a sister-in-law, Rhoda Emerson, who had one child, Corelia Emerson, and to the widow Rhoda, Capt Polk was married in July, 1864 During the time he had recruited fifty men and Gen'l Sterling Price had commenced his march from South of the Arkansas to Missouri Capt Polk rejoined the army, reporting to the regiment with the men he had recruited, and again took command of his Company"

With his command, Capt. Polk marched into Missouri with General Sterling Price, and took active part with him in an aggressive campaign in that State, extending to and North of the Missouri river and westward to the Kansas Line Successful battles took place at Pilot Knob and other points, but Price was forced to retreat back to Arkansas, finally surrendering his army in Louisiana, after Lee had surrendered at Appomattox Capt Polk then rejoined his wife, in Randolph

County, Ark., where he continued for two years. During that time two children were born to them. ¹Christiana Lee, b May 6, 1866; ²John William, b Feb 10, 1868

With this family, in March of the latter year, Capt. Polk returned to his old home in Iron County, Mo, and rejoined his parents

For the benefit of his wife's health, he next removed to California, where, on Dec 14, following, she died On the same day, back in Missouri Capt Polk's mother also died In Nov 1875 he again went back to the old home in Missouri, where he has ever since continued to live

On March 4, 1877, Capt Polk took a third wife, Harriet Isabel Sharp. By his first wife, Sarah Christ, whom he married Nov. 29, 1859, he had no issue By his second wife he had Christina Lee and John William Polk By his third wife, Harriet Isabel Sharp, he had five girls and two boys, viz ¹Charles Henry, b March 30, 1878; ²Hattie Rebecca, b. Sept 11, 1880, ³Euseba Jane, b Feb 12, 1882; ⁴Thomas Benton, b Feb. 8, 1884; ⁵Lula Belle, b. Feb 20, 1885, ⁶Annie Theodosia, b July 15, 1887: ⁷Laura Mae, b Oct 5, 1892.

Christina Lee Polk, eldest child and daughter by Rhoda Emerson, married May 6, 1890, to Lysander Ashlock Issue ¹Charles, b 1891, now in U S Army, ²John William, b 1893, ³Richard Payne, b 1895, ⁴Iil Gerard, b 1898; ⁵Joseph Henry, b 1903, ⁶Frank Dumont, b 1905, ⁷Bertha Alma, b 19— The family resides at Silver Mine, Mo.

John William Polk, son of Capt Chas K Polk, by his second wife, Rhoda Emerson, married Feb 22, 1893, Laura Eliza Miller and they had issue· ¹Archie Elmer, b 1894, ²Effie Lorene, b 1896, ³Raymond Otto, b 1900; ⁴Carrie Edna, b 1902 John William Polk was elected Sheriff of Iron County, in 1902 and again in 1904 While attempting to arrest an outlaw, named William Spaugh, he was shot and killed by another Spaugh No people, it is said by the citizens of Iron County, ever had a better or more popular officer than John William Polk.

Charles Henry Polk son of Capt Charles K Polk, b. March 30, 1878, joined the Baptist church studied for the ministry and was ordained in 1900. He was elected a Representative to the Legislature in 1906 and re-elected in 1908. He resides at Springfield, Mo.

Hattie Rebecca Polk, fourth child of Capt Chas K. Polk, b Sept 11, 1880, married Feb. 1, 1906, Wm L Boatmer, of Arcadia, Mo.

Euseba Jane Polk, fifth child of Capt Chas K Polk, b Feb 12, 1882, married May 2, 1909, Oliver Lesley Yount, of Ironton, Mo.

Thomas Benton Polk, Jr, sixth child of Capt Chas K Polk, b. Feb 8, 1884, is unmarried and lives at the old homestead.

Lula Belle Polk, seventh child of Capt Chas K Polk, b Feb 20, 1885, married April 19, 1908, Francis Otto Thomas, of Granite City, Ill.

Annie Theodosia Polk, eighth child of Capt Chas K Polk, b July 15, 1887, is unmarried.

Laura Mae Polk, youngest child of Capt Chas K Polk, b Oct 5, 1892, is unmarried.

John W Polk, Sr, eldest son of William Wesley Polk, also represented Madison County in the Missouri Legislature several terms, in one of which he secured the passage of a bill through the House erecting Iron County out of a part of Madison. He was also elected member of the State Senate for one or two terms. Altogether, he served in public life for twenty-two years.

Sarah Polk, only daughter of William Wesley Polk, married a Mr Williams and they located at Fort Smith, Ark. Before the Civil War they resided at Ozark, Mo. Their descendants are untraced.

William Polk, second child and son of William Wesley Polk, was a Baptist preacher and lived in Madison and Iron Counties before the Civil War. When quite a young man he was married to Miss Mary Sharp and to them were born six children.

William Polk, b ——, (first child and son of Rev. Wm Polk) married Miss Lucona Hammonds and had six children, four of whom are dead. The two living are Thos B Polk, of

St Louis, a prominent real estate and insurance man, and Sarah Jane, wife of John Sharp, of Flat River, Mo

Thomas Benton Polk, b ——, (second son of Rev Wm Polk), was also a soldier in the Confederate Army Returning home after the war, he married Mrs Jane Irwin, and to them were born two sons while in Missouri, William and Martin Thomas Benton and family then removed to California, where four more children were born to them. [1]Ernest, [2]Julia, [3]Thomas and [4]Etta Martin, Julia and Etta were married Martin's wife died about 1905 He is a Civil Engineer and resides at Chico, Butte Co, California.

James K. Polk, b ——, (third child and son of Rev Wm Polk and wife Mary (Sharp) Polk), was also a Confederate soldier, and resided in Texas County, Mo, where he died He had several children, but their names have not been secured His widow and children still live in Texas County

Trusten Balam Polk, b. ——, of Arcadia, Mo, (fourth child and son of Rev Wm Polk), married Fannie Blanton and they had issue [1]Hattie; [2]Flava, [3]William; [4]Lee, [5]James; [6]Mildred. [7]Edgar [8]Elmer.

Serena Polk b ——, (fifth child of Rev Wm Polk), married Hartford Hammonds To them a son was born, and the father removed with his child to Kentucky after his wife's death.

Fannie Polk, b ——. (sixth and youngest child of Rev Wm Polk), married William Blanton and they removed to Cohasset, Cal Issue unknown

Rev William Polk was prominent during his life, both as a citizen and as a member and leading minister of the Baptist church in Missouri He was one of the organizers of Bethel Associates of United Baptists, the oldest Baptist Association in the State, organized when Missouri was a territory, almost a century ago. Ever since that time he had many of his kinsmen have been active and influential members of the Association There was scarcely a pulpit in Southeast and Southern Missouri that he did n t fill at s me time The c rr ness of his discourses alw ys c   ng l rge audien e   d   transaction of the Civil War was more heinous and unprovoked than that which ended by astrocious murder, the life of this good man

TRAGIC DEATH OF REV. WM. POLK.

The chaotic and troublous times that prevailed in Missouri during the Civil War, when vindictiveness and revenge were rampart on all sides among those holding opposite political opinions, has already been alluded to. Hundreds of murders were committed and among these atrocities was the murder of Rev William Polk, second son of William Wesley Polk, by three Federal soldiers. He lived about eight miles south of Ironton, and on meeting the assassins in uniform, they proceeded to rob him and then informed him that they were going to kill him, and asked if he wanted to pray first. He saw their purpose was to kill him, and in reply said that he had "long before made his peace with God, but he would pray for them." He fell upon his knees, and while asking God to forgive them they shot him in the back, killing him instantly

CHAPTER XLIV.

CHARLES POLKE, THE INDIAN TRADER.

Charles Polke, the Indian Trader, who for a number of years in the forepart of the eighteenth century engaged in trade with the Indians, at his store located at the North Bend of the Potomac River, in Frederick County, Maryland, was the progenitor of a vigorous and adventurous family that crossed the Alleghanies after the Indian barrier to the Ohio Valley had been removed by the battle of Point Pleasant in October, 1774. Descending the Ohio with their families to Kentucky, they planted new homes in the wilderness. Some of them remained in Kentucky the balance of their lives, but others moved on to Indiana, Illinois, Missouri and sections still further to the West and Southwest. So steadily progressive was the march of these Polks that in time they reached the Pacific and the Gulf of Mexico, where many of the latest generation now reside.

Charles Polk, the Indian Trader, judging from data procured concerning him, was one of the two eldest sons of William Polk, Sr., (second son of Robert and Magdalen Polk) by his first wife, Nancy Knox, said to have been a sister of Joanna Knox, second wife of John Polk, Sr., eldest son of the immigrants. Another son of William Polk, Sr., by the same wife, as the proof adduced indicates, was that William Polk who went from Maryland to Carlisle, Pa., where he married Margaret Taylor and moved thence to North Carolina about 1750 and became the progenitor of the Southern branch of the Polk family, which has produced many illustrious sons and daughters. William died west of the Yadkin, a few years after going to North Carolina.

These sons, Charles and William, by the first wife of William Polk 1st, appear to have attained manhood before their father's second marriage, to have been allotted their respective portions of his estate, and then to have turned their faces to other fields for the world that awaited them above.

Charles, after leaving his father's house, proceeded to the North Bend of the Potomac, on the Maryland frontier, where he built a trading house and residence and for a number of years engaged in trade with the Indians, being known as "Charles Polk, the Indian Trader." Here he lived and carried on business until his death in 1753, leaving a widow and six children. He was born in Somerset County, Md., 1700 to 1710, and his brother William just before or after him.

In his will Charles calls his wife "Christian." It is believed that her family name was Matson, and that she was a sister of Ralph Matson, who was co-executor with her of the will of Charles, made the same year in which he died.

Charles Polk's trading store was one of the principal establishments of that kind on the frontier. In Gist's Journal, p. 140, we find that "Charles Polk's name appears in the list of Indian Traders in 1734" (Colonial Archives, Vol. 1, p. 125). On Mayo's Map of 1737 his name is marked, with those of four other settlers, at the North Bend of the Potomac, where Hancock, Maryland now stands. (Also see Colonial Records of Pennsylvania, Vol. 5, p. 760).

Charles Polk and Christian, his wife, were married about 1735, presumably in Somerset County, but of the exact locality of that event, we have no positive proof. In his will of 1753, the six children of Charles and Christian Polk appear as follows: ¹Sarah, b. 1736, ²William, b. 1738, ³Edmond, b. 1740, ⁴Thomas, b. 1742, ⁵Capt. Chas., b. Feb. 2, 1744; ⁶John, b. 1746.

WILL OF CHARLES POLK, INDIAN TRADER.

In the name of God Amen

The nineteenth day of March in the year of our Lord One thousand Seven hundred and fifty-three, I, Chas. Polk of Maryland and County of Frederick farmer being very sick and weak in body but of perfect mind and memory thanks be given unto God therefor calling to mind the Mortality of my Body and knowing that it is appointed for all men once to die do make and ordain this my last Will and Testament, that is to say principally and first of all I give and recommend my soul into the Hands of God that gave it, for my Body I recommend it to the Earth to be buried in a Christianlike and decent manner at the discretion of my Executors, nothing doubting but at the General resurrection I shall receive the same again by the Mighty Power of God, and as touching such wordly estate wherewith it hath pleased God to bless me with in this Life I give devise and dispose of the same in the following manner and form

Imprimis. It is my Will and I do order that in the first place all my just debts and funeral charges be paid and satisfied

Item I give and bequeath unto Christian, my dearly beloved wife, the third part of all my movables and the use of the Plantation as long as she remains a widow, and if she should marry then the Plantation to be sold and disposed of as followeth

Item I give unto my well beloved son William his horse and saddle as he claims now to be his own and his equal share of my Plantation when sold, and it is my desire it should be equally divided among my five sons and one daughter, that is to say William my eldest son, and Edmond my second son, and Thomas my third son, and Charles my fourth son, and John my fifth son, and Sarah my daughter And it is my desire if any of my children should die before they should come of age then their part to be equally divided between the rest of my children.

It is my desire that if my Executors sees proper to send my sons to treads that they should do it, and appoint my beloved wife and Ralph Matson to be my sole Executors of this my Last Will and Testament Ratifying and Confirming this to be my Last Will and Testament. In witness whereof I have hereunto set my hand and seal the day and year above riten

         Charles Polke, (Seal)

Signed, sealed published and declared by the said Charles Polk as his last Will and Testament in the presence of us the subscribers,
Henry Stewart.
John Tictin.
Willaim Gilhil.

On the back of the foregoing will was thus written, viz June the 20, 1753, John Tictin and William Gilliland two of the subscribers to the within Will being solemnly sworn on the holy Evangels of Almighty God depose and say that they saw the testator Charles Polk sign the within as his last Will and Testament and heard him publish and declare the same to be such and at the time so doing he was to the best of their appprehensions of sound disposing mind and memory & John Tictin declares that Harry Stewart subscribed his name at the same time as a witness to the within Will and that they severally subscribed their names thereto at the request and in the presence of the Testator   Taken before

         J Darnall,
         D. Com'sy of Fred Coty.

The above will was recorded in the Orphans Court, Anne Arundel Co., Md in D. B. No 7, folio 494—1751-4

A careful perusal of the foregoing will shows that the person who drew up the document, in the first paragraph wrote the name Polk, but Charles himself signed his name Polke The certificates of probate, made by J Darnall, Deputy Commissary, also has it the latter way   This diversity further illustrates the carelessness with which the name was written in early times, especially by official scribes or copyists

From the will of Charles, it is plain that at the time of his death, between March 19th and June 20th, 1753, none of his children had likely attained to their majority, but Sarah and William were probably almost grown, about seventeen and fifteen years respectively

After the father's death the family no doubt continued for some years to reside on the home plantation and the sons to carry on their father's trading business   Their transactions with the Indians, purchasing furs, for which they gave in exchange other goods, no doubt gave them an extended acquaintance with the savages, an acquaintance that in later years seems to have been of great value to Capt Charles Polke when he rescued his family from captivity, with the aid of Simon Girty, the "White Indian"   No doubt it was at the North Bend that Charles and Simon first met, during such trading.   Later they scouted together around Fort Pitt, after Charles had settled on Cross Creek

THE MURDER OF LOGAN'S KIN.

In 1774, Chas Polk, Jr., was living on Cross Creek, Virginia, (now West Virginia) about sixteen miles from the Ohio river, where Wellsville is now situated. While living there a transaction occurred that set the frontier ablaze with excitement and brought on what is known in history as "Dunmore's War." This transaction was the infamous, unprovoked and inhuman murder of a party of Indians, both men and women, by a band of Christian White Savages, led by one Daniel Greathouse, who later settled in Kentucky. Like the atrocious murder of the Christian Indians at Gnadenhutton, on the Muskingum, in March 1782 by Col Williamson and party from Pa., the act of Greathouse and companions deserves the execration of mankind. The Indians were first made drunk by Greathouse and then ruthlessly killed.

CAPT. CHARLES POLK'S CERTIFICATE.

In Thomas Jefferson's "Notes on Virginia," where he speaks of the infamous conduct of Greathouse and party, he introduces the certificate of Capt. Charles Polke relative to that event. In the Appendix to his Notes, p 26, appears the following.

"The certificate of Charles Polke, of Shelby County, in Kentucky, communicated by Hon Judge Innes of Kentucky; who, in the letter enclosing it, together with Newland's certificate, and his own declaration of the information given him by Baker, says I am acquainted with Jacob Newland, he is a man of integrity. Charles Polke and Joshua Baker both support respectable characters.

Judge Innis, of Frankfort, stated that he had met on the road, November 14, 1799. Joshua Baker, who stated that the murder of the Indians was perpetrated at his house, in 1774, by thirty-two men led by Daniel Greathouse That twelve were killed and six or eight wounded Among the slain was a sister and other relatives of the Indian Chief Logan.

Baker says Capt. Michael Cresap was not of the party That two days before two Indians on their way home were killed by Cresap and a party of land improvers on the Ohio He had the information from Cresap"

The Certificate.

"About the latter end of April, or beginning of May, 1774, I lived on the waters of Cross Creek, about sixteen miles from Joshua Baker, who lived on the Ohio, opposite the mouth of Yellow Creek A number of persons collected at my house and proceeded to the said Baker's and murdered several Indians, among whom was a woman said to be the sister of the Indian Chief Logan The principal leader of the party was Daniel Greathouse To the best of my recollection, the cause which gave rise to the murder was a general idea that the Indians were meditating an attack on the frontiers Capt Michael Cresap was not of the party, but I recollect that sometime before the perpetration of the above fact, it was currently reported that Capt Cresap had murdered some Indians on the Ohio, some distance below Wheeling"

Certified by me, an inhabitant of Shelby County, and State of Kentucky, the 15th day of November, 1799"

CHAS POLKE

Just before the perpetration of their infamous deed Greathouse and party, by agreement met at the house of Capt Charles Polke, but Polk took no part in the bloody work Leaving his house, they passed down to the Ohio on murder bent. Arriving there, they procured a lot of whiskey and enticed a boatload of Indians across from the South side, getting them drunk and then falling upon and butchering them

Among those slain was a sister of Logan the Mingo Chief, who had long been known as "The White Man's Friend" After this infamous transaction, however, Logan ceased to be a friend of the white man. He took up the hatchet, joined his followers with the tribes under Chief Cornstalk, and the frontier families suffered a bloody penalty for Greathouse's infamy

Governor Dunmore called in the surveyors in Kentucky sending Daniel Boone and Michael Stoner to warn them, and on October 10, 1774, after a fiercely contested battle, the embittered savages under Cornstalk were defeated at the mouth of the Kenawha by an army of riflemen under Col. Andrew Lewis.

The tide of emigration to Kentucky set in strong the following year (1775) and Virginia deputy surveyors who had been called back home in 1774, returned to their work in the West, reinforced by others.

Capt. Polk, at his home on Cross Creek, grew restive and determined to follow the tide. He had a wife and two children and with them, his sister Sarah Piety and her children, his brothers, William, Edmond and Thomas, reinforced by quite a party of friends and neighbors, set out in the Spring of 1780 for Kentucky, the party traveling together in flatboats.

A sharp lookout for Indians was kept as they descended the Ohio, but in due time they reached Louisville and landed. For a short time they sojourned at the station of Col. Wm. Linn. Proceeding south from there, Capt. Polk and party located on Simpson Creek, in the present Nelson County. Shortly afterward he built a station of his own, not far from Kincheloe's Station, the latter the principal defense in the neighborhood, and placed his family in it for greater security.

Indian forays into that part of Kentucky from the Wabash tribes of Indians, were quite frequent during that and the two following years. But Capt. Polk's family escaped serious molestation until the early part of September, 1782, when a squad of Wabash Indians, said to be returning from the slaughter of Kentuckians at the Blue Licks, just after the siege of Bryan's Station, near Lexington, appeared in that section.

On the approach of the savages, Col. John Floyd ordered out a scouting party of militia to scour the country. Of this party was Capt. Charles Polk. Some of these scouts were from Kincheloe's and some from Cox's and other nearby stations. The inhabitants at Kincheloe's consisted of six or seven families. After scouring the country for several days, and finding no savages, the militia, on September 1st, were disbanded and returned to their homes, those from Kincheloe's arriving at home late in the evening and retiring to rest. Capt. Polk, wife and four children were among those in the station at the time, but he had not yet arrived home. No signs of attack on a neighboring station

CHAPTER XLV.

CAPTURE OF KINCHELOE'S STATION.

Richard Collins, the Kentucky historian, under the head of Spencer County, p. 724, describing this event at some length, among other statements, says.

"There had been no alarm at Kincheloe's during the absence of the men, and upon reaching home late in the evening, greatly fatigued and without apprehension of danger, they retired to rest At the dead hour of the night, when the inmates of the station were wrapped in most profound sleep, the Indians made a simultaneous attack upon the cabins of the Station, and, breaking open the doors, commenced an indiscriminate massacre of men, women and children The unconscious sleepers were awakened but to be cut down, or to behold their friends fall by their side A few only, availing themselves of the darkness of the night, escaped the tomahawk or captivity Among those who affected their escape, was Mrs. Davis, whose husband was killed, and another woman whose name is not given They fled to the woods, where they were fortunately joined by a lad by the name of Ash, who conducted them to Cox's Station"

After relating the trials and exciting experiences of several other families during the attack, some being slain and others escaping, the historian goes on to say "Several women and children were cruelly put to death after they were made prisoners, on the route to the Indian towns On the second day of her captivity, Mrs. Bland, one of the prisoners, made her escape into the bushes Totally unacquainted with the surrounding country, and destitute of a guide, for eighteen successive days she rambled through the woods, without seeing a human face, without clothes, and subsisting upon sour grapes and green walnuts, until she became a walking skeleton On the eighteenth day she was accidently discovered and taken to Linn's Station where, from kind attention and careful nursing, her health and strength were soon restored

"The situation of Mrs. Polk, another prisoner, with four

children, was almost as pitiable as that of Mrs. Bland. She was far advanced in a state of pregnancy and compelled to walk until she became almost incapable of motion. She was then threatened with death, and the tomahawk brandished over her head by one Indian, when another, who saw it, begged her life, took her under his care, mounted her on a horse with two of the children, and conducted her safely to Detroit. Here she was purchased by a British trader, well treated, and enabled to write her husband, who was absent at the time of her capture.

On the receipt of her letter, the husband immediately repaired to Detroit, obtained his wife and five children, and returned with them safely to Kentucky. After the peace of the succeeding year, the remainder of the prisoners were also liberated and returned home."

The four children of Capt. Charles Polk, captured at Kincheloe's with their mother, were William, aged seven, Elizabeth, aged five, Sally, aged two; and Nancy, aged one year. A second son, Charles, was b. at Detroit shortly after Mrs. Polk arrived there. After the return to Kentucky from Detroit, seven more children, Christiana, Edward, Eleanor, Mary, Thomas, Robert Tyler, and one that died unnamed in infancy, were born to Capt. Charles Polk and wife.

Captain Polk, while living in Virginia at Cross Creek near the Ohio, was married in the winter 1774-5 to Delilah Tyler, a sensible, courageous and self-reliant maiden of that vicinity. One tradition is that she belonged to the Virginia Tyler family that gave to the United States, President John Tyler, but of this we have no positive proof. At the date of their marriage Charles Polk was aged thirty and Delilah nineteen years, and their two oldest children, William and Elizabeth, were born there, before they concluded to emigrate to Kentucky.

There is a family tradition that Charles Polk was at Braddock's Defeat, July 9, 1755, but he could not have been there as a soldier when he was but ten or eleven years of age. If he was present, it must have been as a driver of cattle for the commissary department, a duty   e could very well perform.

In a letter to the writer, of date June 5, 1876, from Wm A. Polk, of Oaktown, Indiana he distinctly states that his great-grandfather, "Capt. Charles Polke was born in 1744 or 45 and was at Braddock's Defeat." Also that "he was a first cousin of Ezekiel Polk, who was the grandfather of James K. Polk." This is additional proof that Charles and William (the latter of whom married Margaret Taylor at Carlisle) were brothers, for their children would be first cousins.

This persistent assertion that Ezekiel and Capt. Chas Polk were cousins has come to the author from several branches of the Polks, who "got it from their grandparents," they all say.

It may also be noted that Capt Bland W Ballard, who was born near Fredricksburg, Va , October 16, 1761, and died in Shelby County, Kentucky, September 5, 1853, aged ninety-two years, married a sister of Edward Tyler, father of Capt. Charles Polk's wife Capt Ballard was a very distinguished Indian fighter in Kentucky's pioneer days He landed at Louisville in 1779, when eighteen years of age, joined the militia, was in nearly every conflict with the savages, and took part in Wayne's defeat of the hostile tribes at Fallen Timbers an event that terminated the Indian War

From the will of Charles Polk the Indian Trader, and from other data, we have approximated the dates of birth of his children, Sarah, William, Edmond, Thomas, Capt Charles, and John. From the family bibles and data of Capt Charles' branch, we learn the following concerning his own family

CAPT. CHARLES POLK'S FAMILY.

Charles Polke was born Feb 2, 1745 in Frederick County, Maryland He died in Knox County, Indiana, September 11, 1823, aged 79 years

Delilah Tyler, wife of Capt Charles Polke, was born in Virginia, February 10, 1755 She died in Nelson County, Kentucky, June 7, 1797. She was a daughter of Edward Tyler and his wife Nancy (Langley) Tyler, of Virginia A sister of Delilah, Priscilla, married Abner Dunn Capt Charles Polk and Delilah Tyler were married in Virginia during the winter of 1774-5, and they had issue.

(1) William, b Sept 19, 1775, d April 26, 1843, in Knox County, Ind

(2) Elizabeth, b about 1777, d in Knox County, Ind

(3) Sarah (Sally), b Sept 9, 1780, d Sept 2, 1818, in Knox County

(4) Nancy, b. about 1781, d ——, in Indiana

(5) Charles, b in captivity at Detroit, Oct 20, 1782, d ——, 1847

(6) Christiana, b Nov. 12, 1784, d ——, 1850, at 'Woodside," Jackson County, Mo

(7) Edward, b ——, 1786, killed in 1814 in the army.

(8) Eleanor, b. ——, 1788, d ——, in Indiana

(9) Mary (Polly) b ——, 1790, d ——. "

(10) Dr Thomas, b Feb 21, 1792, d Feb. 7, 1872, at Gonzales, Tex

(11) Robert Tyler, b about 1796, d in 1844, aged 47 years

(12) A son, b and d in June, 1797, just before the death of his mother, Delilah

From the foregoing it will be seen that Delilah Polk died at the comparatively early age of forty-two years, after giving birth to twelve children, most of whom became noted in their day and time

DESCENDANTS OF SARAH POLK PIETY.

Sarah Polke, married Austin Piety, about 1763, as they had four children, Elizabeth, Nancy, Sarah and Thomas, the youngest born Dec 1770 at Fort Pitt Austin Piety, it is said, was an officer in the British Army and a man of large wealth, a son of Thomas Piety, of Lancastershire, England

After emigrating to Kentucky, Mrs. Sarah Polke Piety resided with her daughter, Mrs Benjamin Cox, and her granddaughter, Mrs James Ballard, until the time of her death in 1835

Of the four Piety children, the eldest, Elizabeth Piety, married a Mr McDonald; the second, Nancy Piety, married a Mr Massey, descendants of these not ascertained. The fourth child Thomas, b Dec 1770, married Mr Mary Duncan, Aug 7, 1792, and d May 1, 1855 His wife Mary Duncan was b Nov. 25, 1771, and d 1846 They lived in Shelbyville, Ky, until after the birth of their last child, then removed to Sullivan County, Indiana, and later, in 1814, to Knox County. Both died there and were buried at old Maria Creek Baptist church, about fifteen miles north of Vincennes They had twelve children, viz

Austin Piety, b Aug 19, 1793; d ———
Elizabeth Piety, b. Dec 10, 1794, d ———
James D Piety, b. May 1, 1796; d. ———
Sarah Piety, b April 6, 1798, d. ———.
Robert Piety, b March 22, 1800; d. ———
Thomas Piety, b May 16, 1801; d ———.
Margaret Piety, b. Jan 8, 1803, d ———.
Samuel D Piety, b June 27, 1804, d ———
Nancy Piety, b. Jan. 11, 1807, d ———.
William D Piety, b March 19, 1808; d ———
Susan D Piety, b Nov. 16, 1811, d ———
Polly Piety, b. Feb 28, 1813, d. ———

Sarah Piety, (third child of Austin Piety, and his wife Sarah Polke), is supposed to have been born about 1769, and married about 1783 Benjamin Cox, who was born in 1767 and was killed by Indians at the mouth of Indian Creek in 1823. He was only sixteen years of age, and she but 14, at the time of their marriage. They had eleven children, viz:

Elizabeth Cox, b ———, 1784, d Nov. ———, 1838; married first Joseph Simpson, second Samuel Miller.

Sarah Piety Cox, b Jan 9, 1785, d Jan. 11, 1860, d. s p single.

Susannah Cox, b Sept 27, 1785, d July 21, 1858, married Col James Ballard, of Shelby County, Aug 2, 1803

Gabriel Squire Cox, b Aug. 7, 1789, d. Nov. 27, 1836; married Nancy Gaston (1815-1863)

Isaac Cox, b ———, d.———.

Joseph Cox, b. ———, d ———, 1862; d. s. p single

Jonathan P. Cox, b. Feb. 18, 1797, d Feb. ———, 1874; married Rachel Lemen Tigert, March 6, 1817

Austin Piety Cox, b ———, 1799, d ———, 1861.

John C Cox, b ———, 1801, d. ———, 1878, married Eliza Garrett, Feb 18, 1830

Benjamin F Cox b ——— d ——— 1887, married Elizabeth Shepherd

Finetta A Cox, b. ——, 1807, d Oct 11, 1872, married Elbridge Arnold, Dec. 6, 1831.

Susannah, (third child of Benjamin Cox and wife Sarah Piety), b Sept 27, 1785, d. July 21, 1858, married Aug 2, 1803, Col James Ballard, of Shelby County, Ky. James Ballard was b Aug. 15, 1763 in Spottsylvania County, Va, and d. on his farm near Shelbyville, Ky., March 26, 1849 He was a son of Bland Ballard, Jr, who was killed in an Indian massacre near Shelbyville, Ky., in 1788, and a brother of Maj Bland W Ballard, the celebrated Indian fighter He had been previously married and by his first wife had a number of children By his second wife, Susannah Cox, he had ten children, viz

Elizabeth Ballard, b June 16, 1804, d Aug 9, 1839; married May 9, 1822, Robert Gregory, Shelby County, Ky, who died about 1840, leaving three sons, the eldest of whom recently died in St Louis Mo

Benjamin Ballard, b. Jan 1, 1806, married twice and lived in Shelby County, Ky, until 1836, when he removed to Green County, Ind, where he d Oct 4, 1844, leaving seven children.

Paulina Ballard, b July 19, 1807; married first her cousin, Benjamin C Simpson, and afterwards Archibald Collings, and d Oct 4, 1881, in Nelson County, Ky, the mother of nine children.

Thomas J Ballard, b. Jan. 19, 1809, d. a bachelor, Nov 10, 1852, in Shelbyville, Ky

Sarah Piety Ballard, b May 12, 1810, d. unmarried Oct 10, 1834, in Shelbyville, Ky.

William Henry Harrison Ballard, b. Oct. 29, 1812, twice married, and d April 5, 1891, on his farm in Shelby County, Ky, the father of seven children

Andrew Jackson Ballard, b Sept 22, 1815 His descendants are given below

Barnett Ballard, b. Nov. 26, 1816, d April 27, 1834 Whilst a cadet at the U. S Military Academy at West Point, N Y., he stood at the head of his class, and was a great favorite, his class mates erecting a monument over his grave at Shelbyville, Ky

Bland Ballard, b. Sept 4, 1819, d. July 29, 1879 He was one of the leading members of the Louisville Bar At the outbreak of the Civil War he was a staunch Union man, and was appointed by President Lincoln as Judge of the U. S District Court for the District of Kentucky During those strenuous times he administered justice with absolute impartiality regardless of personal danger in which he often stood, and lived to command the love and respect of all, some of his warmest friends being those who were opposed to him politically He married Dec 16, 1846, Miss Sarah McDowell, of Louisville, Ky, by whom he had six children, and d July 29, 1879 Josephus Ballard, the youngest child, b Oct 23, 1823, d in infancy. Feb 19, 1824

Andrew Jackson Ballard, (son of James Ballard and his wife Susannah Cox), b. 1815, in Shelby County, Ky., was one of the leading members of the Louisville Bar, and at the outbreak of the Civil War was a staunch Union man, and was appointed by President Lincoln, Clerk of the U S Circuit and District Courts for Kentucky which position he resigned in 1870 ; was at one time member of the Kentucky Legislature and declined a renomination. He married on April 27, 1848 Miss Frances Ann Thruston, of Louisville, Ky, by whom he had five children He d Aug 17, 1885 His children were

Charles Thruston Ballard, b June 3, 1850. Is one of the most prominent business men of the City of Louisville. He married April 24, 1878, Miss Emilina Modeste (Mina) Breaux, of New Orleans, La, by whom he had eight children, five of whom are still living

Bland Ballard, b Oct 29, 1851, d Aug 15, 1852

Abigail Churchill Ballard, b June 24, 1853, d in Mentone, France, April 2, 1874, on the threshold of womanhood

Samuel Thruston Ballard, b Feb 11, 1855. One of the most prominent men of the city of Louisville He married Jan. 25, 1883, Miss Sunshine Harris, by whom he had four children, only one of whom is now living.

Rogers Clark Ballard, b Nov 6, 1858, adopted his mother's family name of Thruston, by order of the Fayette County (Ky) Court, on Oct 27, 1884 He was for some years Assistant on the Kentucky Geological Survey, and has devoted most of his time to scientific and historical subjects He is a bachelor and resides near Louisville, Ky

R. C. BALLARD THRUSTON,
Louisville, Ky., Descendant of Capt. Charles Polk.

Capt. Charles Polk, having served as an officer in the frontier militia, while residing in Virginia, on arrival in Kentucky in 1780, at once took rank among his friends and neighbors as a man of high courage and capacity, filling responsible civic and military positions in Kentucky, and later also in Indiana, after he removed there in 1808 He was chosen as the first Representative from the County of Breckinridge, in the Kentucky Legislature, 1806-7, and immediately after the expiration of his term, followed his sons to Indiana Territory, where he became prominent in public affairs, under General William Henry Harrison He settled in Knox County, near Vincennes Here he lived the balance of his days, active in all that concerned the people, until his death in September 1823

The last regular session of the territorial legislature of Indiana was held at Corydon, in December 1815 On the 14th a memorial was adopted praying Congress for authority to form a constitution and State government, which prayer was granted on April 16th, 1816, and approved by the President In accordance therewith, an election was held to choose members of a convention to form a State Constitution. Two of the five members from Knox County chosen to this convention were William Polke and Benjamin Polke, and from the county of Perry the single representative was Charles Polke The latter was a son of Edmond Polk, brother of Capt. Charles, and was born in 1782 Three of the Polks, therefore, helped to formulate and adopt the first constitution of Indiana

Born on the frontier of Maryland, and taking part in the exciting transactions of his day, during the great struggle between the Red Men and Anglo-Saxon invaders of their domain, Capt. Charles Polk was schooled to hardships and dangers that would have deterred men of a less resolute and energetic character His acquaintance with the Indian character began in childhood, while his father was an Indian trader at the North Bend of the Potomac, and his whole life was devoted, in a greater or lesser degree, to Indian transactions and experiences His association with Simon Girty, at Fort Pitt, before the Revolution, established between them a friendship which later served him well in the recovery of his wife and children from capture That act of Girty's in behalf of Capt

Polk constitutes one of the few humane acts known to have been done toward the whites by the "Frontier Butcher."

SPOKE INDIAN TONGUE WELL.

Charles Polk the Indian trader, being long associated with the Indians in the capacity of a trader, learned to speak their language fluently, as is attested by Capt Christopher Gist, agent of the Ohio Land Company

In his journal, kept by him during his trip down the Ohio, commencing Nov. 4, 1751, Gist says:

"Set out 6 A M and went to an Indian camp and invited them to the treaty at Logstown at the full of the moon in May next. At this camp there was a trader named Charles Polk, who spoke the Indian tongue well Nemecotton, a chief, complained of the white people occupying lands granted to his father Chicoconnecon, and for which he had no pay. Said he: "This trader here, Charles Polke, knows the truth of what I say, that the land was granted to my father and that he or I never sold it, to which said Poke assented"

On another page of Gist's Journal is the following

'Charles Polke's name appears in the list of Indian traders in 1734 (Colonial Archives, Vol. 1, p. 425) On Mayo's Map of 1737 his name is marked with those of four other settlers at the North Bend of the Potomac, where Hancock, Md, now stands (See also Colonial Records of Pa) In 1774, he lived on Cross Creek, W. Va, about 16 miles from the Ohio River, where Wellsville is now situated He was still living in Shelby County, Kentucky, in 1799 (See his deposition in Appendix to Jefferson's "Notes on Virginia," 1801, p 368"

The above statement that Indian trader Chas Polk was living on Cross Creek in 1774, and moved to Kentucky, is a mistake. Indian trader, Chas died in June 1753 His fourth son Capt Chas. Polk, moved to Cross Creek, married there Delilah Tyler, and came to Kentucky in 1780, settling in Nelson County In 1808 he moved to Vincennes, Ind, and died there in 1823 S. Chas Polk, trader, at Loggstown, was the father of Capt Chas the Indian fighter

POLK LAND ENTRIES IN KENTUCKY.

In the list of early land entries made in Kentucky in pioneer days, filed for record at St Asaph's (Logan's) Station, in 1780, appears the following

"Charles Polke, by Thomas Polke, this day claimed a pre-emption of 1,000 acres of land at the State price, in the District of Kentucky, on account of marking and improving the same in the year of 1776, lying on Simpson's Creek, a branch of the Town Fork of Salt River, near the head thereof, to include his improvements. Satisfactory proof being made to the Court, they are of the opinion that the said Polke has a right of a pre-emption of 1 000 acres of land, to include the above location, and that a certificate issue accordingly"

"Richard Connor by Charles Polk a claim of 1,000 acres, by virtue of improving the same in 1776, adjoining land of Charles Polk on Simpson Creek'

"Thomas Polk, 1,000 acres, on account of making and improving same in 1776, lying on the dividing ridge between the Town Fork and Rolling Fork of Salt River, on the head of a branch of Cox's land," etc

"Arthur Poak, by Wm McConnell, this day claimed a pre-emption of 1,000 acres of land at the State price, in the District of Kentucky, on account of marking and improving the same in the year 1776 Rejected"

Who this Arthur Poak was we know not None of the Polk family records name an Arthur Polk, but it looks like he belonged to the Chas Polk line, appearing in Kentucky about the time that Capt. Chas and his brothers did Wm McConnell, who laid in the claim for him, was one of the founders of Lexington, and the tract he sought to enter for Arthur Poak was, no doubt, in Fayette County, near Lexington.

It will also be noticed that the tracts of Chas Polk and his brother Thomas were "marked and improved in 1776" Therefore Charles and Thomas must have first come to Kentucky in that year, making locations on Simpson's Creek Four years later, in 1780, they all came out to Kentucky and permanently located on these tracts

CHAPTER XLVI.

CAPTURE OF CAPT. CHAS. POLK'S FAMILY.

(By Judge William Polk.)

The following account of the capture, near Bardstown, Ky., in 1782, of the family of his father, was written many years ago by Judge William Polk, of Indiana, the eldest of the captured children, and published in The Advocate, a newspaper at Vincennes

William Polk, writer of this account of the captivity of his mother, shared it with her and was the little boy that they dressed in Indian apparel and styled him "the son of the chief."

"Charles Polk, a young man, was among the early adventurers to western Virginia, on the upper branches of the Ohio River Hence we find him in his country's service in 1774, in an expedition against the Indian village on the Scioto, and again with Lord Dunmore, in his celebrated campaign in the latter part of the same year

During the succeeding winter he married and settled as a farmer near what was then called the Mingo Bottom, on the Ohio River, some distance above Wheeling, where he continued to reside with his family during the winter and improve his farm, in the spring removing them to the neighboring fort erected by the settlers for the protection of their families while they cultivated their farms, part performing the labor, while another part acted as spies and guards Having had an improvement made in Kentucky by which he obtained a preemption claim, in what is now Nelson County, about seven miles east of Bardstown, he sold his farm for Continental bills (which depreciated in his hands) and in the spring of 1780, descended the Ohio River with his family, with the intention to settle on and improve his land On landing at Louisville, finding his land so remote and the removal to it dangerous on account of Indian hostilities, at the invitation of his friend and comrade in the days of their boyhood, Col William Linn, one of the bravest among the western sufferers, he settled at Linn's Station, about twelve miles from Louisville

During the summer Mr Polk was frequently engaged, as was usual, in guarding against surprise, and in the pursuit of straggling parties of Indians who infested the settlements, and by that means obtained the confidence of his associates, so that they chose him Captain in the campaign which Gen. G. R. Clark led against the Shawnee towns on the Miami that year, and he acted a conspicuous part in the battle of the Pickaway, where the Indians were signally defeated During the succeeding winter, he removed to his own land, on his arrival he found it occupied by a small band of emigrants from Virginia, who had previously settled there, erected a small fort for the security of their families, and cleared some land and had raised a fine crop of Indian corn the preceding year, not knowing that it was a pre-emption claim Thus situated, he erected a cabin and commenced to improve sufficiently near, in case of an alarm, to take protection in the fort, hunting buffalo for the subsistence of his family and improving his farm to enable him to raise sufficient for their support the approaching season

The early part of the year 1781 passed off without any serious alarm, until near midsummer, when a Mr Ash, who with a large family of sons, having settled a few miles off, alone, on the frontier, being on a visit with his wife and infant son at Capt Polk's on their return early in the after noon, after proceeding about two miles, were met by one of their sons, an active lad of about twelve years of age, who informed his parents that while out at work in their corn field, the Indians had fired upon them and had either killed or taken all the rest of the family; he being a little distance from them, had escaped

The afflicted parents forthwith returned Capt Polk, immediately, with his family, took shelter in the fort, dispatched a runner to the next fort, about four miles, to give the alarm and the same evening with a small party started in pursuit and shortly after dark they arrived at the scene of desolation They found the eldest son, a young m and the youngest and only daughter slain 1   the house had not been burned and on cautiously approaching it, they found the door fastened on the inside. Apprehensive of an ambuscade, they were about to examine, when the voice of a child inquired if it was his father and mother that had come. On their reply the child opened the door and informed them that he was asleep under the bed, wrapped in a buffalo hide to keep off the flies, and that seven or eight Indians came into the house and took off all the things they could carry with them. That when he was first awakened by their noise he was about to tell them his mother would be angry when she came home, but that they looked so ugly he was afraid and lay still until after they were gone. Then he got up and fastened the door to keep them out until his father and mother should come home. The boy was about five years old.

Having thus learned the probable number of the enemy, next morning, on pursuing the trail, they found they had taken the remainder of the family, five sons, prisoners. With the force they had, it was not thought prudent to attempt a pursuit, as it might lead to the massacre of their prisoners. They buried the dead and returned to the fort the same day. The remainder of the season passed without further mischief than straggling parties hovering around the settlement and stealing their horses, which from necessity were permitted to roam through the forests.

Early in the morning, in the beginning of the spring of 1782, four persons left the fort with horses loaded with salt for Harrodsburg, the next station, about thirty miles distant. Having traveled about five miles, they were attacked by about thirty Indians, fortunately but one man was wounded and he not dangerously. By instantly throwing off the loads and mounting their horses, after a warm pursuit they succeeded in regaining the fort. Expecting an immediate attack, the day and night succeeding was passed in repairing the fort and making such preparations for defense as was in their power. Fortunately, no serious attack was made. After remaining two or three days in the vicinity, stealing horses and killing cattle, the Indians dispersed in small bands for the purpose of stealing more horses from the neighboring fort. Captain

Polk, with a small party, pursued one of these straggling bands, overtook them, killed their leader and recovered part of the stolen horses without loss

From this time the remainder of the summer passed off without any serious alarm until August, but the attack on Bryan's Station, near Lexington and the disastrous battle of Blue Licks on the 19th, spread general consternation throughout the country, as no one could conjecture where the next blow would be struck About the time the intelligence of these disasters was received in what was then termed the lower settlements in the vicinity of Louisville, a young man hunting buffalo alone, about twenty-five miles from the nearest settlement, discovered on their march in the direction of the fort, in the vicinity of Louisville (as he supposed) about a hundred warriors. Not being discovered by the Indians, and being on horseback, he hastened to give the alarm and in a few hours apprised his friends of their danger It may be proper here to state that the young man above named, still lives in Shelby County, Kentucky, now upwards of eighty years of age, the highly respected Maj Bland W Ballard, afterwards so well known in the Indian wars and who performed a conspicuous part in the late war, at the celebrated but unfortunate battle of the River Raisin

Col. John Floyd, the officer in command, immediately started an express to give the alarm to the forts in the vicinity of Bardstown, and requesting assistance to meet the enemy, appointed the place of rendezvous nearly midway between the settlements, which were nearly thirty miles apart, on the evening of the next day, the 29th of August, 1782. Col Isaac Cox, the senior officer in these forts, early in the morning of that day, sent an express to Capt Polk, at the weakest and most frontier station in that direction; and that same afternoon, with what men could be spared from the defense of the fort, he started for the appointed rendezvous, where he arrived the same evening about fifteen miles from the fort The arrangements of Col Floyd were most judicious and prudent, as his position was such as to afford assistance to whichever of the settlements might be attacked

Early on the morning of the 30th four of Capt Polk's

men were directed to return to the fort, for the double purpose of acting as spies and of strengthening the fort should it be attacked. Two horsemen were directed to make a circuit entirely around the fort, so that they might discover the trail of the invaders, should they have taken that course; the other two being footmen, were directed to take a more direct route. Unfortunately, the horsemen disobeyed their instructions and after traveling a few miles, made directly for the fort, where they arrived early in the afternoon, thereby quieting in part the alarm of the inhabitants. It was afterwards ascertained that had they pursued their route, as they were directed, they would have discovered the trail of the Indians in time to have advised Col. Floyd, so that he might have reached the Fort previous to its attack and capture.

ATTACK ON THE FORT.

On a clear and bright morning, the moon shining in her meridian splendor, the 31st of August, 1782, about one hour before the break of day, the first alarm to the unfortunate inmates was the war-whoop of the Indians as they assailed the fort from different quarters and obtained immediate possession by climbing the walls and unroofing the cabins, descending from the outside. One man defended his house until his wife and one child were killed, when seizing his other child, a boy about four years old, he made his escape. It was believed that he killed one or two of the Indians. One man and the woman and child, were the only persons slain in the capture. Two white men, four women, and the lad Ash, who had escaped the previous year when his father's family was taken, made their escape in safety. This promising boy grew up highly esteemed and at the early age of 22 fell, bravely fighting for his country at St. Clair's defeat.

The remaining inmates, about thirty in number, were taken prisoners and the fort burned. It was known for many years afterward as the "Burnt Station." On the evening of the day of the calamity, Col. Floyd was advised of the melancholy occurrence. A council was immediately assembled to consult what course would be proper to pursue, and the general opinion was in favor of an immediate pursuit. To this Capt. Polk strongly objected, urging that a pursuit would tend to the massacre of all the prisoners, as the Indians would keep scouts in their rear, on the retreat, so that a surprise could not be calculated upon; and that as it was, it might be possible for him, some time, to recover his family Known as he was for his determined bravery, perseverance and patience, and from his amiable and conciliatory course, being universally beloved, a pursuit was not attempted.

The Indians after taking whatever property of the inhabitants they could travel with, set the houses on fire and consumed the remainder and about daylight retired to their camps Soon after sunrise, they commenced their retreat with their prisoners, in all about thirty, including Mrs Polk and her four children, the eldest, William, a boy of seven years of age, the others daughters, the youngest two years old, and herself in that situation that but faint hopes could be entertained that she could bear the fatigue of a forced march through the wilderness, and her second son was born at Detroit, on the 27th of the ensuing October. On the first day of their captivity, circumstances occurred which, though of minor importance, it is believed, from what was afterwards learned from the Indians, influenced their treatment to Mrs Polk and her children, and probably was the means of preserving her life, which will be detailed in a manner that may appear tedious and unnecessary. The apology is that it is given as an illustration of the Indian character, to show that even among untutored savages there are traits of benevolence and humanity that are worthy to be preserved

At the first assault on the fort, Mrs Polk having her two youngest children in the same bed with her, immediately arose and taking a child under each arm attempted to wake up her two eldest children, but before she succeeded the Indians broke into the house, seized her two children, hurried her out, and shortly after to their camp, within about half a mile of the fort After daylight, in looking over the encampment, she discovered all the prisoners except her own two children, from which she inferred that they had not been discovered in the darkness within the house and been left to be consumed, as she saw them set the house on fire before they left the fort, which added much to her affliction that she had not succeeded in wakening them out of their sleep. It will here be proper to mention that the Indian Chief had arrived in the vicinity of the fort, previous to the departure of Capt. Polk and his men, and from their hiding places had witnessed his leaving for the purpose of joining Col. Floyd. One of the first inquiries in the morning after arriving at their encampment, was for the Chief's (Capt. Polk's) squaw and papooses. When pointed out to them, they appeared much pleased that they had taken them prisoners—said the white Chief would be much disappointed on his return to find his family all taken from him. I have heard Mrs. Polk say she could observe a marked difference in the treatment of her children and others taken. On the second morning, they painted her son in Indian style, decorated him in feathers, and some Indian trinkets, and called him "The Young Chief of the Long Knife," the name given the Kentuckians by the Indians of that day.

Shortly after sunrise they commenced their march, Mrs. Polk carrying her youngest child, and Mrs. Ash, (whose family had been massacred the preceding year, as I have previously named) carrying hers, only a few months old. After traveling a short distance, the Indians took their children from them, for the purpose, as they supposed, of murdering them and directing them to march, Mrs. Ash observing, if they killed her child she would go no further with them. They rapidly pursued their journey for about twelve miles, when they halted. In a short time, the Indian who had taken Mrs. Polk's child, came up to them and handed it to its mother, and, at the same time the two eldest came up and joined her for the first time since their captivity, which much relieved her anxiety on their account. Mrs. Ash repeated that as they had murdered her child she would go no further.

Having crossed no stream of water thus far, Mrs. Polk, from her fatigue and thirst, was so exhausted that she could scarcely breathe. The Indians had brought with them many watermelons from the fort, and while refreshing themselves with them, she held out her hand as a request for a part to relieve her thirst, which was answered by a general laugh and shout of approbation, and some ten or twelve of them handed her slices which she divided among the prisoners around her, offering Mrs Ash a part, saying it would relieve her thirst, which she refused by a shake of the head, without speaking. The Indians countenances immediately changed to anger; they began a conversation among themselves, when one came forward, stripped her of part of her upper garments, and in a few minutes started the prisoners, making signs to Mrs Ash to take her child, a boy two years old and march. After they had proceeded a short distance they distinctly heard the tomahawk strike her head She uttered a scream simultaneous with their war-whoop, and all was silent They continued their march until near sunset traveling this day about thirty miles before they encamped for the night The Indian claiming Mrs Polk and her youngest child as his prisoners, being of a surly temper, proposed killing her that night, saying she could not travel as far next day as they wished to go, to which proposal his brother, of a more humane disposition, objected and proposed to defer the council until the next evening and was joined by two or three others, who assigned as a reason why she should be saved, the circumstances of the watermelons, as related above

The next morning the Indian who had first proposed saving her life, in the council of the preceding evening, by signs informed her that in two days they would cross the big water, as they called the Ohio River, where they had horses, and she then should ride Thus encouraged and stimulated to go as far as she could, a mother's desire to know what would be the fate of her children, the second day passed off as the first, by a rapid march, and contrary to her expectations she made the journey as the day before The same Indian who had interceded for her in council the previous evening, again prevailed in suspending a decision until the next evening

The third day passed off in the same manner, until late in the afternoon, when within a few hundred yards of the Ohio river, her foot slipped in a small hole in the ground and being unable to extricate herself, she quietly sat down to await her fate, which she believed would be immediate death Her ill-disposed master, with a slight kick and surly voice ordered her to march She shook her head signifying she could not

He immediately drew his tomahawk from his scabbard and raised it over her head, for the purpose of dispatching his victim at a single blow, but his more humane brother, who was immediately behind him, caught it in his hand as he drew it back and commenced a conversation in an earnest tone of remonstrance, which Mrs. Polk thought continued two or three minutes, before he let go of the tomahawk, which the other then returned to its scabbard and passed on, while her preserver remained and assisted her to rise and proceed to their bark canoes, in which they had crossed the river in their advances and concealed a short distance up the Kentucky River, above its junction with the Ohio.

He assisted her on board, and observing her feet and legs much swelled, he took his knife and ripped open her moccasins, which they had given her to put on at the commencement of the journey, and which, on account of the swelling, could not be gotten off in any other way. On taking them off, her toe nails came off with a long portion of the skin on the bottom of her feet, which appeared to excite the sympathy of the Indians in the canoe. He then directed her to bathe her feet by pouring water on them while crossing. Having crossed over, he assisted her up the bank and brought her child and blanket to her, then went and brought some oil, or rather, marrow, procured from the bones of buffaloes, which a few Indians who had been left to hunt and take care of the canoes had procured, and directed her to rub her feet with the marrow. He then handed her a large, soft pair of moccasins to put on, after which he said she could sleep and would be better in the morning. From her pain and sufferings, she had but little hopes of living to see the morning light, but to satisfy the kind Indian who appeared to take such an interest in preserving her life, she did as he directed, and, contrary to her expectations, the remedies applied so far relieved her that, for the first night during her captivity, she slept soundly and was so far relieved that I, for many years afterwards, often heard her declare that the whole scene of that afternoon and night still appeared to her a most extraordinary and miraculous interposition of divine goodness for her preservation.

On the same evening, the Indians held another council to

decide on her fate, believing that she could not live to travel to their villages. At this council an elderly Indian who had not before interfered was the first to object, saying she had lived and traveled so far that he believed the Great Spirit would not permit them to kill her and if they attempted it he would be angry with them and they could not prosper. Being joined by others, his advice prevailed and from this time they gave over all thought of killing her under any circumstances. This day being the fourth of their captivity, they traveled but a few miles before they arrived at a camp, where a few old men had remained to hunt during their absence on their war excursion, where they remained the balance of this day; and here were the horses which had been named to Mrs Polk as an encouragement for her to pursue the journey. From this point, the next morning being the fourth of September, the Indians separated into small bands for the convenience of hunting for their support on their journey. Mrs. Polk and her two youngest children being attached to one band and her eldest two belonging to another, they were separated, much to the grief of the afflicted mother.

The party with Mrs Polk proceeded to their villages on the Auglaize River, where they arrived on the tenth of September, where, after remaining four days, they started for Detroit with their prisoners, retaining the youngest daughter, as they informed her, to raise as one of their own squaws, which much increased her grief. At the Rapids of the Miami, or Roche de Bout as it was called, they rested one day. Here was a trader from Detroit, who had been acquainted with Capt Polk previous to the commencement of the Revolutionary War, to whom the Indians related the result of their council in determining on Mrs Polk's case, who informed her thereof and pointed out to her the Indian who so eloquently plead in her behalf at the last council. While waiting here the Indians came up with Mrs. Polk's son, having disposed of her daughter to the Shawnees at one of their villages in the vicinity of Piqua, on the Great Miami, she having been taken sick, and, as they said, they were afraid she would die on the journey and they would get nothing for her. From here they proceeded to Detroit, where they arrived on the th of

September, and gave up such prisoners as they brought with them to Col De Peyster, the commander of the British forces at that point, who treated them with the kindest attention and humanity. In his speech to the Indians, he strongly insisted on their bringing in such prisoners as they had retained, naming in particular Mrs Polk's two children, which they had separated from their mother and strongly remonstrated against their practice of murdering women and children. Such was Col De Peyster's general character for benevolence and humanity, that the prisoners compared him to a kind and indulgent parent in his treatment to his children

A comfortable house was provided for Mrs. Polk and her two children, in common with a small and excellent family of prisoners who had been taken by Col Bird in his celebrated expedition against Ruddell's and Martin's Stations in Kentucky in the year 1780, where she lived as comfortably as the nature of the case would permit.

But the situation of her two children left with the Indians, her anxiety on their account, and her sufferings and exposure on the journey, had much impaired her health, so that fears were entertained for her life. But a short time after her arrival, on the 27th of October, her second son was born, after which her attention to her infant so engrossed her mind, together with the assurance of Col De Peyster, the commander, and Col McKee, the Superintendent of the Indian Department, that they would procure the release of her children from the Indians, she became more reconciled to her situation and her health improved. By industry and economy with the use of her needle, she was supplied with provisions by the British Government. She lived much more comfortably during the winter than could have been anticipated. Early in the spring messengers were dispatched to the Indian country by Colonels DePeyster and McKee in search of her children and such others of the prisoners as the Indians had retained, and on the first of July she had the pleasure of receiving her children under her own maternal care, where we will leave them in the full enojyment of their happiness for the present and return to Capt Polk

No immediate pursuit of the Indians having been attempted, fearing it would lead to a massacre of the prisoners. Capt Polk, with a few friends about ten days afterwards followed on the trails with a view of ascertaining, if practicable, the fate of the prisoners He found the remains of three children and Mrs Ash, who were the only prisoners murdered after they left the fort. From the decayed teeth, he was enabled satisfactorily to ascertain that it was not Mrs Polk who had been murdered

General George Rogers Clark having determined on a campaign against the Shawnee villages on the Great Miami, Capt. Polk was among the first to approve of the measure and he commanded a company in that expedition The Indians having discovered the advance of Gen Clark's army, a few miles from their villages, fled without making any resistance, so that but few were either killed or taken prisoners Detachments were sent in pursuit to destroy the different villages and their corn and vegetables, being the only method whereby they could be made to feel the distress of war Capt Polk took an active part in these excursions, in hopes of recovering some of his family, but was disappointed , a few prisoners were taken and their villages destroyed In one of these excursions, Col McKee, the Superintendent of the Indian Department, narrowly escaped being captured, as he afterwards informed Capt Polk, when at Detroit after his family

On the return of Gen Clark to his headquarters at Louisville, Ky , he was advised there were strong hopes during the winter of peace being confirmed He immediately dispatched a messenger with a flag, accompanied by one of his Indian prisoners, with a letter to Col. McKee, proposing an exchange of prisoners, first of all to release Capt Polk's family , afterwards such other prisoners as Col McKee might select Capt Polk's family, not being under Indian control, he could not comply with Gen Clark's request He detained the messenger until he could send a letter by express to Col De Peyster, the commander at Detroit, who, on receipt of the letter, immediately sent for Mrs Polk, communicated to her the intelligence received and the contents of Gen Clark's letter, at the same time informing her that he could not accede to his proposal for her and her family to return at the he u   tr   as she was now safe, and he could not trust the Indians, and should any accident happen he would be blamed, and should himself feel as if he had been accessory to the massacre of her and her children, that he fully believed peace would be restored during the ensuing summer and that Capt Polk could then safely come for his family, that he would then with pleasure render him the necessary assistance and advised her to write to her husband and the letter should be sent with his own to General Clark

Mrs Polk then named a general order that had been recently issued, directing all the prisoners at that fort to prepare to proceed by the first conveyance to Niagara, on their return to their own country, stating that those who remained behind would not be supplied with provisions from the King's stores, and informed him she could not possibly support herself and children by her own labor He then assured her she need have no fears on that account as the general order was intended for the idle and dissolute among the prisoners, of which he was sorry to say there were too many, and not to drive off helpless women and children He again assured her that he would send into the Indian country and have her children brought in and given up to her, all of which promises he punctually performed Mrs. Polk, as advised, wrote to her husband, which conveyed to him the first certain intelligence of the situation of his family

Early in the spring, Col De Peyster was advised of peace, and was instructed to restrain Indian hostilities on the frontier settlements, and so far succeeded that they were peaceable during the year In the summer following the capture of his family, Capt Polk ascended the Ohio River to obtain some assistance from his friends, who had promised him aid in recovering his family And as the safer route to Detroit was through the Indian country, he procured a passport which was indispensably necessary, from Gen Irwin, who then commanded at Pittsburg. In company with Jonathan Zane, of Wheeling, Va, as his guide, they proceeded through the wilderness to Upper Sandusky, to the residence of the celebrated Simon Girty, so well known at that day as the most active partisan leader of the Indians in their wars on the frontier settlements. They were received with friendship by Girty, and treated with Indian hospitality for two days, while they remained at Sandusky.

Mr. Zane had been the guide the preceding year, to the unfortunate expedition of Col. Crawford, whose melancholy fate at the time excited so much sympathy throughout the country. After conversing freely with Mr Zane on the subject, Girty advised him (as it was generally known among the Indians that he had been the guide to Col. Crawford) not to proceed any further, but to return immediately, as in his opinion it would not be safe to travel through the Indian country, and promised to send a trusty Indian as a guide with Capt Polk to Detroit, and would be responsible for his safety. On the third morning after their arrival at Sandusky, they separated; Mr. Zane to return home, and Capt Polk, in company with his Indian guide, pursued his journey to Detroit, where he safely arrived, the tenth of October, and where he had the satisfaction of meeting all of his family in good health, thirteen months and a few days from the date of their captivity.

The humane and benevolent Col De Peyster reluctantly consented to grant Capt Polk's passport to return through the Indian country, fearing he might be interrupted by hunting parties of Indians he might encounter on his journey. At the earnest request of Capt Polk, he consented, sending a confidential officer as far as Sandusky with a speech to the Wyandotte chiefs, to warn their young men not to molest them while passing through their country. Many other prisoners wished to accompany him on his return, but the commander would not permit any except the family of Mr White, who had resided in the same house with Mrs Polk, and three small daughters were taken, and the son of the only man killed at the taking of the fort, whose wife escaped in company with the widow lady above named, leaving her three small children who were taken, the two youngest were murdered after they had left the fort, which children Col De Peyster put under his care to convey to their parents, furnishing them with and saddle who had lived in his family and been treated as one of his own children.

On the 15th of October, Capt Polk commenced his journey on his return. At Sandusky he remained two days, waiting for Thomas Girty, a brother of Simon, who was on a visit to his brother, as it was believed his company would add to the safety of the party. As a further precautionary matter, he employed an aged Delaware Indian as a guide, and a younger relation of the old man as a hunter.

From Sandusky Simon Girty accompanied them a few miles, passing over the battlefield of the late lamented Col Crawford, pointing out the different movements of the enemy, saying that had Col Crawford continued the pursuit ten minutes longer, at the commencement of the battle, he would have defeated them, as at the time he stopped the advance troops (which he did, fearing an ambuscade), the Indians were about commencing a general retreat. The writer has a perfect recollection of this conversation, though only eight years of age at that time.

No particular accident happened on the journey through the wilderness, but their progress was slow and fatigueing, as the children that were of sufficient ability had to walk. Early in November he arrived among his friends, who resided near the Ohio River, in what is now Brook County, Virginia, and prepared for descending the same, and safely landed at Louisville, Ky, on the evening of the 24th of December, 1783. From thence he removed to his late cabin, which, being some distance from the fort, had escaped conflagration. Having by the captivity of his family, expenses in recovering them, and the destruction of his property, been reduced to poverty, he had to sell the largest portion of his land for what it would bring to enable him to commence again as a farmer.

And having received no compensation for his services, as Captain in the two expeditions under Gen Clark, and at that time in the West, there being but little expectation of ever receiving any thus situated, he assigned his claims on the Government for $200 or $220 worth of goods, at an extravagant price, being all he ever received in a pecuniary point of view, for all his services and sufferings for his country; yet none rejoiced more in her independence, or complained less of the hardships endured. By industry and frugality, he lived to raise a large family of children, who with their descendants, chiefly reside in the States of Indiana and Kentucky.

Mrs. Polk died at the birth of her twelfth child, in Shelby County, Kentucky, on the 7th day of June, 1797. Capt. Polk kept his family together, until several of the eldest children married and removed to Indiana, where he followed them, living among his children as a patriarch of old, beloved and respected by all his acquaintances, and died as he had lived, with Christian resignation and composure on September 11, 1823, in the 76th year of his age.

I have often regretted that more has not been preserved of the early history of the frontier portion of our country. At the request of some friends I have been induced to furnish a plain and unvarnished tale of the captivity of my father's family, as a tribute of respect to my revered parents, and as a drop in the bucket added to the general history of the privations and sufferings of the western pioneers.

WILLIAM POLK.

CHAPTER XLVII.

JUDGE WILLIAM POLK, SON OF CAPT. CHAS. POLK.

The descendants of Capt. Charles Polk and his wife, Delilah Tyler, constitute one of the most numerous branches of the Polk family and they are, and have been, residents of nearly every State and Territory in the Middle West and Trans-Mississippi States and Territories. And wherever found they are generally people of prominence, socially and otherwise.

Judge William Polk eldest of the four children captured with their mother at Kincheloe's Station in Nelson County, in 1782, and who left the foregoing account of that event, was born on Cross Creek, Virginia (now West Virginia), September 19, 1775, a year notable in the annuals of America.

Judge William Polk was therefore five years of age when Capt. Charles Polk, his father, moved from Cross Creek, Va., to Kentucky, and, from the cradle on through a great part of his life, he was in constant contact with Indians and frontier civilization. He and his little sister Elizabeth were the only children of their parents at the time they left Virginia, the others all being born in Kentucky. As William grew to manhood he was given advantage of the best schools in Nelson County and he was an industrious pupil. After reaching manhood, he studied law and was admitted to practice. In the War of 1812 he commanded a company in Major Touissant Dubois' battalion of Kentucky Mounted Spies, and his brother, Thomas, was a member of his company. Born and raised on the border, they were well equipped for such service against the savages.

Settling in Knox County, Indiana, Capt. William Polk soon rose to prominence among the people, by reason of his talents and military services. He is said to have taken part in the battle of Tippecanoe in 1811, and his gallant brother-in-law Capt. Spier Spencer, who had married his sister, Elizabeth fell in that hard-fought engagement.

Indiana was admitted into the Federal Union as a State in 1816 To the convention which formed the constitution of the new State, composed of leading men from each county, Knox County sent John Johnson, John Badollet, John Benefield, Capt William Polke, and Benjamin Polke Perry County sent one representative, Rev Charles Polke, son of Edmond Polke, and also an officer in the Indian War Speaking of these representatives Dunn s Indiana edition of ' American Commonwealths ' Series, says ' The Knox County delegation was the strongest of all in ability, and though it was in a hopeless minority on the party questions that divided the convention, it did a large part of the convention work and was entitled to much of the credit for the result "

JUDGE WILLIAM POLK AND FAMILY.

Judge William Polk, eldest son of Capt. Charles Polk (and also eldest of the four children captured with their mother in Kentucky in 1782), died in Knox County, Indiana, April 26, 1843 In 1806 he moved from Nelson County Kentucky to Knox County. His first wife is said to have been Sally Ashby, of Kentucky, and his second Sarah Cooper By the latter he had. [1]Delilah, b ——, d ——, married Hansbrough, [2]Esther, b ——, d ——, married H D Wheeler; [3]Susan, b ——, d ——, married G Lindsay, [4]Cynthia, b ——, d ——, married W. D. Shepherd; [5]Adam G Polk, b ——, d ——, married Caroline Burnside; [6]Nancy, b.——, d ——, married Hyacinthe Lasalle Jr ; [7]Polly b 1810, d Jan 11, 1892, married Judge Jno. B Niles of Laporte. Ind.; [8]Benjamin, b ——, d ——, family untraced (Benjamin was a member of the Constitutional Convention of 1816), [9]Wm Tyler, b.——, d ——, family untraced, [10]Christiana, b ——, d.——, married Dr Andrews; [11]Eleanor, b ——, d.——, untraced

Judge William Polk was a man of distinguished ability, of great influence among his fellows, and stood in the highest esteem with all who knew him He was also one of the commissioners of the Michigan Road and was Register of the Land Office at Fort Wayne at the time of his death

The inf... ...udge Wm P lk'- m... ...nent

is that he first married Sallie Ashby, in Nelson County, Kentucky. Another is that he married Sarah Cooper. It is possible that he married both of them, Miss Ashby, first, Miss Cooper last

ELIZABETH (POLK) SPENCER

Capt Spier Spencer, b——, was killed Nov 7, 1811, at the battle of Tippecanoe His wife, Elizabeth (Polk) Spencer (a daughter of Capt Charles Polk and Delilah (Tyler) Polk), was born at Cross Creek, Va , in 1777 and when a child of three years came with her parents to Kentucky, settling in Nelson County, on Simpson's Creek, where she, her brother, William, her sisters Sally and Nancy, and her mother, were captured by Indians, Sept. 1, 1782, and carried to Detroit

Elizabeth was born, raised and married on the frontier, and all her early life was in contact with Indians She essentially was a "frontier maiden," and growing to womanhood in Kentucky, was married at sixteen years of age, Feb. 12, 1793, to Spier Spencer, of Nelson County member of a prominent family of that neighborhood.

Between the years of 1800 and 1810, nearly all of the children and near kinsmen of Capt Charles Polk emigrated to Indiana, most of them settling in Perry and Knox Counties, and at other points adjacent The greater part of them settled in the latter county, near Vincennes, at that time the chief military post on the frontier.

With Capt Charles Polk and children also went Spier Spencer and wife, and all of the family took prominent parts in the affairs of the Territory up to and including its admission as a State in 1816.

General Wm Henry Harrison was the Governor and Military Commander of the Territory during that period, and around him were gathered the ablest and bravest of the pioneers. Among these were Capt Charles Polk, his several sons, and his sons-in-law, Capt. Spier Spencer and Capt Wm. Bruce These two latter, together with several of Capt Charles Polk's sons, took part in the battle of Tippecanoe, Nov 7, 1811 the real beginning of the War of 1812—and in that fierce conflict Capt Spencer was killed while fighting with great gallantry at the head of his rifle company. So conspicuous were his services that the counties of Spencer, in Kentucky and in Indiana, were named in his honor.

This battle was a crushing defeat of the savages, led by The Prophet, who, with his brother, Tecumseh, was then engaged in organizing a great coalition of the savages, North and South, with the view of expelling the whites from all parts of the West.

In this battle, besides a few United States troops and the Indiana Militia companies, were a number of men from Kentucky under Col. Joseph Hamilton Daviess, and this gallant officer also fell a short distance from where Capt. Spencer was killed, after being twice wounded and trying to rise again.

Richard Collins, the Kentucky historian, speaking of the gallant conduct of Capt. Spencer, under the head of Spencer County, says:

"This county was named in honor of Capt. Spier Spencer, a young man of ardent patriotism and undaunted courage, who fell at the head of his company in the battle of Tippecanoe. He commanded a fine rifle company in that severe engagement, and occupied a most exposed position. In the midst of the action, he was wounded on the head, but continued at his post, and exhorted his men to fight on. Shortly after he received a second ball, which passed through both thighs and he fell, but still resolute and unyielding, he refused to be carried from the field, and urged his men to stand to their duty. By the assistance of one of his men he was raised to a sitting posture, when he received a third ball through his body, which instantly killed him. Both of his Lieutenants, Messrs. McMahan and Berry, were also killed. Capt. Spencer was a warm friend and bosom companion of the gifted and gallant Daviess, who perished with him in the battle."

Col. Joseph Hamilton Daviess was a former citizen of Lexington, Ky., and a fine portrait of him, executed by a distinguished artist, hangs in the Masonic Lodge in that city.

General Harrison, in his accounts of the intrepidity of the savages at Tippecanoe, said: "The Indians manifested a ferocity uncommon even in them."

By the death of Capt. Spier Spencer his wife Elizabeth,

was left to the sole care and raising of a family of eight children, who grew to manhood and womanhood and became highly respected and most worthy citizens, uniting in marriage with some of the best people in the state.

CHILDREN OF CAPT. SPIER SPENCER.

By his wife, Elizabeth Polk, Capt Spencer had the following issue: [1]George, b ——, d ——, married——, [2]William, b ——, d —— married Caroline Bell, [3]James, b ——, d ——, married, [4]Nancy, b. March 15, 1794, d.——. married Daniel Bell, Dec 24, 1811, [5]Jane, b ——, d ——, married Milo R Davis, [6]Matilda b ——, d ——. married General and United States Senator John B Tipton, [7]Delilah, b ——, d ——, married James B Slaughter, [8]Sarah, b Jan 12, 1809, d July 3, 1885, married Geo P. R Wilson, a son of Joshua Wilson of Kentucky, who settled at Corydon, prior to 1816

Delilah Spencer and James B Slaughter had the following children [1]William, b ——, d ——, married Caroline Pell; [2]Priscilla, b ——, d ——, married Golden, [3]Sarah, b ——, d ——, married Samuel J Wright They had two children that lived, James E and Sarah Wright. James E. married Miss Didelotte and Sarah married David M Rowland The latter had but one child, Mary Rowland, who married William C Adams of Corydon

Thomas C Slaughter married Katherine Jordan and has issue: [1]James L married Lillian Le Mon; [2]Harriet married Andrew M Jones, [3]Clara married William B Clemons, [4]Kate married Harry McGrain.

Sarah Spencer, by her husband, Geo P R. Wilson, had issue [1]James S married Jane Davis, [2]Mary E married Samuel J Wright (his second wife, the first being Sarah Slaughter), [3]Joshua T married Mary C Jordan, [4]George S married Sarah Burnett, [5]Rosa married Charles H Reader, [6]Fanny and Kitty are unmarried

Joshua T Wilson and Mary C. Jordan had issue: [1]Carrie; [2]Lennie, [3]Thomas J, [4]Tilla, [5]Kate, [6]Otway D, [7]Jennings B; [8]Sidney C, [9]George S., [10]Bertha. Only Thomas J, Tilla, Otway D Jennings B. and George S are living

SALLY (POLK) BRUCE'S DESCENDANTS.

James Bruce, accompanied by his brother, George, came from Scotland to America in 1745, and settled at Winchester, Va. His wife's maiden name was Margaret McMahon. From Winchester they moved to the North Branch of the Potomac, in Maryland, where a large family was born to them. One of the sons, William Bruce, married Mrs. Polly (Lucas) Perciful. Soon after marriage William moved to the Monongahela, settling at the mouth of Peter's Creek—"the new store"—now Elizabethtown. Indians prowled throughout that region and forts were the refuge of the people generally, being the only place of safety.

During the Revolutionary War, William was frequently called on to perform military service. He was stationed at a place called Catfish (named for an Indian Chief) near Redstone. He occupied the position of Lieutenant in a company of frontier militia. His next service was under General George Rogers Clark, commanding a company under that great soldier in the Illinois campaign of 1777, by which campaign all the territory between the Lakes, the Ohio and the Mississippi were transferred to the American flag. He was still in the service at Louisville in 1784. Leaving Kentucky, Major Wm. Bruce took part under Harrison, as did his brother-in-law, Capt. Spier Spencer and several of the Polks, in the battle of Tippecanoe.

Major Bruce was married October 23, 1798, to Sally Polk, third child of Capt. Charles Polk and his wife, Delilah Tyler, of Nelson County, Kentucky, and died April 23, 1855, at Bruceville, Ind., leaving many descendants. By his first wife, Sallie Polk, he had twelve children and also a number by his second wife Hettie Richie Holmes.

CHILDREN OF CAPT. WM. BRUCE AND WIFE.

(1) Charles Bruce, b.——, d.——, married first Angeline Wright, of Ohio, by whom he had three children. His second wife was Nancy P. Harrison of Montgomery County, by whom he had ten children.

(2) William D., b ——, d ——, married Betsy Polk. They had six children.

(3) Delilah, b ——, d.——, married Rachael Chambers, by whom he had nine children. His second wife was the Widow Light.

(5) Mary (Polly), b.——, d ——, married Squire Bruce, of Ogle County, Illinois Twelve children

(6) Elizabeth (Betsy) Bruce, b.——, d ——, married John La Follette, Putnam County, Ind., twelve children.

(7) Lucinda b. Feb. 7, 1809, d Feb. 21, 1870, married John Henderson Scroggin, of Knox County, Indiana, and they had six children The Scroggins moved from Kentucky to Indiana [1]Joseph Hamilton, b. May 17, 1836, d ——; [2]William Bruce, b. Sept. 3, 1838, d June 4, 1857; [3]Henry Harrison, b Sept. 11, 1840, d ——, [4]Geo Wilson, b May 5, 1842, d ——; [5]Sally Jane b Jan. 3, 1845, married Dec. 20, 1868, James Wm. Clark, of Nebraska Four children

When the Civil War began in 1861 three of the sons of John Henderson enlisted in the Union Army—Joseph H, Henry H. and George Six months afterward, Henry sickened and died. Joseph H. also fell ill, was in the hospital for over a year, and was discharged George served over three years, but at the battle of Nashville, where Thomas defeated Hood, December 15, 1864, he was severely wounded and died a few days later.

Sally Jane Scroggins and her husband, James W Clark, who was born Oct. 4, 1846, had issue: [1]Geo Edgar, b ——, Oct. 13, 1869; [2]Addie Lucinda, b May 19, 1872; [3]Rebecca Maude, b Dec. 10, 1874, [4]Edith Caroline b Dec. 10, 1876; [5]Ashby Bruce, b. Oct 3, 1879, d. Nov 13, 1880.

JOSEPH HAMILTON SCROGGIN'S FAMILY.

Joseph Hamilton Scroggin, b May 17, 1836, married, 1867, Nancy Gano, b. July 24, 1837. They had [1]Mattie Bruce, b. Feb 15, 1868, [2]Lucinda May, b Nov. 28, 1869, [3]George Washington, b Dec 12, 1871; [4]Sally Ann, b Oct 17, 1873; [5]Rosa, b. July 10, 1875

Capt Joseph Scroggin, by birth an Irishman, was an officer in the English Navy at a time when it was assisting

Spain in one of her wars. While in Spain he met and became enamored with the Princess Fantalina, eldest daughter of Philip V, first Bourbon King of Spain. Philip was a grandson of Louis XIV of France and Maria Louise Gabriella of Savoy. Capt. Scroggin eloped with the Princess to England, where he married her and came to America in 1714, landing at Baltimore. Receiving grants of land, he settled at Snow Hill, Maryland, where both of them died, leaving one child, Joseph Scroggin, Jr., born 1715.

Joseph Scroggin, Jr., married in 1740, in Maryland, Sarah Ann Caldwell, whose sister, Martha was the mother of Hon. John C. Calhoun, distinguished as an American Statesman.

Joseph and Sarah Ann (Caldwell) Scroggin had a family of thirteen children, viz: [1]Nancy, b. May 13, 1741; [2]Capt. John, b. Nov. 13, 1743, [3]Mary, b. Nov. 13, 1745, [4]Joseph, b. June 17, 1747, [5]Samuel, b. June 14, 1749, [6]Sarah, b. Sept. 14, 1750; [7]Robt. Caldwell, b. March 1, 1753; [8]William, b. April 24, 1755, [9]Mildred, b. June 15, 1757; [10]Philip, b. Sept. 5, 1759, [11]Annie Caldwell, b. June 18, 1761; [12]Thomas Clark, b. July 4, 1762, [13]Matilda, b. August 21, 1764.

Sarah Ann (Caldwell) Scroggin, mother of the foregoing children, died Dec. 31, 1770.

Capt. John Scroggin, second child of Joseph and Sarah Ann Caldwell was an officer in the Revolutionary War. He married (in 1767) Eunice Jane Polk, daughter of John Polk, of Deleware, second son of Ephriam Polk, 1st, who was the third son of Capt. Robert Bruce Polk and wife, Magdalen.

In November, 1793, in company with a number of kinsmen, Ephraim Polk, 3rd, the Morris', Nutters', Hopkins', and others he emigrated to Kentucky, all settling not far from each other in the present counties of Fayette, Harrison, Bourbon, Woodford and Scott, where they have many descendants. Many of the latter emigrated to Missouri, Indiana, Illinois and other Western territories, but a large number of their descendants are still to be found in Kentucky.

Being descended from a daughter of King Philip V of Spain, the Scroggins are probably the only family in Kentucky descended from a royal blood.

CAPT. JOHN SCROGGINS' FAMILY.

¹Elizabeth, b. Oct 10, 1768; ²William, b Jan 29, 1770; ³Samuel, b Dec 30, 1771, ⁴John, b May 12, 1774, ⁵Sarah Ann Caldwell, b. Oct 9. 1776, ⁶Joseph, b. Feb. 9, 1779; ⁷Levin Polk, b. March 26, 1782

Joseph, the sixth child of John and Eunice Jane (Polk) Scroggin, married Nancy Jane Holmes, a sister of Hetty R Bruce, and they emigrated to Knox County, Indiana, locating at Bruceville, near Vincennes, where they have many prominent descendants at this day, as also many Bruce kinsmen. Joseph died Nov 4, 1843, and his wife, Nancy (born Aug 20, 1783), died died Dec. 8, 1846 They had the following children ¹Eunice, b. July 23, 1807, in Kentucky, died young; ²John Henderson, b Feb 6, 1809, d March 3, 1848; ³Wm. Weston, b Dec 7, 1810, d. unmarried, Oct 10, 1842; ⁴Ann Elizabeth, b. March 28, 1873, d unmarried, ⁵Josiah Love, b April 8, 1815, d unmarried, ⁶Sallie Jane, b Feb, 16, 1818, married——, and had a son; ⁷Hetty, b. June 15, 1820, d unmarried, ⁸Nancy Ann, b May 23, 1823, died unmarried, ⁹Joseph D, b Dec, 20, 1825.

John Henderson Scroggin married Lucinda Bruce, a daughter of Capt. Wm Bruce and his wife, Sallie Polk, daughter of Capt Charles Polk and Delilah Tyler Lucinda Bruce Scroggin died Feb 21, 1870 John Henderson Scroggin and wife had issue· ¹Joseph Hamilton, b. May 17, 1836, ²Wm Bruce, b Sept 3, 1838, d June 4, 1857; ³Henry Harrison, b. Sept. 11, 1840; ⁴George Wilson, b. May 5, 1842, ⁵Sallie Jane, b Jan. 3, 1845, married James Wilson Clark and lives in Nebraska. They have four children

OF SCOTCH-IRISH BLOOD.

Col John W Polk, of Kansas City, Mo, son of Robert Tyler Polk, and grandson of Capt Charles Polk, in a letter of May 20, 1893, referring to his elder kinsman, stated

"The people named above were all of Scotch descent and formed a Scotch Colony in and around a village named Bruceville about five miles from Vincennes, where they settled soon after Indiana, a part of New France, was acquired by the United States, and many years before the territory was admitted as a state

"William Bruce, for whom the village was named was called "Uncle" by all my aunts and uncles My recollection is that he married a sister of my father's mother Therefore, he must have married a Tyler. I remember him and his wife when I was a small boy say about 1826 They were then old people He was a stately old aristocrat, looked up to by all the family He claimed to be a descendant of the royal blood of Scotland. All the Tylers of Kentucky, most of whom are at Louisville, are of the same family I have met many of them I remember Levi Tyler very well The mother of Isaac Sturgeon, of St Louis, was a Tyler, Capt. Silas Bent, of the Navy, married one

During the Civil War, John Tyler, a son of President Tyler, and myself, served in the same army (Confederate) and were messmates a long time We often talked over our family relations I recall that he was very familiar with his family history, that they were Shropshire people of note and distinction On the Polk side of our family, I have a clear history Both families are entitled to a crest and a coat of arms "

QUARRELED OVER BABY'S NAME.

There is a tradition in the family that Capt. Joseph Scroggin. in abducting the Princess Fantalina from the tower in which she had been confined, in order to prevent her from meeting him, rowed close to the tower and that she lowered herself to him from a window to which she attached a rope

Some months after their arrival in Baltimore, it is said they quarreled over the naming of their child, and she in her anger, threw all their valuable papers into the fire, he being able to rescue only one land grant. The child was named Joseph, and early in youth manifested a most unfortunate temper He possessed all the irascibility of his Spanish-Irish blood When about seventeen years old, he quarreled with his m ther and ... ... Caldwell, a daughter f J ... ... settled.

Sarah's sister, it is said, was the mother of Hon John C Calhoun of South Carolina, the eminent American Statesman.

NANCY RUBY'S FAMILY AND CHAS. POLK, 3rd.

Nancy Polk (fourth child of Capt Charles Polk), born about 1781 in Nelson County, Kentucky, married Peter Ruby and had a family of eight children, viz: [1]Delilah, b about 1804, d ——, married John Keath, [2]Jane, b. about 1806, d.——, married Robt Johnson, [3]Benjamin F, b about 1808, d ——, married Lucy Lemmon, [4]Spier Spencer, b about 1810, d ——, married Polly Shepherd, [5]Charles, b. about 1812, d ——, married Mrs Nichols, 2nd, Mrs Wade, [6]John Ochiltree, b. Oct. 20, 1814; d Oct. 7, 1868, married Deborah Faile, of Vincennes, Ind, June 25, 1836, [7]Sally, b about 1816, d Jan 18, 1817, [8]Robert, about 1818, d Jan 21, 1856

John O Ruby and wife, Debby, had issue [1]Capt William F, La Fayette, Ind, b Dec. 2, 1838, who married Vashti Borden, Sept. 25, 1866, and had issue Aimee J, b Oct. 14, 1878, and Edna Browning, Oct 28, 1879

William F Ruby was a soldier in the Union Army during the Civil War, serving nearly four years in the Tenth and One Hundredth and Fifty-fourth Indiana Infantry as Company Commander, Commissary and Quartermaster After the Civil War he was appointed Quartermaster at the Indiana State Soldiers' Home, La Fayette.

AMTEE J. RUBY AND EDNA B. RUBY.
La Fayette, Ind.

THE NEW YORK
PUBLIC LIBRARY

ASTOR, LENOX AND
TILDEN FOUNDATIONS.

CHAPTER XLVIII.

EDMOND POLK'S DESCENDANTS.

Edmond Polk (second child and son of Charles Polk, the Indian trader of Frederick County, Maryland), was born in that colony in 1740, and died in Nelson County, Kentucky, 1824-5. He was a youth of thirteen when his father died in 1753, leaving a widow, Christian Polk (whose maiden name is said to have been Matson), and six children. As they attained to manhood, these children all appear to have left the old homestead and gone further toward the frontier

Edmond located for a time at Fort Pitt (Pittsburg) or in that vicinity, where he was married in 1765, but we have no record of the maiden name of his wife. It is said that he and his three brothers all took an active part in the American Revolution by service on the frontier as rangers, against the British and their savage allies. Of the children of Edmond and wife, the first six were born in Pennsylvania, and possibly, also, the seventh, Polly, who was born in 1780, the year he settled in Kentucky. The two youngest, James and Nancy, were born in Nelson County, Kentucky

Edmond and brothers, determining to descend the Ohio to find homes in a richer and more fertile land, did so in the spring of 1780, landing at the Falls of the Ohio (now Louisville) where they sojourned a short time. They were accompanied to Kentucky by their sister, Sarah (Polk) Piety, who had married Austin Piety, a British subaltern officer at Fort Pitt some years before, and who deserted her and her children and returned to England when the Revolutionary War began

After a brief sojourn in the vicinity of Louisville, the Polk brothers moved southward and settled on the head waters of Salt river, in what are now Shelby, Spencer and Nelson Counties in which section numerous blockhouses or 'Stations' were erected by an adventurous company of pioneers from Virginia and Pennsylvania, who came just before and at the time of the Polks. There is no doubt, however, that some of the Polks had visited Kentucky before 1780. This is shown by the records of the Virginia Land Office, wherein are recorded grants to people by virtue of locations made for them by Charles, Thomas and other Polks, in 1775 and 1776, on the waters of Cox Creek and Simpsons Creek, in the present counties of Spencer and Nelson and also in Fayette County, near Lexington.

Hence, some of these Polks came with the first parties of pioneers who descended the Ohio the year following the defeat of the Indians under Cornstalk, at Point Pleasant, which event took place in October, 1774. This defeat cowed the Indians and permitted the surveyors and land locators who had abandoned Kentucky in the summer of 1774 on the approach of the Indian War, to come back and resume operations in the Spring of 1775. And with them, as the Virginia Land Office records show, came several of the Polk brothers, who not only picked out locations for themselves, but also marked locations for others, acting as deputy surveyors under the laws of Virginia.

A recent historical sketch in the Kentucky Standard, published at Bardstown, says: "Thomas Polk, David Connor and others settled on Simpson's Creek and built Polk's Station, which was passed into history as the Burnt Station, and stood on the farm of the late W. D. Huston. Cox's Station was settled in the Spring of 1775, by Col. Isaac Cox, who came from Pennsylvania, and Bardstown in 1776 by the Bairds also of Pennsylvania. In 1784, by act of the Virginia Legislature, the County of Nelson was erected out of a part of Shelby County, the latter being one of the original counties of Kentucky District. Isaac Cox and Charles Polke were three of those appointed by the Governor of Virginia as Justices of the Peace, Justices of Oyer and Terminer, and Justices in Chancery of the new county. The first term of court was held in May, 1785, and an order was made for the erection of a prison for debtors, a prison for criminals, a whipping post, pillory and stocks. Capt Charles Polk was one of the magistrates appointed to fix locations and make contracts for such, and Edward was one of the committee of three to report on the character of the work.

Col Wm Polk, of Vicksburg, Miss., writing in 1875, to the author, stated "Grandfather Polk moved from Pennsylvania to what is now Nelson County, Kentucky, about one hundred years ago, where he lived till his death, which occurred near Bardstown in the year 1824 or 1825 His children were Thomas, Charles, Edmond and James on the male side, and Hannah, Kitty, Sally, Polly and Nancy on the female side

"Thomas and Charles moved to Indiana early in life say sixty or seventy years ago, and lived and raised large families upon what was, and is now, called "Polk's Bottom," upon the Ohio river, opposite the mouth of Cloverport, Ky At a later day Edmond, Jr, moved to Illinois with a large family and entered 160 acres of land upon which a part of Chicago now stands

"James lived for many years almost in sight of the place on which he was born and raised, and died near Bardstown James' sons sooner or later all moved to Indiana Grandfather Edmond Polk had a brother, Charles, who lived near Vincennes, and was a conspicuous officer in the army in the first settling of the country The Polks are still numerous in that region, and altogether you may perceive there is a large sprinkling of Polk blood in Indiana

"The members of our branch of the Polk family have never been famous for oratorical powers or talent, nor much inclined toward officers, yet somewhat talented in the way of mechanical genius and general industry, what you may call plain, old-fashioned, sober, good common-sense people almost invariably doing well, very largely Baptists in religion and Jackson and Jeffersonian in politics"

How long the Polks remained in Kentucky after their first visit in 1775, we do not know Doubtless they went back up the Ohio in the late fall to their homes (as most of the pioneers did), and made other locating trips to Kentucky in the years following It is also likely that, the American Revolution coming on in 1776 some of them joined the armies in the frontier service. But we have heard of other services, other than the partially known exploits of Capt Charles Polk, after his arrival in Kentucky, in combatting Indian forays onto the waters of Salt River, in one of which attacks his wife and four children were taken captive in 1782 by a band of Wabash Indians going home from the Blue Lick Massacre of Aug 19, of that year

Edmond Polk died near Smithville, Bullitt County, Kentucky, in 1824-25, and his sons, Thomas and Charles, later followed their uncle Capt. Charles Polk, and his sons, to Indiana Territory Edmond's son, Charles, became a noted Baptist preacher, and located at Polk's Bottom, on the Ohio, in what is now Perry County, Indiana He was an officer under Gen. Harrison in the Indian wars in that section, and was in the battle of Tippecanoe in 1811, also a representative from Perry County in the Territorial Convention of Indiana in 1816 and helped to induct that territory into the Union.

The youngest son of Edmond, James Polk, lived all his life in Kentucky, dying about 1850. As James Polk's eldest child, William, was born in Feb, 1805 his marriage to Nancy Abell must have occurred the year previous, 1804 His tombstone in the family graveyard in Indiana bears only the name "James Polk," without dates of birth or death

James Polk's wife, Nancy Abell, it said, was a sister of Ignatius Abell who married Kitty Polk his sister A number of families who intermarried with the children of Capt Charles and Edmond Polk also emigrated to Indiana, settling near each other in Perry and Gibson, and also in Knox County, near Vincennes, then the military and civic capital of that frontier, presided over by General Wm. Henry Harrison, Territorial Governor Under him the Polks and their kinsmen, the Bruces, Spencers and others served with marked credit in the Indian Wars, and later in the War of 1812

EDMOND POLK'S CHILDREN.

The children born to Edmond Polk and wife were:
(1) Thomas, b 1768, d ——, married Lucy ———.
(2) Rev Charles, b Sept. 26, 1770, d. July 25, 1836, married Willey Dever, Aug 5, 1790

(3) Edmond, Jr., b. about 1772, d. July 28, 1861, at Chicago, Ill.

(4) Hannah, b. about 1774, d. ——, married Adam Guthrie, of Neison County, Kentucky.

(5) Kitty, b. about 1776, d. ——, married Ignatius Abell, of Nelson County, Kentucky.

(6) Sallie, b. about 1778, d. 1825, married Zach Fowler (Some say Thomas Tobin, of Tobinsport, Ind.)

(7) Mary (Polly), b. about 1780, d. unmarried at Bloomfield, Ky.

(8) Nancy, b. about 1782, d. unmarried at Bloomfield, Ky.

(9) James, b. about 1784, d. 1850, married Nancy Abell, of Nelson County, Kentucky.

Of the above children of Edmond Polk, Thomas and Rev. Charles left Kentucky in 1808 and removed to Polk's Bottom, Perry County, Indiana, on the Ohio River, where they purchased and settled on fine tracts of land and raised large families. Charles represented Perry county in the first Constitutional Convention of Indiana, in 1816, when that territory came into the Union. He was a Baptist minister, and a man of recognized ability and influence among his fellows. Edmond Polk, Jr., moved from Kentucky to Indiana, where he married Esther Tobin, and later to Illinois, entering 160 acres of land that is now a part of the site of Chicago. He raised a large family of children and died there.

Hannah Polk married Adam Guthrie, of Nelson County, and had a number of children, one of whom was Hon. James Guthrie, a wealthy financier of Louisville, who was Secretary of the United States Treasury, under President Pierce. Their descendants are numerous in Kentucky and other states. Kitty Polk, who married Ignatius Abell, of Nelson County, had a number of children. They settled at Corydon. Sallie Polk, who married Zach Fowler, also had a number of children, says Col. W. A. Polk, of Vicksburg, Miss. One of Sallie's descendants, however, Mrs. Jacy P. Simons, of Tobinsport, says Sallie married Thomas Tobin. If so, he was likely a second husband.

GRANDCHILDREN OF EDMOND POLK, SR.

Thomas Polk (first child of Edmond, Sr.) married Lucy ———, and had a family, but the name of but one, Edmond, is preserved. The latter married, in 1821, Esther Tobin, and had a son, Edmond, 3rd, b July 31, 1831, who is living at Tobinsport, Ind., where his son, George L Polk, is a merchant In 1856. Edmond married Lucinda Winchell and had issue [1]Lizzie, [2]Abbey, [3]George L., [4]Minnie. The latter married Jarrett Kinder, George L married Susan A Crow, in 1892, and had issue. [1]Lloyd, [2]Mayme; [3]Mabel, [4]Alma. George Polk (second son of Edmond and Esther (Tobin) Polk), b.———, married Amanda Ryan and had issue [1]Riley, [2]Mary, [3]Nancy, [4]Emma; [5]Robert; all of Cloverport, Ky.

Rev. Charles Polk (second son of Edmond Sr), who married Willey Dever, had ten children viz..

(1) Polly, b. Aug. 6, 1791, d Sept 11, 1818.
(2) Edmond, b May 19, 1794, d July 28, 1861.
(3) Richard, b. Oct. 11, 1796, d ———
(4) Greenville, b. Nov. 12, 1798, d. ———
(5) Ilion, b March 14, 1802, d March 5, 1803
(6) Thomas, b. Jan 22, 1804, d. ———
(7) James, b Jan 22, 1806, d. 1873
(8) Aaron, b. Jan 11, 1808, d. Aug. 1, 1815
(9) Ephraim, b Feb. 18, 1810, d July 27, 1815
(10) Helen, b. Dec 5, 1811, d Aug 29, 1815.

Their Children.

Polly Polk (first child of Rev Chas. Polk), married ——— Tobin and had issue

Edmond Polk (second Child of Rev Chas Polk), married Polly Winchell and had Margaret and Avery (twins), b. 1794 Avery still living in June, 1911

Richard Polk (third child of Rev. Chas Polk), married Patsy Sterrett Issue, unknown.

Greenville Polk (fourth child of Rev Chas Polk), married Matilda Sims, Dec 5, 1827, she b June 12, 1806 at Springfield, Ky They had issue: [1] A son, who married and had a daughter, Addie who married a Mr. Payne, of Tobinsport, Ind.;

HON. JAS. GUTHRIE.
Louisville, Ky., son of Hannah Polk, daughter of Capt. Chas. Polk.

THE NEW YORK
PUBLIC LIBRARY

ASTOR, LENOX AND
TILDEN FOUNDATIONS

²Aaron, untraced, ³Edmond and Mary (twins), untraced, ⁴Nancy, married Henry Miller, Feb 8, 1859.

William Henry and Jane, two youngest children, untraced

Nancy and Henry Miller had a daughter, Ada, b March 18, 1860, married James H Payne and they had ¹Nancy Helen, ²Anna Mary, ³Nellie Stewart, ⁴Lloyd Miller; ⁵Jamie Beatrice, ⁶Bernice Taylor.

Thomas (sixth child of Rev Chas Polk), married Malvina Ryan Issue, unknown

James (seventh child of Rev Chas Polk), married Charlotte Humphrey and had· ¹Wm. Riley, ²Rosina; ³Lavinia, ⁴Willia, ⁵Commodore, ⁶Dorinda; ⁷Edwin; ⁸Eliza.

Wm Riley, b. July 14, 1839, married Eliza Gilbert, in 1868 They had issue: ¹Bertha, b——; ²Anna, b——; ³Mary, b——, ⁴Eliza and Jacy (twins), b.—— Bertha is now (1911) living, but the others are dead Wm. Riley's daughter, Jacey, married a Mr Simons and resides at Tobinsport

(8) Aaron (eighth child of Rev Chas Polk), b Jan 12, 1808, d Aug. 11, 1815.

(9) Ephraim (ninth child of Rev Chas Polk), b Feb 18, 1810, d July 27, 1815

(10) Helen (tenth child of Rev Chas Polk), b Dec. 5, 1811, d Aug 29, 1815.

CHILDREN OF JAMES POLK

The children of James Polk and his wife, Nancy (Abell) Polk, were·

(1) Felix M, b about 1803, d. winter 1877-8

(2) William, b. Feb 9, 1805, d Dec 18, 1877

(3) Maria A, b about 1807, d. 1878

(4) Claiborne, b June 20, 1811, d at Fort Branch, Ind., Sept 20, 1901.

(5) Geo. Washington, b. 1813, d ——

(6) Rev Alexander Hamilton, b May 5, 1818, d. at Lakeland, Fla, March 1, 1900

(7) Jas Madison, b July 31, 1820, d Aug 12, 1900

(8) Matilda, b June 22, 1830 d June 16, 18—

Felix married his cousin, Frances Matilda Polk, and left a daughter. His widow married secondly a Mr. Lane. In 1878 his daughter and her mother (Mrs. Lane) resided near Paoli, Ind.

William Polk married Sarah Shoptaw, of Nelson County, Kentucky. They moved to Indiana in 1856 and she died Feb 3, 1890. They had issue. ¹John A., of Greenwood, Ind., b March 12, 1825, d. Feb 13, 1910. He married Martha Embry, of Richmond, Ky., and had issue: ¹Clay, b ——, married Anna King One child, Otta. ²Sallie, b Jan 5, 1862, married Willard Harmon One child, Florence E., b 1895; ³Edward, b 1869. ⁴Robert, b 1873, married Cora Sheeks No issue; ⁵Augusta, b 1867, married Linley Hester One child that died young, ⁶Lee, b. 1877, unmarried in 1910

John A. Polk was a member of the Indiana Legislature and made a large fortune in the canning of vegetables

(2) Col Burr H Polk (second son of Wm. Polk), b Jan 15, 1835, d. May 15, 1887. He married Eliza Ann Montgomery (b Oct 20, 1837, d June 13, 1909) and they had issue. ¹Carrie Sidney, b. Dec 17, 1858, married James McClelland Irwin, of Quincy, Ill., Oct 10, 1883. They had children Annie, b. Oct. 1, 1884, d Aug 18, 1885, Burr Irwin, b Dec 25, 1885; Jas Matthew Irwin, b. March 7, 1889, ²Ida, b May 6, 1861, d. May 8, 1863, ³Frank Montgomery, b Feb 28, 1864 At the beginning of the Spanish-American War he entered the army, with rank of First Lieutenant, and served in the Philippines. He was transferred to the Regular Army as a Second Lieutenant, and died in service, April 30, 1901

(4) Edna, b Dec 31, 1874, married Burton W. Wilson, Attorney-at-Law, June 17, 1902, and they now reside in the City of Mexico They have three children ¹Donald, b Dec 9, 1903; ²Burr Polk, b at Lincoln, Neb, Sept. 25, 1905; ³Mary Elizabeth, b in Mexico City, June 16, 1909

Col. Burr H. Polk was a man of prominence in the Civil War and subsequent thereto In the Army of the Cumberland he bore the rank of Colonel and served on the staffs of General George H Thomas, and others After the close of the war he resided for a time at Vicksburg, as special correspondent of the Cincinnati Commercial, his talents tending strongly to journalism. Later he made a tour of Europe, an account of which, graphic and highly interesting, was published in book form in 1879.

The United States Army Register gives the following data concerning the military positions held by Col. Burr H Polk "Polk, Burr H, Ky.-Ind ; Capt 33d Ind Inf., Sept. 6, 1861; Capt A A G Vols., March 11, 1863; Major A A G. Vols., April 20, 1864. Bvt. Lt Col and Col. Vols., March 13, 1865, for faithful and efficient service Honorably mustered out Feb. 27, 1866.

(3) James Polk, of Waterford, Spencer County, Ky, (third child of Wm Polk and Sarah Shoptaw), b Aug 15, 1837, d. ———, married and had five children: [1]James Guthrie; [2]Nathan; [3]Christopher; [4]Charles, [5]Madison

(4) Eliza Polk (fourth child of Wm Polk and Sarah Shoptaw) b. Feb. 5, 1841, was twice married Her first husband (Dec 10, 1867) was H. C Wood, of Taylorsville, Ky, by whom she had a son, Harry Wood Her second husband was Dr Zachariah Carnes, of Greenwood, Ind By the latter she had a daughter, Floy Carnes. Dr. Carnes died Jan. 10, 1910 Harry is unmarried Floy married Mr Moll, an attorney-at-law of Indianapolis, and they have three children.

(5) Wm Lancaster Polk (fifth child of Wm Polk and Sarah Shoptaw) b May 8, 1844, moved from Indiana to Mississippi in 1869, engaging in planting and the business of a civil engineer. He resided at his death at Vicksburg He married Alice Howe, of Indiana, by whom he had issue: [1]Walter Howe, b in Indiana, Dec. 3, 1867; [2]Paul M, b Nov. 12, 1878, married Alice Garth Downing, of Yazoo City, Miss, Nov 29, 1911; [3]Clara Graham, b March 11, 1882; [4]Lancaster, b Sept 14, 1884, d June 30, 1907.

Walter Howe Polk married (June 14, 1894) Lillian Montgomery, daughter of Major W. E. Montgomery and granddaughter of Chas Clark, War Governor of Mississippi, 1860-1865 Issue: [1]Montgomery Howe, April 4, 1895; [2]Clara May, b Oct. 23, 1896, [3]Walter Howe, Jr, b. Oct. 10, 1898; [4]Lillian Graham, b June 18, 1901; [5]Alice Gertrude, b June 14 1903, d. July 21, 1904, [6]Horace Stuart, b Aug 17, 1905; [7]Wm Paul, b Nov. 16, 1906 Charles and Elizabeth Polk (twins and youngest children of Wm. Polk and Sarah Shoptaw) were born June 16, 1847 Chas. died Aug 7, 1902, and Elizabeth, May 25, 1908 Charles married a Miss Dickerson and had. ¹Dolly, ²Stella, ³Opal, ⁴Nettie. Elizabeth married Daulton Wilson and had ¹Burr, ²Susie; ³Clifton, ⁴Bessie; ⁵Hal. Susie married John Guthrie Hal married Lenore Harmon and they have one child, Jane.

George Washington Polk (fifth child of James Polk, born in Nelson County, Kentucky, about 1816, married Mary Embree and after the Civil War moved to Greenwood, Indiana, where he established a vegetable canning factory and accumulated a fortune The business is still carried on by his son, James Thomas Polk. The children of George Washington Polk and wife were ¹Wm F ; ²Frances Jones, ³James Thomas; ⁴Alice, ⁵Florence, ⁶Perry E

Maria Polk (daughter of James Polk), b. in Nelson County, Kentucky, about 1807, married William Bivin of Hardin County, Kentucky They removed to Princeton, Ind., both dying in 1878, and left issue ——

Matilda Polk (daughter of James Polk), b June 27, 1830, d. June 16, 1850, married first, Jno B Worrell of Jackson County, Missouri. No issue. Secondly, married Jas F Cunningham, a pork merchant of Mobile, Ala, later of Cincinnati, and left issue ——, ——, ——, ——

James Madison Polk, youngest son of James Polk, was born in Nelson County, July 31, 1820, died Aug 17, 1900, in Spencer County, Ky He married Minerva Cochran, born Dec 27, 1824 She died May 20, 1898, in Spencer County.

CHILDREN OF JAMES MADISON POLK.

The children born to James Madison Polk and wife were·
(1) Frances Matilda, b in Jefferson County, Kentucky, Feb. 13, 1849.
(2) James Guthrie, b in Bullitt County, Kentucky, Feb 25, 1851
(3) Nathan William, b in Bullitt County, Dec 24, 1852.
(4) Mary Catherine, b. in Bullitt County, Dec. 10, 1854.

(5) Henry Hamilton, b in Indiana, Feb. 9, 1857

(6) Alvin Crist, b in Spencer County, Kentucky, Dec 4, 1859.

(7) Sarah Isabella, b. in Spencer County, April 16, 1862

(8) Charles Pelham, b in Spencer County, March 23, 1865

(9) Madison Cochran, b in Spencer County, Jan 30, 1868

Sarah Isabella, Chas Pelham and Madison Cochran, living and unmarried.

James Madison and Minerva Cochran were married Sept. 24, 1846. James Guthrie and Mary Elizabeth Baird were married Nov 16, 1874. Frances Matilda and Felix M Polk were married Aug 31, 1882 He was a son of James Polk and Ann Abell. Nathan Wm. and Carrie Cochran (no relation) were married Jan 19, 1887. Henry Hamilton and Rosa Ely were married Sept. 24, 1891 The other children of James M. and Minerva Cochran are yet unmarried

Frances M Polk, who married Felix M Polk, died without issue, at Princeton, Ind, Oct. 15, 1888

James Guthrie Polk and wife had six children, all born in Spencer County, Kentucky: [1]Elida Bertie, b Aug 24, 1875, [2]Annie Elizabeth, b. May 20, 1878; [3]Charles Weldon, b. Jan 1, 1881; [4]William Madison, b Feb 11, 1883; [5]Jacob Boswell, b Sept 28, 1884, [6]Harry Glover, b. July 8, 1887. Elida Bertie, first child of James Guthrie Polk, married Chas Muir, Jan 30, 1900, one child

William Madison Polk, above named, was killed by an accident on board his ship, the U S. S Prairie, at Old Point Comfort, Va, Nov 9, 1904 He was a Naval Apprentice on that ship Elida Bertie Polk, first child of James Guthrie Polk and wife, married Charles Muir Jan 30, 1900 They have one child, Peter Brown Muir, born July 2, 1903.

Nathan W Polk and wife had issue [1]Roy Cochran, b in Spencer County, Jan 8, 1888; [2]Burr Herring, b in Spencer County, Sept. 10, 1889, [3]Mary Ruth, b in Spencer County, Nov 28, 1891; [4]Nellie Lee, b in Spencer County, Sept 16, 1893; [5]Charles Broadus, b in Spencer County, Sept 26 1895. These are all unmarried

Mary Catharine, fourth child of James M and Minerva (Cochran) Polk, died unmarried, Dec 1, 1901

CHILDREN OF HENRY HAMILTON POLK.

Henry Hamilton Polk and Rosa Ely, who were married Sept. 24, 1891, had issue [1]Maude Catharine, b at Louisville, Ky, Aug 1, 1892, [2]Alvin Crist, Jr, b. at Louisville, Ky, Jan 4, 1895, [3]Burley Demsey, b at Louisville, Ky, Feb 16, 1897. None of the above are married. Alvin Crist, sixth child of James M and Minerva (Cochran) Polk, is unmarried Sarah Isabella, seventh child of Jas M and Minerva (Cochran) Polk, is unmarried. Charles Pelham, eighth child of Jas M and Minerva Polk, also his brother, Madison Cochran, the youngest son of James M. and Minerva Polk, are both unmarried

DEATHS.

The family Bible of James Madison Polk shows the following deaths: James Madison, in Spencer County, Kentucky, Aug 17, 1900 Minerva (Cochran) in Spencer County, Kentucky, May 20, 1898 Frances Matilda, at Princeton, Ind, Oct. 15, 1888. Mary Catharine, in Spencer County, Kentucky, Dec. 31, 1904 Mary E, wife of Jas Guthrie Polk, in Spencer County, Aug. 8, 1891. Wm. Madison, by accident on board ship, Nov 9, 1904

NEW SALEM CHURCH.

New Salem Baptist Church, near Samuel's Depot, Nelson County, Kentucky, was organized Nov. 28, 1801. The first members were Emund Polk, Jr, Wm Chenoweth, Mary Chenoweth, Thomas Polke, Lucy Polke, Lucy French, Thomas Polke, Jr, and Mary McNeal. These eight persons met and drafted a constitution Four were subsequently dismissed by letter, Chenoweth and wife, Thos Polke and Mary McNeal died in the fellowship of the church Wm. Chenoweth gave the land on which the church was built Rev Warren Cash was the first pastor, preaching once a month, and Edmund Abell and Thomas Polke were the first deacons The former was a kinsman of Ignatius Abell, who married Kitty Polk and of Nancy Abell, who married James Polk, daughter and son of

Edmond Polk, Sr. For many years the church was known as Wilson's Creek Church, being located at the head of Wilson Creek.

Not long after the founding of Salem Church, some of the Polks of that vicinity (Capt Chas Polk's sons) emigrated to Indiana, followed later by himself (1808), and several of the children of Edmond Polk, Sr. Some of them afterward founded Maria Creek Baptist Church, in Knox County, they and their kinsmen by marriage constituting most of the membership Deacon Edmond Polk, Jr, emigrated from Indiana to Chicago, where he died His farm of 160 acres is now included in the bounds of that city.

CHAPTER XLIX.

CLAIBORNE POLK AND DESCENDANTS.

Claiborne Polk (son of James Polk and Nancy Abell, of Nelson County, Kentucky), born June 20, 1811, married Sept. 25, 1834, at Lexington, Ky., to Rachael Shoptaw. She was born in Nelson County, June 2, 1812, and died Aug. 20, 1855, in Gibson County Indiana Claiborne Polk died Sept 20, 1901, at Fort Branch, Ind The children of Claiborne and Rachael (Shoptaw) Polk were:

(1) Irwin C., b July 4, 1835, in Nelson County, Kentucky.

(2) Mary Catherine, b. Jan 2, 1837, at Taylorville, Ky., d. May 22, 1841, in Gibson County, Indiana

(3) John William, b Feb 18, 1838, at Taylorville, Ky., d July 18, 1839.

(4) Ann Elizabeth, b. May 30, 1840, in Spencer County, Kentucky, d. Aug 22, 1855, in Gibson County

(5) Isabella, b July 20, 1842, in Gibson County, Ind

(6) Theodore, b Jan 29, 1844, in Gibson County, Indiana, d Oct 29, 1844.

(7) Francis Marion, b Oct 25, 1845, in Gibson County

(8) William Albert, b Aug 6, 1848, in Gibson County, Indiana

(9) Caleb Clark, b June 9, 1850, in Gibson County, Indiana

(10) Sarah Jane, b Jan. 13, 1852, in Gibson County, Indiana

(11) Geo Calvin, b Dec 19, 1853, in Gibson County, d Sept 17, 1860.

Claiborne Polk was married to his second wife, Mary McMullen, May 15, 1856 To this union one child was born, Etta A Polk Mary McMullen Polk died Jan. 15, 1899.

Etta A Polk, born July 21, 1858, was married Dec. 8, 1874, in Gibson County, Indiana, to James Thomas Witherspoon. Mr Witherspoon resides at Princeton, Ind Their

CLAIBORNE POLK (top);
ALEXANDER HAMILTON POLK (bottom),
sons of Louis Polk and Nancy Shell, of Lexington.

children, all born in Gibson County, were ¹Cora, b. Dec 28, 1875. Residence, Webster Grove, Mo ; ²Maude, b Feb 19, 1878. Residence, St Louis, Mo , ³George, b March 24, 1880. Residence, Kansas City, Kan , ⁴Charles, b July 3 1882 Residence, 79 Julia St , Edmonton, Canada , ⁵Lucelia, b Jan. 29, 1884, d April 14, 1885. ⁶Eva, b Jan 26, 1886. Residence, 527 Fox St , Edmonton, Canada , ⁷Grace, b. Sept 15, 1888 Residence, No 26 E 44th St , Chicago, Ill , ⁸Mae, b May 2, 1901. Residence, Stony Plain, Canada , ⁹Stella, b Dec. 3, 1898 Residence, Princeton, Ind.

IRWIN C POLK'S FAMILY.

Irwin C Polk, son and eldest child of Claiborne Polk, married Sept 15, 1853, at King Station, Ind., to Elizabeth Marlotte, b Nov 4, 1830. She died Dec 30, 1908, at Harrisonville, Mo Their children were ¹Dovie Estella, b Jan 27, 1852, near Princeton, Ind , married Jan. 27, 1876, James Lewis Pringle, b. near Dayton, Ore , Dec 10, 1853. Residence, 2342 Calumet Ave , Chicago Issue ¹Agnes, unmarried , ²Henry, b——, married Anna Isadore Rapkoch , ³Jessie Pringle, b ——, unmarried , ⁴Lillian Pringle, b——, unmarried. Harry resides at 607 Woodland Park, Chicago These children were all born at Danville, Ill.

²William C , b—— Present address, Roswell, New Mexico , ³Edward J , b.—— Present address, Harrisonville, Mo , ⁴A. B., b,——; ⁵C E , b——, ⁶C L, b,——.

The Pringle family are all musicians and organized the Pringle Concert Company, which has toured the country and delighted lovers of good music Going to Europe to finish their musical education, they studied under the best masters In Berlin, Lillian studied under Anton Hekking Jessie had several eminent voice teachers, among them George Furgeson and Frantz Prochowsky She also studied thoroughly the French, German and Italian languages, which she speaks fluently The present address of the family is Sanford, Fla

ISABELLA (POLK) KENDLE.

Isabella Polk (daughter of Claiborne Polk), b in July 20, 1852, Gibson County Indiana married Sept 16 1862, at

King Station, Ind , to I Robert Kendle, b Sept 14, 1840, and died Jan 5, 1905, at Princeton, Ind They had no children The present address of Mrs. Kendle is Princeton, Ind.

FRANCIS MARION POLK

Francis Marion Polk (son of Claiborne Polk) was born Oct 25, 1845, in Gibson County, Indiana, and died Dec. 29, 1905, at Mound City, Kan He was married Oct 28, 1880, to Miss Emma La Grange of Gibson County They had no children Mrs Polk resides at Mound City, Kan.

WILLIAM ALBERT POLK'S FAMILY.

Wm. Albert Polk (son of Claiborne Polk), born Aug 6, 1848, in Gibson County, Indiana, married Sept 17, 1871, and died Jan 25, 1904, at Fort Branch, Ind His wife Eliza Ann Rycroft, was born March 14, 1851, at Durham, England. Their children were [1]Walter Clyde, b July 20, 1872, in Gibson County, Indiana. [2]Dora Isabella, b. Jan 27, 1874, at Madisonville, Ky, d Aug 24, 1905, at Fort Branch, Ind.; [3]Caleb Claude, b March 22, 1876, at Madisonville Ky.. [4]Robert Kendle, b. Aug. 6, 1878, at Madisonville, Ky, married March 10, 1911, at Geneva, Ill

Claiborne Stanley Polk, b Feb. 4, 1884, at Madisonville, Ky, d. Jan 18, 1899, at Fort Branch, Ind Wm Arthur Polk, b Jan 1, 1886, at Madisonville, Ky . Alice Edmund Polk, b May 17, 1888, at Fort Branch, Ind. Addresses of the above are Fort Branch, Ind, excepting Claude Caleb Polk, who resides at Princeton, that State

CALEB CLARK POLK'S FAMILY.

Caleb Clark Polk (son of Claiborne Polk), born June 9, 1850, in Gibson County, Indiana, was married Nov. 6, 1879, at Westfield, Ind , to Clara Thornburg, b July 30, 1858 Their children were [1]Thomas Claiborne b May 15, 1881, at Crownpoint, Ind . [2]Harry Thornburg, b Sept 25, 1883, at Richmond, Ind . [3]Gertrude Jennie, b. Feb. 23, 1895, at Val-

AGNES AND JESSIE PRINGLE,
daughters of Mrs. ... Polk ...ers of

THE NEW YORK
PUBLIC LIBRARY

ASTOR LENOX AND
TILDEN FOUNDATIONS

paraiso, Ind. The above children are all unmarried and reside at Valparaiso, near Chicago, where Caleb Clark Polk conducts a large school for the teaching of piano tuning

SARAH JANE POLK'S FAMILY.

Sarah Jane Polk (daughter of Claiborne Polk), born Jan 13, 1852, was married June 4, 1872, in Gibson County, Indiana, to Bartlett Bennett Hollis, born April 7, 1843 Their children, all born in Gibson County, were [1]Heber Ernest, b March 3, 1873, [2]Othniel, b Oct 12, 1874. [3]Francis Allen, b. Nov 5, 1876, [4]John Stewart, b March 5, 1880. [5]Rachel, b Feb 5, 1883; [6]Walter, b. Oct. 18, 1885. [7]Charles Edwin, b Jan. 16, 1889: [8]Clarence Vannada, b. June 11, 1891 The present address of these is King's Station, Ind., excepting one, Heber Ernest Hollis, who resides at Vincennes.

ALEXANDER HAMILTON POLK.

Alexander Hamilton Polk (sixth child of James Polk and Nancy Abell, of Nelson County, Kentucky) was born May 5, 1818, and died March 1, 1900, at Lakeland, Fla., to which place he removed from Indiana in 1886 He first moved from Kentucky to Gibson County, Indiana, in 1836, where he engaged in farming and surveying until 1865, when he was ordained as a minister of the Baptist church He continued in the pulpit for seven years, and then quitting it, engaged again in the work of surveying, and was chosen County Surveyor Altogether, he was in the surveying business for over thirty years. On Oct 24, 1839, he was married to Miss Julian Embree, of Princeton, whose family had emigrated to Indiana from Kentucky. She died June 28, 1857 His second wife, Miss Barshaba H Green, he married March 9, 1858 Issue by first wife.

(1) Felix Milburn, b Oct 17, 1841, married in 1872, Julia Brown; 2nd, Fanny Polk, 3rd, Fanny Huddleson

(2) Silas C, b. March 2, 1843, married Dec 25, 1866, Emily J McMullen of Princeton Ind   soldier during the Civil War in the 80th Indiana   was

badly wounded in the head at the battle of Perryville and still suffers from the wound. He settled at Mt. Vernon, Ill., in 1874, engaging in the real estate business.

(3) Mary, b Oct 28, 1845, d. Aug 31, 1906, married Dec 2, 1869, John F Cleveland

(4) Matilda, b Jan 18, 1841, married David M. Wright, of Mt Carmel Ill., about 1867-8, now a widow living at Albion, Ill., no issue

(5) Albert Mills, b Dec. 2, 1849, d Nov. 3, 1860

(6) Sarah, b March 13, 1848, unmarried, and living at Lakeland, Fla

(7) Edward Bates 1st, b Dec 29, 1862, d Feb 11, 1863

(8) Lucius, b Sept 25, 1854, d Dec 12, 1854. Laura and Lucius were twins

(9) Rosetta, b 1855, d in infancy.

(10) A son, b June 4, 1857, d at birth

(11) Fannie B Polk, b Feb. 19, 1859, d Aug 6, 1873

(12) Laura Ellen, b Sept 25, 1854, married Sept 1873, Isaac Spore

(13) Edward Bates, 2d, b Dec 29, 1862 unmarried, and living at Lakeland, Fla Civil Engineer

(14) Olive, b Nov 17, 1864, d Oct 17, 1865

GRANDCHILDREN OF ALEXANDER H POLK.

Silas C. Polk and wife, Emily, had issue:

(1) Vesta, b. 1867, married John F Bogan, an attorney of Mt Vernon, Ill They had no issue.

(2) Julia, b Jan 25, 1870, married C. Elmer Rutherford Issue [1]Raymond E, b April 8, 1895; [2]Dorothy, b April 16, 1899

(3) Lucius, b March 1, 1875, married, 1903, Minnie Hodges, of Cannon City, Col Issue [1]Orville; [2]Harold.

(4) Euseba, b July 4, 1877, unmarried Residence, Birmingham, Ala, school teacher

(5) Laura, b Feb 11, 1879, married Aug 1, 1903, Robt. E L Dickson, of Virginia Issue [1]Albert E, b May 20, 1907, [2]Sidney, b Feb 2 1908, [3]Virginia, b. July 28, 1909

(6) Albert H., b. Sept. 1, 1873, married Sept 1904 to Ollie Lanham, of St Louis, Mo. Issue ¹Lillian; ²Evelyn.

Mary Polk Cleveland, wife of Jno F Cleveland, had issue ¹Roger P , b 1870, married Mary Hopkins. ²Fannie, b Sept 12, 1872, married, 1893, Benjamin Benson; ³Flossie, b 1874, married J Vaden Lee. ⁴Charles, b about 1876, married, 1906, Mabel McDonald

Felix Milburn Polk and his first wife, Julia (Brown) Polk, had one child, Laura Maud

¹Laura Maud, b May 15, 1873, unmarried. ²Frank Embree, b Nov 1875, married Rose——, and has two children, who live in Illinois; ³Fred Harrison, b. Dec 22, 1877, unmarried. ⁴Lester, b. 1880, unmarried Residence, Momence, Ill He is said to be the only child of the family Now at Perdue University, Indiana

Laura Ellen Polk and husband, Isaac Spore had issue. ¹Harvey, b Aug 1874, d July 9, 1876; ²Fanny, b. May 5, 1877, married, 1896, Oscar Woodson, of St Louis, Mo ; ³Florence E , b 1880, unmarried, residence, Owensville, Ind ; ⁴Della May, b 1893 The first ten children of Rev Alexander Hamilton Polk were by his first wife, Julia Embree, the four last by his second wife, Bursha B Green

CHAPTER L.

DESCENDANTS OF REV. ISAAC M'COY AND WIFE.

Rev. Isaac McCoy was born June 13, 1784, at Uniontown, Pa., and died June 21, 1846, at Louisville, Ky. His wife, Christiana Polk daughter of Capt. Charles Polk, was born in what was then Shelby County, Kentucky, Nov. 12, 1787, and died at Woodside, Jackson County, Mo., in 1850. They were married Oct. 6, 1803, in Shelby County, Kentucky, and emigrated to Indiana in 1818, where he enlisted in Indian Missionary work, in which he continued throughout life. He was an earnest, zealous Baptist preacher and in his missionary duties was devotedly assisted by his wife. To them were born thirteen children, viz:

(1) Mahala, b Aug 10, 1804, d Aug 31, 1818
(2) Dr. Rice, b Jan 27, 1807, d May 26, 1833
(3) Dr Josephus, b April 13, 1808, d June 27, 1831.
(4) Delilah, b Nov 24, 1809, d ——.
(5) John Calvin, b. Sept. 28, 1811, d Sept 2, 1889
(6) Elizabeth, b Aug., 1813, d ——
(7) Sarah, b April 13, 1815, d previous to July 30, 1835.
(8) Christiana, b Oct 19, 1817, d Feb 10, 1837
(9) Nancy Judson, b Feb. 26, 1819, d 1850
(10) Eleanor, b July 29, 1821, d. Jan. 11, 1839
(11) Maria Slaughter, b Nov. 29, 1823, d ——.
(12) Isaac, Jr., b April, 1825, d May, 1849
(13) Charles Rice, b Feb., 1827, d in early youth
14, son b ○ ⊢ p. 9, 631

INTERMARRIAGES

The eldest child, Mahala, and the last one, Charles Rice, died in youth, as above shown. Dr Rice, Dr Josephus, Elizabeth, Nancy Judson and Maria Slaughter are said to have all died unmarried. Delilah McCoy married Feb 29, 1828, Dr John t n Lykins. He was of a Virginia family and was born in 1800 in Virginia, dying at Kansas City, Mo, Aug 15, 1856 They had issue ¹William Hall Richardson, b Nov 29, 1828, in Lexington, Ky, died June 15, 1893, at Kansas City. Mo ; ²Sarah, b ——, d.——; ³Charles McCoy, b ——, d. in infancy, ⁴Julia McCoy, b Nov 14, 1839, at Louisville, Ky, d Sept. 14, 1872, at Kansas City, Mo Wm Hall Richardson Lykins was married Dec. 10, 1857, in Kansas City, to Cornelia Victoria Smith, b Jan 16, 1838, at Charleston, S C, now (1911) residing in Kansas City, Mo Sarah Lykins, b ——. married Egbert Freeland Russell Julia McCoy Lykins, b ——, married Oct. 12, 1858, in Kansas City Dr Theodore Spencer Case, b Jan 26, 1832, at Jackson, Ga, d Feb. 16, 1900, in Kansas City

William Hall Richardson Lykins and his wife, Cornelia

NOTES ON THE McCOY FAMILY

Compiled by William H. McCoy in 1915
Edited by Elizabeth Hayward

THE TUTTLE PUBLISHING CO, INC., RUTLAND, VT., 1939 20 pp and Index.

Genealogical and biographical data on 250 descendants of James McCoy, who settled in Pennsylvania before the Revolution Eight generations of this family have lived in the United States The majority of those listed here are from Indiana and other midwestern states.

Outstanding members of the family are: Isaac McCoy, missionary to the Indians from 1817 to 1846, John Calvin McCoy, a founder of Kansas City, Mo, and Col. John C. McCoy, a founder of Dallas, Tex The family has been closely identified with the Baptist denomination, as evidenced by the inclusion of the names of six Baptist ministers, three missionaries and such Baptist leaders as Deacon John McCoy, a founder of Franklin College

Names other than McCoy which figure prominently in this record are: Huston, Little (or Littell), McCormick, Payne and Taggart.

Price: $1 00. Please send remittance with order to:

MRS SUMNER HAYWARD, 224 RICHARDS ROAD, RIDGEWOOD, NEW JERSEY

siding at Kansas City. ⁴Johnson Lykins, b Nov, 18··, residing at Arizona Julia Louis Russell married Samuel Barnhill, and they had four children ¹Wm Allen Barnhill, b ——. ²Claude Barnhill, of L · Angeles b—— ³Harlow Barnhill. b——, ⁴··· · ·· · ll, ·   ·   ·   · married Eli· · ·· · · · · ·   ·   ·   ·   ·son.

CHAPTER L.

DESCENDANTS OF REV. ISAAC M'COY AND WIFE.

Rev Isaac McCoy was born June 13, 1784, at Uniontown, Pa, and died June 21, 1846, at Louisville, Ky. His wife, Christiana Polk daughter of Capt Charles Polk, was born in what was then Shelby County, Kentucky, Nov 12, 1787, and died at Woodside, Jackson County, Mo, in 1850 They were married Oct 6, 1803, in Shelby County, Kentucky, and emigrated to Indiana in 1818, where he enlisted in Indian Missionary work, in which he continued throughout life He was an

The eldest child, Mahala, and the last one, Charles Rice, died in youth, as above shown Dr Rice, Dr Josephus, Elizabeth, Nancy Judson and Maria Slaughter are said to have all died unmarried Delilah McCoy married Feb 29, 1828, Dr John t n Lykins He was of a Virginia family and was born in 1800 in Virginia, dying at Kansas City, Mo., Aug 15, 1856. They had issue: ¹William Hall Richardson, b. Nov. 29, 1828, in Lexington, Ky., died June 15, 1893, at Kansas City, Mo.; ²Sarah, b.——, d.——, ³Charles McCoy, b.——, d. in infancy; ⁴Julia McCoy, b. Nov 14, 1839, at Louisville, Ky., d Sept 14, 1872, at Kansas City, Mo Wm Hall Richardson Lykins was married Dec 10, 1857, in Kansas City, to Cornelia Victoria Smith, b. Jan 16, 1838, at Charleston, S C., now (1911) residing in Kansas City, Mo. Sarah Lykins, b.——, married Egbert Freeland Russell Julia McCoy Lykins, b——, married Oct 12, 1858, in Kansas City. Dr. Theodore Spencer Case, b Jan 26, 1832, at Jackson, Ga., d Feb 16, 1900, in Kansas City

William Hall Richardson Lykins and his wife, Cornelia Victoria has issue ¹Johnston Franklin, b Oct 16, 1838, d unmarried at Kansas City, Feb 3, 1887, ²Susan Elizabeth, b Nov 29, 1860, at Lawrence, Kan., d May 21, 1892, at Kansas City. ³Delilah McCoy, b June 24, 1863, at Lawrence, Kan., now (1911) single and residing at Kansas City

Susan Elizabeth, married Nov 6, 1881, Wm. Whitehead Thacher, of Kansas City. They had two children Nina Etta Thacher, born Feb 10, 1883, died July 17, 1884, and Lilah Case Thacher, born Oct 24, 1885, died November 19, 1904 They live at Pennington, Vt

Sarah Lykins and her husband, Egbert Freeland Russell had issue ¹Zenette Freeland, b ——, d about 1886, ²Wm Lykins, b——, d at 18 years of age, ³Julia Louise, b.——, ⁴Effie, b ——, d in infancy; ⁵Mattie, b——, d. in infancy; ⁶Lillian, b——, d in infancy, ⁷Theodora Case, b ——, residing now (1911) at Independence, Mo., ⁸Cornelia Victoria, b—— Zenette Freeland Russell married Harlow Johnson Boyce, May, 1870 He was b April 17, 1844, at Castalia, Ohio They had issue ¹Chas. McCoy, b Nov 18, 1873, residing at Kansas City, ²Johnson Lykins, b Nov., 1877, residing at Arizona Julia Louis Russell married Samuel Barnhill, and they had four children ¹Wm Allen Barnhill, b.—— ²Claude F. ⸺hill ⸺ ⸺ ⸻, b— ⸺, ³H.⸺ ⸺ B⸺ ill, b ——, ⁴L⸺ ⸺ B⸺⸺ill, ⸺ —— The⸺⸺ Case Russell married Elija H ⸺⸺⸺ ⸺⸺⸺ and issue ⁴L⸺ is All⸺on, b April 11, 1882, married Daisy Barwick, Dec 18, 1909 Residence, Independence, Mo ; ²Sarah Lucas, b ——, d in infancy, ³Alexander Erwin, b Dec 16, 1885, married Mabel Pickett, Oct 30, 1907 They have one child, Russell Huntington, b Oct. 23, 1908; ⁴Zenie Russell, b ——.

Cornelia Victoria married Isaac N Brown, and they have issue ¹Lillian, ²Wm Russell, ³Sarah, ⁴Theodora, ⁵Helen; ⁶Julia, and a son, aged four years

Julia McCoy Lykins and her husband, Dr Theodore Spencer Case had issue ¹Mattie Lykins, b. June 26, 1860, d Jan 20, 1865, ²Emily Arabella, b. Sept. 15, 1861, d March 8, 1865; ³Olive Spencer, b Sept 3, 1865, d Feb 9, 1869, ⁴Delilah McCoy, b Aug. 25, 1867. Delilah married Dec 25, 1889, Geo Carroll Cowles, b Jan 16, 1862, in Butler, Ky., now residing in Kansas City They had issue. ¹Theodore William Cowles, b Sept 21, 1890, d April 26, 1892, ²A son who died at birth, Oct 13, 1895, ³Margaret Cowles, b Oct 29, 1896, d Oct. 31, 1896 ;

Johnston Lykins Case, b Feb 15, 1870, is living in Mexico, and said to be unmarried ⁵Ermine Cowles Case, b Sept. 11, 1871, married June 23, 1898, Mary Margaret Snow, b Aug 9, 1872 They live at Ann Arbor, Mich , and have issue ¹Francis Huntington, b April 4, 1899, is unmarried, ²Theodore Johnston, b March 16, 1911 1920

John Calvin McCoy, fifth child of Rev. Isaac and Christiana (Polk) McCoy, married twice. His first wife, to whom he was united Jan. 23, 1838, in Westport, Mo , was Virginia Chick, b. Dec 22, 1820, d May 28, 1849. Rev. Isaac McCoy, his father, performing the ceremony His second wife, Elizabeth M (Woodson) Lee, was born in Jessamine County, Kentucky She was the widow of Cary Lee By his first wife, Virginia Chick, John Calvin McCoy had issue ¹Josephus, b. Dec 6, 1838, d Sept 2, 1843; ²Eleanor (Nelly), b. July 2, 1840, residence, Rich Hill, Mo , ³Juliette, b Feb 16, 1842, residence, 805 Olive St , Kansas City Mo., ⁴Spencer Cone b. July 25, 1844, killed Jan 8, 1863, in battle at Springfield, Mo , ⁵Wm Chick, b Feb 21, 1846, d. May 12, 1848; ⁶Virginia, b Aug. 22, 1848, living in Texas

By his second wife, Mrs Elizabeth Lee, John Calvin

McCoy had issue ⁷Evelyn Byrd, b Feb. 21, 1851, now living at Kansas City; ⁸Woodson, b Sept 26, 1855, residing at Wilder, Kas. ⁹John Calvin, Jr., b March 8, 1853, d Dec 11, 1905

THE CHICK FAMILY.

William Miles Chick, born Aug 31, 1794; died April 7, 1847 Ann Eliza Smith, b Sept 25, 1796, d July 24, 1876 They were married April 11, 1816, and had issue ¹Mary Jane, b ——, ²Wm Sidney, b ——, ³Virginia, b Dec 22, 1820, married Jno Calvin McCoy, Jan 23, 1838; ⁴Sarah Ann, b March 12, 1823, d Jan 2, 1846, married April 6, 1841, Col Jno W Polk, ⁵Washington Henry, b ——; ⁶Joseph Smith, b ——, ⁷Martha Matilda, b ——, ⁸Pettus Wales, b ——; ⁹Leonidas, b —— No dates of birth, marriage or death was furnished with above names

INTERMARRIAGES OF JNO. CALVIN M'COY'S CHILDREN.

Eleanor McCoy, second child of John Calvin McCoy, married April 14, 1859, Dr Wm Warren Harris, of Rich Hill, Mo, who was born in Bedford County, Va, Oct. 14, 1834 They had nine children, viz ¹Virginia Spencer, b May 28, 1862, residence, Kansas City, ²William Warren, Jr b March 3, 1864, d in infancy, ³Calvin McCoy, b Jan 31, 1866, d Sept 5, 1868, ⁴Thomas Hector, b. Oct 17, 1868, d June 23, 1870; ⁵Catharine Alexander, b. Dec 11, 1870, residence, Kansas City, Mo, ⁶Eleanor Tyler, b June 19, 1873, residence, Rich Hill, Mo, ⁷Harry Innes, b May 17, 1875, ⁸Spencer Francis, b Aug 1, 1877, residence Kansas City, Mo ; ⁹Wm Woodson, b Oct 14, 1880, residence, Kansas City, Mo

Of the foregoing children of Dr. Wm Warren Harris and Eleanor McCoy, Virginia Spencer married March 20, 1883, Robt Taliaferro Thornton, b July 31, 1859, residence. Kansas City Eleanor Tyler married Oct 22, 1902, John Otto Krause, f Rich Hill, M b July 16, 1… ence. Kansas City Harry Innes Harris m……d … 1903, in Nevada, Mo, Helen Byrde Cramer, b Feb 16, 1880 Spencer Francis and Wm Woodson Harris are still untrammeled by matrimonial cares

Robert Taliaferro Thornton and wife had issue ¹Warren Thomas, M D, b Feb 1, 1884, d March 17, 1910, unmarried, ²Harriett, b Jan 21, 1886, married Dec 5, 1908, Laurence Hannan Phister, b April 21, 1885, at Maysville, Ky, residence, Kansas City They have one child, Warren Thornton Phister, b Jan 20, 1910, ³Robt Taliaferro, Jr, b Jan 30, 1888, residence, Kansas City, ⁴Eleanor, b. Feb 19, 1896, residence, Kansas City, ⁵Virginia, b Dec 8, 1892, d Jan 13, 1894

Harry Innes Harris and wife, Helen Byrde Cramer had issue ¹Harry Innes, Jr, b Nov 18, 1904, ²Margaret, b. Jan 14, 1907

Juliette McCoy, third child of John Calvin McCoy and wife, married Feb 16, 1864, at Glasgow, Mo, Robt. Thomas Bass (b Feb 4, 1841), and they had issue ¹Lizzie, b Jan. 13, 1866, in Boone County, Missouri, d July 6, 1872, ²Sally Gay, b May 9, 1867, married Henry Lacy Tomlin (Oct 5, 1888), residence Kansas City, ³Felix Spencer, b Oct 27, 1869, d June 20, 1876, in Kansas, ⁴Calvin McCoy b April 3 1873, married twice First wife, Lalla DeMars (b Aug 1, 1878) in Wyoming, d. July 28, 1901, at Prescott, Ariz By her he had one child, Lalla Margaret, b July 28, 1901 Resides with her father in Arizona Calvin's second wife was Clare Russell, ⁵Robert Thomas, Jr, b Sept 11, 1877, married (Oct, 1908) in Carson City, Nev, Kitty Cavanaugh, b. in Ireland, residence, Golconda, Nev., ⁶Margaret Virginia, b July 12, 1876, d Sept 12, 1876, ⁷Juliette Spotswood, b June 17, 1881, married (July 25, 1905) Levi Wilson, b Nov 16, 1876 They have issue. ¹Robert Lee, b April 20, 1907, ²Virgina, b June 2, 1910, residence, Kansas City Wm Chick McCoy, b Feb 21, 1846, d May 12, 1848

Virginia McCoy, sixth child of John Calvin McCoy and Virginia Chick, b Aug. 22, 1848, married July 3, 1870, Alexander Travis Grimes, of Jackson County, Mo, and they had issue ¹Harvey McCoy, b 1871, in Texas, ²Cora, b 1875, d in infancy, ³Eleanor May, b March 15, 1876, married Nov.

24, 1891, Herbert Hanson He d. Feb 28, 1908, residence, Fort Worth, Texas, ⁴Alexander Travis, Jr, b. April 16, 1878, residence, El Paso Texas, ⁵James Gordon b Sept 4, 1880, at Westport, Mo, residence, Belzonia, Miss, ⁶Chas. Lister, b. Sept 13, 1883, at Kansas City, married (Dec 18 1909) at Memphis, Tenn., Lenora Yancey One child, Gordon Yancey, b Sept 30, 1910. ⁷Virginia Lee, b Sept 25, 1887, at Fort Worth, Texas, married Eugene Ashe, one child, b June 28, 1910, d in infancy, residence, Fort Worth Tex

Evelyn Byrd McCoy b Feb 21, 1852, married (April 29, 1875) James Montgomery Holloway (b. Feb. 10, 1847) and they had issue (1) Elizabeth Scott, b May 15, 1879, at Wichita, Kan., m Oct 1, 1903, Kidder Woodson Woods (b 1875 at Frankfort, Ky) and they had issue ¹Woodson Kidder, b Aug 14, 1904, ²James Holloway, b July 12, 1908, (2) Kate Lee, b July 30, 1881, married (April 26, 1905) Alexander John Atchison Alexander (b 1875) of "Woodburn Farm," Woodford County, Ky They have issue ².Alexander John, b Jan 13, 1907, ²James Holloway, b April 11, 1909

Woodson McCoy, b Sept 26, 1855, married (June 3, 1890) Agnes English of Platte County, Missouri, and they have issue· ¹Spencer English, b Feb 9, 1892, residence, Wilder, Kas, ²Martha, b Aug 18, 1893, d Dec 24, 1894; ³Elizabeth Woodson, b Nov. 15, 1897, residence, Wilder, Kas

John Calvin, Jr, b July 8, 1888, residence, Kansas City, married Florida Mason (b Nov 2, 1854). They have issue ¹John Calvin, Jr, b July 8, 1888; ²Mary Agnes, b Nov. 18, 1890, ³Matt Mason, b July 23, 1892

Sarah, seventh child of Rev Isaac McCoy and his wife, Christiana Polk married Thomas Givens, Fayette Mo Commonwealth Attorney for Eastern District of Missouri, and they had one child, Sarah, Jr, b in 1832, d at 14 years of age Sarah, Sr, d before July 30, 1835

Christiana McCoy, daughter of Rev Isaac and Christiana (Polk) McCoy, married Wm Ward of Howard County, Missouri They had two children ¹Margaret Ward, b 1832, d in infancy; ²Thomas Ward, b 1834, d 1909 Thomas married Miss Talbot, a sister of Bishop Ethelbert Talbot, and they had issue ¹Thomas b   m   M H   n and they have a son and daughters, Alice and Margaret; [2]Margaret, b.——, unmarried, residence, Denver, Colo, [3]Ethelbert, b ——, married Ada Smith, three children, [4]Jno., Episcopal clergyman, b ——, married——, two children, Polly and Peggy. Resides at Wilkesbarre, Pa ; [5]Elsie, a noted sculptress, b ——, married Henry Herring, a sculptor. No issue, [6]William, b ——, married. He is a mining engineer and lives in South America [7]Ralph, b —— Lieutenant in U. S Army. Married in Denver, about 1908. Nancy Judson, ninth child of Rev Isaac McCoy and Christiana Polk, b Feb 26, 1819, d unmarried 1850. Eleanor, tenth child of Rev Isaac McCoy and wife, Christina, b July 29, 1821, d Jan 11, 1839. She married Wm Donahoe, of Howard County, Missouri. No issue recorded. Maria Slaughter, eleventh child of Rev Isaac McCoy and wife, Christiana, b Nov 29, 1823, d unmarried. Isaac, Jr, b April, 1825, d. May, 1849, married Martha Stone, of Jackson County, Missouri. They had a son, Isaac, 3rd, b Aug., 1849, d. 1861. Charles Rice, thirteenth and youngest child of Rev. Isaac McCoy and his wife, Christiana (Polk) McCoy, b. Feb, 1827, d in his youth. The remains of Christiana McCoy, Sr, and of the deceased members of her son John Calvin McCoy rest in the Union County Cemetery, Kansas City. A book entitled "Early Indian Missions," a memorial written by Walter N Wyeth, D. D, of Philadelphia, and published by the Baptist Publication Society, tells of the lives and the mission work of Rev. Isaac McCoy and his wife, Christiana (Polk) McCoy. Another work, "The Eliza McCoy Memoir," written by Calvin McCormick, of Dallas, Tex, tells of the life of Miss Eliza McCoy, a daughter of John McCoy, a brother to Rev Isaac McCoy. And a third work, called "History of Baptist Indian Missions," written by Isaac McCoy, (612 pages) published in 1840, gives almost a complete account of the life of Christiana Polk. In the room of the Kansas Historical Society in the capitol at Topeka, is one of their most prized collections, kept separate in a vault, and called the "Isaac McCoy Collection." It comprises the original manuscript, of the many accounts written by Rev Isaac McCoy concerning the North American Indians, and of pioneer days in the Middle West, then the "Far West." These accounts also tell much about his wife, Christiana (Polk) McCoy

John Calvin McCoy, second son of Christiana, was one of the most noted persons in the early history of Kansas City, and of Western Missouri. He was a Government Civil Engineer, employed to allot lands to the Indians and to act as agent of the United States in transactions with them. A recent history of Kansas City states that if any one was the "father of Kansas City," John Calvin McCoy was entitled to that distinction. He made the first plat of the city and was a member of the original town company. There he lived for more than fifty years, loved and honored to an unusual degree. He was educated at Cincinnati and Transylvania University of Lexington, Ky.

Eleanor McCoy Harris, wife of Dr. W. W. Harris, of Rich Hill, Mo., eldest daughter of John McCoy, by his first wife, Virginia Chick, is a woman of literary taste and ability and has written much for the press and magazines. Although a great grandmother, she is a regular contributor to the Kansas City Star, and is collaborating in the preparation of a history of Jackson County, Missouri, in which Kansas City is situated. She is still alert, vigorous in body and mind, and a good musician.

In his book, "Baptist Indian Missions," published in 1840, Rev. Isaac McCoy says, among other things: "In the forepart of October I attended, at Chicago, the payment of an annuity by Dr. Wolcott, U. S. Indian Agent, and through his politeness addressed the Indians on the subject of our mission. On the 9th of Oct., 1825, I preached in English, which, as I was informed, was the first sermon ever delivered at or near that place. Between our place and Chicago was a wilderness, in which we took five nights lodging on our tour."

CHAPTER LI.

CHARLES POLK, 3rd, AND FAMILY.

Charles Polk, 3rd (fifth child of Capt Charles Polk) was born Oct 27, 1782, in an Indian Camp at Detroit, where his mother and her children, William, Elizabeth, Sarah and Nancy were taken by their savage captors in Sept, 1782. Here the little white papoose remained until his father recovered his family the following year, through the kindly assistance of his old time anti-Revolutionary acquaintance and friend, Simon Girty.

After the return of the family to Nelson County Kentucky, Charles grew up to be a vigorous and active youth, soon becoming skilled as a hunter and alert pioneer, and obtaining the ordinary country school education of that period. He served under General Harrison at Tippecanoe, in 1811, in the Quartermaster's Department, and later was an officer of Indiana Militia, in the War 1812. He took an active part in all the civil and military affairs of his district, and, in 1816, was the single member from Perry County of the first Constitutional Convention of Indiana, when the Territory assumed statehood. He died in Perry County in 1847.

Charles Polk, 3rd, married Margaret McQuaid in 1803, and to them were born thirteen little Polks, viz [1]James, b. in Shelby County, Kentucky, Sept 5, 1804, d 1890. He married Harriett Shepherd, in 1829, [2]Delilah, b Jan 1, 1806, d 1874, married Alexander Blackburn, [3]Lucinda, b Jan. 6, 1808, d Aug, 1872, married Obed Macey in 1826, [4]William Bruce, b about 1810, d 1811, [5]Nancy, b about 1812, d unmarried, [6]Elizabeth, b about 1814, d ——, married Chas Short; [7]Edmond, b. about 1816, d ——, married Jane Elliott, [8]Isabel b about 1818, d 1837, unmarried; [9]Charles, b about 1820, d 1839; [10]Christian, b 1822, d 1848, married first, James Piety Cox, eldest son of Jonathan Cox, of Kentucky. Christian also married two other men — Holden and Samuel Maxwell,

BENJAMIN F. POLK,
of Princeton, Indiana, son of Isaac, son of Charles Polk, 3rd.

[11]Isaac, b Nov 4, 1825, d July 27, 1898 He married first, in 1843, Mary Cox, second, in 1861, Mrs Martha (Couchman) Ferguson By these wives Isaac had twelve children, [12]John M., b Feb 26, 1826, d 1881, was twice married, first to Elizabeth Colton, second to Eliza Jane Hill, [13]Margaret, b 1830, d 1872, married Henry Bartley

Lucinda Polk and Obed Macey had Urania Macey, who married ——Cheeseman A daughter of the latter married Dr George Clark, of California, one of the founders of the San Francisco Geographical Society, and at his death its President

By his first wife, Mary Cox, Isaac Polk had [1]Benjamin F. Polk, whose daughter, Agnes, married Prof R M Tryon, Superintendent Public Schools, Madison, Ind

James Piety Cox and Christiana Polk had issue [1]Isabel, b ——, married George Bond, of Oaktown, Ind. To them were born: [1]Florence, d ——, [2]Grace, married Lee Townland Bond, and they have Imogene and Raymond; [3]Frank, married Miss Holland, [4]Margaret, married John Hammock

[2]Finette, second child of James Piety Cox, married ——Houck, but left no issue, it is said, at her death, [3]Charles, son of James Piety Cox, b ——, d unmarried

John M Polk by his second wife, Eliza Hill, had issue [1]Prentice, b ——, who married Jessie Root and had Robert, Alice and Helen, [2]Mary K., daughter of John M Polk, is Librarian of the U. S. Laboratories at Manilla, Philippine Islands. Margaret (youngest child of Charles Polk, 3rd, and Margaret McQuaid), b 1830 d. 1872, by her husband Henry Bartley, had issue [1]Sylvester, who married Alice Bartley and had Donald and Fay, [2]George, [3]Elizabeth, [4]Nellie; [5]Finette, [6]Bessie

Edward (or Edmond) Polk (seventh child of Capt Charles Polk and Delilah Tyler, b about 1786, was killed in 1814, during the second war of the United States with Great Britain Like all the male members of his family he was an ardent patriot and fought for his country His wife was Achsy Van Meter, by whom he had five children [1]Charles, b ——, d ——, married Miss —— —— —— —— —— —— [2]John Maxwell —— —— —— —— —— —— —— —— n D

Bruce. second, Jonathan Macey; ⁴William V., b ——, d ——, married Polly Haddon. ⁵Isaac, b ——, d.——, married Mrs. Palmer

Eleanor Polk (eighth child of Capt Charles Polk), b. about 1788, John Hollingsworth and had: ¹George, who married Hannah Hill, ²Elizabeth, who married Harry Palmer; ³Joseph, who married Mrs Palmer, ⁴Delilah, who married ——Moore, ⁵Eleanor, who married ——Selby, ⁶Isaac, who married Miss Underwood; ⁷Christiana, who married James McClure

Mary (Polly) Polk (ninth child of Capt Charles Polk), b about 1790, d ——, married Philip Bell and they had ¹Charles, who married Lydia Bartley, ²Emeline, who married David Kipper; ³William who married Nancy Lemmon; ⁴Sallie, who married —— Burns; ⁵Betsy, who married ———

DESCENDANTS OF DR. THOMAS POLK.

Dr Thomas Polk, tenth child of Capt Charles Polk and Delilah (Tyler Polk, was born Feb 2, 1792, in Nelson County, Kentucky, and died Feb 7, 1872, at Gonzales, Texas His wife, Sarah Sloan, was born in Nelson County in 1796, of North Carolina parents, and died March 4, 1872, only thirty-three days after her husband's death Their children were ¹Sarah Ann, b Dec 27, 1831, ²James, b about——, 1833; ³William, b about ——, 1835; ⁴Milam Benjamin, b Feb 29, 1836, ⁵Eliza, b about —— 1837, ⁶——, and d in infancy, 1838; ⁷Elizabeth, b about ——, 1839, ⁸Charles, b about ——, 1840, ⁹——, b and d about ——, 1841 ¹⁰Mary Jane, b ——, 1845, d at four years of age

INTERMARRIAGES

The intermarriages and the descendants of the foregoing of Dr Thomas Polk were Sarah Ann, b. Dec 27, 1831, d June 16, 1876, married James D Anderson, of Gonzales, Texas, Nov 6, 1856. They had issue ¹Thomas James, b Sept 10, 1857, d at one year old; ²Frances Gelhorn, b. Feb 20, 1860, married (Sept. 2, 1874) James D Darst, of Gonzales, Tex,

²Robert Lee, b Aug 9, 1864, married (Feb 21, 1893) Mary Crosby

The children of Robert Lee Anderson and Mary Crosby are ¹Mary Crosby, b Oct 31, 1893; ²J D. Houston, b. April 10, 1896, ³Robert Lee, b June 14, 1897

James Polk (son of Dr Thomas Polk), b about 1833, d at one year old

William Polk, b about 1835, married Jane Campbell and died soon afterward, aged 28 years No issue

Milam Benjamin Polk, b Feb 29, 1836, d July 1894, married Julia Caroline Price, Feb 20, 1873. She was b Jan 7, 1847. They had issue ¹Omi, b. July 26 1874, married Jno Charlton Heaton, Jan. 1, 1900 They had one child, John Polk Heaton, b 1901, d in infancy, ²Charles Stover, b Aug 6, 1876, married Lottie Pickett, Oct 6, 1908, residence, Liberty, Tex ; ³Bessie Thomas, b Feb 3, 1879, married Frank B Salter, June 26, 1907, ⁴Milam Benjamin, Jr, b Feb. 11, 1882, d May 17, 1883; ⁵Patti, b Aug 17, 1885, ⁶Nellie, b Sept 17, 1887

Eliza, daughter of Dr. Dr. Thomas Polk, b about 1837, married Felix Chenault She died Sept 9, 1870, he on Oct 25, 1872 They had issue (1) James Reed, who married Sophia Henson and had issue ¹Edna, b ——; ²LaSalle, b ——, ³May, married Akyle, one child, Bernelle, b ——, ⁴Jefferson, b ——, ⁵Felix, b ——, married Ruby Arnold, ⁶Reed, b —— Felix had two son, Felix, Jr, and Reed

(2) John Bass, b Feb. 14, 1846, married Lilla J Harrison Issue ¹Emma, who married ——Burrows; ²Clarence

(3) Charles Polk, b. Aug 8, 1848, married Jane Testard Issue, ¹Charles Adrian, b ——, 1880, ²Anna Letitia, b Sept 13, 1882, married Wood Caperton, ³Whitson, b Oct 16, 1884, married Lula Simmons

(4) Benjamin Peck, b Feb 20, 1852, unmarried.

(5) Lucien La Salle, b Dec 15, 1853, married Narcissa De Witt, Sept 16, 1874. Issue ¹Cora, b May 20, 1877, married Herbert Green Issue Herbert, b Dec 2, 1906, Wilfred, b March 18, 1910, ²Clinton, b May 28, 1881, unmarried, ³Lucien James, b Oct 6, 1883; ⁴Dora, b April 15, 1885, d May 28, 1886

(6) Medora, b May 7, 1855 married Jno Louis Hous-

ton, Dec. 1873. Issue: ¹Augusta, b Dec 28, 1874, d March 12, 1885, married August Kline; ²George L, b ——, married Alice Thompson. Issue ¹Kennon, b Sept 26, 1895, d March 8, 1896, ²Doris, b Aug, 1896, ³Aileen H B, Oct 18, 1898; ⁴Katharine, b . Oct 12, 1906

Letitia Chenault, b Aug 9, 1857, married Samuel L Fore, of Gonzales, Tex , Feb 20, 1889. Issue ¹Blake Davidson, Cuero, Tex., b. Jan. 9, 1890, ²Sam Lane, Cuero, Tex., b. May 3, 1891 Blake Davidson Fore and Mary Lease were married Nov 28, 1909 Loren Blake Fore son of Blake and Mary Fore, b July 7, 1910, residence, Florasville, Tex

Eizabeth Polk, daughter of Dr Thomas Polk, b about 1838, aged 66 years, married William B Cavitt, and they had ¹Cora Millie, b ——, d ——, ²Miles Edward, b ——, married Mollie Booth, and had a daughter, Elizabeth Booth.

Frances Gelhorn Anderson, b Feb 20 1860, married James D. Darst, of Gonzales, Tex , Sept. 2, 1874 They had issue (1) Imogene E , b July 31, 1876, married W G Mulligan, of High Prairie, Alberta, Canada Their children are . ¹Lucille Annie, b July 3, 1895; ²Thelma Sue, b June 27, 1897; ³Imogene, b Dec 13, 1900

(2) James Anderson, b Sept 19, 1878, married Aug 11, 1908, Mary Lou Hogan, of Lufkin, Tex They have one child, Dorothy, b Nov 6, 1909

(3) Sue Lee, b Oct 3, 1880, married J Wm Cobb, of St Louis, Mo Their children are: ¹Frances Cobb, b Aug 19, 1900; ²B N. Darst, b June 27, 1902; ³J. Wm , Jr , b Aug 18, 1904, ⁴Susan Lee, b ——, 1905, ⁵Whitfield, b Dec 23, 1907, ⁶Mary Ethel, b.——, 1909

John Jacob Darst, b June 27, 1885, unmarried

Sarah Ethel Darst, b Dec 30, 1882, married J G McRea, Aug 29, 1906 They have one child, Wm Darst, b June 18, 1909,

Thomas Roswell Darst, b Sept 8, 1888, married Lucille Lois Houston Jan 28, 1909

Eleanor Alma Darst, b July 6, 1890, married James C Smith, Hearne Texas, April 18, 1908

Mary Jane Polk (daughter of Dr Thomas Polk), b about 1845, d at four years of age

SKETCH OF DR. THOMAS POLK.

(By his Grandaughter, Mrs Frances G Darst)

Dr Thomas Polk, tenth child of Capt Charles Polk and his wife, Delilah (Tyler) Polk, was born in Nelson County, Kentucky, Feb 2, 1792 He died Feb 7, 1872, at Gonzales, Texas, where he had resided for over fifty years When Thomas was 16 years of age, his father, Capt Charles Polk, removed from Kentucky to near Vincennes, Ind, where he and his sons became prominent in civil and military affairs in that Territory Amid the stirring scenes of the frontier Thomas grew to manhood, studied medicine and began practice In 18— he married Miss Sarah Sloan (b. 1796 in Nelson County, Kentucky), who proved through a long life on the frontiers a brave and loyal helpmate Like his father and uncles, however, Thomas could not resist the lure of the fields that lay toward the setting sun, with their opportunities for adventure and wealth He decided to go to the Southwest, and in 1820 emigrated to Arkansas Territory The following year, 1821 attracted by the marvelous stories concerning the Republic of Texas, to which a strong tide of hardy emigrants flowed, he moved forward to that country and settled permanently

Descended from an adventurous line, Dr Thomas Polk was soon absorbed into the exciting transactions of that period under Col Stephen F Austin and General Sam Houston As a surgeon he served in the ranks of the army of the Republic and acquitted himself with bravery and distinction He was in the whole of the long struggle between the Texan patriots and the Mexican forces that opposed them On the column that stands in the Statehouse at Austin, erected to the memory of the "Heroes of Texas," his name is inscribed with those of other prominent actors in that struggle

The story of Dr Thomas Polk's life and adventures in the Southwest is most interestingly told in a letter to the author, by his granddaughter, Mrs Frances G Darst, of Gonzales, Texas Her account furnishes a striking picture of the trials and sufferings of Americans who formed the Texas Republic and battled long against the Mexicans to hold it, finally planting the Stars and Stripes over all the rich territory north of the Rio Grande. Says Mrs Darst

"Dr Thomas Polk and wife, with several small children, left Vincennes, Ind., and emigrated to Arkansas Territory in 1820, where they sojourned for about a year. Texas was then a part of Mexico. Lured by adventure and prospective land grants, they came to this state in 1821 and were a part of Col Stephen F Austin's Colony, settled near Bahia Crossing, near what is now Austin County. There they lived until after the Mexican Revolutionary War.

"Dr. Polk was a surgeon in the Army of the Republic, but he had practiced medicine and engaged in farming and ranching for many years previous to the war. The country was full of wild animals, and also Indians, the latter making frequent raids on the settlers, stealing horses and cattle, and killing and capturing all the white people they could. Yet, these savages were always friendly to the Polks, because grandma Dr Thomas Polk's wife, often gave them food and aid. There was a cane brake near Dr. Polk's house and one day when the family were at dinner—one of the seldom days when they had a pudding—an immense Indian in war paint and feathers came out of the cane brake and stood in the door, uttering a loud grunt 'W-a-a-u-g-h.' The children all screamed and ran away and hid, some of them crawling under the bed. Grandma was not excited a bit, and going to the big chief, led him to a seat at the table, inviting him to eat. She helped him liberally to everything. He was particularly pleased with the pudding, and after eating what was given to him, helped himself to the rest of it. Then after dispatching it, he patted himself on the stomach, exclaimed, 'Heap good' and became playful. Seeing Eliza's little bare toes sticking out from under the bed, whither she had fled for safety at first appearance, he reached down and pulled her out by the foot, seemingly greatly pleased by her screams and frantic efforts to get away. Grandma ran to her rescue, but the Indian patted her on the shoulder and left the house.

"Grandpa Dr Polk, afterwards learned that the canebrake was full of Indians, with hostile intentions, but because this one was treated so kindly, they never molested the family at that or any other time. The big Indian often came afterwards, sometimes bringing another with him and frequently brought presents of game and fish, and grandma always cooked a goodly portion for him to eat He would signify his satisfaction by patting and rubbing his stomach

I will now tell you how this particular pudding was made. and all cakes and sweets at that time· Grandma sifted the cornmeal through a muslin cloth, to obtain the finest flour. She then shortened it with bear s fat and sweetened it with wild honey This was before the day of baking powder, or even soda, so when grandma had no saleratus she dripped strong lye from wood ashes, which, combined with sour milk, made a very good leaven She was a good manager and a hospitable housekeeper She often regaled the wayfarer and sometimes guest, with this cake and refreshing drink made of cold water poured on preserves made by stewing wild plums in honey Game was plentiful—bears. deer, turkeys, duck, quails and an abundance of honey was to be found in the hollow trees Also berries, pecans. grapes and various wild fruits in their season Grandpa killed several bears in the yard and grandma also killed one that was trying to kill a shoat

"As all supplies were shipped from New Orleans, and often delayed unaccountably, the people were obliged to subsist mainly on the game which they found in the woods, and fear of the Indians made it difficult to kill game Once during a corn famine, they were a long time—many weeks—without bread But their most serious misfortune occurred about the close of the war for Independence

'Grandpa was at home. on a furlough, to welcome the arrival of Milam Benjamin, the youngest child The people had not recovered from the fear and gloom cast over the country by the terrible Goliad Massacre. when came the direful news of the fall of the Alamo, with a necessity for every family between San Antonio and Houston to leave their homes and flee for their lives—the "Great Runaway." as it has been called

"Just at daylight, one morning. Mr Brown, a faithful nearest neighbor who lived two miles away, galloped to the door shutting, Get up D   ' Get up   ' ' The Mexicans are coming.' People d'   · g or at   ·   ·   d you and came back. Hurry! Hurry!" Within two hours they had secreted the cooking utensils and such bedding and provisions as they could, in hollow trees and logs, and packed up the few things they could carry, and set out. Grandma, with an infant of but a few days old in her arms, and a son behind her, Grandpa and Charles on the pack horses, and three little girls on a bobtailed pony that hitherto had been regarded as perfectly safe, but, he may have scented danger, for he ran away at the outset and scraped his precious burden from off his back as he ran under the swinging limb of a black-jack tree. The children were not hurt much; the pony was captured, all three piled on again, and they hurried forward to catch up with their fleeing neighbors. Recent heavy rains had made travel difficult, and when they reached the Brazos River it was out of its banks and unfordable. So the men set about building a raft to carry the women, children and baggage over. The horses swam across. Grandma was sitting on a fallen tree, with her babe on her lap, when her children were placed on the raft for the first trip across the swollen, rushing stream. She threw up her hands, screaming "Bring them back to me! My children will be drowned." But she was assured the danger was far less than if they remained on that side, to be butchered by the Mexicans. All were finally rafted across safely and they trudged on through the woods for life and liberty. At length night came upon them, a dark, starless night—and rain pouring in torrents. The men cut brush and piled it high, for the women and children to sleep on. The water ran ankle deep on the ground and they cut large pieces of bark from a fallen tree and threw it over Grandma in lieu of an umbrella, to keep her and her little babe dry. The next day the party reached Donahue's Ranch, tired, wet and hungry, but comparatively safe, and found a large number of people already encamped. Here they met Uncle William who had marched with the Regular Army. But in a few days he was thrown from a horse, which fell on him, striking him in the breast with the pommel of the saddle from which he suffered greatly. He had several hemorrhages of the lungs, for several days, and Grandpa was detailed with him, and other sick soldiers, when the San Jacinto battle took place

On the eve of the battle, General Sam Houston was pressing horses into service to draw cannons to the battlefield. An orderly came for the horse grandma had ridden from home; their best horse, a splendid animal. But grandma remonstrated. Nevertheless, he led the horse away. Shortly afterward, grandma followed with a butcher knife, and seeing her horse hitched to a cannon, proceeded to cut him out of harness. General Houston saw her in the act, and said 'Madam, I fear this is a bad omen.' But she told him her husband and son were in the army, and she needed the horse to help earn a living for her little children. So when General Houston saw she was determined to have her horse, he assisted her to mount and she rode the animal back to camp.

San Jacinto was the victorious decisive battle. Santa Anna was captured and Texas became a Republic. But as the country was still in an unsettled, dangerous condition, many families returned to the States. Grandma was urged to go with them; but she would not leave grandpa, and Uncle William was too ill to leave Donahue's Ranch. But when he was convalescing, she did return (alone, except for her little children) to her home in Austin County, as grandpa's services as surgeon were needed elsewhere, and with Uncle William, and was fortunate to find that their home had been passed by the Mexicans, who pillaged and burned every other house and village in their way. On account of their exposure and many deprivations, the children sickened with typhoid fever soon after their return home. Two of them were dangerously ill and grandma attended them unaided for weeks, with no means of communicating her distress to grandpa. One day Mr Brown (who had also been detained at San Jacinto) and a Mexican rode up to the gate, supporting a man between them, on a horse, a man limp from sickness, with his head swollen to immense proportions. When grandma went to the door, Mr Brown asked. 'Mrs Polk, do you know this man?' She shook her head and answered that she had never seen him before. 'Oh, yes you have, this is Dr P lk.'

"Grandpa had badly

salivated, and his head and face were swollen until he was unrecognizable. They carried him into a room apart from the children. The next day, Irvin, a boy of twelve years, died. Mr Brown and a more distant neighbor, named Alford, dug a grave in a thicket below the house. They placed Irvin in a little board coffin, put it on a slide to which a rope was attached, and dragged it to the grave.

"Eliza finally recovered, but all of her hair came out. In time, grandpa got well, but was never able to hear well again. They finally became dissatisfied and moved away, living a short time at Brazoria, San Philippi and Cuero and at last located in Gonzales County, where he ceased to practice medicine and engaged in farming and stock raising to a ripe old age.

A great part of the time during those experiences, Dr Thomas Polk was busy professionally. The country being but sparsely settled he made long journeys on horseback, so that his practice and his services as Surgeon in the Texas Revolution kept him away from home much of the time. While he had many thrilling adventures, he was reticent on the subject at home, perhaps to keep grandma from being anxious when he was away. He evaded, rather than sought honors or publicity in any form. Grandma could never quite forgive him for bringing her to raise her family in a wilderness, and tears would course down her cheeks when she lamented their want of schools religious and social advantages; yet she was a staunch helpmate, standing loyally by him through every battle of a long life, and died of grief a few months after his death. Grandpa would look upon his broad acres, fine stock, and handsome, healthy children, and declare he had nothing to regret.

"As are the other Polks, we are nearly all Presbyterians, and all Democrats. Some have wealth and some have not, but all are comfortable. There are two old bachelors on our branch, but no old maids, only one divorce and never a case of insanity."

CHAPTER LII.

EPHRAIM POLK, 1st, AND DESCENDANTS.

Ephraim Polk, 1st, progenitor of most of the Polks in Delaware, Kentucky, Iowa, Ohio California, and some other of the Western and Southern States, was the third son of Capt Robert Bruce Polk and his wife, Magdalen (Porter) Polk, nee Tasker

Ephraim Polk, 1st, was born in Ireland about the year 1671 and was a child of tender age when his parents emi-

(Polk Family and Kinsmen)

p. 449.

Charles Williams was brother of Elizabeth wife of Ephraim Polk.

Elizabeth Williams (no relation to Henry Williams, as shown by his will), daughter of Michael and Ann his wife, was born May, 29, 1674, at Anamessix, Md. (Stephney Parish Records, at Somerset Co., Md.)

Information supplied by

Dec. 11, 1933

salivated, and his head and face were swollen until he was unrecognizable. They carried him into a room apart from the children. The next day, Irvin, a boy of twelve years, died Mr Brown and a more distant neighbor, named Alford, dug a grave in a thicket below the house They placed Irvin in a little board coffin, put it on a slide to which a rope was attached, and dragged it to the grave

'Eliza finally recovered, but all of her hair came out In time, grandpa got well, but was never able to hear well again They finally became dissatisfied and moved away living a short time at Brazoria, San Philippi and Cuero and at last located in Gonzales County, where he ceased to prac-

CHAPTER LII.

EPHRAIM POLK, 1st, AND DESCENDANTS.

Ephraim Polk, 1st, progenitor of most of the Polks in Delaware, Kentucky, Iowa, Ohio, California, and some other of the Western and Southern States, was the third son of Capt. Robert Bruce Polk and his wife, Magdalen (Porter) Polk, nee Tasker.

Ephraim Polk, 1st, was born in Ireland about the year 1671, and was a child of tender age when his parents emigrated to America settling in Somerset County, Maryland. Ephraim died in 1718, as shown by the fact that on March 19th of that year his widow gave bond in the Somerset Court as Administratrix of his estate, with Charles Williams (presumably her father, or a brother) and Dennis Driskett as sureties, in the sum of two hundred pounds each. Her maiden name was Elizabeth Williams, a descendant of Henry Williams, a Virginia planter, who settled there in 1618, and who had property in Somerset County, Maryland. Many of this Williams family resided on the Eastern Shore, their ancestors being among the first colonists who came over with Lord Baltimore. Elizabeth is also said to have been a sister of Mary Williams, wife of her husband's brother, James Polk. Ephraim and Elizabeth were married about the year 1700, when he was a little less than thirty years old, as their eldest child, Magdalen Manlove Polk, who died unmarried, was born in 1702.

After Ephraim's death his widow married John Laws, of another prominent colonial family, several of whose members were intermarried with the Polks, and she was his wife in 1724, as the records show.

Judging from the entries of record in the Land Office of the Colony at Annapolis, and also from other official documents in the Clerk's office of Maryland and Delaware, Ephraim appears to have been in his day a thrifty, rising of the sons of Capt Robert Bruce Polk in the acquirement of real estate and other property. The Colonial Land Office records show the following grants from Lord Baltimore to him:

Ephraim Poalk, "Clonmell," 100 acres, lying in Somerset County, between Manokin Branch and Pidgeon House or Little Creek, Sept 20, 1700 Recorded in Liber D D No 5 folio, 73.

Ephraim Poalk, "Long Delay," 274 acres, lying in Somerset County, in Dame's Quarter, on W side of Ball's Creek, March 26, 1705 Recorded in Liber D D No 5, folio 366.

Ephraim Poalk, "Chance," 200 acres, lying on E side of Chesapeake Bay, in Dorchester County, May 27, 1715 Recorded in Liber E E No 6, folio 235

Ephraim Polack, "Poak's Chance," 200 acres E side Chesapeake Bay, Dorchester County, Sept 10, 1715 The different spellings of the name were evidently due to the carelessness of entry clerks or officials at that day These four grants make an aggregate of seven hundred and seventy-four acres entered by Ephraim Polk, between the years 1700 and 1715, the last entry being less than three years before his death In addition to these entries, he owned large bodies of other lands by purchase, and valuable ore deposits in Cedar Creek Swamp A good deal of his property was located in the part of Maryland that fell into Delaware after the readjustment of the lines of those provinces

The issue of the marriage of Ephraim Polk, 1st, and Elizabeth Williams, was five children [1]Magdalen Manlove; [2]Charles, 1st, [3]John; [4]Joseph, [5]Ephraim, 2d Magdalen Manlove, the first child, b about 1702, d single In the Pa. Archives, Series I, Vol 3, p 644, she is mentioned in 1759 as a "spinster," aged 57 years

CHARLES POLK, 1st, SON OF EPHRAIM, 1st.

Charles Polk, first son of Ephraim Polk and Elizabeth Williams, was born March 16, 1704, and died Aug 28, 1784 He married Patience Manlove, on July 8, 1738 She was born in 1711 and died Sept 23, 1776 Her family was also a numerous one in Maryland, the men of which held prominent civic positions and were large land owners, the women were noted for their fairness of face and good housekeeping.

Like his father, Charles Polk, 1st, was an enterprising and successful business man, and a prominent citizen of his community. According to one biographer, "he ranked with the first people of his day, filling several positions of honor and trust." Being the eldest son, and, under the then existing English law of primogeniture, "heir-at-law" of his father, Charles inherited the bulk of the family estates. Selling his lands in Somerset, he moved to Dorchester County, where his father had entered "Polk's Chance" in 1715, and remained there for some years. In 1740 he again sold out, and following the Nanticoke River to its source in the "Territories of Pennsylvania" settled in what is now Sussex County, Delaware. Here he remained and reared and educated his children, dying Aug. 28, 1784, near Bridgeville, highly esteemed and respected by all. He was a man of engaging personality, great force of character, and acquired a goodly fortune by his industry and excellent business talents.

By his wife, Patience, Charles Polk had six children, three sons and three daughters.

CHILDREN OF CHARLES POLK, 1st

The children of Charles, 1st, and Patience (Manlove) Polk, were: [1]Mary Magdalen, b May 3, 1739, d ——. [2]Judge Charles, b. Oct 26, 1740, d. Aug. 28, 1795, [3]Priscilla, b. Nov 15, 1742, d ——, 1816; [4]Anna (called "Nancy"), b Jan 10, 1744, d ——, [5]George, b Nov 15, 1746, d Dec 1795, [6]John, b March 10, 1748, d ——, 1782.

Anna Polk, born Jan 10, 1744 (fourth child of Charles Polk, 1st, and Patience Manlove) was generally called "Nancy." She married Mathew Morine, a man of noted physical strength, by whom she had issue [1]Charles, [2]Mary, [3]Matthew, [4]Nancy, [5]Priscilla, [6]William, [7]Manlove.

George Polk, fifth child of Charles, 1st, and Patience Manlove, born Nov 15, 1746, married and had issue [1]Charles, [2]George, [3]Elizabeth, [4]Margaret, [5]Harriet.

Mary Magdalen Polk the eldest child, married first, Henry Bowman in 1761, by whom she had one child, Nathaniel Bowman, b Feb 23, 1762 Secondly, she married Robert Minors, by whom she had six children ¹Sarah Seymour, b Aug 17, 1764, d Feb 25, 1813, ²Priscilla, b Aug 21, 1765, d ——, ³Nancy (Ann), b Jan 1, 1767, d July 13, 1815, ⁴Mary, b July 14, 1710, d April 16, 1851, ⁵Charles, b Feb 26, 1774, ⁶Robert, b 1777, d ——

Nathaniel Bowman married Lovey P Vickers and had one daughter, Henrietta, who married John Hall. The children of this union were Mary Ann Hall and Governor John W Hall The latter born Jan. 1, 1817 He accumulated a large estate and resided at Frederica, Delaware Being highly successful in business, and very popular, he was elected Governor of Delaware, serving from 1879 to 1883 Governor Hall married ————, and had issue ¹Samuel W, ²John W, Jr; ³Carrie W and S ——, etc

SKETCH OF GOVERNOR JOHN W. HALL.

John W. Hall, Governor of Delaware, 1879-1883, was b. Jan 1, 1817, in Frederica, Kent County where he resided until his death He was a son of John Hall, Sr, who died when his son was but nine years of age The wife of the latter was Henrietta Bowman, daughter of Nathaniel Bowman and Lovey P Vickers. Nathaniel's father, Henry Bowman, married Mary Magdalen Polk, daughter of Charles Polk, son of Ephraim 1st Mary Magdalen's brother, Judge Charles Polk, was the father of Governor Charles Polk, of Delaware, and so this branch of Ephraim s line has produced two governors of Delaware.

As John W Hall grew to manhood he entered the mercantile business, and when twenty-one he began business on his own account, soon acquiring a large trade, and branching out into lumber, grain and shipping He acquired a number of farms, carried on extensively agricultural pursuits, and acquired a large fortune.

Politically, John W Hall was a Whig, but later he allied himself with the Democratic Party In 1866 he was elected

(Polk Family and Kinsmen)
p. 452.

Nathaniel Bowman, son of Henry Bowman and Mary Magdalen Polk, married Sarah Draper, and had three daughters: Miriam, Esther and Henrietta. The latter married married John Hall of Kent Co., Delaware. Their son, Gov. John Wood Hall married Caroline Warren. Their children were: 1. Samuel Warren Hall, 2. John Wood Hall, Jr., 3. Caroline Warren Hall, 4. Sarah Henrietta Hall.

No descendants except for Samuel. Samuel Warren Hall married Anna Sullivan, and had: 1. Frank S. Hall, who married Frances Davies; 2. Samuel Warren Hall, Jr., who married Mary Gertrude Scott, and had: Samuel Warren Hall, III.; William Scott Hall who m. Catherine Elizabeth Read; Gertrude Anna Hall.

Information supplied by
Dec. 11, 1933

Mary Magdalen Polk, the eldest child, married first, Henry Bowman in 1761, by whom she had one child, Nathan-

Politically, John W. Hall was a Whig, but later he allied himself with the Democratic Party. In 1866 he was elected

GOV. JOHN W. HALL,
of Delaware.

THE NEW YORK
PUBLIC LIBRARY

ASTOR LENOX AND
TILDEN FOUNDATIONS.

a State Senator, and in 1876 a delegate to the National Democratic Convention. In 1874 he barely missed the nomination for Governor, and in 1878 was nominated by acclamation for that office and was duly elected by a very large majority. After the expiration of his gubernatorial term he devoted himself to the comforts of home the balance of his life.

JUDGE CHARLES POLK

Judge Charles Polk, second child of Charles Polk, 1st, and Patience (Manlove) Polk, was born Oct 26, 1740, died Aug 28 1795; married May 29, 1786, to Mary Manlove, a cousin, daughter of Jonathan and Elizabeth Manlove, of Sussex County, by whom he had three children ¹Gov Charles, ²Elizabeth; ³John The two latter died in infancy

Judge Charles Polk was a man of prominence in Delaware, and held several positions of trust and honor. On Oct 25, 1790, he was elected Judge of the Common Pleas Court for the County of Sussex, commissioned on Nov 8 following, and qualified Feb 9, 1791. On Oct. 1, 1791, he was elected to a convention held for the purpose of "framing a Constitution for ye State of Delaware," and when the convention met was chosen President of the body During the sitting of the convention he was taken ill, left its deliberations, and did not afterwards serve in its work

GOVERNOR CHARLES POLK.

Governor Charles Polk, second child of Judge Charles Polk, was born Nov 15, 1788, and died Oct 27, 1857 He married Mary Elizabeth Purnell, daughter of John Purnell, of Sussex, on September 4, 1811. She died in July, 1865 The issue of this marriage was fifteen children ¹Mary Elizabeth Manlove, b Jan 14, 1815, ²Wm Alexander, b June 10, 1816, d Feb 7, 1899, ³John Purnell, b. May 22, 1818, d Aug 21, 1881, ⁴Caroline, b March 19, 1823, d. March 5, 1895, ⁵Sallie Maria, b June 3, 1825, d Sept 14, 1846, unmarried, ⁶Annie May, b Dec 9, 1832; ⁷Dr. Charles George, 2d, b July 31, 1835, d Jan. 24 1911 ⁸James Henry, b Feb 7, 1838 ⁹Joseph-ine Purnell, b Feb 10, 1840, [10]Theodore Albert, b Nov 21, 1842

The children of Governor Charles Polk that died young or unmarried, were Dr Chas George, d July 1, 1820, Chas Edward, d in 1833, George Frederick, d June 1, 1832, Ellen Ann, d Dec 14, 1832, Anna May, d Aug 4, 1893, unmarried

Of those who attained to manhood or womanhood, Mary Elizabeth Manlove married Jan 14 1845, to John Bailey of Kenton, Del. Issue [1]Charles, b June 3, 1848, [2]Wm Andrew, b. Aug 18, 1849. [3]Mary Anna, b April 19, 1857

James Henry Polk married in 1858 Mary Masten He died Oct, 1867 Offspring: [1]Sallie Maria, b Aug. 23, 1861, [2]Theodore E, b Oct 13, 1862, [3]John P b. Feb. 17, 1864

Wm Alexander Polk born June 10, 1816, died unmarried, at Georgetown, Del, Feb 7, 1899 He was a farmer, but a man of fine intelligence and greatly esteemed He was elected a Representative in the Legislature of Delaware in 1866, and chosen speaker of that body His residence was in Nanticoke Hundred In 1841 he was an Aide to Governor Cooper, Deputy Register of Wills, 1841 to 1853, Commissary U S A, 1864-5, to General Sully, Register of Wills for Sussex County from 1881 to 1871

John Purnell Polk was appointed Nov 1, 1849, to the position of Clerk in the Department of State, at Washington City, serving about thirty years, or until a short time before his death By steady promotion he became Chief Clerk of Division C, having charge of correspondence with the Barbary States, China, Ecuador, Egypt, Greece, Hawaiian Islands, Japan, Liberia, San Domingo, Turkey, and other countries not assigned, and miscellaneous correspondence relating to those countries

John Purnell Polk never married He resided for many years, from 1849 until his death, Aug 2 1881, at the National Capital with his maiden sisters He was a most genial and lovable man, and highly popular with all who knew him He took great interest in the family history and furnished the author with much of the data of his own experience in his own line, as well as others

DR. THOS. JEFFERSON PYLE, WIFE AND DAUGHTER.

Caroline Polk, born March 19, 1823, died March 5, 1893 She married May 26, 1860, William Virden, of Frederica,

Charles George Polk, born July 31, 1835, died Jan 24, 1911, at the home of his son, James L. Polk, Merchantville, N. J He studied medicine, and became a prominent physician in Philadelphia, also filling the chair of Pharmacy in the University of Pennsylvania During the Civil War he was Assistant Surgeon, U S. A, and Post Surgeon in charge of hospitals He also served on the staff of the Surgeon General He married ———, and had issue. [1]Charles; [2]J Levingood, [3]Carrie

Josephine Purnell Polk (daughter of Gov Charles Polk) married, in 1867, John O Truitt, of Milford, Dela, and had issue [1]John E, b Oct 17, 1868; [2]Leo O, b April 28, 1871

Theodore Albert Polk, Pharmacist and Chemist (youngest child of Governor Charles Polk) was b Nov 21, 1842, at Ellersley, Milford Neck, Dela. He was married in 1868 to Miss Mary Fawcett Issue [1]Albert Fawcett, b Oct. 11, 1869, [2]Mary Turner, b. Sept. 9, 1871, married Dec 20, 1888, to Dr Thos Jefferson Pyle, of Baltimore, in which city he has large business interests They have issue [1]Frances Polk, b Oct 21, 1889; [2]Sarah Albert, b July 5, 1891; [3]Wm. Stanton, b Dec. 28, 1894; [4]Charles Polk, b Aug 1, 1897, [5]Mary Elizabeth, b Feb 15, 1899, [6]Theodora, b April 27, 1905

Albert Fawcett Polk is a prominent lawyer and leading Democratic politician of Delaware. On Dec 29, 1897, he was united in marriage to Miss Martilla Evans, daughter of James A Evans, of Georgetown, Dela, a lovely and accomplished woman. They have no issue

George Polk (second son of Charles Polk, 1st, and Patience Manlove), b. Nov 15, 1746, married a Miss Rian, and died in 1795 They had issue [1]Charles, [2]George, [3]Elizabeth; [4]Margretta, [5]Sally; [6]Anna. Charles was thrown from a sleigh and killed in 1815. He married a Miss Minors and left a daughter, who died unmarried George married Miss Laws and left one son, Charles James, unmarried, near St Johns Town, Dela Elizabeth married Wm Ro- nm and they had issue [1]Peter unmarried; [2] both married,

²Margaretta, married, first, Robert Miners, by whom she had one child, secondly, she married James S Knowles. Issue one child, William Sally married Henry Bowman, by whom she had several children

Anna married Alexander Polk Laws He participated with Commodore Stephen Decatur in the recapture of the United States frigate, Philadelphia, and her destruction under a hot cannonade by the forts at Tripoli. He was the third man to leap onto the deck of the frigate on that occasion, and for his gallant conduct received a sword from the State. Alexander and Ann left a son, Robert, in North West Fork Hundred, who inherited the sword

CHAPTER LIII.

SKETCH OF GOVERNOR CHARLES POLK.

The following sketch of Governor Charles Polk, of Delaware, was written about twenty years ago, by a leading gentleman of that State, who was well acquainted with the Governor and knew him intimately.

Governor Charles Polk, son of Judge Charles Polk, of Sussex (who was the son of Charles, the first, son of Ephraim), was born near Bridgeville, Dela., Nov. 15, 1788, and died near Milford, Kent County, Oct. 27, 1857. On Sept 4, 1811, he was married to Mary Elizabeth Purnell, daughter of John Purnell, of Berlin, Worcester County, Maryland, by whom he had fifteen children, nine of whom survive him, including Ex-Register of Wills William A Polk; Dr Charles G Polk, late Assistant Surgeon U A S, and Theodore A. Polk. He was the fourth Charles in his immediate line His father, Judge Charles Polk, dying when he was in his eighth year, the boy's training and education devolved upon his mother, whose piety and intellectual strength were to the son of inestimable value Her maiden name had been Mary Manlove. She was a Quakeress, a woman of high culture, of rare intellectual and moral worth She instilled into the mind of her only surviving child those principles of right and honor which guided him through the vicissitudes of many years of political life and left his name adorned with many virtues and untouched by a word of reproach

At an early age the boy was placed at the Western Boarding School, at Smyrna, where he obtained his preliminary education At the age of fourteen he began his classical education at Lewes, Dela., and there was formed the strong regard between himself and Hon John M Clayton, and which terminated only in death At the age of eighteen he began the study of law with Kensey Johns, Sr devoting three years to it, and acquiring a knowledge of common and statute law attained by very few persons, but he never actively engaged in the practice of his profession, having a strong aversion to its exacting duties. As an orator, he possessed the finest qualities. But few men have lived who held their ideas so well elaborated and ready for promulgation, and comprehended more fully the science of government. Had he yielded to the wishes of his party and accepted the position of United States Senator, there is no doubt that he could have achieved a high national reputaton, and added another name to the list of master minds which Delaware has furnished to the Councils of the Nation. It may not be out of place to remark here that he also declined to accept the position of Chancellor of the State of Delaware, offered to him by Governor Hazzard, about the year 1831. About 1816 he moved to Kent County and purchased a tract of 1,100 acre sof land lying along the shore of Delaware Bay, near Milford, upon which he resided for many years, and at the time of his death, and which land is still held in the family undivided. As an evidence of the acuteness of his mind, it may be stated that on the day immediately preceding his death he dictated his "last will and testament" and signed it without making any alteration whatever in the instrument. His power of memory was remarkable, and until within a few weeks of his death there seemed to be no deterioration in his intellectual strength. He could repeat by rote nearly the whole of Virgil, Horace and Livy, in Latin, and Xenophon's "Anabasis" and "Memorabilia" and "Thucydides" in Greek. A few months before his death he repeated wthout error, either in Latin or English, Cicero's first oration against Cataline.

In politics, Governor Polk was a Federalist, and afterwards a Whig. In his views he was Conservative, more inclined to cling to the traditions of the past than to partake in untried innovations. The American Constitution was his ideal of a basis of laws; the perfect instrument for the government of the Nation; the concentrated wisdom of all nations and all times.

During his administration, efforts were made to alter the Constitution, and which he strongly opposed in his message to the Legislature in January, 1829. "I applaud," said he

GOV. CHARLES POLK,
of Delaware.

THE NEW YORK
PUBLIC LIBRARY

ASTOR, LENOX AND
TILDEN FOUNDATIONS

"the policy which holds up that instrument to our country as too sacred to be made the subject of experimental alterations; too dear to become the victim of political essayists it is daily growing more dear to us as the Magna Charta of our liberties. As Delaware was the first to adopt the Constitution, may she be the last to desert it May it remain unimpaired by the lapse of time, unfettered by illiberal construction, unchanged by the restless spirit of internal faction or the ruthless violence of external foes" Noble words; concretely and powerfully expressed, and worthy of the greatest minds that have illumined the annals of the Anglo Saxon race

Governor Polk was one of the most prominent and active men in Delaware He was exceedingly affable and engaging in his manner, of strikingly handsome appearance, and regarded as a man of pure mind and sterling integrity He was a strong friend, intimate companion and zealous supporter of Hon. John M Clayton, whom he made his Secretary of State, and by whom he was thoroughly liked and trusted

Following is a list of the positions of trust and honor held by Governor Polk Elected to the House of Representatives from Sussex County, Oct , 1813, and re-elected in 1815. Moved into Kent County in 1816 and was chosen as Representative from that County in 1817 Elected to the Levy Court, 1819; to the State Senate in 1824, and chosen Speaker of that body Elected Governor in 1826 by the Federal party over David Hazzard. Was a member of the State Senate in 1832 and Speaker thereof in 1836, when by the death of Governor Bennett he again became Governor In 1831 was elected a member of the Constitutional Convention, and chosen as President of that body Elected again to the Senate in 1838, and chosen Speaker in 1840 Appointed Register of Wills for Kent County in 1843, and served for a term of five years He was appointed Collector of the Port of Wilmington, Dela , in 1850, and resigned in 1853

SKETCH OF HON ALBERT F. POLK.

Hon Albert Fawcett Polk of Georgetown Del , a scion of one of the most virile branches of the Polk family His great-grandfather, Judge Charles Polk (son of Charles, 1st, son of Ephraim) was a man of eminence in his day. He was President of the first Constitutional Convention of Delaware. Albert F. Polk's grandfather, Charles Polk, 3d, was twice Governor of that State, and one of the best lawyers and ablest statesmen of his day. He was also President of the second Constitutional Convention of Delaware, in 1831, which framed the instrument that was superseded by a third one in 1897.

Theodore Albert Polk, father of Albert F. Polk, was the youngest son of Gov. Charles Polk, and held several public positions, among them Deputy Register of Wills for Sussex County, succeeding his son, Albert. The latter was born at Frederica, Kent County, Del., Oct. 11, 1869. When he was one year of age his father moved to Seaford, where they resided four years. They then moved to Georgetown, the County seat of Sussex, where Albert F. attended the public schools, graduating from the High School in June, 1885. The following September he entered the Freshman Class and took a classical course at Delaware College, Newark, graduating therefrom in June, 1889, as valedictorian of his class, and with the military honors of the College, giving his name a place in the Official Army Register for January, 1890, and securing the gold medal. In the fall of 1889 he entered the office of the Register of Wills of Sussex County as a deputy, and at the same time registered as a student at law under Hon. Alfred P. Robinson, who was made Chief Justice of Delaware in February, 1893. After a close study of the elementary principles of the profession, Albert F. Polk was admitted to the bar as a practitioner, in October, 1892, and since that time has steadily advanced into a lucrative practice. In March, 1894, he was appointed City Solicitor, which position he held for two terms, declining further service.

In politics, Albert F. Polk has always been a pronounced Democrat, taking an active part in the various contests of his party. For two years he was editor of the Delaware College Review, and Delaware staff correspondent of the Philadelphia Press for one year. In the campaign of 1892 he was political editor of the Sussex Countian. He is a prominent member

HON. ALBERT F. POLK,
Georgetown, Del.

and officer in the Masonic Order, having filled several of the highest offices of the order in his State. On December 29, 1897, he was united in marriage to one of the most charming young women of Georgetown, Miss Martilla Evans, daughter of Mr. and Mrs James A. Evans. They have no children.

Albert F. Polk has represented Sussex County in the State Legislature, and served as Counsel for the Senate. He was also chosen as one of the three Legislative Attorneys to revise the laws of the State so as to conform to the new constitution. He is a member of the Delaware Historical Society, and also takes part in all movements promoted for the betterment of society. In the recent Taft-Bryan campaign, he was chairman of the Democratic Committee and performed effective services for his party.

ALLIED FAMILIES.

Among the leading Colonial families that became related by intermarriage with the Polks and Morris' of Maryland and Delaware, were the Manloves, Hayes, Brinckles, Curtis', Bowmans, Coverdales, Scroggins, Beswicks, Purnells, Minors, Herings, and others.

Some of these families came to America before the Polks, settling first in Virginia, and moving thence to Maryland and Delaware, when the latter province was claimed by both Wm Penn and Lord Baltimore, which contention was finally settled by the erection of the "Three Lower Counties" into Delaware Colony.

These families were intermarried principally with the descendants of Ephraim, third son of Robert and Magdalen Polk, and were settled principally in Kent and Sussex.

Charles Polk, the eldest son of Ephraim Polk 1st, married Patience Manlove, in 1738, and their son, Judge Charles Polk, a prominent man of his colony, married Mary Manlove. The latter were the parents of Governor Charles Polk, who married Mary Elizabeth Purnell.

Mary Magdalen Polk, a sister of Judge Charles Polk married Henry B. wines first and Robert Mitt... Ephraim Polk 2d married Polly Manlove, Prisilla... oughter of Charles Polk 1st, married Richard Hayes, and Joseph Polk, a brother of Charles Polk 1st, married Sarah Coverdale

MINORS' AND BESWICK'S.

Robert Minors (son of Robert and Sarah Minors), b Dec 26, 1737, d ———, married Mrs Mary (Polk) Bowman, daughter of Charles Polk 1st, and Patience Manlove. Mary was b. May 3, 1739. By her first husband, Henry Bowman, whom she married in 1761, she had one child, Nathaniel Bowman, b Feb 23, 1762. By her second husband, Robert Minors, whom she married in 1763, she had issue. ¹Sarah Seymour; ²Priscilla, ³Nancy (Ann), ⁴Mary; ⁵Charles; ⁶Robert

(1) Sarah Seymour, b 1764, d Feb 25, 1813, married first Capt Levin Hill, second, John Purnell. By her first husband, Sarah had no issue By her second she had twins William Thomas and Sarah Seymour Purnell, b July 25, 1805, d July 21, 1865 The latter married Curtis Brinckle Beswick and d. in 1865 (See Beswick line).

William Thomas Purnell, twin brother of Sarah Seymour married first Henrietta Brown, second Henrietta Spence, daughter of U S Senator Spence of Maryland William Thomas read law under Hon John M Clayton and later removed to Mississippi While a resident of that State he was appointed by President Taylor as U S Consul to Brazil, and afterwards Special Counsel of the U S Government, in sundry cases He d at Snow Hill, Md., in 1862 By his first wife, Henrietta Brown he had issue: ¹Josephine, who d young; ²Charles T, who married Clara Bertron, daughter of Rev. S R Bertron, of Mississippi Charles T. was a captain in the Confederate Army By his second wife, Miss Spence, William Thomas Purnell had two children, Clayton Purnell, attorney-at-law, Frostburg, Md , and Louise The other descendants of this line from William Thomas Purnell have not been traced

Priscilla Minors (daughter of Robert Minors and Mary Polk Bowman), b Aug 21, 1765, married George Beswick, son of John and Phoebe Beswick Among her descendants are Mrs Ella Marshall, of Dover, Del , of heirs of Wilson Lee Cannon, deceased.

Nancy or Ann (third child of Robert Minors and Mary Polk Bowman), b Jan. 1, 1767, married Curtis Beswick, son of John Beswick and Phoebe Brinckle and d July 18, 1815

Nancy and Curtis Beswick had issue ¹Mary Minors Beswick, b. 1794, d March 23, 1853; ²William, b Jan 28, 1801, d Jan 11, 1855; ³Curtis Brinckle Beswick, ⁴Lovey Polk Beswick, ⁵Susannah Lochman Beswick Mary Minors Beswick, b about 1794, d unmarried in 1853 Curtis Brinckle Beswick, b 1796, d 1880, married Sarah Seymour Purnell, daughter of John Purnell and Sarah S Minors-Hill Lovey Beswick, married Nathaniel Oliver Bowman and d in 1823 Nathaniel was a son of Mary Magdalen Polk by her first husband, Henry Bowman (see Chas Polk descendants)

Susannah Lockerman (fourth child of Nancy Minors and Curtis Beswick), b June 9, 1798, d Jan. 21, 1846, married Nathaniel Luff, Aug 31, 1823 by whom she had issue:

(1) William B. Luff, b June 25, 1824, d July 14, 1824. } Twins.
(2) Mary Ann Luff, b. June 26, 1824, d. Oct 2, 1825

(3) Annie Elizabeth Luff, b Oct 12, 1826, married Isaac Preston, 185—

(4) Nathaniel Peterson Luff, b Jan 13, 1829, d Sept 25, 1901, married Mary C Moore, Dec 8, 1857

(5) Caleb Lockerman Luff, b Feb 12, 1832; married Elmira Moore in 1866

(6) Susan Luff, b June 24, 1834, married Andrew Logan

(7) Joshua Beswick Luff, b Jan 23, 1837, d Aug 5, 1888, married Emma Harrington in 1858

(8) William Joseph Luff, b. Aug 23, 1841, drowned in spring, April 11, 1843

Nathaniel Peterson Luff was a very successful business man He was one of the adventurers in the West, and to the California gold fields in 1849, and lived there several years Returning to Delaware, he settled down and married in 1857, applying his talents to active business affairs

Mary Minors (fourth child of Mary (Polk) Bowman and Robert Minors, b July 19, 1770, d April 16, 1851, married Vincent Lockerman Beswick, son of John and Phoebe Beswick Their only representative so far traced is Caleb J Smithers, Frederica, Del.

Charles Minors (son of Robert and Mary (Polk) Bowman Minors), b Feb 26, 1774, untraced.

Robert Minors (son of Robert and Mary (Polk) Bowman Minors), b 1777, untraced except as to two descendants, Mrs. G. Layton Grier and Mrs Dr. P T Carlisle, of Milford, Del

Curtis Brinkle Beswick (son of Nancy Minors and Curtis Beswick), b 1796, d Jan 11, 1880 He married June 2, 1825, Sarah Seymour Purnell, daughter of John Purnell and Sarah S Minors-Hill They had issue:

(1) John Edward Beswick, b Aug 6, 1826, d. March 1, 1828

(2) Wm Purnell Beswick, b Jan 7, 1828, d June 12, 1892.

(3) Angeline Brinkle Beswick, b Dec 7, 1830, d April 29, 1904, married Wm G Hering, Jan 25, 1855

(4) Robert John Beswick, b July 7, 1834, d April 19, 1907, unmarried.

(5) Sallie Ann Beswick, b Feb 14, 1838, d. April 21, 1899, married Hezekiah Masten, half brother of Ex Governor Jno W Hall She had no issue

(6) Geo Washington Purnell Beswick, b March 22, 1841, d. Oct 20, 1855

(7) Mary Elizabeth Beswick, b March 4, 1845, d in infancy

Robert John Beswick, son of Curtis B. Beswick and Sarah S Purnell, was president of the Town Council of Milford, Del , member of the Levy Court of Kent County, and Justice of the Peace and Notary Public at Milford

William Purnell Beswick, b. in 1828 (son of Curtis Brinckle Beswick), married Susan Slaughter, and they had issue

(1) Sallie May Beswick, b 1861, married John F Hammond ; no issue

(2) Annie Purnell Beswick, unmarried.

(3) John Brinckle Beswick, unmarried

(4) Edward S Beswick, married Harriet E Jackson, daughter of Rev L H Jackson Issue [1]Wm Purnell, [2]Mary Louise, [3]Edward Lawson Beswick, [4]Thomas C. Beswick (son

of Wm Purnell Beswick and Susan Slaughter), married Florence Beaumont

Angeline Brinckle Beswick (daughter of Curtis Brinckle Beswick and Sarah S Purnell), b. 1830, d 1904, married William G Hering They had issue.

(1) Sallie Purnell Hering, b 1855, d. in infancy
(2) Mary Elizabeth Hering, b 1857, d 1881
(3) John W Hering, b 1861 Resides at Milford, Del
(4) Georgiana, b. 1866, married Jas H. Salmons Issue ¹James H, d in infancy, ²Ethel, ³Marion
(5) William Beswick Hering, b 1869, married first Fanny Roach-Fowler, second Edna Bickel By the first wife he had Robert John, b 1899, and William, who died in infancy By the second wife, Mary Elizabeth.

The foregoing Minor family data is copied largely from the Beswick Bible, dated 1768 and containing entries back to 1723, now in possession of John W Hering, of Milford, Kent County, Del Susannah Lockerman Beswick, daughter of Curtis and Ann Beswick, and wife of Nathaniel Luff, was b June 9, 1798, d Jan 21, 1846 William Beswick, son of Curtis and Ann Beswick, was b Sept 23, 1799, and d Oct. 19, 1800 Mary Minors Beswick, daughter of Curtis and Ann (Nancy) Beswick, d March 23, 1853, unmarried.

BESWICK BIBLE RECORDS

In addition to the foregoing Beswick data, the following is recorded in the old Beswick family bible

Phoebe (Brinckle) Beswick, wife of John Beswick, was b Dec 22, 1733, d Feb 25, 1801.

Mary Beswick, daughter of John and Phoebe, b March 13, 1754.

Susannah Beswick, daughter of John and Phoebe, b Aug 12, 1756.

Sarah Beswick, daughter of John and Phoebe, b Jan 10, 1759

Curtis Beswick, son of John and Phoebe, b Jan 17, 1762, d. May 26 1812

George Beswick, son of John and Phoebe, b   1764.

Vincent Lockerman Beswick, son of John and Phoebe, b April 27, 1767, married Mary Minors, and d Aug 21, 1804

Polly Minors Beswick, daughter of Curtis and Ann (Nancy) was b Feb 24, 1795, d March 15, 1799.

Curtis Brinckle Beswick, son of Curtis and Ann (Nancy) b March 3, 1796, d Jan 11, 1880

Love Minors Beswick, daughter of Curtis and Ann (Nancy) b April 15, 1797, d. Feb. 19, 1823; married Nathaniel Oliver Bowman.

Robert Minors, who married Mrs Mary (Polk) Bowman (daughter of Chas Polk 1st, and Patience Manlove), progenitor of the foregoing five generations of that name, owned a tract of land on Mispillion River, in Mispillion (now Milford) Hundred This tract now belongs to Miss Annie Purnell Beswick

William G Hering, who married Angeline Brinckle Beswick, was postmaster at Milford, Del, by appointment of Presidents Grant and Hayes, and at sundry times member of State and County Republican committees

John W Hering, son of Wm G and Angeline B. Hering, was educated at Delaware College; member of the Convention that formed the last Constitution of Delaware, 1896-7 At the present time he is Secretary of the Milford Building and Loan Association

THE MANLOVE FAMILY.

The Manlove family is an extensive one in Maryland, Delaware and Pennsylvania, and in numerous instances were inter-married with the Polks of those states

Mark Manlove, "The First Comer," as he is denominated by his descendants, came over from England and settled before 1652 in Northampton County, Virginia, locating in that section, which was later erected into Accomac County, adjoining the Maryland line From Northampton he is said to have removed in 1660-5 over into Somerset County, Maryland, or, perhaps, the readjustment of the line between the two colonies threw him into Maryland without removal He received from the "Lower County" 150 acres of land for

JOHN W. HERING,
Milford, Del.

"head-rights." Here he continued to reside until his death in 1666, which was a few years anterior to the arrival of the Polks and their location in Somerset. The will of Mark Manlove, on file in the Clerk's Office of Somerset County, was probated Sept. 14, 1666. He came, it is said, from Staffordshire, England.

Mark Manlove Sr., the "first comer," was twice married and had nine children by his first wife and three by his last, Eliza ————. Some of his children moved to Kent and some to Sussex County, Del.

These children were: [1]John, [2]Thomas, of Sussex, who d. 1709; [3]Ann, who married first Thos. Nixon of Kent, secondly ———— Robinson; [4]Mary; [5]Mark Jr., of Kent, who d. 1694, [6]William, [7]Christopher, [8]George, [9]Luke, [10]Hannah, [11]Abijah, [12]Percy.

William Manlove, son of Mark Sr., d. 1694. He married Alice Robbins, of Kent County. He was a Justice of the Peace in 1688-90; member Pennsylvania Assembly 1689-93. He received a grant of one thousand acres of land.

The children of William and Alice Robbins Manlove were [1]Mark, [2]William; [3]Mary; [4]Hannah, [5]Elizabeth, [6]Samuel.

William (son of William), married Elizabeth ———— and had issue: [1]William, [2]Elizabeth (who married Peter Brinckle), who d. 1765, [3]Mary ————. Their children were [1]Wm., [2]Jesse; [3]Peter, [4]Mary, who married Jas. Gregory.

Mary Gregory had issue: [1]James, [2]Mary, who married Felix Thibault, b. 1791, and descended from an ancient family of France, [3]Julia, who married Guy Bryan, a descendant of Sir Guy Bryan.

Mary Thibault had one child Cecelia Julia Thibault, who married J. Creagh Smith, of Revolutionary descent. They had issue: [1]George, [2]M. Cecelia; [3]Amelia Holmes, [4]Felix; [5]J. Creagh.

WILLIAM MANLOVE, SR.

William Manlove Sr., ancestor of the Manloves of Delaware, v... ... ... had six bro... ... ... f his children were Rowland and Mark. The latter was known as the "first comer" of the family to America about 1650, settling first in Northampton County, Virginia, and later in Maryland, about 1666.

Rowland Manlove was born at Wern, in Shropshire, and was in the naval service under Sir Walter Levison. He obtained sufficient wealth to enable him to buy of Sir Walter Chetwind, "Wanfields," in the parish of Rynston, near Uttoxeter, County Stafford, and d. there in 1652, or about the time his brother Mark emigrated to Virginia.

Rowland Manlove married Magdalen, daughter of William Wyke and they had issue. [1]Sarah, who married Wm. Bartlett, [2]Mary, who married Morgan of Whitechurch; [3]Elizabeth, who married Thomas Manlove; [4]Alice, who married Roger Fowke, of Snowshall, [5]Margaret, who married Thomas Challonan, of Chedle.

Matthew Manlove (second son of Matthew and Susannah), was a Captain in Col. Samuel Patterson's "Flying Camp" Regiment of the Revolution. Capt. Matthew Manlove's will is dated Feb. 11, 1811, probated Dec. 19, 1811. The devisees in his will were his nephew, Governor Charles Polk, and his sister Jemima (Manlove) Molleston.

Curtis Brinckle and Mary Manlove had one child, Phoebe Brinckle, b. 1733, d. 1801. She married John Beswick, who d. 1771. She then married Smith Bassett, by whom she had no issue. By her first husband she had issue: [1]Mary; [2]Susannah; [3]Sarah, who married ———— Laws; [4]Curtis, b. 1762, married Ann (Nancy) Minors, and d. 1812, [5]George, b. 1764; [6]Vincent Lockerman, b. 1767.

THE CURTIS FAMILY.

The Curtis family came to America from Bristol, England. John Curtis the reputed first immigrant of the name to these shores and progenitor of the Delaware branch that intermarried with the Morris and other kinsmen of the Polks, was descended from an ancient family resident in Applefore, in County Kent, England.

As far back as he can be traced, John was a wealthy land

owner in the County of Kent, on Delaware, in the "Province of Pennsylvania " He was a prominent and influential man in his community and was frequently honored by official preferment He was a member of the Governor's Council in 1687, '89, '90, '93, '98, member of the Assembly, from Kent, 1682, '83, 84, '85. He d. April 30, 1698 The Curtis family was related to the Rodneys, of whom Caesar A. Rodney, one of the Delaware Signers of the Declaration of Independence was a distinguished representative.

On arrival in Delaware, John Curtis obtained a patent from Governor Andros for "Aberdeen," May 5, 1769 (Duke of York's Record 189). Also see Duke of Yorks Book of Laws, p 509, '23, 31, '34, 569, '76, 485, '95 He was Justice of the Peace for Kent County, Feb 28, 1685, and again in 1690 (Scharf's Hist Del 1089, 30 Also Register Soc. of Colonial Wars)

John Curtis married first Elizabeth Cubley, daughter of John Cubley of Kent County, by whom he had four children After her death he married Nov 27, 1689, Priscilla Bowers, widow of George Bowers At the time Priscilla married him she was the widow of Nathaniel Hunn, who had d about 1718

The children of John Curtis were: [1]Caleb, [2]Ann, [3]Elizabeth, [4]Winlock; [5]Ruth. Caleb is supposed to have died young and unmarried. Ann married Richard Curtis, of Mispillion, Kent County, March 1, 1687 (See Deed Book B, p 65)

Richard Curtis was a member of the Assembly from Kent County in 1690 and d 1695 Their daughter Elizabeth, who d. in 1743, married Peter Brinckle Sr , who d April 15, 1728 Peter was a Justice of the Supreme Court of the "Three Lower Counties," April 2, 1717 Also a commissioner to lay off the town of Dover, and was in America before 1695 (Kent Will Book, D p 52, also Book F p 6, and Deed Book C. p 208)

Winlock Curtis, fourth child of John Curtis by his first wife, married Ann Bowers, sister-in-law of his stepmother. Winlock was administrator to his wife Ann, Feb 9, 1698 He and Ann his wife had a daughter Ann, b Nov 15, 1690, who married Robert Clay. (For this line see Robert Burton Genealogy, Maryland Hist.

Ruth, fifth child of John Curtis, by his second wife, Priscilla Bowers, is untraced

The children of Richard and Ann Curtis were ¹Elizabeth, who married Peter Brinckle; ²Samuel. Elizabeth survived her husband about thirteen years (Kent County Will Book, II p 129, April 9, 1741) Elizabeth d in 1743, and Peter on April 14, 1728, and letters of administration were granted to his wife Elizabeth (See Book Y p. 10) Samuel died young or single, and is untraced

Elizabeth Curtis (daughter of John and Elizabeth Cubley Curtis) and William Brinckle, her husband, had issue· ¹Winlock, ²John; ³Mary, who married Jehu Curtis, Associate Justice Kent County, April 1743: b Oct 19, 1692, d Nov 18, 1753; ⁴Sarah, who married Col ————, ⁵Miriam, who married ———— Highland, ⁶Elizabeth, who married John Clarke Jr, son of John Clarke Sr, and Elizabeth Green Manlove

Elizabeth Curtis Jr. (daughter of Ann and Richard Curtis), was a niece of the foregoing Elizabeth She was married Jan 5, 1687-8 to Peter Brinckle, and had issue ¹Curtis, d 1767; ²Daniel, b 1754, ³William, d 1748; ⁴Peter, d 1764; ⁵Richard, d 1788, ⁶Elizabeth, who married first Van Brinckle, second ———— Davis

Curtis married Mary Manlove, daughter of Matthew Manlove and Susannah Williams (See Elizabeth Green Manlove)

Curtis Brinckle,. son of Peter and Elizabeth Brinckle, d 1767 Curtis and his first wife, Mary Manlove Brinckle, had one child, Phoebe, b 1733,, who married John Beswick and d in 1801 Curtis, second wife was Sarah ————, by whom he had no issue After his death she married Geo. Ogle

Phoebe Brinckle, b 1733, d 1801 and her husband John Beswick had issue ¹Mary, ²Susannah, ³Sarah, who married ———— Laws, ⁴Curtis, b 1762, married Nancy Minors, and d 1812; ⁵George, b 1764, married Priscilla Minors; ⁶Vincent Lockerman, b 1767, married Mary Minors, and d 1804

Curtis Beswick (son of John and Phoebe Beswick), married Nancy Minors and d 1812 They had: ¹Mary M, who d unmarried, 1853; ²Curtis Brinckle, b 1796 married Sarah

S Purnell, and d 1880; ³Susannah Lockerman, who married Nathaniel Luff, ⁴Lovey, who married Nathaniel Oliver Bowman

Curtis Brinckle Beswick, second child of Curtis and Nancy (Minors) Beswick, was b in 1796, and d 1880 He married Sarah S Purnell and had issue: ¹John E , ²William P , who married Susan Slaughter; ³Angelina B , who married Wm G Hering, ⁴Robert J., ⁵Sallie A , who married H Masten; ⁶Geo W P ; ⁷Mary E (For descendants of William P and Angelina B , see Minors' Chart)

BARRATT FAMILY.

Philip Barratt Sr , settled on Sassafras river, Cecil County, Maryland, before 1678 and d Aug 1733 He married Jane Merritt, daughter of Thomas and Elizabeth Merritt, of the same county After Philip's death his widow Jane, married Joseph Price, of Kent County, Delaware Philip Barratt, Sr , and his wife Jane had one child, Philip Barratt, Jr , who married Miriam Sipple Philip Barratt Jr , was a prominent man in his day He was b in Cecil, Oct 12, 1730, and d Oct 28, 1784 He was sheriff of Kent County in 1775; member of Assembly 1779-1784 He was the founder of Barratt's Chapel, Kent County, where the American Methodist Episcopal Church was started (See Conrad's History of Delaware, p 892)

Miriam Sipple (wife of Philip Jr), the daughter of Wartman Sipple Jr , b. 1737, married 1755 After the death of Philip Barratt Jr , she married Dr Edward White, of Maryland, and d Aug 3, 1800

Philip Barratt Jr , and Jane Merritt, his wife, had two children, Caleb Barratt, who married Mary Neall, daughter of Jonathan Neall of Talbott County, Maryland, and Andrew Barratt, who married Ann Clarke, daughter of John Clarke 3d, and Elizabeth McNatt.

Ann was b. Feb 28, 1759, married Dec. 10, 1778, and d Oct 9, 1811. Her husband, Andrew Barratt, was b in Kent County, Sept 22, 1756, and d April 18, 1821 He was Judge of the Court of Common Pleas for Kent County in 1 10,

Speaker of the Delaware Senate, in 1812, '13, 14; Presidential Elector 1816, '20; Sheriff of Kent County 1790, '92, member of the Assembly from Kent in 1792.

Andrew and Ann (Clarke) Barratt had a daughter Ann, who married Dr Robert Dill, Ann was b Oct 18, 1781, and d Feb 13, 1814 She and Dr Dill were married Dec 27, 1804 Dr Dill was Adjutant General of Delaware in 1814 He was b about 1778, and d. Dec. 19, 1819. They had a daughter, Ellen Leighton Dill, b. Dec. 1, 1805, d. Dec 25, 1868. She was married Dec 2, 1823 to James Barratt Sr, of Kent, who was b. in that County in 1797, and d in Philadelphia, Feb. 3, 1862 In 1859 he was President of the Corn Exchange in that city

James Barratt Sr, and his wife Ellen Leighton Dill had a son, James Barratt Jr, who married Mary Irvine Cummings The latter couple had a son, Judge Morris S. Barratt, b Aug 23, 1862 He was admitted to the Philadelphia Bar Dec. 1, 1883, and is at the present time Judge of the Philadelphia Court of Common Pleas No 2. Judge Barratt was married to Ellen Levering, b 1874, and they have three children, [1]Norris Stanley Jr, b 1895, [2]Thomas Levering, b. 1899, [3]Edith b 1907

THE CLARKE FAMILY.

John Clarke, a prominent citizen of Delaware, bought land in Kent Jan 10, 1701 (see Book F. p 57). His will is dated Nov. 29, 1727 and was probated Jan 12, 1729 (See Will Book S p. 34).

John Clarke married Elizabeth (Greene) Manlove, widow of Mark Manlove of Kent County. John Clarke d. 1694, while Justice of the Peace for Kent County He conveyed to his wife, Elizabeth, 200 acres of land in Kent County, and after her death he married Catharine ———.

John Clarke and Elizabeth (Greene) Manlove, his wife, had a son John Clarke Jr, who married Elizabeth Brinckle. She was a daughter of William and Elizabeth (Curtis) Brinkle John Clarke Jr., d. early in 1755, and letters of administration were granted to his widow, Elizabeth, Jan 25, 1755.

Elizabeth, after John's death, married Peter Lawler,

(after April 1, 1722 and before Oct. 31, 1825), and in 1741 bought 348 acres "Peter's Neck Farm."

John Clarke Jr., and his wife Elizabeth Brinckle had a son, John Clarke 3d, who married Elizabeth McNatt. John 3d was a member of the General Assembly, from Kent. Oct 1769; Judge Court of Common Pleas of Kent, 1777. He d Dec 18, 1781.

Elizabeth McNatt, wife of John Clarke 3d, was a daughter of John McNatt. Judge Andrew Barratt's bible, in possession of John W Hering, gives the name of the wife of John Clarke Jr, as Elizabeth. John Clarke's will calls his wife Ann; hence the latter must have been the name of a second wife.

John Clarke 3d, and his wife, Elizabeth McNatt had seven children: [1]Ann Clarke, who married Andrew Barratt, as heretofore stated, [2]William; [3]Winlock, Lieutenant U S Navy, d in 1810; [4]Clement, [5]Elizabeth; [6]Sarah; [7]John The latter was a member of the Delaware House, from Kent, 1910, '11, '13, '14, '15 He married —————, and had two children [1]Elizabeth, who married Robert C Pennewill, and [2]Anna, who married Caleb H Sipple Anne Clark Barratt, was b Feb 28, 1759; married to Andrew Barratt Dec 10, 1778, d Oct. 9, 1811.

BRINCKLE'S IN MILITARY SERVICE.

The following members of the Brinckle family who were in the military service of Pennsylvania Colony are copied from Penn. Archives, Vol 1, 5th Series

"List of officers of the Lower Regiment, Newcastle County, 1756 'Col Jacob Van Bibber,' who married Mary Brinckle of Mispillion Hundred, Kent County"

"List of officers for the regiment of Militia for Kent upon Delaware, 1756: 'Lieut Col John Brinckle.'" p. 51

"Lower part of Little Creek Hundred, Kent County, Capt. John Brinckle, 1756." p 55

"Lower part of Mispillion Hundred. Capt Benjamin Brinckle; Lieut John Molleston," p 55

"Names and dates of enlistment of Capt French Battell's Company of ye Lower County Pro m al 1   1 ph Brinckle May 24th p 1 "

MEMBER OF PENN'S COUNCIL.

John Brinckle, of Kent County, Delaware, b. about 1644, was a member of William Penn's Council; member of the Assembly at various times; Associate Justice, Captain of Colonial Militia; etc. His will was probated at Dover in Dec. 8, 1721. In it he makes a devise to his "cousin Peter Brinckle," who married Elizabeth Curtis, etc. (For continuation see Curtis genealogy.)

The aforenamed John Brinckle married ———————— and had a daughter, Elizabeth. She married Arthur Meston and d. in 1821. Her daughter Elizabeth married Rev. Thomas Crawford, of Glasgow, Scotland, the first minister in Delaware, and was buried in the Chancel of Christ Church, Dover.

The children of Elizabeth and Rev. Thomas Crawford were:

Elizabeth, who married Caesar Rodney and had issue: ¹Caesar A. Rodney (signer of the Declaration of Independence), ²George, ³William; ⁴Daniel, ⁵Thomas.

THE HAYES FAMILY.

One of the prominent families of Delaware connected by marriage with Ephraim's branch of the Polk family is that of Hayes. Richard Hayes, the immigrant, was b. in England in 1679. He came to Delaware in 1696 and d. in 1773, at the age of 77 years. Five years after coming to Delaware he was married to Dolly Manlove, by whom he had a son, Captain Nathaniel Hayes, b. 1703, d. 1786. Capt. Hayes married Elizabeth Carlisle, and had a son Richard Hayes, b. 1743, d. 1796, who married Priscilla Polk, b. Nov. 15, 1742, d. 1816, daughter of Chas. Polk 1st, and grand daughter of Ephraim Polk 1st.

Richard d. in 1796 and Priscilla married secondly Pemberton Carlisle. By his wife, Priscilla, Richard Hayes had issue: ¹Manlove, b. 1767, d. 1849, ²Mary, b. about 1769, never married, ³Betsy, b. about 1771 never married, ⁴Alexander, b. about 1773, never married; ⁵Charles, b. about 1775, never married, ⁶Sarah, b. about 1777, never married.

Manlove Hayes, the eldest of the children, as if determined to make up for the celibacy of his two brothers and three sisters, married three times; first Zipporah Laws in 1792; second to Mary Laws; third to Ann Emerson, nee Bell, in 1811 By his first wife, Zipporah Laws, he had issue ¹Judge Alexander Laws Hayes, b 1793, d 1875, married Mrs Isabella McClay, nee Patterson; ²Mary Hayes, b. 1795, married W. K. Lockwood. Issue ¹John A , ²Henry H , ³Anna E , married H Goodwin.

Judge Alexander Laws Hayes and his wife, Mrs Isabella McClay had issue. ¹Edmund, b ———, married ———, d without issue, ²Mary E, b ———, married J Bowman Bell; ³Charles, b ———, d unmarried; ⁴Catharine, b. ———, untraced, ⁵Louisa, b ———, married Alexander Cummins; ⁶Harriet, b. ———, untraced

By his second wife, Mary Laws, Manlove Hayes had a daughter Eliza M Hayes. She was twice married, first to Dr Thomas Stout, by whom she had one child, Peter F Stout Her second husband was William F Boone, of Philadelphia, by whom she had William M and Charles Boone William M married Sally Kennedy of Baltimore

By his third wife, Ann Emerson, nee Bell, Manlove Hayes had issue· ¹Harriet Sykes, b ———, untraced , ²Col Manlove, President Delaware Railway, b ———, married Rebecca C Howell. Issue: ¹Mary, ²Edith, ³Anna Bell; ³Charles Polk, b ———, married Julia F Blake Issue Anna Bell, deceased

WILLIAM POLK'S DESCENDANTS.

William Polk (son of Lieut John Polk, son of Joseph Polk and Sarah Coverdale), was b. in Sussex County, Jan 30, 1781, and d ——— William was twice married, first to Elizabeth Tatman, daughter of Purnell Tatman, secondly to Miss Margaret (Pennington) Cochran, (widow of John T. Cochran), in Dec 1825

By his first wife William Polk had issue

(1) Cyrus Polk, b Jan 3, 1810, d June 27, 1859 Cyrus married Mary Jane Flintham, daughter of Benjamin Flintham

(2) Elizabeth (or Eliza, daughter of William Polk by first wife, was b ———, married at Cantwell's Bridge (now Odessa, Del), to John P Cochran April 1 1833 and d July 24, 1855 Their children were Wm F L Ip " 1831,

²Rebecca, b Nov 2, 1836, married Dr T R Gilispie, ³Charles P., b March 27, 1839, ⁴John, b June 28, 1841, d ——; ⁵Eliza, b Oct 5, 1843, married Wm Green, ⁶Juliana, b. Dec 17, 1848, ⁷Cyrus, b Dec 25, 1852, d. 1853

Julia Polk daughter of William Polk and his second wife, Mrs Margaret (Pennington) Cochran, b. ——, married June 29, 1852, David J. Cummins, President of the Smyrna National Bank They had issue ¹William Polk Cummins; ²Mary P Cummins, ³Susan F Cummins, ⁴Juliet Agnes Cummins; ⁵Edith J. Cummins; ⁶Albert W. Cummins

Charles Tatman Polk, youngest son of William and Elizabeth (or Eliza) Polk, b. Dec 18, 1818, d. March 21, 1863, married in 1852, Sarah Eliza White, daughter of George White, a wealthy farmer near Milford, Del, by whom he had four children ¹Cyrus Polk, b at Odessa, June 15, 1853; ²George White Polk, b Sept 23, 1854, ³Chas T. Polk, b March 27 1856; ⁴William Polk, b. Nov 19, 1857.

THE LUFF FAMILY.

The first one of the Luff family to come to America was Hugh Luff, from England, in 1685. On arrival he secured warrants from Wm Penn for lands in Delaware, on which he settled, and where his descendants have contiued to reside to the present day The first warrant accorded to him was dated August 20, 1685, as appears by the records at Dover, Kent County.

Hugh had two sons, Nathaniel 1st, and Caleb, and these names have come down through succeeding generations. Nathaniel also had a son, Nathaniel Luff 2d, and the latter two sons, Nathaniel P and Caleb Luff

Nathaniel 2d, was married four times. First to Ailsey Fawcett; second to Susannah L. Beswick, third to Mary E Thompson, fourth to Rebecca McCalley A son by the first wife was John S Luff, who served in the Mexican War as First Lieutenant of the First Pennsylvania Regiment He was wounded at Vera Cruz and Cerro Gordo Later he accompanied his half brother, Nathaniel P. Luff, to California during the gold fever.

DR. J. M. LUFF,
Felton, Del.

The second wife of Nathaniel 2d, Sussannah Lockerman Beswick was the progenitress of Dr J. M Luff They were married Aug 31, 1823. She was a daughter of Curtis and Nancy Beswick, who was a daughter of Mary (Polk) Minors, daughter of Charles Polk 1st, and Patience Manlove Nathaniel was b in 1791 and d April 3, 1859 Susannah was b June 9, 1798, and d June 21, 1846

The old Luff plantation in Milford Neck adjoined that of Governor Charles Polk, and a part of the latter, when sold in 1836 was purchased by Nathaniel P, who devised it to his son, Dr J. M Luff, of Felton. Caleb Luff 2d, was in the Delaware Legislature during the Revolution He had a son, Dr Nathaniel Luff, who was a surgeon in Washington's army

Nathaniel P Luff married Mary C Moore, daughter of Thos Jefferson Moore, and sister of Dr. John A Moore The latter's son, John Bassett Moore, was a distinguished international lawyer and counsel to the Paris Commission The Luffs have always been extensive land-holders and leading business men Nathaniel P. owned seven beautiful farms at his death The children of Nathaniel 2d, and Susan L. Luff were:

(1) William B. and Mary Ann Luff, twins, b June 25th and 26th, 1824, and died in infancy

(2) Annie Elizabeth Luff, b Oct 12, 1826 Living in Chicago She married Isaac Preston and had issue: ¹Herbert Preston, who d July 25, 1907. He married Beatrice Bruce. No issue. ²Thomas C Preston, who married Alice Carley Williamson

(3) William N Luff, b Sept 23, 1862, married Jean Allen and they have William Thomas and Robert Allen The Prestons all reside in Chicago

(4) Nathaniel Peterson Luff, b Jan 13, 1829, d Sept 25, 1901, married Mary C Moore

(5) Caleb Lockerman Luff, b Feb. 12, 1832, married Elmire Moore

(6) Susan Luff, b. June 21 1834 married Andrew Logan.

(7) Joshua B Luff, b Je... married Emma Harrington

(8) Wm. Joseph Luff, b Aug. 23, 1841. Drowned April 11, 1843.

The children of Nathiel Peterson Luff and Mary C Moore were. ¹Dr. Jefferson Moore Luff, b Dec. 1, 1858, ²Annie Mary Luff, b. March 20, 1864; ³Addie Beswick Luff, b July 7, 1870. All unmarried

Caleb Lockerman Luff married Elmire Moore, in 1866, and had issue ¹Herbert P Luff, b Oct 26, 1867; ²Katie Moore Luff, b July 7, 1870 She married Wm Case and had a child Milla Natalie Case, b Aug. 27, 1893.

Susan Luff and her husband, Andrew Logan, had issue ¹Henry C Logan, b ———, d. March 6, 1894; ²Thomas C. Logan, b ———, d Aug 9, 1909; ³William B Logan, b ———, married Grace ————, ⁴Elliott Logan, b ——— None of these had children

Joshua Beswick Luff, who married Emma Harrington, first, and Susan A. Callahan second, had by the first. ¹Nathaniel H Luff, b Nov 24, 1859, d single Nov. 1, 1895; ²Sarah M. Luff, b Nov 7, 1862, d in infancy, ³Caleb B Luff, b Feb 2, 1861, d in Petaluma, Cal , March 9, 1902, married Evelyn Dalton and left two children, Genevieve and Hale Harper Luff; ⁴Emma H Luff, b Feb 4, 1864, married first Oliver J Hart, second Thomas Sliter. No issue by either husband, and the widow now resides in Washington, D C.

By his second wife Susan A Callahan, Joshua B Luff had. ¹Dr. Joshua Homer Luff, b ———, who married Clara Shoemaker Johnson She d. May 29, 1907, leaving children. ¹Elizabeth; ²Gertrude and ³Virginia Gertrude married John Harrison Rathman, no issue

Dr. Joshua Homer Luff is a successful practition at Hudson, N. Y. Caleb B Luff, his half-brother, went to California when a young boy and became in time manager of Hale Bros store at Petaluma and died there He had a very successful business career, was making a large salary, and was highly esteemed in the community.

Dr Jefferson Moore Luff, of Felton, son of Nathaniel P Luff, is a prominent and wealthy man in his town, and has frequently been solicited to offer himself for political preferment. In 1879 he commenced the study of medicine, graduating in 1881 from Jefferson Medical College, at Philadelphia He at once entered upon a lucrative practice and also owns and conducts a drug store in Felton.

JOHN POLK, SON OF EPHRAIM, 1st.

John Polk (second son of Ephraim and Elizabeth (Williams) Polk, was born about 1705, and died in 1782. He married Sarah Vaughan, daughter of Lt Col. Joseph Vaughan, the distinguished commander of "The Blue Hen's Chickens the only Continental infantry regiment from Delaware in the Revolutionary War, and which, by its valor on many fields, won imperishable renown It participated in all the battles of Washington at the north, and its ranks were sadly decimated, under Gates and Green in the Carolinas, being finally reduced to a handful It lost heavily at both the Cowpens and Camden. Its first two commanders were Col John Haslett, from Jan. 19, 1776, to Jan 3, 1777. Col David Hall, from April 5, 1777, to Dec 14, 1779 Col Haslett fell at the hard fought battle of Princeton

At the battle of Germantown, Oct 4, 1777, Col Hall was severely wounded and incapacitated for further service In the same battle were other Polks—Lt Col. Wm Polk, of North Carolina, whose regiment had come North in the brigade of Gen Francis Nash, who was killed in the battle. Ephraim Polk, 3d, of Sussex County, Delaware, who was a member of Capt Joseph Rhoad's Company, Col Wm Wills' Philadelpha regiment, Joab Polk (brother of Ephraim, 3d) of Capt Bateman Lloyd's company, Second New Jersey regiment ,and several others of the name

Col Thos Polk (of Mecklenburg Declaration fame, father of Lt Col Wm Polk) commanded a squadron of North Carolina Cavalry and was not in the battle, being detailed to escort the American baggage and supply train of seven hundred wagons, from Philadelphia to a place of safety at the Moravian settlement, Bethlehem All the bells of the city were taken along, including the famous Liberty Bell, which, the Moravian church records at Bethehem say, fell from its wagon onto the street before the wagon train was parked

Colonel Hall's wound being so severe that he could not

continue in the service, on Dec 14, 1879, Lt Col Joseph Vaughan was placed in charge of the regiment and continued in command of it until the close of the war In the battle of Camden, Aug 16, 1780, it was sadly depleted, the brunt of the fighting in that sanguinary conflict being sustained by it and the Maryland regiment Before the end of the war its numbers were reduced to about two companies or less It entered the service with full ranks, received many recruits during the war, and the small remnant of it that survived the long struggle mournfully attested the valor of its rank and file.

John Polk and Sarah Vaughan left six children, viz [1]William, [2]John, [3]Levin; [4]Eunice Jane; [5]Betsy, [6]Sally William was a leading Whig in his neighborhood He was one of the Minute Men and a member of the Committee of Vigilance during the Revolution, and afterwards Surveyor General of Delaware. He married, first Rachel Bell, second, Leah Marshall William was a man of great enterprise and acquired a large fortune in lands and mills in Sussex County He owned three or four mills at his death, and also large tracts of land in Harrison County, Virginia which, by his will, executed on Nov 20, 1786, he devised equally to his four children. His lands in Sussex adjoined those of the Calloways. Fienys, Williams, Greers, Kennys and Bacons, as recited in his will William died about 1796 His children were · [1]Robert; [2]Anne, [3]Leah [4]Sally Andrews Robert married Elizabeth Kinney and left one child, Nichola, who died in 1846, unmarried Anne married William Ready They moved to Ohio and had several children. Leah married Wm. Polk, her first cousin (son of John Polk, son of John, son of Ephraim), and left four children [1]Eliza; [2]John; [3]Southey Andrews, [4]Washington The latter was lost at sea in 1839. Sally Andrews Polk, the last daughter of William, 1st, son of John, second son of Ephraim, married Levin Collins, an eminent surveyor Their children were [1]Luther, [2]Sally; [3]Luraine, [4]Hiram [5]Leah; [6]Levin Luther Collins married, first, Luraine, daughter of John Collins Their children were: [1]Levin P, [2]Mary E His second wife was Eleanor Cannon, a widow, whose maiden name was Leonard, of Somerset County Maryland Their children were Luraine and George Hamilton Sally

Collins married Anthony Collins, and they had issue ¹William Henry; ²Leah Anne; ³Cyrus Edwin. They moved to Ohio. Luraine Collins, second daughter of Sally Polk and Levin Collins, married Capt Elisha Purnell, and they had issue ¹William Thomas, ²Emeline, ³Sally; ⁴Hiram T, ⁵Phillip Cannon. Hiram Collins, second son of Sally Polk and Levin Collins, married Susan Armstrong, of Laurel, Del. Their children were ¹Martha, ²Eliza J.; ³Euphemia,⁴Edwin, ⁵Caleb Polk, ⁶Joshua Dallas, ⁷Cyrus. Levin Collins, third son and youngest child of Levin Collins and Sally Polk, married Julia Ann Moore, daughter of Luther Moore, of Sussex. They had but one child, a daughter, George Anne.

John Polk, who was the second son of John Polk and Sarah Vaughan, was also a leading Whig and Minute Man of Sussex County. On several occasions these brothers shouldered their guns and assisted in quelling Tories bent on mischief. William was particularly bold and aggressive toward the enemies of his country. John first married Betty Moore, daughter of Thomas Moore, of Sussex, and had one child, William. John married, secondly, Polly Dolbee, and had: ¹William; ²John, ³Josiah. Polly was a sister of the mother of Judge James Robbins, of Worcester County, Maryland. William, son of John Polk and Betsy Moore, married Leah Polk, daughter of his father's brother, William, and had ¹Eliza, ²John, ³Southey Andrews, ⁴Washington. John died before he was 21, unmarried. Washington was drowned at sea in 1839. Southey Andrews resided at Laurel, Sussex County, and was engaged in business there as a merchant. He was a man of fine character and intelligence. Eliza, b ——, d 1846, married Isaac Williams, and left one child, Elizabeth Polk. The second wife of William, son of John and Betty Moore, was the widow Hetty Glover, of Philadelphia. They had two sons, who died in infancy. William died in 1821, aged 44 years. He was a man adorned with almost every virtue. He inherited a good estate, and made two fortunes afterwards. But through his kindness to and confidence in all men, he died in r I b n I l m h ae own to sue any He mi and the suavity of his manners and the purity of his heart made him a favorite wherever he went and gave him uncommon popularity

John Polk, son of John Polk and Polly Dolbee (and half brother of William afore-mentioned), was born in 1779 and died in 1842, a bachelor. He was a merchant in Laurel. No man, perhaps, ever enjoyed the confidence and affections of those who knew him, in a higher degree. He possessed a very vigorous mind, and business habits that crowned his labors with a handsome fortune. He died in 1842, at the age of 63.

Josiah Polk, second son of John Polk and Polly Dolbee, was a farmer in Sussex and Captain of militia. He marched to Lewistown during the war of 1812, to defend it against the attacks of the enemy. He was born about 1781, and died in 1839, unmarried. Levin Polk, third son of John Polk and Sarah Vaughan, died at the age of twenty-two years, unmarried.

Eunice Jane Polk, eldest daughter and fourth child of John Polk and Sarah Vaughan, was born Oct. 2, 1743, in Sussex County, and died in Woodford County, Kentucky, May 12, 1809. On account of her primness and amiable manner she was popularly called "Nicey" Polk. She married Capt John Scroggin, one of seven gallant brothers who were officers in the Revolution. In the fall of 1793, Capt. Scroggin and family emigrated to Kentucky with several kinsmen—Ephraim Polk, 3d, the Morris, Nutters, Coverdales and others.

Betsy Polk, second daughter of John Polk and Sarah Vaughan, married Lowder Sirman, of Sussex County, Delaware. Their children were ¹Lowder; ²Betsy; ³Levin; ⁴John Lowder Sirman, Jr., married Sally Calloway, of Essex, and they had issue ¹William; ²James; ³John Polk; ⁴Lowder; ⁵Nancy; ⁶Maria; ⁷Sarah. William married Lovey Smith, and they had but one child, Sarah Elizabeth. William, second wife was Polly Smith, sister to Lovey, by whom he had William L and Lovey Ellen. James Sirman, son of Lowder Sirman, Jr., married Lovey Elliott and had issue: ¹Eleanor; ²Samuel; ³Wm Spicer; ⁴Benjamin. John Polk Sirman, son of Lowder Sirman Jr., married Elizabeth Staten, daughter of Rev. Thomas W Staten, of Worcester County Md. Issue:

¹Isaac Warner, ²John William, ³Sarah Ellen. Betsy Sirman, daughter of Betsy Polk and Lowder Sirman, Sr., died unmarried Levin Sirman married Betsy Vaughan and had. ¹George; ²Joseph, ³Elizabeth, ⁴William H.; ⁵John C., ⁶Eleanor; ⁷Mary

George married Miss Leonard, of Somerset County, Maryland Joseph married, first, Sarah Morris, of Sussex; second, Ann Thompson. William H. married Hannah Morris Elizabeth married Stewart Shockley, of Somerset County. Eleanor married Levin Sullivan, of Sussex. Mary married John Leonard, of Somerset County.

John, the youngest son of Betsy Polk and Lowder Sirman, Sr., married Mary Derickson, daughter of General Samuel Derickson, of Sussex, a man of distinction John died without issue

Sally Polk, youngest child of John Polk and Sarah Vaughan, married John Bacon, of Sussex, and had one child. Henry Bacon, a substantial, highly respected farmer and citizen, who was three times married, first, to Mary Parker, daughter of George Parker, of Somerset County, Maryland, by whom he had issue: (1) Sally Bacon, who married Wm Knowles, of Laurel, Del They had issue: ¹George, ²Mary A ; ³Martha J , ⁴Sally, ⁵Olivia, ⁶Emma; (2) George Bacon married and settled in Missouri, and had a family, (3) Mary Bacon married David A Moore and died without issue; (4) William Bacon married Maria Dashiel, daughter of Winder Dashiel, of Laurel Del, and settled in Somerset They had issue· ¹John; ²Mary, ³Winder; ⁴Rebecca, (5) Nancy Bacon married Thos Philips, of Seaford, Del., and had one child, James, (6) Elizabeth married Henry Brereton, of Somerset. and emigrated to the Southwest. Issue not known. Henry Bacon's second wife was Priscilla Fookes, of Worcester, Maryland, by whom he had issue ¹Henry, died unmarried, ²Jonathan, who married a widow Vickers, daughter of Thomas Fookes, of Delaware He died leaving a daughter. Henry Bacon's third wife was Mary Hearne, of Sussex County, Delaware Issue ¹James, ²John; ³Thomas ⁴Samuel, ⁵Levin, ⁶Lavenia, ⁷Henry Central Kentucky

CHAPTER LIV.

POLK-SCROGGIN KINSHIP.

On the arrival of Capt John Scroggin and Eunice Jane (Polk) Scroggin, his wife, in Kentucky in the fall of 1793, they established themselves on a fine farm in Bourbon County, about twelve miles from Cynthiana There they lived, prospered, raised their children and died, and their bodies were interred in the family burying ground on the farm It is said that Capt Scroggin's brother, Samuel, accompanied by Ephraim Polk, 3d, and several others from Sussex, had previously come to Kentucky (in 1786) to view the land and fix on locations for their respective families And when they came in 1793, they fixed their homes not far apart, some locating in Bourbon and some in Woodford County John and Samuel settled in what is now Harrison—then a part of Bourbon—and Robert and other brothers in Woodford County All the related families that came—the Scroggins, Nutters, Polks and Morris—brought with them from Delaware slaves and live stock

The descendants of the Scroggin family are among the very few people in Kentucky or the West who can claim that royal blood flows in their veins, as they descend directly from the Princess Fantalina, daughter of Philip V, of Spain. The genealogy of the Scroggin family, which has been carefully preserved, and a copy of which was given to the author of this book a quarter of a century ago, is as follows

GENESIS OF AMERICAN SCROGGIN FAMILY.

An Irish naval officer, named Joseph Scroggin, who was in the service of Philip V, of Spain, became enamored of that monarch's daughter, the Princess Fantalina She reciprocated the affection of the impetuous Hibernian, who abducted her, took her on board his vessel, and sailing away, married her

In 1714 they came to America, landing at Baltimore, bringing land grants, diamonds, gold snuff boxes and other jewels. Having several grants of land, Joseph settled near Snow Hill, in the Colony of Maryland, where he died. Their only child, Joseph Scroggin, Jr., was born in 1715. In 1740, at the age of twenty-five, Joseph Scroggin, Jr., was married to Sarah Ann Caldwell, whose sister, Martha Caldwell, was the mother of Hon. John C. Calhoun of South Carolina, one of America's greatest men.

Doubtless, by reason of the fact that the high temper of both the Irish and Spanish races were united in him, Joseph Scroggin, Jr., appears to have been a self-willed and uncontrollable youth, falling out with his mother, leaving her, refusing to speak to her, or to submit to her control, and, it is said, not even the taming yoke of matrimony could cool his fiery nature.

Joseph Scroggin, Jr., and his wife, Sarah Caldwell, had thirteen children: [1]Nancy, b. May 13, 1741, [2]John, b. Nov. 13, 1743; [3]Mary, b. Nov. 13, 1745; [4]Joseph, b. June 17, 1747, [5]Samuel, b. June 14, 1749, [6]Sarah, b. Sept 14, 1750; [7]Robert Calwell, b. March 1, 1753, [8]William, b. April 24, 1755, [9]Mildred, b. June 15, 1757, [10]Philip, b. Sept 5, 1759; [11]Annie Caldwell, b. June 18, 1761; [12]Thomas Clark, b. July 4, 1762, [13]Matilda, b. Aug 21, 1764. Princess Fantalina, the mother of Joseph Scroggin, Jr., died Dec 31, 1770.

Of the foregoing "baker's dozen" of children. Nancy married James Polk, in Delaware. Capt John, as stated, married Eunice Jane Polk. Mary married Capt Revel Wharton, who was killed on his own vessel in an engagement with the British, in the War of 1812. She afterward married Wm F. Boone, of Philadelphia. Mary's only child (by her first marriage) married Elisha English, of Kentucky, grandfather of Hon. Wm. H. English, of Indiana, who was candidate for Vice President on the ticket with General Hancock. Mr English's daughter, Rosa English married Dr Willoughby Walling, formerly of Louisville, now of Chicago, who was United States Consul at Edinburgh, Scotland, under President Cleveland. Dr. and Mrs Walling have two sons, Willoughby George and Capt Wm F English. Capt Wm F. English resides at Indianapolis, and is a very wealthy man. Hon. Wm. H. English left a large fortune, devising $750,000 to Mrs. Rosa Walling, his daughter, and the balance of his property, in realty, to his son, William. The latter served as Captain in the U. S. Army, in the Spanish-American War. He was on the staff of Maj. Gen. Joe Wheeler. At the battle of San Juan his horse was shot and fell on his leg, badly injuring him. Taken to the field hospital, he contracted fever and came near dying. He refused to take pay for his services in the army.

Samuel Scroggin married Betty Collins. He was a Lieutenant in the Revolution, from Delaware. He came to Kentucky, as stated, first in 1786, to view the country, and again in 1793, and located in Bourbon County.

Sarah married Samuel Davis, of Fayette County, Ky., and lived in or near Lexington. Robert Caldwell Scroggin, born 1753, married Ann Culver. Robert was an Ensign in the Revolution and emigrated to Woodford County in 1790, coming from Snow Hill, Md., the same locality where his father, Joseph Scroggin, Jr., had settled. Mildred Scroggin was devotedly attached to an officer who was killed in the Revolutionary War, and faithful to that attachment, she died unmarried. Philip Scroggin, also a Captain in the Revolution, came to Kentucky in 1793. In the War of 1812 he again joined the army to fight the old enemy, the British, and was killed in battle. Annie Caldwell Scroggin married James Davis, a brother of Sarah's husband, and lived in or near Lexington, Ky. Thomas Clarke Scroggin, who was a Lieutenant in the Revolution, married Isabella Buchanan and emigrated to Kentucky. Mathilde Scroggin married a Methodist preacher, Rev. Joseph Collins, of Baltimore. The seven Scroggin brothers were all over six feet in height and all were officers in the Revolution. They seemed to inherit the religious tendencies of their mother (Sarah Caldwell), who was of a French Huguenot family, grafted onto Scotch-Irish Presbyterians. Her descendants generally followed the latter faith.

An interesting incident is related of Capt. John Scroggin, while he was on his way to Kentucky in 1793, which showed his courage and kindness of heart. The Indian War was then in progress under General Anthony Wayne, and emigrants bound down the Ohio River were in constant peril from bands of savages who infested the north shore of that stream. Frequent attacks were made on the boats of emigrants, and many were killed. White men who had been captured in childhood by the Indians, and raised up to become veritable savages, were employed as decoys.

While descending the Ohio, a white man appeared on the Ohio shore, and begged piteously to be taken aboard. Although vigorously opposed by his companions, who suspected the purpose of the appeal, Capt. Scroggin insisted on succoring the man, saying he could not find it in his heart to leave a fellow creature in distress. The boat was turned toward the shore, and when close to it a band of ambushed Indians fired on the party, wounding several, but killing none. The boat immediately put off and its occupants escaped further injury. Capt. Scroggins' wife, Eunice Jane Polk, urged him to secure a large body of land, but he said it was useless, there being so much land, which he could get at any time. Robert Caldwell Scroggin's grand-daughters, Miss Scroggin and Mrs. Judge Haviland, reside at Cynthiana, Ky. They are children of Robert Culver Scroggin. Robert had a grandson, John Henderson Scroggin, son of Joseph Scroggin, whose wife, Lucinda Bruce, was a daughter of Capt Charles Polk's daughter, Sallie, who, with her mother and three other children were captured by Indians in Aug., 1782, in Nelson County, Ky., and taken to Detroit and sold to the British Commandant. For account of this capture, and of the Bruce kinsmen, see chapter relating to Capt Charles Polk, the Indian fighter, who came from Pittsburg to Louisville in 1780 and afterward moved to Indiana and died near Vincennes, 1823.

The muster roll of troops from Kentucky in the War of 1812, show the following. "Levin Polk Scroggin, First Corporal in Capt. Maurice Langhorne's Bourbon County Company, First Rifle Regiment Kentucky Militia, commanded by Lieut. Col John Allen. Mustered in Aug 15; mustered out Oct. 14, 1812."

Levin Polk Scroggin was the seventh child of

Eunice Jane Polk and Capt John Scroggin On May 20th, Robert Scroggin again joined the army to fight the British, and Indians, with the rank of First Lieutenant of Capt. Richard Matson's Bourbon County Company, Col. Richard M Johnson's Kentucky Mounted Infantry. He was in the battle of the Thames (Oct 5, 1813) won by the army of Kentuckians under Gen. Wm. Henry Harrison and Governor Isaac Shelby. Col. Allen's regiment, the First Regiment Kentucky Rifles, of which Levin Polk Scroggin was a member, was in the battle and massacre at River Raisin (Jan. 22, 1813), where Col Allen, Capt McCracken and many others were barbarously slain after being made prisoners The late John A Scroggin, of Versailles, Ky., a prominent merchant of that place, was a son of Levin Polk Scroggin

GALLANT OFFICERS OF THE REVOLUTION.

All the seven Scroggin boys (sons of Joseph Scroggin, Jr) joined the patriot army under Washington and were officers in the Revolutionary Army, acquitting themselves with distinction. Capt. John Scroggin died at his home in Woodford County, Kentucky, Dec 14, 1812 In a letter to the author, of date Feb 25, 1892, J. H. Scroggin, of Bruceville, Knox County, Indiana, says·

"Capt John Scroggin married one of my grandmothers, Eunice Jane Polk, daughter of John, and grand-daughter of Ephraim Polk, 1st, third son of Capt Robert Bruce Polk and Magdalen (Tasker) Porter Eunice was born Oct 2, 1743, in Maryland, and died in Kentucky, May 29, 1809 They had the following children· [1]Elizabeth, b Oct 10, 1768, [2]William, b Jan 29, 1770, [3]Samuel, b Dec 30, 1771; [4]John, b May 12, 1774, [5]Sarah Ann Caldwell, b Oct 9, 1776, [6]Joseph, b Feb 9, 1779; [7]Levin Polk, b. March 26, 1782

"Joseph Scroggin (sixth child of John and Eunice Jane (Polk) Scroggin married Nancy Jane Holmes, an elder sister of Hetty R Bruce, my stepmother, in Kentucky. Joseph died Nov. 4, 1843 Nancy Jane, his wife, born Aug. 20, 1783, died Dec 8, 1846 They had the following children, born in Kentucky: [1]Eunice Jane, b. July 23, 1807 d young in Kentucky, [2]John Henderson (my father), b Feb 6, 1809, [3]William Weston, b Dec. 7, 1810, d. unmarried, Oct 10, 1842; ⁴Ann Elizabeth, b. March 28, 1813, never married, ⁵Josiah Love b April 8, 1815, never married; ⁶Sallie Jane, b Feb. 16, 1818, married and raised one son, all dead; ⁷Hetty, b June 15, 1820, never married, ⁸Joseph D, b Dec. 20, 1825; ⁹Nancy Ann, b March 23, 1828, never married There is but one left to represent my grandfather's family, and that is myself

"John Henderson Scroggin, son of Joseph and Nancy Ann Scroggin (nee Holmes), and grandson of John and Eunice Jane (Polk) Scroggin, and great-grandson of Joseph and Sarah Ann Scroggin (nee Caldwell), and great-great grandson of Capt Joseph and Fantalina Scroggin, is the record of descent. The Princess Fantalina was the eldest daughter of Philip V, first Bourbon King of Spain Philip V was a grandson of Louis XIV of France, and married Marie Louise Gabriella of Savoy

'John Henderson Scroggin married Lucinda Bruce, a daughter of William and Sally Bruce (nee Polk) My father was born Feb 6, 1809, and my mother one day later, but he died many years before she did—he on March 3, 1848, she on Feb 21, 1870 They had issue. ¹Joseph H, (myself), b May 17, 1836; ²William Bruce, b Sept 3, 1838, d June 4, 1857, ³Henry Harrison, b. Sept. 11, 1840, ⁴George Wilson, b May 5, 1842, ⁵Sallie Jane, b Jan. 3, 1845 The latter was married Dec 20, 1869, to James William Clark, of Nebraska, and they have four children.

'In the War of the Rebellion, brothers Henry and George and myself enlisted in the Union Army Six months later, Henry fell sick and died I was laid up in hospital for over a year and then discharged as an invalid Brother George served on for more than three years, but on the second day of the battle of Nashville, between the armies of Hood and Thomas, Dec 16, 1864, and late in the evening, he was shot and died in a few days

'My own family consists of Joseph Hamilton, born May 17, 1836, married Nancy Jane Gano, born July 24, 1837 Issue ¹Mattie Bruce, b Feb 15, 1868, ²Lucinda May, b Nov 28, 1869, ⁰⁰ ⁰⁰⁰ ⁰⁰⁰⁰ ⁰⁰ ⁰ ⁰⁰ ⁰⁰ ⁰⁰⁰⁰ ⁰ ⁰ Ann, b Oct ⁰⁰ ⁰⁰⁰⁰ ⁰⁰ ⁰⁰ ⁰ July ⁰⁰ ⁰⁰⁰⁰

"Nancy Scroggin, eldest child of Joseph and Sarah Ann (Caldwell) Scroggin, b May 13, 1741, married a Mr. Polk, of Philadelphia. Her husband and Eunice Jane Polk, who married Capt John Scroggin, were cousins"

JOSEPH POLK, SR., SON OF EPHRAIM, 1st.

Joseph Polk, third son of Ephraim Polk 1st, b. 1720, d in Delaware in 1812 He married Sarah Coversdale and they had issue.

(1) Isaac, b 1751, d. 1824 unmarried

(2) John, b April 1, 1754, d Aug 12, 1811, married March 3, 1776 Amelia Hurst

(3) Joseph Jr, b. 1758, d 1823; married first Miss Layton; second Miss Neal

(4) Jesse, b 1761, went west and never heard of again

(5) Priscilla, b 1763, said to have gone to South Carolina She is believed to have been the second wife of Capt. Wm Polk, of Accomac County, Va, who, after the Revolutionary War, settled and died in South Carolina, some of his children emigrating to Ohio and Indiana

(6) Ann, b 1765, also said to have gone to South Carolina

JOSEPH POLK, JR., SON OF JOSEPH POLK, SR.

Joseph Polk Jr, (third son of Joseph Polk and Sarah Coverdale), b. 1758, d 1823, was twice married His first wife was Miss ———— Layton, of Sussex, by whom he had one child, Layton Polk His wife dying soon after, Joseph married secondly Miss Neal, of Sussex, by whom he had five or six children. The name of but one of these is preserved—Margaret Neal Polk, who married her cousin Geba, next to the youngest son of John Polk and Amelia Hurst, and had by him six children

Jesse Polk (fourth son of Joseph Polk Sr, and Sarah Coverdale), born 1761, went west and was never heard from afterwards

The two last children of Joseph Polk Sr. and Sarah Coverdale were Priscilla, b 1763, and Ann, b 1765. What became of them is not certainly known. Josiah F Polk, in 1849, in a letter to Col Wm H Winder, said: "They are said to have gone to South Carolina"

In this connection it may be stated that a Capt. William Polk, who was an active Whig and commanded the local militia company, resided in Accomac County, on the Eastern Shore of Virginia, for some years before and during the Revolution He had a sister named Martha, but who the parents of Capt William and Martha were, the writer has not ascertained. The second wife of this Capt. Wm. Polk is said to have been Priscilla Polk possibly the above mentioned daughter of Joseph Polk

Geba (ninth child of John Polk and Amelia Hurst), b 1794, d Sept. 6, 1881, emigrated in 1812 to Logan County, Ohio, where his uncle, Joseph Polk and family had settled a short time before In 1818 he was married to his cousin Margaret Neal Polk, daughter of Joseph Polk by whom he had six children. The record in the family Bible reads

Geba Polk, b Sept 6, 1851, aged 56 years. Margaret Neal, wife of Geba Polk, d. Aug. 20, 1882, aged 87 years, 3 months and 20 days

The children of this marriage were·

(1) Robert Neal Polk, b March 5, 1824.

(2) Sarah Amelia Polk, b Oct. 15, 1825

(3) William Geba Polk, b ———, d at Lexington, Ky, in hospital, Dec 3, 1862, aged 34 years, 11 months and five days.

(4) Margaret Miranda Polk, b 1837, d Oct. 16, 1868

(5) Layton Polk, d Aug. 28, 1851, aged 20 years, 10 months and 13 days

(6) Mary Elizabeth Polk, b Aug 20, 1834, d Dec 7, 1861

The intermarriages of the above children were

Robert Neal Polk to Sarah Jane Harper, Feb 21, 1852. She d Dec. 17, 1858 Issue, one child Margaret Jane Polk, b March 5, 1856 The latter married Irwin Hawkins, and had issue· [1]Alexander [2]Ovid, [3]Charles Hawkins Ovid and Charles are living at Springfield, Ohio

Robert Neal Polk married secondly to Elizabeth Ann Wren-Fuson, in July, 1859, by whom he had

(1) Ada Elizabeth Polk, b May 7, 1860.
(2) Charles William Polk, b April 7, 1863.
(3) Mary Amelia Polk, b Dec. 18, 1865.
(4) Elmer Geba Polk, b Nov 28, 1867
(5) Eva Christine Polk, b. April 8, 1873.
(6) Joseph Robert Polk, b June 22, 1875

Ada Elizabeth married S E Caldwell, Nov. 29, 1882. Issue

(1) Edward Raymond Caldwell, b July 15, 1884, d. Oct. 16, 1887
(2) Estelle Maud Caldwell, b Dec 13, 1885
(3) Ada Mae Caldwell, b Nov. 8, 1888
(4) Oro Evelyn Caldwell, b April 4, 1892.
(5) Eva Lillian Caldwell, b Jan 15, 1895.
(6) Marion Christine Caldwell, b Feb 21, 1903, d Aug 26, 1903.

Charles William Polk (son of Robert Neal Polk), married Aug 6, 1885, Maria Pope Issue

(1) Franklin Robert Polk, b. Aug 20, 1886
(2) Helen Elizabeth Polk, b Sept. 21, 1889
(3) Florence Polk, b. March 25, 1892
(4) Charles Kenneth Polk, b Nov 18, 1896, d Nov 22, 1897

The above family reside at Zanesfield, Ohio

Mary Elizabeth Polk(daughter of Robert Neal Polk), married John M Barger, Aug 25, 1907

Eva Christine Polk (daughter of Robert Neal Polk), married Charles Otho Frields, Dec. 24, 1896 He d Jan 8, 1899; no issue

Joseph Robert Polk (son of Robert Neal Polk), married Marion J Porter, Feb. 18, 1903 Issue

(1) Pauline Frields Polk, b April 18, 1905
(2) Wesley Porter Polk, b Aug 14, 1907

Sarah Amelia Polk (second child of Geba Polk and Margaret Neal Polk), married Aaron Allebaugh, March 1, 1855; no issue They reside at Quincy, Ohio.

William Geba Polk (second son of Geba and Margaret

Neal Polk), 15th Ohio Infantry, who died in hospital at Lexington, Ky., Dec 3, 1862, the second year of the Civil War, was not married. His remains rest in the Federal burying ground, within the Lexington Cemetery, in which are interred nearly one thousand men who fell in battle or died of disease in hospitals. A tombstone marks his grave.

Margaret Miranda Polk (fourth child of Geba and Margaret Neal Polk), married Benjamin Cretcher, Aug 14, 1855, and d Oct 16, 1868. They had issue:

(1) Robert Cretcher, b May 29, 1857, married April 18, 1880 to Hettie May Melhorn.

(2) Nannie Cretcher, b Oct 19, 1859, married Frank McCormick, June 24, 1879. Issue ¹Ora Maria, b June 10, 1883, married Logan W Hale, July 27, 1904; ²Warren, b Aug. 14, 1905

(3) Ben W Cretcher, born April 13, 1864, married Elsie Hamilton, June 10, 1895

Layton Polk (fifth child of Geba and Margaret Neal Polk), d Aug 1851, aged 21 years, and unmarried

Mary Elizabeth Polk (sixth child of Geba and Margaret Neal Polk), married John C Cretcher, Sept 27, 1857, and had issue.

(1) Lutrecia Cretcher, b. July 3, 1858, d March 4, 1880, married June 10, 1879 George R Null

(2) William Harrison Cretcher, b. March 20, 1860, d in infancy.

(3) Margaret Elizabeth Cretcher, b. Nov 14, 1861, d. March 1884, married William Bronson, April 1880.

Robert Neal Polk and his daughter Mrs Emma C Fields, reside at Fall River, Mass. Elmer G and Joseph Polk, and Mrs Ada Caldwell, at Alliance, Ohio, Mrs. Mary A Barger at Urbana, Ohio

ROBERT POLK AND FAMILY.

Robert Polk (tenth child of John Polk and Amelia (Hurst) Polk), b June 25, 1797, d ——, 1854. He married in 1827, Margaret Reybold, the accomplished daughter of Major Philip Reybold, of Delaware. Their children

(1) William Reybold Polk, b. ———, married May 30, 1855, Kate Rothwell, Summit Bridge, Del.

(2) Anna Eliza Polk, b ———, d in infancy

(3) Anna Louisa Polk, b ———, d Feb. 2, 1886

(4) Margaret Polk, b ———, d 1837, unmarried

(5) Robert Polk, b ———, d 1896, unmarried, at Richmond, Va

(6) Albert H Polk, b ———, d young

(7) Matilda Reybold Polk, b ———, d. young, in 1843

(8) Henry C Polk, b. ———, d ———, unmarried

(9) John Philip Reybold Polk, b. Oct 18, 1845, d ———, 1901, at Charlotte, N C, unmarried

(10) Elizabeth Polk, b ———, d at 16 years of age, unmarried

Of these ten children Robert Polk and Margaret Reybold, only five attained to maturity, and only one, William R., married and reared a family.

John Philip Reybold Polk, the writer is greatly indebted for data of the Polk family An elegant, accomplished and courteous gentleman, distinguished in appearance and universally esteemed, he had few equals He took great pride and interest in the family history, unlike some with whom the writer has had to deal with during the preparation of this work

John P R Polk was assiduous in the collection of data, and prompt in reporting it During the correspondence between himself and the writer, he fell ill of grippe, at Charlotte, N C, in 1901, and suffering a relapse after getting up and believing himself recovered, he fell ill again and died quite suddenly Receiving no answer to a letter sent him, the writer inquired of his brother Wm R Polk, of Birmingham, Ala, concerning him and received in reply the news that he was dead

"When the Civil War was declared, the Federal gunboats burned four of Mr Polk's vessels He was a Southern sympathizer, and offered for active service, but on examination, was pronounced physically incapacitated for bearing arms. He became a blockade runner, a position for which only a few intrepid spirits were fitted, but he combined those elements,

JOHN P. R. POLK.
Wilmington, Del.

THE NEW YORK
PUBLIC LIBRARY

ASTOR, LENOX AND
TILDEN FOUNDATIONS

a brave heart and a cool head. In six weeks he had forty-six thousand dollars in gold, or its equivalent, and had made for himself a great reputation as a blockade runner. There was a thousand dollars offered for his capture and the gunboats were keeping a close watch. His adventures and hairbreadth escapes would fill a volume.

CHILDREN OF WM. REYBOLD POLK.

"The children of the marriage of William Reybold Polk and Kate Rothwell Polk were five:

(1) Robert Edgar Polk, d young
(2) Annie Amelia Polk, d aged 11 years.
(3) William Rothwell Polk, b 1862
(4) Robert Henry Polk, b 1865
(5) Catherine Gertrude Polk, b. 1869, d. 1893, unmarried

"William Rothwell Polk (third child of William Reybold Polk and Kate (Rothwell) Polk), b 1862, married 1898, Katerina Stella Henry, of Delaware. He owns and operates a manufactory of electrical motors and dynamos, etc , and resides in Atlanta.

"Robert Henry Polk (fourth child of William Reybold Polk and Kate (Rothwell) Polk), is General Superintendent of the Bell Telephone Exchange at Savannah, Ga. He is a brilliant young man with a bright future before him. He married December 25, 1893, Agnes Ayars, nee Hoeyt."

CHAPTER LV

CHILDREN OF EPHRAIM POLK, 2nd.

As before stated, Ephraim Polk, 2d, was born about 1709 His marriage to Mary Coverdale, (a sister of Sarah Coverdale, wife of his brother Joseph Polk), evidently took place about 1740, as his eldest child was born in 1742. His children were

(1) Emanuel, b about 1742, d Sept. 1, 1797; will dated Sept 6, 1793, probated Nov 16, 1797, d unmarried

(2) Joseph, b about 1744, d ——.

(3) Jehosephat, b. about 1746, d ——.

(4) Joab, b about 1748, d ——

(5) Mary (Polly), b about 1750, d ——, unmarried

(6) Esther, b. about 1752, d ——, married Mr. Owens

(7) Elizabeth, b. about 1754, d. ——, unmarried

(8) Nancy, b about 1756, d ——, unmarried

(9) Ephraim, 3d, b Nov 24, 1758, d March 24, 1814 in Scott County, Kentucky

In a letter to the author, of date February 7, 1873, from Mrs Sarah (Polk) Adkins, a daughter of Ephraim 3d, she says: "Only three of grandfather Ephraim Polk's children were married, I have been told, the rest dying single Those who married were my father, Ephraim 3d, his brother Joseph, and his sister Esther Owens"

WILL OF EPHRAIM POLK, 2nd

In the name of God, Amen, I, Ephraim Polk, of the County of Sussex in Delaware, being at this time in good health, as also of sound and perfect mind and memory praised be God, do make this my last will and testament as followeth:

Imprimis—I give and bequeath to my son Emanuel Polk, two hundred acres of land, being part of ye tract whereon stands my dwelling House, and Manner plantation, beginning at ye run of ye Branch on the North side of ye afores'd plantation, including the dwelling House and two thirds of ye Orchard, so continuing to run Southerly so as to lay off ye afors'd two Hundred acres on the East and South-East part of ye tract to him, and the Heirs lawfully begotten of his body forever, or for want of such issue, my further Will is at ye decease of my Emanuel, ye land and premises shall fall to and be the right of my son Ephraim Polk and his heirs lawfully begotten of his body forever; or should my son Ephraim decease without issue, the land and premises shall fall to my son Joab Polk, and the heirs lawfully begotten of his body forever. The whole of the above Claus so conditioned that my daughter Esther Owens is to have ye house she now lives in, with five acres of land round it, also timber to support it and firewood sufficient for one fire, during ye absence of her husband, or should she be now a Widow, during widowhood

Item—I give and bequeath to my son Ephraim Polk the remaining part of my tract of land afores'd left my son Emanuel Polk, with all the appertainances thereunto belonging to him and the Heirs lawfully begotten of his body forever. I also give to my son Ephraim one hundred acres of a tract of land called Coverdale's New Design adjoining the land afores'd, being ye South West part of s'd tract called Coverdale's New Design, to him and the heirs lawfully begotten of his body forever, or for want of such heir my further will is the one hundred acres of land afores'd, as well as the land and premises in the same track with my Emanuel shall fall to and be the right of my son Emanuel Polk, and the heirs lawfully begotten of his body forever, or should Emanuel decease without issue lawfully begotten of his body, my will is the land and premises afores'd shall fall to and be ye right and property of my son Joab Polk, and the heirs lawfully begotten of his body forever. Conditioned is ye above Claus that my daughter Elizabeth Polk shall have a lot in afores'd premises in the Southwest corner of my dwelling plantation of five acres, with the privilege of Timber to build a House, as also to support it and sufficiency of firewood for one fire.

Item—I give and bequeath to my son Joab Polk the use of the plantation he now lives on and I possest on I hath

hitherto occupy'd, with the land already laid off to him, by
a marked line, being one hundred acres of the west part of
the Tract of land called New Design during his natural life
and should his wife be the longest lived, I leave the premises
afores'd to her during her widowhood, and at the decease of
my son Joseph or should his wife be the longest lived, at her
decease or marriage, my further will is the afores'd land and
premises left to my son Joseph his lifetime, should descend
to and be the right of my Grand Son William Polk, son of
Joseph Polk and the heirs lawfully begotten of his body forever, etc., the aforesaid Clause is so conditioned that my
daughter Elizabeth Polk is to have a lot of five acres within
ye afores'd Hundred acres left to my son Joseph his lifetime
which five acres is to be laid off on the southwest part of said
land adjoining ye fence of the afores'd Joseph, also Capt
Nathaniel Hayes fence She is also to have the privilege of
timber to build a House, as also to support the place firewood for one fire, etc., during the time she continues single
or unmarried

Item—I give and bequeath to my son Joab Polk the remaining part of my Tract of land called Coverdale's New
Design being nearly one hundred acres be the same more or
less lying between the land already bequeathed to my son
Ephraim and that left Joseph his lifetime, to him and the
lawful heirs of his body forever, or should he leave no such
issue living my will further is ye afores'd premises should
descend and go to my son Ephraim and the Heirs lawfully
begotten of his body forever.

Item—I give and bequeath to my daughters, Elizabeth
and Mary one hundred and thirty-five acres of land and Marsh,
lying on the West side of Cedar Creek, adjoining Lands of
Edward Stapleford, Simon Lewis and the heirs of Ephraim
Holeager S'd survey begins opposite to the mouth of a Gut
makes out of ye afores'd Creek and on ye east side near a
Landing formerly called John Richards Landing, ye aforesaid
Tract to be equally divided between my two daughters Elizabeth and Mary, afs'd and their Heirs forever

Item—I give and bequeath to my son Emanuel Polk,

one Negro Man named Peter, as also one Sorrel Mare to him and his Heirs forever

Item—I give and bequeath to my son Ephraim his riding Mare as also her two year old Colt, being both commonly called his, to him and his Heirs forever.

Item—I give and bequeath to my four children now living with me viz Emanuel, Joab, Ephraim and Elizabeth, my six Negroes not yet mentioned, viz Cloe, Dinah, Cate, Sal, Leah and Caesar, with the whole and every part of my estate not before willed to be equally divided amongst them, to them and their Heirs forever.

Item—My further Will is my daughter Elizabeth shall have free privilege of eating and keeping apples out of either or every of my three Orchards left Emanuel, Joab and Ephraim free and without control during the time she is single or unmarried, etc

Item—My further Will is one quarter of an Acre together with the prize Tree where I have made my Sider the Ground afores'd to lay in a Circle round the Tree, shell be free to my Sons Emanuel and Ephraim to make their Sider, forever, etc

And I do hereby Constitute and appoint my sons Emanuel and Ephraim to be the sole Exrs of this my last Will and Testament, revoking and disallowing all other Wills heretofore made by me In Testimony whereof I have hereunto set my hand and Seal this 5th day of January, 1789

Sign'd Seal'd and Delivered   Ephraim Polk. (Seal)
in presence of us John Polk Sen'r
Robert Shankland, Edward Polk,
Charles Polk.
Sussex County, L. S

Memorandum, the 22d day of March, 1791, before me, Phillips Kollock, Register appointed for the probate of Wills and granting Letters of Administration for the County of Sussex, appeared Robert Shankland and Charles Polk, two of the Witnesses to the within Will, who being duly sworn on the Holy Evangels of Almighty God, did severally depose and say that in their sight presence and hearing the Testator Ephraim Polk did sign, seal, publish and declare the same to be his Last Will and Testament and that at the time thereof he was of a sound and perfect mind, memory and judgment, and that they and each of them together with John Polk Senior and Edward Polk subscribed the same as Witnesses in presence of the Testator and at his request

PHILLIPS KOLLOCK, Reg'r

By the foregoing it will be observed that Ephraim Polk 2d, who was born about 1709, executed his will on January 5, 1789, and died at about the age of 82 years, a short time before March 22, 1791, on which date the document was presented to the Register of Wills for Sussex County for probate. As he makes no mention of his wife, whose maiden name was Mary Coverdale, it is fairly inferable that she was then dead. Had she been alive, he would have made some provision for her

The children still under his roof at the time he executed his will, and whom he names, were Emanuel, Joab, Elizabeth and Ephraim. The rest of his children five in number, Joseph, Jehosephat, Mary, Esther and Nancy, had evidently left the parental home, Joseph and Esther marrying and establishing homes of their own. He does not mention Nancy, who probably died single and before his will was executed. He refers to Jehosephat and Joab in a way which suggests that they also were married. He had already settled Joseph on a plantation of one hundred acres, part of the Coverdale tract called "New Design"

Esther, whose husband (Mr Owens) appears to have been long absent and his whereabouts not known, is referred to as living in a house by herself, which residence, with five acres of land attached, he confirms to her. Elizabeth, evidently then single, is also given a five acre tract, with timber for a house and its maintenance. Esther Owens at that time had two children, Phillis and Esther Jr, but Ephraim does not mention them. Their names we secure from the will of Emanuel Polk, who died unmarried nearly five years later. Perhaps they had not been born at the date of Ephraim's will and therefore could not be mentioned by him

In Ephraim' will he mentions but one child of Joseph whose name was William, and to him he makes a conditional bequest In Emanuel Polk's will, executed September 6, 1793, probated November 16, 1797, he mentions Joseph's children as William, Sallie, Elizabeth, Augusta and Molly M. Emanuel dying without issue, under Ephraim's will his (Emanuel's) lands fell to Joseph. Probably with a view of breaking or nullifying the entail by Ephraim of the two hundred acres lying on Bowman's Branch, or for some other reason not now known, before Emanuel's death he sold this two hundred acres on Bowman's Branch to his nephew Augusta Polk, one of the sons of Joseph. This name is written Augusta in the will, but as Augusta is the feminine of Augustus, it is evident that it should have been spelled the latter way

Augustus Polk dying intestate and without issue, some time after Emanuel's death, his sisters, Sallie Polk Elizabeth Polk and Molly M. Polk on October 22d, 1801, for a valuable consideration sold their respective interests in this tract to their brother William Polk

CHAPTER LVI.

EPHRAIM POLK, 3rd.

Ephraim Polk 3d (youngest of the eight children of Ephraim Polk 2d and Mary Coverdale), was b in North West Fork Hundred, Sussex County, Delaware, November 24, 1758 Just as Ephraim attained to manhood the troubles between the American Colonies and the mother country had culminated in armed conflict British fleets ravaged the coasts of Delaware, bombarding towns, while British soldiers and their Tory allies in Sussex and other counties harried the patriot inhabitants The hastily embodied American soldiers consisted of militia regiments, later put on Colonial establishment, with little drill, discipline or equipment.

The close of the first year of the Revolution (1776) found the American cause shrouded in gloom The army of Washington had been defeated in a number of battles Menaced by the proximity of the enemy, on December 12th, the Continental Congress quitted Philadelphia and retired to Baltimore Notwithstanding reverses sustained, the firmness of the patriots was unshaken and the Colonies exerted themselves to sustain Washington with added troops. Foremost in this work was the little Colony of Delaware Many of her sons also went to other colonies and entered the service. Among this class were Joab Polk and his youngest brother, Ephraim Polk 3d, the latter then just past the age of eighteen. Joab was ten years the senior of Ephraim, and with his elder brothers, Emanuel, Joseph and Jehosephat, had been serving the patriot cause as members of the Sussex Militia, and were chiefly employed in the repression of Toryism

An opportunity was soon presented the following year (1777) for Joab and Ephraim to gratify their desire for a larger field of action Washington, then at Philadelphia, being in need of horses, some of these animals was dispatched by Ephraim Polk 2d to that place in charge of his sons Joab and

Ephraim. On arrival at the Quaker City, the animals were duly delivered to the proper officials. Joab then crossed the river into New Jersey and enlisted in the service, apparently for a short term each time. The Colonial Records of New Jersey show that he first joined the company of "Captain Joseph Pancoast, First Regiment, of Burlington." He next appears as a "Corporal in the First Battalion, Second Establishment, also Militia." Finally he is registered: "Joab Polk, Captain Bateman Lloyd's Company, Second Regiment Continental Troops."

According to the statement of Dr. Jefferson J. Polk, of Perryville, Ky., a son of Ephraim Polk 3d, the latter and his brothers all served throughout the war, returning home only at the conclusion of peace. This fact, Dr. Polk stated, he heard from the lips of his father, when, with his family seated around he would recount instances of the long struggle for American freedom.

Soon after Joab and Ephraim reached Philadelphia, the British army under Lord Howe defeated Washington (Sept 11th) at Brandywine. The following day Washington's army fell back to Philadelphia, retreating further to Reading. On Sept 26th Howe occupied Philadelphia, the Continental Congress having migrated to Lancaster. Howe stationed the main division of his army outside of the city, at the village of Germantown, while Washington was twenty miles away awaiting developments. Finally he decided to attack the British division at Germantown, which he did on October 4, the contest lasting nearly three hours, the Americans losing about 1,000 men in killed and wounded. Among the troops engaged in this battle was Nash's Brigade, from North Carolina, in which was Lieutenant Colonel William Polk, a descendant of William Polk 2d, son of Robert and Magdalen Polk. Also his father, Col Thomas Polk, of "Mecklenburg Declaration" fame, who commanded a squadron of two hundred cavalry and escorted the American baggage train of seven hundred wagons out of the city to Bethlehem for safety. Among the articles carried away were the bells of the city churches and public buildings, including the State House bell, now known as the Liberty Bell. Let the reader, on opening the city, all citizens capable of bearing arms were embodied into a regiment commanded by Colonel William Will, known as the Fourth Class Philadelphia Militia. With this raw organization Col Will joined Washington's army. In this regiment, beside Ephraim Polk 3d, was Capt Charles Wilson Peale, one of the most noted artists of his day, founder of Peale's Museum of that city, and whose sister, Elizabeth Digby Peale, married Capt Robert Polk, of Maryland, Commander of the privateers "Black Jake" and "Montgomery" fitted out at Annapolis, and who was killed on board his vessel by a British cannon shot. Capt Polk was a descendant of Robert Polk, fifth son of Robert Bruce Polk and Magdalen Porter

Ephraim Polk 3d enlisted Sept 10, 1777, in Capt Joseph Rhodes' Company, Col Will's Regiment, receiving his "Baptism of fire" at Germantown on October 4th following. As a matter of interest to his descendants and kinsmen, the following partial muster roll is copied from "Pennsylvania Archives, Second Series, Vol 13, p 675

CAPTAIN RHOADS' COMPANY.

Captain Joseph Rhoads, commissioned Sept 10, 1777

First Lieutenant Adam Bohl, commissioned Sept 10, 1777

Second Lieutenant, Conrad Rubert, commissioned Sept 10, 1777

Sergeant, William Henry, appointed, commissioned Sept 10, 1777

Corporal, Henry Kains, appointed, commissioned Sept 10, 1777.

PRIVATES.

Paradon Peterson, enlisted Sept 10, 1777
Ephraim Polk, enlisted Sept. 10, 1777.
Anthony Hanna, enlisted Sept 10, 1777.
Thomas Robinson, enlisted Sept 10, 1777
William McElroy, enlisted Sept 10, 1777

Then follows a list of 32 other privates whose names we omit. Ephraim Polk, it will be seen, was the second man on the list of privates of his company

As the Third Pennsylvania Regiment of Foot, Col Will's regiment passed into the Continental Line and served throughout the war. The powder-horn which Ephraim put on when he enlisted at Philadelphia in September, 1777, was presented to the writer by his aunt, Mrs Polly Wolfe of Indiana, in 1873, and by him in 1913 to Harry H Polk, of Des Moines, Iowa.

VALLEY FORGE.

The battle of Germantown was practically a "drawn fight." While the British held the field, it was at the expense of a heavy loss of officers and men. The Americans fell back leisurely to their camps on Skippack Creek, retiring later to White Marsh. Here began the sufferings of the patriot army for food and clothing. Early in December the British essayed an attack on the American army, but they changed their purpose and retreated. After another council of war, it was decided to remove the American army to a greater distance from the enemy. Three days later it crossed the Schuylkill—many of the soldiers marching through the deep snow with bare feet—and on December 19th commenced building winter quarters at Valley Forge. There they erected log huts and spent that long, bitter winter freezing, starving and suffering as no troops on earth ever before had suffered.

Congress being unable to alleviate the desperate situation of the suffering troops at Valley Forge, Washington turned to one man who indeed proved a succoring angel to his country in her hour of greatest need. That man was Robert Morris, the merchant prince of Philadelphia, a large ship owner, who also maintained a fleet of privateers. Robert Morris was at that time the wealthiest man in America, his fortune being estimated at eight millions. He had already advanced large sums to the Congress for war expenses, but, when appealed to by Washington, he raised by great effort the funds requested. This great benefactor of his country, but for whose monetary aid at critical junctures the American cause would doubtless have been a failure, was a kinsman to Rhoda Morris, the wife of Ephraim Polk, of the Polk family of Kent and Sussex Counties, Delaware.

EPHRAIM EMIGRATES TO KENTUCKY.

At the close of the Revolution Joab and Ephraim Polk returned to their home in Sussex. After their return both of them remained for a time under the parental roof, assisting their father in his affairs until his death in March, 1791. This event necessitated a separation of the family. The old homestead was sold and the proceeds distributed in accordance with the will of Ephraim 2d. The eyes of the younger Ephraim, some years before his father's death, had been turned toward the region which lay beyond the Alleghanies, and stretched westward beyond the Mississippi. Determined to first explore it, he set out for Kentucky in the spring of 1785, accompanied, it is said, by some of the Scroggins, and Nutters, kinsmen, and others. Arriving at Limestone (now Maysville) they fell into the "Great Buffalo Road," which crossed the Ohio at that point and led South into the rich grazing lands of Central Kentucky. Following this general route into Kentucky, they arrived at Bryan's Station, the scene of a siege by Canadian troops and Indians, in August, 1782. They also visited Lexington and adjacent stations, and explored on the waters of North Elkhorn and the upper branches of Eagle Creek. Ephraim chose a location on Lain's Run, a branch of the North Elkhorn, in what is now Scott County, a few miles north of Georgetown. The others also satisfied themselves as to locations and the party returned to Delaware.

Events at home, however, delayed Ephraim in his purpose of emigration from Sussex. After his return from Kentucky, Ephraim cast his glances about for a partner in his joys and sorows of the future. His gaze finally rested on a fair cousin, Rhoda Ann Morris, daughter of Daniel Morris, Jr., and Ann Polk his wife, of Sussex. Daniel's father was also named Daniel—(Daniel Morris, Sr.), who had a biblically named progeny, viz: Hezekiah, Daniel Jr., Nathaniel, John Masten Martin, Deborah, Comfort and Mary Morris. Ephraim Polk 3d and Rhoda Morris were married on March 8, 1792.

A year before this event Ephraim's father had died, and the estate had to be settled by himself and his brother Emanuel, executors named under the will. This work was not finally disposed of until the summer of 1793 had passed. Ephraim now began his preparations for emigration to Kentucky. Before this, on February 16, of that year, Asenath, their first child, was born. The company of emigrants, in addition to Ephraim and his family, consisted of a number of kinsmen, persons related by blood or marriage. Among these were: Captain John Scroggin, a brave soldier of the Revolution, who had married Eunice Jane Polk, David and Thomas Nutter; one of the Coverdales, several of the Morris family, kinsmen of Rhoda, and others.

In the fall of 1793, Ephraim Polk and wife, and the other members of their company, took up their line of march for Kentucky. Good wagons, with strong teams, carried such household effects as were considered indispensable. Other horses were ridden by members of the party and they bid farewell to the old homes in Sussex and started toward the West. With Ephraim went the negroes received from his father's estate, and Capt Scroggin and others also took slaves with them. Several kinds of stock, fruit and garden seeds, were also taken along, the people and animals all forming quite a little caravan. Ephraim Polk, Capt Scroggin and others of the party being veterans of the Revolution, were not disconcerted by rumors of danger from Indians on the Ohio. They were all well armed and prepared for any emergency.

Traveling by steady stages the immigrants passed through the northern part of Maryland and thence into Pennsylvania. Falling into "Braddock's Road," they pursued it westward past Chambersburg and Bedford, across the Alleghanies, and on to Redstone Old Fort, (now Brownsville) on the Monongahela. At this point where a large boat-yard was turning out covered flat-boats known as "Kentucky Broadhorns," for sale to those bound down the Ohio, the party purchased a commodious craft, put aboard their animals, farm implements, wagons, household effects and slaves, and started by water to accomplish most of the distance yet to be travelled. Accompanying them, also, was a squad of friendly Delaware Indians who joined them at Redstone. Reaching the Ohio and entering that stream, in due time they arrived at a l.. .ping murder at the han.. . .

It is said that while descending the Ohio they came near being entrapped and slain. At a point on the river a white man appeared on the north bank of the stream and called to them, claimed to have escaped from the Indians, and begged piteously to be taken on board. Captain Scroggin, not wishing to leave a fellow man in distress, urged that they take the supplicant aboard. Some of the others, suspecting a ruse, opposed the suggestion. But at last the boat was turned toward the shore and when near it a band of ambushed savages arose and fired a volley into the boat, slightly wounding one or two, but killing no one. The boat was urged out into the stream again and pursued the balance of the journey to Limestone unmolested.

At the latter place the party disembarked, sold their boat, and loading their plunder again into the wagons, and on packhorses, they followed the "Great Buffalo Road" to the waters of Lam's Run. Here at the head of this small tributary of North Elkhorn, Ephraim Polk "drove his stake." And while the negro men felled trees for the cabin, and it was in course of erection, the squad of Delaware Indians who came with them and had camped nearby hunted game and maintained the most friendly relations. By this time they had become quite attached to the party, and adopting the name of "Polk" they returned to the Ohio by the way of Kentucky River and pursued their course down that stream and on beyond the Mississippi.

After Ephraim had completed a substantial log house, all hands set to work vigorously to clear a cornfield, burn the brush and prepare for planting a crop the ensuing spring. And while Ephraim was busy in these matters, the other members of the emigrant party had dispersed to different localities and were similarly employed.

AN INDIAN RAID

Kentucky at that time had quite a numerous population and Indian invasions or attacks were no longer feared. But, notwithstanding this fact, while Wayne's Indian War was in progress, small parties occasionally crossed the Ohio and

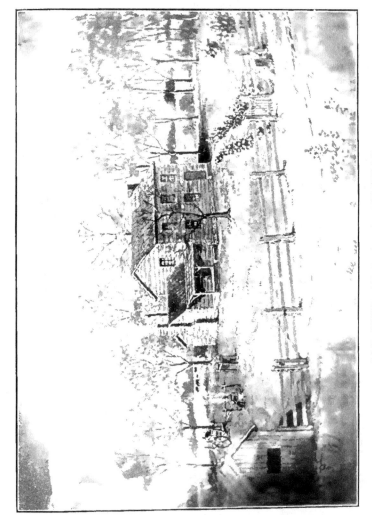

OLD EPHRAIM POLK HOMESTEAD.

stealthily approached the frontiers of the central part of the State, travelling by night, and here and there stealing horses and murdering people in exposed situations. Such a party ascended the Licking and attacked a family just over the ridge, at no great distance from Ephraim Polk's home, killing all the family but two women whom they took captive. Ephraim had been out hunting, and nearing home at the close of the day, noticed feathers scattered along the trail. On seeing the feathers along the trail Ephraim suspected an Indian foray and shortly after news of the massacre was received. He quickly joined a well armed party of men and pursued the savages, but they escaped down the Licking with their prisoners, and the pursuers returned. That was about the last Indian raid into Kentucky. Wayne's victory over the allied British and Indians at Fallen Timbers, in August 1794, ended the Indian War in the country lying between the Alleghanies and the Mississippi, and the settlers of Kentucky were no longer harassed by a stealthily, savage foe.

In their new home Ephraim Polk and his wife industriously exerted themselves to render their situation as comfortable as possible, and in a few years had their plantation well cleared and fenced. They planted the seeds of fruits, which they had brought from Delaware, and in the course of time their apple orchard became famous as the finest in Kentucky.

Dr Jefferson J Polk, of Perryville, Ky, fifth child of Ephraim, 3rd, and Rhoda (Morris) Polk, a man of keen intellect and fine intelligence, published his autobiography in 1867, a few years before his death.

Speaking of Ephraim Polk, 1st, Dr Polk says: "Shortly after his arrival in America he dropped the l-o from his name, (Pollock) and from that time his proper cognomen became Polk. This change may have been accidental, but is was most probably designed. In his new home his family increased in number, and enjoyed all the sweets of domestic happiness. At his death his youngest son, who was also named Ephraim, became possessor of the old manor house. He married and became the father of four sons and two daughters." In this Dr Polk .... Ephraim Polk 2d ..... But he was writing from memory of what he had heard in childhood.

"Like his father," says Dr. Polk, "he was for the times, a rich man. His youngest son he likewise named Ephraim. He had scarcely seen all the members of his family reach the years of maturity before the struggle between the colonies and the mother country began. At the first sound of war, father and sons flew to arms in defense of their homes. Through the whole contest they bore unflinchingly their full share of dangers and privations.

"Victory had hardly crowned our arms and peace been declared, when the family was scattered, each member of it seeking a new home. A number of them came to the West, to peril their lives again in a war with the red men of the forest. My father Ephraim Jr., was among the emigrants. After a tedious and dangerous journey, three families arrived at what was then called Limestone (now Maysville) in the then Territory of Kentucky. Following the most direct trail of emigration, the path made by the wild buffalo as he moved from the Ohio to the saline regions of the interior, they found their way to Bryan's Station, near Lexington. Here separated those who had traveled together eight hundred miles on a flat-boat, and many miles through unbroken forests.

"My father moved northeast and located on Lain's Run, in Scott County, five miles north of where Georgetown now stands. The family at that time consisted of father, mother, and one daughter. Hostile Indians were frequently seen in the neighborhood, and about the time of his settlement they murdered two members of a family a mile from his house, and carried the remaining two into captivity. One of these, a woman, having made her escape some time afterward, returned to the neighborhood, the fate of the other was never known. As soon as it was known that the murders had been committed, pursuit was made, but without overtaking the savages. Their danger from that source was now at an end, but new hardships from another quarter. The dense forests were to be cleared, and the virgin soil prepared, before proper sustenance could be obtained for the family.

"Soon the parents were blessed with another daughter,

then a third, and afterwards a son. When two years had elapsed, a deep gloom was thrown around them by the accidental drowning of this son, (Ephraim) in a spring near the house. Another son was given them in the place of the one that was taken, Jefferson J. Polk, b. March 10, 1802."

In the second chapter of his autobiography Dr Polk says: "My first recollections of parental government and teachings commenced at six years of age. My father, still bearing implacable hatred to kings and kingly power, took great pains to instill the same spirit into the minds of his sons. His leisure hours and the long winter evenings were employed in rehearsing the conflicts between the Whigs and the Tories, and in giving an account of the hard fought battles in which he and his brothers had participated during the Revolutionary War. He was very particular to make his sons pledge fidelity to the government constitution, and laws of the United States, and especially to Mr Jefferson's administration. Taught by such a father, and imbibing such principles, it might reasonably be expected that my infant mind would be completely **Americanized** Love of country, hatred of George III, of British red-coats, and of American aborigines, were the first emotions of my young and patriotic heart

"Only a few years passed before I witnessed in person the drilling of soldiers for another sanguinary conflict with the British and Indians I was then ten years old The crowning victory was the battle of New Orleans, and the news of Jackson's triumph over Packenham determined my father to join the Southern Army in the Spring He set about making suitable preparations for the intended campaign But Providence interposed, and before the middle of March, 1815, the disease called the **cold plague** deprived the army of an experienced soldier and his family of its head. It was the first death I had ever witnessed"

CHAPTER LVII.

THE MORRIS FAMILY.

The Morris family was quite a large one in Maryland and Delaware, many of them residing in Sussex, and it was the latter branch which intermarried with the Polks. They were all of original Quaker stock that came over with William Penn. One of the most distinguished patriots of the American Revolution, Robert Morris, the Philadelphia financier and millionaire, was of the same family.

As before related, Ephraim Polk 3d and Rhoda Morris, daughter of Daniel Morris Jr., and Ann (Polk) Morris, of Sussex County, Delaware, were married March 8, 1792, and their first child, Asenath, was born some months before they emigrated to Kentucky. Rhoda Polk's father, Daniel Morris Jr., who married Ann Polk in 1754, was a son of Daniel Morris Sr., of Kent County, adjoining Sussex, who died about 1785, leaving children ¹Hezekiah; ²Daniel, Jr.; ³Nathaniel, ⁴John; ⁵Masten; ⁶Deborah; ⁷Comfort; ⁸Mary Clifton; ⁹David.

Hezekiah evidently deceased before his father, judging from the fact that Elizabeth Morris, widow and administratrix of Curtis Morris, of Sussex, in a petition filed by her against the estate of Ann (Polk) Morris, August 27, 1812, in the Fayette County, Kentucky, Circuit Court, sets forth that Daniel Jr., "was the eldest son of said Daniel Morris deceased, having by the laws of Delaware the right to his father's lands, upon paying the co-heirs the value of their respective portions." From this statement it appears that Curtis Morris and his wife, Elizabeth, (whose maiden name is said to have been Wright), did not come to Kentucky; but remained in his old home, and died there, his widow instituting suit in the Fayette Circuit Court for an equitable share in the estate of his mother, Ann (Polk) Morris, who had devised most of her property to her youngest son, David Morris, who had charge of her during her great affliction from paralysis for some years before her death. The fact that a subpoena issued for Elizabeth to appear in the Fayette Court was returned "Not found; not a resident of this Commonwealth," further proves that she and Curtis did not come to Kentucky with the others in 1793. In her petition Elizabeth also states that Curtis was "a resident of the State of Maryland," probably in the same neighborhood with the Morris and Polk families of Deleware, but just across the State line

So it appears that Daniel Morris, Jr., inheriting his father's manor place, sold it in 1793 and came to Kentucky, his brother, Curtis, remaining in Maryland, and dying there in 1804, as stated by his widow. Elizabeth also deposed that 'Wm McNitt married a daughter of Daniel Morris, Sr., and brought suit for a part of the latter's estate' and that David Morris, another son of Daniel, Sr., also filed suit against the estate and they recovered the amounts asked for

Daniel Morris, Jr., and his wife, Ann, prospered after coming to Kentucky, being an industrious and frugal couple. Daniel Morris, Jr., did not remain in Deleware until he could satisfy the respective claims of the co-heirs of his father's estate, but delegated that duty to his eldest brother, Curtis, and the latter dying before this satisfaction was rendered, the co-heirs brought suit against the estate of his mother, he also having previously died at his home in Scott County, in 1805.

In November, 1807, Ann (Polk) Morris, widow of Daniel, Jr., purchased a beautiful tract of land near Payne's Station, Fayette County, Kentucky, from Hayden Edwards, and the following year erected thereon a substantial two story brick residence, where she continued to reside until her death. She was a member of old Bethel Presbyterian Church, one of the first churches established in Fayette County after the settlement of Lexington in 1779. In the old family graveyard, on this farm, Ann, her husband, their children—Rebecca, Robert, Mary, Ann, John, William, Sarah, David—and a number of the grand children were buried.

CHILDREN OF DANIEL MORRIS, JR.

The children of Daniel Morris, Jr., were

(1) Daniel Morris b Sept 18, 1755; d Dec 1806, in Kentucky

(2) Curtis Morris, b. May 31, 1757, d 1801, married Miss Wright, a relative of the wife of Joseph Polk Issue unknown

(3) Rebecca Morris, b. November 2, 1759, d unmarried.

(4) Robert Morris, b August 17, 1761; d unmarried

(5) Brinkley Morris, b September 15, 1763; married, and moved to Rush County, Indiana, in the '30's, and left descendants

(6) Mary (Polly) Morris, b July 2, 1765, d in Scott County, Kentucky. Married John Hopkins and had issue. ¹John, Jr, ²Robert, ³Betsy; also several others untraced

(7) Ann Morris, b. November 23, 1767; d unmarried

(8) John Morris, b November 26, 1769; d. 1817; married Miss Loflin Issue ¹William, ²Thomas, ³Daniel

(9) William Morris, b June 6, 1772, d ———, married Miss Beauchamp, of Scott County, daughter of Jesse Beauchamp Issue ¹John, ²William, ³Jesse William last named removed to Rush County, Indiana, during the '30's He married and left a family

(10) Rhoda Morris, b October 27, 1773, d October 22, 1839, married Ephraim Polk 3d For issue see list under heading "Children of Ephraim Polk 3d."

(11) Sarah Morris, b August 12, 1775, d —————. married William Beauchamp (brother of Jesse Beauchamp, father of Wm. Morris' wife) of Scott County Issue. ¹Jesse, ²Susannah, ³Betsy, ⁴John, ⁵Mrs Rucker, ⁶Agnes Gray, ⁷Hettie Hopkins, ⁸Polly Morris, ⁹William

(12) David Morris, Jr, b. January 14. 1779; d ———, married Hannah Risque, of Scott County Issue ¹Daniel, ²John R, ³James, ⁴David C, ⁵Wesley, ⁶Julia Ann, ⁷Robert The four last all died unmarried, at the old home place, near Payne's Station, Scott County

Of the children of the foregoing sons and daughters of Daniel Morris, Jr and Ann Polk

Robert Hopkins (son of Polly Morris and John Hopkins) was married twice; first to——————————, by whom he had issue John Hopkins, who married Lizzie Dougherty, and Robert Hopkins, who married Alice Dunnington, daughter of Dr Dunnington, of Paris, Kentucky Their children were --- Robert Hopkins, Jr, before the Civil War, was a large owner of stage lines in Kentucky, noted for his enterprise and elegance of dress at all times Broken in fortune by the Civil War, he went to Texas, and later to Vinita, Indian Territory, where he established stage lines and owned a hotel. He left several children

By his second wife, Almira Risque (or Risk), Robert Hopkins, Sr, who was a wealthy farmer and distiller of Woodford County, had issue. [1]Henry Hopkins, of Payne's Station, who married Miss Josie Nichols, [2]George Johnson Hopkins, who married Miss Griffith, [3]William Hopkins, who did not marry, [4]Cabell Breckinridge Hopkins, who married Miss Van Pelt, of Lexington, [5]Mary Hopkins, who married James Gaines of Fayette County, [6]Thomas Hopkins, who married Miss Lowry, [7]James Hopkins who married Miss Moore of Midway, Ky.

Daniel Morris (son of David Morris, Jr, and Hannah Risque (or Risk) married Miss Tilford, a daughter of Col. Tilford, of Lexington, Ky, by whom he had issue [1]Lizzie, who married first, James Brown, secondly, Wm Payne No issue by either.

William Morris, son of James and Davidella (Messick) Morris, was a soldier in the Confederate Army during the Civil War, in General John H Morgan's Cavalry brigade His elder brother, James C Morris, served in the Union Army as Captain of Company "D" Twentieth Kentucky Infantry

CHILDREN OF JAMES MORRIS, SR

James Morris, Sr, married Davidella Messick, of Lexington and had issue

(1) Zephaniah Morris, b March 6, 1836, married Mary E Spencer, of Warsaw, Ky They had [1]Preston Hampton; [2]Sarah C, [3]Wm B.; [4]Margaret R., [5]James Messick; [6]Frank C, [7]Charles S.

(2) Jas C. Morris, b July 7, 1838, married Lillie Reed, of Maysville, Ky, and they had: [1]James L, [2]Lillie R, [3]Martha D, [4]Mary B; [5]Allen B; [6]Carrie M

(3) Wm Henry Morris, b O.. .d 1'.. .. .. Annie Martin He d Aug .. ..

(4) Margaret Hannah Morris, b April 6, 1848, married John Russell, no issue. He d March 19, 1890.

(5) David Morris, b Feb 5, 1847, married Mary Moore, of Midway, Ky, she dying he next married Miss Lou Reynolds, of Indiana. Issue ¹David R ; ²Mary Moore; ³Hunter

(6) John Morris, b July 26, 1852, married Tillie Gilbert, of Lexington One child, Margaret R.

(7) Alfred Russell Morris, b May 7, 1855, married Ora Bell Durham, of Danville, Ky They had issue ¹Milton W.; ²Robert M, ³Alfred C ; ⁴Chas W, ⁵Mary D

James Morris Sr., (son of David Morris and Hannah Risque) was for many years a leading merchant of Lexington Of his other sons beside Rev James C Morris, William was engaged in the chinaware trade; Zephaniah was a merchant at Beards, Ky John, cashier of a bank at Miltonvale, Kansas, David and Alfred R were popular and widely known traveling representatives of wholesale houses

CHILDREN OF EPHRAIM POLK, 3rd.

The children born to Ephraim Polk 3d and his wife Rhoda (Morris) Polk, were

(1) Asenath Polk, b. in Delaware, February 16, 1793 d October, 1842 at Madison, Indiana She married Wm A Burch and left one child, Anderson Burch, who was a soldier in Col Marshall's Kentucky Cavalry, in the Mexican War, and also in the Confederate Army in the Civil War He was wounded at Buena Vista

(2) Mary (Polly) Polk, b in Kentucky, October 12, 1794 · d August 22, 1874, at Liberty, Indiana, leaving a family of eight children

(3) Ann (Nancy) Polk, b. August 9, 1796; d March 11, 1850, near Greenfield, Indiana, leaving a large family.

(4) Ephraim Polk 4th, b in 1798, drowned in big spring near house, in May, 1801, in Scott County, Ky

(5) Jehosephat Polk, born May 3, 1800, died October 25, 1864, at Spring Station, Woodford County, Ky

(6) Jefferson J Polk b March 10, 1802, d May 23, 1881, at Perryville, Ky He had a family of eight children.

(7) Daniel Polk, b. June 25, 1804; drowned at Frankfort in Kentucky River, September 17, 1862. He was twice married and had nine children

(8) Hester D Polk, b June 14, 1806; d August 13, 1867, at Danville, Kentucky

(9) Clement Madison Polk, b September 11, 1808; d. May 2, 1849, at Springfield, Ill

(10) Gilead Polk, b. August 10, 1810, d May, 1855, at Midway, Woodford County, Ky.

(11) Sarah Polk, b June 21, 1812, d. at Liberty Union County, Indiana

(12) Ephraim Polk 5th, b August 10, 1814, died unmarried, September 3, 1840, at Springfield, Ill

FAMILY OF MARY POLK WOLF.

Mary Morris (Polly) Polk, second child of Ephraim 3d and Rhoda (Morris) Polk, was born October 12, 1794, in Kentucky, at the pioneer home of her parents, on Lam's Run the year following their emigration from Delaware On July 10, 1816, she was married to Jesse Wolf, son of Jacob Wolf, who was among the early emigrants to Kentucky, from Pennsylvania Jesse Wolf was b. October 29, 1795 In 1835 Jesse and Polly Wolf emigrated to Union County, Indiana, where their children grew to the ages of maturity, and lived there until they died, she on August 12, 1874, he several years later

CHILDREN OF POLLY AND JESSE WOLF.

(1) Eliza A Wolf, b April 19, 1819, d ——

(2) Jacob Harrison Wolf, b May 10, 1820, d January 14, 1893

(3) Harvy J Wolf b June 26, 1822, d July 26, 1883

(4) Hattie Eveline Wolf, b October 10, 1825, d November 20, 1856.

(5) Nancy A Wolf, b January 26, 1827 d ——

(6) Thomas Jefferson Wolf, b February 11, 1829; d ——

(7) Mary Susan Wolf, b December 21, 1831, d. January 6 1859

(8 ...

INTERMARRIAGES.

The intermarriages and children of Jesse and Polly (Polk) Wolf were

Eliza A. Wolf (1) married August 21, 1838, to William Sands, by whom she had

(1) James Sands, b. ——, d. ——, married Mollie Rogers. Issue unknown.

(2) Charles W. Sands, b. ——, d. ——, married Nannie Israel Issue unknown.

Jacob Harrison Wolf married twice His first wife whom he married on March 12 1844, was Eliza J Lorimer She was b March 15, 1826, and d July 26, 1900 By her he had five children, viz:

(1) John Wesley, b January 6, 1845; d August 24, 1845

(2) Mary Susan, b June 16, 1847 She was twice married Her first husband was James W Bedel, whom she married March 23, 1870 To them was born one child, Albert Bedel, on July 3, 1871. Albert married October 13, 1901, Louise Louvilla Bishop Issue unknown

James W Bedel d. March 23, 1870, and on October 9, 1878, his widow, Mary Susan, married John Davison, a prominent farmer near Rushville Mr Davison was b January 7, 1835, and d. June 30, 1896.

(3) Martha Caroline Wolf, b August 26, 1849, (third child of Jacob Harrison Wolf), was universally called "Mattie" She was married July 13, 1876, to Thackery K. Galbreath, of Greenfield, Indiana, who was b. November 7, 1849, at Cynthiana, Kentucky. They had issue

Clara Leota Galbreath, b May 20, 1877, married July 29, 1896, to Harry Davison, b April 23, 1872 They had two children [1]Louella Maria, b. March 31, 1898, [2]Lillian Isabel, b October 3, 1901

(2) Claude Galbreath, b August 11, 1879

(3) Rosaline M Galbreath, b April 19, 1882

(4) Edmond P Galbreath, b April 28, 1885

(5) Nancie Marie Galbreath, b December 21, 1891.

(4) Rosaline Wolf, b December 4, 1852 (fourth child of Jacob Harrison Wolf), married July 1, 1876, to Hamlin Morris, of Rushville Indiana, a distant kinsman. At last

MRS. MARY (POLLY) WOLFE,
daughter of Ephraim Polk, 3rd.

accounts they were living at Ponca City, Oklahoma, having no children. The marriage of Mattie and Rosaline Wolf was a double ceremony at their home in Indianapolis

(5) Francis Albert Wolf, b March 18, 1855 (fifth child of Jacob Harrison Wolf) married November 16, 1882, Mary E. Frazier, b September 28, 1864 They had issue [1]Minnie Lee Wolf, b July 6, 1884, [2]Otho Francis Wolf, b June 9, 1895

By his second wife, Jacob Harrison Wolf had one child, Clara May, b March 6, 1889

Harvey J. Wolf, (third child of Jesse and Polly (Polk) Wolf) was twice married His first wife was Mary A Larimore, a sister of Jacob Harrison Wolf's wife Harvey and Mary were married June 9, 1846, and she d. October 31, 1854 Harvey next married Rachael Bryant, in 1856, and she d February 19, 1885 By his first wife, Harvey J Wolf had issue: [1]Florida Wolf, b August 10, 1851; married December 26, 1872, to Albert Stanly Brown, of Lyon's Station, Indiana, by whom she had issue: Rozzie May Brown, b January 26, 1874 She married Charles N Huber, February 22, 1900. Issue· Charles Albert Huber, b June 12, 1902

The second child of Harvey J. Wolf was named Frank, b in 1854, untraced

Mary Francis (third child of Harvey J Wolf), b June 16, 1853, married in 1877, Mr Titrington, of Lyon's Station, Indiana, by whom she had issue. [1]Harvey Clide Titrington, b. April 9, 1879; [2]Ethel May Titrington, b August 13, 1883, d November 2, 1898, [3]Della Belle Titrington, b December 15, 1887, d in infancy

Jessie Wolf (fourth child of Harvey J Wolf, and the first by his wife, Rachael Bryant), b November 26, 1860, d. April 22, 1885 A second child by this wife, Eliza Jane, was b August 23, 1862, d. January 8, 1878.

Hester Eveline Wolf, (fourth child of Jesse and Polly (Polk) Wolf), married October 29, 1846, Dr Aaron Talbert of Union County, Indiana, by whom she had three daughters Susan, Anne and Belle, all of whom died young at Dayton, Ohio Dr Talbert removed from Dayton to Lexington, Kentucky, where his wife Hester Eveline d November 20, 1856

Nancy A Wolf (fifth child of Jesse and Polk (Polk)

Wolf), married August 29, 1856, Mahundra Hollingsworth, by whom she had five children: ¹William, ²Belle, ³Edward, ⁴Charles E, ⁵Ettie No dates of birth or marriages obtained Belle married a Mr Micham, of St. Joe, Mo

Thomas Jefferson Wolf (sixth child of Jesse and Polly (Polk) Wolf), was twice married, first, February 1, 1856, to Mary Weatherow by whom he had issue ¹Ida, ²Thomas J., ³Issa, ⁴Emmet, ⁵Anna, ⁶Charles, ⁷Bertie. By his second wife, Adeline Price, Thomas Jefferson had no issue

Mary Susan Wolf (seventh child of Jesse and Polly (Polk) Wolf), married Samuel N Minor, November 11, 1850 They had issue ¹Levin R. Minor, b January 12, 1852; ²Clara E Minor, b September 27, 1853, d June 29, 1884 The latter married April 7, 1874, to William Wallace, an editor of Rushville, Indiana

Ida Belle Minor, b May 28, 1854; d February 28, 1876 Married December 2, 1872, Earnest Mason, son of Alonzo Mason, of Wabash, Indiana Earnest Mason d December 2, 1902. They had two children ¹Blanche, b December 1, 1873, who married July 2, 1901, to Chas. W O'Donnell, of Detroit. ²Hinda, b February 14, 1875, d January 1, 1876

The children of Clara E Minor and William Wallace were

(1) Janie Wallace, b April 2, 1875, married June 13, 1898, Ralph Payne They had issue ¹William Wallace Payne, b April 30, 1899; ²Lawrence Wesley Payne, b. February 14, 1901

(2) Levin E Wallace. b December 14, 1876, untraced

(3) Zetta Wallace, b June, 1882, d in infancy

(4) Mattie Wallace, b September 16, 1883, d in infancy

Sarah Elizabeth Wolf (youngest child of Jesse and Polly (Polk) Wolf), married twice Her first husband was William Hart, whom she married February 19, 1850 Her second husband, by whom she had no issue, was Jacob Frink By the first she had four children · ¹Alice, ²Frank, ³Minnie, ⁴Sadie

JESSE WOLF'S CAPTURE

Jesse Wolf, the husband of Polly (Polk) Wolf, was a man of great determination and a stranger to fear He was but seventeen years of age when the War of 1812 began. In the summer of 1813 General William Henry Harrison, sorely pressed for soldiers with which to prosecute his Northwestern campaign, because of the opposition manifested in the Eastern States toward the war, came to Kentucky and appealed to Governor Isaac Shelby for aid. The old hero of King's Mountain, who had just been chosen a second time to fill the gubernatorial chair, turned over the administration of its duties to Lieut. Governor Hickman and summoned his fellow Kentuckians to his standard.

There lurked in the breast of every Kentuckian a deep, inherited hatred of British and Indians, because of their infamous deeds in pioneer days.

Nine regiments of Kentuckians rallied to the standard of Shelby, and being mounted at Newport, marched with him to Lake Erie, arriving just in time to hear the booming of Perry's guns as they demolished Barclay's British fleet. Shelby's army crossed over to Canada on Perry's ships, and by a rapid march overtook Proctor's army of British and Indians at the Moravian Towns and signally defeated them on October 5th, in the battle of the Thames. One of the slain was the noted Indian Chief Tecumseh.

Among those who went from Kentucky on this campaign and took part in the battle were the brothers Conrad and Jesse Wolf, who had enlisted in Capt. Jacob Stucker's Company of Col. Richard M. Johnson's regiment. They were enrolled on May 20, 1813, and mustered out at Newport, Kentucky, November 19, 1813. In the battle of the Thames Jesse Wolf was twice wounded—in the forehead and in the breast—and captured by the Indians. Some days after the battle, his captor, an Indian Chief, directed him to accompany him to a creek nearby to wash out a kettle. Wishing to get a drink of water, the chief handed his tomahawk to Jesse to hold while he got down on his knees to drink from the stream. While he was so engaged, Jesse sank the tomahawk into his skull, killing him instantly, and made his escape to Detroit river, crossing it and rejoining his regiment.

CHAPTER LVIII.

FAMILY OF NANCY (POLK) ADAMS.

Ann (Nancy) Polk, (third child of Ephraim 3d and Rhoda Morris Polk), born at the old homestead on Lain's Run, in Scott County, Kentucky, August 9, 1796, died in Shelby County, Indiana, March 11, 1850. Isaac Adams was also born in Scott County, August 13, 1799, and died in Shelby County, October 8, 1851. Isaac and Nancy Polk were married in Kentucky, in 1819, and emigrated with other kinsmen to Indiana in the fall of 1826, settling on Blue River.

In the spring of 1840 Isaac Adams and family removed to Rush County, and in 1848 to Shelby County, Indiana. Thence they removed to Hancock County. Most of their eleven children were born in Kentucky.

The following record is from the family Bible of Ephraim Polk 3d, which was inherited by his daughter, Nancy Adams, and taken by her to Indiana:

Ephraim Polk 3d, d. March 24, 1814, in Scott County, Kentucky.

Ephraim Polk, Jr., d. May, ——, 1801, drowned in spring.

Rhoda Polk d. October 23, 1839, in Scott County, Kentucky.

Ephraim Polk (son of Ephraim and Rhoda Polk), d. September 3, 1840, in Springfield, Illinois.

NANCY ADAMS' FAMILY.

Nancy (Polk) Adams, b. August 9, 1796; d. March 11, 1850.

Isaac Adams, b. August 13, 1799; d. October 7, 1851.

Nancy and Isaac had eleven children viz:

(1) James M. Adams, b. Jan. 15, 1820; d. September 20, 1891.

(2) Amanda Adams, b. March 17, 1831, d. February 26, 1872.

(3) Edward P. Adams, b August 21, 1822, d November 18, 1899
(4) Mary Adams, b November 26, 1823; d October 26, 1897.
(5) Hester Adams, b January 1, 1825, d. October 6, 1892
(6) Malinda Adams, b. April 26, 1826; d March 26, 1827
(7) A son, b January 24, 1828, d January 27, 1828
(8) Daniel Adams, b. May 26, 1829; d. January 21, 1845.
(9) Rhoda Adams, b February 19, 1831; d. January 5, 1893.
(10) Sarah Jane Adams, b April 10, 1832; d ——
(11) Marcellus Martin Adams, b November 12, 1834, d. ——

MARRIAGES.

James M Adams, and Phoebe J. Johnson, were married January 19, 1841

Amanda Adams and John White were married February 11, 1841

Hester Adams and Allen McMichael were married January 25, 1844.

Edward P Adams and Elizabeth Six were married February 7, 1847

Mary (Polly) Adams and Dr James M Ely were married June 11, 1847

Rhoda Adams and Hiram Hufford were married April ——, 1851.

Sarah J. Adams and Thos A Gant were married August 17, 1864.

Marcellus M Adams and Miranda V Bailey were married October 20, 1858 He was married secondly to Nancy Hinchman, March 12, 1874

James M. Adams married December 20, 1864 to Belinda Johnson, a sister of his first wife.

DR JAMES M. ELY'S FAMILY.

Dr James M Ely, b September 18, 1821, at Columbia, Tenn d December 1, 1907 No Palestine

Mary Adams Ely, b November 26, 1823; d October 26, 1897.

Dr Ely and Mary Adams married June 11, 1847, and had the following children

(1) Manora Arabella Ely, b March 29, 1848

(2) Lucien C. Ely, b March 1, 1855

(3) Ada Mae Ely, b July 10, 1859.

Manora Arabella Ely was married November 5, 1868, to Dr Chas H Kirkhoff, who was b February 15, 1847, and d. February 11, 1899 They had issue

(1) Charles Kirkhoff, b April 13, 1869

(2) Anna Kirkhoff, b December 10, 1874, died January 4, 1881

(3) Harry Kirkhoff, b April 30, 1883.

Harry Kirkhoff and Fanny H Studa, were married June 8, 1903. Fanny was b in Cincinnati, Ohio, October 5, 1881 They had issue ¹Maxine Kirkhoff, b September 18, 1903, ²Mary Kirkhoff, b June 29, 1905

Dr Lucien C Ely, b March 1, 1855, was married October 10, 1878, to Ida J Anderson, b November 13, 1857 They had issue

(1) Harry Ely, b August 5, 1879, married December 25, 1901, to Myrtle Hunter, by whom he has one child, Kenneth Ely, b June 14, 1904

Ada Mae Ely, b July 10, 1859, married March 11, 1878, to W H Garver, b August 11, 1857, in Hamilton, Butler County, Ohio To them was born a daughter who died shortly after birth

FAMILY OF DR. JAMES M. ADAMS

Dr James M Adams (eldest child of Isaac and Nancy (Polk) Adams), was b in Scott County, Kentucky, Jan 15, 1820, and d in Shelby County, Indiana, September 20, 1894 He was married twice, his wives being sisters His first wife, to whom he was united January 14, 1841, was Phoebe J. Johnson, of Shelby County, b April 22, 1824 By her he had issue

(1) Sarah Ann Adams, b May 17, 1843

(2) Mary Melissa Adams, b February 16, 1846,

(3) John Quincy Adams, b November 26, 1848; d. July 29, 1850
(4) Marcellus W. Adams, b September 30, 1851
(5) Martha B. Adams, b June 6, 1854.
(6) Emma Adams, b February 15, 1857; d ——.
(7) Frank Adams, b June 2, 1861, d December 13, 1862

Phoebe J Adams died in Shelby County, June 18, 1864, and on December 20, 1864, Dr Adams was married to Belinda Johnson who was born May 15, 1832. By the latter he had.

(8) Charles W Adams, b March 21, 1866
(9) Will Cumback Adams, b April 6, 1868
(10) Dr Ovid Adams, b April 8, 1871.
(11) Catherine Adams, b March 26, 1873; d December 18, 1879.
(12) Jesse Adams, b. ———, 1875

Most of these children live at Shelbyville, Indiana

INTERMARRIAGES.

Mary Melissa Adams, married Theodore F Vandergrift, March 28, 1871, and to them were born: [1]Harry Vandergrift; [2]Kitty Vandergrift

Marcellus W. Adams was married December 28, 1871, to Sarah Chapler, and to them was born seven children [1]Fred, [2]Arthur, [3]Earl, [4]Emma, [5]Roland, [6]Bessie, [7]James They all reside in Wabash, Indiana.

Martha B Adams married John Calvin Tyner, of Wabash County, August 21 1873, and they had issue [1]Cora, [2]Fred, [3]Frank, [4]Oma, [5]Jack Cora married Elva Signs They have one son, aged nine years, and they reside at Butler, Indiana, All the other children of John C Tyner and wife live at Wabash

FAMILY OF JOHN WHITE.

Amanda Adams, b. March 17, 1821, d. February 26, 1872, was the second child of Isaac and Nancy (Polk) Adams She was married February 11, 1841, to John White, a most excellent gentleman of Wabash, Indiana. He was b December 19, 1815, and d March 29, 1870 They had issue

(1) Mary Jane White b January 11 ... ember 25, 18..

(2) Parmelia Alice White, b. June 30, 1843.
(3) Daniel White, b. January 28, 1845
(4) Ann Marie White, b April 1, 1847
(5) Lealdis White. b December 29, 1848 d ———, 1880
(6) John W White, b October 12, 1858, killed in 1877 by highwayman, in Rush County
(7) Lydia White. b December 14, 1851.
(8) Mattie Amanda White, b January 17, 1854
(9) Sarah India White, b July 29, 1869, d in 1881

Parmelia Alice White (second child of John and Amanda Adams White), married on July 10, 1872, Lieut Harry H Wheeler of Wabash, a veteran officer of the Seventy-fifth Indiana Vol Infant in the Civil War, who was b August 5, 1819. They had issue ¹Gertrude Wheeler, b August 26, 1874, d. January 30, 1908, ²Anna Wheeler, b October 16, 1877, residence Lexington, Ky, ³Lee H Wheeler, b March 16, 1881; d July 18, 1881

Anna Wheeler was married February 22, 1899, to Homer H Lamport, of Wabash, a son of Rev A W Lamport of Pasadena, Cal They have no children Homer Lamport removed from Wabash to Lexington, Ky, in 1902 and was made General Foreman of the Mechanical Department of the Lexington & Eastern Railway Company

Lieut Wheeler was a widower at the time he married Parmelia Alice White His first wife was a Miss Martha Lessig, of Wabash, to whom he was married July 10, 1863 They had one child, Edith Wheeler, b February 16, 1865 She married Bland Baldwin, a leading jeweler of Wabash, and they removed a few years later to Winchester, Kentucky, his native place They have three children ¹Lee Wheeler, 18, ²Cora, 16, ³Albert Rand Baldwin, 10

Daniel White (third child and eldest son of John and Amanda (Adams) White), was married November 10, 1869, to Ellen Tyner of Hancock County, Indiana, by whom he had issue

(1) Bessie Tyner White, b July 31, 1872 She married Frank Porter and they have no children Residence Enid, Oklahoma

(2) Earl White b January 4, 1876

ELIZABETH TYNER WHITE,
granddaughter of Nancy (Polk) Adams, La Fayette, Ind.

THE NEW YORK
PUBLIC LIBRARY

ASTER, LENOX AND
TILDEN FOUNDATIONS.

(3) Grace White, b April 11, 1884 Single and resides with parents in La Fayette, Indiana

Earl White grew to manhood in La Fayette, and took a course in Perdue University, graduating therefrom in June, 1896 When the Spanish-American War began he enlisted in the army, joining an Indiana battery, but his company did not reach the seat of war, its services not being necessary After being mustered out, he took a position with a leading manufacturing firm in Chicago He was sent to Bremen, Germany, to look after the firm's business there, where he remained for five years Coming back to America, he located in Indianapolis While living at Bremen, Earl married a German lady, Lottie Hess, and they have one child, William

Bessie Tyner White, Earl's sister, also attended Perdue University

Ann Marie White (fourth child of John and Amanda (Adams) White), was married October 5, 1865, to Alden Newsom, who was b June 7, 1842 The issue of this union was

(1) Winona Newsom, b January 30, 1867

(2) Samuel Lee Newsom, b February 15, 1869

(3) Cora Belle Newsom, b July 16, 1872 Winona is not married

Samuel Lee Newsom married Anna Henley, of Carthage, Ind, and they have one child, Catherine, now grown

Cora Belle married Frank McCarthy, of Carthage, but they have no children

Lealdis White, (fifth child of John and Amanda (Adams) White), married December 7, 1871 to Sarah Boone He d in 1880, leaving no issue

John W White, (sixth child of John and Amanda (Adams) White), was murdered and robbed by a highwayman named Foxwell in 1877, in Rush County, Indiana His murderer was captured, tried for the crime, but escaped from the penitentiary and fled

Lydia White, (seventh child of John and Amanda (Adams) White), was married Sept 18, 1872, to Samuel Shank, and to them were born two children

(1) Clarence Shank, b

(2) Bernice Shank, b Feb. 24, 1892 Bernice married Dec 24, 1908, Mr Shelby, of Beatrice, Nebraska

Mattie Amanda White (eighth child of John and Amanda (Adams) White), married Feb 22, 1873, James Williams, of Sigourney, Iowa They have three children ¹Ora, b 1878; ²Ray, b 1882, ³Alice, b 1885.

Sarah India White, b July 29, 1869, d Nov 4, 1873, when twelve years of age

FAMILY OF ALLEN McMICHAEL

Hester Adams, (fifth child of Isaac and Nancy (Polk) Adams), was b. Jan 1, 1825, and d Oct 6, 1892. She was married Jan 25, 1844 to Allen McMichael, by whom she had issue

(1) James Madison McMichael, b Dec 28, 1844, d. April 27, 1884

(2) William J McMichael, b Sept 8, 1846, d Oct 19, 1853.

(3) Nancy Ann McMichael, b Jan. 20, 1884, d Feb. 9, 1870.

(4) Marcellus McMichael, b Oct 17 1850, residence, Des Moines, Iowa.

(5) Alonzo McMichael, b. April 1, 1853, residence, Des Moines, Iowa

(6) Mary J McMichael, b April 5, 1856.

(7) Sarah Alice McMichael, b July 23, 1858

(8) Martha A McMichael, b. Oct. 5, 1861

(9) Laura L McMichael, b April 5, 1866.

MARRIAGES

James Madison McMichael married in 1868 to Eliza C Howard, of Des Moines, Iowa, and had issue: ¹Anna, ²William N , ³John Wesley; ⁴Charles, ⁵George. The latter is dead but the others live with their mother at Des Moines, Iowa.

Nancy Ann McMichael was married in 1859 to W. H. Hendrix and died without issue.

Marcellus N McMichael is Chief Engineer and Superintendent of the Des Moines Water Company, Des Moines, Iowa, and is regarded as a highly efficient officer. He was married in 1874 to Miss A. F. Houstin, and had issue ¹Minnie M.; ²Lucien P., ³Winfield S., ⁴Marcellus M. Lucien P. lives in New York, the others in Des Moines, Iowa.

Marcellus M. McMichael was married secondly, in 1893 to Hattie E. Savage, by whom he has no issue.

Alonzo McMichael was married in 1875 to Araminta Hobson, by whom he had one child.

Mary J. McMichael was married Feb 22, 1877 to George G. Carter, (b. Nov 23, 1853) and they live at Nevada, Iowa. To them were born nine children, viz.

(1) Alta Carter, b. March 4, 1878
(2) Daisey L. Carter, b. June 23, 1879
(3) Frederick Carter, b. April 3, 1881
(4) Edwin O. Carter, b. May 18, 1883
(5) Clarence Carter, b. Jan 15, 1885.
(6) Bessie Carter, b. Jan. 28, 1886, d. March 8, 1887
(7) Frankie Carter, b. Dec 23, 1888, d. Aug 25, 1893.
(8) Laura Carter, b. Sept 28, 1890
(9) Laurence Carter, b. Sept 11, 1897.

Alta Carter married Ed Hague, June 29, 1898.

Frederick Carter and Halley ——— were married April 19, 1906, residence, Tacoma, Washington.

Daisy Carter and Dr W. D. Mason were married Dec. 20, 1907 Residence, Ogden, Utah

Edwin O. Carter and Anna Addison were married Nov 5, 1908 Edwin is a graduate of Iowa University, and a prominent physician of Iowa Falls, Iowa

Clarence Carter was married to Ruth McCollum, Dec. 30, 1908 Residence, Tacoma, Washington.

Sarah Alice McMichael was married Sept 27, 1876, to George Miller Breeding, of Winterset, Iowa, and they had issue:

(1) Lulu Breeding, b. Aug 31, 1877.
(2) George Allan Breeding, b. April 30, 1879.
(3) Elinor Breeding, b. July 9, 1880

George M. Breeding, d. Sept. . . . . was married July 11 . . . .

(4) Martha Peak, b Jan 18, 1886
(5) Frank Peak, b July 20, 1888
(6) Ralph Peak, b July 20 1891
(7) Bruce Peak, b Nov 28, 1892
(8) Ruth Peak, b June 15 1897
(9) Hugh Earle Peak, b April 22, 1900

Martha McMichael was married to William Conway, Nov 3, 1885 They had issue
(1) Laura Conway, b Dec 30, 1887
(2) Frank Conway, b July 20, 1889
(3) Edward Conway, b. Sept 12, 1890
(4) Fred Conway, b June 25, 1898

William Conway, d Nov 3, 1885, and his widow was married Dec 23, 1908, to a Mr Sinke They all reside in Des Moines

Laura McMichael married William Kimball, in October, 1883, and they had issue
(1) Bessie Kimball, b May 7, 1885
(2) Nellie Kimball, b. Dec 6, 1886
(3) Myrtha Kimball, b Aug. 15, 1889
(4) Katherine Kimball, b Sept 4, 1892
(5) Clyde Kimball, b Dec 30, 1901; d July 24, 1902.

Bessie was married in November 1908 to Hartley Worden and they reside on a ranch near Wibeau, Montana The other children live in Des Moines

JOHN H. HUFFORD'S FAMILY

John H Hufford, b Dec 25, 1828, in Rush County, Indiana. Rhoda A Adams, b Feb. 19, 1831 They were married April 10, 1851 Issue·
(1) Nancy E Hufford, b July 7, 1852, d March 17, 1853
(2) Arkansas Hufford, b July 18, 1854, d Dec. 14, 1859.
(3) Ann M Hufford, b Sept 19, 1855, d Sept 24, 1855
(4) Laura Hufford, b March 24, 1857, married, lives in Rushville
(5) John M. Hufford, b July 10, 1859, residence, Greenfield, Indiana
(6) Amanda F Hufford, b May 3, 1861, married ——— Havens, Greenfield

(7) Lot Adams Hufford, b Sept 3, 1863. Prof College
(8) William T Hufford, b Dec 5, 1865
(9) Bennie O Hufford, b Dec 13, 1867
(10) Edward Polk Hufford, b Oct 10, 1872

Edward P Adams and his wife Elizabeth Six, had born to them a son, John W Adams, ———, 1850

FAMILY OF THOMAS A GANT.

Sarah Jane Adams, (popularly called "Sadie"), was the tenth child of Isaac and Nancy (Polk) Adams. She was b April 10, 1832, and was married Aug. 17, 1861 to Thomas A Gant, a grocer, of Greenfield, Ind , by whom she had five children

(1) Annie Lile Gant, b July 4, 1865, d Sept 2, 1866
(2) Minnie Gant, b. April 10, 1868; d Sept 30, 1869
(3) Dora Gant, b July 29, 1869
(4) Marcellus Frank Gant, b Feb 11, 1872
(5) John Gant, b July 4, 1874

DR. MARCELLUS M. ADAMS' FAMILY.

Dr Marcellus M Adams, b Nov 12, 1834, was the eleventh and youngest child of Isaac Adams and his wife Nancy (Polk) Adams Dr Adams was twice married His first wife was Miranda V Bailey, of Freeport, Ind , to whom he was united Oct 20, 1858, and by whom he had the following children

(1) Clara Adams, b Oct 19, 1859, d Dec 2, 1863
(2) Fannie B Adams, b Jan. 28, 1862, d March 13, ——
(3) Nettie V Adams, b Dec 1, 1866, lives in Los Angeles, Cal

Miranda (Bailey) Adams d June 11, 1873, and on March 11, 1874, Dr. Adams married Nancy Hinchman, of Rush County, Indiana., b. Oct. 17, 1847 Her family emigrated from Virginia to Indiana. Issue

(4) Olive Adams, b Jan. 15, 1875, married Sam'l Brown, firm of Brown Bros , beef and pork packers, Indianapolis, Ind
(5) Mary Hester Adams b Feb 1, 1877
(6) Ellen May Adams b Jan 8, 1881

FANNIE STUTSMAN'S FAMILY.

Fannie B. Adams, b. Jan 28, 1862, d. March 13, 1895, (second child of Dr Marcellus M. Adams by his first wife, Miranda V. Bailey), married M. P Stutsman, Jan. 2, 1885, by whom she had issue

(1) George Edgar Stutsman, b Aug 5, 1885
(2) Nancy Hazel Stutsman, b October 24, 1886
(3) Benjamin H Stutsman, b Aug 12, 1888
(4) Nellie Stutsman, b Nov 25, 1891; d at 2 years of age
(5) Fred Adams Stutsman, b March 7, 1893
(6) Nettie Leona Stutsman, b February 10, 1895.

SKETCH OF DR MARCELLUS M. ADAMS.

Dr Marcellus Martin Adams, of Greenfield, Indiana, b Nov 12, 1834, was the eleventh and youngest child of Isaac and Nancy (Polk) Adams

Marcellus grew to manhood on the farm, taking an active part with his brothers in all the duties incident to an agricultural life

Marcellus read medicine with Dr James M Ely, while living at his house, and attended lectures at the Rush Medical College, Chicago, in the winter of 1860 He later attended the Medical College of Indiana, from which he was graduated

The Civil War breaking out, and Dr Adams being a zealous friend of the Union, he enlisted in a three monthe regiment, but the quota of Indiana in the 75,000 call of Mr Lincoln was filled before his company had time to don the habiliaments of Mars. Dr. Adams was postmaster at Freeport at that time and returned for a short time to the sale of postage stamps and delivery of letters.

After a call was made by Mr Lincoln for 300,000 more troops, Dr Adams again enlisted (in July, 1862), going to Camp Joe Reynolds, at Indianapolis On arrival there he was put on duty as Dispensary Sargent with three barracks full of volunteers to look after and also draw rations for. In September following he was detached from his company (First Indiana Cavalry) and put in charge of recruits and drafted men as surgeon. He served in that capacity for about a year

ELLEN, MARY, OLIVE AND NETTIE ADAMS
daughters of Dr. M. M.

at Camp Carrington, Indianapolis and was then commissioned as Assistant Surgeon of the 116th Indiana Volunteer Infantry, six months troops, performing the entire medical duties for that organization until their return home in February, 1864

At the close of the war Dr. Adams returned to Indiana setting up in practice at Greenfield, where he accumulated a competency and resided thereafter. giving a portion of his time to his farm near that city

Dr Adams was recognized as one of the ablest physicians in the State of Indiana, and for many years he enjoyed a large practice He was quiet, genial and agreeable of manner, somewhat inclined to humor, and very popular Dr Adams, in addition to his medical researches and duties took great interest in paleontology. He had one of the largest private collections of the kind in the West, including skeletons, armor, and implements of prehistoric and Indian races; enough Indian bones and relics and curios of all kinds to equip a large museum. Dr. Adams died at his home in Greenfield, Ind

DR. JEFFERSON J. POLK AND DESCENDANTS.

Dr Jefferson Johnson Polk (sixth child and third son of Ephraim 3d, and Rhoda (Morris) Polk), was b. at the old Polk homestead on Lain's Run, Scott County, March 10, 1802, and d at Perryville, Kentucky, May 23, 1881 His wife, whose maiden name was Eliza Tod, was a daughter of Wm Tod, a leading manufacturer of Lexington. She was born in that city and d April 13, 1867

Jefferson first attended the neighborhood school and being apt and clear headed, soon mastered the simpler studies, working on the farm in season and going to school in the fall and winter months The balance of his education Jefferson Polk obtained in a printing office, one of the best schools a boy can attend, a school in which he learns not only spelling, punctuation, the meaning of words, grammatical construction of sentences, geography, history, etc, but in which he is daily brought into contact with the best thought and intellect of the day, and current even -

At the age

mother, Rhoda Polk to Colonels Richard M and James Johnson, who owned the Georgetown Patriot (Major Wm Sebree, editor), to "learn the art and trade of a printer"

The paper suspending publication after he had worked on it for three years, Jefferson was given a release and an excellent letter of recommendation to all editors and printers Armed with this, he went to Lexington in 1820, securing employment on the Kentucky Gazette, which had been founded by John Bradford in August, 1787, the second newspaper established west of the Alleghanies Mr Bradford was a man of great erudition He also published almanacs, books and pamphlets This position presented a broader field of the printing art, and Jefferson Polk soon learned every intricacy of the "art preservative of arts"

Jefferson now began a regular course of reading, procuring books on all subjects from the library of Transylvania University, which contained several thousand volumes Being an omnivorous reader, he explored the domains of history, art, science, literature, and other departments of human knowledge With a view of making medicine his profession, he read up on that science and attended lectures at the Medical Department of Transylvania After he had completed the necessary length of service imposed by the craft he took charge as foreman of the office of Wm Gibbs Hunt, publisher of The Modern Monitor, and later assumed a like position with Thomas T Skillman, publisher of the Western Luminary, a Presbyterian journal, and also of books, pamphlets and bibles

About this time Jefferson concluded to don the matrimonial yoke Miss Eliza Tod was the name of the fair one whose lovely face and form transfixed his palpitating heart. The preacher, the celebrated Rev Nathan H Hall, fastened on the yoke

In February, 1826, Jefferson Polk moved to Danville and purchased the Olive Branch printing plant, of Edmund Shipp At the time Kentucky was just emerging from the excitement of the Old and New Court question, but a fiercer controversy soon ensued Henry Clay had voted in Congress for John Quincy Adams, in preference to General Jackson, for President, and was appointed by Mr Adams Secretary of State

DR. JEFFERSON J. POLK,
of Perryville, Ky., son of Ephraim Polk 3rd.

"Bargain and corruption" were charged. The Olive Branch had been a Jackson sheet, but Jefferson Polk now hoisted the banner of Mr. Clay.

The great cholera scourge of 1833 killed many citizens of Danville and great numbers of others fled, but Jefferson Polk remained, waiting on the sick, giving them medicine, praying with them, and helping to bury them. He sold his newspaper and printing plant to S. S. Dismukes, who conducted it for some time, aided by Clement Polk, also a printer, and brother of Jefferson Polk.

James G. Birney, a strong advocate of Abolitionism and then a resident of Danville, induced Dismukes to print an Abolition sheet, he, Birney, writing the editorials. The populace was incensed; a mob was organized, and it proceeded to the office with a view of destroying the plant and driving the editor and printer from the town. Dismukes had purchased the paper from Jefferson Polk on credit, after which the latter purchased a book store and added to it a stock of drugs.

While the mob was assembling, Jefferson Polk demanded the keys of the office from Dismukes and received a hasty transfer of the property back to himself. Then mounting a balcony, he announced to the mob that he had re-purchased the property that he had sold it on credit and it had not been paid for by Dismukes. This appeased the crowd and it quietly dispersed. Birney in deep disgust, left Kentucky, went to Michigan, and was afterward the first candidate of the Abolition Party for the Presidency. Clement Polk, who favored peacible, not forcible emancipation, was also disgusted, and emigrated to Springfield, Illinois, where he bought a farm, established a newspaper and erected a large grist mill. And there he died in 1849. During his residence there he was an intimate friend and associate of Abraham Lincoln, then a young lawyer at that bar.

After taking back the Olive Branch and plant, Jefferson Polk conducted the paper for fifteen months and again disposed of it. He also disposed of his book and drug store and purchased a farm near Danville. The Methodist Quarterly Conference licensed him   p   his he commenced at the same   tudies

In November, 1839, he matriculated in Transylvania Medical College at Lexington, and after much hard study graduated therefrom

In 1840 Jefferson Polk sold his farm, removed to Perryville, and commenced a regular practice of medicine The citizens of Perryville, in 1831, led by Dr Polk, organized the first temperance society in Kentucky

Dr. Polk's eldest son, William Tod Polk, also studied medicine, graduating from Transylvania Medical School in 1848, and entering into partnership with his father The latter's son, Thomas Polk, and his daughter Margaret Polk, also became physicians Thomas removed to Kansas, and practiced and died there. Margaret graduated at the Women's Hospital of Philadelphia, became a Missionary Doctor, and for many years she has been at the head of a big Methodist Hospital at Soo-Chow, China Her neice, Miss Ethel Polk, daughter of her brother, Dr Thos Polk, deceased, also graduated at the Philadelphia Woman's Hospital, and went to China as a Missionary Doctor, at the same hospital with her Aunt Margaret Jefferson Polk's family is largely a family of doctors and lawyers

When the Civil War began, Dr. Jefferson Polk strongly espoused the cause of the Union, his views being supported by his daughters. The sons all sympathized with the South, but took no active part in the armed conflict The battle of Perryville, October 8, 1862, brought the horrors of war to their doors There were Polks on both sides in that battle. Lieut General Leonidas Polk of Louisiana, commanded the Confederate troops, the Commander-in-Chief, General Braxton Bragg, being absent Under General Polk were numerous other descendants of Robert and Magdalen, belonging to Southern commands. On the Union side was Col. Burr Harrison Polk, of Indiana, and others of the name from that state, and Illinois

Dr Polk and his son, Dr Wm Tod Polk, rolled up their sleeves and worked hard in aid of the wounded Dr Polk's house was filled with wounded men and he was put in charge of them He and his son continued their aid to the wounded for some time after the battle

DR. WM. TOD POLK,
Perryville, Ky., son of Dr. Jefferson J. Polk.

THE NEW YORK
PUBLIC LIBRARY

ASTOR, LENOX AND
TILDEN FOUNDATIONS

Dr Jefferson Polk retired from active practice on account of the precarious condition of his health, and died May 23, 1881

FAMILY OF DR. JEFFERSON J. POLK.

The children born to Dr Jefferson Johnson Polk and his wife, Eliza (Tod) Polk were:

(1) Martha F Polk, b October 15, 1824; d. July 8, 1911.

(2) William Tod Polk, b January 3, 1827, d April 24, 1890

(3) Ephraim Jehosephat Polk, b January 16, 1829, d June 17, 1896

(4) Jefferson B Polk, b March 3, 1831, d February 5, 1833

(5) Margaret Grant Polk, b. March 7, 1833; d unmarried, July 9, 1911

(6) John M Polk, b. November 22, 1835, d May 2, 1898

(7) Rosa F Polk, b September 5 1839, d May 23, 1888

(8) Thomas Jefferson Polk, b March 17, 1842, d January 18, 1886

(9) Eliza Bell Polk, b October 18, 1845; living at Perryville, unmarried.

Dr Jefferson J Polk, b. March 10, 1802, d at Perryville, Ky., March 23, 1881

Eliza (Tod) Polk, his wife, d April 13, 1867

The intermarriages and families of Dr. Jefferson J. Polk s sons and daughters were as follows

MARTHA F. DUNCAN'S FAMILY.

Martha F. Polk, b. at Lexington, eldest child of Dr Jefferson J Polk, was married February 11, 1852 to Rev William W Duncan, teacher and Presbyterian minister Mr Duncan was a graduate of Center College, Danville, Ky He filled a number of pulpits in different parts of the State and for a number of years conducted an academy at Taylorsville, Kentucky

Th... ldred
Duncan... most

lovable woman and married Samuel H Wakefield, of Nelson County Mr Wakefield died at Chattanooga. Tenn, May 6, 1899, and Lila's father, Mr Duncan, April 7, 1900.

To S H Wakefield and his wife, Lila, were born two children ¹Steel Duncan Wakefield, and ²Tod Wakefield

FAMILY OF DR. WILLIAM TOD POLK.

Dr Wm Tod Polk (eldest son and second child of Dr Jefferson J Polk), was b at Lexington, Ky, January 3, 1827. Before he had attained to his majority he commenced reading medicine under his father He next took a course of lectures at the Medical College of Transylvania University, graduating therefrom in the class of 1848. He then settled in practice with his father, at Perryville, continuing in partnership until the latter retired in 1859, on account of failing health He practiced at Perryville during a period of forty-two years, or until his death, and none had a reputation for higher professional skill

Dr William Tod Polk was twice married. First, on December 18 1851, to Miss Maggie A Briscoe, of Boyle County, who d June 23, 1881 Second, to Mrs. Lou Wharton, of Danville By the latter he had no issue

By his first wife Dr Wm Tod Polk had issue

(1) John B Polk, b December 2, 1852; d April 6, 1858

(2) Dr Thomas P Polk. b September 15, 1855, d ———

(3) Margaret H Polk, b March 13, 1862, living at Soo Chow, China

(4) Jefferson Polk, Vet Surgeon, b 1864.

Dr Thomas Polk the second son, after graduating in medicine, practiced for some time at Perryville with his father. He then moved to Kansas, establishing himself near Kansas City, where he died He was twice married His first wife was Miss Catharine Camp, of Boyle County, by whom he had issue ¹Paul Eve Polk, ²Jennie Polk By his second wife, Jennie Camp, sister of Catharine he had ³Ethel Polk ⁴Fay Polk Paul Eve died young Ethel graduated at the Scarritt Bible and Training College, Kansas City She next entered the Philadelphia Woman's Medical College and after graduating in medicine went to China in September, 1912, as a Doctor-Missionary, to join her aunt Margaret Polk, who has charge of the large Methodist Hospital at Soo-Chow.

It will be observed that she makes the fifth physician in her line, including her grand-father, Dr Jefferson J. Polk

CHAPTER LVIX

FAMILY OF EPHRAIM J. POLK.

Ephraim Jehosephat Polk, (son of Dr Jefferson J. Polk), b. January 16, 1829, at Lexington, Kentucky, d suddenly from heart trouble in his law office, June 17, 1896, at Harrodsburg, Ky, where he had resided and practiced law for many years, with the exception of a few years residence at Louisville While residing at Louisville he made a race for Congress, on the Prohibition ticket

After attending the schools of Perryville, Ephraim was a student at Center College and graduated therefrom He then went to Georgetown and read law under his cousin, Marcellus Polk, a leading attorney at that bar Locating at Harrodsburg, he was admitted to the Mercer County bar in 1858, and soon enjoyed a good practice

On Jan 15, 1858, Ephraim J Polk was united in marriage to Miss Mary Ellen Newton, only child of Mrs. Kitty Newton, and a member of one of the pioneer families of Kentucky The young wife was a beautiful girl, whose personal charms were equalled only by her amiability and loveliness of character in every respect

CHILDREN OF EPHRAIM J. POLK.

(1) Martha Ferguson Polk, b December 2, 1859
(2) Eliza Catharine Polk, b August 21, 1861
(3) John Newton Polk, b November 17, 1863
(4) Jefferson Johnson Polk, b. October 8, 1866.
(5) Ella Polk, b December 3, 1868
(6) Margaret Scott Polk, b November 24, 1870
(7) William Goddard Polk, b December 24, 1872

Martha, the eldest child, was married December 30, 1886, to Prof Harry Asbury Evans, of Harrodsburg, Ky After marriage Prof Evans and wife went to Texas, establishing a female academy at Sulphur Springs. His wife, who was

WM. GODDARD POLK,
Louisville, Ky., son of Ephraim J. Polk.

very proficient in mathematics, taught that department While conducting this school. Prof Evans died. August 15, 1898. They had no children Mrs Evans continued to conduct the school for some years after the death of her husband, then retiring and returning to Kentucky She now resides at Louisville

Eliza Katharine ("Kitty") Polk (second child of E J and Mollie (Newton) Polk), was married March 16, 1882, to Leslie I Coleman, of Harrodsburg, a young man of the highest character, and a fine business man, who for a number of years was engaged in the commission business at that place Later he removed to Louisville, where he was General Agent for several big coal mines of Tennessee, and from there to Knoxville, where he is now engaged in coal mining

Leslie I. and Kitty Coleman had issue
(1) Mary Coleman, b July 30 1883
(2) Julius Polk Coleman, b June 2, 1885
(3) Nellie Birnie Coleman, b November 9, 1887

The latter graduated at the Semple Collegiate School, Louisville, in the class of 1905

John Newton Polk (third child of Ephraim J Polk and Mary Ellen Newton), was married November 24 1886, to Julia Phillips, of Lebanon, Kentucky, daughter of a prominent citizen and proprietor of the large Roller Mills at that place John was engaged in commercial business for some time, but later purchased a farm near Salvisa, in Mercer County, where he lived until his death

To John Newton Polk and wife were born:
(1) Elizabeth Seymour Polk, b October 13, 1887; d November 22, 1891
(2) George Latimer Polk, b May ——, 1889
(3) Leslie Coleman Polk, b December 30, 1892
(4) Ephraim John Polk, b September 2, 1896
(5) Annie McChord Polk, b August 21, 1899

Jefferson Johnson Polk 2d, (fourth child and second son of Ephraim J and Mary Ellen Newton), was married January 3, 1889, to Miss Louise Wheat, by whom he had issue:

(3) Emily Louise Polk, b November 30, 1898.
(4) Charles Edward Polk, b October 17, 1901
(5) Elizabeth Polk, b. September 6, 1892.

Mary Lynn, the eldest, a lovely young woman, is instructor in Expression and Physical Culture, at Louisville, in connection with a prominent Seminary

Ella Polk (fifth child of Ephraim J and Mary Ellen (Newton) Polk), married Harry Crump Montgomery, of Louisville, October 19, 1892 At the time of their marriage, Mr Montgomery had charge of one of the departments of the large jewelry establishment of Wm Kendrick & Sons, and afterward became one of the firm, with his wife's brother, William Goddard Polk, in the Southern Optical Company. They had issue

(1) Harry Polk Montgomery, b. January 3, 1895.
(2) Eugene Jefferson Montgomery, b March 31, 1897
(3) Eleanor Montgomery, b. March 12, 1900
(4) Mary Catharine Montgomery, b March 26, 1902

Margaret Scott Polk (sixth child of Ephraim J and Mary Ellen (Newton) Polk), is unmarried. She is an accomplished artist and was for several years, art teacher at Margaret Hall, a female seminary at Versailles, Ky

William Goddard Polk (seventh and youngest child of Ephraim J and Mary Ellen (Newton) Polk), is unmarried He is a prominent business man of Louisville, largely interested in Kentucky and Tennessee mountain lands and coal mines, in which he has accumulated a handsome fortune

Margaret Grant Polk (fifth child of Dr Jefferson J and Eliza (Tod) Polk), b March 7, 1833, never married She lived, until her death, at the old homestead, in Perryville. For a number of years she was a teacher of mathematics in Godby Institute, Perryville, and also in an Academy conducted at Taylorsville by her brother-in-law, Rev William W. Duncan She died July 8, 1911. Maggie, as she was called, was an amiable and highly educated woman and universally beloved

John M Polk (sixth child of Dr Jefferson J and Eliza (Tod) Polk), after a good education embarked in the dry goods business at Danville, and later at Harrodsburg He married Miss Mary Tiliord, of Danville, and going to Elizabethtown, Ky., during the 80's, became cashier of a bank, and also a partner in same. After continuing in the banking business for some years, John M. retired and removed in May 1887, to a farm near Clarksville, Tennessee, where he embarked in the Jersey cattle business, and died May 2, 1898.

CHILDREN OF JOHN M. POLK.

The children of John M. and Mary (Tilford) Polk were:
(1) Tilford Polk, b. June 10, 1873, d. June 13, 1873.

(2) John Proctor Polk, b. September 26, 1875; residence Nashville, Tenn.

(3) Anna Tilford Polk, b. August 15, 1877, d. November 30, 1877.

(4) Minnie Tod Polk, b. December 13, 1886, living with mother at Mt. Pleasant, Tenn.

John Proctor Polk, was for some time L. & N. R. R. Station Agent at Columbia, Tenn., and later Chief Night Operator of that road at Nashville. He married at Columbia, November 12, 1902, to Miss Anne Fleming, of that place. Issue:

(1) John Proctor Polk, Jr., b. September 18, 1904; d. July 29, 1906.

(2) Kate Polk, born August 4, 1907.

Rosa F. Polk (seventh child of Dr. Jefferson J. and Eliza (Tod) Polk) b. September 5, 1839, d. May 23, 1888. Gentle of manner, sweet and amiable always, she was loved by every one who knew her. After an excellent academic education she engaged for some years as a teacher in Godby Institute, at Perryville.

On May 12, 1868, Rosa was married to George R. Latimer, a dry goods merchant of Perryville, who later was engaged in business at Kansas City, but returned to Kentucky and opened a dry goods store at Lebanon, where he now resides. No issue.

Thomas Jefferson Polk (eighth child of Dr. Jefferson J. and Eliza (Tod) Polk), b. March 17, 1842, d. January 18, 1886. After attending the local Academy, he matriculated at Center College, Danville, where he finished his course. He then located at Harrodsburg and engaged in the business for some years He next studied law at Harrodsburg with his brother Ephraim J Polk and entered practice at that bar in partnership with him Thomas was a most excellent man in every respect

On March 10, 1869, Thomas J Polk was married to Miss F Alice Walker, daughter of Rev Walker, a prominent minister of the Methodist Conference of Kentucky They had issue

CHILDREN OF THOS. J. POLK AND WIFE.

(1) William Tod Polk, Jr , b ——, 1871 d June 9, 1888.
(2) Edward B Polk, b about 1873; d in Texas———
(3) Rose Latimer Polk, b about February, 1875, married Clarence Hancock and to them was born a son, Marcus A Hancock
(4) Anna Coleman Polk, b ————.

Eliza Belle Polk (ninth and youngest child of Dr Jefferson J and Eliza Tod Polk), b October 18, 1845, in Boyle County, is unmarried and lives at the old homestead in Perryville She received a fine academic education at Godby Institute and is a woman of wit and intelligence

CHAPTER LX.

DANIEL POLK AND DESCENDANTS.

Daniel Polk (seventh child and fourth son of Ephraim 3d, and Rhoda (Morris) Polk), was b June 25, 1801, at the old Polk plantation on Lain's Run, Scott County, Kentucky He was drowned in Kentucky River, near Frankfort, Sept 16, 1862, while that city was occupied by the Confederate forces under General Kirby Smith He had loaned his seine to a party of soldiers, who were fishing It became hung on a snag and Daniel went into the river to loosen it In this attempt he became entangled in it, and being a large man he was drowned

On the day following Daniel Polk's death, and while all the family were absent attending his burial, the Confederate forces at Frankfort retreated across Kentucky River and out toward Lawrenceburg, followed closely by General Sill's division of Gen'l Buell's army In this division were a number of new regiments of Federal troops that had joined Buell at Louisville, and who, with little training or discipline, committed many outrageous depredations on the people of Kentucky, not stopping to inquire whether such citizens were loyal or disloyal Following the retreating Confederates, and reaching the house of Daniel Polk while all the family were absent at his funeral, a number of uniformed vandals broke into the house, robbed it of all they could carry away and destroyed all else

Daniel Polk was twice married, first, on Oct 6, 1829, to Sally Ann Tanner, (b Jan 24, 1812), daughter of David Tanner, of Cane Ridge, Bourbon County, Ky She was a first cousin of Joel Tanner Hart, the noted American Sculptor, who died in Florence, Italy in 1877, where he had lived and wrought for many years His celebrated masterpiece, "Woman Triumphant," purchased by the ladies of Lexington for $5,000, was destroyed in the burning of the court house, May 14, 1897. Joel T. Hart was the

Losing his parents when he was a child, he was adopted by his uncle David, and he and Sally Ann grew up together as foster brother and sister, until they were separated by her marriage to Daniel Polk.

DANIEL POLK'S CHILDREN

By his first wife, Sally Ann, Daniel Polk had issue

(1) Luvisa Polk, b Oct 21, 1830, d. Oct 26, 1837

(2) David Tanner Polk, b Mar 16, 1832, d May 30, 1904.

(3) Rhoda Ann Polk, b Dec 15, 1833, d Sept. 1, 1901.

(4) Thomas P D Polk, b Feb. 4, 1836; residence, Indianapolis

(5) Willis Webb Polk, b May 12, 1838; d Nov. 29, 1906.

(6) Sardius Gilead Polk, b Nov 21, 1840, d May 24, 1882.

(7) Mary Jane Polk, b. June 26, 1843; d March 29, 1875

(8) Margaret E Polk, b April 14, 1845; residence, Louisville, a widow

(9) Sarah C ("Kitty") Polk, b Aug 10, 1847, d Dec 13 1891

(10) James K Polk, b March 27, 1850, residence, Louisville

Sally Ann (Tanner) Polk dying on June 15, 1851, Daniel Polk married his second wife, Ann E White, May 6, 1852 She was b. April 27, 1827, d ——, 1912 at Frankfort. She was the daughter of Judge David White, of Donerail District, Fayette County

By his second wife, Ann (White) Polk, Daniel Polk had issue

(11) Charles L Polk, b March 27, 1853; residence, Louisville He married Bettie Sue Franklin

(12) John C Breckinridge Polk, b Aug 3, 1854

(13) Luretta Polk, b. April 18, 1859, d Jan 25, 1872

After the death of Daniel Polk, his widow, Ann Polk married Thomas Dunlap

FAMILY OF DAVID TANNER POLK

David Tanner Polk, second child and eldest son of Daniel Polk, was married May 12, 1858 to Elizabeth Guthrie, of Platte

County, Mo., daughter of W. A. Guthrie, a kinsman of Hon James Guthrie, of Louisville, Ky., Secretary of U. S. Treasury, under President Pierce. She was b. Oct. 16, 1844, and d. Aug. 18, 1901. They had issue

(1) Mary Polk, b. Nov. 30, 1859; married Sept. 22, 1880 to Canby Hawkins, of Platte County, banker and farmer. Mr. Hawkins is a kinsman of Gen'l Canby, at one time a distinguished officer of the United States Army. Also of Major Gen'l Hawkins, U. S. A.

(2) Veva Polk, b. Oct. 20, 1861, d. Nov. 14, 1881

(3) Eliphalet Polk, b. Nov. 24, 1863, d. Sept. 26, 1864.

(4) Ida Polk, b. Aug. 15, 1865, d. Feb. 24, 1870

(5) David Tanner Polk Jr., b. July 20, 1871, married Nov. 24, 1898 to Elnora Cox.

(6) Lee Polk, b. Sept. 17, 1867, d. Feb. 22, 1870.

Of the six children of David Tanner Polk, the only two surviving are Mary Hawkins and David Tanner Polk Jr., of Excelsior Springs, a prominent dental surgeon

FAMILY OF DAVID TANNER POLK, JR

Dr. David Tanner Polk Jr., (son of David Tanner Polk Sr., and his wife Elizabeth Guthrie), was b. July 20, 1871, and married Nov. 24, 1898 to Elonora Cox, b. Sept. 22, 1877. They had issue: [1]Graham Polk, b. Feb 9, 1900, [2]Elizabeth Jane Polk, b. Aug. 27, 1902, [3]Lucille Merideth Polk, b. Nov. 11, 1904, [4]Iris Lenore Polk, b. Oct. 15, 1906

Dr. David Tanner Polk Jr., resides at Excelsior Springs, Mo.

FAMILY OF RHODA ANN RODGERS.

Rhoda Ann Polk (third child and second daughter of Daniel Polk and Sally Ann (Tanner) Polk), born Dec. 15, 1833, was married Aug. 1, 1854 to James Hardin Rodgers (b. Aug. 11, 1832) a farmer of Franklin County, by whom she had issue.

(1) William Rodgers b. June 23, 1855, d. April 2, 1878

(2) Eliza Rodgers, b. . . . . ried

(3) James R. . . . .

(4) Thomas J Rodgers, b Aug. 24, 1861, unmarried, living in South America

(5) Benjamin F. Rodgers, b April 11, 1863

(6) Henry C Rodgers, b Nov 19, 1865; unmarried, residence, Louisville, Ky

(7) Hugh Allen Rodgers, b Aug. 7, 1868, d May 19, 1885

(8) Mary Latham Rodgers, b. June 28, 1870; unmarried.

(9) Hardin Rodgers, b Feb 8, 1872; unmarried, residence Louisville, Ky.

(10) Sally Tanner Rodgers, b Feb 28, 1874, unmarried

(11) Elizabeth C Rodgers, b Oct. 21, 1876.

(12) Forrest Rodgers, b March 14, 1880, unmarried

MARRIAGES.

Elizabeth C Rodgers (generally called 'Katie"), a very popular and handsome woman, was educated in the schools of Frankfort and engaged in teaching for several years. She then took a course in the Commercial College of Kentucky University, at Lexington, graduating therefrom During attendance at this college she met Charles Carter, of West Virginia, also a student of the same institution, and while she was in New York City on a visit, the young man went there and on Jan 29, 1902 they were married at the home of Mrs Carrie Tatum, a first cousin of her mother Mr Carter engaged in business at Fairmont, West Virginia, where they resided for several years They now reside at Pittsburgh, Pa To them have been born four children, two of whom are dead and two living, George and an infant

Mr Carter is a splendid man He enlisted in the army, from West Virginia, during the Spanish-American War, and in a skirmish with the Philippinos was shot through one of his lungs He crawled into a thick chapparel at the roadside and thereby escaped death, the bolomen rushing past him only a few feet away, in pursuit of the pickets they had driven in After a stronger force of Americans had repulsed the enemy, Mr. Carter was rescued by his comrades and finally recovered and returned home, entering the college at Lexington.

ROY RODGERS 2d, U. S. A.,
son of Ben F. Rodgers.

FAMILY OF BEN F RODGERS.

Ben F Rodgers (fifth child of Hardin Rodgers and Rhoda (Polk) Rodgers) was married Dec 15, 1886, to Margaret Evans (b Dec. 26, 1869) of Henry County, Ky, daughter of Lucian Evans To them were born five children
  (1) William Evans Rodgers, b Sept 21, 1887
  (2) Roy Rodgers, b May 6, 1889
  (3) Eleanor Rodgers, b April 22, 1890
  (4) Aline Rodgers, b Oct 18, 1891
  (5) Lillian Rodgers, b. July 5, 1893

William E Rodgers, eldest of the above, was married Feb 25, 1908, to Bessie Kavanaugh Bright, of Louisville, (b Sept 30, 1888) They have two children, ¹Wm Evans Rodgers Jr, b. Feb. 22, 1909, ²Bernice, b Dec 29, 1912 Wm Evans Rodgers is a Civil Engineer in the employ of the Louisville & Nashville Railroad and resides at Louisville, Ky. Roy Rodgers, the second son, is a member of Battery F, Second Field Artillery, U S A

FAMILY OF THOMAS P. D. POLK.

Thomas P D Polk (fourth child of Daniel and Sally Ann (Tanner) Polk), was born Feb 4, 1836 On May 31, 1857, he was married to Mary Eliza Pollock, of Jeffersonville, Indiana She was b May 5, 1839 in Clark County Indiana, and d January 23, 1901 They had issue:
  (1) Charles Oscar Polk, b. July 22, 1858, d Aug. 8, 1895.
  (2) Margaret Evaline Polk, b March 7, 1860, untraced.
  (3) William Daniel Polk, b June 8, 1862, d July 6, 1887.
  (4) Harriet Frances Polk, b Nov 21, 1865, married James Biggert, residence, Jeffersonville, Ind
  (5) Nellie Polk, b. Feb 14, 1868 married Forest Sampson, family untraced
  (6) Laura Polk b April 5, 1870: married George Smith: family untraced
  (7) John Polk b Feb 12, 1872, drowned July 28, 1888, while bathing in the Ohio
    Charles Oscar Polk

(1) Viola Polk, b Nov 25, 1883
(2) Oscar Polk, b. ——, 1885; d. April 19, 1885
(3) Inez Polk, b ——, 1887; d Sept 8, 1892

Thomas P. D Polk and family reside at Indianapolis

FAMILY OF WILLIS W POLK

Willis Webb Polk (fifth child of Daniel and Sally Ann (Tanner) Polk), was b May 12, 1838, on the farm in Scott County, Kentucky He d in Southern California, Nov 29, 1906

When Willis was four years of age (1842) his father removed to Winchester, Kentucky, residing there six years, pursuing his architectural business He then returned to Scott County, buying a farm on Eagle Creek, near Muddy Ford While living there, Sally Ann (Tanner) Polk, Daniel's wife, died and was buried in the family graveyard at the old Ephraim Polk place, a few miles distant There the eldest child of Daniel, Luvisa, had also been buried, in Oct 1837, beside her grandparents, Ephraim 3d and Rhoda Ann Polk

In 1853 Daniel Polk sold his farm in Scott County and purchased one in Franklin County, lying on the Lawrenceburg pike, about a mile from Frankfort, and but a short distance from the present new State Capitol building On Cedar Creek, which ran through the place, Daniel built a saw and grist mill

Here Daniel's family grew to maturity, and here he was living when he was drowned in 1862 Willis, who was very studious and a great reader, attended school in Frankfort, and was particularly fond of ancient history, art and literature

Willis left home, on New Years' Eve, 1856, and started for the West, assisting in driving stock to Sangamon County, Illinois, reaching his destination at Buffalo Heart Grove, Jan 1, 1857. After a few months sojourn in Sangamon County, Willis departed for Weston, Mo, where his eldest brother, David Tanner Polk, had located some years before.

On June 27, 1857, Willis reached Weston, where he engaged in contracting and building, meantime falling a victim to cupid's well-aimed darts. The fair one in the case was Miss Parthenia Frances Dye sixth daughter of John Kenneth Dye,

THE NEW YORK
PUBLIC LIBRARY

ASTOR, LENOX AND
TILDEN FOUNDATIONS.

who had emigrated from Mayslick, Kentucky, to Missouri a few years previous. She was born at Mayslick July 30, 1840. On Oct 10, 1858, Willis and Miss Dye were united in marriage. The children born to them were:

(1) Annie Polk, b Oct —, 1859, d Dec —, 1868.

(2) William Chinn Polk, b Nov 23, 1860, resides at Weston, Mo. William C is a most excellent man and for a number of years has been bookkeeper and cashier in a Weston bank. He married Sept 16, 1891, to Miss Minnie Hillix, of Weston, a daughter of Wm Walker Hillix, formerly of Midway, Ky., and his wife Rebecca (Whittington) Hillix. To them was born a daughter that died in infancy, Nov 22, 1898.

Willis W. Polk's wife died in 1866, near Weston and not long after the birth of their second child. On Jan 1, 1867, after the Civil War, Willis was again married, his second wife being the widow Endemial Burch, nee Drane, of Kentucky. She was a daughter of Rev J T Drane, a noted Baptist preacher and brother of Judge Drane of Frankfort.

Willis W. Polk Sr., and his second wife had issue

(3) Willis W. Polk, Jr., b Oct 3, 1867, residence, San Francisco

(4) Daniel Polk, b May 25, 1869; d in 1909

(5) Endemial Polk, b Nov. 15, 1872, d. May 20, 1890, in Paris, France

(6) Daisey Polk, b April 23, 1874, living in San Francisco

(7) Trusten Polk, b Sept 18, 1876, d Nov 20, 1877.

Mrs Endemial Polk, d in July 1906 at Blakely, Cal., and her husband, Willis W Polk Sr., followed her to the grave not long after, Nov 29, 1906

Willis W Polk Jr., was married at San Francisco to Mrs Christine Moore, nee Barada a Spanish lady and niece of the wife of President Diaz, of Mexico. They have no issue

Daniel Polk, brother of Willis, was married Dec. 25, 1897 in Brooklyn, New York, to Miss Alice Grimm, of Topton, Pa. He died in New York City in 1909. They had a daughter, Endemial. Daniel was also an architect, his specialty being classic work. . . . . He was also a noted musician, playing . . . .

Miss Daisey P H . . . . and-some woman, and also a fine musician, playing on the violin with remarkable skill She was a pupil while in Italy of Caesar Thompson and other noted violin teachers

Prompted by the artistic inclinations of his children, while residing at St Louis, Willis W. Polk Sr , took his family to Europe in order to give them the best advantages in art and music culture, spending about seven years there. After a short residence in London he went to Rome and finally located at Florence, the great art center, where his sons could study the classic styles of architecture, and the daughters pursue their studies in music Here the eldest daughter, Endie, at the age of eighteen became known as a young woman of extraordinary musical talent, her voice being conceded the equal of that of Patti or any other great singer, according to statements of her teachers. She was the idol of her parents and family A date was fixed for her debut in grand opera, at Paris, France. She was heralded by critics and the press as "a coming great prima donna "

But, alas' the fond hopes of her devoted family were doomed to disappointment A few days before her intended debut the Angel of Death waved his dark wand over the happy, expectant ones of Willis Polk's household, and the voice of the beautiful and idolized daughter was stilled forever She died in Paris, France, May 20, 1890, from a sudden attack of appendicitis Crushed and sorrowing, her father and family returned to the United States the following year, going to San Francisco and erecting on a hill overlooking the sea a beautiful residence which was destroyed by the great earthquake.

During his residence in St Louis, Willis W Polk, Sr , was President of the Mechanics Exchange In the early 80's he was a candidate for Congress, being defeated by Thomas Allen Referring to his death, the St. Louis Globe-Democrat of Dec 1, 1906, paid him a flattering tribute as a man of high intelligence and decided talents

Of the Civil War record of Willis W Polk, lack of space prevents a full account Like his father, Willis was a strong Southern man and decided to follow the Stars and Bars He joined a company of the Missouri State Guard, and was with General Sterling Price at the battle of Lexington, where the Federal troops under Col Mulligan surrendered. Several months later he entered the regular Confederate service as a member of Company K, Third Missouri Volunteers and was appointed Second Sergeant of the Company. At the battle of Pea Ridge, a Federal bullet gave Willis a scalp wound and his comrades jokingly told him the missile would have killed him, but it happened to strike a Hard-Shell Baptist, which religious faith he professed. He was one of a small force that captured a Union battery at Elkhorn Tavern, together with a big supply of Commissary stores. He was in all the battles of General Price's command—Farmington, Iuka, Corinth, and others. At Iuka a stalwart Federal knocked him senseless with the butt of a gun, believing he had killed him. But Willis revived and escaped capture. After the war was ended, Willis settled at Lexington, Ky., in the business of architect, later going to Hot Springs, Arkansas and afterwards locating in San Francisco.

FAMILY OF SARDIUS G. POLK

Sardius Gilead Polk (sixth child of Daniel and Sally Ann (Tanner) Polk), was b Nov 21, 1840 near Newtown, Scott County, Kentucky, and died at Plattsburg, Mo., May 24, 1882. As he grew to manhood, Sardius divided his time between farming and managing the mill, which was chiefly employed in the production of lumber. He also attended school at Frankfort during the fall and winter months. In 1858 he also decided to emigrate to the West and went to Weston, Platte County, Missouri, where his elder brother, David Tanner Polk, had settled some years before.

Sardius engaged for some time in contracting and building and afterward located in Fort Scott, Kansas, where he formed a partnership with a man named Grant and continued the same line of business with marked success. During the Civil War he was connected for a time with the U S Quartermaster's Department. After the war he resumed contracting, which business he continued until his death. On Feb 28, 1865 Sardius w... i-sell
(b Oct ...

eral times State Representative of that order at its annual conventions

The children of Sardus G and Nancy (Russell) Polk were

(1) Carrie Polk, b Dec 27, 1865
(2) Mary Ann Polk, b Feb 29, 1868.
(3) Oscar Polk, b March 2, 1870
(4) John Edward Polk, b Dec 8, 1872; d Feb 15, 1873
(5) Jessie, b ————, married Edward Zink.
(6) Frank Polk, b ————

INTERMARRIAGES.

Carrie Polk, the eldest child, married John Oliver Johnson, of Erskin, Clinton County, Mo They have two sons, Ellis and Oliver Mary Ann married George Ellenberger, a Dunker preacher, of Turney, Clinton County, Mo, and they have a number of children They now reside at Peru Nebraska

Jessie, the third daughter, married Edward Zink They have no children Mr Zink is a railroad station agent and telegraph operator in Nebraska.

FAMILY OF JAMES KNOX POLK

James Knox Polk, b March 27, 1850 (tenth and youngest child of Daniel and Sally Ann (Tanner) Polk), was twice married His first wife was Mattie Dicks, who d March 4, 1874 By her he had one child, Sardius, b Oct 11, 1873 His second wife was Mrs Alice Howard, of Utica, Ind., by whom he had four children, viz, [2]Maud Ellis Polk, b July 4, 1885, [3]George Howard Polk, b Jan 12, 1887; [4]Mary Durbin Polk, b. June 4, 1889, [5]James Orville Polk, b. Dec 16, 1891 The family all reside in Louisville.

SARAH (KITTY) POLK'S FAMILY.

Alice Everett Anderson, daughter of John H and Sarah Catharine (Polk) Anderson, b Oct 7, 1868 at Jeffersonville, Ind, married Aug 16 1890 Joseph V Zartman and they had issue: ¹Joseph Zartman, b Sept. 29, 1894. ²Paul Zartman b ———, 1903; ³Joseph Zartman, b Feb. 21, 1905.

Clarence Crawford Anderson, son of John H and Sarah Catharine (Polk) Anderson, b April 22, 1871, at Jeffersonville, Ind., married March 23, 1892, Annie McMann, and they had issue ¹Ralph Clarence Anderson, b September 10, 1893, ²Myrtle Marie Anderson, b August 1, 1896, ³Clarence Anderson, b July 28, 1899; ⁴Frank Anderson, b August 21, 1901.

Arthur Field Anderson, son of John H and Sarah Catharine (Polk) Anderson, b September 19, 1873, at Jeffersonville, Ind., married March 11, 1896, Caroline Magdalena Kunkel, and they had issue ¹Mildred Louise Kunkel, b February 24, 1899; ²Edward John Kunkel, b March 26, 1901, ³Dorothy Anna Kunkel, b Dec 24, 1904.

Laura Maud Anderson, daughter of John H and Sarah Catharine (Polk) Anderson, b February 21 1875, at Jeffersonville, Ind., married January 31, 1901, Oliver P Morton Lane

Estella Blanche Anderson, daughter of John H and Sarah Catharine (Polk) Anderson, b March 31 1878, d May 15 1880.

Ellis Ezra Anderson, son of John H and Sarah Catharine (Polk) Anderson, b March 6, 1884, at Jeffersonville, Ind., not married

Charles L. Polk, son of Daniel Polk and his second wife, Ann (White) Polk, was born March 27, 1853 He married Mrs. Bettie Sue Duke, nee Franklin, who died suddenly December 25, 1908

John Breckinridge Polk (youngest son of Daniel Polk by his second wife, Ann (White) Polk, was twice married His first wife was Fannie Watts, of Woodford County, whom he married December 5, 1878 By her he had one child, Henrietta Polk, b December 25, 1879, d March 28 1881 Fannie (Watts) Polk died February 12 1891, and on February 16, 1892, John Breckinridge Polk was married to Susan Godsey, of Hazel Green, Ky John resides at Frankfort, Kentucky

Margaret ... child of Daniel ... Pollock

Feb 27, 1835 and d Feb 28, 1903 They had no issue. She lives at Louisville.

Sarah Catharine (Kitty) Polk (ninth child of Daniel and Sally Ann (Tanner) Polk), was b. Aug 10, 1847 and d Dec 13, 1891, at Indianapolis She married March 21, 1866, John H Anderson, of Jeffersonville, Ind He was b Sept 18, 1842, and d Jan 10, 1901. They had issue. [1]Harry E, [2]Alice E, [3]Clarence C., [4]Arthur F., [5]Laura M, [6]Estelle B, [7]Ellis E

Mary Jane Polk, b June 26, 1843, d March 29, 1875 (seventh child of Daniel and Sally Ann (Tanner) Polk), was married to Cornelius Anderson, of Jeffersonville, Ind, and they had issue: [1]Geo W Anderson, residence, Lewiston, Mont, [2]Kitty Anderson, who married first a Mr. Smith, second a Mr. Anderson, [3]Nettie Anderson, who married a Mr McAdoo, and lives at Hamilton, Mo; [4]William Anderson, who married Nannie Anderson and is dead

CHAPTER LXI.

FAMILY OF HESTER D. COLLINS

Hester D Polk (fourth daughter and eighth child of Ephraim Polk 3d, and Rhoda (Morris) Polk), b Jan 11, 1806, d at Danville, Kentucky, ———, 1885 She married George W Collins, a hardware merchant of that city, a highly respected man, beloved by everybody

To George W. and Hettie (Polk) Collins two children were born [1]John Ephraim Collins, b July 30, 1831. [2]George W Collins Jr b ——— John Ephraim Collins, during his youth, attended the private schools of Danville, followed by a course at Center College Later he finished his educational course at the Kentucky Military Institute, Frankfort, where he became quite proficient in military drill and tactics He next went to St Louis, Mo, where he was engaged in business for some time, going thence to Woodbury, N J In the latter place he was married, April 12, 1854, to Miss Emma Clarissa Tatum, of St Louis, some of whose family were extensively engaged in the steamboat business when steamboating on the Mississippi and Ohio rivers when traffic by water was at its height and few railroads had been built in the West

When the Civil War came on George W Collins and wife espoused with intense earnestness the cause of the Union When Col Fry's Fourth Kentucky Infantry Regiment was mustered into service and joined General Burnsides' Army, it followed a beautiful silk flag that was made by Mrs Collins and other Union ladies of Danville

Shortly after the war began Battery B, Capt John M Hewett, a company of light artillery was raised and mustered into service George Collins Jr, the youngest of the two sons, joined it and he was made Trumpeter, serving with it throughout the war

John E Collins
and Hetty (Polk) Collins

listing in the Twenty-third Pennsylvania Infantry. His commission as Adjutant of the regiment bore date of Aug. 2, 1861. On Sept. 25, of the same year, he was transferred as First Lieutenant to Company I. On October 31, 1861, he resigned his office and went back to Missouri, where he assisted in raising the 8th Missouri Cavalry, of which he was commissioned Major on June 24, 1862. With this regiment he served in the Western Department, attaining to the Colonelcy, and was mustered out of service on April 3, 1863.

FAMILY OF COL. JOHN E. COLLINS.

The record of Col. John E. Collins, as furnished by his son, Harry S. Collins, of St. Louis, is as follows:

John Ephraim Collins, b. at Danville, Ky., July 30, 1831; married Emma Clarissa Tatum, of St. Louis, at Woodbury, N. J., April 12, 1854. Emma Clarissa (Tatum) Collins, b. Jan. 18, 1836, in St. Louis, d. Nov. 1, 1870, in Kansas City, Mo.

COL. JOHN COLLINS' CHILDREN.

[1] Cora Emma Collins, b. in Philadelphia, Pa., March 13, 1855, married in St. Louis April 23, 1877, Mathew Ryan Draper, of Dodge City, Kansas; d. in Dodge City, Nov. 2, 1881.

[2] May Collins, b. in St. Louis, Nov. 5, 1857, d. Nov. 22, 1857.

[3] Bertha Clara Collins, b. in St. Louis, Sept. 23, 1859; married Henry Lovell, of Billings, Montana, d. in Oakland, California, March 22, 1887. He died in the winter of 1892.

[4] Harry Stiles Collins, b. in St. Louis, Dec. 22, 1861, married Emma Matlock Murdock, Oct. 25, 1882. Residence, St. Louis.

[5] Joseph Tatum Collins, b. July 14, 1864, d. July 16, 1864.

GRANDCHILDREN.

Mabel Lucille Draper, b. March 18, 1878, d. Oct. 9, 1878.
Cora Edith Draper, b. Feb. 18, 1881, in Dodge City, Kansas. Residence, Colorado Springs, Col.

William Tatum Lovell, b in Billings, Montana, July 26, 1885 Living on his ranch in Wyoming. Willard's father, Matthew Ryan Draper, was born in Cincinnati, O, and died Aug 4, 1891, at Colorado Springs where his daughter Cora, by his first wife, and two other daughters by his second wife, reside

Roy Murdock Collins son of Henry Stiles Collins, b in Potosi, Mo, March 9, 1884 Residence. St Louis.

After the death of his first wife, Matthew Ryan Draper was married in 1886 to Sarah Watson Clark, by whom he had two children ¹Lulu Wilcox Draper, b Sept. 7, 1887, in Warsaw, Ill , ²Matthew Ryan Draper, b Oct 10, 1889, at Colorado Springs

The latter is also a girl, and being born only two months after her father's death, she was named for him, but is called Mattie Mrs Lulu Wilcox Sawyer, a cousin of the second wife of Matthew Ryan Draper, was made executrix of the estate and guardian of the children, and they all reside in Colorado Springs

Cora Edith Draper, the only living child of Matthew Ryan Draper by his first wife, was a lovable and popular young woman of Colorado Springs, Col She gew to womanhood and was educated there, graduating from the Colorado College in June, 1902, with the degree of Ph B She afterwards took up kindergarten work and engaged in teaching it in a private school She was an active member of the Woman's Club of her city and was made Secretary of the Art and Literature Department Several years ago she joined the Catholic church and taking the veil, became a sister in the convent of that city

DESCENDANTS OF CLEMENT M. POLK.

Clement Madison Polk (fifth son and ninth child of Ephraim Polk 3d, and Rhoda (Morris) Polk), was b Sept 11 1808, at the old Polk place at the head of Lain's Run, Scott County, Kentucky, and died at Springfield, Ill , May 21, 1849 Like his brothers, ... taking part in all its duties . . . . ents of education in the schools of the neighborhood, he was apprenticed to "learn the art and trade of a printer," manifesting a preference for that occupation, as his brother Jefferson had done

He began his trade in a printing office at Georgetown, later going to Lexington, and thence to Danville At the same time he commenced a regular system of reading and soon acquired a knowledge of history, political and general, and of literature and other departments of learning Clement was an apt student and his mind readily grasped and assimilated all that came within its reach Politically, he became an Emancipationist of the Cassius M Clay school, but was opposed to forcible emancipation In person Clement was the tallest of his father's family, measuring six feet two inches His brothers were also above the average, most of them six feet high and over.

Some time after his brother Jefferson removed from Lexington to Danville and purchased the Olive Branch, which he sold later to S S Dismukes in 1833 after conducting it for seven years, Clement also went there and was engaged on the paper

While a resident of Danville, Clement Polk was married, in 1835 to Mrs Susan Ford Dinwiddie, nee Richardson, daughter of Tandy Richardson, of Jessamine County whose wife was Lucy Burton, member of a prominent family of that county

CHILDREN OF CLEMENT POLK.

The children of Clement M. and Susan (Dinwiddie) Polk, by this union, were.

(1) James Burton Polk, b ——, 1836; d at Danville, Aug 20, 1860.

(2) Sarah Elizabeth Polk, b ——, 1838, d at Oskaloosa, Iowa, ——, 1871

(3) Charles Ephraim Polk, b Dec 6, 1839, d at Petaluma, Cal., June 6, 1891

(4) Susan Caroline Polk, b Feb 3, 1843 at Springfield, Ill., and d in New York City, Jan 30, 1908

THE NEW YORK
PUBLIC LIBRARY

LENOX AND
TILDEN FOUNDATIONS.

(5) William Henry Polk, b March 24, 1841, d at Watsonville, Cal, Oct. 22, 1879.

The three first named were born at Danville, Kentucky, the two last at Springfield Ill

Of the foregoing sons and daughters of Clement Polk and wife Sarah Elizabeth, married in 1859, Isaac Hensley, of Greencastle, Ind, by whom she had a son, Charles P Hensley, b in 1860, residing at Burlington, Iowa Isaac Hensley died in the army, in which he enlisted at the beginning of the Civil War She married secondly Henry Henley of Rush County, Indiana, by whom she had issue [1]Alice, [2]William, [3]Mary, [4]Edward, [5]Carrie, [6]Josie. Their intermarriages and children are untraced, except Alice, who married Almer Long.

Charles Ephraim Polk, was married November 27, 1873 to Miss Josephine Thompson, daughter of James D and Mary E Thompson, of Petaluma, California She was b in that city, August 25, 1853 The children of this union were

(1) James K Polk, b October 23, 1874 Residence San Francisco

(2) Mary E Polk, b April 7, 1878; d May 8, 1878

(3) Clement M Polk, b April 11, 1879, d May 10, 1901

(4) Charles E Polk, Jr., b ———— residence Burlington, Iowa

(5) Edward Hubbert Polk, b ————

(6) Ella S Polk, b ————

The four sons are all in business at San Francisco

daughter of Susan C Tatum and granddaughter of Clement Polk

Susan Caroline Polk was married February 4, 1866, to Charles Frederick Tatum, of St Louis Missouri The Tatums were a prominent family of that city They had issue:

(1) Ella S Tatum, b February 14, 1867.

(2) Frederick Tatum, b ————, 1871, d in infancy.

(3) Charles Robyns Tatum, b October 25, 1876

(4) Edward Hubbert Tatum, b December 24, 1878

(5) Ruby Tatum, b June 3, 1881

Ella S Tatum was married April 1886, to Walter Bishop Manny of St. Louis Issue [1]Mildred Lucille Manny, b July 21 ———, d ——————— August 26, ————, ———— ——— ————

Walter Roy Manny graduated at Yale College in 1910 Now at Cornell College. Ralph is a student at Hotchkiss School

Charles Robyns Tatum married in San Antonio, Tex, in Nov, 1908, Mary B Dalby Residence, Berkeley, Cal Issue ¹Chas E, b Aug., 1909; ²Mary Ella, b Aug, 1910, ³David, b Sept, 1912

Edward Hubbert Tatum graduated from Yale in 1900, later from Columbia Law School and in practice in New York City He married June 3, 1908, Mary Brincherhoff, of that city

Ruby Tatum was married January 7, 1902, to LeRoy Brewster, of New York City

William Henry Polk (fifth child and third son of Clement M Polk), born at Springfield, Illinois, March 24, 1843, was married at Greencastle, Indiana, March 22, 1866, to Elizabeth Snider, b September 15, 1845 She d. October 12, 1902, at Watsonville, California They had issue

(1) Caroline Elizabeth Polk, b at Greencastle, March 1, 1867

(2) Rhoda Florence Polk, b at Oskaloosa, Iowa, April 30, 1869

(3) Charles William Polk, b at Oskaloosa, October 12, 1871, d October 7, 1902

(4) Maud Lula Polk, b at Watsonville, California, November 11, 1876

Caroline Elizabeth Polk, the first child, was married December 21, 1887, at Santa Cruz, California, to Joseph Henry Card They have one child, Elva Merle Card, b at Watsonville, February 27, 1890 Their residence is Salinas City, Monteray County, California Rhoda Florence Polk married September 30, 1888, Wallace L Hoyt, of Watsonville Charles W and Lula are still single

CHARLES EPHRAIM POLK.

Charles Ephraim Polk was born in Boyle County, Kentucky, December 6, 1839 In 1840, his father, Clement Madison Polk, emigrated to Springfield, Illinois, where he was engaged

WALTER B. MANNY AND WIFE, ELLA TATUM MANNY.

THE NEW YORK
PUBLIC LIBRARY

ASTOR LENOX AND
TILDEN FOUNDATIONS

both as a farmer and journalist till his death, which occurred in 1849. The subject of this sketch and his younger brother, then went to live with their uncle, Jehosephat Polk, in Scott County, Kentucky, where Charles spent his time working on the farm and going to school till he arrived at the age of fourteen. He was then apprenticed to Edward Clark, of Lexington, Kentucky, to learn the watch and jewelry trade. After working there for four years, he engaged with a larger house, that of Thos G. Calvert, where he remained till 1864.

Business in the border States at that period was rather hazardous, owing to the Civil War then in progress, and Charles Polk determined to join some friends who were about to make a journey overland to California. The trip across the plains was a long and tedious one, and part of the way quite dangerous on account of the presence of the hostile Sioux Indians, who, when a favorable opportunity presented itself would attack and kill the emigrants and steal their stock. On July 12th Charles and his companions had a narrow escape. A large band of savages were concealed in the bushes on Horseshoe creek, and attacked a train a little in advance of theirs, killing the men, six in number, destroying their wagons, and carrying off two women, and a little girl, and all the stock.

The party reached Virginia, Nevada Territory, October 8th, where Charles remained about six weeks, but not finding profitable employment, he pushed on to San Francisco. For four years he was connected with A. G. Medley, of that city, and on November 8, 1871 commenced on his own account the watch and jewelry trade at No. 35, Main Street, near English.

Charles E. Polk, like his father, Clement M. Polk was very tall, being about six feet two inches in height. Old citizens of Lexington who knew him intimately say he was a man of fine intelligence, a great reader especially of history, and universally esteemed by all. An evil star seemed to hover over the pathway of Clement Polk. In 1848 his wife fell sick and died. He brought her remains to Kentucky and interred them in the old Gillespie graveyard, near Danville. The Gillespie .... remain .... months

later he too was stricken, dying May 2, 1849. The remains of Clement Polk were interred in the Springfield cemetery.

At the time of Clement's death his brother, Jehosephat (Hosea) Polk, was a resident of Indiana, to which state he had emigrated for the purpose of securing cheap lands on which to raise hemp. Receiving intelligence of the death and burial of his brothe rClement, Hosea Polk drove from Indiana to Springfield, Illinois, secured the children and brought them back to his home. The eldest son, James Burton, emigrated to Arkansas, engaging there in the book trade. He died in 1860, while on a visit to Danville. Sarah and her sister were educated at the schools of Danville, the former returning to Indiana, where she married. Susan Caroline also went to Arkansas and made her home with her Uncle B. F. Richardson, a planter, where she remained during the Civil War and until married. Her sons are graduates of leading colleges and her daughters beautiful and accomplished women.

Just before the outbreak of the Civil War William H. Polk, son of Clement M. Polk, went to Indiana, where he enlisted in the Twenty-second Indiana, a heavy artillery, which saw such service in the Southern campaigns. By reason of his conspicuous gallantry in battle, William rose to the rank of Captain of his battery. Ill health, however, compelled him to quit the service before the end of the conflict and he removed to California with the purpose of trying to benefit his health. Those who served with him in the army all unite in saying that he was a man of distinguished bravery.

DESCENDANTS OF GILEAD POLK

Gilead Polk (sixth son and tenth child of Ephraim 3d and Rhoda (Morris) Polk) was born at the old Polk homestead, in Scott County, August 10, 1810, and died suddenly of heart disease at Midway, Woodford County, in April, 1855. He attended the neighborhood school, taught in a log schoolhouse near his home, and being an apt student, acquired a knowledge of reading, writing, arithmetic, geography and grammar. When eighteen years of age, Gilead was appren-

EDW. HUBBERT TATUM.

THE NEW YORK
PUBLIC LIBRARY

LENOX AND
TILDEN FOUNDATIONS

ticed to learn the trade of architecture, building, and bridge construction He planned and built some of the finest old Colonial residences in Kentucky during the middle of the last century, and was especially skilled in bridge building Some of the most noted bridges across Elkhorn and its tributaries were planned and built by him, and many of them are still in use, though erected nearly three quarters of a century ago

Gilead Polk's first wife was Marietta Givins, a daughter of John Givens, a farmer of Harrison County, who resided near Jacksonville, and whose wife was a Miss Craig, member of a prominent pioneer family Her kinsman, Capt John Craig, commanded the defenders of Bryan's Station when it was besieged in August, 1782, by British Canadians and Indians John Givins' father, Major Alexander Givins, came from Virginia to Kentucky in pioneer days and settled in Harrison, then a part of Bourbon County John Givins was a member of the Kentucky Legislature in 1817

Gilead Polk and Marietta Givins were married in the winter of 1836 To them was born one child, Ephraim, who died in infancy Marietta also died, two years after marriage, in 1838. Gilead Polk's second wife was Margaret Ann Johnson, (born July 27, 1815, died October 11, 1851), daughter of Joseph and Ann (Alexander) Johnson (b 1789, d. 1850) of Newtown, Scott County, Kentucky.

Joseph Johnson was born in Virginia He was a soldier in the war of 1812, and was wounded in the head and arm, at the battle of the Thames His wife Ann, whom he married in 1817, was a daughter of William Alexander, Sr , who also came from Virginia to Fayette County, Kentucky, about 1786 The latter's wife was Margaret Creswell, of Maryland Her family came to Kentucky about the time the Alexanders did, settling near Bryan's Station in Fayette

CHILDREN OF GILEAD POLK

The children of Gilead and Margaret (Johnson) Polk were:

(1) Ann Eli ... r 12, 1851

(2) William Harrison Polk, b March 4, 1843; residence Lexington, Ky

(3) Theodore Clay Polk, b January 6, 1845, residence Denver Colorado

(4) John Knox Polk, b August 25, 1847; d July 27, 1912, at Los Angeles, Cal.

(5) Mary Hester Polk, b January 13, 1850, d. February 5, 1850.

(6) Malvina Alice Polk, b May 20, 1851, d October 7, 1851

Margaret (Johnson) Polk d October 9, 1851, only two days after the death of the last named child Her husband, Gilead Polk, d suddenly of heart disease, four years later, April—, 1855, leaving his three sons to the guardianship of his brother Daniel Polk

Of the sisters of Margaret (Johnson) Polk, two of them married brothers named Walker Jane Johnson (b October 22, 1825, d March 9, 1854), married William A Walker, a woolen manufacturer of Leesburg, Ky They had three children, ¹Joseph, ²Mattie, ³William Joseph Walker married Buena Lail, and had a number of children, and moved to the Indian Territory Mattie Walker, a very handsome woman, married P P Cummins, for many years a merchant of Leesburg, and later a banker and farmer. They have no issue William Walker, Jr, d in early youth

Amanda Fitzallen Johnson (b March 23, 1827 d. March 24, 1851), married John Lyle Walker, of Paris, brother of William, by whom she had two children, Jennie and Joseph Jennie b May 3, 1846, was married in 1864 to Newton B Rion, Jr, of Paris, and d October 4, 1866, without issue Joseph Walker (b 1848), second child of John L and Amanda Fitzallen Walker (called "Little Joe," to distinguish him from his cousin "Big Joe," son of Wm A Walker), married Lizzie Pullen, second daughter of B F Pullen, Mayor of Paris They had two children, Frank and Bessie The latter d in childhood Frank is a prominent business man of Paris He married, ——————, and has issue

The Walker brothers, Wm. A and John L, were sons of Joseph Walker Sr, and his wife (a McPheeters), who emi-

THE NEW
PUBLIC LIBRARY

ASTOR, LENOX AND
TILDEN FOUNDATIONS

grated to Kentucky, from Augusta County, Va , in pioneer days

Bettie Johnson (b. June 9, 1831, d. July 9, 1860), sister of Margaret Johnson Polk, was considered one of the handsomest woman in Bourbon County, as beautiful in character as she was fair in person, she was a universal favorite

Coming to Paris in 1828, John Lyle Walker learned the trade of printer, in the office of the "Western Citizen," a paper founded in 1808, and which, after the Civil War was consolidated with The True Kentuckian and the name changed to "The Kentuckian-Citizen" This is the oldest newspaper of continuous circulation in Kentucky, or in the West

John L Walker purchased an interest in the paper and printing office, and for a period of nearly forty years he and his partner, Wm C Lyle, conducted it The latter was successor of his father, Rev John Lyle, who founded the paper

CHAPTER LXII

THE JOHNSON FAMILY.

The record of the Johnson family is incomplete, as to some of the dates of marriages and deaths. The names of the children of Joseph and Ann (Alexander) Johnson, and the years of their birth, are as follows

Joseph Johnson, b about 1785; d 1846 Ann Alexander, b 1789, d. at Paris, Kentucky, May 21, 1850 Joseph Johnson and Ann Alexander were married in 1816 Their children were

(1) Zarada Johnson, b 1817, d 1830
(2) Louann Johnson, b 1819, d July 14, 1872
(3) Robert Johnson, b. 1821, d. ———.
(4) William Harrison Johnson, b 1823; d ———
(5) Mary Prudence Johnson, b 1824, d November 2, 1843
(6) Eliza Jane Johnson, b October 22, 1817, d March 9, 1854
(7) Apaulean Johnson, b 1826, d October 12, 1843
(8) Margaret Ann Johnson, b 1827, d October 9, 1851
(9) Amanda Fitzallen Johnson, b March 23, 1828; d March 24, 1851
(10) John Johnson, b ———, 1829, d ———, 1874
(11) Bettie Johnson, b June 9, 1831 d July 9, 1860
(12) Malvina Curry Johnson, b ———, 1837, d May ———, 1904.

John L Walker, b January 22, 1807, d March 19, 1873
William A Walker, b September 22, 1805, d April 19, 1878
William Walker, Jr, son of Wm A. Walker, b January 28, 1854, d October 11, 1864
Jennie (Walker) Rion, b May 3, 1846, d October 4, 1866.
Joseph Walker, son of Jno L Walker b ———, 1848; d —

Bessie A Walker daughter of Joseph Walker, b November 29, 1871; d July 10, 1871

THE ALEXANDER FAMILY.

The Alexanders were a prominent family of Bourbon County, one of whom was the late Charlton Alexander Sr, a wealthy and influential financier and large land owner who for many years was Cashier of the Paris Branch Northern Bank of Kentucky William Alexander, Sr, father of Ann (Alexander), Johnson, mother of Gilead Polk's second wife, was a manufacturer of hemp rope and bagging for cotton baling, shipping it South in large quantities William Harrison Johnson was also a large manufacturer of hemp at Paris

Another prominent member of the family was William W Alexander, son of William Alexander, Jr William W Alexander married Jane Stamps, his cousin, daughter of Wm Stamps, and a niece of Jefferson Davis, President of the Confederate States, to whom she bore a most striking resemblance William W Alexander was a brilliant lawyer and noted advocate at the Paris Bar

THE HOLLADAY FAMILY.

William Holliday, son of Capt John Holliday emigrated to Kentucky about 1795, settling in Fayette County, where, shortly after, was born to him a son Thomas Holladay While the latter was quite a youth the War of 1812 commenced and he and his brother, William Holladay, Jr, enlisted in the army

The Holladays were intermarried in Virginia with the Lewis, Littlepage and Hawes families Major Lewis Holladay (b 1751), served through the Revolution Lewis Littlepage, going to Spain with the United States Minister, quitted the Legation, joined the Spanish army, and took part in the siege of Gibralter Later he fought against the Turks In the conquest of Poland by Russia, he sided with Poland and was made a General by King Stanislaus He was private secretary to that monarch when dethroned That Stenislaus loved him as a son ⸺ ⸺ son of this ⸺

Col Samuel Hawes, of the 4th Va Continentals, received a grant of 1,200 acres of land in Bourbon County. His daughter married Capt Robt Buckner, and the latter's daughter, Charlotte Buckner, married Thomas Holladay, grandfather of Mrs Wm H Polk, of Lexington, Ky On this large tract at the old Holladay mansion, Mary Holladay, mother of Mrs Polk, was born

Thomas Holladay's brother, Benjamin Holladay, went to Utah as an army contractor in the 50's with Col. Albert Sidney Johnson's army He made a large fortune in the West and founded the Overland Stage Line and Pony Express. He built the Portland & California Railroad, established a steamship line, and engaged largely in mining John Buckner Holladay, son of Thomas Holladay, was a Major in Col Ezekiel Clay's Kentucky regiment, C S A, and after the war served several terms as sheriff of Bourbon County. He married Sally Morgan, of Carlisle, Ky, and left issue [1]Lulu, [2]Lottie, [3]Katy, [4]Bruce, [5]Mayme. Lula married John Miller and died The others live at Paris, Ky

FAMILY OF WILLIAM H. POLK.

William Harrison Polk (eldest son of Gilead Polk), was married September 24, 1867, to Charlotte Buckner Talbutt, oldest daughter of Col Jesse H Talbutt and his wife, Mary (Holladay) Talbutt, of "The Meadows," near Lexington Col Jesse H Talbutt's father, Charles Talbutt, Sr, was a noted hotel keeper at Paris, Ky, in the early part of the last century, and represented his county in the Kentucky Legislature in 1848

The Talbutt family was one of the largest in Bourbon County, their ancestors coming in pioneer days from Virginia Chas Talbutt's son, Dr Chas Talbutt, a surgeon in the Confederate Army, married Iva Wharton, daughter of Gen'l Thos. J. Wharton, Attorney General of Mississippi

Jesse H. Talbutt, father of Mrs Wm. H Polk, though a strong Whig and residing in a Democratic county, on account of his great popularity was elected several times to the office of Sheriff of Bourbon County He accumulated a fortune

MARY (POLK) BOULDIN AND WM. C. POLK

in trade, at Paris and in Cincinnati. After the war he purchased the beautiful old Elisha Warfield estate, "The Meadows," near Lexington, which he lost by security debts for others.

To Wm. H. Polk and his wife, Charlotte Buckner (Talbutt) Polk, were born seven children, viz:

(1) Jesse Talbutt Polk, b. September 23, 1868, residence Lexington, Ky.

(2) William Clay Polk, b. December 10, 1870, residence Lexington, Ky.

(3) John Early Polk, b. August 25, 1873, d. January 18, 1895.

(4) Tasker Polk, b. November 25, 1875, residence Washington, D. C.

(5) Mary Alice Polk, b. August 2, 1879, d. February 27, 1910.

(6) Lillie Bryan Polk, b. December 23, 1881; residence Lexington, Ky.

(7) Margaret Polk, b. August 4, 1884, d. September 11, 1888.

William Clay Polk was married to Eva Miller, of Irvine, Kentucky, February 6, 1904. Their first child, Mary B., b. October 9, 1904, d. in infancy. Their second, Myrtle Lee, was b. September 3, 1911.

John Early Polk was married June 16, 1892, to Linda B. Wooldridge, of Versailles, Ky., daughter of John Major Wooldridge, a prominent lawyer. They had one child, a son, Maurice Wooldridge Polk, b. March 30, 1893. He is a student at Center College, Danville, Ky., and his mother resides in Colorado. John Early Polk d. at Houston, Texas, January 18, 1895, from injuries received in a fall down an elevator shaft.

Mary Alice Polk was married April 8, 1902, to Powhattan Wooldridge Bouldin, a son of Col. David Bouldin, of the Confederate Army. Col. Bouldin was one of the pioneers of Sedalia, Mo. His wife was a sister of John Major Wooldridge, father of Linda B. Wooldridge, wife of John Early Polk. Mary (Polk) Bouldin had no issue.

Tasker Polk . . . . was married N . . . . rette

County. He resides in Washington City. They have one child, Henry Tasker Polk, b. July 29, 1908. Tasker was a member of Company C, (of Lexington), Second Kentucky Infantry, and enlisted with it in the Spanish-American War. The Kentucky troops were mobilized at Lexington, and proceeded to camp at Chicamauga battlefield, near Chattanooga, to await orders for transfer to Cuba, which orders were never issued. The services of the regiment not being needed, it was mustered out at Lexington.

The other living children of Wm. H. Polk, Jesse T., and Lillie B., are unmarried and reside with their parents at Lexington, Ky.

CHAPTER LXIII.

WILLIAM H. POLK

William Harrison Polk (second child and eldest son of Gilead and Margaret (Johnson) Polk), b March 4, 1843, spent his boyhood mostly at school, in Midway, and after the death of his parents was taken by his guardian to Illinois where he resided until 1861

When Fort Sumpter was fired on, William, like all excitable, patriotic youths, enlisted in the army, making three attempts before he succeeded. He joined Company D, 21st Ills. Inft. This company was from Tuscola, Douglas County, and was commanded by Capt James E Calloway. The 21st was a three months regiment, whose Colonel was David S Goode, a Kentuckian and ex-soldier of the Mexican War, and of Walker's Nicaraugua Expedition. The 21st was mustered into the three months service at Mattoon, in April, 1861. It was then taken to Springfield, where it was mustered June 14 for a term of "three years, or during the war." Its new Colonel was Captain U S Grant, then a Mustering Officer on the staff of Governor Yates. Col. Grant, after drilling the regiment diligently, punishing all infractious, and well disciplining his men, marched to Quincy, Illinois, where it crossed the Mississippi into North Missouri. There it campaigned for several months and then went to Ironton, in Southeast Missouri, campaigning in that section and down into Arkansas. Its first "baptism of fire" was at the battle of Fredericktown, October 21, 1861, where the Confederates were defeated

During his services in the army Wm H Polk was never off duty a day or wounded, though he had some "close calls." The last two years of his service he was detailed as bodyguard and also as orderly to generals Jeff C Davis and Davis S Stanley division commanders and was chiefly employed .... he .... nd in battles vice, came back from the front, and was mustered out at Chattanooga, and paid off at Louisville. And when the regiment started to Illinois for disbandment, William left it and proceeded to his "Old Kentucky Home," where he was introduced to his two brothers and kinsmen. Not long afterward he was appointed clerk in the Paris post office, and shortly after, on recommendation of President Andrew Johnson and General U. S. Grant, was made postmaster. He was reappointed after the latter became President, but resigned and went to Kansas, and thence to Sherman, Texas, taking the position of City Editor on the staff of the Sherman Daily Register.

After three years experience in Texas journalism he returned to Kentucky, and took the position of City Editor on the Lexington Daily Transcript. Shortly afterwards he was made Managing Editor. Some months later he purchased the Daily Transcript, in partnership with Major P. P. Johnston, an ex-Confederate officer of Lee's Army, continuing as Managing Editor. Selling his interest to his partner, he founded The Evening News. He next sold his interest in that paper and went back to the staff of the Daily Transcript. In boom days he founded The Middlesboro Daily Democrat. By the collapse of the big boom, his enterprise was swamped, along with others. Returning to Lexington, he purchased The Drummer and tried to conduct a "funny paper." Exhausting his stock of "fun" which did not produce any deaths from laughter among his subscribers, he launched the Weekly Globe, and later the Weekly Observer. Heavy competition induced him to suspend his publications and he went on the staff of the Daily Leader. In July, 1908, he "reformed the error of his ways," and quit journalism to engage in literary work.

1. THEODORE C. POLK JR., 2. THOS. BARLOW POLK,
sons of Theodore C. Polk Sr.
3. JAMES WILLIAMS,
Chief Turret Capt. U. S. N., grandson of Theodore C. Polk Sr.

THE NEW YORK
PUBLIC LIBRARY

ASTOR, LENOX AND
TILDEN FOUNDATIONS.

CHAPTER LXIV.

FAMILY OF THEODORE C. POLK.

Theodore Clay Polk (second son of Gilead Polk), was married September 9, 1867, to Maggie Hart Barlow, of Midway, Kentucky, second daughter of Capt Milton Barlow, an officer who served in the Confederate Army. She died at Denver, Colo., January 1, 1911.

CHILDREN OF THEODORE CLAY POLK.

Theodore Clay and Maggie (Barlow) Polk had issue.
(1) Lottie Barlow Polk, b December 28, 1868, living at Denver, Colorado
(2) William Milton Polk, b October 25, 1870, living at Denver, Colorado
(3) John Milton Polk, b. February 9, 1874, d March 29 1907
(4) Theodore Clay Polk, Jr., b February 8, 1876, living at Goldfield, Colorado
(5) Milton Barlow Polk, b ———, 1878, d in childhood, at Great Bend, Kansas
(6) James Knox Polk, b August 10, 1882, living in Denver
(7) Thos. Barlow Polk, b August 26, 1886, real estate Agent, Seattle, Washington
(8) Archie Duncan Polk, b ———, d in infancy.
Lottie Barlow Polk was twice married, first on March 23, 1887, to George Williams, of Denver, a son of Dr Malcomb Williams of New Orleans. They had two children: [1]James Malcomb Williams, b January 29, 1888, [2]Marguerite Barlow Williams, b. December 17, 1890.

United States Navy. He enlisted a second time, was promoted to the position of Chief Turret Captain, U S Navy.

Enlisting with him at the same time, and serving on the same ships, was his uncle, Thos Barlow Polk, only two years his elder

Thomas Polk was married September 26, 1907, after quitting the Navy, to Miss Carita Nedrey, of Denver They have one child, Margaret Esther Polk, b June 27, 1909

Theodore C Polk, Jr, (son of Theodore C Polk Sr), was twice married His first wife, to whom he was united February 8, 1876, was Miss Viola Brown, of Denver; no issue. His second wife was a widow, Mrs. Emma Williams, of the same city They live at Cripple Creek, Colorado.

John Milton Polk (son of Theodore C. and Maggie Barlow Polk), a splendid and handsome young man, who measured six feet two inches, enlisted in the Colorado Heavy Artillery, in the Spanish-American War His regiment saw hard service in the Philippines At the close of the war he returned to Colorado and settled at Pueblo While ascending a stairway he accidentally dropped a pistol, which was discharged, producting a mortal wound from which he died. He was Drill Master of several secret orders having a military corps

Marguerite Barlow Williams (daughter of Geo W Williams and Lottie Barlow Polk), married in 1910 Dr. Caypless, and afterwards, in September, 1912, to Frederick Lewis Samuels of Denver

THEODORE C POLK.

Theodore Clay Polk, after the emigration of his brother William H Polk, to Illinois, continued for several years to reside with his Uncle Daniel At the beginning of the Civil War, he enlisted in Captain Daniel Garrard's Company F, Twenty-second Kentucky Infantry, Col. Daniel W. Lindsay The battalion of which company F formed a part was sent to Camp Swigert, in Greenup County, Eastern Kentucky, where other companies from that section were added until the regiment was completed The regiment then joined the division of Gen'l James A Garfield, operating in the Big Sandy Val-

JOHN MILTON POLK,
Denver, Col., son of Theodore C. Polk Sr.

ley. It took part in the battle of Middle Creek and other engagements. It then went to Cumberland Gap and joined the division of Gen'l Geo. W. Morgan, assisting in fortifying the Gap. Here they remained until Bragg started from Chattanooga on his invasion of Kentucky, in August, 1862. From Cumberland Gap, Morgan's Division proceeded to West Virginia, campaigned there for some time, after which it was ordered South, going by steamers to Memphis. Joining General Sherman's forces, it was in the campaign on the Yazoo and at Chickasaw Bayou. In assaulting the enemy's works at Hayne's Bluff, the Twenty-second lost heavily. Among the killed was Capt. Garrard of Theodore C. Polk's Company. Lt. Col. Monroe and a number of other officers were wounded. Theodore C. Polk was also severely wounded by a ball through the right groin and hip. Falling, when shot, he placed his knapsack in front of his head to protect it, and several balls lodged in the folded blanket. He laid under fire for several hours, until night permitted of his removal from the field. Taken to Paducah, Kentucky, Theodore lay in hospital for nearly a year, and in February, 1863, he was discharged from the service.

After recovery Theodore entered a dry goods store at Frankfort, later engaging as a traveling salesman with a Philadelphia house. In March, 1873 he removed to Great Bend, Kansas, where he located a land claim, and was elected the first District Clerk of Barton County, serving as such for several years, then resigned, sold his farm, and engaged in the commission business at Colorado Springs. Retiring from this, he went to Denver. He now resides in that State.

FAMILY OF JOHN KNOX POLK.

John Knox Polk (b. August 25, 1847), third and youngest son of Gilead and Margaret (Johnson) Polk, after the death of his father lived for several years with his uncle and guardian, Daniel Polk. He attended the public schools of Frankfort, acquiring a good education, after which he entered a store in that   He was but   an, too young to enlist as a soldier. Zealous, however, to enter the service in some capacity, he sought and obtained a position in the Quartermaster's Department, at Lexington, then military headquarters for the Federal forces in Kentucky, where he continued until the close of the war.

After the war John settled in Paris, Kentucky, where his oldest brother resided and engaged as salesman in a shoe store. Later he was made U. S. Storekeeper in the Revenue service. While a resident of that city he was married, August 29, 1872, to Miss Amanda Burford, a handsome young lady of Harrodsburg. The result of this union was four children, viz: [1]Davis H. Polk, b. September 4, 1873; [2]Effie Polk, b. ———, [3]Howard Polk, b. ———, [4]Percy Polk, b. ———

While the family resided in Kansas City, the eldest son, Davis H. Polk, clerked in the post-office for several years, at the same time taking up the study of medicine. After graduation from the Medical College of that city, he began practice. At the outbreak of the Spanish-American War he was appointed to the position of Contract Surgeon at the Presido, near San Francisco, where he remained during the war, ministering to the sick and wounded.

Effie, only daughter of John Knox and Amanda (Burford) Polk, was educated at Kansas City. After graduation she was appointed to the position of teacher in one of the city schools.

SARAH ATKINS AND EPHRAIM POLK, 5TH

Sarah Polk (next to the youngest child of Ephraim and Rhoda (Morris) Polk), b. June 21, 1812, removed to Liberty Indiana, about 1830 with her sister, Mrs. Polly Wolf. She was married to a gentleman named Atkins, and had one daughter. The latter was married and had a son named John, born about 1862, but the writer is informed that all of them are now dead.

Ephraim Polk 5th (twelfth and youngest child of Ephraim and Rhoda (Morris) Polk) was b. at the old Polk place in Scott County, August 10, 1814. Going to Springfield, Illinois, to reside with his brother Clement, he died there unmarried on September 5, 1840.

MRS. SARAH (POLK) ATKINS,
Liberty, Ind., daughter of Ephraim Polk 3d.

THE NEW YORK
PUBLIC LIBRARY

ASTOR, LENOX AND
TILDEN FOUNDATIONS.

CHAPTER LXV.

DESCENDANTS OF JEHOSEPHAT POLK.

Jehosephat Polk (or Hosea as he was generally called), fifth child and second son of Ephraim, 3d, and Rhoda (Morris) Polk, was born at the old homestead on Lain's Run, Scott County, Kentucky, May 3, 1800, and died at Clifton Farm, near Spring Station, Woodford County, Oct 25, 1864 The child preceding Hosea, Ephraim, b in 1798, was drowned in 1801 in a large spring near the house. This death leaving Hosea the eldest son, and his father dying in 1814, as he grew to manhood he was accorded the management of the farm by his mother and attended to her business affairs

Soon after the death of Ephraim Polk, 3d, his widow Rhoda, being of Quaker stock and opposed, like all Quakers, to slavery, set free her slaves and placed her sons at trades, two becoming printers, several architects and builders, and Hosea a cabinetmaker This trade he plied with great vigor and acquired a considerable competence He then bought a farm near Oxford, Scott County, and soon became known as the most successful planter in Kentucky, making a specialty of raising and water rotting hemp for the Southern cotton planters use in baling cotton, and for ship cordage He also established a bagging factory and rope walk and when at the pinnacle of success lost all by security debts for others

Having such a great reputation as a farmer, and as a man of great business capacity, Hosea accepted the position of general manager, for Robt A. Alexander, of the extensive Woodburn Farms in Woodford County, which position he still occupied at the time of his death Oct 25, 1864

In 1840 Hosea, before he lost all by security endorsements, sold his farm and bought the Peak farm, near Georgetown, in order to h i children convenient to colleges While living there his I graduated there

In 1822 Hosea Polk married Sarah Jane Moore, daughter of James Moore, Sr, of the same neighborhood, a family from Virginia. Hosea's wife, like himself, was a person of great energy and business ability, an ideal wife, mother and manager of the home. She was born Oct. 12, 1795 and died March 1, 1882, in S Pasadena, California. The remains were brought to Kentucky and interred beside those of her husband in Georgetown cemetery

FAMILY OF HOSEA AND SALLY POLK.

The children born to Jehosephat and Sarah J (Moore) Polk were

(1) Marcellus Polk, b Jan 11, 1824, d Sept. 11, 1885 at St. Joseph, Mo.

(2) Sally Ann Polk, b Aug 19, 1825; married June 4, 1846 to Joseph G Deming, of Edinburg, Ind.

(3) James E. Polk, b. Aug 16, 1827, d June 16, 1808

(4) Melissa Polk, b July 21, 1829, married Edw M Hubbert, Sept 9, 1852.

(5) Jefferson Scott Polk, b Feb 18, 1831, d. Nov. 3, 1907.

(6) Mary Susan Polk, b Nov 29, 1833, d Dec. 1910 at Orange, Cal.

(7) Elizabeth Jane Polk, b. April 3, 1836, d Jan 1, 1843

(8) Margaret Polk, b June 29, 1839, d March 2, 1909, at Los Angeles, Cal

INTERMARRIAGES.

On June 4, 1846, Sally Ann Polk to Jos. G Deming, of Edinburg, Ind.

On March 4, 1852, Jas E Polk to Margaret Y Payne, of Lexington, Ky

On Sept 9, 1852, Melissa Polk to Edward M. Hubbert, of Edinburg, Ind.

THE NEW YORK
PUBLIC LIBRARY

ASTOR, LENOX AND
TILDEN FOUNDATIONS

On Oct. —, 1853, Marcellus Polk to Ella G Samuell.

On Jan 25, 1854, Jefferson Scott Polk to Julia A Herndon

On Sept 9, 1867, at New Albany, Ind, Mary S Polk to Rev Alexander Parker, of Connersville, Ind

On Aug 13, 1875, at Columbus, Ind, Margaret Polk to O. R Dougherty, of Indianapolis

MARCELLUS POLK'S FAMILY.

Marcellus Polk, eldest child and son of Hosea and Sarah J. (Moore) Polk, was married Nov 10, 1853 to Ella G Samuell, of Scott County, and to them were born eleven children, viz

(1) Nannie Polk, b Aug 12, 1854, d. unmarried, July 11, 1877

(2) James Scott Polk, b April 16, 1856; married Olivia Ford, of St Joseph, April 9, 1885

(3) Wm. Barber Polk, b Sept 1, 1857; married Lillian Stewart, of St Joseph, May 8, 1883

(4) Sallie Polk, b July 7, 1859

(5) Ella Offut Polk, b Feb 22, 1861, married Wm H Brown, of St. Joseph, Feb. 5, 1884

(6) Samuel Polk, b Dec 25, 1862, married Josephine Wakefield, of Savannah, Mo., Oct. 29, 1890

(7) Maggie Polk, b. Dec 8, 1864, married Thos. W. Pack, of St. Joseph, Dec 29, 1886

(8) Edmonia W Polk, b March 24, 1866, d June 25, 1882 at St Joseph.

(9) Melissa Hubbert Polk, b June 10, 1868, married July 13, 1893, Robert C Whittinghall, of St Joseph

(10) Mary Lou Polk, b Dec. 7, 1869

(11) Lillie Belle Polk, b Sept 25, 1871.

All these children were born at Georgetown, Ky.,

SKETCH OF MARCELLUS POLK

Marcellus Polk was raised on the farm and took an active part in . . . . g the fall an. . . . . . . Peak farm near Georgetown. Marcellus entered Georgetown College and his sister Sally Ann attended Miss Tuck's Female Seminary, both graduating with honors of their classes

After graduation, Marcellus accepted the position of tutor to the children of Col June Ward, who, besides a splendid Kentucky home, owned a large plantation at Lake Washington, Miss, at which latter place Marcellus conducted most of his work while a tutor He next returned to Kentucky and read law under Hon Jas F Robinson, later Governor of Kentucky While so employed he was offered the chair of Mathematics in a college at Shelbyville, Ky, but deciding to stick to the legal profession opened a law office in Georgetown, securing a large practice He was also devoted to farming, adjoining the town A few years after the Civil War, he removed to Winterset, Iowa, and later in 1884 to St Joseph, Mo, where he practiced law until he died in Sept, 1885

Marcellus Polk's wife, nee Ella Samuell, was from one of the leading pioneer families of Scott County, a handsome, lovable woman and devoted mother, and with her children she still lives at St Joseph, Mo.

SARAH A. DEMING'S FAMILY.

Sarah (Sally) Ann Polk (second child of Hosea Polk), b Aug 19, 1825, was married June 4, 1846 to Joseph G Deming, of Edinburg, Ind, and they had issue

(1) Mary Melissa Deming, b. March 9, 1847, d Sept 1, 1859

(2) Cornelia Florence Deming, b Jan 18, 1849; married June 12, 1879 to Rev H. L Nave

(3) Zannetta C Deming, b March 11, 1851, d Feb 4, 1852

(4) Marcellus G Deming, b. Jan. 2, 1853, married 1st in 1887 to Hattie Rowley, who d March 30, 1889; 2nd May 19, 1892 to Ida Landis

(5) Joseph J Deming, b Sept. 23, 1854, married Aug 1, 1881 to Nettie Morey

MARCELLUS POLK AND WIFE, ELLA SAMUELL POLK, AND SIX DAUGHTERS.

THE NEW YORK
PUBLIC LIBRARY

ASTOR, LENOX AND
TILDEN FOUNDATIONS.

SARAH ANN DEMING AND ...ING.

ASTOR, LENOX AND
TILDEN FOUNDATIONS.

(6) Margaret Deming, b Feb 4, 1856, d ———.
(7) James E. Deming, b Sept 9, 1858, d. March 31, 1878
(8) Charles Deming, b April 6, 1862, d July 8, 1863
(9) Janie Polk Deming, b May 6, 1864.
(10) Julia H. Deming, b Aug 13, 1866.

By his second wife, Ida Landis, Marcellus G had issue. [1]Miriam, b June, 1895, [2]Dorothy, b March, 1900

Joseph Jefferson Deming and wife had issue [1]Horace, [2]Jane, [3]George and [4]Edward, twins

Cornelia Florence (Deming) Nave had issue
(1) Marcellus Deming Nave, b April 3, 1880
(2) Henry Dewey Nave, b April 13, 1881
(3) Karl Kondit Nave, b. Oct 1, 1882
(4) Mary Grace Nave, b April 6, 1885, d April 9, 1900

JAMES E. POLK.

James Ephraim Polk, third child and second son of Hosea Polk, b Aug. 16, 1827, on attaining manhood entered the mercantile business at Lexington, Ky., where his affable manners made him many friends Later he became a partner in the wholesale drygoods house of McAlpin, Polk & Hibbard, Cincinnati, amassing a fortune Selling his interest, he and his wife went to Europe and lived for a number of years in France Returning to America, he lost a fortune on Wall street.

James married March 4, 1852, Miss Margaret Y Payne, of Lexington, Ky., daughter of Judge Henry Payne, but they had no issue She died June 29, 1901, in New York City, and he 1908 at Des Moines, Iowa, at the home of his brother, Jefferson S. Polk The remains of both were entombed in his family vault in Lexington, Ky., cemetery.

FAMILY OF EDWARD M AND MELISSA HUBBERT.

Edward M Hubbert, b Sept 25, 1828 at Martinsburg, N Y Melissa, b in Scott County, Ky, July 21, 1829 Their children were
(1) James E. Hubbert, 17, 1853

(2) Charles H Hubbert, b in New Albany, Ind, Feb. 8, 1856

(3) Cornelia Hubbert, b at New Albany, Ind., Oct 31, 1858

(4) Mary Hubbert, b at New Albany, Ind, March 1, 1863

(5) Marc Hubbert b at New Albany, Ind, Nov 25, 1864

(6) Ella Polk Hubbert, b at New Albany, Ind, Jan 11, 1867

MARRIAGES

At New Albany, Ind, Oct 5, 1880, James E Hubbert to Libbie B Gorsuch

At Birmingham, Ala, April 30, 1884, Thos O Smith to Cornelia Hubbert

At Louisville, Ky, July 5, 1888, Marc Hubbert to Caroline Tellon

BIRTHS

Hubbert Smith, in New Albany, Ind, Jan 17, 1885

Chas Edward Hubbert, in New Albany, Ind, July 26, 1882

Julia Smith, in Birmingham, Ala, July 15, 1890

Frances Hubbert, in New Albany, Ind, June 17, 1891

Thos O Smith, Jr, in Birmingham, Ala, Nov 25, 1891.

DEATHS.

John Hubbert, in Columbus, Ind April 25, 1869, aged 72½ years.

Cornelia Hubbert, in Columbus, Ind, Nov. 23 1888, aged 86 years

Mary Hubbert, in New Albany, Ind, Sept 4, 1864

Chas Edward Hubbert, at Sweet Springs, W. Va, June 25, 1891.

Edward M Hubbert, at New Albany, Ind., Aug 4, 1897

James E. Hubbert at Chicago, Ill, Feb 4, 1911

JAMES . POLK AND . . . LK.

MELISSA (POLK) HUFF-ETT AND HUSBAND
LEWIS HUFF-ETT

THE NEW YORK
PUBLIC LIBRARY

ASTER, LENOX AND
TILDEN FOUNDATIONS

MARY SUSAN POLK'S FAMILY.

Mary Susan Polk (sixth child of Hosea and Sally Polk), b. Nov 29, 1833, d. Dec —, 1910 at her home in California She was married Sept 9, 1868, to Rev. Alexander Parker, Presbyterian minister, of Connersville, Ind They removed to Orange California, where he was pastor of a church for a numbe of years, and also engaged in fruit culture They had issue
(1) Jesse Parker, b. March 12, 1870, d Jan 8, 1871.
(2) Wm. Edward Parker, b Nov 26, 1872
(3) Zinnetta Griffith Parker, b July 20, 1874

Rev Parker was b at Georgetown, Brown County, Ohio, July 17, 1829

MARGARET DOUGHERTY'S FAMILY.

Margaret Polk (eighth and youngest child of Hosea and Sally Polk, b June 29, 1839, d March 3, 1909 at Los Angeles, Cal), was married Aug. 13, 1875, at Columbus, Ind , to O. R Dougherty, of Indianapolis, Ind In March, 1877 they removed to California, engaging in fruit culture. She died there in Nov., 1909, leaving a son and a daughter The son, Paul Dougherty, was b Aug 21, 1877; the daughter, Ruth, was b June 28, 1880 Residence, South Pasadena, Cal

FAMILY OF JEFFERSON SCOTT POLK.

Jefferson Scott Polk and Julia Herndon were married at Georgetown, Ky , Jan 25, 1854 Issue.
(1) Mary Blanton Polk, b. Dec 22, 1854, d May 22, 1863
(2) John Scott Polk, b June 14, 1857, residence, Des Moines, Iowa
(3) Lutie Lee Polk, b Aug. 8, 1861, d March 10, 1871.
(4) Mildred L Polk, b Jan 8, 1866
(5) Daniel S Polk, b March 8, 1870, d March 12, 1871
(6) Sarah Jane Polk b April 21, 1872
(7) Harry H ,   Des Moines

MARRIAGES.

John Scott Polk married Miss Maud Haskitt June 30, 1879 Issue ¹Jefferson Haskitt Polk, b July 3, 1880, ²Elizabeth Caroline Polk, b March 31 1883, d March 31, 1883

Mildred L Polk married Geo B Hippee (b Jan 1, 1860), on March 16, 1887 Issue ¹George Polk Hippee, b. Dec 24, 1887; ²Herndon Page Hippee, b Nov 18, 1889; ³Mildred Hippee, b June 20, 1892, ⁴Mary Hippee, b June 23, 1898

Sarah J Polk married Albert G Marsh (b Oct 13, 1867), on Feb 13, 1895 Issue ¹George Herndon Marsh, b June 17, 1897; ²Albert Polk Marsh, b Nov 25, 1900

Harry Herndon Polk married Alice Kauftman (b Aug. 12, 1878), Jan 3, 1900 Issue ¹Mary Barr Polk, b Oct 30, 1900; ²Julia Herndon Polk, b July 17 1903

George Polk Hippee, son of Mildred and George B Hippee was married at Des Moines, April 30, 1910 to Ruth Easton

SKETCH OF JEFFERSON SCOTT POLK.

No man in America bearing the name of Polk stood higher in the estimation of his friends and acquaintances, or left a more enduring impress on his time and environments, than Jefferson Scott Polk, son of Jehosephat and Sally Ann (Moore) Polk, who was born in Scott County, Kentucky, Feb 18, 1831, and died at Des Moines, Ia, Nov 3, 1907, where he located in the practice of law in 1855, just after marriage to Julia A Herndon, a daughter of John Herndon, son of one of Kentucky's pioneers

Going to Iowa shortly after marriage, they began life in a modest way, she attending to household duties while he hung out his shingle and awaited clients "Seventy-five cents, for drawing up a deed,' said he in an interview published in a Des Moines newspaper a few years ago, was the first fee I received after I entered practice"

In a few months, however, the people were impressed by the quiet, clear headed, plain spoken and modest young attorney and business flowed in on him steadily, finally resulting in one of the largest law practices in the Northwest

Left—O. R. DOUGHERTY, WIFE, MARGARET (POLK) DOUGHERTY, SON AND DAUGHTER

JEFFERSON SCOTT POLK AND H[...]

THE NEW
PUBLIC LIBRARY

ASTOR, LENOX AND
TILDEN FOUNDATIONS

ADMITTED TO BAR IN KENTUCKY.

Jefferson S. Polk earned his first money by teaching school during his early manhood, at odd hours reading law books. Quitting teaching, he entered the law office of his brother, Marcellus Polk, who had a fine practice at Georgetown. By close and persistent study and after a course at Transylvania Law School at Lexington, Jefferson had mastered the principles and judicial procedure of his profession and on May 9th, 1854, before Hon. Alvin Duvall, Judge of the Ninth Judicial District of Kentucky, he was admitted to the bar, passing the ordeal with much credit.

The following year he married and emigrated with his bride to Des Moines, then a village of about one thousand people. Here he drove his stake, and when he died the modest village had grown to a city of nearly one hundred thousand people. And in this astonishing growth and development, by reason of the push and enterprise of its people, he was one of its most active and important factors, always at the front with his keen business perceptions and advice, and also his money to help carry out any helpful enterprise. Because of his clear brain and sound advice, he soon was looked up to as a safe leader in whatever would enhance the interests of the town.

Jefferson steadily accumulated a fortune and established the gas works and waterworks of the city. Selling these properties, he purchased the street railway, equipped with ordinary cars and horses. He gradually extended the lines to all parts of the city and suburbs and finally installed an electric plant for motive power. A large number of up-to-date cars were put on and the street car system and service became one of the best in the United States.

The real estate operations of Jefferson S. Polk were also on a large scale. By purchasing surburban ground, opening new additions to the city, and extending the car lines to them, he made a great deal of money. So the and improved properties a in deeds on n of several millions.

He was also embarked in the building and operation of suburban car lines. These he placed under the presidency and management of his son Harry Herndon Polk, who exhibited much of the business ability of his father. The City Railway presidency and management he gave to his son-in-law, Mr. George B. Hippee, a gentleman every way qualified for such duties.

As his years increased and his declining health suggested less business activity and mental effort, he relegated all railroad affairs to his son Harry and Mr. Hippee.

Several times during the latter years of his life Jefferson visited the old homesteads of his father and grandfather in Scott County, Kentucky, meeting and greeting kinsmen. Although a multi-millionaire, and listed as one of the wealthiest men in Iowa, his plainness and unpretentious manner impressed all who met him.

During his early business career in Iowa, Jefferson was also an active promoter of steam railway lines in that state, with General Crocker and others helping to forward the construction of several now great railway lines. His health gradually declining, he died at his home in Des Moines, on Nov. 3, 1907.

TRIBUTES TO HIS LIFE AND CHARACTER.

The tributes of citizens of Des Moines to the life and character of Jefferson S. Polk were doubtless the highest ever accorded to any citizen of that city. All the newspapers published full sketches of his life and achievements, his usefulness and enterprise, his modesty and moral example, and his generosity to the needy on all occasions. Resolutions embodying their opinion and appreciation of the man, were passed by all the public bodies of the city, and high estimates of his character were written and published in all the papers. Lack of space here forbids even a short brief of what was said of him in print, commendatory of his life, character and achievements.

After the death of Jefferson Polk his large business interests devolved upon his son Harry Herndon Polk, who, with

THE NEW YORK
PUBLIC LIBRARY

ASTOR, LENOX A D
TILDEN FOU

ASTOR, LENOX AND
TILDEN FOUNDATIONS.

MRS. SALLIE (POLK) MAISH AND HUSBAND.

Mr Hippee, has built one of the finest business blocks in Iowa, in the center of the city, and the son exhibits a business capacity that bids fair to equal that of his father

SKETCH OF HARRY HERNDON POLK

Harry Herndon Polk, b Nov 30, 1875, in the city of Des Moines, Polk County, Iowa, received his youthful education in the best schools of Des Moines He then entered the Pennsylvania Military College in Sept, 1892, and later attended Amherst College, Amherst, Mass He then went abroad for six months, and upon his return entered the office of his father and studied law

In 1898, Harry, with his father and brother-in-law, George B. Hippee, formed a syndicate to build inter-urban lines in and around Des Moines He was elected President and General Manager of the Inter-urban Railway Company, and served in that position until they sold these properties

In 1896 Harry was appointed First Lieutenant of the Lincoln Hussars, a local cavalry organization At the breaking out of the war with Spain, he was made an aide on the staff of General James Rush Lincoln, who commanded the Iowa troops However, he did not see any active service, the war being ended before he could get to the field In 1899 he was appointed Captain of Troop A, Iowa National Guard, in which organization he served for four years

HERNDON HALL, HOME OF JEFFERSON POLK

One of the most beautiful and elegant homes in Iowa is "Herndon Hall," in Des Moines, built by Jefferson S Polk for his wife and children, and named for her, in commemoration of her family name It is situated on a spacious tract of land in the "West End," on Grand Avenue, one of the the principal avenues of the city The house was planned by a celebrated Eastern architect and completed in 1883 The style is that of an "English country house," built largely of red sand stone and pressed brick The interior is divided into spacious reception and ... ... lining rooms, ... hall, etc. The interior is finished in natural woods, and every part is done in the highest style of the builders art. The ceilings were all frescoed by a noted German artist and rare tapestries hang in graceful folds on the walls.

Speaking of his elegant home, Jefferson Polk said:

"When we built 'Herndon Hall,' we built it for our children. Here they grew up to vigorous young man and womanhood. The shadow of death has never entered its portals."

In a little printed brochure, composed during his hours of quiet and reflection, and dedicated to his sons and daughters, Jefferson Polk said:

"Love, my dear ones, begets love. As you love your children so will they love you. Get, I beseech you in close touch with your little ones. Get your arms around them, press their dear little hearts up to you and keep them there. Do not let business or other pleasures cause you to neglect this duty. Your children's love for you is worth more to you than gold or diamonds, and your love, to and for them, is the greatest legacy you can leave them. These memories, these shadows, these dreams of a loved father, mother and home, will do more to make of your children good men and women, good citizens and good christians, than all other influences combined.

"In neglecting to build up your homes with order, love and justice, you violate your first and greatest duty to yourselves, your children, your country and your God. However troublesome these memories may be you can neither blot them out nor banish them. Your happiness, as well as the happiness of your children now and hereafter, depends largely upon your home and home influences."

Such words as these could only have emanated from a tender heart, filled with the loftiest conceptions of right and justice, and imbued with the tenderest affection and solicitude for those bound to him in his home life. And as the shadows were slowly enveloping his own life he wrote and put in enduring form, that they might not be soon forgotten, these suggestions and admonitions a-

Residence of Herndon Stuart Polk, Raleigh, N.C., "HERNDON HALL"

THE NEW YORK
PUBLIC LIBRARY

ASTOR, LENOX AND
TILDEN FOUNDATIONS

CHAPTER LXVI

DR. ED. POLK'S BRANCH OF FAMILY

A few years after Ephraim Polk, 3d and kinsmen emigrated from Delaware to Kentucky (1793), another family of Polks from the same locality followed him to the vicinity of Lexington, locating near Paynes Depot. The leader of these was John Polk, and from information secured it appears that they came about 1810.

It is said that John's wife, whom he married in Delaware was Elizabeth Saltinge. They had issue

(1) Lucille Polk, b ———, d ———, who married first a Mr Graham, second a Mr Miller. Issue, unknown

(2) Major William Polk, b ———, d. ———, married Nancy Mitchell. Said to have gone to South Carolina

(3) Edward Polk b 1750, d 1808 married Margaret Piper. Issue

    (1) John T Polk, b ———, d ———, married Betsy Hopkins, of Scott County

    (2) Wm Polk, b ———, d ———, untraced.

    (3) Eliza S Polk, b. ———, d ———, untraced

    (4) Mary (Polly) Polk, b ———, d ———, untraced

    (5) Ruth Polk, b 1797, d ———; married in 1818 Wm Cox. No issue

    (6) Edward, Harriett, Margaret and "Sally" Adams Polk, all untraced

John Polk and Betsy Hopkins had a son Dr Ed T Polk, born June 13 1813. d Feb 27, 1891, who married Sarah Marshall

Tasker fourth child of John Polk and Elizabeth Saltinge, went w— t m ————— ———— ———— short time b— ————— ————— ————— isville.

and later to his farm near Jeffersontown, where he died His children were

(1) Bettie Polk, b Jan 21 1843, d Aug. 30, 1899, who married Capt. Lawson, of Louisville

(2) Lizzie M Polk, b Jan 21, 1843, d Aug 30, 1889; who married George Fulton, of Louisville

(3) John R M Polk. b March 21, 1851, d Dec. 23, 1893 who married a Miss Addie Rice, daughter of Capt Rice, of Louisville John R M. had a daughter Sadie, b Sept 7, 1881, d Dec 8, 1897, and a son John, b July 20, 1885. John R M. was a well known Louisville lawyer, and his son is also an attorney.

John Polk, the emigrant to Kentucky in 1810 is said to have been from the family line of Wm Polk, Sr

DR. EDWARD T. POLK

As above stated, Dr Edward T Polk's first wife was Lizzie Marshall, of Scott County, Ky His second wife was Sophronia Hooton, who had two children: Mrs Charles H. Wilson, of Smithfield, Ky., and a son who died young Mrs Wilson had a family of eight children, six of whom are living

For a third wife, Dr Ed Polk was united to Mrs Frisbee, a widow, who survived him By her first husband, Capt Frisbee, she had a daughter, Ella (Mrs Coleman), with whom she resides near Middletown, in Shelby County

John R M Polk (son of Dr Ed Polk), married Addie Rice They had two children, Sarah and John the attorney.

Elizabeth Marshall (Polk) Fulton had issue

(1) Sarah Fulton, who died young

(2) Mattie Lee Fulton, b Oct. 2, 1866, married Dec. 14, 1899 to Henry Otto Hausgen, of Washington, Mo No issue Mrs Hausgen is a popular writer and a woman of fine literary taste

(3) Joseph Galt Fulton, b Sept 6, 1868; married Sept. 13, 1890 to Gertrude Linker, of Connecticut They have two

R. L. POLK,
Detroit, Mich.

ASTOR, LENOX AND
TILDEN FOUNDATIONS

children ¹Edward Irving, b Jan 4, 1892; ²John Drake, b Sept 17, 1900

(4) Mary Jeanette Fulton, b Sept 2, 1873, married Scott Prather. No issue

The author received a good deal more data concerning this branch of John and Elizabeth Saltinge Polk, but it came in such confused shape that it could not be used so as to insure accuracy

FAMILY OF R. L. POLK.

There is no name in America, perhaps, better known than that of R L Polk, of Detroit, Michigan, publisher of city directories His father dying in New Jersey and devising his property equally to his two children, it is said, the son R L Polk made over most of his part to his sister and emigrated to Detroit and commenced the publication of city directories This business he continued for years with such success that he is now rated a millionaire His life has been such a busy one that he can tell little of his remote family antecedents

Both his father and grandfather were named David Polk, and an examination of the descendants of Wm Polk, Sr, of Somerset County, Maryland, indicates that David Polk, Sr (his grandfather) was of that line He moved to Baltimore, where David, Jr, was born and after a good education entered the Presbyterian ministery, after graduating at Jefferson College and at Princeton Theological Seminary He had a brother George, who lived either at St. Louis or Louisville. David, Jr, died at Brookville, Pa, in 1857, at the age of about 48 years

David Polk, Sr, had a family of six children, viz: ¹John; ²George, ³Eliza, ⁴Jane, ⁵Margaret; ⁶Rev David, Jr

In a letter to the author, R L. Polk states

My father did not preach in Baltimore. He moved to Western Pennsylvania and died in Brookville, Jefferson County, that state, in 18—   After his m   er he became estranged from his family   little intercourse with them

"My father, David Polk, was born in Baltimore in 1809 While he was attending the Theological Seminary in Princeton, N J he met Mary Charlotte Warner, who was visiting some relatives in that locality, and afterwards married her She was born in Trenton, N. J. in 1813 My father was ordained a Presbyterian Minister in Baltimore about 1833, some time after which he moved to Wheeling, West Virginia, and was later sent by the Presbytery to Bellefontaine, Ohio, where I was born Sept 12, 1849 Later he was sent by the Presbytery to Brookville, Pa, where he died in 1857, leaving my mother with six children She returned to her father's home in Trenton, N. J, where she lived until her death in 1890 My mother had seven children, as follows [1]Margaret, [2]David, [3]Charles C, [4]Mary, [5]Susan, [6]Louisa B, and [7]Ralph L

The first three were named after my father's, and the last four after my mother's relatives

My brother, Judge Charles C Polk, resides in Los Angeles, Cal

CHAPTER LXVII.

ROBERT POLK, JR., AND DESCENDANTS

Robert Polk, Jr., (fifth son of Capt. Robert Bruce Polk and his wife Magdalen), was b. in Somerset County, Maryand, about 1675, or shortly after his parents landed in America

Robert Polk, Jr., was a very active, enterprising planter and citizen, and possessed great force of character. About 1699 he was married to Miss Grace Guillette, by whom he had a considerable family, only part of which he mentions in his will. Robert d. in 1727. His will is dated Feb 21, 1725, and was probated in Dorchester County, May 10, 1727, the same year in which the wills of his mother, Magdalen Polk and his brother James Polk were probated in Somerset County

According to data secured from the Maryland offices of record, Robert Polk, Jr., and his wife Grace had issue ¹Thomas, ²William, ³Robert; ⁴Mary; ⁵Grace and three other daughters whose names he does not call. The tracts of land devised by Robert in his will were "Venture," "Hazard," "Folorn Hope" and "Bally Hack." No executor named. Witnesses William Polk, Daniel Harrison, Robert Polk

To his son Thomas, Robert Polk, Jr., devised "Venture," the "dwelling plantation." To his son Robert, then under fourteen years of age, he gave "Hazard." And said Robert was to be a free man at 14 years, if his mother should marry again.

To his brother, Joseph Polk, (youngest son of Robert and Magdalen), Robert devised part of a tract called "Forlorn Hope"

FAMILY OF ROBERT POLK, JR.

The estimated dates of births of the children of Robert Polk, Jr., were

(1 Thomas b. 11 b. d in 1702   L..   Lauviah —

(2) Col William Polk, b about 1705, d Oct 28, 1788; married Mrs. Mary (Vaughan) Woodgate

(3) Robert Polk, 3d, b about 1707, d Dec 1770, married Alice Nutter

(4) Mary Polk, b about 1714, d. ———

(5) Grace Polk, b about 1716, d ———

Three other daughters are mentioned in his will, making five daughters in all, but three names are not given

According to data procured between 1810 and 1818, by Josiah F. Polk and Col. Wm. H. Winder, of Maryland, and others interested in the preparation of the Polk tree published in 1849, and since that time by others who made careful research, the line of Robert Polk, Jr, down to the Revolution was as follows.

(1) Robert Bruce Polk and wife, Magdalen, who came to America about 1672.

(2) Robert Polk, Jr, b about 1675, d 1727, married Grace Guillette in 1699

(3) Robert Polk, 3d, b about 1709-11, d 1771; married Alice Nutter

LAND GRANTS TO ROBERT'S LINE.

As heretofore stated, Robert Polk's father, Capt Robert Bruce Polk, received two grants of land, "Polk's Lott" and "Polk's Folly" from Lord Baltimore on March 7, 1687 The next grant was to Ephraim Polk, for "Clonmell," on Sept 20, 1700 And shortly after, on Nov 8, 1700, Robert Polk, Jr., was granted "Bally Hack," 200 acres, lying in Somerset County, marsh ground This grant is of record in the Maryland Land Office, at Annapolis, in Book D D. No. 5, folio 73 In this grant Robert's name is written Poalk, owing doubtless to the carelessness of the entry clerk

No more grants from Lord Baltimore to Robert Polk, Jr, appeared on the list and the other tracts acquired by him were no doubt by private purchase His brothers received numerous grants from the Colonial office, but Robert was apparently satisfied with one from that source

One of the tracts mentioned in his will by Robert Polk,

Jr., "Folorn Hope," appears later, in 1738, as granted to Joseph Polk This was about the time Joseph is said to have returned from Ireland, whither he had gone soon after his mother's death in 1727, to possess the estate of "Moneen" which she had devised to him in her will of 1726.

The Dorchester County records show a number of land transactions in the name of Robert Polk Those before 1727 were by Robert, Jr. Those after that year (in which he died) by his son Robert Polk, 3d, who appears to have been a very large land proprietor, purchasing many tracts

Other interesting entries on the Dorchester records are

Appraisement of land of Clement Polk, under fourteen years old, orphan and child of Robert Polk, deceased, now under the guardianship of Manuel Manlove, made Sept 7, 1712, of following tracts: Horseys Swamp," 100 acres, "Little Goshem," 250 acres This Clement Polk was doubtless a son of Robert Polk, Jr, and Grace Guillette, as Robert 3d was then but a small boy

Wm Polk appointed guardian to Caleb and Mary, orphans of Christopher Nutter, August —, 1773

ROBERT POLK, 3D, A COLONIAL OFFICIAL

Robert Polk, 3d was a Justice of the Peace in Dorchester County from 1750 to 1770 (See History of Dorchester County, Md, p 422, 23 and 24) His wife, Alice Nutter, was a daughter of Christopher Nutter, Sr, of Somerset, who came to America a number of years earlier than the Polks The Nutters and the Polks of Roberts branch were several times intermarried and two of that family, Thomas and David Nutter, came to Kentucky in 1793 with Ephraim Polk, 3d, and other kinsmen, settling near Lexington, where they have numerous descendants

Alice Nutter Polk wife of Robert Polk, 3d, d in 1772 Her will (, 16, 1773 I , ther Russum, granddaughters, Esther Nutter and Sarah Nutter

The tract of land named was "John's Settlement" Daniel Polk Executor Witnesses Wm Bradley, Joseph Bradley and John Smith.

In his will (June 12, 1770, probated Jan. 15, 1771, Robert Polk, 3d, names as his legatees, sons Daniel, John, William and granddaughters, Esther Nutter and Sarah Nutter His wife, Alice and his son Daniel Polk are named as executors In the division of estate he devised to Daniel tracts "Lone Poplar," 168 acres; "Smith's Chance," 50 acres; "Addition,' 57 acres, "Daniel's Lot," 80 acres Daniel also to have part interest and title in bonds of Wm Neel for 375 acres, also in bond for conveyance of another tract of 108 acres, and £200 lawful money.

To his son John Robert 3d, gave "Polk's Fancy," the home plantation, and six other tracts

CHILDREN OF ROBERT POLK 3D.,

of Dorchester County Maryland.

The children of Robert Polk, 3d, son of Robert Polk, Jr, were

(1) Capt Robert Polk, b about 1744, killed 1779 on board privateer Montgomery He married Elizabeth Digby Peale

(2) David Polk, b about 1746, untraced

(3) John Polk, b about 1748, untraced

(4) Daniel Polk, b Feb 28, 1750, d March 29, 1796

(5) Wm Polk, b about 1752, d 1788.

CHAPTER LXVIII.

COL. WILLIAM POLK'S DESCENDANTS

Col William Polk left more descendants than any other child of Robert Polk, Jr., and wife (nee Grace Guillette), and they included a large number of leading citizens of Maryland and Delaware

Col Wm Polk was b about 1705 and d in Oct, 1788 His will is dated Dec 27, 1787, and was probated Oct 17, 1788 He was twice married The name of his first wife is not known. His second wife was a widow, Mrs Mary (Vaughan) Woodgate, daughter of Edward Vaughan, an ironmaster of Sussex County, Delaware By her first husband Mrs Woodgate had a son, Jonathan Woodgate, who emigrated to Kentucky in 1808 and settled in Scott County, near Polk kinsmen who had come out in 1793

Col William Polk's wife d Feb 20, 1789 Her father, Edward Vaughan, was a brother of Col Joseph Vaughan, of the famous Delaware Continental Regiment, and these, with Johnathan Vaughan another brother, owned Deep Creek Iron Furnace and Nanticoke Forge, in Sussex

Col Wm Polk was also a wealthy planter In 1773 he was appointed by the court, guardian of Mary and Caleb Nutter, orphans of Christopher Nutter, and in April, 1782, his son Trusten Laws Polk married Mary

CHILDREN OF COL. WM POLK.

To Col Wm Polk were born twelve children, but we know not how many were by the first wife Probably most of them were The names of these children were

(1) Trusten Laws Polk, b about 1741, d June 15, 1796, intest.

(2)

(3) Robert Polk, b

(4) Alexander Polk, b about 1750, d ———, was an officer in the U. S Navy
    (5) Clement Polk, b 1752, d before 1802
    (6) Esther H Polk, b about 1754, d ———.
    (7) Sarah Nutter Polk, b. about 1756, d ———
    (8) Anna Polk, b about 1758, d ———
    (9) Nancy Polk, b about 1760, d ———.
    (10) Elizabeth (Betsy) Polk, b. about 1783, d about 1805.
    (11) Polly (Mary) Polk b about 1785, d. in 1808
    (12) Kitty (Ketura) Polk, b. about 1787. d. ———.

INTERMARRIAGES.

Trusten Laws Polk, eldest son of Col. Wm. Polk, married Mary Nutter, daughter of Christopher Nutter

Wm Polk, second son of Col Wm Polk, married Sarah Robinson, eldest daughter of Judge Peter Robinson, of Sussex

Robert Polk, untraced.

Alexander Polk married ———————, and had a son Robert. Alexander, was a Midshipman in the U. S Navy, and for distinguished gallantry at Tripoli in 1803 was voted a sword by Congress

Esther Polk married Nathaniel Russum. Issue, unknown

Sarah Nutter Polk, untraced

Anna Polk married ——— Gossens. Issue twins

Nancy Polk married Peter Brown Issue [1]Margaret Nutter Brown, [2]James Brown. The latter had. [1]Priscilla; [2]Margaret (Peggy) Nutter; [3]Elizabeth, who married Wm Clarkson; [4]——— who married ——— and was the father of Mrs Louisa A. Kemper, of Mississippi, who married Dr Andrew C Kemper, of Cincinnati, O, a surgeon in the U S Army during the Civil War

Betsy Polk married Rev James M Round (b. 1777), of Snow Hill, Md. They had a daughter Elizabeth Polk Round, who died in Ohio in 1847 She married David West, and their daughter, Henrietta S. West, married Wm. Clark, by whom she had

    (1) Adelaide Clark, who married Judge Wheeler

(2) Sarah Virginia Clark, who married Judge Barber. The latter had issue ¹Dolly, ²Herbert; ³Helen

Dolly married Mr P C Patterson and they had issue ¹Margaret F, ²Helen, ³Winona; ⁴Sam'l Lee and one other.

Polly Polk, daughter of Col Wm Polk and Mrs Mary Woodgate Polk, and who d in 1808, married Zach Hatfield

Kitty (Ketura) Polk, the youngest child of Col Wm Polk, untraced

After Trusten Laws Polk's death his widow married Thomas Sorden

WILLIAM POLK, SON OF COL. WILLIAM, SON OF ROBERT POLK, JR.

William Polk (second son of Col William and Mary (Vaughan-Woodgate) Polk, was born in Sussex County, at the homestead "Polks Defense," near Bridgeville, Feb 19, 1746, and died April 10, 1801

Williams' mother, Mary Vaughan, was the daughter of Edward Vaughan, as appears from Col Wm. Polk's will in which he says, "I give unto my beloved wife, all my right and title and demand of all the lands, goods, and chattels that were of the property of Edward Vaughan, deceased, that now is at Deep Creek Furnace, and my desire is that my wife shall have full power and authority to settle the estate of Edward Vaughan deceased," etc

Edward Vaughn was interested in the Iron Works at Deep Creek Furnace. He was a brother of Jonathan and Joseph Vaughan who came from Ashton, Chester County, Pa, organized a Company, and founded the Deep Creek Iron Works in Nanticoke Hundred, Sussex County On January 28, 1763 the Compay applied for 5,000 acres of land, and soon had 7,000 acres upon which they carried on an extensive iron business This industry was almost broken up by the Revolution, which carried off many of the men as soldiers, and some of them as officers Among the latter was Lieutenant Colonel Joseph Vaughan the distinguished ... of the Del... regiment after the retirement ... ived at Germant... v...

It was probably before 1792 that William Polk married Sarah Robinson, oldest child of Judge Peter and Arcada (Milby) Robinson Sarah was born on November 8, 1770, on the Robinson plantation near St George's Chapel She died May 3, 1815 The Robisons were among the earliest settlers of Sussex County, William, the ancestor of the family, having taken up land in Indian River Hundred, on Angola Neck, in 1693 In Colonial times the family were large landed proprietors, and carried on extensively, for the period, a milling business, then one of the most productive industries of the country They however, early entered public life, as we find that Parker Robinson, William's grandson, was a Justice of the Peace from 1765 until 1775 [Scharf II 1212, Pa Arch 2d Ser X 81,217]

Peter Robinson, Parker's brother on November 4, 1756, was appointed Lieutenant of the Sussex County Militia, in Col Jacob Kollock's Regiment, which was organized for service in the French and Indian War [Pa Arch. 2d, Ser II 578]

Lieutenant Peter Robinson married Catharine Burton, of Indian River Hundred The Burtons also were among the first settlers of Sussex County They held extensive tracts of land, and have ever been distinguished in the history of the State

Among the children of Lieutenant Peter Robinson and Catharine (Burton) Robinson were Thomas and Peter, Jr.

Thomas has come down to us as "The Loyalist," a man who took an eminent part in the opening Revolution, "a gentleman of high character, of superior education, and of great talents and influence" He married also a Burton (Priscilla), and they resided at the "Chapel" Their son, Judge Peter Robinson, was an eminent lawyer, Secretary of State, Representative, State Senator, and Third Associate Justice of Delaware Peter Robinson, Jr, Lieutenant Peter's second son began his official life in 1771 as Sheriff of Sussex County, and was again appointed in 1772 [Pa. Arch, 2d Ser IX 662]

On November 29, 1791 he was a member of the State Constitutional Convention that convened at Dover and adopted the new State Constitution [Scharf II 1213]

On February 1, 1792 Peter Robinson was appointed Justice

of the Peace of Sussex County (Scharf II, 1243) and on October 30, 1793, he was appointed Associate Justice of the Supreme Court of Sussex County, under the Constitution of 1792. This office Judge Robinson filled ably for many years, holding Court in Georgetown which became the County seat in 1791. [Scharf I 223, 537, II 1269.]

Sarah Robinson's mother, Arcada Milby, was also of an old Sussex County family of note in Colonial and Revolutionary times. From her descended later and by intermarriage, Gen. Alfred A. Torbert, U. S. A., a distinguished officer of the Civil War.

From the Census of 1800, and various deeds, we learn that William Polk resided with his family on his own property in Lewes and Rehoboth Hundred. Here he died intestate in May, 1801, leaving his widow and three girls, to whom descended certain lands and tenements in Lewes and Rehoboth Hundred and Northwest Fork Hundred.

William and Sarah (Robinson) Polk had issue:

(1) Elizabeth Polk, b about 1795. She married Peter Fretwell Wright.

(2) Arcada Polk, b Nov 21, 1798. She married Stephen Marshall Harris in 1824, in Georgetown, and d on Sept 8, 1846, in Grand Detour, Ill.

(3) Sarah Polk, b in 1799. She married Robert Burton and died in Philadelphia in 18——

In 1810 Sarah (Robinson) Polk married Gen. Thomas Fisher of Sussex and Kent Counties, a man of great eminence and influence in the public life of Delaware. By him she had no issue.

In Gen Fisher's Bible is the record "Sarah Robinson, second wife of Thomas Fisher and daughter of Peter and Arcada Robinson, was born Nov 8, 1770. At the time of her marriage with Thomas Fisher, she was the widow of Wm Polk, deceased."

In the War of 1812, General Fisher commanded a brigade of Sussex County Militia and was present at the bombardm... also spectat... tell her childr...

At this time Gen. Fisher resided on his farm near Dover Here Sarah (Polk) Fisher died in 1813 She was buried on the farm and her neglected grave be seen to-day (1908)

DESCENDANTS OF ELIZABETH (ROBINSON) POLK.

Elizabeth Robinson Polk (eldest child of William and Sarah (Robinson) Polk), was born in Lewes and Rehoboth Hundred about 1795 She married about 1815 Peter Fretwell Wright. On April 12, 1813, Mr Wright was commissioned Captain of the First Company, Eighth Regiment, Sussex County Militia, part of one thousand men called for the defense of Lewes In 1817, he was appointed one of the Trustees of Education for Lewes and Rehoboth

On March 5, 1816. Peter F. Wright petitioned the Court of Sussex in behalf of his wife Elizabeth, for a division of the 'lands of which Sarah Fisher, late Sarah Polk, died intestate," in 1813 The said intestate Sarah, in her lifetime, having been the wife of Wm. Polk, survived him, and married Thomas Fisher, Esq., and died in the lifetime of said Thomas Fisher without issue by him. That the said Sarah left three children· Elizabeth, now the wife of the petitioner; Arcada Polk, and Sarah Polk, offspring of her (Sarah) and her former husband. the said Wm Polk

Elizabeth Polk and Peter Fretwell Wright had issue·

(1) Arcada Wright, who married George Dufour Both died at Clover Plain, near Philadelphia, no issue.

(2) Elizabeth Wright, d unmarried.

(3) Charles Wright, d unmarried

(4) Wilhelmina Wright, who married William Kennedy, deceased They had. [1]George Kennedy, deceased, [2]Noel Kennedy, married and had family, [3]Samuel Kennedy, married and had family

(1) Arcada Polk (second daughter of William and Sarah (Robinson) Polk), was b on Nov 21, 1798, near Lewes The "beautiful Kitty Polk" as she was called, married in 1824, Stephen Marshall Harris son of Major Benton Harris, an officer of the War of 1812 Mr. Harris was a descendant of the Rev Robert Harris son of Stephen of Chesterden,"

Cheshire, England Robert came to Accomac County, Virginia, early in 1700, and took up lands there. His son Abraham, removed to Sussex County, Delaware, and became a large land owner. It was upon fifty acres of his property with an additional twenty-six acres, that Georgetown was founded in 1791, the land being purchased by the Commissioners (Scharf II, 1207)

Benton Harris, Abraham's son, was one of the most noted business men in the community, and was identified with the growth of Georgetown for many years. In 1813 Benton was appointed a Major in the volunteer service of Sussex County, which was on military duty for the State of Delaware in the War of 1812 He was present at the bombardment of Lewes by the British, on April 6-7 1813.

Benton's eldest son, Stephen Marshall, was born in Georgetown January 7, 1797. He became a partner in his father's mercantile business, was a generous supporter of St Paul's Church, and in civic affairs served as Recorder of Sussex County, in 1821, and Director of the Farmers' Bank 1826 and 1827. In 1830 he removed to Philadelphia, where he established a wholesale commercial house, and was one of the original members of the Church of the Epiphany, founded by the Rev. Stephen H. Tyng.

Mr Harris was a rover, and in 1846 removed to the West and settled with his family in Grand Detour, Illinois. Here his wife, Arcada Polk, d Sept 8, 1846 Mr Harris conducted business for many years after in Rock Island and Chicago He d Oct 31, 1881, in Dixon, Ill, at the home of his daughter, Mrs Cumins

Arcada Polk and Stephen Marshall Harris had issue:

(1) Ann Elizabeth Harris, b in Georgetown, Del, in 1826, a beautiful girl, gifted with a fine voice. She d in New Orleans, Louisiana, in 1865, and was interred beside her father and mother in Grand Detour, Ill

(2) Sarah Polk Harris, b in Georgetown, Del., in 1828 These two older sisters were known in the Western home as the "*, u* *" * * * their beauty until the l* * * *

In 1* * * * * John

Henry Langley, a descendant of the Langleys of Boston, Mass. They resided at Rock Island, Ill., where Mr Langley was engaged in the shipping business, for many years He died in 1880, and was survived by his wife until May 1, 1886 They had a son, Louis Pierpont. A daughter survived them · Ida Langley, who was b in Rock Island in 1852 She married Morris J. Sheppard, of New York They now reside at Saugerties, Pa

(3) Maria Louisa Harris, b September 10, 1830, in Philadelphia, married George Sumner, whose ancestors were among the early settlers of Albany, New York For many years he was a Commission merchant in Chicago, where he d. in 1888 They had one child, Beulah Sumner, who died at the age of seven. Mrs Sumner d in New York City, December 17, 1908

(4) Josephine Polk Harris, b in Philadelphia, Sept 1, 183— removed with the family to Grand Detour, Ill , in 1846 On May 24, 1854, she was married to Theron Allen Cumins, a prominent business man They removed to Dixon, where they had a beautiful home and largely entertained Mrs Cumins has the distinctive features of the Polk family, which reappear in individuals of each generation She has traveled much at home and abroad, and has written some amusing "Reminiscences of Western and Southern Life" Her husband Theron A Cumins, was b in Tembridge, Vermont, July 12, 1825, was the son of Joseph and Hannah (Converse) Cumins, who were married Oct 8, 1808 His maternal great-grandfather, Lieutenant Joshua Converse, was one of the Minute men of Vermont and he was in the battle of Bunker Hill. Lieutenant Joshua's son was Col Israel Converse, a distinguished officer of the Revolution, serving to the close. He was born in Stafford, Conn , Aug 7, 1743, married Hannah Woolbridge, died at his home in Randolph, March 28, 1806, where he was buried with military honors

One of Col Israel Converse's children was Judge Converse, who resided in Parkham, Ohio, and left descendants there Col Israel's daughter, Hannah Converse, married as we have seen, Joseph Cumins Their son, Theron A. Cumins, was a man of extraordinary business ability He early sought his

MRS. JOSEPHINE POLK CUMINS,
granddaughter of Wm. Polk, son of Col. Wm. Polk, son of
Robert Polk, Jr.

THE NEW YORK
PUBLIC LIBRARY

ASTOR, LENOX
TILDEN FOUN A

fortune in the West and engaged in the manufacture of Agricultural implements, in Grand Detour, a village whose brilliant future was never realized The 'Grand Detour Plow' became noted, not only in this country, but in Europe, and laid the foundation for Mr Cumin's immense fortune. He removed to Dixon, where he founded the "Dixon Plow Works" and built a beautiful home He died there in August, 1898 and lies in the cemetery beside his three children

Josephine Polk Harris and Theron Allen Cumins had issue

(1) Theron Lawrence Cumins, b May 11, 1855, d Jan. 11 1870; buried in Dixon.

(2) Arcada Polk Cumins

(3) Harris Converse Cumins, b June 23, 1861, d on Oct 6th, following, buried in Dixon

(4) Joesphine Harris Cumins, b Dec 19, 1863, d Feb 18, 1870, buried in Dixon

(5) Nina Estelle Cumins b July 9, 1866, d March 5, 1897

(6) Arcada Polk Cumins was b. in Grand Detour, Ill.

Arcada was graduated from St Agnes' School, Albany N Y, in the class of 1878. On the 20th of December, 1883, she was married to Mahlon Nugent Hutchinson, in St Luke's Episcopal Church, Dixon, by the Rev John Wilkinson Mrs Hutchinson is a woman of fine presence add keen wit They now reside in Philadelphia, the home of the Hutchinson family for over 130 years

Randall Hutchinson, son of John Hutchinson, had two sons, James and Mahlon

James, b 1752, was the most distinguished member of the family. He studied medicine in the University of Pennsylvania and in Europe Upon his return to America in 1777, he became an active supporter of the struggle for Independence, and served with eminence as a Surgeon in both the army and navy until the close of the war He was appointed in 1787 Surgeon and Physician General of Pennsylvania Radical in his views upon public questions, Dr Hutchinson naturally b.   c of
as it   ted a
member of the Committee of Correspondence upon its re on-

ganization in 1793. He died Sept 5, 1793, in Philadelphia of yellow fever, at his post of duty. He was twice married and left descendants.

Mahlon Hutchinson, the younger brother, and son of Randall and Catherine (Rickey) Hutchinson, was born Dec 24, 1754. Removing to Philadelphia, he became one of the wealthiest merchants there, the first great merchant of the family. In 1794 he was a member of the Committee of Relief for the families of soldiers sent by President Washington to suppress the western Pennsylvania Whiskey Insurrection. From 1809 to 1813 he served as Director of the Pennsylvania Company for Insurance on lives and granting annuities. On January 7, 1779, he married Sarah Palmer, daughter of John Palmer, Jr., and Sarah Walker, whose ancestors early settled in Bucks County, Pa. Sarah Palmer died in 1808 and her husband May 7, 1836.

Mahlon, their eldest child, 1783-1862, received a mercantile training in Stephen Girard's Counting house and amassed a fortune as a merchant. He married 15th of December, 1813, Elizabeth, daughter of Daniel and Elizabeth Lovett. Elizabeth died in 1835.

Of their seven children, John Palmer Hutchinson is in direct line. His older brother, Daniel Lovett Hutchinson, born in 1816, was a prominent banker and stock broker, of Philadelphia.

John Palmer Hutchinson, b in Philadelphia, Oct 27, 1823, d there Dec 30, 1872. On November 24, 1857 he married Maria Nugent, of Norristown, Pa.

John Palmer and Maria (Nugent) Hutchinson had issue [1]Mahlon Nugent, who married Arcada Polk Cumins; [2]John Palmer, b Jan 10, 1860, d Jan., 1896, [3]Anne, b Nov. 30, 1861, [4]George, b 1865, d 1871.

(1) Mahlon Nugent Hutchinson, the eldest child, was born in Philadelphia, Aug. 30, 1858. He was graduated from Harvard University, Class 1879, and from Bellevue Hospital Medical College in 1881. Dr and Arcada Polk (Cumins) Hutchinson have no issue.

Nina Estelle Cumins, daughter of Theron A. and Josephine (Polk) Cumins, was born July 9, 1865. She was edu-

DR. MAGILL

PUBLIC

ASTOR, LENOX AND
TILDEN FOUNDATIONS

cated at St Agnes' School, Albany, N Y and subsequently spent some time in Paris with her mother, in order to perfect herself in the French language. Later, while they were spending the winter at Asheville, N. C, Nina was married there in Trinity Church to Major Augustus Cleveland Willcoxen on Jan. 15, 1896 She was a young woman of rare personal charms, but died Aug 5, 1897, the following year, in their home at Atlanta She left no issue

(5) Lydia Harris, born in Philadelphia in 18——, was graduated from the New York Conference Seminary, near Albany, in 1855, and died in Chicago in 1895

(6) Thomas Benton Harris, born in Philadelphia on Feb 28, 1836, died Nov 14, 1903, in Idaho Springs, Colorado, unmarried

(7) Emma Polk Harris, born in Philadelphia, was graduated from the New York Conference Seminary, later from the Normal School of New Orleans, La, and from the Philadelphia School of Oratory on June 11, 1878. For a number of years she was engaged in literary work in New York City, as Assistant Editor of Dio Lewis's Magazine, special correspondent of various journals, biographical writer for 'Appleton's Cyclopedia of American Biography;' also for White's National Cyclopedia Recently (1908) she has compiled a 'Genealogy of the Wilkins Family of Amherst, New Hampshire," of "The Robinson Family of Sussex County, Delaware," and of 'Harris Family," also of Sussex She married Charles R Brainard, son of Dr Linus B Brainard, a Surgeon in the United States Army during the Civil War, and a descendant of the Brainards of New England

Mr Brainard was a graduate of Racine College in 1861, from which he received the degree of Master of Arts in 1867. He was admitted to the Bar in Boston in 1876, and to the United States Bar two years later Although he built up a successful practice. Mr. Brainard eventually became absorbed in literary work, first as contributor to leading periodicals In New York he became connected with some of the principal publishing houses, especially Appl...   ...istori-
cal ar...   ...   1897,

at Waupaca, Wis. He left no issue. Mrs. Brainard resides now, (1908), in New York City.

(8) George Washington Doane Harris, was born in 1838. He was a successful man in Rock Island, a man of brilliant parts and a great favorite in the society of that gay city. He died there unmarried in 1893.

Sarah Polk, youngest daughter of William and Sarah (Robinson) Polk, was born in, or near Lewes, Delaware, in 1799. She married Robert Burton, of Milton, where they resided. He died after 1830 and his widow removed to Philadelphia with her two children after that date. Here she lived to a serene and beautiful old age, and died in 1880. Robert Burton's great grandfather was William, son of Thomas Burton, of Longner Hall, Shropshire, England who was a lineal descendant of Sir Edward Burton, from whom descended the family of Coningham, which was knighted by Edward Fourth in 1460.

Daniel Burton, born in 1768, married Arcada Milby. Among their children was Robert, above mentioned. Robert and Sarah (Polk) Burton had five children of whom two survived:

(1) Mary Robinson Burton, born in Milton in 1822 and has resided many years in Philadelphia in a beautiful home.

(2) Arthur Milby Burton, born in Milton Jan 14, 1829. He was admitted to the Bar in Philadelphia, Oct. 11, 1851, and until his death was actively engaged as an attorney in Philadelphia and built up an extensive practice, much of which was freely given to the needy.

CHAPTER LXIX.

TRUSTEN LAWS POLK'S DESCENDANTS.

Trusten Laws Polk (eldest son of Col Wm Polk, son of Robert Polk, Jr), was b about 1711 and d Jan 15, 1796, intestate Another account says he died Oct. 28, 1798 On April 18, 1782 he married Mary Nutter, orphan daughter of Christopher Nutter, Sr and ward of his father, Col Wm Polk

The children of Trusten Laws Polk and wife, Mary (Nutter) Polk were

(1) Wm Nutter Polk, b March 20, 1786, d April 22, 1835
(2) Daniel Polk, b ———, 1788, d unmarried
(3) Eleanor Polk, b. about 1790, d in Kentucky
(4) Sinah Polk, b about 1792, d ———.

Wm Nutter Polk married Lavenia Causey, July 17, 1809 She was b. Jan. 12, 1791, d March 24, 1825 William inherited the homestead of his father, "Polk's Defence" Lavenia was a daughter of Gov. Causey, of Delaware

Daniel Polk, second child of Trusten Laws Polk, d unmarried it is said

Eleanor, third child of Trusten Laws Polk, married her cousin, Daniel Polk, Jr , son of Daniel Polk, Sr , in 1812, and the same year they emigrated to Louisville, Ky , where she d. ———, 18—, and he afterwards married Catherine W. Hite By the latter he had no issue

Sinah, fourth child of Trusten Laws Polk, married Dr. John Cary, of Bridgeville, Del , and had issue Names not furnished.

CHILDREN OF WM. NUTTER POLK.

(1) Governor Trusten Polk, b May 29, 1811, in N. W Fork Hundred, Sussex County, Del., d April 16, 1876 at St Louis, Mo He married Elizabeth N Skinner, Dec. 26, 1837, she b in Connecticut Feb 17, 1819 and d March 22, 1896

(2) .... 25, 1832 -

(3) Wm Causey Polk, b July 12, 1815, d. Dec 28, 1893 He married Jan 16, 1838 at Bridgeville, Del., Sarah A. Tharp. b. 1821, daughter of Governor Tharp, of that state In 1870 his venerable widow was still living, aged 88 years Wm. Causey Polk inherited from his father the old homestead, "Polk's Defence," with its many slaves.

(4) Mary Causey Polk, b July 30, 1818, d ———, married April —, 1838, Daniel Currey

Louisa Caprion Dorsey (second wife of Capt Trusten Polk, son of Wm. Causey Polk and Sarah Tharp), was a great granddaughter of Deborah Ridgely, daughter of John Ridgely, the first owner of Hampton, Va.

INTERMARRIAGES.

Governor Trusten Polk and wife had issue·

Anna Polk, b. Sept. 14, 1839, d Oct. 1902, married April 13, 1864 Hon Wm. F Causey, of Milford, Del., son of Gov Peter F Causey They had issue·

(1) Anna Causey, b ———, married Dec 14, 1892 Wm R Aldred, of Milford, Del, Issue: Elizabeth N, b Jan. 24, 1894.

(2) Trusten Polk Causey, b. ——— at St. Louis. Attorney-at-law, Suffolk County, Virginia Bar

(3) Foster Causey, b ——— Resides at Washington, D C

(4) Maria Causey, b ——— Residence, Milford, Del

(5) Bessie Causey, b. ———. Residence, Milford, Del.

Mary Polk, daughter of Gov Trusten Polk, b April 22, 1841, married April 21, 1870 Dr James Avery Draper, of Wilmington, Del Issue:

(1) Elizabeth Draper, b March 23, 1871.
(2) Cornelia Draper, b May 13, 1872.
(3) James Avery Draper, b Oct 31, 1874
(4) Madeline Draper, b Nov 3, 1878
(5) Trusten Draper, b. Oct 20, 1880

All were born in Wilmington, Del

Cornelia Bredell Polk, third child of Gov Trusten Polk. b. Oct. 2, 1844, d. Oct. 28, 1895, married first, in Oct 1870, James E Drake, of Selma, Ala, second, John C Kennard, of St. Louis. She had issue

(1) Gaston Drake, b ———, married ———
(2) Trusten Drake, b ———, who married Alice Hocker, Dec 3, 1902.
(3) Bertrand Francis Drake, b ———
(4) James Erle Drake b ———, married Aug 1902, Leila Golson.

Elizabeth Polk, fourth child of Gov Trusten Polk, b June 26, 1852, married Oct 1880, Thomas S McPheeters, of St Louis, and had Thomas S , Jr

Trusten Polk, fifth child of Gov Trusten Polk, b Aug 2, 1856, d. March 5, 1860

ELIZABETH SHOCKLEY'S FAMILY.

Elizabeth Causey Polk (second child of Wm Nutter Polk), b. April 13, 1813, d Aug 25, 1832. By her husband Elias Shockley whom she married Jan 16, 1838, she had issue: William and Lavenia

WM. CAUSEY POLK'S FAMILY.

Wm Causey Polk and wife Sarah (Tharp) Polk, had issue:

(1) Capt Trusten Polk, b Aug. 4, 1840, d July 12 1902 He was married twice, first to Grace George, Dec 17, 1867, second to Louisa C Dorsey, Feb 9, 1870. He served three years in the Confederate Army.

(2) Caroline Polk, b Aug. 26, 1842, married Chas W Kalkeman, Oct 26, 1869   They had: [1]Wm P Kalkeman, [2]Chas Von H Kalkeman; [3]Eleanor Kalkeman, who married J. H. Wheelwright

(3) Elizabeth Polk, b Dec 15, 1847, married Joshua D Warfield, Oct 26, 1869   They had seven children four boys and three girls, names not secured

(4) Eleanor Polk, b May 5 1849, married Dr Thos B Owings, Feb 21, 1871   No issue

(5) Wm T. Polk, b May 7, 1853, unmarried He possessed m

They had one child, Mary Currey, who married Gen'l Alfred T A Torbert, U S A.

SKETCH OF GOVERNOR TRUSTEN POLK.

Trusten Polk, Governor and United States Senator, was born April 16, 1811, in Sussex County, Delaware, son of William N Polk, who was a direct descendant of Robert and Magdalen Polk, from whom likewise were descended the late President Jame K Polk, Gen. Thomas Polk, of Mecklenburg fame, and Bishop Leonidas Polk. His mother belonged to the influential Causey family, of that State. He attended the Academy at Cambridge, Md, preparatory to entering Yale College, where he graduated at the age of 19 with distinguished honors He studied in the office of John Rodgers, then Attorney-General of Maryland, and afterward attended two courses of lectures in the law department of Yale University In 1835, without influence and with comparatively little means, he came to St Louis. In 1843 he was City Counselor. Some years after coming to St Louis a pulmonary trouble developed and he visited the South in 1844 In the following year he traveled in the northern parts of the United States and Canada Whilst absent he was elected on the Democratic ticket for member of the State constitutional convention His health now restored, Mr Polk returned to his profession in St Louis In 1848 he was one of the Cass and Butler Presidential electors, but took no other prominent part in public affairs until 1856, when he was elected Governor Ten days after his inauguration the General Assembly elected him United States Senator, and he resigned the executive chair in October, 1857 In the Senate he followed the course of the Southern Democrats In 1861 he resigned and went to New Madrid, and subsequently became Judge-Advocate-General of the Army under Gen Stirling Price, with the rank of Colonel In 1864 he was taken prisoner and was confined for several months on Johnson's Island before he was exchanged During his absence his property in St Louis was confiscated by military order, but was at length restored At the close of the war he returned to St. Louis and resumed the practice of law, continuing until his death, which was somewhat sudden April 16, 1876

GOVERNOR AND U. S. SENATOR TRUSTEN POLK,
of Missouri.

THE
PUBLIC L.

ASTOR, LENOX AND
TILDEN FOUNDATIONS

CHAPTER LXX.

THE WHITE FAMILY.

Family tradition says the White family, which intermarried with the Polks, of Sussex County, Delaware, made its advent into America about 1700, the first one of the name being Dr. John White, said to have been from Durham County, England Dr. White was a single man when he came and entered the medical practice in Sussex and adjoining sections of Maryland

From tradition it appears that he had decided before leaving England on marriage to an attractive young lady, daughter of wealthy parents, whose first name was Elizabeth Her family name has not been preserved. Elizabeth was so much smitten with the doctor that she ran away from home to an English seaport, took passage on a ship, and came across the briny deep to her lover. Shortly after her arrival they were united in marriage, and to them was born a considerable family. Some time after their marriage a ship arrived from her family in England, laden with goods and household effects consigned to her and her husband

The regular order of birth of the children of Dr John White and wife, Elizabeth, is not known, nor all their names Those whose names have been preserved were Col Thomas White (who was the second child), Dr Edward White, Mrs Mary Morris, Margaret Nutter Polk, Sarah Cook and Anna White.

Col Thomas White was the father of Judge Samuel White, U S Senator, of Bishop White, of Pensylvania and of Mrs Mary White Morris, wife of Robert Morris, the distinguished Philadelphia financier and patriot of the Revolution, who sacrificed his large fortune to the needs of Washington's ragged and starving soldiers at Valley Forge, and died in poverty him··· 'f   q'   ···ested very l··· ···   ··· ··· ·. ',   , and was u··· ·l.   · the statutory English law of imprisonment for debt, which then existed in the Colonies, he served in prison for three years and a half, his faithful wife spending much of her time with him in his confinement

To Mrs. Morris was first given the title of "First Lady of the Land."

The appointment of Mr Morris as Superintendent of Finance, with his wealth and social distinction, made his home the center of all the amenity and civility of the day, and as hostess Mrs. Morris shone pre-eminent. The Marquis de Chastellux, the Abbe Robin, Citizen Mazzei, the Prince de Broglie, the Chevalier de la Luzerne, and others, have each recorded some agreeable memory of Mrs Morris. Washington on more than one occasion made her house his home. When Mrs Washington journeyed from Mt Vernon to New York, after the inauguration of the first President, she stopped in Philadelphia and took Mrs. Morris with her, in her carriage, to New York and at the first levee Mrs. Morris was given the place of honor on the right of the President's wife, a distinction always accorded her at public functions during Washington's administration. When the capital was removed to Philadelphia, it was Mrs Morris' home that was given up for the President's house.

Mr Morris survived his imprisonment five years, and Mrs Morris survived him twenty-one years. It was said of her that, "without the attraction of great personal beauty, Mrs Morris was tall, graceful, and commanding, with a stately dignity of manner, which ever made a controlling impression upon all with whom she was brought in contact." Stuart's portrait of her is said to have been the last female head that he painted. This portrait, bought by James Lennox, hangs in the Lennox Gallery, New York Public Library.

Col Thomas White was commissioned as one of the Justices of the County Court and Orphans Court of Kent County, by Governor John McKinley, March 8, 1777 On July 22, 1786, he was commissioned by Governor Vandyke as Third Justice, and on Feb 15 two years later, was made Second Justice by Governor Collins Later he was made Chief Justice Judge White died in 1795 aged 67 years.

Samuel White, son of Judge Thomas White, after the Revolution in which he was an officer, was appointed U. S Senator from Delaware, by Governor Richard Bassett, to succeed Dr Henry Latimer, who had resigned

Senator Samuel White was b in 1777, in Kent County, Del From his father Samuel received the home plantation, "Belisle" After a good education, Samuel studied law and was admitted to practice at Dover, in March, 1793 In 1806 he sold his farm and removed to Wilmington He was a Federalist in politics, but held no office until appointed U. S Senator on Feb 28, 1801. On Jan 11, 1803, at the regular session of the General Assembly, he was elected for the full term of Senator, beginning March 4, 1803. On Jan 11, 1809, he was re-elected for a second term While still a member of that body, he died on Nov 4, 1809

Samuel White died a bachelor His father, Judge Thomas White, left to survive him, a widow named Margaret, a daughter of David Nutter of North West Fork Hundred, Sussex County, the one son, Samuel, and three daughters, Margaret Nutter Polk, Sarah Cook and Anna White The latter it is said, never married Margaret Nutter White, the eldest daughter, married Daniel Polk, of Sussex County, and by him had a numerous family all of whom married members of prominent families. Daniel Polk's parents were Col. Wm. Polk and Alice Nutter; Col Wm Polk, a son of Robert Polk, Jr and Grace Guillette; Robt Jr, fifth son of Robert and Magdalen Polk the immigrants of 1672 Margaret Nutter, who married Daniel Polk, was the eldest daughter After marriage they resided first in Sussex, later removing to Kent County.

DANIEL POLK, SR., OF DELAWARE.

Daniel Polk, Sr, of Sussex County, Delaware was b Feb 28, 1750, and d March 29, 1796 Daniel was the fourth child of Robert Polk, 3d, and Alice Nutter, and he died on his plantation, the "Bonum Farm," near Wilmington, and his wife on September following

D . . . . ity in the S . . . . . eld in 1792

On Feb 9, 1775, Daniel was married to Margaret Nutter White, a daughter of Judge Thomas White and sister of U. S Senator White.

DANIEL POLK SR'S., FAMILY.

Daniel Polk, b. Feb 28, 1750, d. March 29, 1796
Margaret Nutter White, b April 11, 1758, d Sept 23, 1796
(1) Elizabeth Polk, b Sept 30, 1776, d Nov 11, 1836.
(2) John Polk, b Oct 20, 1778, lost at sea in 1800
(3) Margaret (Peggy) White Polk, b. Sept 26, 1780, d. June 16, 1826 She and Sarah were twins.
(4) Sarah Polk, b Sept 26, 1780, d Oct 5, 1781
(5) Daniel Polk, Jr , b. June 13, 1783, d June 14, 1838.
(6) Thomas White Polk, b April 1, 1784, d Feb 26, 1794
(7) Robert Polk, b March 13, 1786, d Sept 20, 1795.
(8) Anna Polk, b March 14, 1788, d Sept 29, 1860.
(9) Samuel White Polk, b Nov 2, 1790, d Oct 17, 1849
(10) Maria McClauster Polk, b. Sept. 26, 1795, d Oct 1798.

INTERMARRIAGES.

Elizabeth Polk married Dr James L Clayton, Dec 6, 1795

Peggy (Margaret) married Dr. George W. Logan, of Charleston, S. C , Oct 28, 1802

Anna married Wm G. Tilghman, of Talbot County, Md , Dec 13, 1809 She d in 1860, aged 70 years.

Samuel White Polk married Mrs Margaret Fidelite Fletcher (nee Ducournau), May 22, 1824.

CLAYTON FAMILY.

James Lawson Clayton, b July 15, 1769, d March 19, 1833. Elizabeth Polk, b Sept 30, 1776, d Nov. 11, 1836 The above were married Dec. 6, 1795 and had
(1) Rachael Clayton, b Jan 4, 1797
(2) John Laws Clayton b April 20, 1798

(3) Margaret Clayton, b Dec 11, 1799, d Oct 28, 1800
(4) Hester Clayton, b. Feb 27, 1802, d same day
(5) Amelia Eliza Clayton, b March 14, 1803.
(6) Anna Clayton, b Sept 2, 1805.
(7) Susanna Clayton, b March 7, 1808, d April 16, 1813
(8) James Clayton, b March 5, 1810, d Aug. 10, 1815

Governor Joshua Clayton, father of Dr Jas L Clayton, d Aug 11, 1798, in his 54th year

Rachael Clayton, wife of Joshua Clayton, d Jan 7, 1821. Rachael was married to Nathaniel Smithers, July 26, 1826, by Rev. I Wilson

Gov Joshua Clayton was a son of James Clayton, a descendant of Joshua Clayton who came over with Wm Penn and settled on "Bohemia Manor," in Cecil County, Md, where Joshua, the Governor was born in 1744 His mother was Rachael McCleary, an adopted daughter of Governor Richard Bassett.

SAMUEL WHITE POLK'S FAMILY.

Samuel White Polk (son of Daniel Polk, Sr, and Margaret Nutter White), was born in Dover, Del., Nov 2, 1790, d Oct 17, 1849.

Margaret Fidelete Ducournau (widow of James Fletcher), was b. Feb. 17, 1797 The above were married May 22, 1824. Their children were:

(1) Louise Polk, b Oct 25, 1825, d Dec 1, 1857

(2) Oswald Howard Polk, b Sept 21, 1827, d June 11, 1858

(3 M   1830
(4

(5) Edward Polk, b June 11, 1832, d Aug 1834
(6) Authur Louis Polk, b Feb 2, 1834, d Oct 21, 1864
(7) Felix Polk, b Sept 19, 1836
(8) Frederick Polk, b Aug 8, 1838, d July 27, 1840
(9) Maria Victoria Polk, b Jan 8, 1842, d Jan 23, 1844
Of the above children, three were married, viz.
Louise married Morgan May, May 31, 1853

Arthur Louis married Anna, daughter of E J Forstall, Feb 2, 1861 Neither of these left any surviving children

Jules married June 11, 1866 Mary Victoria Rees and had one son, Samuel Polk, b May 28, 1867.

Samuel White Polk, when a young man emigrated to New Orleans, and was a prominent business man of that city During the Civil War several of his sons served in the Confederate Army

When Samuel went to New Orleans, he carried with him the family bible of his father Daniel Polk, Sr , and after his death it fell into possession of Mr Theobold Forstall, Secretary of the New Orleans Gas Co., who transcribed for the author the foregoing data of Daniel Polk's family The widow Fletcher, whom Samuel White Polk married, was the grandmother of Mr Forstall

MIDSHIPMAN JOHN POLK.

John Polk (second child and eldest son of Daniel Polk, Sr), and his brother Daniel Polk, Jr., were both appointed in 1799 as Midshipmen in the U S. Navy, by President John Adams, on the recommendation of Caesar A. Rodney. John was lost at sea in 1800, in the sinking of the U S frigate "Insurgante " His brother Daniel resigned his commission in 1804, married in 1808 his cousin Eleanor Polk, daughter of Trusten Laws Polk and in 1812 emigrated to Louisville, Ky. Later he settled in Shelby County, where his wife died. He married again in 1823, his second wife being Catherine W.

Hite, by whom he had no issue By his wife Eleanor Polk he had twelve children She died in Shelby County in 1841.

Daniel died in Shelby County, June 11, 1838. The services of himself and brother John Polk while in the Navy, were mostly on Mediterranean stations. From a "List of Officers of the U S Navy and Marine Corps 1775-1900," we copy p 439 , Daniel Polk, Midshipman, March 16, 1799, resigned Jan 24 1804 John Polk, Midshipman Dec 5 1799, lost on the Insurgante, 1801

FAMILY OF DANIEL POLK, JR.

Daniel Polk, Jr , Midshipman, and his wife, Eleanor Polk, who married Sept 27, 1808, had issue

(1) Eliza A Polk, b Sept 25, 1809, d Feb. 11, 1886, married Burr G Powell, of Virginia

(2) Mary Polk b Aug 3, 1811, d Aug 3, 1813

(3) Dr. Louis Polk, b May 17, 1813, d ———; married Margaret B Metcalfe, Oct 5 1848

(4) Samuel Polk, b July 5, 1815 d Nov. 1 1823.

(5) Daniel Polk, b. Dec 31, 1816, d ———. married Elizabeth Rucker, of Georgetown, Ky.

(6) Margaret Polk, b Oct 12, 1818, d Jan. 11, 1822

(7) Henry Clay Polk, b May 5, 1820, d June 30, 1830

(8) Amanda L Polk, b Dec 3, 1822, d Oct 1890, married T M Davis, of Shelby County, Ky No issue.

(9) Sarah J Polk, b Jan. 27, 1825, d Oct 19, 1885, married Oct 11, 1845 R T. Conn, of Bourbon County Ky

(10) Sophronia Polk, b Feb 2, 1827 d ———, married T W Hornsby

(11) Ellen Maria Polk b Jan 21, 1829 married May 26 1858, Landon A Thomas Sr , a banker of Frankfort, Ky He d. Oct. 2, 1889, and she on Feb 6 1911

(12) Leah Polk b April 8, 1831, d in infancy

D   after the death of his wife Eleanor Polk, was
Feb 7

FAMILY OF ELIZABETH POWELL.

Burr G Powell, who married Eliza A Polk, daughter of Daniel Polk, Jr, was born in Virginia in Sept 1800, died Jan 1895 They had issue:

(1) Kate E Powell, b Feb 22, 1835, d. Jan 27, 1895; married Wm P Tyree, of Tennessee, Aug 17, 1853

(2) William H Powell, b Aug 25, 1842, married Martha A Grant, June 12, 1879. She d in 1881 No issue.

(3) Henry Clay Powell, b May 13, 1844, never married

(4) Edward B Powell, b March 4, 1846, married Elizabeth S. Emmerson, Nov 17, 1881

(5) Amanda Polk Powell, b. Aug. 31, 1847; never married

FAMILY OF KATE POWELL TYREE.

Kate E Powell, who married Wm P Tyree, had issue:
(1) Lena Leoto Tyree, b June 11, 1854
(2) Elizabeth E Tyree, b. April 27, 1856
(3) Albert Tyree, b May 30, 1860
(4) Clem Tyree, b July 10, 1861
(5) Eugene Tyree, b Nov 25, 1862
(6) William P Tyree, b. July 13, 1866
(7) Nellie Tyree, b Oct 31, 1868
(8) Stella Tyree b July 27, 1871

FAMILY OF EDWARD B. POWELL

The children born to Edward B Powell and Elizabeth S Emmerson were
(1) Ralph E Powell, b Oct 15, 1882
(2) Thruston Powell, b April 1, 1884
(3) Weston Powell, b Dec 31, 1885
(4) Amanda Powell, b Nov. 16, 1887
(5) Samuel G Powell, b Feb 23, 1890.
(6) Edna Powell, b April 5, 1892.

FAMILY OF DR. LOUIS POLK.

Dr Louis Polk (third child and eldest son of Daniel Polk, Jr., of Shelby County, Ky.), was married Oct 5, 1848 to Margaret B Metcalfe, by whom he had issue

(1) Edwin Polk, b Oct 23, 1849   Residence, San Antonio, Tex.

(2) Baylor Polk, b March 4, 1851   Residence, Silver City, N M

(3) Daniel Polk, b Nov 16, 1852, married Anna Reed and had issue: Zillah and a son

(4) Louis Polk, b Sept 21, 1855, d ———; married Mary Guthrie   Issue ¹Margaret, ²Jennie; ³Louise, ⁴Guthrie

(5) Lura Polk, b Jan 19, 1858, d Nov 19, 1858

(6) Fannie B Polk, b Oct 19, 1859   Residence Texas

(7) Lillian May Polk, b Oct 18, 1862; married J A Baker and had a son, Robert Baker   Residence, Ardmore, Okla

(8) Trusten Polk, b Nov 29, 1864, married Maggie Guthrie   Issue ¹Edwin, ²William, ³Margaret

(9) Eloise Polk, b Oct 19, 1866, married ——— McGill, of Ardmore, Okla

FAMILY OF MRS. LANDON A. THOMAS, SR.

The children of Landon A. Thomas and wife, Ellen Maria (Polk) Thomas were:

(1) Landon A Thomas, Jr., b June 5, 1859, married Oct 21, 1885, Mary C Fleming, of Augusta, Ga   Residence, Augusta

(2) Anne Thomas, b June 7, 1860, unmarried residence Frankfort, Ky

(3) Edmond Pendleton Thomas, b Nov 18, 1861, d July, 1862

(5) Western D. Thomas, ... , 1891

FAMILY OF LANDON A THOMAS, JR.

The children of Landon A Thomas, Jr of Augusta, Ga, and his wife, Mary (Fleming) Thomas are

(1) Landon Thomas, b Dec 28, 1886
(2) Ellen Polk Thomas, b Mar 14, 1895
(3) Emily Hame Thomas, b May 28, 1897
(4) Anne Thomas b Oct 30, 1901

Richard T. Conn and his wife, Sarah J Polk Conn (daughter of Daniel Polk, Jr, and wife Eleanor, of Shelby County, Ky), had issue

(1) Anna V Conn, b. 1846 married Feb, 1870, Sam'l W Forder, of St Louis, Mo

(2) Florence E Conn b Nov 25, 1862, married Nov. 9, 1887, Taylor Stith, of St Louis, Mo

The children of Sam'l W and Anna C Forder were:
(1) Conn Forder, b Dec 28, 1871; married June, 1900
(2) Mary Alice Forder, b July 12, 1875, d Nov., 1904.
(3) Dr Carver W Forder, b July 17, 1878; unmarried
(4) Sam l W Forder, b Nov 1, 1880, unmarried.

The children of Taylor and Florence E Stith were:
(1) Madeline Florence Stith, b. Sept. 9, 1888
(2) Richard Taylor Stith, b Feb 6, 1890.
(3) Harold Joseph Stith, b. Jan. 16, 1899.

FAMILY OF DANIEL POLK, OF DENVER.

Daniel Polk, fifth child of Midshipman, Daniel Polk and wife Eleanor, was b in Shelby County, Dec 31, 1816 and d at Denver, Col, Aug ——, 1895. By his wife, Elizabeth Rucker who d Sept, 1894, he had issue.

(1) Alice Polk, b. March 22, 1845; married Nov. 3, 1868, Wm. C Hill Issue I Wm Hill, b Jan 31, 1871; married Anna A Bent, Nov 4 1907 Issue: Alice Polk Hill, b Sept.

22, 1908 Mrs. Alice Polk Hill has for a number of years been one of the most prominent women in Denver, in social and literary life, and is author of a book entitled, "Pioneers of Colorado." She was the only woman in the convention that made the charter for the city and county of Denver

(2) Ellen Polk Hill, b Dec 31, 1852, married Herman Ruff, Aug 27, 1878 Issue, Alice Polk Ruff, b Aug 31, 1885

(3) Louis Polk, b Sept, 1847, d July, 1890; unmarried

PEGGY LOGAN'S FAMILY

Peggy, or Margaret Polk, third child of Daniel Polk, Sr, with her twin sister Sarah was born Sept 26, 1780 Sarah died when a year old

On Oct 28, 1802, at the home of Dr James Clayton in Wilmington, Peggy was married to Dr George Logan, Jr, of Charleston, S C Peggy d June 16, 1826 and Dr Logan took as a second wife, Ann Turner

Peggy and Dr Logan met while she was attending school in Philadelphia, Dr Logan at that time being a student of Medicine at the University of Pennsylvania Peggy at the time was a ward of Hon Caesar A Rodney, one of Delaware's "Signers," who had been a very close political friend of her father's Dr Logan and wife lived at Charleston, S. C., until her death in 1862, at the age of 46 years, leaving six children Mrs Logan was accounted the beauty of her family Dr Logan's ancestor, Col George Logan, of the British Army, came to Charleston in 1690, in command of a regiment of Horse to protect the colony from its enemies

The children born to Dr George Logan and wife, Peggy (Polk) Logan were:

(1) George William Logan, b July 10, 1804

(5) Caesar A. Rodney Logan, b Aug 3, 1815, d Sept. 7, 1853.

(6) William Logan, b Sept 23, 1818, d in 1841

These sons all became prominent citizens, the first, George W Logan, became a distinguished Judge General Thomas Logan of Richmond, Va, a distinguished artillery officer of the Confederate Army, was of this family

THE TILGHMAN FAMILY.

Anna Polk, daughter of Daniel Polk, Sr., was b March 14 1788 and d Sept 9, 1860 On Dec 13, 1809, she married Wm Gibson Tilghman, of Talbot County, member of a distinguished Maryland family, and to this union were born nine children, five of whom grew to maturity and married, and have numerous descendants

CHAPTER LXXI.

CAPT. ROBERT POLK, NAVAL OFFICER.

Captain Robert Polk, son of Robert Polk, 3d and Alice (Nutter) Polk, was born in Dorchester County, Maryland in 1744 and was killed in 1779, during the Revolution, on board his ship the privateer Montgomery, in a desperate engagement with a British ship. It is said that he greatly distinguished himself in the engagement, and that he received a mortal wound from a large splinter that was knocked off by one of the enemy's cannon balls and entered his body. His will is on file at Baltimore.

Capt. Robert's commissions as commander of the privateers "Black Jake" and "Montgomery" were issued by the State of Maryland. He sailed from Annapolis, scoured the seas for British merchantmen, and took his prizes, of which he made quite a number, into the port of Norfolk for disposal. The records of the U. S. Navy contain accounts of his exploits and captures while in command of the ships named.

Capt. Robert Polk was married in 1765, when twenty-one years of age, to Elizabeth Digby Peale, of Philadelphia (b. Jan. 20, 1747), a sister of Charles Wilson Peale, the distinguished artist, and founder of Peale's Museum of that city. Of the youth of Robert little is known beyond the statement that he was early inclined to seafaring. When the Revolution came on he was in the full vigor of manhood and eagerly entered the ranks of his country's defenders, as did others of his kinsmen.

Mrs. Polly Wolf, of Indiana, in 1874, telling the author about her father Ephraim Polk's enlistment in Philadelphia, in 1777, stated that "while there he visited a cousin, Capt. Robert Polk, who was a naval officer and was afterwards killed on his ship." This she got from her father when she was a little ... ire of winte ... ences and recollections of the Revolution.

DESCENDANTS OF CAPTAIN ROBERT POLK.

(Data furnished by Peale Family.)

Capt Robert Polk, b in Maryland 1744, killed in Navy, 1779 Elizabeth Digby Peale, b Jan 20, 1747 at Charlestown Md They were married in 1765 and had issue

(1) Margaret Polk, b June 4, 1766, d ———
(2) Charles Peale Polk, b March 17, 1767, d 1822
(3) Elizabeth Boardley Polk, b Aug 1, 1770, d ———

The portrait of Capt Robert Polk in uniform, painted by his wife's brother, Chas Wilson Peale, was taken by his widow to Virginia, where it was destroyed by Federal soldiers during the Civil War

FAMILY OF CHARLES PEALE POLK.

Charles Peale Polk, son of Capt. Robert Polk and Elizabeth Digby (Peale) Polk, was three times married His first wife was Miss Ruth Ellison of New Jersey, about 1785. His second wife was a Mrs. Brockenbrough, of Fredericksburg, Va, in 1811 His third was Miss Ellen B Downman, in 1816.

By the first wife Charles Peale Polk had·

(1) Elizabeth Polk, b 1786, d. 1874
(2) Robert Polk, b Dec 9, 1788, married Penelope Johnson Maury.
(3) Josiah Polk, b ———, d ———
(4) David P Polk, b about 1790, d 1835 Was an officer in U. S Army in war of 1812 He was appointed an Ensign in the Twelfth Infantry June 22, 1812; 3d Lieut March 20, 1813, 1st Lieut Aug. 24, 1814 Honorably discharged June 15, 1815 He married Letitia Jane Stewart.
(5) Anna M Polk, b about 1792, d ———
(6) Edward B Polk, b about 1794 d. unmarried Was also an officer in U S Army
(7) Theodore Polk, b about 1796, d ———
(8) Caroline Polk, b about 1798, d ———
(9) Franklin Polk, b about 1800, d ———
(10) Ruth Polk, b. about 1802, d - —

Robert Polk by his first wife Penelope J Maury, had issue 'Mary, b ——— d — , married J J Brown, of

Virginia, ²Gabriel Duval, b ———, d 1835 ³Susan, b ———, d ———, married Rev H Haverstick at Philadelphia in 1839, ⁴Robert Isaac Watts, b March 28, 1818 at Washington, D C, d Oct. 11, 1861

By his second wife, Mrs Brockenbrough, of Fredericksburg, Va, whom he married in 1811, he had:

(11) Columbus C Polk, b about 1812-13 He went to sea and was never heard of again

By his third wife, Ellen B. Downman, whom he married in 1816, Charles Peale Polk had

(12) Ellen B Polk, b ———, d ———

Elizabeth Boardley Polk, third child of Capt Robert Polk and Elizabeth Digby Peale, married twice, first to Septimus Claypool, no issue Second to Rev Dr Bend, the Rector of St Paul's P E Church of Baltimore No issue

Robert Isaac Watts Polk and his wife Sarah J (Somerville) Polk were married May 10, 1838, in Fredericksburg City, Md They had issue

(1) Elizabeth Polk, b. April 14, 1839, at Woodstock, Va, Charles Cochran.

(2) Penelope Maury Johnson Polk, b Aug 17, 1843, at Winchester, Va, married Philip Leidy, M D, a distinguished physician, paleontologist and scientist of Philadelphia, who has a world-wide reputation

(3) Laura Polk, b Dec 23 1849, married first James Ladson Hall, 2nd, George Nelson Gregg

(4) James Fontaine Polk, b Jan 15, 1846, d Jan. 11, 1869.

(5) Duvall Polk b Oct 15, 1852, married Lillie Bancroft Caldwell

(6) Robert Polk, b Jan 9, 1855

Duval Fontaine Polk, son of Robert Isaac Watts Polk b Oct 15, 1852, at Winchester, Va married Oct 8, 1874, at Philadelphia, Lillie Bancroft Caldwell (daughter of Robert and Ja
¹Helen
1877.

CHARLES PEALE POLK, ARTIST.

Among the distinguished artists of the Revolutionary period was Charles Wilson Peale, of Philadelphia, whose industry was probably not equaled by any other person of his profession, both in oil portraits and miniature work. His son, Rembrandt Peale, and his nephew Charles Peale Polk (son of Capt. Robert Polk), both inherited the artistic talent and also produced pictures of distinguished subjects of the time. It was the habit of Peale to encourage the talents of his son and nephew all he could.

On one occasion, having secured the consent of President Washington for a sitting, he took along his son and nephew, and all three sketched Washington at the same time, whereat other artists expressed their disgust at Peale "making a family affair of the sitting."

Would be critics of the present day have attempted to discredit Charles Peale Polk's ability as a painter, but the numerous specimens of his work still extant attest his skill with the brush. Some have asserted that Polk was a mere copyist and have tried to belittle his work, but the latter speaks for itself when viewed by the unprejudiced critic. All the great artists of the world have been set upon by hypercritical faultfinders, but their work still lives.

A very beautiful portrait of Washington painted by Charles Peale Polk and signed on the back in his characteristic manner "Cs Polk, Painter No 53" is now in possession of Mrs Mary G von Tschudi Price, of 357 West 118th Street, New York. The portrait is of head size three quarters length, in perfect condition and still in the original frame. With colors mellowed by time it is most interesting as a work of superior merit by Polk, as well as a contemporary Washington picture. It has never been out of the present owner's family and, according to its traditions, was painted from life, and was given by Washington to Col Wm Clemm, a prominent citizen of Baltimore, who was among the first to go from that town to fight for American Independence.

Washington is here represented in Continental uniform, with three stars on the epaulettes, his hand holding a chapeau,

PORTRAIT OF WASHINGTON.
By Charles Peale Polk, son of Capt. Robt. Polk and Elizabeth Digby

rests on the hilt of his sword In the background, on one side, are Princeton and the college buildings On the other side a sentinel on duty, before a camp over which floats an American flag As Polk, in a letter to Washington, of date Aug. 6, 1790, states that during the last year, (1789-90) he had completed 50 portraits, wishes a sitting, asking that Washington grant him one, and as this portrait is signed No 53, it is more than likely that this was an original portrait, executed perhaps about 1795, when Polk was one of the three painters, including Rembrandt Peale, who availed themselves of this opportunity to paint Washington, who had granted a sitting

CHARLES PEALE POLK'S LETTER TO WASHINGTON.

The following is a copy of the letter written by Charles Peale Polk to George Washington requesting of him the favor of a sitting

New York, Aug 6, 1790

Sir

Encouraged by your Excellency's known Affibility and admirable Condescention, a Citizen of Philadelphia Humbly requests the Indulgence of an Interview His Errand tho' far from being disinterested to himself, He hopes will be very far from being displeasing or offensive to your Excellency His Object is if Possible, to obtain the Honorable privilege of One Short Sitting from the President, to enable him to finish a portrait of your Excellency, (in head size) Prepared with that design

He has in the Course of the last year Executed fifty Portraits tho his advantages were not what he wished, But Imag   I per
mit (Just

and finished performances—the resemblance of Him whose Character will never be obliterated from the hearts of true Americans

Should this request meet your Excellency's favor, not only will the desires of many Respectable Citizens be gratified, but the Interests of a depending family greatly promoted And the Pleasure Vastly Increased of your

    Excellency's
      most Obedient and
      devoted Servt.
     CHARLES PEALE POLK.

His Excellency the President.

Copied from the Manuscript Division Library of Congress, Nov. 27, 1910

CHAPTER LXXII.

POLKS OF ACCOMAC COUNTY, VIRGINIA

Capt. Wiliam Polk, of Accomac County, Virginia, married Sabra Bradford, Jan. 25, 1764 and had issue

(1) Sally Polk, b March 13, 1766
(2) Margaret Polk, b Jan 24, 1768
(3) Nathaniel Polk, b May 15, 1770
(4) Bridget Polk, b June 3, 1772.
(5) James Polk, b April 4, 1774.
(6) Jane Polk, b. April 5, 1776
(9) Robert Polk, b June 2, 1778.
(8) Martha Polk, b. Sept. 27, 1780.
(9) Amelia ("Milly") Polk, b. Oct. 13, 1782
(10) William Polk, b July 5, 1784
(11) John Polk, b March 10, 1786

INTERMARRIAGES.

Sally Polk married three times, first to Jacob Lurton, second to Littleton Townsend; third to Thomas Sturgis How many children she had by these three husbands is not known By Mr Townsend she had a daughter Sabra Polk Townsend who married first John Scarborough, second Capt. Samuel Waples in 1822, son of Paul Waples, of Delaware Two sons by the first died young By Capt. Waples she had Edward B. Waples; a daughter (name unknown) who married Wm Robertson and had three sons, also another daughter untraced Capt Waples was a Lieutenant in the company of Capt Wm Polk, in the Revolution.

Edward B Waples, son of Capt Samuel Waples, b Jan 17, 1825 married —————— and had·

(1   · ·i n   i i   iertie
Lee W   '· ·

(2) John S Waples, who had Sarah, Sabia and Mary Robertson Waples

(3) Jennings Wise Waples, who had Wm Jennings and Sarah Waples

(4) Edward B, Jr, and Charles S Waples, both of whom married but left no issue

Capt Samuel Waples was a soldier in the Revolution, in the Ninth Virginia Continentals, Col Chas Scott's brigade, and was one of the suffering patriots at Valley Forge.

SALLIE POLK'S DESCENDANTS.

Sallie Polk (daughter of Capt Wm. Polk, by her last husband, Thomas Sturgis), had a daughter Mehala Sturgis, who married first Joseph Gunter, second Con Laws By the first she had

(1) Benjamin Thomas Gunter, married Ellen Frances Fisher

(2) Elizabeth S Gunter, married Thomas C Pitts By the second husband Sallie had Joseph Gunter Laws

Benjamin Thomas Gunter and wife Ellen 'had· ¹Mahala Gunter, married John Edmonds Issue Alfred B G, John Willis, Ella Tabitha, James Frederic, and May Edna Edmonds, ²John Joseph Gunter, b ———, d Oct 2, 1889, married Florence M Custis and had Ellen Custis, ³Alfred Benjamin Gunter, b ———, d unmarried, ⁴Joseph Fisher Gunter also d unmarried, ⁵Wm Frederick d unmarried, ⁶Benjamin Thomas Gunter married Anne Eastburn He is an eminent lawyer and for many years was Circuit Judge of his district

Thomas C Pitts and wife, Elizabeth (Gunter) Pitts had issue.

(1) Robert C Pitts, untraced

(2) Wm B Pitts, married Ella K Hopkins, no issue

(3) Alice T Pitts, married Spencer F Rogers Issue ¹William Pitts Rogers, ²Alfred B G Rogers; ³John T Rogers, ⁴Susie P Rogers; ⁵Spencer F Rogers, ⁶Elizabeth ("Bessie") Rogers, married Lewis J Harmonson, ⁷Louis P Rogers; ⁸Anne Louis Rogers

MARGARET POLKS DESCENDANTS

Margaret Polk (second child of Capt. William Polk), married Revel Colburn. He was born in Virginia Sept 16, 1764 and died in Henry County, Indiana, Feb 24, 1844. She died Nov 26 1837, in the same county. Revel and Margaret (Polk) Colburn were well educated and though advanced in years he taught school for several terms after settling in Indiana. His wife was a physician and engaged in active practice. A sovereign remedy administered by her for the prevalent disease of malaria was "Rock Oil," put up in small bottles, and now known as petroleum, which was skimmed from the surface of springs.

The children of Revel and Margaret (Polk) Colburn were: [1]John; [2]Sally (Hobson); [3]James; [4]William, [5]Henrietta Rhoads, [6]Sabra (Twiford), [7]Jane (Webster), [8]Mary (Leonard). John was a Methodist preacher. He married Elizabeth Petty and had [1]Jesse, [2]Sally; [3]William, [4]Martha [5]Caroline. The latter married James Alired Current May 8 1851. He was born at Grafton Va. June 25, 1824.

Sally (daughter of Margaret and Revel Colburn), married George Hobson, Sept 7, 1807. Sally was born in Chatham County N. C., Dec 27, 1789.

George and Sally Hobson had issue
(1) William P Hobson, b ———, d ———
(2) Revel C Hobson, b Sept. 13, 1810, d Jan 20, 1819
(3) Polly B Hobson, b March 1, 1813, d a week later
(4) Bale B Hobson, b March 24, 1814, d April 11, 1815
(5) Jose K Hobson, b ———, d ———
(6) Margaret K. Hobson, b ———, d ———
(7) Jemima D Hobson, b ———, d ———
(8) Eliza J Hobson, b ———, d ———
(9) James R Hobson, b ———, d ———
(10) George W Hobson b Aug. 12, 1828, d Nov 1839
(11) Sarah A Hobson, b ——— d ———

Eliza J Hobson, daughter of Sally (Colburn) and George Hobson married Samuel J Current and they had a number of ch   , Ind
auth   ulies,
the Hobsons all being descendant   lk, of

Accomac, through his daughter Margaret, who married Revel Colburn

Bridget Polk (daughter of Capt Wm Polk), married Thomas Clegg, who died in North Carolina in 1827. They had issue

(1) Wm Clegg, who d. young
(2) Esther C. Clegg, married Wm. Arens.
(3) John Clegg, emigrated to Georgia, untraced.
(4) Elizabeth Clegg married Mr Bixman
(5) David Clegg, married Miss Bixman

The others, all untraced as to issue, were Nathaniel, Thomas, Jr, Peggy, Nancy, Mary, Luther and Baxter Clegg

James Polk (son of Capt Wm Polk and Sabra (Bradford) Polk, married Elizabeth Hutchison He removed to Chatham County, N C James died near Guilford, C H, in May 1824, and his sons decided to remove to the Ohio Valley James and Elizabeth had issue

(1) Hugh Polk, b Feb 1, 1799, who married Jeretta ——————, and had [1]Wm P, [2]James; [3]Martha, who married Wm Shelby; [4]Elizabeth, who married —————— Wilson, [5]Abijah, who married Miss Wright; [6]Rebecca, [7]Peter and [8]Stran Polk

(2) Robert H Polk (son of James and Elizabeth Polk), b June 13, 1800 in Accomac County, Virginia, married Hannah Hodgen, Dec. 11, 1823 She was born Feb 25, 1802 and died Feb 12, 1875 In 1841 Robert H Polk removed from North Carolina to Henry County, Ind. He had issue

(1) Col Babel N Polk, b Nov 19, 1824, married Louisa Northum He had five children, one of whom, Sophronia, married Lindsay Vestal, of Madison, Ind

(2) Milton D Polk, b. Aug 7, 1826, d Nov. 9, 1849.

(3) Rebecca Polk, b Sept 11, 1828, married Jacob Kennard

(4) Rachel Polk, b Sept. 9, 1830, married Quinton Vinchow and had a daughter Ruth and two more children.

(5) Caroline Polk, b. ———, married George Kern Issue unknown

(6) Robt Polk b. ———, d —— Residence, Madison, Ind,

MRS. SARRA POLK JOYNES AND DAUGHTER

THE
PUBLIC

ASTOR, LE X A
TILDEN FOUNDATIONS

The youngest child, Elizabeth, b Nov 6, 1811, married David F Woods Preceding her in date of birth were Mary J., Emma, Joseph and Mary, but their dates are not preserved

Rebecca Polk Kennard had a son Milton M Kennard, of Knightstown, Ind.

Margaret ("Peggy") Polk (daughter of James and Elizabeth Hutchison Polk), b in 1802, married first Rutherford Petty, second P Garner By the first she had ¹Robert Petty, who married Rachael Vestal; ²Elizabeth Petty, who married Wm Armfield, ³Nancy Petty, who married Lewis Swindle. By the second husband, Mr Garner, Margaret had three sons, Edmond, Tasker and ——————— who had a son Samuel

James Polk (son of James and Elizabeth Hutchison Polk), b 1804 in Accomac, married Finnell Stewart, of North Carolina They had Col J Robert Polk, b 1833, who was Auditor of Wabash County Indiana, dying in 1875 He had several children, names not furnished

John Polk (son of James and Elizabeth Hutchison Polk), married and had a son Robert who went to California

Nancy Polk (youngest child of James and Elizabeth Hutchison Polk), married Peter Ruby

Jane Polk (daughter of Capt Wm Polk and Sabra Bradford Polk, b April 5 1776, married first George Handover, second Zorobabel Edwards Issue, untraced

Robert Polk (son of Capt Wm. Polk and wife), b June 2, 1778, emigrated from North Carolina to Henry County, Ind Issue, if any, not recorded

Martha (Patsy) Polk (daughter of Capt Wm Polk and wife), b Sept 27, 1780, married Joshua Fitchett and located in Northampton County, Virginia They had a number of descendants, among them

(1) Mary Fitchett, who married William Dixon

(2) Emily Fitchett, who married Thomas Duncan.

(3) Sabra Polk Fitchett, who married June 5, 1819, Tully A T Joynes, of Onancock, Va

(4) William Fitchett, untraced.

it had issue

(1) Alexander T Joynes, who married Mary Wilkins. They had a daughter, Lessie, who married A Fuller

(2) Wm F Joynes, who married Jennie Hopkins They had a daughter, Tabitha and a son T H. Joynes, the latter of Baltimore Tabitha married Nov 27, 1900, E Thomas Waters

Tully A. T Joynes, Jr., (son of Tully A T, Sr), married Mary Hamilton and had ¹Evelyn and ²Julia A Evelyn married Nov. 25, 1908, Chas. C. Womach Julia A. married May 6, 1909, Dr Shipley, of Baltimore

Tabitha Joynes, daughter of Tully A T Joynes, Sr, married first Dr Jno C Laurence, of North Carolina; second Samuel B Hance, of Baltimore

Goodwin Joynes, b Sept. 6, 1856 (youngest son of Tully A. T Joynes, Sr.), married Sally W. Northam, Nov 25, 1880. They had·

(1) Louise, b Feb 2, 1882
(2) Blanche N, b. Jan. 20, 1886
(3) Helen G, b Oct 26, 1888
(4) Tully A T, b Nov 27, 1890
(5) George Goodwin, b. Jan. 6, 1896

Louise, married Mosby G. Perrow, of Lynchburg, Va, Nov. 11, 1902.

WILLIAM POLK'S DESCENDANTS.

William Polk (tenth child of Capt Wm. Polk and wife, Sabra), b July 5, 1784, married Hannah Hobson, March 30, 1809, she was b Oct 10, 1776 They had five sons and two daughters, viz ¹James, ²William; ³Robert; ⁴Nathaniel, ⁵John; ⁶Sarah and ⁷Martha Ann The latter married first, Mr Bloom, second, Mr. McConnell

James Polk, eldest son of Wm Polk and Hannah (Hobson) Polk, was quite an artist in silhouette pictures, executing them with great skill His father, Wm Polk, removed from North Carolina to Clinton County, Ohio, about 1807, where he died, and where he left a number of descendants A daughter of James Polk, Mrs Annie Darbyshire, resides at Sabina, Cinton County

Of the other children of William and Hannah (Hobson)

Polk, Robert settled at Muncie, Ind Nathaniel removed to Missouri Sally died when grown John and Sarah untraced.

Amelia ("Milly") Polk (ninth child of Capt William Polk and wife), b Oct 13, 1782, married Littleton Harmon, of Chatham, N C, and removed to Indiana, settling near the Polks who had preceded them They had issue ¹James; ²Sally, ³Reuben, ⁴Sina; ⁵Thomas; ⁶Nancy

John Polk (youngest son of Capt Wm Polk and wife, Sabra (Bradford)) Polk), b March 10, 1786, was drowned while in bathing, aged about 20 years.

By his second wife (who is said to have been Priscilla Polk, of Maryland, a cousin), Capt Wm Polk had a daughter Priscilla Polk, b. April 21, 1793 She d in 1810

CAPT. WM. POLK'S ANCESTORS

Among the most active and patriotic participants in the American Revolution was Captain William Polk, of Accomac County, Virginia, whose residence was on the seashore, where he carried on the business of making salt from sea water Close by he had a fine residence built of bricks said to have been brought in a ship from England Here he was living when the Colonies threw off the yoke of England and war came on.

William Polk raised a company of troops of which he was made Captain, and with them he did good service When the British ravaged the Virginia coast, under the traitor Benedict Arnold, they burned his residence and salt works, his wife barely escaping capture

Who were the parents of Capt William Polk is not positively shown by the data at the author's command All of it must be classed simply as inferential proof.

A few of the Maryland and Delaware Polks moved south into Accomac County, Virginia, and Capt William Polk may have been from one of these families In several of the Polk branches appear data that points toward Capt. William as one of their line, but none are full enough on that point to con:

Mary

Winder Garrett, of Williamsburg, Va., in October 1897 issue of the American Historical Magazine, page 383, she names the children of William Polk and Priscilla Roberts, as shown on the Polk tree published in 1849. Of William, eldest of these children, she says he was twice married, but cannot give names of his wives. But she gives two of his children, Col Thomas and John, by his first wife, and Ezekiel by second wife Shelby. Son of Col Thomas, married a Colburn. The names of Thomas John and Ezekiel do not appear in the Bible record list of Capt Wm Polk's family. Hence the conclusion that William Polk, eldest son of William and Priscilla, besides Thomas and John, also may have had a son William, who was Captain William Polk, of Accomac.

It will also be noticed that Margaret Polk, second child of Capt Wm Polk, married Revel Colburn, and that a son of Wm Polk, first child of William shown on 1849 Polk tree, also married a Colburn.

CHAPTER LXXIII.

THE POLLOCKS OF AMERICA.

Rev Horace Edwin Hayden, of Harrisburg, Pa, in 1888, published in pamphlet form a "Pollock Genealogy," containing an extended sketch of Col Oliver Pollock, of Carlisle, Pa, a distinguished man of his day in financial transactions and of great wealth, all of which he placed at the disposal of his country during the Revolutionary War, when he was Commercial Agent of the government at Havana and New Orleans. But for his efforts in securing supplies and ammunition for the army and navy, and for Gen'l George Rogers Clark for his Illinois Campaign, the American arms possibly may have failed of success

Says Rev. Hayden· 'The Pennsylvania Pollocks are all of Scotch-Irish descent, and supposed to have had but one origin, in "Petrus, son of Fulbert, who succeeded his father and assumed as a surname the name of hereditary lands of Pollock in Renfrewshire He lived in the reign of Malcolm IV, who died in 1165, and was a man of great eminence in his time and a benefactor of the Monastery of Paisley This donation was confirmed by Joceline Bishop of Glasgow, who died 1199 Besides his estates in Renfrewshire, he held the barony of Rothes in the county of Aberdeen, which he gave to his daughter, Mauricle de Pollock who married Sir Norman Lesley and was ancestor of the Earls of Rothes (Burke) Although the arms differ, the crests of the Scotch and Irish Pollocks are the same, "a boar passant, or and vert, transfixed with a dart, proper"

"The Pennsylvania Pollocks embrace descendants of James and Oliver Pollock of Carlisle, Pa, comprising family names of Alger, Bradford, Briggs, Dougherty Dady, Foley, Gibson, Morrison, McKay, O'Brien, Pharis, Penninmen, and Rob and settled in Pennsylvaia as well as descendants of Samuel Pollock, of Chester and Dauphin Counties, Pa

"The North Carolina Pollocks were intimately connected with Aaron Burr Rev Johnathan Edwards, D D , son of the great Johnathan the Divine of New England, had eleven children. Of these the third, Esther, b 1732, married Rev Aaron Burr, President of Princeton College and father of Aaron Burr, Vice President of United States Eunice, sister of Esther, married first Thomas Pollock, of Newbern, N. C.

"George Pollock, son of Thos Pollock and Eunice Edwards, was an intimate friend of Aaron Burr, his first cousin He lived in Philadelphia from 1800 to 1806 Burr was his guest when he visited Philadelphia (see life of Blennerhasset) Four men named Pollock were among the early settlers of Cumberland County, Pa

(1) James Pollock, of East Pennsboro
(2) Oliver Pollock, of Carlisle, brother of James (1)
(3) James Pollock, of Hopewell Township, whose will, dated May 25, 1773, mentions six children, viz ¹John Pollock; ²Jean, married Mr Hinchman, ³Martha, married Mr Dobson, ⁴James Pollock, ⁵William Pollock; ⁶Robert Pollock

"The descendants of James and Oliver comprise the family names of Alger, Bradford, Briggs, Dougherty, Dady, Foley, Gibson, Morrison, McKay, O'Brien Pharis, Penniman and Robinson

"James and Oliver Pollock, brothers, emigrated from Ireland to America and located at or near Carlisle, Pa , before 1760 The private papers, miniature and coat of arms of Oliver Pollock, including all his official documents, commissions from, and correspondence with the Continental Congress, etc , were destroyed during the Civil War—partly at Vicksburg, Miss , and partly by the United States gunboat Essex, when it shelled Bayou Sara, La , in 1863

"James Pollock settled in East Pennsboro township, Cumberland County, Pa He married Ann Lowry. James Pollock died Sept. 1, 1800, at Carlisle, and his will was probated Nov 2, following His widow, Nancy Pollock, resided there in 1809. Oliver Pollock was administrator of the estate. James Pollock certainly had two sons possibly four

COL. OTIS W. POLLOCK, U. S. A.
San Francisco.

THE
PUBLIC LIBRARY

ASTOR, LENOX AND
TILDEN FOUNDATIONS

"(1) Thomas Pollock, whom Oliver Pollock mentions in a letter to the President of the United States Congress, dated New Orleans, Sept 18, 1782, thus 'I dispatched my nephew, Thomas Pollock, with fifteen volunteers, and Captain La Fitte with twenty-six armed men to Captain Willing's assistance' Nothing more is known of this Thomas

(2) John Pollock must have been born before 1756 and possibly emigrated with his father. He was sent to Philadelphia in 1776 by his father to draw £600 from the Committee of Safety for use of the Commissioners of Cumberland County His will, on file at Carlisle contains all that is known of his family From this it appears that John Pollock married Grace ——————, and had one daughter Margaret, who married Hanse Morrison, and had in 1807 two sons, John Pollock Morrison and Lucas Morrison Hanse lived at Pittsburgh and married Margaret Pollock (or Peggy, as the Pennsylvania archives have it), Nov 12, 1795 He is said to have been a Captain in 1813 in Gen'l Claiborne's brigade of Mississippi and Louisiana Territory Volunteers Jno Pollock d Feb 18 1807, at Carlisle, probably over 60 years of age, as he calls himself in his will 'old and infirm

'Hamilton Pollock of Tunica, La, in 1804, was Oliver Pollock's nephew and agent, looking after and managing the latter's extensive interests in that section If he was married it is not known

"Lieutenant Colonel Otis W. Pollock, U S A, retired, now residing in San Francisco, Cal, in a communication to the Pennsylvania Magazine some years ago, stated

"The ancestors of President James K Polk, and those of Ex-Governor James Pollock of Pennsylvania, and those of another family of Pollocks, came from the north of Ireland, some place in the neighborhood of Coleraine or Londonderry and located in Chester County, not far from 1719 Ex-President Polk's name was Pollock They acquired the habit of spelling it Polk, subsequently the apostrophe was dropped and the name became Polk

Col Pollock says further "The emigrants of the other famil   s and
Char   urival

in this country and became a doctor of medicine and remained there. John settled at Carlisle, in Cumberland County, James in Ligonier Valley, Westmoreland County, and Charles in Northumberland County

"The John Pollock referred to above is probably the John Pollock who came from Ireland with three brothers, one of whom is said to have become rather wild and returned to Ireland This last John Pollock changed his name to Pogue some years after he came to this country He married Elizabeth Neal, at Carlisle, and had sons named William, James, Samuel, George, Robert and David, and a daughter named Sarah Of these, James married Frances Baker and George married Nancy Davis Robert married Sarah Patterson, and Sarah married John Curry William and Samuel died unmarried

JUDGE JOHN C. POLLOCK'S LINE.

Hon. John C. Pollock, U S Judge for the District of Kansas, contributes the following data regarding his paternal line·

"My great, great grandfather, Samuel Pollock, was born and reared in Scotland and there married Jane   (name unknown) prior to the Revolutionary War They came to this country, were among the earliest settlers, and patented a tract of land in North Strabane Township, Washington County, Pa. They were members of the Covenanter Church The date of their coming to this country I do not have I am going to endeavor to get hold of a copy of this patent. Samuel Pollock appears to have been a man of considerable education and intelligence At his death he left three sons, John, Samuel and William, and four daughters, Margaret, Jane, Nancy and Grizella.

"The second son of Samuel and Jane Pollock, Samuel Pollock 2d, was my great grandfather He married Ellen Young They had four sons and five daughters The sons were John, James, Robert and Samuel The daughters were named Jane, Betsy, Sarah, Margaret and Martha

"The eldest son of Samuel Pollock and Ellen Young, John Pollock, was my grandfather He married Nancy Hayes and located on Wheeling Creek, near Uniontown, Belmont County, Ohio. To these good people there were born fourteen children, Samuel, William, Robert, James, James II, John and Calvin, and daughters, Ellen, Margaret, Mary, Sarah, Agnes, Jane, and another, the name I do not remember. I can give you the history, in full, of course, of all my uncles and aunts if you desire it, who they married, when, and full information.

"My father's name was Samuel Pollock, the oldest son of John Pollock and Nancy Hayes. He was born Jan. 11, 1818, died March 2, 1882. He married Jane Scott, my mother. There were seven children born to Samuel Pollock and Jane Scott, four sons and three daughters. James, John (myself), Joseph, William, Margaret, Ellen and Nancy. The youngest daughter, Nancy, died of diphtheria at two and one-half years of age. My brother Joseph is also dead. My mother was born Dec. 3, 1820 and died Dec. 3, 1899."

JAMES AND WILLIAM POLLOCK.

(Data from Leland W. Pollock.)

James Pollock and his brother, William Pollock, came to this country about the close of the Revolutionary War, shortly after the surrender of Lord Cornwallis at Yorktown. Both being farmers, they bought land and settled in the Wyoming Valley of the Susquehannah River, in Northumberland County, Penn. Both were married after coming to this country and were the heads of large lists of descendants.

(1) James Pollock had at least one son, Samuel, whose wife Margaret bore him issue: ¹William, ²Thomas, ³James, ⁴John, ⁵Richard, ⁶Margaret, ⁷Jane, ⁸Ann, ⁹Mary.

William, eldest of the above, b. 1769, married Sarah Wilson. Children: ¹Sarah, married James S. Dougal; ²Fleming Wilson, married Mary Armstrong; ³Thomas Caldwell; ⁴Margaret, married Wm. McCleery; ⁵Samuel, b. 1808, married Elizabeth S. Sterling and they have a son, Thomas Chalmers; ⁶Mary   burn, had s   rried Chas

William, the immigrant brother of James, had at least one son, Joseph. It is not known whether he had any more or not.

Joseph Pollock was born in Northumberland County, Pa., receiving a very good education. He married Mary Smith of Lancaster County, Pa., and by her he had three sons. After her death the family moved to a point on the Big Beaver River west of Fort Pitt, now Pittsburg, and 18 miles from its junction with the Ohio River, 20 miles below Fort Pitt, and 18 miles from Beavercourt, the county seat, and five miles from New Castle, now the county seat of Loraine County. Here he married Margaret Gray, a native of New York, by whom he had eleven more children.

Joseph was a good farmer, highly respected by all the neighborhood. He was an elder in the Presbyterian Church until his death in 1827, when he was buried in the old family cemetery on the farm.

Joseph Pollock had issue: ¹John; ²Samuel, ³James; ⁴Joseph; ⁵David; ⁶Davis, ⁷John 2nd, ⁸William, ⁹Benjamin Smith; ¹⁰Jane, married Wm. Pollock, a distant relative; ¹¹Polly, ¹²Margaret.

Samuel Pollock 2nd, was born in Northumberland County. He received a very thorough education, graduating from Darlington College, in Beaver County, and continuing his study to prepare himself for the ministry until his health failed. His first wife was a Miss Lesley, of Beaver County, who bore him three children. In 1814 he married again, to a widow, Margaret Morrow Henan, a native of Wilmington, Del., daughter of Thomas and Margaret Morrow. By her he had four children. He died in 1837 at Maravia, Lawrence County, and was buried in the family cemetery on the old farm in that county. He had issue: ¹Samuel, married Joseph Zimerman, ²Mary Ann, married Joseph Zimerman, ³Hanah, married Robert Hineman, have one child, ⁴James Harvey, ⁵Polly, married John Smith; ⁶David Smith, ⁷Eleanor.

Joseph (son of Joseph and Margaret Gray), was born in Beaver County. He also was well educated, going through Darlington College, intending to study to be a Presbyterian minister, but finally deciding he was not a good enough christian, he took up the study of medicine, and practiced his profession many years in Williamsport, Pa He was a polished scholar in Hebrew, Latin and Greek, had a strong intellect and was a man of great judgment. He was supervisor of the Beaver Valley Canal, and was twice elected as a representative to the legislature in Harrisburg His wife's name was Rachel Morehead, by whom he had the following children, all dead now

(1) Perryander, b ———, never married, went to Old Mexico in 1835 where he purchased a gold mine with which he did very well until a band of Mexican robbers, coming upon him, murdered him, taking all his money

(2) Milo married a Vanhorn and settled on a farm in Jackson County, Iowa

Both are dead The latter had issue: [1]Hiram, [2]Camillow; [3]Hisaferno, [4]Berlinda Clendenning, d. 1898 at age of 93; [5]Laura, [6]Adoline, [7]Caroline, [8]Josephine

James Harvey Pollock married Lydia Phillips and had issue: [1]David Wells; [2]Joseph Philip, [3]Samuel Harvey, [4]Charles [5]Robert Martin, [6]Milton DeWitt, [7]Grant, [8]Emma

David Wells Pollock, married Barbra Lewis, a merchant in central Illinois for many years, now a farmer near Durango, Col They have children [1]Wells, [2]Helen, [3]Bertha, [4]Ethel; [5]Lewis

Joseph Philip Pollock married Ida Ball Issue [1]Leland Wells, [2]Milton Wayne [3]Ruth Janet

Samuel Harvey Pollock, married Janet Carlyle One son, Harvey Carlyle

Robert Martin Pollock, married Jennie Maltby Issue: [1]Lloyd, [2]Floss, married Walter Kellog, [3]Cary.

Milton Dewitt Pollock married Emma Miles

Ulysses Sydney Grant Pollock married Ivy Miles Issue. [1]Willard, [2]Marie, [3]Ruth.

Emma Pollock, married Wm Hinton, d 1909 Issue: [1]Stanley; [2]Virgil, [3]Vivian.

Polly, daughter of Samuel Pollock and Miss Lesley, married John Smith Issue [1]Mary Ellen, [2]Rebecca Ann; [3]James Harvey [4]John Liget [5]Marcus

His mother was left a widow when he was but twelve years old. October 18, 1847 he married Sarah Jane Kuhn, at Sewekly, a daughter of John Kuhn and his wife Katherine Schapher, b. July 29, 1830.

In 1865 the family moved to the west, settling first in Iowa, then going to a farm near Jefferson City, Mo From here he moved to New Bloomfield, Calloway County, where he lived for fifteen years. On February 5, 1896, his wife died at the age of sixty-five For sixty years and more he was an Elder in the Presbyterian Church, an active worker in all kinds of religious activity. Like all the Pollocks, as far back as anything is known of them, he was a strict Presbyterian. He is still living in 1911 a venerable old man of over eighty-six, highly respected by all his relatives and acquaintances His children are as follows

(1) Frank Pollock, b July 25, 1849, married Oct 5, 1897, to Katie Shepherd Present address, Hamilton, Illinois No children

(2) Margaret Pollock, b March 10, 1851, married Feb 18, 1875 to George H Gordon Present address, (near) Jefferson City, Mo Issue ¹Luella, married Eugene Campbell; ²Edgar, has two children, Harvey and Dorothy.

Charles E Pollock b March 1, 1853, married Feb 26, 1886 to Mattie Mahan Present address, (near) Jefferson City, Mo Issue ²Mildred; ³Edward; ⁴Robert.

William H Pollock, b March 13, 1856, married October 31, 1900 to Mollie Hyten. Present address, Fulton, Mo. Issue·

Sue M Pollock, b May 13, 1856, married Aug 7, 1881 to Norman P. Bruce Present addres, (near) Jefferson City, Mo Issue ¹David, ²Sadie, ³Clarence, ⁴Ozetta

Nannie A Pollock, b Oct 16, 1861, married Nov 19, to John C. Renner Present address, New Bloomfield, Mo Died Oct 2, 1904 Issue ¹William, ²Johnnie

Sarah Emma Pollock, b Feb 17, 1866, married Aug 6, 1885 to Jefferson P Bailey Present address, (near) Jefferson City, Mo Issue. ¹Ella, ²William

CHAPTER LXXIV.

DR THOMAS POLLOCK'S DESCENDANTS.

(By Col. Otis W. Pollock, U. S. A.)

Dr. Thomas Pollock, of Coleraine, County Derry, Ireland, married Mary Cochran, of the same place, and raised a large family, all of whom were born there. They were

(1) John Pollock, b March 3, 1724, d July 16, 1794, at Carlisle, Pa.; married first Catharine Campbell, second Eleanor Scull.

(2) Thomas Pollock, M. D., b 1726, d unmarried at Coleraine

(3) Robert Pollock, b (twin with Thomas) 1726

(4) James Pollock, b 1728, d 1812, married Mary Heron

(5) Charles Pollock, b 1732, d 1795, married Agnes Steele

(6) Jane Pollock, b about 1734, d Feb 17, 1797; married ——— McLean

(7) Eliza Pollock, b about 1736, d ———, married ——— Sheriff

(8) Mary Pollock, untraced

(9) ——— Pollock, b ———, d ———, married first Mr Colwell, second Mr Allison, removed to Nova Scotia

(10) Elizabeth Pollock, b ———, d. ———, at Coleraine

(12) ——— Pollock, b ———, d ———; married Davis Barber, of Northumberland County, Pa Possibly came to America with her brothers

John settled at Carlisle, Pa, and had the following children, by first marriage, all born at Carlisle ¹Eleanor Pollock, b Feb 7, 1760, married Jas Armstrong, ²Thomas Pollock, b March 22, 1762, lawyer, d unmarried 1812, ³Alexander Pollock, b Jan 30, 1764, d 1801, married Jane Sheriff, ⁴John Pollock, b Dec 11, 1765, d Feb 18, 1772.

Thomas the immigrant, returned to Ireland, where he studied medicine, practiced and died

James settled in Ligonier Valley, Westmoreland County, Pa, and had the following issue ¹Thomas Pollock, b 1772, d. 1847, married first Rachael Hendricks, second Susan Henderson, ²Elizabeth Pollock, b about 1774, d ———, married John McCoy; ³Mary Pollock, b about 1776, d ———, married David Knox; ⁴James Pollock, b about 1779 d unmarried; ⁵John Pollock, b 1783, d 1862, married Elizabeth Hamill, ⁶David Pollock, b 1784-5, d probably Jan 20, 1807, killed by French robbers in the Alleghany Mountains, ⁷Nancy Pollock, b 1789 d 1845, married William Lytle

Charles, settled in Northumberland County, Pa He lived in White Deer Township, Buffalo Valley, and had the following children, all of whom were born in Northumberland County: ¹John Pollock, b ———, d unmarried March 1795; ²Adam Pollock, b 1767, d 1815, married 1801 Elizabeth Gilliland, ³James Pollock, b August 8 1769, d May 24, 1857, married June 2, 1801, Mary Steele, ⁴Thomas Pollock, b 1772, d Sept. 29, 1844, married first in 1796, Margaret Fruit, second, in 1820, Eleanor Knox; ⁵William Pollock, b 1773, d ———, married Sally Fruit, ⁶Richard Pollock, b ———, d unmarried young, ⁷Charles Pollock b 1780, d Aug 1798, death caused by over-exertion in lifting sacks of grain, ⁸Mary Pollock, b 1782, d 1784, ⁹Jane Pollock, b 1784, lived only six weeks, ¹⁰Robert Pollock, b May 22, 1785, d Feb 22, 1844, married Margaret Anderson

Adam, James, Thomas, William and Robert, sons of Charles, after their father's death, which occurred in Northumberland County in 1795, removed with their mother to Erie County, Pa where with the exception of Thomas and William, they settled and remained The latter two brothers subsequently removed to Clarion County, Pa , where their descendants now live

PATERNAL LINE OF LT COL OTIS WHEELER POLLOCK

(1) Dr Thomas Pollock, Coleraine County, Derry, Ireland

(2) Charles Pollock, Northumberland County, Pa.

(3) Adam Pollock, Erie County, Pa

(4) Charles Pollock, Erie City, Pa

(5) Otis Wheeler Pollock, Lt Col U S Army

CHAPTER LXXV.

VISIT TO SCOTTISH ANCESTRAL HOME.

Col Otis W. Pollock, U S A, retired, of San Francisco, has always manifested great interest in the genealogy of his family and the personal history of its members

In a letter to the author, in Jan 1911, Col Pollock says.

"I have the "Irish Pedigrees" by John O'Hart; David Scott's History of Scotland; George Crawford's History of Renfrewshire, and the Family of Stewart, and Burke's Peerage and Baronetage, from which I have worked out the pedigree back to Adam O'Hart, in his work, has the pedigree of Queen Victoria traced to Adam the first man I was able to trace mine until it became co-incident with hers. When we come to Robert Pollock of that ilk, the first Baronet, your genealogy and mine back to Adam are identical.

'I visited Europe in 1888, and while there called at Pollok Castle, and had a very pleasant interview with Mr Ferguson Pollok, and his family. He showed me over the castle and told me many things You probably may know that the last Baronet, Sir Hew Crawford Pollok, was a wild boy. He ran away from home, came to the United States, enlisted as a private soldier in the Fourth U. S. Cavalry, served three years, re-enlisted for a second term, and at one time, in 1867, while the regiment was serving in Texas, and they were in camp, he picked up an old newspaper and stuck a corner of it in the fire to light his pipe Extinguishing the fire, he spread it out to look it over, when he discovered a notice of the death of his father

"He immediately made himself known to his commanding officer (he had enlisted under the name of Johnston) and through the influence of the British Minister at Washington, procured a discharge from the army He then returned to Scotland and assumed the title and estate He married and finally died in London in 1885

"While in Scotland, I also visited the estate of Mountainstown, and met the proprietor, a young man since dead His name was John Napier George Pollok I also became acquainted with Captain Arthur Williamson Alsager Pollok, from whom I received a full record of the family of Pollock Carlisle Pollock Patterson, Chief of the U S Coast and Geodetic Survey, was from the family whose genealogy I enclose

The genealogy here referred to by Col Pollock and which he received from Captain Arthur Williamson Alsager Pollok, is omitted, it being the same that appears on the first pages of this book

THE POGUE FAMILY.

Another American family whose genesis begins in the Pollok family of Scotland and Ireland, is that of Pogue The first of them emigrating to America assumed that style of writing their name after their settlement in Virginia and Pennsylvania These families, like their Pollok and Polk kinsmen, spread out into the American Colonies some going to the Carolinas, and thence West and South to Tennessee and Kentucky, producing sons and daughters who were eminent socially and otherwise, attaining to prominence in civic and military affairs

The first of the Pogues (or Poages), of whom we have a record were Robert and John Poage, brothers, who came from County Derry, Ireland, in 1740, to Virginia, settling near Staunton, where Robert was made a member of the first County Court of Augusta County He had nine children, whose importation he proved May 22, 1740, soon after arrival Such action was a necessary step to settlers procuring lands John, the younger brother did not marry until he came to Virginia and settled in Rockbridge County, near the Natural Bridge He raised a considerable family, one of whom, Martha, married Col James Moore. They moved with other families to Abb's Valley, Southwest Virginia, where he and most of his family were slain by Shawanee Indians raiding in from Ohio His w..tivity in Oh   d at the st.

John Poage after settlement in Augusta County, married Mary Blair, and was also a Magistrate of his county. He was High Sheriff in 1778, and later County Surveyor, which office became hereditary in his family. Martha, daughter of Robert Poage, married Andrew Woods and died at Ripley, Ohio, in 1818. One tradition is that Robert Poage was a nephew or a grand nephew of Capt. Robert Pollok, who settled in Maryland about 1672, changed his name to Polk and became progenitor of the extensive American family of that name.

One of Robert Poage's sons, Wm. Poage, moved from Southwest Virginia in 1775, coming with Col. Richard Calloway to Boonesboro. In 1758, and at other times, he was in active service against the Indians. In 1762 he married Mrs. Ann (Kennedy) Wilson, settling near Black's Fort, now Abingdon. In August 1774 he was a Sergeant in command of Fort Russell, with twenty men, and Lieutenant Daniel Boone was in command of Fort Moore, four miles west of Fort Russell. Shortly after Wm. Poage came to Kentucky he settled at Harrodsburg, where he was slain by the Indians. According to tradition Elizabeth, the wife of Robert Poage the immigrant to Virginia, was a Sheridan and a cousin of Richard Brinley Sheridan. Others say she was a Preston. Soon after the War of 1812 John and Joseph Pogue and family moved from North Carolina to Tennessee.

The first settler on the site of Indianapolis was a George Pogue, who was killed by Indians in 1819. He had moved from North Carolina to Fayette County, Indiana.

Col. Robert Pogue commanded a Kentucky regiment in the War of 1812, and left a number of descendants in Mason and Bracken Counties.

This ends the author's labors on his history of the Polk family, on which he has been engaged at intervals for forty years. That there are errors in it he does not doubt, and he leaves to future historians of the family, if any should appear, the task of sifting them out and correcting them. The data collected amounted to much more than it was possible to make use of, and consequently much had to be omitted which the author would like to have included in the work.

"POLK FAMILY AND KINSMEN"

HISTORY of the Polk family since its settlement in Maryland in 1672, copiously illustrated with portraits of prominent members of the various branches, is now ready for distribution to members of the family and others desiring it. It represents many years of persistent labor by the editor and compiler. The narrative begins with the family's Scotch genesis in 1053, and comes down through Ireland, from whence Capt. Robert Bruce Polk and family came to America. Great care was exercised in its compilation and the facts it contains will be of the utmost interest to every member of the family. A full history is given of each branch in America, and of its dispersion into the States of the Union, North, South, East and West. Among its features are highly interesting accounts of frontier, Revolutionary and Civil War experiences of various members. Only a limited number of copies have been printed and these will be furnished to applicants for $6.00 per copy, plus 26 cents for expressage. Remittance by draft or P. O. Money Order preferred. Direct all orders to

W. H. POLK,
LEXINGTON, KY.

COMPLIMENTARY NOTICES

From a number who have received and perused the book, highly commendatory letters have been received by the author.

Dr. Wm. Mecklenburg Polk, of New York, son of Bishop and Lieut.-General Leonidas Polk, ordered seven copies, and says: "From all who have seen it I have heard only the highest praise."

District Judge A. B. Watkins, of Athens, Texas, ordering three copies, after reading book, writes: "I have examined with much interest the volume, and I think it but deserving that I express to you my appreciation of the work which you have so safisfactorily completed. It is far beyond the commonplace of family succession. And one is the more pleased, because it gives the entire stamp of verity, by reciting facts and events which add an interest to the correctness of the matters set out. It seems to me a work of most infinite detail and toil, and I only regret that your modesty prevents you from saying something more of yourself, and the boundless patience and labor that you must have given to it through so many years. The entire family connection owe you a debt of gratitude. I know, of course, that it would not be possible to compensate you personally for your work; it has taken too great a part of your life, and you will have to content yourself with the thought that you, of all the members, have happily completed what so greatly interested Colonel William Polk, of North Carolina, his father, General Thomas Polk, President James K. Polk and General Leonidas Polk, while they were yet alive."

Many other letters of like tenor have been received.

On account of the   t to subscribers by express.

CPSIA information can be obtained
at www.ICGtesting.com
Printed in the USA
LVHW080806050323
740708LV00019B/308